American National Security

American National Security

Seventh Edition

MICHAEL J. MEESE
SUZANNE C. NIELSEN
RACHEL M. SONDHEIMER

Foreword by
GENERAL JOHN P. ABIZAID,
US ARMY (RETIRED)

Johns Hopkins University Press
Baltimore

Printed in the United States of America on acid-free paper
2 4 6 8 9 7 5 3 1

Johns Hopkins University Press
2715 North Charles Street
Baltimore, Maryland
21218-4363
www.press.jhu.edu

Library of Congress Cataloging-in-Publication Data
Names: Meese, Michael J., author. | Nielsen, Suzanne C., author. | Sondheimer, Rachel M., author.
Title: American national security / Michael J. Meese, Suzanne C. Nielsen, Rachel M. Sondheimer.
Description: Seventh edition. | Baltimore : Johns Hopkins University Press, [2018] | Includes bibliographical references and index.
Identifiers: LCCN 2018007463 | ISBN 9781421426938 (hardcover : alk. paper) | ISBN 9781421426778 (pbk. : alk. paper) | ISBN 9781421426785 (electronic) | ISBN 1421426935 (hardcover : alk. paper) | ISBN 1421426773 (pbk. : alk. paper) | ISBN 142142678I (electronic)
Subjects: LCSH: National security—United States. | United States—Military policy.
Classification: LCC UA23 .J66 2018 | DDC 363.340973—dc23
LC record available at https://lccn.loc.gov/2018007463

A catalog record for this book is available from the British Library.

To
Amos A. Jordan and William J. Taylor Jr.

Two exceptional scholars, educators, mentors, policy makers, and US Army officers, who taught and inspired generations of national security professionals

Contents

Foreword

A successful approach to the challenges and opportunities that we face in a dynamic and complex world must be based on an informed discussion of the issues that is open, clear, and unambiguous. This book, *American National Security*, provides an impressive, comprehensive discussion of the issues, actors, policies, and history that have influenced national security policy in the past and will shape its direction in the future. Just as America and the world are continuously evolving, the authors have significantly revised this edition based on recent US history, some of the initial policy approaches of the Trump administration, and changing global dynamics.

A comprehensive approach to American national security policy is necessary to avoid the strategic myopia that can often afflict policy makers. It is not sufficient to conduct a "soda straw" examination of issues using a country-by-country or issue-by-issue approach. It is important to look at regions and strategies holistically to understand trends and to anticipate how actions in one area will reverberate throughout the world.

For example, in the Middle East, the world is facing a number of challenges that have affected and will continue to have implications for US national security. First, Sunni Islamic extremism, which is embodied in al-Qaeda, the Islamic State in Iraq and the Levant (ISIL), and their affiliates, continues to motivate and support violent attacks that foment instability. Second, Shia Islamic extremism, as led by Iran and its proxy forces fighting throughout the Middle East, exacerbates conflicts in the region and exploits state weakness to further Iran's strategic ends. Third, the Arab-Israeli conflict remains salient throughout the region, in spite of significant efforts of the United States and others to achieve a long-term solution. Finally, in spite of recent increases in US energy production, the world remains dependent on energy resources from the region, which is why the Middle East will continue to be strategically important. These trends are difficult to discern if one only examines particular incidents, but they become clearer through a more comprehensive review of the issues. Circumstances are changing in the Middle East and opportunities abound, but considerable strategic dangers remain.

The information revolution is affecting security and political stability throughout the Middle East, as well as the broad array of US national security interests in that region and beyond. More individuals throughout the world have greater access to information, which compresses decisionmaking cycles and accelerates the effects of any particular action, either by the United States or by those who would oppose US policy. Individuals and organizations are networked globally and have the ability to see beyond the local areas in which they live, which can be positive, as it opens opportunities, but also negative, as it raises expectations and enhances perceptions of relative deprivation. Moreover, ubiquitous technology empowers and connects individuals, corporations, and others in ways that can be extremely unpredictable and potentially harmful to American interests and to the ability of states to influence the trajectory of events.

The United States led the West during the Cold War, and US policy was the driving force behind many global issues, especially after the attacks of September 11, 2001. Today, American leadership remains essential to global security and to developing and executing strategies to confront challenges. That does not mean that the United States should have policies that only employ American assets, but it does mean that there should be an American commitment to lead so that other countries understand there are some enduring policies that the United States will continue to support over time. To manage costs, the United States will need to demonstrate its sustained commitment to allies and to international peace and security through means that do not always include a large-scale deployment of US forces. The Trump administration's *National Security Strategy* recognizes the continuing challenges in the Middle East but also clearly points to the growing strength of America's near-peer competitors, China and Russia. When these issues are considered alongside persistent and emerging security challenges in places such as North Korea and parts of Africa, it becomes clear that the United States will face an extremely complex security environment for the foreseeable future.

It is important to understand the perspectives and approaches that provide the context for American national security policy making. As discussed in part I of this book, "National Security Policy: What Is It, and How Have Americans Approached It?," one of the strengths that the United States brings to policy making is its values. Those values are represented both by the ideals enshrined in the Constitution and Declaration of Independence and by the strength and dedication of the American people to do the hard work necessary to make the United States and the world a stronger, safer, and better place for future generations. A successful and sustainable approach to national security will rest on these values, which should continue to influence policy choices in the future.

With national security policy, it is sometimes difficult to understand all the players involved, which is addressed in part II, "National Security Policy: Actors and Processes." During my career as a military leader, I worked with all the actors discussed, often engaging with the White House and Congress. With the intelligence, diplomatic, and homeland security communities as partners with the military, the challenge was to integrate our efforts in support of shared strategies. Understanding the proper role of the military, the vital importance of the budget process, and the intricacies of national security decision making are crucial to the effective formulation of security policy. There is no substitute for learning about all of these actors and agencies firsthand, but studying their history, culture, organization, and practices is a great first step toward understanding their important roles in American national security.

Recently, the United States seems to have had an overreliance on the military element of power. As this book describes in part III, "Ways and Means of National Strategy," it is critical to understand and incorporate all elements of power when developing a successful long-term strategy. Our overreliance on the hammer of military power has created a dynamic that makes every problem look like a nail. While military action can gain time for political activity to take place, it is vital that we incorporate economic, diplomatic, informational, educational, intelligence, law enforcement, and other aspects of power in the development of a sustainable strategy. All elements of national power need to be adequately resourced so that we can most effectively advance American interests in the world.

Finally, understanding the history and dynamics of global security issues, examined in part IV, "International and Regional Security Issues," is particularly important. There is a tendency to view the issues in a particular country or region in only their current circumstances, without understanding the historical context or perceptions of past US policy in the region. Many of the issues that policy makers deal with today are the legacy of previous, seemingly well-intentioned decisions that may not have adequately reflected the underlying reality of the various groups on the ground. Only by being willing to listen to the issues from the perspective of those who live with them will US policy makers be able to understand how to develop an effective, sustainable strategy over the long term.

American National Security is an ideal resource that ties together theory, actors, instruments of power, and regions of the world, with clear, detailed explanations that facilitate understanding of international relations and security policy. The people who are likely reading this book—students of national security policy, diplomats, policy makers, military officers, intelligence professionals, engaged citizens, and others—collectively provide the strength, insight, and hope for America going forward. The challenges that we face are great, but the wisdom in this book will help its readers develop a comprehensive understanding of the issues affecting national security policy. That understanding can lead to effective, long-term strategies that will serve US national interests while enabling the United States to continue to lead allies and other international partners in fighting for shared prosperity and peace.

General John P. Abizaid, US Army (Retired)

Preface

The seventh edition of *American National Security* continues the rich tradition of providing a single authoritative book that describes and explains US national security policy, actors, processes, and issues in a comprehensive and understandable way. This edition has been substantially rewritten to account for significant changes in the national security environment in the past decade. It is intended to provide a foundation of understanding for teachers, students, and practitioners of national security policy, one of the most important and least understood subjects in public policy.

This book provides this foundation in a logical structure that introduces the reader to the subject and provides a topically organized reference for immediate or future use. The first part of the book explains what national security policy is and how Americans have approached it over time. Understanding the theory, history, and evolution of American national security policy helps explain existing institutions and strategy. Part II describes each of the major actors and processes, including the president, Congress, homeland security, intelligence, the military, budgeting, and the national security decision-making process. Part III explains the ways and means of national strategy, including diplomacy, information, economics, and military power. Part IV tours the globe with chapters on each major region of the world, which examine the history of American engagement, current US interests and policies, and enduring issues likely to affect American national security policy in each area. Finally, part V encourages the reader to consider major dynamics that may shape American national security decisions in the future.

All seven editions of this text are the result of the dedicated scholarship and unparalleled knowledge and experience of the two men to whom we dedicate this book: Amos A. Jordan and William J. Taylor Jr. Brigadier General Joe Jordan graduated as the highest-ranking cadet in the West Point Class of 1946, studied at

Oxford University as a Rhodes Scholar, earned his PhD from Columbia University, and served on the faculty in the Department of Social Sciences at West Point for twenty years, eventually retiring as the Professor and Head of the Department. He continued to serve in senior civilian positions in the Department of Defense and the Department of State and was a member of the President's Intelligence Oversight Board. He served as President and Chief Executive Officer of the Center for Strategic and International Studies (CSIS), President of the CSIS Pacific Forum, and as a Senior Advisor at the Wheatley Institution at Brigham Young University. Colonel Bill Taylor was commissioned through the US Army Officer Candidate School (OCS) in 1955 and was later elected to the OCS Hall of Fame. He earned his PhD from American University and served on the faculty in the Department of Social Sciences at West Point for sixteen years. At the time of his retirement, he was serving as the Director of National Security Studies. He then became an Adjunct Professor at Georgetown University's School of Foreign Service and served at CSIS, where he led the International Security Program, was a Senior Advisor, and helped lead the professional development program. These men provided a tremendous legacy of excellence, precision, rigor, and clarity—one that continues to inform this seventh edition of *American National Security.*

As faculty in the Department of Social Sciences in the 1970s, Jordan and Taylor recognized the need for a textbook that would explain US national security to an audience with renewed interest in security issues after the Vietnam War. The first edition was published in 1981 and quickly became the most relied-upon text in national security policy courses at institutions serving undergraduates, graduate students, and military and civilian government professionals. Subsequent editions of the book followed the same basic approach—identifying the history, continuities, and trends in American national security policy that provide context for the contemporary challenges that policy makers face on a daily basis. Jordan and Taylor combined their efforts with Lawrence J. Korb of the Brookings Institution for the third and fourth editions, and Michael J. Mazaar of CSIS for the fifth edition. The sixth edition returned partial responsibility for the book's authorship to the Department of Social Sciences at West Point, as Jordan and Taylor recruited Michael Meese and Suzanne Nielsen, previous and current Department Heads, respectively, to co-author that edition. Rachel Sondheimer, an Associate Professor who teaches American politics at West Point, has joined Meese and Nielsen to co-author this seventh edition.

The Department of Social Sciences at West Point is responsible for teaching the disciplines of political science and economics to cadets, and it is also home to the Combating Terrorism Center, which provides cutting-edge research on the terrorist threat, as well as the Office of Economic and Manpower Analysis, which supports the Army's senior leaders as they shape the future force. It is a national resource of talented military and civilian faculty who teach cadets about the national security policies that they will observe, encounter, help develop, and execute throughout their professional careers. Classrooms at West Point are the ideal laboratory to test the concepts from this text, and the current version has benefited greatly from the insights of faculty and students as it was developed. Indeed, this work would not have been possible without this collaboration at the United States

Military Academy, which is among the reasons why proceeds from the sale of this book are donated back to West Point. Several faculty members leveraged their considerable national security expertise to help draft significant revisions to many chapters. In particular, we would like to acknowledge the work of Terry Babcock-Lumish ("Putting the Pieces Together: National Security Decision Making" and "Nuclear Policy"), Jordan Becker ("Europe"), Ruth Beitler ("The Middle East"), Ryan Bell ("Putting the Pieces Together: National Security Decision Making" and "Nuclear Policy"), Steven Bloom ("Economics"), Roxanne Bras ("Irregular Threats: Terrorism, Insurgencies, and Violent Extremist Organizations"), Tania Chacho ("East Asia"), Robert Chamberlain ("Latin America"), Meghan Cumpston ("The International Setting"), Joe DaSilva ("The Evolution of American National Security Policy" and "Congress"); Brian Dodwell ("Homeland Security"), Dean Dudley ("Planning, Budgeting, and Management"), Brian Forester ("Presidential Leadership and the Executive Branch" and "South Asia"), Jim Golby ("The Role of the Military in the Policy Process" and "Military Power"), Jessica Grassetti ("Planning, Budgeting, and Management"), Liesl Himmelberger ("East Asia"), Seth Johnston ("Europe"), Bonnie Kovatch ("Sub-Saharan Africa"), Patrick Kriz ("Latin America"), Charlie Lewis ("The Evolution of American National Security Policy" and "Congress"), David Myers ("Latin America"), Rob Person ("Russia"), Don Rassler ("South Asia"), Adam Scher ("Traditional Approaches to National Security" and "Intelligence and National Security"), Nathan Strickland ("The Evolution of American National Security Policy"), Mike Walker ("Economics"), Ray Walser ("Latin America"), Tom Walsh ("Diplomacy and Information"), Jason Warner ("Sub-Saharan Africa"), and Richard Yon ("Presidential Leadership and the Executive Branch" and "Congress").

We would like to express our appreciation to the Department of Defense Minerva Project, which supported the completion of this volume. We would also like to recognize Brandon Mohr, whose significant cartographic design assistance is reflected in the maps in part IV. Teresa Lawson provided exceptionally helpful editorial assistance as the manuscript was being developed that improved it significantly. The book would not have been possible without the help of Lauren Straley and Julie McCarthy at Johns Hopkins University Press, who oversaw its development and production. Copy edits and indexing under the supervision of Kim Giambattisto improved the final text. Of course, any errors or omissions remain the responsibility of the authors. Additionally, the views expressed in this book are those of the authors and do not reflect the official policy or position of the Department of the Army, Department of Defense, or the US Government.

With the cacophony of information that bombards practitioners, teachers, and students of national security policy, it is critical that individuals from all backgrounds have a good understanding of the history, concepts, institutions, processes, and policies that provide essential context. We hope that this book serves as a foundation that will help students and practitioners to understand better the important issues that affect American national security. The more that individuals learn, the better they will be able to contribute to effective national security policy development and implementation.

Abbreviations and Acronyms

A2/AD	anti-access/area denial
ABM	anti–ballistic missile
ACDA	Arms Control and Disarmament Agency
ACRF	African Crisis Response Force
ACRI	African Crisis Response Initiative
AFRICOM	US Africa Command
AGOA	African Growth and Opportunity Act
AIPAC	American Israel Public Affairs Committee
AMISOM	African Union Mission in Somalia
ANZUS	Australia, New Zealand, United States Security Treaty
APC	armored personnel carrier
AQAP	al Qaeda in the Arabian Peninsula
ASEAN	Association of Southeast Asian Nations
ATACMS	Army Tactical Missile System
AU	African Union
AVF	all-volunteer force
AWACS	Airborne Warning and Control System
BCA	Budget Control Act
BMDS	ballistic missile defense system
BRAC	Base Realignment and Closure Commission
Brexit	British exit from European Union
C4I	command, control, communications, computers, and intelligence
CAFTA-DR	Dominican Republic–Central America Free Trade Agreement
CARICOM	Caribbean Community
CARSI	Central American Regional Security Initiative

CBO	Congressional Budget Office
CBRN	chemical, biological, radiological, and nuclear
CBSI	Caribbean Basin Security Initiative
CCP	Chinese Communist Party
CENTCOM	US Central Command
CENTO	Central Treaty Organization
CFE	Conventional Forces in Europe (treaty of 1990)
CFIUS	Committee on Foreign Investment in the United States
CIA	Central Intelligence Agency
CJTF-HOA	Combined Joint Task Force-Horn of Africa
COIN	counterinsurgency
COM	chief of mission
COMINT	communications intelligence
CPA	Coalition Provisional Authority
CSCC	Center for Strategic Counterterrorism Communications
CSCE	Conference for Security Cooperation in Europe
CSSTA	Cross-Strait Services Trade Agreement
CTR	Cooperative Threat Reduction
CVE	countering violent extremism
CYBERCOM	US Cyber Command
DC	Deputies Committee (of the National Security Council)
DCA	Defense Cooperation Agreement
DCI	Director of Central Intelligence
DCS	defense commercial sales
DEA	Drug Enforcement Agency
DHS	Department of Homeland Security
DIA	Defense Intelligence Agency
DISA	Defense Information Systems Agency
DMZ	demilitarized zone (Korean peninsula)
DNI	Director of National Intelligence
DoD	Department of Defense
DoDIN	Department of Defense Information Network
DOJ	Department of Justice
DPP	Democratic Progressive Party (Taiwan)
DPRK	Democratic People's Republic of Korea (North Korea)
DSCA	Defense Security Cooperation Agency
DTRA	Defense Threat Reduction Agency
ECOWAS	Economic Community of West African States
ELINT	electronic intelligence
ESDP	European Security and Defense Program
EU	European Union
F3EAD	find, fix, finish, exploit, analyze, and disseminate
FATA	Federally Administered Tribal Areas
FBI	Federal Bureau of Investigation
FDI	foreign direct investment

FDR	Franklin Delano Roosevelt
FEMA	Federal Emergency Management Agency
FIRE	Firefighter Investment and Response Enhancement
FISA	Foreign Intelligence Surveillance Act
FISINT	foreign instrumentation signals intelligence
FMF	foreign military financing
FMS	foreign military sales
FSB	Federal Security Service (Russian)
FTAA	Free Trade Area of the Americas
FY	fiscal year
G7, G8, or G20	group of seven, eight, or twenty (international economic forums)
GAO	Government Accountability Office
GATT	General Agreement on Tariffs and Trade
GDP	gross domestic product
GEOINT	geospatial intelligence
GNP	gross national product
GPS	global positioning system
HASC	House Armed Services Committee
HPSCI	House Permanent Select Committee on Intelligence
HSC	Homeland Security Council
HUMINT	human intelligence
IADB	Inter-American Development Bank
IAEA	International Atomic Energy Agency
IBRD	International Bank for Reconstruction and Development
ICBM	intercontinental ballistic missile
IED	improvised explosive device
IGO	intergovernmental organization
IMF	International Monetary Fund
IMINT	imagery intelligence
INF	Intermediate-Range Nuclear Forces (treaty of 1987)
IOB	Intelligence Oversight Board
IRBM	intermediate-range ballistic missile
ISAF	International Security Assistance Force
ISIL	Islamic State in Iraq and the Levant
ISR	intelligence, surveillance, and reconnaissance
JCS	Joint Chiefs of Staff
JSTARS	Joint Surveillance Target Attack Radar System
JTTF	joint terrorism task force
KGB	Committee for State Security (Russian)
KMT	Nationalist Kuomintang Party (Chinese)
MAD	mutually assured destruction
MASINT	measurement and signature intelligence
MCC	Millennium Challenge Corporation
MERCOSUR	Common Market of the South (Spanish)

MIRV	multiple, independently targetable reentry vehicle
MISO	military information support operations
MNC	multinational corporation
MOOTW	military operations other than war
MWe	megawatt
NAFTA	North American Free Trade Agreement
NATO	North Atlantic Treaty Organization
NCTC	National Counterterrorism Center
NEC	National Economic Council
NGA	National Geospatial-Intelligence Agency
NGO	nongovernmental organization
NIE	National Intelligence Estimate
NORAD	North American Aerospace Defense Command
NORTHCOM	US Northern Command
NPR	Nuclear Posture Review
NPT	Nuclear Nonproliferation Treaty
NRO	National Reconnaissance Office
NSA	National Security Agency
NSC	National Security Council
NSDD	National Security Decision Directive
NSR	National Security Review
NSS	National Security Strategy
OAS	Organization of American States
OAU	Organization of African Unity
OBOR	one belt, one road
OCO	overseas contingency operations
ODNI	Office of the Director of National Intelligence
OHS	Office of Homeland Security
OMB	Office of Management and Budget
ORHA	Office of Reconstruction and Humanitarian Assistance
OSCE	Organization for Security and Cooperation in Europe
OSD	Office of the Secretary of Defense
OSINT	open source intelligence
PA	Palestinian Authority
PC	Principals Committee (of the National Security Council)
PCC	policy coordination committee (of the National Security Council)
PDD	presidential decision directive
PDVSA	Petróleos de Venezuela, SA (Venezuela's National Oil Company)
PEO	peace enforcement operations
PEPFAR	President's Emergency Plan for AIDS Relief
PfP	Partnership for Peace
PIAB	President's Intelligence Advisory Board

PKK	Kurdistan Workers' Party
PKO	peacekeeping operations
PLA	People's Liberation Army
PLO	Palestinian Liberation Organization
POM	Program Objective Memorandum
PPBE	Planning, Programming, Budgeting, and Execution
PPBS	Planning, Programming, and Budgeting System
PRC	People's Republic of China
PREACT	Partnership for East African Counterterrorism
PRI	Institutional Revolutionary Party (Mexico)
PSI	Proliferation Security Initiative
PSUV	United Socialist Party of Venezuela
QDDR	Quadrennial Diplomacy and Development Review
QDR	Quadrennial Defense Review
QHSR	Quadrennial Homeland Security Review
R&D	research and development
R2P	responsibility to protect
RMA	revolution in military affairs
ROC	Republic of China (Taiwan)
ROK	Republic of Korea (South Korea)
SALT	Strategic Arms Limitation Talks
SASC	Senate Armed Services Committee
SCAF	Supreme Council of the Armed Forces (Egypt)
SDF	Self-Defense Forces (Japan)
SDI	Strategic Defense Initiative
SEATO	Southeast Asian Treaty Organization
SIGINT	signals intelligence
SLBM	submarine-launched ballistic missile
SOCOM	US Special Operations Command
SOF	special operations forces
SORT	Strategic Offensive Reductions Treaty (2002)
SOUTHCOM	US Southern Command
SSCI	Senate Select Committee on Intelligence
START	Strategic Arms Reduction Treaty (1991)
TCO	trans-national criminal organization
TPP	Trans-Pacific Partnership
TSCTP	Trans-Saharan Counterterrorism Partnership
TTIP	Transatlantic Trade and Investment Partnership
UAV	unmanned aerial vehicle
UN	United Nations
USA PATRIOT	Uniting and Strengthening America by Providing Appropriate Tools Required to Intercept and Obstruct Terrorism
USAID	United States Agency for International Development
USIA	US Information Agency

VEO	violent extremist organization
VTC	video teleconference
WMD	weapons of mass destruction
WTO	World Trade Organization
YPG	Kurdish People's Protection Units

1

National Security Policy
What Is It, and How Have Americans Approached It?

1

The International Setting

Every day, newspapers, television news channels, and Internet sites cover a wide variety of political, economic, and military developments around the world. Given this vast volume and variety of information, it can be difficult to determine which events and trends are most likely to affect the national security of the United States. Although deriving a constant set of generic criteria may be impossible, theories and concepts from the discipline of political science can help concerned observers analyze and assess a complex strategic environment.

No "silver bullet" or simple answer holds the key to understanding domestic and international developments. However, reliable conclusions are more likely when an analyst explicitly acknowledges assumptions, is unambiguous about the meaning of key concepts, and can clearly state the logic of his or her arguments. This approach best prepares the analyst to examine the evidence and test assessments in light of competing views and explanations. Of course, all analyses of important issues are likely to be accompanied by uncertainty. Analysts should estimate the degree of uncertainty associated with their assessments, explore potential implications, and recommend ways to hedge against key uncertainties wherever possible. Although a sound understanding of the strategic environment is not sufficient to ensure good national security decisions, it is an essential starting point.

National Security

The term *national security* refers to the safeguarding of a people, territory, and way of life. It includes protection from physical assault and in that sense is similar to the term *defense*. However, national security also implies protection, through a variety of means, of a broad array of interests and values. During the administration of President Barack Obama, these national interests were:

- The security of the United States, its citizens, and U.S. allies and partners;
- A strong, innovative, and growing U.S. economy in an open international economic system that promotes opportunity and prosperity;
- Respect for universal values at home and around the world; and
- A rules-based international order advanced by U.S. leadership that promotes peace, security, and opportunity through strengthened cooperation to meet global challenges.[1]

Although core national interests may be articulated differently by different presidential administrations, and prioritizing them may be difficult and controversial, many of the key themes persist over time. In addition to physical security and economic prosperity, preservation of the national security of the United States requires safeguarding individual freedoms and other US values, as well as the laws and institutions established to protect them. In the post–World War II period, the protection of these interests has generally been thought to require US action on the world stage to help create a favorable international environment. At their core, judgments about national security are decisions about the protection of the fundamental values and core interests necessary to the continued existence and vitality of the state.[2]

Traditional conceptions of national security, which focus on preserving the state from external threats, have been called into question from several directions. Some believe that past approaches to national security have focused too much on threats from other states and have paid inadequate heed to a variety of transnational challenges, including migration, narcotics trafficking, transnational crime, and terrorism. Whereas human beings are the main actors in these challenges, other transnational phenomena, such as environmental degradation, critical resource shortages, and infectious diseases, might not be the result of human intention, yet they still pose threats to states. Advocates for a focus on this broader security agenda—an agenda that has received greater emphasis since the end of the Cold War—believe that these issues deserve a place next to the traditional focus on the security competition among states as national security priorities.[3]

A second question, which is related but even more fundamental, is raised by scholars and policy advocates working in a field known as *human security*. These advocates question the adequacy of the concept of national security itself by disputing the presumption that the state rather than the individual is the key unit of concern. Particularly in predatory, failing, or failed states, security from external threats may not be the most urgent consideration. Human security is also related to transnational security challenges. According to the United Nations (UN), "Human security is needed in response to the complexity and the interrelatedness of both old and new security threats—from chronic and persistent poverty to ethnic violence, human trafficking, climate change, health pandemics, international terrorism, and sudden economic and financial downturns. Such threats tend to acquire transnational dimensions and move beyond traditional notions of security that focus on external military aggressions alone."[4] Threats to human security vary across time and are highly context-specific. Human security scholars vary in the definitions that they use; some focus on the full range of threats to personal well-being and dignity, while others focus more narrowly on political violence. However, they agree on putting the welfare of individuals at the center of their analyses.[5]

The term *national security* is an elastic one; its meaning and implications have expanded, contracted, and shifted over time. Reminiscent of Dr. Samuel Johnson's definition of patriotism as "the last refuge of scoundrels," protection of national security has sometimes even been invoked to justify or conceal illegal acts. Because national security issues can involve high stakes, it is especially important to analyze critically any argument that employs national security as a justification for a position or action. It is also useful to remember that national security policy in the US context serves both material interests and nonmaterial values and to return occasionally to first principles. Does a particular policy further US security or economic interests or values while preserving the US Constitution and the framework it establishes for the American way of life? If the answer to that question is uncertain, then so may be the grounds on which a particular policy rests.

Perspectives on International Politics

Three of the most important intellectual perspectives in the field of international relations are realism, liberalism, and constructivism.[6] These three worldviews reflect different basic assumptions about which phenomena are truly important and how the world is expected to operate. It is useful for both scholars and policy makers to be self-conscious about their perspectives so that they understand the likely strengths and weaknesses of their approaches to international events and developments. Clarity about core assumptions may also help policy makers anticipate circumstances under which their various initiatives may be mutually reinforcing or might instead be contradictory.

Realism. The oldest and perhaps the predominant view of the nature of international politics is *realism*, which has intellectual roots dating back to Thucydides and Machiavelli. Realists see international politics as a dangerous, conflict-prone realm in which security is far from guaranteed. States are the primary actors and can be analyzed as if they were unitary and rational actors whose core national interest can be defined as power. Given the presence of anarchy—defined as the lack of a single authority having sovereign power over the states in the international system—realists assert that states must pursue self-help strategies in order to survive. Although some states may strive only to maintain their positions in the system, others may pursue domination. To preserve independence and prevent destruction, states seek to balance the power of other states either through alliances or through internal means of increasing their relative power, such as arms buildups or economic mobilization. Although alliances may be useful forms of cooperation, they should be expected to last only as long as the common threat that initially brought the allies together remains relevant.

An important contribution of the realist school of thought is its emphasis on the central concept of *power*. Although it can be tempting to define power as influence or as the ability to get one's way, this approach can easily become misleading. For example, a Canadian victory in a trade dispute with the United States does not make it reasonable to conclude that Canada is more powerful. Seeking to give the term a more scientific and measurable formulation, political scientist Kenneth Waltz argues that power is a combination of seven components: size of population, territory, resource endowment, economic capability, military strength, political stability, and competence.[7] All of these elements must be considered in any assessment, although the weighing of the elements varies in different contexts. Waltz's central prediction is that states can be expected to react to the power of other states by engaging in balancing behavior. He argues that if "there is any distinctively political theory of international politics, balance of power theory is it."[8]

In an effort to refine Waltz's approach, Stephen Walt argues that power is important but not fully adequate to explain what motivates state behavior. States respond not just to the power of other states but also to the level of *threat* they pose, with threat defined as encompassing material capabilities as well as geographic proximity, offensive power, and aggressive intentions.[9] This formulation suggests that states can influence how others respond to their power through the extent to which they develop offensive means and through the manner in which they convey their intentions. Although Waltz and Walt differ slightly on the key motivator for balancing behavior, they have in common most of the assumptions that characterize the realist school of thought: that the world is a dangerous place in which each state must ensure its own survival by obtaining and competently applying power.

Although realism has proven itself an enduring and valued paradigm with many strengths, it also has weaknesses. Realists have traditionally emphasized the primacy of the state and the relative importance of relations among the great powers.[10] The current era, marked by the decreasing relevance of state boundaries and by critical transnational threats stemming from weak and failed states, presents a challenge to the primacy that realists give to great power competition. A second issue is the priority that realists give to power and security, especially military security. Realists may be right in regarding these state concerns as central, but this may make realism a less valuable approach to explaining state policies in other issue areas. For example, although a realist perspective may help to explain international trade issues in some cases, other variables—such as domestic interests, domestic and international institutions, the structure of the international economy, and the interactions of state and non-state actors—are frequently significant as well.[11]

Finally, realism does not contain within itself an adequate explanation of change. To a great extent, realists have taken pains to point out continuity in international politics. For example, realists might claim that the same fear that Sparta had of an increasingly powerful Athens—which, according to Thucydides, contributed to war between those powers more than two thousand years ago—could serve as a powerful explanation for war today.[12] This dual emphasis on the balance of power among states and on states as key actors makes realists less likely to explore such potential system-transforming phenomena as the rising importance of transnational actors and the impact of the process of globalization on the international system.

Liberalism. A second major international relations tradition has its roots in the political writings of Immanuel Kant and other Enlightenment thinkers. Whereas the core value for realists is state security, the core values for liberals are individual liberty and moral autonomy. Although states may still be seen as the key actors in international politics, their status rests on whether or not they can reasonably be seen as the legitimate guarantors of the rights and aspirations of their populations. This perspective underpins the right to rebel found in the political theory of John Locke and other important liberal thinkers.[13] Where a realist may be content to assume that a state is unitary and may not carefully analyze domestic institutions or politics, a liberal sees societal actors as having central importance.[14] According to the liberal tradition, democratic institutions, as well as liberal democratic values within a population, will have an important impact on foreign policy behavior.

With regard to US national security, perhaps the single most important international relations insight stemming from the liberal tradition is *democratic peace theory*. This theory seeks to explain the empirical fact that liberal democracies have rarely gone to war with one another.[15] Although the exact mechanisms that have contributed to preventing such wars are the focus of ongoing research, explanations generally focus on the nature of democratic institutions and norms. Democratic institutions require consensus and therefore create time for debate, thus averting wars for unpopular purposes (such as, presumably, war with another liberal democracy). Democratic norms emphasize peaceful conflict resolution and compromise, especially with another democratic government, which is seen as the legitimate custodian of the interests of its people.[16] Although a democratic state may not be more peaceful in general, it is less likely to go to war with another state that shares its democratic institutions and norms.

In addition to focusing greater attention on the domestic characteristics of states, liberalism also differs from realism in the mechanisms it suggests for the maintenance of international peace and stability. Realists would likely dismiss any suggestions that a permanent peace among states is possible, but they would hold that periods of relative peace and stability can be achieved if states prudently look to their interests (defined as power) and pay adequate attention to maintaining a balance of power in the international system.[17] Liberals, on the other hand, would be more likely to look to the mechanisms identified by Kant in his 1795 political essay "Perpetual Peace: A Philosophical Sketch." There, he hypothesizes that a permanent peace among states would have three characteristics: all states would have representative, elected governments; these governments would form a federation among themselves to resolve differences and to ensure an overwhelming response to any state's aggression; and individuals would have the basic right not to be automatically treated as an enemy when arriving in a foreign land.[18] This last provision, a minimal human right that opens the door to commerce, identifies a mechanism for the development of peaceful relations, which is explored more fully in Kant's 1784 work "Idea for a Universal History with a Cosmopolitan Purpose."[19] According to this essay, trade will increase the interconnectedness among societies, which will in turn increase the benefits of peaceful relations and heighten the costs of increasingly destructive wars.

Though scholars working within the liberal tradition have refined these basic arguments and developed more specific propositions, Kant's central ideas still underpin much of the liberal approach. Democratic peace theorists explore the possible benefits of democracy in terms of peace and security. Kant's notion of a federation of states was an early articulation of the focus of modern liberal theorists on the roles that international institutions and international law can play in furthering common interests among states.[20] Finally, the idea that increased trade can promote peace continues to inform liberal thinking. For example, political scientists Robert Keohane and Joseph Nye developed an approach called *complex interdependence* that sees the mutual dependence between states created by economic interconnectedness as making conflict less likely.[21]

For most liberals, these ideas are underpinned by concepts of universal human rights and the view that the freedom and moral autonomy of the individual are central values. A classic statement of this viewpoint can be found in the US Declaration of Independence: "We hold these truths to be self-evident, that all men are created equal, that they are endowed by their Creator with certain unalienable Rights, that among these are Life, Liberty and the pursuit of Happiness. That to secure these rights, Governments are instituted among Men, deriving their just powers from the consent of the governed."[22] The liberal desire to protect the individual is also embodied in international law, such as the "Universal Declaration of Human Rights" adopted by the United Nations in 1948, as well as in the Geneva Conventions and other laws of warfare.[23]

Like realism, liberalism has both strengths and weaknesses. It is a historical fact that liberal democracies have rarely if ever fought one another, although the process of democratization can itself be quite dangerous to international peace and security.[24] International law can be useful in defining standards and in establishing a mechanism to punish individuals when domestic systems cannot, but its most significant shortcoming is the lack of guaranteed enforcement. Similarly, international institutions have been significant in helping states to achieve mutually beneficial outcomes—the General Agreement on Tariffs and Trade (later the World Trade Organization, or WTO) has facilitated free trade and global economic growth, for example—but they, too, are limited by uncertain enforcement. Finally, increased international commerce has improved individual welfare around the world—if unevenly—and the mechanism of mutual dependence has been used in efforts to make war less likely between states. As an example, in the early post–World War II years, Germany and France established the European Coal and Steel Community (which later evolved into the European Union [EU]) with the intent of making war between them less likely. However, even in the area of trade, there have been disappointments. In 1910, Sir Norman Angell argued in *The Great Illusion* that economic interconnectedness had made war obsolete and conquest counterproductive; World War I broke out only four years later. Overall, the world wars in the middle of the twentieth century were great setbacks to the liberal vision. Enlightenment did not necessarily mean progress, and economic interdependence, democracy, and international institutions were not adequate to preserve the peace.

Perspectives and Practice. In the actual practice of American national security policy, it is often possible to discern a combination of realist and liberal influences at work. For example, an American school of thought known as *neoconservatism* achieved prominence and influence in the early twenty-first century. Neoconservatives, in common with realists, see the international environment as dangerous and as characterized more by conflict than by cooperation. Like realists, they put power at the center of their analyses and see it as the responsibility of the great powers—or, more precisely, the United States, as the world's only remaining superpower—to manage world affairs and to provide what peace and stability can be attained.[25] They are skeptical of the notion of an international community and of the idea that consensus among states that uphold different values confers meaningful legitimacy on foreign policy action. They also question the value of international law and international institutions, especially the United Nations, which has proven itself, in their view, to be the "guarantor of nothing."[26]

Despite these commonalities with a realist perspective, neoconservatism also incorporates strands of liberal thought, especially in viewing realism as ultimately inadequate because of its lack of moral vision. The use of US power should always be guided by moral values and should be used to promote "democracy, free markets, [and] respect for liberty."[27] Like many liberal-tradition thinkers, neoconservatives have argued that doing the morally right thing—such as supporting the development of liberal, democratic governments abroad—would also be the best way to promote US interests. Neoconservatives also share with at least some liberals the notion that the condition of international affairs is improvable, although their chosen means to do so is through the use of US power rather than through efforts to strengthen mechanisms of global governance. International institutions and international law, in the neoconservative worldview, often merely mask efforts of weak or undesirable actors to restrict US freedom of action.

The reader can evaluate the degree to which the neoconservative outlook reflects traditional American approaches to national security by consulting chapter 2. Here, it is sufficient to note that both realists and liberals challenge the neoconservative outlook, but for different reasons. As a first example, take the neoconservative claim that "America must be guided by its independent judgment, both about its own interest and the global interest."[28] Realists dismiss the notion of a "global interest" and would question the claim of any state that it possesses universal moral values and will act in accordance with them. Liberals question both the legitimacy of US claims to this decisionmaking authority and the ability of the United States to exercise it well. A second example is the neoconservative assertion that the United States is a uniquely benign global hegemon whose status validates its claim to world leadership.[29] Realists, who might question the importance of a benign status, are even more skeptical of the notion that the United States is capable of remaking the world in its own image. Liberals question whether the unilateral use of US power, particularly US military power, can succeed at promoting democracy and whether such an approach would preserve global perceptions that the United States is benign.

Whatever its future, neoconservatism has been charged with being excessively realist for its focus on material power and US national interests, as well as excessively idealist in its agenda of democracy promotion abroad.[30] It has also been widely criticized for providing the rationale for increased unilateralism and the justification for the US decision to invade Iraq in 2003. Although US policy makers seeking practical solutions to complex problems might draw on insights from a combination of the realist and liberal traditions, it is useful to probe the contradictions that a blending of these two worldviews can create.

Constructivism. In addition to realism and liberalism, a third worldview is *constructivism*. Scholars working within this paradigm examine the potential importance of nonmaterial as well as material factors in shaping situations and affecting outcomes. For example, Alexander Wendt rejects the realist emphasis on the distribution of material capabilities, arguing instead that relative material capabilities affect behavior only in the context of amity or enmity between the actors involved. For example, the imbalance of power between the United States and Canada does not foster the same sense of insecurity that is created by the imbalance between India and Pakistan (a topic explored further in chapter 19). Shared knowledge and the practices of the actors involved are also important to understanding how states will behave in any given situation.[31]

Besides illuminating the potential importance of nonmaterial factors in shaping the relations among states, an additional constructivist contribution is its ability to provide an explanation for change. The constructivist asserts that identity not only shapes but is also shaped by social interactions over time. Because change may occur at a level of values and fundamental interests rather than just at the level of behavior, the fundamental character of international politics could change due to interactions among states affecting the identities of the actors involved.

The constructivist view of international relations aids in the examination of a number of issues of potential significance to national security. For example, constructivism focuses attention on questions of identity, such as the content of a state's strategic culture, which may help to explain a state's behavior.[32] Similarly, constructivists consider the role of international norms, such as those that govern state intervention into the affairs of other states, to evaluate how these norms may shape behavior as well as how they have evolved over time.[33] Constructivists also examine socialization processes—such as the interaction of states in international institutions—for their potential explanatory power.[34] Constructivism offers an additional worldview for understanding the behavior of key actors in international politics.

Key Concepts

This section introduces five concepts that are essential tools to critical and analytical thinking about international politics: anarchy, sovereignty, levels of analysis, power, and non-state actors.

Anarchy. As used in international relations, the term *anarchy* refers not to mere disorder but instead to a lack of formal and authoritative global government. It is the existence of anarchy that distinguishes international politics from the domestic realm. Although international institutions may provide some degree of governance within particular issue areas, in the world today, there is no single authority that can arbitrate disagreements and enforce the decisions that result from such arbitration.

The traditions of international relations discussed above agree on the existence of anarchy; they disagree on its implications. For such realists as Thomas Hobbes, where there is no overarching authority, there is no law and no peace, because individuals must constantly compete with one another merely to survive.[35] Among states in a condition of anarchy, one should expect constant suspicion and the ever-present possibility of war. For liberals such as Locke, on the other hand, society is possible in the absence of a common authority. Instead of constant war, the state of nature is one of inconvenience because enforcement is uncertain. An implication of this view is that states can form some type of rudimentary society in which, even in the absence of world government, they can cooperate to achieve mutual gains.[36] For constructivists, either the realist or the liberal outcome is possible, depending on the identities of the states involved and the social context of their interactions.

Sovereignty. The contemporary conception of *sovereignty* dates to the Peace of Westphalia in 1648, which many mark as the origin of the modern state system. A series of treaties intended to bring to a close a bloody period of religious conflict, the Peace of Westphalia also reflected a desire to limit future wars by establishing the principle of sovereignty. In essence, sovereignty means that each state has total authority over its own population within its own territory. Modern recognition of sovereignty can be found in the UN Charter. This document recognizes the "sovereign equality" of all of the member states of the United Nations and affirms that "nothing contained in the present Charter shall authorize the United Nations to intervene in matters which are essentially within the domestic jurisdiction of any state."[37]

Many important national security issues involve the concept of sovereignty. First, the idea of sovereignty implies the formal legal equality of the world's more than 190 states. Although this is recognized in the UN General Assembly, where each state gets one vote, it is qualified in the UN Security Council, where each of the five permanent great-power members gets a veto. States may be legally equal, but relative power also shapes how they interact. Another issue is the contrast between the ideal of sovereignty and the fact that many of the world's states lack sufficient capacity to exercise full control over their own populations and territories. This shortcoming in governance creates a variety of transnational and human security concerns, and it also makes it more difficult to resolve them. Limits to sovereignty are another area of concern. For example, the Convention on the Prevention and Punishment of the Crime of Genocide, which went into force in 1951, commits the contracting states to "undertake to prevent and to punish" acts of genocide.[38] This international agreement makes clear that genocide, perhaps the most egregious form of human rights violation, will justify an intervention by states into another state's affairs.

In the twenty-first century, notions of the extent and limitations of sovereignty have continued to evolve with the introduction of the "Responsibility to Protect" (R2P). According to this concept, "Sovereignty no longer exclusively protects states from foreign interference; it is a charge of responsibility that holds states accountable for the welfare of their people."[39] This idea reinforces sovereignty by placing the primary onus on states to ensure the security and well-being of their populations. When a state fails to do so, however, R2P calls for other member states of the United Nations to take action against that state; R2P thus sets a limit on state sovereignty.

As a matter of practice, state sovereignty has never been absolute. Long after the Peace of Westphalia, there have been countless examples of strong states pursuing their national interests by involving themselves in the affairs of weaker ones. In the twentieth and early twenty-first centuries, sovereignty has increasingly come into question in cases where states are predatory toward their own populations or simply unable to protect them. As states decide when to intervene in the internal affairs of other states, in response either to security concerns or to violations of human rights, the value of preserving the ideal of sovereignty as a limiting force in international conflict should be carefully weighed.

Levels of Analysis. Introduced by Waltz in *The Man, the State, and War* in 1959 as the three "images" of international relations, the concept of *levels of analysis* has become a common organizing framework for thinking about the causes of outcomes in international politics.[40] In simplified terms, the causes of international developments can be thought of as stemming from individuals, from domestic factors, or from the international system as a whole. Although one or another may have greater explanatory power in a given instance, all may bear on a given case. Clarity about the source—or sources—of the key influences at work in any given situation is important, as it will have implications for potential policy responses and will aid in assessing their likely effectiveness.

Individual Level of Analysis. One place to look for causes of events is at the individual level of analysis. For example, some argue that war will always be a part of the human experience because the tendency toward competition and violence is intrinsic to human nature. A number of leading realist thinkers, from Thucydides to Hans Morgenthau, have expressed this view. Although perhaps plausible, this perspective cannot provide a complete account, because an unchanging human nature cannot explain variations in war and peace over time. Other explanations that can be more helpful in accounting for variation draw upon the role of psychological factors or even specific personalities. As a case in point, analysts argue that Saddam Hussein's personal characteristics played a role in the defeat of his regime at the hands of US-led coalition forces in 2003.[41] Caution is called for here as well: although the characteristics of individuals may often be important, a focus upon them must be accompanied by an explanation of the process through which individual motivations and dispositions are able to affect state action.

Domestic Level of Analysis. A second approach suggests that actions in international affairs are best understood as the product of the internal character of states. Vladimir Lenin's view of the imperialistic activities of capitalist states and his conviction that these tendencies would produce their downfall is an example of looking to the organization of the domestic political economy to explain state behavior.[42] He believed that tendencies toward wealth concentration and overproduction in capitalist states would inevitably lead them to exploit and dominate the underdeveloped areas of the world in an international struggle for markets, resources, and profits. As the potential colonial territory of the world diminished, Lenin predicted that increased competition would ultimately result in destructive wars among the imperial states and the end of the capitalist system.

Other possible characteristics of states that have been hypothesized to affect international behavior include their political institutions, culture, ideology, and bureaucratic and organizational politics. Democratic peace theory provides an example of the first two. Analysts seeking to explain why liberal democratic states do not war with one another emphasize either the characteristics of democratic institutions or the shared norms and values that promote the peaceful resolution of differences. Domestic political systems and political culture can also provide explanations for more aggressive foreign policy behavior, such as that of Russia under President Vladimir Putin.[43] The third characteristic mentioned above, ideology, can be defined as a set of "beliefs that give meaning to life" and "an explicit or implicit program of action."[44] An ideology that had particularly significant consequences for international peace and security was Nazism as exemplified in the German Third Reich. Finally, numerous scholars have examined the manner in which bureaucratic politics within a government and the characteristics of large government organizations can influence state behavior.[45]

International Level of Analysis. A third way to understand actions or outcomes in international politics is in terms of the international system as a whole. Accepting anarchy as a starting point, those who look to the international system generally focus on one of two categories—process or structure.

Those who look to *process* examine the interactions of states or the transnational forces that are not clearly motivated by or confined within particular states. An example of the focus on state interaction is provided by theorists who examine the ways in which international institutions can affect state behavior. Given the existence of self-interested states in an anarchic system, it may nevertheless be possible to structure their interactions through institutions so that cooperation is more likely.[46] An example of the focus on transnational forces is provided by scholars and policy makers who argue for the importance of globalization. Although there is no single agreed-upon definition, *globalization* is generally seen as an ongoing process that decreases the significance of state borders.[47] Enabled by reductions in costs of transport and communication, new technologies, and the policy choices of many of the world's political leaders, international trade is increasing, international flows of capital are on the rise, the nature of international business activity is changing, and there is a tremendous diffusion of cultural forms. It may be difficult to point to globalization as the specific cause of any one event or outcome, but its processes are arguably changing the character of international politics by altering the relative economic power of states, raising the salience of certain transnational concerns, increasing the challenges of global governance, and empowering new actors. As globalization offers new opportunities for individuals, organizations, and states, it also brings new security challenges.[48]

In addition to process, analyses of the *structure* of the international system can also be useful for understanding international politics. The clearest formulation of this is in Waltz's *Theory of International Politics* (1979). He argues that as long as anarchy exists and two or more actors seek to survive, it is possible to understand a lot about the nature of international politics merely by knowing the number of great powers in the international system.[49] For instance, in a world with one great power that outstrips all others, or *unipole* (as is arguably the case with the United States today), other powers will seek to balance against that dominant state. At the same time, the unipole will be tempted into an overactive role in the world because its power is unchecked.[50] Waltz's argument is helpful in illuminating general tendencies, but it is unlikely to yield the specific, context-sensitive prescriptions needed by policy makers.

Power. Despite the central importance of the concept of power, there is no universally accepted definition. This stems in part from four aspects of power that make it difficult to settle on a single formulation. First, power is dynamic. New instruments of power have appeared continuously over the centuries, and new applications for old forms are always being found. The collapse of the Soviet Union in the early 1990s provides an example of the manner in which a particular state's power can change dramatically over time.

In addition to being dynamic, power is also relative, situational, and at least partially *subjective*. Power is relative because its utility depends in part on comparing it with whatever opposes it, and it is situational because what may generate power in a particular set of circumstances may not do so in another. Even a less-developed country can achieve surprising results under a strong political leadership that is able to engender sacrifice and a sense of purpose among its people. The defeat of the French in Vietnam in 1954 and the subsequent failure of the US intervention to support South Vietnam, which fell to North Vietnam in 1975, are classic cases. Large, capable conventional military formations may struggle in irregular warfare, and long-range, precision strike capabilities, which may be very effective against an adversary's armor formations, can prove less useful in trying to stop an adversary who is conducting ethnic cleansing. Finally, power is at least partially subjective in that a reputation for being powerful may be sufficient to achieve results without an actual application of that power.

In spite of these complexities, it is nevertheless possible to consider power in terms of its relatively objective characteristics—that is, in terms of specific capabilities. One of the classic definitions of power comes from Hans Morgenthau in *Politics among Nations* (1954). Power, he says, is a product of: geography, natural resources, industrial capacity, military preparedness, technology and innovations, leadership, quantity and quality of armed forces, population, national character, national morale, quality of diplomacy, and quality of government.[51] Morgenthau argues that an assessment requires analyzing each factor, associated trends, and how these trends are likely to interact over time.[52] Waltz, in his definition introduced above, emphasizes only seven elements. Although simpler, Waltz's formulation is similar to Morgenthau's in that neither can fully resolve difficulties in assessment stemming from imperfect information, weighting, and aggregation. Because of these difficulties, even careful efforts to assess and measure relative power will always be accompanied by uncertainty.

In the parlance of some observers of international relations, power defined as capabilities is also known as *hard power*, to distinguish it from a competing concept, *soft power*. Originally coined by Nye, the term *soft power* refers to "the ability to achieve desired outcomes in international affairs through attraction rather than coercion." He explains that "it works by convincing others to follow, or getting them to agree to, norms and institutions that produce the desired behavior. If a state can make its power legitimate in the perception of others and establish international institutions that encourage them to channel or limit their activities, it may not need to expend many of its costly traditional economic or military resources."[53] Urging that power need not be thought of as an end in itself, but rather as a means to further US interests and values, Nye argues that the power of attraction and legitimacy can help the United States to secure these interests and values at lesser cost. Skeptics, on the other hand, argue that soft power will tend to have little or no force in shaping the behavior of other states when they have important interests at stake.

In 2007, Nye was the co-chair of a bipartisan group of distinguished policy practitioners who argued that hard power and soft power were each inadequate when deployed alone. What the United States needed instead was a "skillful combination of both," in what the group called "smart power."[54] To make the most of its power resources, a state should seek to integrate the use of hard power capabilities such as military force with soft power instruments such as diplomatic efforts to build coalitions and to enhance legitimacy. According to Nye, smart power "refers to the ability to combine hard and soft power into effective strategies in varying contexts."[55]

Assessing national power is an art, not a science; any specific assessment will be open to a variety of challenges. National security analysts in and out of public office cannot escape the task of identifying an ill-defined and moving target and of accounting for that which is often not adequately measured. Policy makers in Washington and the rest of the world must act, however scant and unreliable their information may be. Power, in one sense or another, is generally a central feature of the analyses behind their actions.

Practical Assessments of Power. When decision makers actually assess power, they do so in specific contexts. They do not engage in some general theoretical exercise but in a specific situational analysis: *who* is involved, over *what issue*, *where*, and *when*? Taking each of these questions in turn, the *who* element is crucial. States differ in both the quantity and quality of resources available to them. Health, education, motivation, and other factors confound attempts to establish reliable equivalency ratios between and among different states. Although no government can make something from nothing, some have the organizational, managerial, technical, scientific, and leadership skills that enable them to make much more with equal or lesser amounts of similar resources. Israel, for example, has held its own during several wars against adversaries many times its size.

This leads to the second element of situational analysis, namely, the issue. Whatever it may be, whether or not national leaders are able to pursue it depends largely on public support or lack thereof. All governments depend on at least the passive support of their citizens in order to function, and none can expect to endure once it has lost that minimum loyalty embodied in the term *legitimacy.* As long as a government satisfies the minimum expectations of the politically active or potentially active members of its society, there is little chance of internal upheaval.[56] Mobilizing resources to apply to national security tasks requires more than passive support, however; it necessitates some degree of sacrifice and active involvement. For some issues, such support may be difficult to muster; others have an almost electrifying effect upon a nation's consciousness, eliciting enormous willingness to sacrifice. The attack on Pearl Harbor in 1941 had such an effect on the American people; the terrorist attacks on 9/11 arguably did as well, at least initially. The morass of Vietnam had little such support even at the outset and, like the war in Iraq begun in 2003, gradually generated opposition rather than support. Most national security issues lie between these extreme poles of support and dissent. In these cases, leaders must build support for those tasks they believe important or else resign themselves to impotence.

The third situational feature of power is geographic: *where* events take place. All states are capable of making some sort of splash somewhere in the pool of world politics, normally in their own immediate neighborhoods. No matter how large the splash, however, its effects tend to dissipate with distance from the source.

The ability to apply resources at a distance sufficient to overcome the resistance generated by those closer to the conflict has always characterized great powers; it continues to provide a useful test to appraise claimants to that status.

This introduces the final situational feature of power, *time*. The interplay of leaders' ambitions and creativity, changes in resources, technological developments, and the public response to challenges all work to effect a continual redistribution of global power. Empires acquired to the great satisfaction of their builders have overtaxed successors' abilities to maintain them, resulting not only in the loss of domain but in the collapse of the founding unit as well. The Soviet Union's demise makes this point dramatically. Similarly, the haphazard and unfocused expenditure of resources in a variety of smaller-scale foreign ventures may ultimately produce a long-term drain that adversely affects areas of national life not originally thought vulnerable. This latter concern about a gradual dissipation of national power motivated some domestic critics of US activism abroad during the 1990s and into the early twenty-first century.

Application of Power. Power for its own sake can be likened to money in the hands of a miser; it may delight its owner, but it is of little consequence to the world because it is applied to no useful purpose. The American experience between the two world wars in many ways resembles such a situation. In profound isolation, the United States forfeited its initiative in world affairs to other states, principally to the traditional European powers and Japan. The reputation of the United States as a significant military power, established in the Spanish-American War and World War I, plus its geographic advantage of being separated from other great powers by oceans, protected the country and its interests during this period. But reputation is a fleeting thing, especially for great powers that are identified in their own time with the existing world order. Opponents' steamship and bomber technology could partially overcome the protective barrier of the oceans, while a foreign policy of isolationism eroded the American military reputation. Pearl Harbor and four very expensive years of war were the result of ignoring the relevance and uses of power.

The purpose of power is to overcome resistance in order to bring about or secure a preferred order of things. When the resistance is generated by other human beings, the purpose of power is to persuade those others to accept the designs or preferences in question or to destroy their ability to offer continued resistance. Depending upon the importance attached to the goal, the capabilities available to the respective protagonists, the skills they possess in applying those capabilities, the vulnerabilities each has in other areas, and the history of conflict between them, the techniques of persuasion can take two principal forms: rewards or punishments. *Rewards* are of two types: the presentation of some benefit in exchange for the desired reaction or the willingness to forgo negative behavior in exchange for compliance. Threats can be a component of this latter use of rewards to persuade because unless and until the threatening actor delivers on its threat, no actual harm has occurred. Either type of reward will work as long as all parties concerned feel they are getting something worthy of the exchange or are minimizing their losses in a situation where all the alternatives appear worse.

When nations in a dispute decide to carry out a threat, or to initiate negative action without prior threat, they are seeking to persuade through *punishment* or *coercion*. Such persuasion works only if the actor being punished can avert its predicament by compliance. Therefore the threatened punishment, its timing, and its application must be chosen carefully in order to achieve the desired effect. To punish indiscriminately not only squanders resources, thereby driving up costs, but may also be counterproductive in that it antagonizes and sharpens resistance by forcing a change in the perception of stakes.

Since the early 1990s, US negotiations with North Korea over the status of its nuclear weapons program provide examples of rewards and punishment. The United States has been willing to offer North Korea aid and other incentives for verifiable disarmament. At the same time, the United States has imposed an economic embargo and various degrees of economic sanctions on North Korea as punishment for its nuclear weapon and missile testing activities. (For more on the North Korean nuclear situation, see chapter 18.)

Nonstate Actors. Globalization has increased the significance of non-state actors to American national security. Key non-state actors include intergovernmental organizations (IGOs), nongovernmental organizations (NGOs), multinational corporations, the media, and religious groups. This category also includes groups once primarily thought of as subnational, such as labor unions and political parties, which now have extensive international connections. Violent entities, such as criminal organizations and terrorist groups, are also non-state actors.

Intergovernmental Organizations. An IGO is a multinational body whose members are states. These organizations may be relatively global in scale, as exemplified by the United Nations (193 members), the World Bank (188), the International Monetary Fund (188), and the World Trade Organization (162). However, IGOs can also be regional organizations, such as the European Union (28), the African Union (54), and the Association of Southeast Asian Nations (ASEAN, 10).[57] The purposes of IGOs vary widely and may include the coordination of policies relating to security, trade, currency exchange, communications, or economic development.

Nongovernmental Organizations. NGOs are non-state entities that may operate domestically or abroad. Some NGOs rely on financial support from donor states, while others raise funds through individual and corporate donations. Well-known NGOs include humanitarian aid organizations such as Médecins Sans Frontières (Doctors Without Borders) and the International Committee of the Red Cross. Many NGOs focus on specific goals, such as providing vaccinations for children, reducing communicable diseases, or expanding educational opportunities for girls. NGOs play a critical role in international development, as they often address problems that less-developed states are unable or unwilling to tackle on their own. NGOs may disburse funds on behalf of a developed state when local authorities are not trusted to spend foreign aid appropriately. The United States Agency for International Development is the primary liaison between the US government and a number of NGOs with which it shares certain goals and which it supports financially.

Multinational Corporations. Multinational corporations (MNCs), such as Coca-Cola, Royal Dutch Shell, and De Beers, are motivated primarily by profits. Accordingly, MNCs tend to be more loyal to their shareholders than to the states in which they operate. Due to their sheer size and wealth, MNCs can be powerful actors. Many underdeveloped states provide tax benefits and waive financial restrictions, environmental regulations, and labor laws to attract them. The resulting arrangement can spark local resentment at the power of the MNCs and constrain the local government's ability to pursue other socially desirable goals.

The Mass Media. The mass media play an important role in raising awareness of international security issues. Television coverage of humanitarian disasters, for example, often mobilizes private donations to relief organizations, such as the International Committee of the Red Cross. As relief organizations often arrive on the ground long before any other form of international response, the media's role in attracting attention to a brewing crisis is critical. Media coverage can often spur donor states into action as well, as voters exert political pressure on their government to "do something" about the horrendous images of starving children or devastated villages appearing on their televisions. The media are a fickle presence, however; their goal is to keep consumers interested, and thus coverage tends to decline rapidly once the initial reporting begins to lose its impact.

Religious Groups. Religion will likely continue to play an important role in international affairs, as well as in the domestic affairs of various states. Obvious examples from the perspective of US national security are al Qaeda and the Islamic State in Iraq and the Levant (ISIL), which have invoked particular interpretations of Islam as the justifications for their actions. Another example comes from before the end of the Cold War, when the Catholic Church in Poland played a critical role in the delegitimization of communism in that country. Religious groups may also compete over treasured holy sites, which is part of what makes competing Israeli and Palestinian claims over Jerusalem seem so irreconcilable (see chapter 20 for more on this conflict).

Subnational Groups. Multiple interest groups exist in every state, large or small. These groups may be organized around social or economic class, ethnicity, religion, geography, trade, or other identity. Some of these groups fit neatly within the borders of a particular state, but many do not. Ethnic groups are often dispersed across several states, and in some cases, an individual's sense of ethnic identity may be stronger than his or her identity as a citizen of any state. Social unrest and political instability may result when the majority of people in an interest group feel that their group identity is more important than their national identity. In some cases, the actions of such interest groups may undermine state sovereignty. For example, in many states that gained their independence after colonization, political borders were often determined by negotiation between great powers with little to no consideration of ethnic groups. As a result, the traditional homelands of many ethnic groups now sit astride two or more states. (See chapter 20 for the impact of this in the Middle East and chapter 21 for a discussion of sub-Saharan Africa.)

Violent Nonstate Actors: Political Opposition, Terrorism, and Crime. It is critical to understand the role of violent non-state actors, because the very existence of such groups poses a direct challenge to international stability and state authority.[58] Globalization has facilitated the growth of such groups, which, like businesses, have benefited from advances in information technology and transportation. Secure communications, ready availability of arms and other supplies, access to global financial markets, global recruitment opportunities, and the increasing ease of international travel have allowed these groups to operate as transnational entities. The increasing sophistication of violent non-state actors—including violent political opposition groups, terrorist organizations, and international criminal networks—has created new dangers and a greater need for cooperation among states. Terrorism as a national security challenge is discussed in greater depth in chapter 14 and in several of the regional chapters in part IV of this volume.

International Relations Theory and National Security Policy

Most international relations theories can be associated with the traditions of realism, liberalism, or constructivism, but theories are more specific than these broad perspectives. A theory consists of assumptions, key concepts, propositions about causal relationships, and an articulation of the conditions under which the theory can be expected to hold. These elements should be sufficiently clear so that the theory can be subjected to testing. Two examples from the realist perspective include balance of power theory, which looks at expectations of state behavior given different relative power situations, and the theory of hegemonic stability, which examines the manner in which a single dominant power in the international system can foster an open system of international trade.[59] Two liberal tradition examples are neoliberal institutionalism, which examines the role of international institutions in fostering cooperation, and democratic peace theory, which seeks to explain peaceful relations among democracies. A theory is useful to the extent that it contributes to describing, explaining, and predicting international events and has implications for policy prescription.

When approaching a particular national security problem or situation, every policy maker has a theory. It may be held more or less consciously and be more or less carefully specified, but it always exists. According to Walt, "Theory is an essential tool of statecraft. Many policy debates ultimately rest on competing theoretical visions, and relying on a false or flawed theory can lead to major foreign policy disasters."[60] As an example, Walt gives the "infamous 'risk theory'" of German Admiral Alfred von Tirpitz before World War I. His theory held that Germany's ability to threaten British naval supremacy would cause Great Britain to accept Germany's preeminence on the continent. In fact, the opposite proved to be true. As a more recent example, advocates of the US war in Iraq in 2003 "believed war would lead to a rapid victory, encourage neighboring regimes to 'bandwagon' with the United States, hasten the spread of democracy in the region, and ultimately undermine support for Islamic terrorism. Their opponents argued that the war would have exactly the opposite effects."[61] As Walt goes on to explain, theories can help to illuminate propositions about the fundamental dynamics of international relations.

A contemporary situation that shows the significant policy implications of theoretical differences is the rise of China. A realist balance-of-power theorist would expect an increasingly powerful China to become more assertive and begin to pose a possible threat to its neighbors. As a counter, the theorist would argue that the United States should shore up regional alliance arrangements and potentially increase various facets of its own power. A neoliberal institutionalist, on the other hand, might focus on China's increasing engagement in regional and international institutions and thus recommend policies to encourage and reward this engagement as a way of fostering the cooperative pursuit of common interests and reinforcing the value that China places on peaceful relations. A constructivist might argue that China's future behavior will be decisively governed by the dominant Chinese "national ideas about how to achieve foreign policy goals" and the extent to which these ideas are achieving success.[62] If China's current policies meet setbacks, and alternative national ideas are present within important Chinese domestic constituencies (emphasizing, for example, separation from or the revision of the international system), China's policy approach could be expected to change in potentially dangerous or disruptive ways. (For more on China, see chapter 18.)

Although it might be frustrating for a policy maker to be given such contrasting visions of important policy problems, the preservation of multiple perspectives is invaluable. These competing explanations and prescriptions suggest a continuing need to engage with available evidence and to test reality when making critical policy choices.

Characteristics of the Current International System

One way to examine the nature of the international system today is to focus on globalization and its effects. The economic, cultural, and political processes associated with globalization are likely to lessen the significance of state borders over time, change the relative power among states, increase the importance of non-state actors, and contribute to the challenges associated with global governance. Although a state can still decide to close itself off as much as possible to the outside world—North Korea is a dramatic example—the costs of doing so are increasing (see chapter 18).

The forces of globalization do not have purely positive or purely negative effects. In economic terms, although technological diffusion, increased trade, and increasingly international capital flows have improved the welfare of millions of people around the world, all countries and individuals are not able to benefit equally. Even within countries, the benefits from an increasingly open international trading system are not evenly shared. In addition to economic effects, the forces of globalization can be disruptive or even unwelcome to traditional societies in which rapid change may be difficult to assimilate and can empower violent non-state actors.[63]

Despite the importance of globalization, states will remain the key actors in international politics for the foreseeable future. For one thing, both independently and through actions in such international institutions as the World Trade Organization, the decisions made by states will affect the pace and nature of globalization. In addition, until or unless more effective institutions of global governance are constructed, states will remain the actors most capable of solving most problems.[64] Even individuals or groups with a transnational agenda generally need to work with or through states to realize their goals. Any who are tempted to take a determinist view of the impact of globalization would be wise to keep in mind the capabilities and political choices of states.

Even as the process of globalization continues, competing conceptions of international order persist. As former Secretary of State Henry Kissinger points out, "Our age is insistently, at times almost desperately, in pursuit of a concept of world order. Chaos threatens side by side with unprecedented interdependence: in the spread of weapons of mass destruction, the disintegration of states, the impact of environmental depredations, the persistence of genocidal practices, and the spread of new technologies threatening to drive conflict beyond human control or comprehension."[65] Kissinger argues that the closest thing to a global order today stems from the mechanisms of the Peace of Westphalia, which included an embrace of sovereignty and an acceptance of the need to maintain state independence through the preservation of a balance of power. In the centuries that followed the initial agreements in 1648, the countries of Western Europe played a critical role in expanding these ideas to other continents. However, he also points out that these were practical solutions to the problems of a specific region of the world at a particular moment of its history. Even at the time, competing conceptions of the basis of international order existed in Russia, China, and the Muslim world; challenges to the principles embedded in the Westphalian system continue today.[66]

In recent decades, a diffusion of power among the major states in the international system has further fueled questions about the legitimacy of current mechanisms for global governance. Kissinger writes:

> A reconstruction of the international system is the ultimate challenge to statesmanship in our time. The penalty for failing will be . . . an evolution into spheres of influence identified with particular domestic structures and forms of governance—for example, the Westphalian model as against the radical Islamist version. At its edges each

> sphere would be tempted to test its strength against other entities of orders deemed illegitimate. . . . A struggle between regions could be more debilitating than the struggle between nations has been.[67]

Kissinger notes that the United States, which has played a central leadership role in advancing a particular conception of international order since the mid-twentieth century, has an important role to play in the development of an international order that responds adequately to the demands of the twenty-first century.

The US government has recognized the significance of these issues to American national security, as the 2015 edition of US *National Security Strategy* explains in a chapter entitled "International Order": "The modern-day international system currently relies heavily on an international legal architecture, economic and political institutions, as well as alliances and partnerships the United States and other like-minded nations established after World War II." The document asserts that the United States must "reaffirm" this system as well as help it to evolve.[68] Whether or not the international system that the United States helped build can be adapted in the coming decades of the twenty-first century to continue to serve US national interests—as well as to serve as a basis for international order on a global scale—remains to be seen.[69] There are early indicators that the presidential administration of Donald J. Trump, with its "America First" foreign policy, will place less value on multilateralism in US foreign policy than the administrations that preceded it (see chapter 25).

Despite important changes in the international strategic environment of the United States over time, there are also constants. One of the most important of these is that the United States always has and always will face the need to balance the limited means it is willing to devote to national security policy with the ends it seeks to pursue. The traditional American approaches likely to shape this balance are the subject of chapter 2; the manner in which the United States has managed, or not managed, to strike this balance over time is the subject of chapter 3. Whether one assesses the current and future international environment as extremely threatening or relatively benign, the challenges faced by US policy makers in balancing US national security needs with other interests and domestic priorities remain great.

Discussion Questions

1. Define the terms *national security* and *human security*. Are there any tensions between these two concepts?
2. What is the realist worldview? What are strengths and weakness of the realist perspective on international politics?
3. What does balance of power theory predict? Provide examples of balance of power theory in action.
4. What are the main mechanisms through which adherents of the liberal tradition believe that peace can be furthered in international politics? What are their strengths and weaknesses?
5. What is the constructivist critique of the idea that anarchy causes security competition among states?

6. What is *national power*? Can you quantify national power? How?

7. What is *soft power*? Is soft power important in explaining the US role in the world? Why or why not?

8. Given the rising significance of non-state actors in a globalizing world, how would one argue that states remain the primary actors in international politics?

9. How important are theories of international relations to policy makers? Should they be? Why or why not?

10. What are the most important characteristics of the international strategic environment of the United States today?

Recommended Reading

Allison, Graham T., and Philip Zelikow. *Essence of Decision: Explaining the Cuban Missile Crisis*. 2nd ed. New York: Longman, 1999.

Art, Robert J., and Robert Jervis. *International Politics: Enduring Concepts and Contemporary Issues*. 12th ed. Boston: Pearson, 2014.

Bhagwati, Jagdish. *In Defense of Globalization*, with a new afterword. New York: Oxford University Press, 2007.

Bull, Hedley. *The Anarchical Society*. 4th ed. New York: Columbia University Press, 2012.

Doyle, Michael W. *Ways of War and Peace: Realism, Liberalism, and Socialism*. New York: W. W. Norton, 1997.

Fukuyama, Francis. *America at the Crossroads: Democracy, Power, and the Neoconservative Legacy*. New Haven, CT: Yale University Press, 2006.

George, Alexander. *Bridging the Gap: Theory and Practice in Foreign Policy*. Washington, DC: US Institute of Peace Press, 1993.

Keohane, Robert O. *After Hegemony: Cooperation and Discord in the World Political Economy*. Princeton, NJ: Princeton University Press, 2005.

Keohane, Robert O., and Joseph S. Nye Jr. *Power and Interdependence*. 4th ed. Boston: Longman, 2011.

Kissinger, Henry. *Diplomacy*. New York: Simon & Schuster, 1994.

———. *World Order*. New York: Penguin, 2014.

Mearsheimer, John J. *The Tragedy of Great Power Politics*. New York: W. W. Norton, 2001.

Morgenthau, Hans. *Politics among Nations: The Struggle for Power and Peace*. 2nd ed., rev. and enl. New York: Knopf, 1954.

Nye, Joseph S., Jr. *The Future of Power*. New York: PublicAffairs, 2011.

Russett, Bruce M. *Grasping the Democratic Peace: Principles for a Post–Cold War World*. Princeton, NJ: Princeton University Press, 1995.

Thucydides. *History of the Peloponnesian War*. Translated by Rex Warner. New York: Penguin, 1972.

Walt, Stephen M. *Origins of Alliances*. Ithaca, NY: Cornell University Press, 1987.

———. *Taming American Power: The Global Response to U.S. Primacy*. New York: W. W. Norton, 2005.

Waltz, Kenneth N. *Man, the State, and War: A Theoretical Analysis*. New York: Columbia University Press, 1959.

———. *Theory of International Politics*. New York: McGraw-Hill, 1979.

Wendt, Alexander. *Social Theory of International Politics*. New York: Cambridge University Press, 1999.

Internet Resources

The United Nations, www.un.org
US Central Intelligence Agency *World Factbook*, www.cia.gov/library/publications/the-world-factbook/index.html
US Department of State, www.state.gov
The White House, www.whitehouse.gov
World Trade Organization, www.wto.org

Notes

1. The White House, *The National Security Strategy of the United States of America* (Washington, DC: The White House, February 2015), 2.

2. For a helpful discussion, see "Appendix I: Guidelines for Strategy Formulation," in *U.S. Army War College Guide to National Security Policy and Strategy*, 5th ed., ed. J. Boone Bartholomees Jr. (Carlisle Barracks, PA: Strategic Studies Institute, 2012), 2:413–18.

3. See, for example, Thomas F. Homer-Dixon, *Environment, Scarcity, and Violence* (Princeton, NJ: Princeton University Press, 1999); Ole Waever et al., *Identity, Migration, and the New Security Agenda in Europe* (New York: St. Martin's Press, 1993); and National Intelligence Council, *Global Trends 2030: Alternative Worlds*, NIC 2012-001 (Washington, DC: NIC, December 2012).

4. United Nations Trust Fund for Human Security, *Human Security in Theory and Practice: An Overview of the Human Security Concept and the United Nations Trust Fund for Human Security* (New York: United Nations, 2009), 5.

5. For a brief overview of the human security agenda, see Des Gasper and Oscar A. Gómez, "Human Security—Twenty Years On," December 16, 2014, http://hdr.undp.org/en/content/human-security-%E2%80%93-twenty-years.

6. In the interests of space, and because of its decline over time, Marxism is not discussed here. For its basic tenets, see Robert Gilpin, "Three Ideologies of Political Economy," in *Understanding International Relations*, 5th ed., ed. Daniel J. Kaufman et al. (New York: McGraw-Hill, 2004), 426–28. For its translation into a theory of international relations, see V. I. Lenin, *Imperialism: The Highest Stage of Capitalism* (New York: International Publishers, 1939). Perhaps the Marxist perspective persists most strongly among dependency theorists who examine the role of the capitalist developed world in contributing to underdevelopment in other parts of the world. See Theotonio Dos Santos, "The Structure of Dependence," *American Economic Review: Papers and Proceedings* 9, no. 2 (1970): 231–36, and Kema Irogbe, "Globalization and the Development of Underdevelopment of the Third World," *Journal of Third World Studies* 22, no. 1 (2005): 41–68.

7. Kenneth N. Waltz, *Theory of International Politics* (New York: McGraw-Hill, 1979), 131.

8. Waltz, *Theory of International Politics*, 117.

9. Stephen M. Walt, *Origins of Alliances* (Ithaca, NY: Cornell University Press, 1987), 21–26.

10. See, for example, John J. Mearsheimer, *The Tragedy of Great Power Politics* (New York: W. W. Norton, 2001).

11. Peter J. Katzenstein, Robert O. Keohane, and Stephen D. Krasner, "International Organization and the Study of World Politics," *International Organization* 52, no. 4 (1998): 684–85.

12. Thucydides, *History of the Peloponnesian War*, trans. Rex Warner (New York: Penguin, 1972), 49.

13. John Locke, *The Second Treatise of Government*, ed. Thomas P. Peardon (New York: Macmillan, 1952), esp. 119–39.

14. Andrew Moravcsik, "Taking Preferences Seriously: A Liberal Theory of International Politics," *International Organization* 50, no. 4 (1997): 516.

15. Michael W. Doyle, "Kant, Liberal Legacies, and Foreign Affairs," *Philosophy and Public Affairs* 12, no. 3 (1983): 205–35; Michael W. Doyle, "Kant, Liberal Legacies, and Foreign Affairs, Part 2," *Philosophy and Public Affairs* 12, no. 4 (1983): 323–53.

16. Bruce Russett, *Grasping the Democratic Peace* (Princeton, NJ: Princeton University Press, 1993), 24–42.

17. Hans Morgenthau, *Politics among Nations: The Struggle for Power and Peace*, 2nd ed., rev. and enl. (New York: Knopf, 1954), 10.

18. Immanuel Kant, *Political Writings*, ed. Hans Reiss (Cambridge: Cambridge University Press, 1991), 41–53.

19. Kant, *Political Writings*, 93–130.

20. Robert O. Keohane and Lisa L. Martin, "The Promise of Institutionalist Theory," *International Security* 20, no. 1 (1995): 39–51; Robert O. Keohane, "Twenty Years of Institutional Liberalism," *International Relations* 26, no. 2 (2012): 125–38.

21. See Robert O. Keohane and Joseph S. Nye Jr., *Power and Interdependence*, 4th ed. (Boston: Longman, 2012), 19–21.

22. Declaration of Independence, www.archives.gov/national-archives-experience/charters/declaration_transcript.html.

23. United Nations, Universal Declaration of Human Rights, December 10, 1948, www.un.org/Overview/rights.html. For a discussion of contemporary challenges to the law of war, see Gary Solis, *The Law of Armed Conflict: International Humanitarian Law in War* (Cambridge: Cambridge University Press, 2010).

24. See Edward D. Mansfield and Jack Snyder, "Democratization and the Danger of War," *International Security* 20, no. 1 (1995): 5–38; and Edward D. Mansfield and Jack Snyder, *Electing to Fight: Why Emerging Democracies Go to War* (Cambridge, MA: MIT Press, 2005).

25. Charles Krauthammer, "The Unipolar Moment," *Foreign Affairs* 70, no. 1 (1990/1991): 29.

26. Krauthammer, "The Unipolar Moment," 25.

27. William Kristol and Robert Kagan, "Toward a Neo-Reaganite Foreign Policy," *Foreign Affairs* 75, no. 4 (1996): 27.

28. Charles Krauthammer, "The Unipolar Moment Revisited," *National Interest* 70 (Winter 2002/2003): 16.

29. Krauthammer, "The Unipolar Moment Revisited," 14.

30. Francis Fukuyama, "The Neoconservative Moment," *National Interest*, no. 76 (Summer 2004): 57–68. See also the response by Charles Krauthammer, "In Defense of Democratic Realism," *National Interest*, no. 77 (Fall 2004): 15–25.

31. Alexander Wendt, "Constructing International Politics," *International Security* 20, no. 1 (1995): 77–78.

32. For one example, see Alastair Iain Johnston, *Cultural Realism: Strategic Culture and Grand Strategy in Chinese History* (Princeton, NJ: Princeton University Press, 1995).

33. Martha Finnemore, *The Purpose of Intervention: Changing Beliefs about the Use of Force* (Ithaca, NY: Cornell University Press, 2003); for another examination of the role

of international norms, see Jeffrey W. Legro, *Cooperation under Fire: Anglo-German Restraint during World War II* (Ithaca, NY: Cornell University Press, 1995).

34. For a case study that tests this, see Alastair Iain Johnston, "Learning versus Adaptation: Explaining Change in Chinese Arms Control Policy in the 1980s and 1990s," *China Journal*, no. 35 (January 1996): 27–61.

35. Thomas Hobbes, *Leviathan*, ed. Michael Oakeshott (New York: Macmillan, 1962), 101.

36. See Hedley Bull, *The Anarchical Society*, 4th ed. (New York: Columbia University Press, 2012).

37. Charter of the United Nations, June 26, 1945, www.un.org/aboutun/charter.

38. The Office of the United Nations High Commissioner for Human Rights, Convention on the Prevention and Punishment of the Crime of Genocide, January 12, 1951, http://www.ohchr.org/EN/ProfessionalInterest/Pages/CrimeOfGenocide.aspx.

39. United Nations Office on Genocide Prevention and the Responsibility to Protect, "Responsibility to Protect," http://www.un.org/en/genocideprevention/about-responsibility-to-protect.html. This website references the Report of the International Commission on Intervention and State Sovereignty, *The Responsibility to Protect*, December 2001, http://responsibilitytoprotect.org/ICISS%20Report.pdf.

40. Kenneth N. Waltz, *Man, the State, and War* (New York: Columbia University Press, 1959), 12.l.

41. Kevin Woods, James Lacey, and Williamson Murray, "Saddam's Delusions: The View from the Inside," *Foreign Affairs* 85, no. 3 (2006): 2–26.

42. Lenin, *Imperialism*. See also John Hobson, *Imperialism* (London: Allen & Unwin, 1916).

43. See, for example, Andrei P. Tsygankov, "Assessing Cultural and Regime-Based Explanations of Russia's Foreign Policy: 'Authoritarian at Heart and Expansionist by Habit'?" *Europe-Asia Studies* 64, no. 4 (2012): 695–713.

44. Jerome D. Frank, *Sanity and Survival: Psychological Aspects of War and Peace* (New York: Random House, 1967), 109.

45. See the bureaucratic politics and organizational process models in Graham T. Allison and Philip Zelikow, *Essence of Decision: Explaining the Cuban Missile Crisis*, 2nd ed. (New York: Longman, 1999).

46. Robert Axelrod and Robert O. Keohane, "Achieving Cooperation under Anarchy: Strategies and Institutions," *World Politics* 38, no. 1 (1985): 226–54.

47. James Rosenau, "The Complexities and Contradictions of Globalization," *Current History* 96, no. 613 (1997): 360–64.

48. A particularly important shaper of opinion regarding globalization has been *New York Times* columnist Thomas L. Friedman; see Friedman, *The Lexus and the Olive Tree* (New York: Farrar, Straus and Giroux, 1999); and Friedman, *The World Is Flat: A Brief History of the Twenty-First Century* (New York: Farrar, Straus and Giroux, 2005). For an exploration of globalization's benefits, see Jagdish Bhagwati, *In Defense of Globalization*, with a new afterword (Oxford: Oxford University Press, 2007). For an example of the relationship between globalization and one specific transnational threat, see Fathali M. Moghaddam, *How Globalization Spurs Terrorism: The Lopsided Benefits of "One World" and Why That Fuels Violence* (Westport, CT: Praeger Security International, 2008).

49. Waltz, *Theory of International Politics*, 118.

50. Kenneth N. Waltz, "Structural Realism after the Cold War," *International Security* 25, no. 1 (2000): 5–41.

51. Morgenthau, *Politics among Nations*, 102–37.

52. Morgenthau, *Politics among Nations*, 138–52.

53. Joseph S. Nye Jr. and William A. Owens, "America's Information Edge," *Foreign Affairs* 75, no. 2 (1996): 21, fn. 1. See also Joseph S. Nye Jr., *Bound to Lead* (New York: Basic Books, 1990).

54. CSIS Commission on Smart Power, *A Smarter, More Secure America* (Washington, DC: Center for Strategic and International Studies [CSIS], 2007), 7.

55. Joseph S. Nye Jr. *The Future of Power* (New York: PublicAffairs, 2011), xiv.

56. Klaus Knorr, *Military Power and Potential* (Lexington, MA: Heath, 1970), 143.

57. Membership numbers are as of March 2016.

58. See Audrey Kurth Cronin, "Behind the Curve: Globalization and International Terrorism," *International Security* 27, no. 3 (2002/2003): 30–58.

59. The theory of hegemonic stability has both realist and liberal variants.

60. Stephen M. Walt, "The Relationship between Theory and Policy in International Relations," *Annual Review of Political Science* 8, no. 1 (2005): 23.

61. Walt, "The Relationship between Theory and Policy," 28–29. See also David A. Baldwin, "Success and Failure in Foreign Policy," *Annual Review of Political Science* 3, no. 1 (2000): 167–82.

62. Jeffrey W. Legro, "What China Will Want: The Future Intentions of a Rising Power," *Perspectives on Politics* 5, no. 3 (2007): 516.

63. For a discussion of the limitations and risks associated with globalization, see Stanley Hoffmann, "Clash of Globalizations," *Foreign Affairs* 81, no. 4 (2002): 104–15.

64. For an examination of increased intergovernmental cooperation as a response to globalization, see Anne-Marie Slaughter, *A New World Order* (Princeton, NJ: Princeton University Press, 2004).

65. Henry Kissinger, *World Order* (New York: Penguin Press, 2014), 2.

66. Kissinger, *World Order*, 4–8.

67. Kissinger, *World Order*, 371.

68. The White House, *National Security Strategy*, 23.

69. For the US role after World War II, see G. John Ikenberry, *After Victory: Institutions, Strategic Restraint, and the Rebuilding of Order after Major Wars* (Princeton, NJ: Princeton University Press, 2001), esp. 163–75. Expressing optimism that this order can be preserved even as power in the international system becomes more diffuse is G. John Ikenberry, "The Future of the Liberal World Order," *Foreign Affairs* 90, no. 3 (2011): 56–68.

2

Traditional American Approaches to National Security

Generalizations about distinctly American approaches to national security matters should be advanced with the same caution as all large generalizations. Americans are a heterogeneous group and tend to differ on policy issues along lines that may include age group, sex, party affiliation, region, socioeconomic status, education levels, religion, and ethnicity. Americans vary in their opinions on, for example, defense spending. At times of low defense budgets, some citizens have argued for greater armament; high defense budgets always have their antagonists. Even when the United States has been committed to war, a portion of society has been dedicated to pacifism. Invariably, some segment of the population has felt that the United States has committed to war at the wrong time, for the wrong cause, or in the wrong place.

Despite wide divergence in individual opinions, some central trends recur in the American approach to national security. For instance, except in times of war, Americans have traditionally focused much of their energy on the pursuit of private interests and consequently have viewed national security as a secondary matter. In part, this attitude has its roots in the political outlook of the country's founders, who—as Thomas Jefferson so famously articulated in the Declaration of Independence—saw that the purpose of government was to secure the rights of individuals to "Life, Liberty, and the pursuit of Happiness" as determined by each citizen.[1] For substantial periods of American history, a focus on private interests and domestic affairs was enabled by a geographic situation that left the United States relatively secure from great power competition and conflict. Once conscious of a threat, however, US attitudes have tended to shift quickly and dramatically.

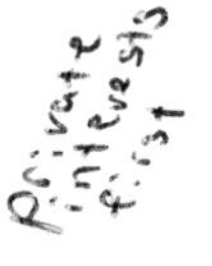

American attitudes toward foreign policy and national security affairs are affected both by "changes in the domestic and foreign political-economic situation involving the presence or absence of threat in varying degrees" and by "the character and predisposition of the population."[2] This chapter focuses on the latter variable, briefly examining certain tendencies of thought and action arising from the American experience and its historic context. The effects of domestic and foreign political developments, as well as economic trends, are examined elsewhere, especially in chapter 3.

Public Involvement and National Security Policy

Before discussing specific influences on US national security policy that flow from the historical experience and beliefs of Americans, it is useful to explore—in more general terms—the role that public opinion plays and should play in the national security policy process. Some view the involvement of the public in national security policy as detrimental. The realist position, for example, typically argues that foreign policy making should be reserved for the elites in society who are capable of making decisions secretly, effectively, and coherently.[3] Elites should either lead the public to support their chosen policies or ignore the public's preferences altogether.[4] The reasons for this are twofold. First, national security policy is so important that it must be controlled by the most knowledgeable people, who will make decisions based on rational calculations of the national interest. Public opinion is all too often uninformed and based on emotion. Second, decisions in the areas of foreign policy and national security are sometimes urgent and at other times require policy makers to take a long-term perspective. Public opinion will be an inadequate guide to action in either of these cases: it will be too slow to crystalize to be of use in a crisis and too mercurial to be of benefit in long-term strategic planning.

Of course, there are always multiple sides to important issues, and there are those who argue that public involvement not only is essential to democracy but can also improve policy formulation and sustainability. Although realists emphasize rational calculation, the starting point for the liberal view is the normative argument that policy should reflect the will and values of the people. A process that is open to democratic participation and accountability will not only be best for a particular society but may also produce more mutually beneficial interactions with other states. It is a core proposition of the liberal tradition in international affairs, for example, that liberal democracies tend to be more peaceful than nondemocracies, at least in their interactions with one another. This is in part because the public plays a constructive role in constraining policy makers.[5] A second way in which the involvement of the population can be beneficial is that public debate can help to clarify major issues. Some scholars have argued that public opinion is more stable and rational than the realist perspective allows.[6]

In addition to aiding policy formulation, public involvement may also be an asset in policy execution and sustainability. Public involvement is more likely to create harmony between popular opinion and government policy, which will tend to enhance legitimacy.[7] In addition, involvement of the public can help sustain support for the sacrifices that foreign and national security policies may entail.

The Importance of Values. Whatever the position taken on the desirable degree of public involvement, it is clear that any US security policy requiring sustained national sacrifices must be founded, in large part, upon basic public values. Although values are often imprecise, diverse, and apt to change, policy makers have a responsibility to clarify, interpret, synthesize, and articulate them as they bear upon particular foreign and national security issues. Policy makers must reconcile diverse perspectives and competing values in relation to a particular aspect of national security; a degree of compromise is often necessary. However, the values at stake in policy formulation cannot be ignored.[8]

One time-tested means of generating consensus, especially for the executive branch, is to couch policy in terms that command broad support within American society. Political leaders may seek to articulate their initiatives in terms of values so cherished by the polity that it would appear "un-American" to challenge them. This practice is generally recognized by policy makers as desirable and, on occasion, politically necessary. Examples include President Woodrow Wilson's call for moral action in foreign affairs, President Jimmy Carter's stress on human rights in American foreign policy, and President George W. Bush's declaration in 2002 that the United States would "actively work to bring the hope of democracy, development, free markets, and free trade to every corner of the world."[9] In remarks about the ongoing civil war in Syria in 2013, President Barack Obama conceded limits to US action abroad even as he acknowledged the imperative created by US values: "Our ideals and principles, as well as our national security, are at stake in Syria. . . . Terrible things happen across the globe, and it is beyond our means to right every wrong. But when, with modest effort and risk, we can stop children from being gassed to death, and thereby make our own children safer over the long run, I believe we should act. That's what makes America different. That's what makes us exceptional."[10] In these remarks, Obama appealed both to interests and to values as he sought support for his policy—a common rhetorical approach for US political leaders.

Public Opinion and Its Impact on National Security Policy. Although values are a significant influence on public opinion, current events and myriad sources of information, mostly outside of government, also have a profound impact. From within the government, it is the executive branch that traditionally has had the greatest ability to shape mass opinion. This corresponds to the leadership role of the president in national security affairs and reflects the information advantages held by the president as well as his or her ability to speak with a single voice.

The relative influence of the president may also be affected by the tendency for executive prerogative to grow in times of war or crisis. During the Cold War, for example, the decades-long threat of the Soviet Union and its satellites demanded focused leadership in Washington. This dynamic strengthened the presidency in its legislative and policy battles with Congress.[11] Likewise, immediately after the terrorist attacks on US soil of September 11, 2001, Congress again tended to defer to presidential leadership. The American public tends to unite—at least initially—behind decisive national security actions of the president in a phenomenon known as the "rally around the flag" effect. Good examples include the spike in public approval for President George H. W. Bush after he initiated the first Gulf War to expel the Iraqis from Kuwait in 1991 and the similar gains experienced by President George W. Bush after the initial invasion of Iraq in 2003.[12] However, these surges in support will be influenced by subsequent developments and often prove temporary.

In historical terms, public opinion has played a relatively limited role in the national security policy process—with a few notable exceptions. One of these exceptions is that, during periods not characterized by a single overriding security concern, public opinion can make the formulation of clear priorities and a coherent agenda problematic. Some have argued that this was characteristic of the 1990s.[13] Public opinion can also become powerful when particular national security policy issues become significant due to their perceived cost. The public's role and interest in American national security policy, for example, took a dramatic turn in the spring of 1968, when the casualties of the Vietnam War received significant publicity after the Tet offensive.[14] Although the Tet offensive was not a success in military terms for the North Vietnamese or their Viet Cong allies within South Vietnam, "It resulted in the critical turning point on the U.S. domestic front. Substantial numbers of prominent and influential figures became convinced that the American people were no longer willing to pay the price in casualties and dollars for continuing the war indefinitely in Vietnam."[15]

Although public opinion may be important to national security decision making, it is much too simple to say that it will have a decisive impact on policy choice. An interesting example is the relationship between public opinion and US military involvement in the Iraq War, which began with the US-led invasion in 2003. By December 2006, a CNN poll showed that 70 percent of Americans disapproved of the president's handling of the war, 54 percent thought that US troops should be withdrawn immediately or within the next year, and 50 percent said that they did not believe victory in Iraq was possible.[16] These numbers did not prevent George W. Bush from announcing what became known as the "Iraq surge" in January 2007, which involved sending additional military forces to Iraq, as well as other changes in strategy.[17] When Obama announced that he was pulling all US forces out of Iraq in 2011 (except for advisors attached to the US embassy in Baghdad), 75 percent of Americans approved this decision.[18] In the face of fairly consistent negative popular views on the Iraq War, two consecutive presidents nevertheless made different choices about US strategy and levels of investment in that conflict.

An influential study of past US popular support for war policy "demonstrates the importance of leadership and objective events and conditions in the level of the public's commitment to an ongoing military operation."[19] The study suggests that the most important sources of influence on US public opinion during a war are the actual progress of events, expectations for overall success, and the extent to which national leaders are united or divided on war policy. In turn, public opinion influences the future actions of elected leaders. The government both affects and is affected by many different voices over time.[20]

When the public becomes engaged in national security issues, Congress tends to respond with increased involvement in the national security policy process. For example, as the political salience of the Vietnam War grew in the late 1960s and early 1970s, many members of Congress became concerned with the erosion of congressional authority relating to the initiation and execution of the war. In response, Congress passed legislation specifically prohibiting the funding of US efforts in portions of Southeast Asia, as well as the War Powers Act.[21] As the legislation prohibiting funding demonstrates, Congress can shape ongoing military operations through the power of the purse. However, a prohibition on funding is a blunt instrument and a difficult one to wield when US armed forces are already in combat. A member of Congress can oppose a war and yet feel duty bound to vote for supplies for the troops, as Representative Abraham Lincoln did during the Mexican War in 1848.[22] As for the War Powers Act, though its original purpose was to ensure that Congress and the president would share in making decisions that could get the United States involved in armed hostilities, assessments of its actual impact are mixed at best.[23] (For more on the issue of Congress and the War Powers Act, see chapter 5.)

Public interest in US military operations has varied widely, particularly in the last thirty-five years. Some interventions, such as Panama in 1989 and Desert Storm in 1991, attracted sustained public scrutiny, while others, such as Bosnia in the mid- to late 1990s, attracted only moderate and fleeting public interest. Despite these variations, the potential importance of public opinion in national security policy is something US policy makers cannot afford to neglect.

Primacy of Domestic Affairs

Throughout US history, domestic affairs have generally taken priority over foreign and security policy. To some extent, this has been a product of good fortune and circumstance. For much of the nation's history, great distances and ocean barriers made it possible for physical security to be largely taken for granted. In 1796, the country's first president, George Washington, encouraged his fellow citizens not to "forego the advantages of so peculiar a situation" by getting needlessly entangled in European affairs.[24] The fact that British sea power was committed to preserving the status quo in North America for most of the nineteenth century was further reason for complacency. In addition, much of early American history took place during a century of unprecedented world peace, from the Congress of Vienna in 1815 to the outbreak of World War I in 1914. For Americans, of course, there was the bloody domestic experience of the Civil War midway through that period, and there were also several great power wars abroad. Relatively speaking, however, the world was generally peaceful, and there was no general war. Although few Americans gave much thought to the exceptional nature of this era, the extended period of peace allowed Americans to focus almost exclusively on things close to home, including continental expansion and consolidation of hemispheric interests.

Although domestic affairs have traditionally taken precedence, in the nineteenth century many Americans embraced the idea of "Manifest Destiny," a phrase popularized in 1845 by journalist John O'Sullivan, who argued that it was the mission of the United States "to overspread the continent allotted by Providence for the free development of our yearly multiplying millions."[25] At the time, O'Sullivan was specifically arguing for the US acquisition of Texas, California, and Oregon; the United States expanded to encompass all three of these territories during the 1840s. The Spanish-American War near the end of the nineteenth century began a new period of expansion into the Caribbean and the Pacific and marked a shift in the foreign involvement of the United States. The size of the US army almost doubled from 1898 to 1901, as the United States emerged from its "Splendid Little War" as a great power with some imperial possessions in both the Pacific and the Caribbean. These holdings were unrelated, however, to the events that drew the United States into World War I. Violation of American rights as a neutral power, especially the sinking of the *Lusitania* by German submarines in 1915 and revelation of German plots in Mexico, ended the great debate over America's involvement in a European war: the United States entered World War I in 1917 as an "associated power" of the Allies.

Following World War I, America tried again to turn its back on the world outside the Western Hemisphere, rejecting President Woodrow Wilson's hopes for the League of Nations, pushing for rapid disarmament, and renouncing war "as an instrument of national policy" in the Kellogg-Briand Pact of 1928. Americans focused on a return to "normalcy"—that is, getting on with domestic concerns. The Great Depression in late 1929 and the 1930s ensured that public attention would remain riveted on internal problems. Meanwhile, the United States sought to legislate itself out of foreign political entanglements through the Neutrality Acts of 1935, 1936, and 1937, which barred sales or shipments of munitions to belligerent nations. A popular "lesson" derived from World War I was that the United States had been unwittingly dragged into war by the deceit and trickery of European diplomats. The response: "Never again!"

Separation of Power and Diplomacy

To Americans, not only does "normalcy" refer to the primacy of domestic affairs, but it also reflects a belief that tranquility is the normal condition of the world order. This is not surprising when one recalls that, until the twentieth century, the United States did not engage in major wars with the world's great powers. The political philosophy that informed the founding of the United States also encouraged a belief that order is the norm. The American political heritage has been strongly influenced by Enlightenment philosophers and particularly by John Locke, whose basic precepts were well known to the Founding Fathers of the United States and were important in both the American Revolution and in the framing of the Constitution.[26] Locke conceived of the state of nature as a condition of peace, mutual assistance, and preservation.[27] He posited the ability of people to arrive at a conception of "the right" through their innate humanity—a view that reflected a degree of trust in the rationality and even goodness of human beings. Rational people would not want war, he believed; therefore, states that adequately represent the will of their peoples could and should resolve their differences through discussion and compromise.

Americans have tended to ignore the contrary views of an earlier English philosopher, Thomas Hobbes, who wrote in *Leviathan* that, in the state of nature, human life is "solitary, poor, nasty, brutish, and short."[28] Without a central controlling power, there would exist a war "of every man against every man," which would leave no room for industry, culture, or any real society.[29] Because states are not governed by a common power, he reasoned, they interact much like individuals in the state of nature: "In all times, kings and persons of sovereign authority, because of their independence are in continued jealousies, and in the state and posture of gladiators; having their weapons pointing, and their eyes fixed on one another; that is, their forts, garrisons, guns upon the frontiers of their kingdoms; and continual spies upon their neighbors; which is a posture of war."[30] States must constantly seek power to secure themselves, and therefore the normal state of affairs among states is, if not actual war, at least the ever-present possibility that war will break out. Embracing Locke and rejecting Hobbes, the traditional American view is that diplomacy should represent a process of ironing out differences through discussion, with eventual agreement based on rational accommodation of reasonable interests.[31] In this view, power in relation to diplomacy is at best largely irrelevant and at worst immoral.

Diplomacy itself has long been suspect in many American minds because of diplomats' reputation in the Western world for deviousness, duplicity, and secrecy. Both during and after World War I, for example, widespread opinion held that it was the secret dealings of diplomats that had been largely responsible for the war.[32] Committed to this view, Wilson was instrumental in the development of a new diplomatic procedure for "registering" and publishing treaties. "Open covenants, openly arrived at" became his credo. But the principles of open methods "almost wrecked diplomacy on the shoals of impotence."[33] As public negotiations often proved nonproductive, little wonder that politicians began to load formal instruments of agreement and public statements with platitudes while leaving the important details to secret exchanges. A recent example is the 2015 international agreement limiting Iran's nuclear programs: almost a decade of open multilateral negotiations involving the five permanent members of the United Nations Security Council, Germany, and Iran were unsuccessful until, through parallel rounds of secret bilateral talks, the United States and Iran were finally able to achieve key breakthroughs.[34]

Idealism

The Judeo-Christian ideals and the philosophy of the Enlightenment embedded in the Western political heritage have affected not only American values and goals but also the means Americans typically embrace for attaining national goals. Presumptions of humanity's innate goodness and natural preference for peace have tended to condition the American approach to issues of national security.

The standards by which Americans judge the world have arisen organically out of their own experience. By the early twentieth century, the United States had become not only a great power but also a relatively satiated power that enjoyed phenomenal economic growth and social harmony. The United States had become a status quo country, its people essentially satisfied with life as they knew it, holding their condition at home as the ideal for rational people everywhere. They believed in the virtues of democracy and took it for granted that democracy should be viewed as beneficial and as a meaningful goal by all people throughout the world.[35]

Given this experience and the important role of religion in the origins of the republic, it was only natural that the American people early on developed a sense of mission that was idealistic, messianic, and hopeful of divine favor for national aspirations.[36] Since the time of the Puritan theologian Cotton Mather (1663–1728), Americans have tended to use biblical metaphor in viewing their country as a "city on a hill," a beacon for all to see and emulate. In 1847, weighing in publicly on the pending peace treaty that would conclude the Mexican War, former US congressman and elder statesman Albert Gallatin appealed to this American sense of mission when advocating a just peace with Mexico: "Your mission is to improve the state of the world, to be the 'model republic,' to show that men are capable of governing themselves, and that the simple and natural form of government is that which also confers most happiness on all, is productive of the greatest development of the intellectual faculties, above all, that which is attended by the highest standard of private and political virtue and morality."[37] This sense of mission arose again in the 1880s, this time to check the baser rationales of American imperialism. It held back outright imperialist designs in Hawaii and in the Caribbean until 1898, when its defenders were overcome by the patriotic fervor of the Spanish-American War. This messianic drive reappeared in 1917 as a national sense of responsibility to save democracy in Europe. Wilson became its champion, taking the lead after the war to form the League of Nations. It gave short-lived impetus to the "Good Neighbor Policy" in Latin America in the 1930s and helped give birth to the concept and realization of the United Nations (UN) and the Marshall Plan after World War II. Even during times when the sense of mission was undercut by the forces of realism or imperialism, the leaders of such forces clothed their designs in terms of American ideals. They knew that the American self-image was a powerful block to any program expressed purely in terms of power or material gain.

For much of the twentieth century, many Americans were occupied with a long series of projects for shaping a better international system and for returning the world to the presumed natural order of peace and harmony. Hopes rested on various formal legal codes and international institutions. In addition, a common perception of the proper American role was that of providing leadership by example rather than by significant participation in cooperative international projects. Many people continued to think that the sheer weight of American example would exert a decisive influence upon the rest of the world.[38] But, as discussed further below, this traditional idealism has increasingly given way in recent decades to the realization that, while they are still vital, ideals and examples by themselves are not enough.

Aversion to Violence and Implications for Military Policy

The Judeo-Christian gospel, which has been central in forming American values, teaches that "thou shalt not kill," and the liberal culture of Western civilization has applied that ideal to people in the collective entities called states. The Enlightenment philosophy of secular perfectionism further strengthened this belief, emphasizing that violence is not only morally wrong but irrational and unnatural. There have been counterexamples, such as bursts of patriotic enthusiasm for what many now regard as having been an unjust war, such as that waged by the United States against Mexico in the 1840s, as well as the military campaigns against Native American populations during continental expansion. Nevertheless, Americans have generally been unwilling to consider war as anything other than a scourge. It kills, maims, and separates families and friends. War and preparedness for war also interrupt the routine cycle of self-directed materialism and prosperity.[39]

In the traditional American view, war and peace are viewed as polar opposites. Resorting to war or threatening violence are seen as aberrations from the normal, peaceful course of international affairs. Thus, many Americans have difficulty processing military theorist Carl von Clausewitz's famous proposition that "war is merely the continuation of policy by other means."[40] War cannot be a legitimate instrument of policy, in a typical American view, for it is a pathological aberration.

Related to this view, Americans tend to regard peace as the responsibility of civilian policy makers and war as the province of the military. This dichotomy leads to the further notion that the military should have no peacetime function in policy making and that civilian policy makers should not have detailed involvement in the execution of military operations.[41] As a consequence, until US intervention in World War II, military policies were often formulated largely without knowledge of relevant political objectives or consequences, and political decisions were reached without professional military advice about military capabilities.[42] (For more on the role of the military in national security policy, see chapter 8.)

Traditionally, the American approach to war has leaned on one main proposition: the United States should participate only in a *just war*—a "war fought either in self-defense or in collective defense against an armed attack."[43] Fighting in any other type of war is considered "unjust." Among other things, this proposition has historically ruled out preventive war, which is defined as striking an adversary who may become a future threat but does not pose an imminent danger.[44] President Harry Truman made the point explicit: "We do not believe in aggressive or preventive war. Such war is the weapon of dictators, not of free democratic societies."[45]

The American aversion to violence, along with the traditional devotion to the status quo in the international order, has also tended to deny the legitimacy of violent revolution against sitting governments. Somehow, Americans have been inclined to forget that their own founders were steeped in Lockean philosophy, which recognized the legitimacy of "the right to rebel," and that the United States was itself born of revolution.

Distrust of Standing Military Forces

Given the traditional view, which sees no necessary connection between diplomacy and armed might, it is not surprising that until recently Americans have accorded little importance to the military other than in exceptional periods. In fact, one could go even further and argue that American liberalism is fundamentally hostile to the military and its functions.[46] Dating back to the colonial era and the Revolutionary War, this distrust is related to a long-standing fear of militarism and the possibility that the military could displace civilian government or impose military values, perspectives, and ideals on the rest of society. Unbridled militarism could become a threat to freedom and democracy.

In addition to concerns over militarism, Americans have also believed strongly that a military force of *citizen-soldiers*—citizens called to arms in times of crisis—would be sufficient to defend the nation, and that in their hands freedom would be most secure. Although Washington called for a "moderate, compact force, on a permanent basis," during the Revolutionary War,[47] an almost unquestioning faith in a citizen-soldier militia predominated afterward. Indeed, this faith was reinforced by the United States' ability to call upon its citizen-soldiers to fight victorious wars against foreign foes in 1812, 1846, 1898, 1917, and 1941.

Because America's wars were to be fought by a force raised for that purpose in times of crisis, peacetime conscription, or a draft, has generally been viewed as "un-American." This belief has also had the effect of limiting standing military forces. In wartime, conscription was used late in the Civil War and again in World Wars I and II. However, the first peacetime conscription law was not passed until September 1940. Even with substantial threats looming over the horizon, this legislation barely passed in Congress. Following World War II, in August 1945, Truman asked Congress for a peacetime draft for an indefinite period to replace overseas veterans. A two-year conscription bill was finally passed in June 1948 and was renewed each year thereafter until 1972.[48] Overall, the United States has conscripted standing forces in the absence of a declared war during only about 10 percent of its existence.

Except in crisis, Americans traditionally have wished that the minimum essential military establishment would do whatever it had to do with the smallest possible diversion of public attention and funds. Once a crisis has passed, Americans have sought to demobilize as soon as possible. A dramatic illustration is the hasty deactivation of the Continental Army in 1784. The Continental Congress directed the commanding officer "to discharge the troops now in the service of the United States, except twenty-five privates to guard the stores at Fort Pitt, and fifty-five privates to guard the stores at West Point and other magazines, with a proportionate number of officers; no officer to remain in service above the rank of captain."[49] The rush to "bring the boys back home" after World War II was another dramatic example of this same phenomenon. In less than two years, the United States demobilized almost 11 million soldiers, sailors, and airmen, leaving a scattered residual force of about 10 percent of its wartime strength to safeguard the victories in Europe and Asia.

War as a Battle of Good versus Evil

Because the United States rejects the notion of war as an extension of policy, it cannot logically use the military as an instrument to restore a balance of power, to protect economic interests abroad, or to serve other interests that are merely material in nature. Instead, America goes to war as a last resort and in the name of moral principles: "to make the world safe for democracy" or "to end all wars." This strand in American political thought received expression again in 2003, when George W. Bush praised the military for its successful invasion of Iraq with these words: "And wherever you go, you carry a message of hope, a message that is ancient and ever new. In the words of the prophet Isaiah, 'To the captives, come out; and to those in darkness, be free.'"[50] The United States gives its sons, daughters, and treasure to a cause only in righteous indignation or outrage, and almost always while claiming to serve purposes broader than its own interests.

Although aversion to violence may be one of America's best characteristics, it can also cause the American people to react with moral outrage to the violent actions of others. This moral outrage can then spur the United States into resisting proportionality or restraints in its response. After all, if a conflict is one of good versus evil, with Americans on the side of good, all actions would seem to be justified and only the unlimited objectives of unconditional surrender or total destruction of an enemy are acceptable. Yet Americans do not have a tradition of glorifying violence, per se. The problem has always been the relationship of ends to means: a cause that is noble enough is seen to justify unlimited, violent means. The sufficiency of some causes has, however, been a matter of considerable retrospective debate among American historians and philosophers. In addition, a disposition to wage war in an unlimited fashion may make more difficult the compromises of practical statecraft and diplomacy that are likely to be necessary in fostering a postwar peace that serves US interests at the lowest possible cost.

The requirements of political mobilization can also make it difficult for US national security policy makers to calibrate the use of means and the scale of objectives in accordance with the national interests and values that are at stake in a given situation. To engender public support for war—to get the public to sustain the dangers and privations—policy makers often couch their causes in black-and-white terms. Atrocious behavior of US enemies has often made it easy to explain and justify the outbreak of war against what is construed as the criminal conduct of an inhuman and perhaps degenerate foe.[51] This has obvious benefits for the war effort, but it is very hard to turn off the public's emotions once they have been aroused. If the president mobilizes support for specific military interventions abroad, he or she may later find that options become restricted or foreclosed by the emotional stakes and simplified expectations of the public. It becomes difficult to fight a war for limited objectives when the process of limitation involves negotiating with ultimate evil, represented by the enemy. Once policy makers have advocated total victory, it tends to become a driving goal, and progress toward such a goal must be demonstrated. Protracted war with limited objectives tends to obscure victory. Highly competitive by nature, Americans do not relish tie games.[52] They want to win big, early, and quickly.

Impatience

Americans believe that with a little common sense and know-how, things can be done in a hurry.[53] In part, this belief may rest on a simplified and idealized version of American history, one that does not fully take into account the country's own long struggles with human rights issues, such as slavery, and its long debates about the proper role of government in the economy and society. Whatever the source of American impatience, a protracted limited war does not fit this temper any more than costly and sustained military preparedness does. Hence any prolonged conflict demanding self-sacrifice that is inadequately related to a clear vision of overriding national interest is likely to produce public outcry for cessation of American involvement. Such was the case in the Vietnam War, as well as the smaller-scale US intervention in Somalia in the early 1990s.

A more recent example involves US public attitudes toward the large and costly ground wars that the United States waged in Afghanistan and Iraq beginning in 2001 and 2003, respectively. As these expensive conflicts continued into the second decade of the twenty-first century, American investment in and attention to them declined. While 46 percent of Americans surveyed claimed to be following the events in Iraq closely when George W. Bush made the surge announcement in 2007, only 19 percent said they were doing so by December 2010.[54] In his cover letter to the 2015 National Security Strategy, Obama may have been tapping into this public sentiment as he pointed out that the United States had "moved beyond the large ground wars in Iraq and Afghanistan that defined so much of American foreign policy over the past decade. Compared to the nearly 180,000 troops we had in Iraq and Afghanistan when I took office, we now have fewer than 15,000 deployed in those countries."[55] However, American impatience may not always be conducive to wise strategy and policy. By 2015, some analysts worried that a lack of popular support and declining media coverage would lead to a termination of US military involvement in the war in Afghanistan on terms that would fail to serve US national interests and would bring greater long-term costs.[56] In spite of this concern, the Trump administration has been able to continue deployments in Iraq and Afghanistan, albeit at reduced numbers with correspondingly reduced casualties.

Impatience, the primacy many Americans place on domestic affairs, and the complexity of many international security challenges may also make it difficult for US political leaders to obtain or sustain support for nondramatic policies focused on long-term objectives. For example, though many would agree that the greatest direct military threat to the security of the United States is in the nuclear realm, the American public tends to ignore this danger. Despite occasional peaks of public attention sparked by specific events, such as the international agreement to limit Iran's nuclear program, it is difficult to get public support mobilized for longer term policies related to such issues as control over fissile materials in Russia.[57]

Policy makers can also expect to find it challenging to sustain public support for nonmilitary actions to counter efforts by other states to develop chemical and biological weapons.[58]

Old Traditions and New Realities

The American experience since World War II has transformed some important aspects of the traditional American approach to national security. Driven by factors that have included relative US power, the Cold War threat of the Soviet Union, the accelerating processes of globalization after the end of the Cold War, and the rising importance of transnational concerns such as international terrorism, the sustained engagement of the United States abroad reflects a realization that Americans can no longer seek security by focusing only on the affairs of the Western hemisphere and otherwise pursuing isolation. A second area of transformation in the traditional American approach to national security relates to the salience given to military affairs. Important aspects of traditional attitudes toward the military that seem to have changed in the latter half of the twentieth century and early part of the twenty-first include higher levels of public trust in the military, increased involvement of uniformed personnel in national security policy making, a willingness to devote continuing substantial resources to defense even in the absence of a declared war, a greater reliance on professional soldiers, and an expansion of the circumstances under which Americans are willing to use force abroad. A third area of transformation is an enhanced appreciation of the role of power in diplomacy and the increased salience of a multilateral approach to managing international affairs.

Although there has been change, there have also been important elements of continuity in American approaches to foreign policy and national security. American tendencies toward idealism and the casting of international conflicts in terms of good and evil appear to persist. The United States continues to explain its overseas military actions and foreign policies in terms that reflect moral concerns and purposes that are broader than merely American self-interest. Importantly, although the United States has remained engaged in global affairs for over seventy years, domestic concerns are still primary for many Americans.

Despite the continuing pull of old traditions, after World War II Americans reluctantly and gradually came to accept the new role of the United States as a world power with global responsibilities. The experiences of the 1920s and 1930s suggested that US disengagement from the world had not served US interests, but had instead contributed to a global economic downturn and the rise of fascist, expansionist states. As World War II drew to a close, the specters of communism as a global challenge and of Soviet acquisition of nuclear capability destroyed Americans' traditional sense of continental security. Past reliance on geographic location and the US military's capacity to protect the physical integrity of the North American homeland gave way to an assumption that the security of the United States depended upon the balance of power and the role played by actors operating outside the Western Hemisphere. This belief that events and developments around the world affect US security and prosperity has remained a basic underpinning for American foreign and national security policy since World War II.[59]

Changes in the American Approach to Military Affairs. The post–World War II changes in the nation's approach to military affairs include an increased confidence in the military as an institution. In fact, a 2017 poll showed that the US institution in which the public had its greatest confidence was the military. Survey data reveal that 72 percent of Americans had "a great deal" or "quite a lot" of confidence in the military, while the next most trusted institution was small business, at 70 percent. The presidency was at 32 percent, and Congress at 12 percent.[60] The military has topped this poll since 1998, and during the decade prior was displaced only twice: by "small business" in 1997 and by "organized religion" in 1988. In fact, the position of the military in American society today has even caused some to write with concern about the phenomenon of a "new American militarism."[61] As a smaller and far from representative portion of US society serves in uniform, Americans have come to have increasing respect for an institution that they generally know less and less about.

A second change relates to the traditional American tendency to isolate the military from decisions about war and peace. The systematic involvement of the US military in the national security process, which began during World War II, continued to grow after victory in 1945. The National Security Act of 1947 signaled an enduring conceptual overhaul in that, through its provisions, military views became integrated into overall defense and policy planning. A new organization, the National Security Council, was established to determine, at the highest level of government, the relationships between national objectives and military policy in peacetime, in war, and in the gray area in between. In the decades following, the national security policymaking process has been continuously adjusted by executive order and by legislation, including the highly significant Goldwater-Nichols Department of Defense Reorganization Act of 1986. Among its many important provisions is one that mandated that the president develop and set forth a national security strategy to guide the entire national security system according to a set of shared priorities. (For more on the organization of the national security policymaking system over time, see chapters 3 and 10.)

A third change is a reduction of the traditional American aversion to devoting significant resources to national security. From the 1950s through the 1980s, the Soviet threat drove Americans to allocate a substantial share of the nation's wealth to defense. Although the armed forces faced significant budget stringency in the years following the Vietnam War, the last few years of the Carter administration again saw budget growth. Defense spending grew significantly during the Reagan years, from $415 billion in fiscal year (FY) 1980, before Reagan took office, to a high of $618 billion in FY 1989 (all figures are inflation adjusted in 2019 dollars). With the subsequent demise of the Soviet threat worldwide, Americans began to expect a peace dividend. President George H. W. Bush began downsizing the military as well as cutting the budget during his administration, and these cuts were accelerated during the early years of the Clinton administration. However, the end of the second Clinton administration again saw defense spending on the rise. During FY 2000, the second consecutive year of defense increases, outlays totaled $468 billion. After the terrorist attacks of 9/11, George W. Bush dramatically increased defense spending. Including all supplemental and war funding, annual defense outlays peaked at $783 billion in FY 2010. After withdrawing most forces from Iraq and Afghanistan, Obama oversaw budget reductions, to $622 billion in FY 2016. President Trump reversed the decline in the defense budget, increasing outlays to $689 billion in his 2019 budget request.[62] Although this is a relatively small proportion of US gross domestic product in historical terms—only 3.3 percent—it is the largest single category of discretionary spending in the US federal budget. By some necessarily imprecise calculations, it is also approximately equal to the military expenditures of the next seven largest military spenders combined.[63] There have been important fluctuations in defense spending since the end of World War II, but when the first century and half of the country's existence is compared with the last seven decades, it is clear that Americans have become much more willing to make significant investments in standing military forces even during times of ostensible peace.

A fourth change has been to US military manpower policy, which shifted away from conscription during the Nixon administration and has remained essentially constant since. In 1968, during his first presidential campaign, Richard Nixon announced his intention to end the draft and to create an all-volunteer force. The debate in American society and in Congress was wide ranging and reflected views on the Vietnam War, the duties of citizens, and conceptions of fairness as they related to conscription. Appropriate legislation was eventually passed, and the last conscript left the force in November 1974. Since that date, the United States has relied on professional volunteers, often long-serving, to constitute its standing military forces. Although by the early twenty-first century the all-volunteer force (AVF) has become widely accepted, there are still recurring concerns about the separation of the military from the society it serves and the relative merits of compulsory military service.[64]

A fifth change in traditional American attitudes toward military policy relates to the conditions under which the United States is willing to use force abroad. The United States has tended to articulate its reasons for war in terms of moral principles and, based on these, to have sought total victory over unjust enemies. But the period after World War II saw the country repeatedly engaged in small wars for limited purposes, such as in Korea in the 1950s and Vietnam in the 1960s and early 1970s. To some extent, the constraints that policy makers imposed on US means devoted to these wars reflected a desire to avoid a broader conflagration that might have brought the United States into direct armed conflict with the Soviet Union. However, restrictions on the use of force also reflected the fact that the US interests at stake were limited. Given the traditional American approach to armed conflict—and especially the idea that America wages wars on the side of good against evil adversaries—US political leaders will continue to find it hard to articulate to the American people why the use of force is sometimes in the national interest even if total war is not.

Moreover, the motivations for armed intervention have also evolved. In the past, war has been seen as justified only by an attack upon the United States or in support of collective defense in response to an act of aggression. This latter justification can, in part, explain US leadership in the Gulf War in 1991, which was prompted by Iraq's invasion of Kuwait. However, new justifications for the use of force have arisen since the end of the Cold War. Internal conflicts involving massive humanitarian disasters in Somalia, Haiti, Bosnia, and Kosovo in the 1990s and in Libya in 2011, or state sponsorship of terrorist attacks—Afghanistan in 2001—have been seen as justifying armed intervention. In addition, the historical US aversion to preventive war was challenged in the wake of the 9/11 terrorist attacks.[65] As stated in the 2002 National Security Strategy: "We must be prepared to stop rogue states and their terrorist clients before they are able to threaten or use weapons of mass destruction against the United States and our allies and friends. . . . In an age where the enemies of civilization openly and actively seek the world's most destructive technologies, the United States cannot remain idle when dangers gather."[66] This statement constitutes a portion of the intellectual justification for what many characterize as a US preventive war against Iraq in 2003. A second portion of the justification was the conviction that the regime of Saddam Hussein simply could not be trusted and that the key to lasting peace was total regime change, from dictatorship to democracy. It remains to be seen whether the option of preventive war becomes an enduring component of the American approach to national security. (See chapter 3 for a more extensive discussion of this case.)

Changing US Approaches to Diplomacy and Engagement. Several facets of the US approach to diplomacy and international engagement have also been transformed in the post–World War II era. One is that Americans have come to have a greater appreciation of the relationship between power—including military force—and diplomacy. Secretary of State Henry Kissinger during the Nixon administration and Secretary George Shultz during the Reagan administration, among others, sought to use this relationship to further US interests. In a 1984 speech, Shultz argued that "power and diplomacy are not alternatives. They must go together, or we will accomplish very little in this world." Shultz acknowledged an American tendency to believe that diplomacy and military options were "distinct alternatives" but saw this viewpoint as expressing a flawed understanding of international politics.[67]

A second important change relates to a historical tendency toward unilateralism and wariness of foreign commitments, which was sometimes accompanied by the idealistic belief that the force of American example would be enough to bring about desired changes in world affairs. Since World War II, however, the approach of the United States to international affairs has been explicitly multilateral in many issue areas. The United States played a critical role in building a system that would better enable it to address challenges in international affairs in cooperation with other states. On issues of security, the United States participated in the formation of the United Nations in 1945, the foundation of the North Atlantic Treaty Organization (NATO) in 1949, and an expanding set of bilateral and regional security relationships throughout the next several decades. On issues associated with the international economy, the United States was a key player in the Bretton Woods Agreement in 1944, which laid the foundation for international institutions of economic governance in the areas of postconflict reconstruction, economic development, finance, and trade. As it fostered these agreements and participated in the resulting international institutions, the United States was agreeing to be bound by international commitments while also laying the groundwork for exercising leadership—at least among a significant number of the countries of the world—through consent.[68]

American multilateralism has varied in degree and in its specific manifestations in the decades since World War II, but it nevertheless marks a significant departure from early US history. In the latter half of the twentieth century, there was an enduring consensus among national security policy makers that it would be easiest to secure American liberty and security within a rule-governed system, even if US freedom of action were to be somewhat constrained. In the early years of the twenty-first century, many have seen the administration of George W. Bush as straying from this consensus in, for example, the US rejection of the Kyoto Protocol on global warming, the International Criminal Court, and a new protocol to enhance enforcement of a biological weapons convention.[69] Even so, many forms of US multilateralism persisted during the George W. Bush administration, and multilateralism was again affirmed as central to the US approach to international affairs during the subsequent Obama administration. As President Obama declared in the 2015 National Security Strategy: "We will continue to embrace the post–World War II legal architecture—from the UN Charter to the multilateral treaties that govern the conduct of war, respect for human rights, nonproliferation, and many other topics of global concern—as essential to the ordering of a just and peaceful world, where nations live peacefully within their borders, and all men and women have the opportunity to reach their potential."[70] The emphasis appears to be changing again under President Donald J. Trump, who declared an "America First" approach to foreign policy and whose early actions included withdrawal from the Trans-Pacific Partnership multilateral trade deal and the Paris climate accord. However, Trump also reaffirmed the mutual defense article in the NATO Treaty, suggesting the potential durability of the international institutions created after World War II.[71]

The Persistence of Idealism as an Influence on US Policy Abroad. Although there have been significant departures from traditional American approaches to national security in some areas, other trends persist. For example, a traditional American faith that rational people can peacefully resolve conflicts through dialogue was expressed in the US effort to create the United Nations in 1945. Through other means, however, such as the military alliances formed during the next several decades, the United States hedged its bet on the ability of the United Nations to contain communist expansion. In part, too, American idealism was reflected in the rebuilding of a shattered Europe through the Marshall Plan and in the impulse to foster economic development through foreign assistance. However, these initiatives were also integral to the US policy of containing global communism by buttressing the economic vitality and social stability of America's democratic allies.

This mixture of idealism and pragmatic concern for US national security remains characteristic of the US approach to the world in the twenty-first century. For example, the traditional American desire for moral clarity may help explain the approach of the administration of George W. Bush to diplomacy in which it avoided "rewarding bad actors," such as North Korea, Syria, and Iran, by refusing to accept bilateral talks.[72] However, that idealism was often blended with pragmatism, as reflected in these May 2009 remarks by Bush's successor, Obama: "We uphold our most cherished values not only because doing so is right, but because it strengthens our country and it keeps us safe. Time and again, our values have been our best national security asset—in war and peace; in times of ease and in eras of upheaval. Fidelity to our values is the reason why the United States of America grew from a small string of colonies under the writ of an empire to the strongest nation in the world."[73] In other words, acting in accordance with American values is right, and it also promotes US prosperity and security.

In addition to idealism, a second American tendency that persists into the twenty-first century relates to the primacy of domestic affairs. This point should not be overstated and is in fact contradicted by some of the points made above: the perception of many Americans that the United States must be globally engaged to preserve its prosperity and security, the willingness of Americans to devote significant national treasure to defense even in the absence of declared war, and the occasional US willingness to use force abroad for humanitarian purposes. However, as is the case with many countries, domestic politics remain important and often play a primary role.[74]

One example of the primacy of domestic affairs may be the fate of the presidential reelection bid of George H. W. Bush in 1992. Although the 1991 Gulf War had led to a quick and decisive victory, and the president's subsequent poll numbers soared, he still lost office. Clinton's winning 1992 campaign, remembered for the guiding idea of "It's the economy, stupid," illustrates that, although national security is important, domestic affairs often take precedence. Similarly, in the 2000 election, George W. Bush ran and won on a platform of a more modest US foreign policy, including decreased American involvement in nation building. Even after the terrorist attacks of 2001 and during ongoing military operations in Afghanistan and Iraq, a 2006 survey on US foreign policy attitudes found that 55 percent of Americans felt that the government should be paying more attention to domestic issues.[75] Of course, much depends on exactly how the questions are asked: another poll in 2013 showed that while 52 percent of Americans agreed that "the U.S. should mind its own business and let other countries get along as best they can," a larger majority, 72 percent, wanted "the U.S. to play a shared world leadership role."[76] Nevertheless, international relations and national security received relatively little attention in the 2012 and 2016 presidential elections. While broad acceptance of the need for US international engagement persists, the tendency to give primacy to domestic affairs seems to be a natural one to which Americans will return in the absence of major international conflict.

Discussion Questions

1. What aspects of the American historical experience continue to influence US views toward national security policy?
2. How important is public opinion in national security policy formulation today?
3. How could public opinion both enhance and inhibit an effective national security policy?
4. How have the ideas of Locke and Hobbes been reflected in American national security policy? Which school of thought provides better insight into today's security environment?
5. If Americans are traditionally averse to war, what explains the fact that the United States has been involved in numerous wars and maintains a large military establishment?
6. Does American idealism make US national security policy more or less effective?
7. Do current US leaders still make arguments about the use of force in terms of good versus evil? If so, what are possible consequences of this behavior?
8. How would you describe the historical role of the military in peacetime national security policy? How has it changed?
9. What has been the traditional American approach to diplomacy? How has it changed?
10. Do you believe that Americans today continue to focus more on domestic than on international affairs? On what evidence do you base your assessment?

Recommended Reading

Bacevich, Andrew J. *The New American Militarism: How Americans Are Seduced by War.* New York: Oxford University Press, 2005.

Baum, Matthew A. *Soft News Goes to War: Public Opinion and American Foreign Policy in the New Media Age.* Princeton, NJ: Princeton University Press, 2003.

Boot, Max. *The Savage Wars of Peace: Small Wars and the Rise of American Power.* New York: Basic Books, 2003.

Elshtain, Jean Bethke. *Just War against Terror: The Burden of American Power in a Violent World.* New York: Basic Books, 2003.

Finnemore, Martha. *The Purpose of Intervention: Changing Beliefs about the Use of Force.* Ithaca, NY: Cornell University Press, 2003.

Fukuyama, Francis. *America at the Crossroads.* New Haven, CT: Yale University Press, 2006.

Gaddis, John Lewis. *Strategies of Containment.* New York: Oxford University Press, 1981.

———. *Surprise, Security, and the American Experience.* Cambridge, MA: Harvard University Press, 2004.

———. *The United States and the End of the Cold War.* New York: Oxford University Press, 1992.

Haass, Richard N. *Foreign Policy Begins at Home: The Case for Putting America's House in Order.* New York: Basic Books, 2013.

Hobbes, Thomas. *Leviathan.* New York: Collier Books, 1962.
McDougall, Walter. *Promised Land, Crusader State: America's Encounter with the World since 1776.* Boston: Houghton Mifflin, 1997.
Mead, Walter Russell. *Special Providence: American Foreign Policy and How It Changed the World.* New York: Routledge, 2002.
Rosenthal, Joel H., and Christian Barry, eds. *Ethics and International Affairs: A Reader.* 3rd ed. Washington, DC: Georgetown University Press, 2009.
Russett, Bruce M. *Controlling the Sword: The Democratic Governance of National Security.* Cambridge, MA: Harvard University Press, 1990.
Sestanovich, Stephen. *Maximalist: America in the World from Truman to Obama.* New York: Alfred A. Knopf, 2014.
Shy, John W. *A People Numerous and Armed: Reflections on the Military Struggle for American Independence.* Ann Arbor: University of Michigan Press, 1990.
Silverstone, Scott A. *Preventive War and American Democracy.* London: Routledge, 2007.
Walzer, Michael. *Just and Unjust Wars.* 4th ed. New York: Basic Books, 2006.
Weigley, Russell F. *The American Way of War.* New York: Macmillan, 1973.

Internet Resources

Center for Strategic and Budgetary Assessments (CSBA), www.csbaonline.org
The Gallup Poll, www.gallup.com
PollingReport.com, www.pollingreport.com

Notes

1. Thomas Jefferson, "Declaration of Independence," July 4, 1776, http://www.archives.gov/exhibits/charters/declaration_transcript.html.

2. Gabriel A. Almond, *The American People and Foreign Policy*, 2nd ed. (New York: Praeger, 1977), 54.

3. Gabriel A. Almond, "Public Opinion and National Security Policy," *Public Opinion Quarterly* 20, no. 2 (1956): 371–73.

4. Ole R. Holsti, "Public Opinion and Foreign Policy: Challenges to the Almond-Lippmann Consensus Mershon Series: Research Programs and Debates," *International Studies Quarterly* 36, no. 4 (1992): 440.

5. Holsti, "Public Opinion and Foreign Policy," 440.

6. Benjamin I. Page and Robert Y. Shapiro, *The Rational Public: Fifty Years of Trends in Americans' Policy Preferences* (Chicago: University of Chicago Press, 1992), 1.

7. Philip J. Powlick, "The Sources of Public Opinion for American Foreign Policy Officials," *International Studies Quarterly* 39, no. 4 (1995): 428.

8. Joseph S. Nye Jr., "Redefining the National Interest," *Foreign Affairs* 78, no. 4 (1999): 24.

9. The White House, *National Security Strategy of the United States of America* (Washington, DC: The White House, September 2002), v.

10. Barack Obama, "Remarks by the President in Address to the Nation on Syria," September 10, 2013, https://www.whitehouse.gov/the-press-office/2013/09/10/remarks-president-address-nation-syria.

11. Charles B. Cushman Jr., *An Introduction to the U.S. Congress* (Armonk, NY: M. E. Sharpe, 2006), 41.

12. William M. Darley, "War, Public Support, and the Media," *Parameters* 35 (Summer 2005): 124–25.

13. See Nye, "Redefining the National Interest," 22–35.

14. Ralph B. Levering, *The Public and American Foreign Policy, 1918–1978* (New York: Morrow, 1978), 134–37.

15. Mark Lorell and Charles Kelley Jr., *Casualties, Public Opinion, and Presidential Policy during the Vietnam War* (Santa Monica, CA: RAND, 1985), 60.

16. CNN, "Poll: Approval for Iraq Handling Drops to New Low," December 18, 2006, http://www.cnn.com/2006/POLITICS/12/18/bush.poll/index.html.

17. George W. Bush, "President Bush Addresses Nation on Iraq War," January 10, 2007, CQ Transcripts Wire, http://www.washingtonpost.com/wp-dyn/content/article/2007/01/10/AR2007011002208.html.

18. Pew Research Center, "Iraq and Public Opinion: The Troops Come Home," December 14, 2011, http://www.pewresearch.org/2011/12/14/iraq-and-public-opinion-the-troops-come-home/.

19. Eric V. Larson, *Casualties and Consensus: The Historical Role of Casualties in Domestic Support for U.S. Military Operations* (Santa Monica, CA: RAND, 1996), xix.

20. Powlick, "The Sources of Public Opinion for American Foreign Policy Officials," 430.

21. Wallace Earl Walker, "Congressional Resurgence and the Destabilization of US Foreign Policy," *Parameters* 18 (September 1988): 58.

22. Abraham Lincoln, "To William H. Herndon," June 22, 1848, in *The Portable Abraham Lincoln*, ed. Andrew Delbanco (New York: Penguin, 2009), 28–30.

23. Richard F. Grimmett, "War Powers Resolution: Presidential Compliance," Congressional Research Service Report to Congress (RL33532), September 25, 2012.

24. George Washington, "Farewell Address (1796)," in *American Political Thought: A Norton Anthology*, ed. Isaac Kramnick and Theodore J. Lowi (New York: W. W. Norton, 2009), 322.

25. John O'Sullivan, "Annexation," *United States Magazine and Democratic Review* 17, no. 1 (1845): 5–10.

26. Carl Becker, *The Declaration of Independence: A Study in the History of Political Ideas* (New York: Knopf, 1942), 76–78.

27. Lee Ward, "Locke on the Moral Basis of International Relations," *American Journal of Political Science* 50, no. 3 (2006): 692.

28. Thomas Hobbes, *Leviathan* (New York: Collier Books, 1962), 100.

29. Hobbes, *Leviathan*, 100.

30. Hobbes, *Leviathan*, 101.

31. Robert E. Osgood, *Ideals and Self-Interest in America's Foreign Relations* (Chicago: University of Chicago Press, 1953), 433.

32. Frederick H. Hartmann, *The Relations of Nations*, 4th ed. (New York: Macmillan, 1973), 101–2; Kenneth W. Thompson, *American Diplomacy and Emergent Patterns* (New York: New York University Press, 1962), 45–46.

33. Hartmann, *Relations of Nations*, 102.

34. Laura Rozen, "Inside the Secret U.S.-Iran Diplomacy that Sealed Nuke Deal," *U.S. News and World Report*, August 12, 2015, http://www.usnews.com/news/articles/2015/08/12/inside-the-secret-us-iran-diplomacy-that-sealed-nuke-deal.

35. Harry R. Davis and Robert C. Good, *Reinhold Niebuhr on Politics* (New York: Scribner's, 1960), 308–13.

36. See Frederick Merk, *Manifest Destiny and Mission in American History* (New York: Knopf, 1963), 261.

37. Albert Gallatin, quoted in Merk, *Manifest Destiny*, 262–63.

38. See Charles O. Lerche Jr., *Foreign Policy of the American People*, 3rd ed. (Englewood Cliffs, NJ: Prentice-Hall, 1967), 110–11.

39. See Davis and Good, *Reinhold Niebuhr on Politics*, 140.

40. Carl von Clausewitz, *On War*, trans. and ed. Michael Howard and Peter Paret (Princeton, NJ: Princeton University Press, 1976), 87.

41. Lerche, *Foreign Policy*, 117.

42. Robert E. Osgood, *Limited War: The Challenge to American Strategy* (Chicago: University of Chicago Press, 1957), 31.

43. Robert W. Tucker, *The Just War: A Study in Contemporary American Doctrine*, 2nd ed. (Baltimore, MD: Johns Hopkins University Press, 1979), 11.

44. See also Michael Walzer, *Just and Unjust Wars* (New York: Basic Books, 1977), 76–78.

45. Harry S. Truman, quoted in Walzer, *Just and Unjust Wars*, 15.

46. For an expression of this position, see Samuel P. Huntington, *The Soldier and the State* (Cambridge, MA: The Belknap Press of Harvard University Press, 1957).

47. George Washington, quoted in Daniel J. Boorstin, *The Americans: The Colonial Experience* (New York: Random House, 1958), 368.

48. James Gerhardt, *The Draft and Public Policy* (Columbus: Ohio State University Press, 1971), 83–122.

49. Resolution, Continental Congress, quoted in Huntington, *The Soldier and the State*, 144.

50. Jarrett Murphy, "Text of Bush Speech," May 1, 2003, http://www.cbsnews.com/news/text-of-bush-speech-01-05-2003/.

51. John W. Shy, *A People Numerous and Armed: Reflections on the Military Struggle for American Independence* (Ann Arbor: University of Michigan Press, 1990), 238–42.

52. Almond, *The American People and Foreign Policy*, 30–31, 48–50.

53. Almond, *The American People and Foreign Policy*, 51.

54. Pew Research Center, "Iraq and Public Opinion: The Troops Come Home," December 14, 2011, http://www.pewresearch.org/2011/12/14/iraq-and-public-opinion-the-troops-come-home/.

55. The White House, *The National Security Strategy of the United States of America* (Washington, DC: The White House, February 2015), i.

56. See, for example, Dominic Tierney, "Forgetting Afghanistan: Americans Are Debating Whether to Fight ISIS, without Acknowledging that They're Already at War," *Atlantic*, June 24, 2015, http://www.theatlantic.com/international/archive/2015/06/afghanistan-war-memory/396701/.

57. For one call to action, see Graham T. Allison, Owen R. Cote, Richard A. Falkenrath, and Steven E. Miller, *Avoiding Nuclear Anarchy: Containing the Threat of Loose Russian Nuclear Weapons and Fissile Materials* (Cambridge, MA: MIT Press, 1996).

58. Andrew Newman, "Arms Control, Proliferation, and Terrorism: The Bush Administration's Post–September 11 Security Strategy," *Journal of Strategic Studies* 27, no. 1 (2004): 59.

59. John A. Thompson, "Conceptions of National Security and American Entry into World War II," *Diplomacy and Statecraft* 16, no. 4 (2005): 671–72.

60. Frank Newport, "Americans' Confidence in Institutions Edges Up," June 26, 2017, http://news.gallup.com/poll/212840/americans-confidence-institutions-edges.aspx.

61. Andrew J. Bacevich, *The New American Militarism: How Americans Are Seduced by War* (New York: Oxford University Press, 2005).

62. Office of Management and Budget, *Fiscal Year 2019, Efficient, Effective, Accountable: An American Budget* (Washington, DC: Office of Management and Budget, February 2019). Calculations based on tables 6.1 and 10.1. Figures reported are for all national defense outlays converted into FY 2019 dollars.

63. National Priorities Project, "Federal Budget Tipsheet: Pentagon Spending," FY2015, https://www.nationalpriorities.org/guides/tipsheet-pentagon-spending/.

64. For both sides of the debate, see Charles Rangel, "Should the All Volunteer Force Be Replaced by Universal Mandatory Military Service?" *Congressional Digest* 85, no. 7 (2006): 206–8.

65. See, for example, Scott A. Silverstone, *Preventive War and American Democracy* (London: Routledge, 2007). For a challenge to the idea that consideration of preventive war is unprecedented in the United States, see John Lewis Gaddis, *Surprise, Security, and the American Experience* (Cambridge, MA: Harvard University Press, 2004).

66. The White House, *The National Security Strategy of the United States of America* (Washington, DC: The White House, September 2002), 14–15.

67. George Shultz, "Address before the Trilateral Commission on April 3, 1984," *Department of State Bulletin* 84, no. 2086 (1984): 13.

68. Gaddis, *Surprise, Security, and the American Experience*, discusses these developments.

69. Robert Jervis, *American Foreign Policy in a New Era* (New York: Routledge, 2005), 87. For a different perspective that argues that the national security strategy of President George W. Bush was actually more multilateral than that of his predecessor, see John Lewis Gaddis, "A Grand Strategy of Transformation," *Foreign Policy* 285, no. 4 (2000): 50–57.

70. The White House, *The National Security Strategy of the United States of America* (February 2015), 23.

71. Peter Baker, "Trump Commits to Defending NATO Nations," *New York Times*, June 9, 2017, https://www.nytimes.com/2017/06/09/world/europe/trump-nato-defense-article-5.html?mcubz=0&_r=0.

72. For a critical perspective, see Barbara Bodine, "Channel Surfing: Non-Engagement as Foreign Policy," *Audit of the Conventional Wisdom* 6, no. 12 (2006): 1–3.

73. Barack Obama, "Remarks by the President on National Security," May 21, 2009, https://www.whitehouse.gov/the-press-office/remarks-president-national-security-5-21-09.

74. Stanley Hoffmann, "Clash of Globalizations," *Foreign Affairs* 81, no. 4 (2002): 105.

75. Ana Maria Arumi et al., *Americans Wary of Creating Democracies Abroad* (New York: Public Agenda, 2006), 18.

76. Andrew Kohut, "Americans: Disengaged, Feeling Less Respected, but Still See U.S. as World's Military Superpower," April 1, 2014, http://www.pewresearch.org/fact-tank/2014/04/01/americans-disengaged-feeling-less-respected-but-still-see-u-s-as-worlds-military-superpower/.

3

The Evolution of American National Security Policy

National security strategy and the instruments of power available to pursue it are shaped by the interaction of a number of influences, many of which defy precise identification. However, there are three principal categories of variables through which the evolution of strategy and structure can be traced: international political and military developments, domestic priorities, and technological advancements. This chapter follows these variables through the evolution of American national security policy since World War II, revealing patterns of continuity and change. This history goes far in explaining today's national security policy challenges and the capabilities and limitations of current instruments of power.

A brief clarification of terms is necessary. As used here, the term *strategy* refers to "a prudent idea or set of ideas for employing the instruments of national power in a synchronized and integrated fashion to achieve theater, national, and/or multinational objectives."[1] A national security strategy provides the conceptual framework within which a state pursues its security. The term *instruments of power* refers to "all of the means available to the government in its pursuit of national objectives. They are expressed as diplomatic, economic, informational, and military."[2] The military instrument that is available to policy makers at any given time is also referred to as *military structure*, which comprises the size, composition, disposition, and capabilities of the armed forces. In an ideal situation, the instruments of power available to national policy makers would be optimized to support the achievement of their strategic vision, but for reasons discussed below, that is often not the case. The term *national policy* is used to refer to "a broad course of action or statements of guidance adopted by the government at the national level in pursuit of national objectives."[3] Policy can therefore relate to either strategic objectives or the development of instruments of power, depending on the issues at hand.

The National Security Environment

The history that follows traces the evolution of US national security policy since World War II, with a focus on the interaction of three types of developments: those that occur outside the United States, those that occur in the domestic arena, and those that stem from technological change.

International Political and Military Developments. The international environment is an important and constantly changing influence on US policy. National security strategy is largely a response to perceived threats and opportunities in the international arena that affect American interests. One important characteristic of the international environment is the presence or absence of alliances, because the security efforts of friendly and allied states affect US security problems and the type and size of the US effort required. In addition to security challenges posed by other states, today's policy makers must also address threats and opportunities that stem from global economic developments, the actions of non-state actors, and transnational threats, such as infectious disease. (See also chapter 1.)

Domestic Political and Economic Developments. American national security policy is heavily influenced by domestic politics, domestic policy goals, and perceptions of the health of the US economy. These influences can shape every aspect of the US national security agenda but may have their most tangible impact on the budgetary process. Defense budgets and programs may not determine strategy, but national security options are significantly influenced by the nature and extent of the resources available.

Domestic (and international) mass media organizations also play important roles in shaping US national security policy. The tremendously varied media sources currently available to Americans provide continuous access to information and images from all over the world. Although members of the media do not make national security policy, they can influence the agenda and frame issues for debate.

Technological Change. Technological advancements dramatically influence security concerns and calculations. One need only look at the carnage of World War I to see the results if policy does not keep pace with technology. There had been a century of unparalleled technological advancement between 1815 and 1914, yet a century of relative peace in Europe had left military strategy and tactics largely as they were at the time of the Congress of Vienna. The military plans of 1914 simply were not adequate for the proper employment of existing technological capabilities, and the bloody stalemate that developed on the Western front was due in large part to failure to adapt military strategy and tactics to new technological capabilities.

A more contemporary example concerns the rapid advance of information-related technologies. In the few short decades since the Internet came into existence, individuals and organizations have rushed to exploit the potential of rapidly improving information technologies, increasingly turning to cyberspace to communicate, to make and store wealth, to deliver essential services, and to perform vital national security functions.[4] By 2009, as President Barack Obama explained, "This world—cyberspace—is a world that we depend on every single day. . . . America's economic prosperity in the 21st century will depend on cybersecurity. And this is also a matter of public safety and national security."[5] Concern about the impact of developments in cyberspace on national security continued into the Trump administration, most notably in relation to questions over the extent of Russian interference in the 2016 presidential election. The dependence of modern societies on cyberspace for their way of life constitutes a structural change in the security environment with significant national security implications.

What is possible in American national security is in part determined by the technological capabilities of the United States relative to those of its potential adversaries. During the Cold War, the security of the United States and its allies relied upon the strength and invulnerability of US strategic nuclear weapons. Today, perceptions abroad of the US capability and willingness to employ its nuclear arsenal are still relevant to deterring potential threats from other states. However, a lessening of tensions between the United States and Russia since the end of the Cold War, the growing risks of nuclear proliferation, and increased concerns about the possible employment of nuclear weapons by terrorists have shifted the focus of US nuclear policy toward the latter two issue areas in the early twenty-first century.[6] (See chapter 17 for more on US nuclear policy.)

Strategy and Structure

National security strategies are implemented using instruments of power, with the military instrument often playing a significant role. Because international relations and domestic politics are intertwined, national security policy exists in two worlds. Decisions about strategy are made largely in response to perceived threats and opportunities in the international environment and are largely the domain of the president; they primarily shape diplomatic and economic commitments, deployment and employment of military forces, and the development and readiness of a variety of capabilities. Decisions pertaining to the development of instruments of power are more strongly influenced by domestic politics and are heavily influenced by Congress; they deal primarily with investment decisions as reflected in the national budget. In terms of defense policy, key investment decisions are those related to personnel, equipment, and readiness.[7]

Decisions relating to strategic objectives and to structure interact at all levels. The country's policy goals determine the instruments needed, while the instruments that have previously been created limit current strategic options. Moreover, ongoing programs created through structural decisions can have a dynamic of their own in shaping future strategy. At any moment in time, there is likely to be some disconnect between strategy and structure; strategy can change rapidly and is primarily the domain of the US executive branch, whereas structure takes time to build and key decisions are in the hands of Congress. (See also chapters 4 and 5 for more on the role of the president and Congress in US national security policy).

The closely intertwined yet ever-changing relationship between strategy and structure is a central dynamic in the evolution of US national security policy. After touching briefly on efforts during World War II to shape the postwar economic and security environment, this chapter progresses through each presidential administration and focuses on the relationship between strategy and structure and how international political and military developments, domestic priorities, and technological advances have affected this relationship for more than seven decades.

Postwar Planning during World War II

Even before World War II ended, diplomats and statesmen began to look beyond the war to the subsequent peace. The deep worldwide economic depression of the 1930s and the concomitant rise of aggressive militaristic states such as imperial Japan and fascist Germany made these statesmen aware that international peace and security would be intertwined with economic prosperity in the postwar world. Two of the developments that stemmed from this realization were the 1944 agreements at Bretton Woods, New Hampshire, which sought to develop mechanisms to regulate the postwar international economy, and the 1945 conference in San Francisco, California, that resulted in the United Nations (UN) charter. As suggested by the physical location of both of these conferences, the United States, along with its allies, played a leading role in forging these agreements. (See also chapter 25.)

With the broad aim of fostering global economic stability and growth, representatives of forty-four countries met at Bretton Woods in July 1944 to develop mechanisms that would support currency stability, economic reconstruction and development, and free trade. Their negotiations resulted in the creation of the International Monetary Fund to foster currency stability and the International Bank of Reconstruction and Development (also known as the World Bank) to support economic reconstruction and development. Trade issues proved the most difficult to address; a 1947 conference in Geneva, Switzerland, resulted in the General Agreement on Tariffs and Trade (GATT), which proposed rounds of trade negotiations to reduce barriers to trade worldwide. Only much later, in 1995, did the GATT evolve into the World Trade Organization.[8]

In addition to addressing economic issues, international negotiations conducted as World War II was drawing to an end sought to create an institution that could help foster international peace and security. To this end, representatives of fifty countries met in San Francisco from April to June in 1945 to draft the UN Charter. President Franklin D. Roosevelt was concerned not to repeat President Woodrow Wilson's failure to bring the United States into the League of Nations after World War I, so he had obtained advance congressional endorsement for the eventual membership of the United States in such an organization. Congress ultimately voted to ratify the UN Charter on July 28, 1945; the organization came into existence in October 1945, after the charter was ratified by twenty-nine countries.[9]

President Harry S. Truman and the Origins of Containment

The end of World War II saw the United States emerge as the most powerful nation on earth. Its homeland was untouched by war, and its enormous industrial potential had served as the "arsenal of democracy" for itself and its allies. The collapse of Germany and Japan led to visions of a prolonged peace implemented through the collective security machinery of the new United Nations. Technologically, the United States was also in an unchallengeable position. The US creation and use of the atomic bomb was probably the single most important development affecting postwar international relations.[10]

Rapid Demobilization, 1945–1946. With victory came enormous public and congressional pressure for the United States to bring the troops home. This domestic pressure led to one of the most rapid demobilizations in history. On the day that Japan surrendered and after the defeat of Nazi Germany, the Army had more than 8 million soldiers; less than a year after the end of the war, that number was down to less than 2 million.[11] By 1947, the United States had drawn down its armed forces from a wartime peak of 12 million soldiers, sailors, and airmen to a low of 1.4 million.[12]

This massive disarmament occurred even though the wartime alliance between the United States and the Soviet Union had been replaced by rapidly increasing tension. American policy makers, confronted with what they perceived to be aggressive Soviet intentions in Eastern Europe, Greece, Turkey, Iran, and East Asia, came to agree on the need for a tougher line. In 1947, US diplomat George Kennan expressed this emerging consensus when he advocated a policy of containment: "The main element of any United States policy toward the Soviet Union must be that of a long-term, patient but firm and vigilant containment of Russian expansive tendencies."[13]

Containment became the conceptual framework that structured American strategic policy for the next four decades. Opposition to communist expansion became the fundamental principle of American foreign policy. Despite disagreements over the means to achieve this goal, there was little disagreement on the goal itself. The policy of containment would lead in turn to reliance on the concept of *deterrence.*

New Strategy and Old Structure. Successful implementation of the policy of containment required ready forces sufficient to deny the Soviets the ability to expand their empire. For this purpose, having existing forces ready to meet immediate needs was clearly more useful than mobilization potential. In December 1947, Secretary of Defense James Forrestal listed the "four outstanding military facts of the world" as the predominance of Russian land power in Europe and Asia, the predominance of American sea power, exclusive US possession of the atomic bomb, and superior US production capacity.[14] The ground and air units of the United States and its allies were inadequate to contain the Soviet Union's conventional force capabilities, and the United States lacked doctrine appropriate for countering this Soviet superiority with its tiny atomic arsenal. The United States could threaten the Soviet homeland with atomic attack if Soviet armies marched into Western Europe, but the atom bomb was of little help in other defense tasks, such as preserving the integrity of Iran, deterring an attack on Korea, or suppressing guerrillas in Greece.[15] Conventional ground and air power seemed essential for these latter tasks, yet the US force structure was weakest in precisely those respects.

Implementing the policy of containment raised the difficult problem of how to deal with domestic political constraints on the size of the military effort. Overriding a presidential veto, Congress passed a general income tax reduction bill in early 1948, thereby limiting the revenue available for domestic and military expenditures. Despite the president's requests, no substantial tax increases would be approved until after the outbreak of the Korean War. Because President Harry Truman was determined to balance the budget, the administration imposed a ceiling on military expenditures consonant with the reduced resources available. Domestic political priorities left inadequate monies for the forces-in-being that were assessed as needed to contain Soviet power. Thus, by default, reliance on mobilization continued.

A second constraint on the successful implementation of the policy of containment was the doctrinal orientation of the military. American military thinking was still preoccupied with preparations to mobilize forces to win a major war if one should occur.[16] The goals of each of the armed services had been set prior to the end of World War II, and because there was no unified force design or budgetary process, each service became locked into its own vision of its future role and mission. As political scientist Samuel Huntington observed, "The two great constraints of effective military planning, the doctrinal heritage from the past and the pressure of domestic needs, combined to produce a serious gap between military policy and foreign policy."[17]

In response to these challenges, the Truman administration secured passage of the National Security Act of 1947. Among other things, the act separated the Air Force from the Army and consolidated the military services into a unified defense establishment. In addition, the act empowered the new secretary of defense to be able, in theory, to neutralize service biases by crafting an overall strategic vision that the services would be required to support. However, despite a revision to the act in 1949 that created the Department of Defense (DoD) and was designed to give the secretary of defense more power, the service chiefs remained focused on their own agendas. Other important provisions in the 1947 legislation created the Central Intelligence Agency (CIA) and the National Security Council (NSC), which provided potentially powerful tools for presidents to formulate and shape national security priorities.

The Truman Doctrine. On March 12, 1947, Truman appeared before a joint session of Congress and outlined his views on the necessary US response to communist pressure in Greece and Turkey. In what came to be known as the Truman Doctrine, the president argued that the United States must help other states to maintain their political institutions and national integrity when threatened by aggressive attempts to overthrow them. This was no more than a frank recognition, Truman declared, that totalitarian systems imposed their will on free people, by direct or indirect aggression and that, by thus undermining the foundations of international peace, they threatened the security of the United States.[18]

The Truman Doctrine represented a marked departure from the US tradition of minimal peacetime involvement in international affairs. Although the 1904 Roosevelt Corollary to the Monroe Doctrine had articulated a rationale for US intervention in the Western Hemisphere, the Truman Doctrine justified US military and economic aid programs to any state around the globe that faced communist aggression. The justification it contained for American intervention in foreign lands was used repeatedly by subsequent administrations.[19]

The Marshall Plan. The Marshall Plan, a massive US economic aid program launched in 1948, was designed to help restore the war-shattered economies of Europe. American leaders believed that the ability of Europe to resist communist aggression was dependent on its rapid economic recovery.[20] In conjunction with the establishment of the Bretton Woods institutions and the United Nations, the Marshall Plan marked the emergence of the United States as a country willing to devote considerable resources to the promotion of international stability. The Marshall Plan and the Truman Doctrine also heralded a new US willingness to adopt an activist role to protect US interests abroad.

Events soon solidified the US view of the communist threat and affected the formulation of US security strategy. In 1948, the forced communization of Czechoslovakia and the blockade of surface access routes to West Berlin intensified Western perceptions of the Soviet Union as an overtly hostile state. In August 1949, the Soviet Union exploded its first nuclear device, and in October, communist forces won the Chinese civil war, dramatically shifting the balance of power in Asia and creating the perception of a monolithic adversary stretching from Prague to Beijing.

NSC 68 and Its Implications. The disturbing events of 1948–1949 highlighted inadequacies in US military posture. Awareness of these shortcomings led to the first serious attempt to reconcile strategy with structure—that is, to balance the strategy of containment with a force designed to implement that strategy. A joint committee of the State and Defense Departments was instructed "to make an overall review and reassessment of American foreign and defense policy."[21] Its report, labeled "NSC 68" and delivered to the NSC on April 1, 1950, advocated "a much more rapid and concerted build-up of the actual strength of both the United States and the other nations of the free world" to counter the Soviet threat through means other than war.[22] NSC 68 called for a substantial increase in defense expenditures, warning that the United States must be capable of dealing with both limited war and all-out war. The problem was how to sell a substantial increase in the defense budget to an administration committed to a policy of economy and balanced budgets. The problem was solved on June 25, 1950, when North Korea invaded South Korea.

War and Rearmament. The invasion of South Korea was the immediate crisis that generated public support for vastly increased defense spending. Expenditures for national security programs nearly quadrupled between FY 1950 and FY 1953, rising from $13 billion to $50.4 billion.[23] Nevertheless, important differences of opinion remained concerning Soviet intentions in South Korea and elsewhere. Some felt that the North Korean attack was part of a general Soviet plan for worldwide expansion, while others saw it as a feint designed to divert resources from Europe.[24] Despite these differences, Communist China's entry into the war in late 1950 solidified US perceptions of an aggressive, monolithic communist threat.

The outbreak of the war found the United States with an extremely limited conventional capability. The rearmament effort was characterized by three competing, but complementary purposes: immediate prosecution of the Korean War, creation of a mobilization base for the long term, and development of active forces to balance Soviet strength and to deter further Soviet aggression.[25] In short, the war in Korea made rearmament possible, but rearmament was not directed solely at the problem of fighting the war; forces were also developed for worldwide deterrence purposes.[26]

NATO: The Institutionalization of Containment. The Soviet Union's political pressure on its neighbors and the great size of its conventional forces caused widespread and increasing concern about the security of Western Europe. As a consequence, the United States deemed it necessary to enter into a peacetime alliance and for the first time to deploy forces on the territory of allies in the absence of armed conflict. In the North Atlantic Treaty, which was signed in April 1949, the twelve parties from Europe and North America agreed that an attack on one would be considered an attack on all. The North Atlantic Treaty Organization (NATO) was the expression of the US effort to contain communism by military means, and Europe became America's first line of defense.

An initial goal of ninety NATO divisions (half active, half reserve) by 1954 was deemed by experts and agreed by political leaders to be necessary for a conventional defense of Europe, but it quickly became obvious that the goal would not be met. By 1952, European members of NATO, already less fearful than they had been about the possibility of Soviet military aggression in Europe, began to reduce defense budgets, cut terms of service for draftees, and stretch out arms procurements. NATO members subsequently approved a drastic reduction in force goals and came to rely much more on the tactical and strategic nuclear weapons of the United States to deter Soviet aggression.

Conflicting Priorities. With continuing casualties and costs in Korea, as well as a stalemated military situation, the American public became increasingly sour on the war. It had also become evident that the war was not the beginning of a general Soviet assault on the West. Public resentment over military spending rose and, by 1952, the Truman administration made a marked shift toward domestic priorities. At the same time, however, US policy makers and the public believed that the international communist threat to US and European security was real and immediate. Acceptance of the strategy of containment and the necessity for forces-in-being reflected the realities of international and technological affairs. The challenge for President Dwight Eisenhower, when he took office in 1953, would be to reconcile conflicting demands for increased spending on domestic priorities with the needs of national defense.

The Eisenhower Administration, 1953–1960: Massive Retaliation and the New Look

From the outset, Eisenhower regarded the threat to US security as dual: both military and economic. The military threat posed by the communist powers was obvious, but Eisenhower also believed that continued high levels of defense spending threatened the health of the US economy and were, therefore, also significant long-term threats. To counter this dual threat, domestic and military expenditures would have to be properly balanced for an extended period.

Domestic Priorities and Strategic Reassessment. To preserve US economic vitality, Eisenhower was determined to reduce military expenditures and balance the federal budget. An impasse developed between the administration and the military, as the Joint Chiefs of Staff (JCS) were committed to a substantial military buildup in line with NSC 68. Eisenhower replaced the members of the JCS, and in May 1953 the new JCS assumed the task that their predecessors had refused: wrestling with the difficult problems of strategic reassessment.

In a study labeled "NSC 162," the NSC Planning Board made an effort to define future national security policy in the broadest sense. The paper recommended the continuation of the policy of containment but with greater reliance on nuclear weapons, strategic air power, and air defense capabilities that could protect the continental United States. The Sequoia Study conducted by the JCS concurred; it recommended further development of strategic retaliatory forces and the withdrawal of some US troops from overseas. Allies would form the first line of defense, buttressed by American air and naval power; the majority of US forces would be held in reserve.[27]

The Strategic Impact of Technology and the New Look. Technological advances provided the means by which Eisenhower sought to implement a strategy of global containment on a discount budget. The overwhelming superiority of the American nuclear arsenal would provide cost-effective strategic options, which in turn would allow the administration to cut expensive conventional capabilities in favor of domestic programs.

The Eisenhower "New Look" defense program made a number of assumptions about the international environment: that there would be no significant increase in international tensions and no significant change in the relationship between US and Soviet power. The New Look relied heavily on nuclear weapons and the threat that aggression would be met with massive retaliation.[28] Strategic air power became the mainstay of the US deterrent posture, and tactical nuclear weapons were to be used to replace the reduced levels of conventional forces in forward defense areas.

The critical strategic change was expressed by Secretary of State John Foster Dulles on January 12, 1954: "There is no local defense which alone will contain the mighty land power of the Communist world. Local defenses must be reinforced by the further deterrent of massive retaliation power."[29] Therefore, Dulles stated, the president had made the basic decision "to depend primarily upon a great capacity to retaliate instantly and by means and at places of our own choosing."[30] In sum, America would rely on nuclear weapons to meet even those military contingencies threatening less than general war. The member countries of NATO subsequently agreed to the deployment of tactical nuclear weapons in Western Europe and authorized military planners to assume that nuclear weapons would be used in the event of hostilities.

Extending Containment. Given deep and widespread concern in the United States about communist aggression, the presumption that US nuclear weapons could and would serve to deter both large and small aggressions, and the desire for a balanced budget, it appeared to make sense in the 1950s to strengthen governments on the periphery of the communist bloc. Extending the American military alliance system beyond NATO became an integral part of containment strategy.

One principal lesson of the Korean War, as perceived by US policy makers in the 1950s, was that American disengagement and equivocation had tempted the communists to invade Korea. America's commitment to defend friendly territories adjacent to communist countries must be made explicit through military alliances. The United States therefore began to include Asia in its ring of containment by knitting the states of the region into a network of military alliances under US leadership.

In 1951, the United States negotiated a security treaty with Japan that guaranteed the defense of Japan and granted the US military the right to maintain military bases on its territory. A similar mutual defense treaty was signed with the Philippines. Also in 1951, the United States signed the Australia, New Zealand, United States Security Treaty, or ANZUS, pledging US support for the security of these countries. In 1953, following the armistice, the Republic of Korea and the United States signed a security pact pledging consultation in the event of armed attack and establishing the disposition of land, sea, and air forces in and around South Korea. In 1954, the United States signed a treaty with Taiwan that called for joint consultation in the event or threat of armed attack and specified the disposition of US forces on Taiwan and the nearby islands of the Pescadores.

In 1954, the United States established the Southeast Asian Treaty Organization (SEATO) with Australia, France, New Zealand, Pakistan, the Philippines, Thailand, and the United Kingdom. Each of these members committed to "act to meet the common danger" in the event of hostilities in the treaty area. In addition to joining SEATO, the United States also sent millions of dollars in military aid to Indochina to help finance the French war with the Viet Minh. In 1954, as the French position in Vietnam became tenuous, the French government requested the commitment of American troops, but Eisenhower refused.

In 1959, the Central Treaty Organization (CENTO), which the United States supported but did not formally join, was also launched. The alliance, intended to prevent Soviet expansion southward, linked the United Kingdom, Turkey, Iran, and Pakistan. The United States also signed bilateral defense agreements with Pakistan and with Iran.

Covert Action. In addition to reliance on nuclear weapons and the extension of alliances, Eisenhower turned to the CIA, under Director Allen Dulles, for another relatively low-cost means to protect US national interests and gain advantage in the Cold War struggle against the Soviet Union and other countries that could become Soviet allies.[31] In addition to conducting its mission to provide intelligence, the CIA undertook covert operations in the 1950s in support of the coup against Iran's Prime Minister Mohammad Mossadegh in 1953, the overthrow of Guatemala's President Jacobo Arbenz in 1954, and other activities against regimes around the world that were perceived to embrace communism.[32]

Near the end of the Eisenhower administration, the CIA began to plan for the ouster of Fidel Castro in Cuba. Castro had overthrown the US-friendly regime of Fulgencio Batista at the beginning of 1959.[33] One element of the CIA program approved by Eisenhower involved the training of Cuban exiles in Guatemala with the intent that they would return to Cuba to lead a revolution to depose Castro. The Bay of Pigs invasion was launched by Eisenhower's successor in 1961; its failure resulted in the firing of Allen Dulles as CIA director. The Bay of Pigs disaster, as well as the second- and third-order effects of other CIA covert action missions in the 1950s, ultimately sparked a debate that continues to this day about the utility of covert action as an instrument of US foreign policy.[34] (For more on intelligence, see chapter 7.)

The "New New Look," 1956. When the policy of massive retaliation was formally established in 1954, the United States possessed the ability to destroy the military forces of the Soviet Union with little likelihood of serious retaliatory damage. By 1956, however, this was no longer the case. Major Soviet catch-up efforts and technological innovations had led to an arms race; in an astonishingly short time, mutual vulnerability to nuclear devastation had become a fact.[35] The rapid growth of Soviet strategic nuclear power had undermined the New Look's two key assumptions: that the earlier ratio of Soviet-to-American nuclear power would not be radically altered and that US nuclear retaliatory forces could deter both large and small aggressions. Even at the outset, the doctrine of massive retaliation had been criticized by analysts who argued that the threat of massive nuclear retaliation would not be effective in deterring communist countries from participating—either overtly or covertly—in relatively small-scale wars around the world because the use of nuclear weapons in such situations was simply not believable. Only conventional forces, they held, could deal effectively with such relatively low-level conflicts.

The administration began to look for a strategy that permitted greater flexibility. The resulting "New New Look" adjusted existing programs without increasing military expenditures. Its dominant characteristics included continuing efforts to stabilize military spending; downgrading of mobilization, readiness, and reserve forces; accepting that US strategic retaliatory capability was just sufficient to deter a direct attack on US territory or equally vital interests; and recognizing, if reluctantly, the need to build and maintain capabilities for limited war.[36]

It should be noted that the New New Look continued to treat tactical nuclear weapons as a credible means of waging limited war. Indeed, one of the major distinctions of the new approach was the direct integration of tactical nuclear weapons into the strategy of limited war.[37] Writing in the October 1957 issue of *Foreign Affairs*, John Foster Dulles explained that "in the future it may . . . be feasible to place less reliance upon deterrence of vast retaliatory power," because the "nations which are around the Sino-Soviet perimeter can possess an effective defense [through tactical nuclear warfare] against full-scale conventional attack."[38]

Eisenhower's programs were shaped by the twin pressures of Soviet and American technological achievement and an American economy that was plagued by both continuing recession and inflation. Largely as a result of inflation, defense costs were rising. Confronted with a choice between increasing the national debt and reducing military spending, the Eisenhower administration chose the latter. In constant dollar terms, military spending was less in 1960 than it had been in any year since 1951.[39]

The final years of the Eisenhower presidency saw a number of international and technological pressures on US national security policy. In August 1957, the Soviets announced the successful test of an intercontinental ballistic missile (ICBM). In October of that year, the Soviets launched the first artificial satellite, Sputnik, causing an intense reexamination of US strategic programs. The Gaither Committee, appointed early in 1957 by Eisenhower to study a fallout shelter program for the United States, presented its report shortly after the launching of Sputnik. Defining its mandate broadly, the committee recommended a substantial increase in the defense budget aimed primarily at improving the US strategic posture.[40] Although the committee's recommendations were largely rejected, the discussion of strategic capabilities that it triggered helped make the charge that a "missile gap" existed in favor of the Soviet Union into an issue in the 1960 presidential campaign.

The Kennedy-Johnson Years, 1961–1968: Flexible Response

As the new decade began, changes in both the external environment and technology dictated a reappraisal of national strategy. The growth of Soviet nuclear capabilities cast doubt upon the wisdom and credibility of US retaliatory threats, and the missile-gap controversy raised questions about the adequacy of US nuclear force levels. Western awareness of the increasingly bitter dispute between China and the Soviet Union aggravated the problem of deterrence as China came to be viewed as a potential power center and threat in its own right.

Changes in weapons technology and force structure also made a reexamination of US policy imperative. Reliance on tactical nuclear weapons, particularly in Europe, was increasingly viewed as dangerous for two main reasons. First, the relatively weakened US strategic position meant that deterrence might fail. If it did, escalation to all-out nuclear war would be hard to check because, while there tends to be a clear "firebreak" between the use of conventional and nuclear weapons, there is no such discernible break between the deployment of tactical and strategic nuclear weapons. Second, should a crisis arise, shortages of conventional forces would present decision makers with a difficult choice between nuclear retaliation and inaction. Turbulence in the developing countries of the world also demonstrated the shortcomings of US retaliatory strategy: the Soviet Union and China were giving military and economic assistance to "wars of national liberation" in Asia, Africa, and Latin America. The policy of massive retaliation was inadequate to deal with these complexities. Just a few years earlier, technology had been seen as a panacea capable of ensuring containment while limiting military spending. Now, however, the domestic political debate focused on the potential dangers of reliance on nuclear technology.

Military Structure and the McNamara Pentagon. Despite the goals of the National Security Act of 1947 and subsequent reforms, the missions of the various armed services were still determined largely independently of one another when Robert McNamara became President John Kennedy's secretary of defense in 1961. Monies were allocated among the services on a "fair share" basis, and each service developed programs within its budget constraints with little regard for what the others were doing. "Army planning, for example, was based, largely, on a long war of attrition, while the Air Force planning was based, largely, on a short war of nuclear bombardment."[41] Each service developed its strategic nuclear program independently, as if the programs of other services did not exist.[42] McNamara was determined to control and rationalize the development of US military forces. He received two instructions from the president: "Develop the force structure necessary to our military requirements without regard to arbitrary or predetermined budget ceilings. And secondly . . . procure it at the lowest possible cost."[43] McNamara set out to increase US combat strength measurably and quickly, even as he developed a new military strategy.

Flexible Response. The strategy of Flexible Response was developed to give the president the capability to respond effectively to any challenge with the appropriate level of force. Flexible response within the strategic nuclear posture provided policy makers the options of massive retaliation, limited nuclear countervalue attacks (that is, against population centers), or counterforce strikes (against military targets). The Kennedy and Johnson administrations increased the strategic inventory dramatically, developing the capability to inflict "unacceptable damage" on the Soviet Union even after absorbing a surprise first strike.[44]

Although these changes were significant, it was in the area of conventional forces that the doctrine of Flexible Response departed most drastically from the concept of massive retaliation. To provide adequate options, conventional force capabilities had to be improved and modernized. The Army was increased from twelve to sixteen divisions, the Navy surface fleet was enlarged, and the reserves and National Guard were revitalized. Special operations forces were also enhanced. In general, the United States sought a "two-and-a-half" war posture: that is, the United States sought to be capable of fighting a large-scale war in Europe, another sizable war somewhere else in the world, and a third, smaller-scale conflict, all simultaneously.

American efforts to introduce a Flexible Response doctrine into NATO initially encountered allied resistance. The increased reliance on conventional forces caused uneasiness among Europeans, who feared erosion of the nuclear deterrent. The Eisenhower administration had asserted that nuclear weapons might well be used, but by the end of the Johnson administration, the United States was reluctant to contemplate the use of nuclear weapons in limited wars.

Conventional Forces and Intervention. Improvements in capabilities were not matched by the development of clear doctrines to govern intervention and the application of force. In his inaugural address, Kennedy had made his famous pledge: "Let every nation know, whether it wishes us well or ill, we shall pay any price, bear any burden, meet any hardship, support any friend, or oppose any foe to assure the survival and the success of liberty."[45] Such an open-ended commitment was, of course, unrealistic, for it did not provide any useful guidance for deciding when the use of force was in the national interest and when it was not. In 1965, the United States deployed ground combat troops to the Republic of Vietnam and also intervened in a civil upheaval in the Dominican Republic. As the Vietnam War lengthened and deepened, popular dissatisfaction grew, and domestic dissent and economic pressure began to play a significant role in the formulation of US strategy. By FY 1968, defense spending had climbed to $78 billion, $20 billion of which represented the direct cost of the war in Vietnam.[46] After a deeply divisive presidential election season, the incoming Nixon administration faced the prospect of strategic nuclear stalemate and an unpopular war.

The Nixon and Ford Administrations, 1969–1976: A Strategy of Realistic Deterrence

By 1969, the national consensus on US national security policy had seriously weakened. The prolonged and costly US intervention in Vietnam raised doubts about the ability of the United States to deal with insurgencies around the world, and the nature of the strategic balance dictated a reassessment of American defense policy.

The policy of containment no longer seemed to reflect a realistic appraisal of the international situation.

Reassessment of the Strategic Environment. By 1968, the Soviet Union had achieved rough nuclear parity with the United States. Either side could inflict unacceptable damage on the other even after absorbing a first strike. Under these conditions, the United States and the Soviet Union seemed to realize that it was in their best interests to limit the possibilities of confrontation. From such reasoning, at least on the US side, came the concept of *détente* and the associated Strategic Arms Limitation Talks (SALT).

At least two other important factors informed US thinking about military policy. First, public and congressional disenchantment with the war in Vietnam dictated a reevaluation of where and how US conventional forces might be used. Second, economic constraints also had an impact: the position of the dollar in the world economy had deteriorated as wartime inflation increased, and domestic social and economic problems seemed to demand greater investment.

Strategic Sufficiency. Given the Soviet Union's nuclear arsenal and its demonstrated ability and willingness to match improvements in American strategic forces, the Nixon administration concluded that nuclear superiority would be impossible to maintain.[47] Any attempt to do so would only escalate the arms race without increasing security for either side. However, President Nixon was also unwilling to allow the Soviet Union to achieve a position of nuclear dominance. Planning for US forces thus focused on "strategic sufficiency." Reflecting an acceptance of nuclear parity, this doctrine included a number of precepts:

- *Assured destruction:* The United States would maintain three separate and independent offensive systems: ICBMs, submarine-launched ballistic missiles (SLBMs), and manned bombers. This "triad" would ensure that even if the United States were struck first, it would be able to inflict unacceptable levels of damage on the enemy through destruction of its population and economy.[48]
- *Flexible nuclear options:* Flexibility of forces and targets would allow the president to tailor any US strategic response to the nature of the provocation.
- *Crisis stability:* Enhanced and flexible capabilities would reduce Soviet willingness to stage a less-than-all-out attack and would eliminate a Soviet incentive to strike first.[49]
- *Perceived equality:* A rough balance of strategic capabilities would prevent coercion or intimidation of the United States or its allies.

Conventional Force Policy. In 1974, the Nixon administration's appraisal of conventional war policy reaffirmed one traditional commitment and modified another. The US commitment to NATO was reaffirmed and strengthened following the US withdrawal from Vietnam. Although the overall size of the US Army was reduced by 50 percent, US NATO forces—which had been deprived of personnel and equipment during the Vietnam War—were strengthened and re-equipped. Additionally, the United States abandoned the so-called two-and-a-half-war strategy and began to maintain forces based on a one-and-a-half-war strategy. (In reality, this change was not that dramatic, since the United States had never acquired the level of forces needed for two-and-a-half wars.) The NATO commitment became the primary planning contingency for structuring US conventional forces.

A major reappraisal of US policy also centered on the feasibility of deterring or fighting local conflicts in developing countries. The resulting policy, known as the Nixon Doctrine, concluded that the United States would no longer automatically intervene against externally supported insurgencies. The Nixon Doctrine could be expressed as three essential principles: self-help, primary regional responsibility, and residual US responsibility.[50] The principle of self-help dictated that the country being threatened must take responsibility for its own security. Further, in the case of insurgency, the United States would expect the local government to initiate vigorous programs of economic and political development.[51] The second principle, regional responsibility, meant that the United States expected neighboring countries to work together to eliminate or deal with causes of instability in their area. Finally, the principle of residual US responsibility indicated that while the United States might provide military assistance, it would intervene directly only if vital American interests were threatened. President Gerald Ford and later President Jimmy Carter endorsed this policy of strictly limited US involvement as the basis for US action in dealing with insurgencies in developing nations.

The Carter Administration, 1977–1981: Strategic Reassessment

As is customary with a new administration, President Carter initiated a reappraisal of US national security policy when he took office in January 1977. Such reappraisal was clearly warranted, for much had changed. The steady strengthening of Soviet nuclear forces underscored the momentum of the strategic arms race and the importance of moving forward with arms control. A second important dynamic involved the People's Republic of China: Nixon's reestablishment of the US-China dialogue in 1972 had reversed a longstanding policy of treating that country as a prime danger. A third trend related to the proliferation of newly independent countries since World War II and the increasing demands made by these countries for a more just international order.

Another important cause for reassessment concerned past US policy. Détente, a central theme of the Nixon administration's approach to foreign affairs, had been discredited. The original goal of détente was to lessen tension and hostility between the superpowers. By the beginning of the Carter administration, however, it appeared that the Soviet Union had interpreted détente as mere acknowledgment of the new power balance and a license to expand its influence. Americans were unhappy with a policy that seemed incapable of checking the adventurism of the Soviet Union and its allies in the noncommunist world.

The United States had also changed dramatically on the domestic front. The wars in Korea and Vietnam seemed to illustrate the reduced utility of military force, feeding renewed skepticism about defense spending and worldwide military deployments. The recession of 1974–1975 led to a reemphasis on domestic priorities and raised further questions about the extent to which resources should be channeled into expensive defense programs. As a presidential candidate in 1976, Carter made clear his intent to reduce military spending in favor of domestic priorities. Despite evidence of a continuing massive Soviet military buildup, there was sufficient uncertainty to permit both presidential candidates to downplay the specter of future Soviet adventurism.

Technology also had, to some extent, restructured the security environment. Continued technological advancements—such as multiple independently targetable reentry vehicles (MIRVs) for nuclear weapons; cruise missiles; and anti-satellite capabilities—threatened to upset perceptions of nuclear stability. Improvements in conventional weapons, including video-guided bombs and laser-guided artillery shells, had enhanced military capabilities, but the consequences for the stability of conventional force balances were not yet fully understood.[52]

The Carter administration crafted its foreign policy strategy based on each of these factors and in light of its own comprehensive assessment of the comparative strengths of the United States and the Soviet Union. In 1977, the administration reaffirmed the importance of maintaining a balance in strategic nuclear forces, choosing the label of "essential equivalence." It continued to rely upon the concept of massive retaliation but backed away from plans for limited nuclear options that had been considered during the Nixon administration. In the context of essential equivalence, the Carter administration picked up the lagging SALT II talks and pressed them forward vigorously. The subsequent treaty signed by Carter and General Secretary Leonid Brezhnev in Vienna in 1979, although never ratified by the US Senate, continued to define the upper limits of essential equivalence into the 1980s.

The Carter administration underscored the key role of NATO in Europe and reaffirmed the existing forward strategy. The overall concept of having forces sufficient to fight a major war in Europe and simultaneously a smaller war elsewhere—the one-and-a-half-war construct of the Nixon administration—was endorsed as the guiding principle behind the size and character of the defense forces. In part as a response to fears about energy security stemming from the oil crisis of 1973, special attention was focused on the Persian Gulf as the possible site of the "one-half" war. Although measures to create the force projection capability required to respond to crises in the Persian Gulf were slow to get under way, the administration's declared policy accorded the region higher priority than it had earlier received.

In a bid to stabilize the power balance in Asia and to create a more satisfactory framework for US-Soviet relations, the administration proceeded with the normalization of American relations with the People's Republic of China. Formal recognition occurred in early 1979, immediately preceding a visit to the United States by Vice-Premier Deng Xiaoping. In fulfillment of Carter's campaign promises, the administration also began preparations to withdraw American ground forces from the Republic of Korea; congressional opposition, however, forced the administration to leave those US forces in place.

In terms of overall national security policy, the 1970s ended on a somewhat surprising note. The Soviet Union's impressive and continuing defense buildup, its invasion of Afghanistan in 1979, and its gains in a number of other regions—generally propelled by Soviet arms and advisors and sometimes by Cuban proxies—had so alarmed large sectors of the public and Congress that a stronger defense policy and increased spending were pressed on a reluctant president. This was exacerbated by the results of the Islamic revolution in Iran earlier in 1979, which included an ongoing American hostage crisis and the loss of a US ally in a strategic region. As a result of these changes in the security environment, Carter's final defense budget and five-year defense plan contained substantial increases.

The Reagan Administration, 1981–1988: Redressing the Military Balance

America entered the 1980s with a new administration committed to strengthening US power, to resisting further Soviet-supported communist expansion, and to leaving Marxism-Leninism on "the ash heap of history." From 1981 to 1988, the US defense budget almost doubled in the largest peacetime military buildup in American history. The United States moved rapidly to deploy a new-generation triad of strategic nuclear systems, to expand the US naval fleet from about 479 to 600 ships, and to modernize US conventional land and air forces.[53] One of the more dramatic developments in US national security policy during this period came in March 1983, when the president called for the development of a system to defend the United States against ballistic missile attack. Called the Strategic Defense Initiative, or "Star Wars" by the media, it could radically alter the forms of future military confrontation.[54]

In the developing world, the Reagan administration turned to a more activist policy of American support for noncommunist insurgencies against Soviet-supported communist regimes. This policy, which came to be known as the Reagan Doctrine, enjoyed several successes. In 1983, an American military intervention in Grenada stopped the threat of a communist-supported takeover. American aid to anti-communist forces probably contributed to the Soviet Union's decision to withdraw its support for the Marxist government in Angola and, in part, to the Soviet decision to withdraw from Afghanistan in 1989. More problematic were efforts by Reagan administration officials to funnel aid to anticommunist "Contra" guerillas in Nicaragua. The manner in which high-ranking officials provided aid to the Contras violated US law and became known as the Iran-Contra scandal. Reagan's national security advisor resigned, and another member of his staff was fired in an affair that called into question the president's management of White House personnel.[55]

In the midst of confrontation, the 1985 emergence of Mikhail Gorbachev as the leader of the Soviet Union presented the opportunity for beginning a new dialogue.

The Reagan administration's strategy of deferring major efforts at arms control until it was in a position to negotiate from strength began to pay off in a series of Soviet concessions that eventually led to the Intermediate Nuclear Forces (INF) Treaty of 1987. With subsequent dramatic changes in Eastern Europe and the breakup of the Warsaw Pact, other negotiations would eventually yield the Conventional Forces in Europe (CFE) Treaty of 1990 and the Strategic Arms Reduction Treaty (START) of 1991.

Goldwater-Nichols. Although the preceding decades had seen numerous shifts in national security policy as the threat evolved, many in Congress and the executive branch believed that the formulation and communication of national security strategy remained flawed. Past national security policies had generally failed to focus adequately on national values, interests, and goals. Moreover, these strategies still did not provide the integration that the 1947 National Security Act was meant to foster. In response, Congress passed the most significant legislation on national security since the 1947 law. The Goldwater-Nichols Department of Defense Reorganization Act of 1986 required the president to report the administration's national security strategy to Congress on an annual basis. In this document, the president would codify the values, national interests, and key objectives that would drive security and defense policies. The report would also allow Congress to evaluate the coherence and feasibility of the administration's reconciliation of ends, ways, and means.

In addition to providing focus, Goldwater-Nichols sought to integrate the US armed services better with one another. Despite the intent of the 1947 legislation and McNamara's reforms, interservice rivalry still dominated budget allocation, weapons programs, and the planning and execution of military operations. In response, the 1986 act strengthened mechanisms for integrating service-specific budget programs and streamlined the operational chain of command from the president through the secretary of defense to theater commanders. The legislation also sought to improve military advice by making the chairman—rather than the Joint Chiefs of Staff as a corporate body—the president's principal military advisor. In the past, consensus-based decisionmaking processes had tended to dilute the military advice the Joint Chiefs of Staff provided to the president. The Goldwater-Nichols legislation also addressed weaknesses in joint war-fighting capabilities, which were revealed in a failed attempt to rescue US hostages in Iran in 1980 and during the 1983 military operation in Grenada, by mandating improved service interoperability.[56] (For more on the role played by Congress in US national security affairs, see chapter 5.)

The George H. W. Bush Administration, 1989–1992: Toward a New World Order

The NSC staff under President George H. W. Bush began a review right after he took office in 1989, but events in the Soviet Union and Eastern Europe were moving so fast that publication of the administration's national security strategy had to be delayed. By 1989, Gorbachev's policies of *glasnost* (openness) and *perestroika* (restructuring) and the sheer force of his personality, combined with deep domestic economic problems, led to the end of the Cold War and, ultimately, to the demise of the Soviet Union. The United States and its allies had effectively contained the Soviet Union for forty years. After an aborted putsch in Moscow in August 1991 aimed at overthrowing Gorbachev and his reforms, the old Soviet Union was finished, although the future of its fifteen former republics remained to be settled.

In 1989, after the newly appointed leadership of East Germany declared its borders with the West to be open, West German Chancellor Helmut Kohl sought to unify Germany for the first time since 1945. In the midst of a rapidly changing situation in Europe, George H. W. Bush achieved a major diplomatic triumph. Through astute diplomatic engagement with allies in Europe as well as the Soviet Union, the administration was able to help bring about German unification and to ensure the newly reunified Germany's membership in NATO.[57]

The Bush administration soon faced another crisis in the Middle East when Saddam Hussein's Iraq sent its military forces into Kuwait in August 1990. Although this invasion was a surprise, the Bush administration responded with robust diplomacy and firm military action.[58] With the acquiescence of the Soviet Union and the backing of a UN Security Council resolution, the United States led a coalition of more than thirty states that included approximately 500,000 American troops to a swift and decisive defeat of the Iraqi Army and the liberation of Kuwait.

In the midst of these dramatic international developments, the Bush administration's 1991 national security review called for fundamental changes. These changes included: a focus on regional conflict; a need to shift future arms control efforts from the US-Soviet balance to a broader, global focus on nuclear nonproliferation; and the need to take economic issues into account in national security planning.[59]

Reflecting new realities, and anxious to satisfy domestic cravings for a "peace dividend" in the wake of the Cold War, Secretary of Defense Richard Cheney and Chairman of the Joint Chiefs of Staff Colin Powell appeared before the Senate budget committee in January 1991 to propose a multi-year 25 percent reduction in American forces from 1990 levels. By 1995, those cuts would reduce active-duty Army divisions from eighteen to twelve, the Air Force from thirty-six fighter wing equivalents to twenty-six, the Navy from 546 ships to 451, and reserve forces and Department of Defense (DoD) civilian employees by over 200,000 each. In addition, Cheney and Powell announced plans to cancel one hundred weapons programs and to close or realign over two hundred bases and facilities worldwide. As Cheney later explained, "The cuts would reduce the US military to its lowest end strength since before the Korean War; they would cut our [DoD] share of the Federal budget, once as high as 57 percent, to 18 percent, the lowest level in forty years. The defense budget would fall by 1997 to 3.4 percent of GNP, by far the lowest level since before Pearl Harbor."[60]

The new military strategy guiding this "defense build-down" reflected the shift from containing the spread of communism and deterring Soviet aggression to a

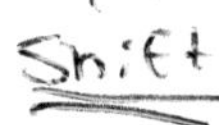

more varied and flexible approach. The major force structure requirements included strategic deterrence and defense; a forward but reduced presence of US conventional forces in regions vital to US national interests; a crisis response capability that could meet short-notice demands either unilaterally or with multilateral partners; and, given longer warning times, a military and industrial capacity to reconstitute forces against major threats.[61] In 1992, as the FY 1993 defense budget was being debated on Capitol Hill, it appeared that Congress largely agreed with the administration—for the time being—that US military capabilities would be reduced but would not be allowed to plummet as had occurred after earlier wars.

Although the George H. W. Bush administration met with considerable foreign and national security policy success, the weight of domestic affairs was evident in the president's failure to win reelection in 1992. Earning only lackluster support among some Republicans, who failed to forgive him for reneging on a promise not to raise taxes, George H. W. Bush was defeated by Democratic candidate Bill Clinton, who famously capitalized on the economic recession then plaguing the country with a campaign that was focused on the economy.

The Clinton Years, 1993–2000: Cautious Change

President Bill Clinton's administration sought to respond to the complexities of a post–Cold War world with a defense strategy organized along three basic lines: first, the United States would prevent threats from emerging; second, the United States would deter threats that did emerge; and third, if the first two lines of defense failed, the United States would have the capability to defeat threats using military force. The first category emphasized a range of confidence-building measures and the strengthening of democratic societies, as well as the maintenance of strong alliances, efforts to counter the spread of weapons of mass destruction (WMD), the forging of a pragmatic partnership with Russia, engagement in multilateral security dialogues, and the pursuit of comprehensive engagement with China. On the second line of defense, deterrence, the Clinton administration asserted that only the United States could deter threats worldwide. To do so, the United States required a reduced but effective nuclear force; strong, ready, forward-deployed conventional forces with a clear power projection capability; and the demonstrated will to use those forces when vital interests were threatened. Third, as the final line of defense, the United States needed dominance built on readiness, high technology weapons, and superior information systems to ensure victory.[62]

Military Structure. The Clinton administration did not make any dramatic changes to military force guidance or structure to implement this strategy. Beginning in 1993, the defense drawdown begun by the preceding administration continued as defense spending remained relatively stable. The Clinton administration's two major reviews of defense policy, the Bottom-Up Review of 1993–1994 and the Quadrennial Defense Review (QDR) of 1996–1997, basically enshrined the status quo. Both reviews required the US military to be able to fight two nearly simultaneous major theater wars, such as a second Persian Gulf War as well as a war on the Korean peninsula, without major allied assistance. Force structure and budgetary requirements flowed from this concept. DoD proposed to fight these wars along conventional lines, funding each military service in fairly traditional percentages and avoiding major doctrinal changes.

Critics found much to dislike in this thoroughly customary approach to defense planning. Initially, some worried about a major mismatch between forces and budgets. Projected budgets could not provide sufficient new tanks, planes, and ships to keep the overall force prepared for conflict. These observers began to worry about the "defense train wreck" that would occur when the current generation of military hardware reached its maximum service life and there was no new generation to take its place.[63] Other critics pointed to a so-called revolution in military affairs—a revolution based on real-time battlefield intelligence, precision sensors and strike systems, information warfare, new weapons such as unmanned aerial vehicles and stealth ships, and other elements—and claimed that the Clinton administration was doing nothing to make it a reality for the US military. Some worried the United States was doing what all leading powers had done through history: assuming that the next war would be like the last. Finally, a host of critics from across the political spectrum argued that the Clinton administration was not doing enough to reverse the Cold War nuclear arms race that had left each side with thousands of nuclear weapons. They called for faster action before the continuing US-Russian nuclear standoff once again undermined East-West relations.

Clinton administration officials had ready answers to these criticisms. Beginning in the mid-1990s, they added money to defense budgets to help redress the force structure–budget imbalances and argued that it made little sense to embark on a new round of equipment modernization before the new revolutionary generation of hardware was fully ready. They indicated that they were experimenting with radical new equipment and tactics but that integrating them into the military in a stable and effective way would naturally take some years. Finally, they pointed out that the United States and Russia could destroy only so many nuclear warheads in any given year and that their nuclear reductions were proceeding as fast as technology allowed. In a retrospective defense of the Clinton administration's stewardship of the armed forces, defense analyst Michael O'Hanlon argued that "the Clinton Pentagon oversaw the most successful defense drawdown in US history—cutting military personnel by 15 percent more than the previous administration had planned while retaining a high state of readiness and a strong global deterrence posture. It enacted a prescient modernization program. And the military it helped produce achieved impressive successes in Bosnia and Kosovo."[64]

Military Intervention. Although the Clinton administration took a cautious approach to structural change of the armed forces, it was more activist in its willingness to use force abroad. Having inherited the Somalia operation from his predecessor, Clinton later intervened with US armed forces in humanitarian crisis situations in Haiti (1994), Bosnia (1995), and Kosovo (1999). Many critics questioned whether these interventions represented a wise use of US military power, given the uncertain relationship between these situations and vital US national interests. Others were concerned about the legitimacy of these endeavors, given the norm of state sovereignty, which discourages intervention in another state's domestic affairs. From a US domestic perspective, there were concerns over cost and the impact of a greatly increased pace of operations on a smaller, all-volunteer military that was still structured largely along Cold War lines. This debate became louder during the 2000 presidential election season.[65]

As the twentieth century came to a close, US defense policy was clearly in transition. Debates over the significance of international political developments, competing forces within domestic politics, and the impact of technology continued to play significant roles in national security policy. However, a broadly satisfactory response was difficult for US national security policymakers to craft, in part because the United States did not face a clearly defined threat or unifying crisis.

The George W. Bush Administration, 2001–2009: Crisis and Transformation

Much like its predecessors, the incoming Bush administration struggled to articulate US national security policy goals in the post–Cold War environment. As a presidential candidate, Governor George W. Bush had formulated a modest agenda and argued for scaling back the foreign policy activism of the Clinton years. Key advisors to his campaign had criticized the Clinton administration for failing to prioritize, for overusing the military and taking "thinly stretched armed forces close to a breaking point," and for embracing multilateralism at the expense of the US national interest.[66] In an April 2000 debate, George W. Bush had promised to pursue a "humble" foreign policy.[67] However, the terrorist attacks of September 11, 2001, suddenly presented the United States with a genuine crisis and a concrete threat. This event had a dramatic impact on the American people and spurred the US government to take a new approach to national security.

New Threats and a New Strategy. Surprise attacks on US territory are rare in American history. As historian John Lewis Gaddis points out, the only other examples are "the British burning of the White House and Capitol in 1814 and the Japanese attack on Pearl Harbor in 1941." Gaddis argues that such attacks can set the stage for radically new national security strategies by seeming to show that previous policies had failed.[68] Throughout the Cold War and into the 1990s, the policy of containment and the strategy of deterrence had informed US national security policy. After devastating terrorist attacks on US soil, and given challenges from non-state armed groups and the risk of WMD proliferation, these traditional approaches appeared obsolete. In his May 2002 graduation speech at West Point, President George W. Bush was explicit: "New threats also require new thinking." He went on to say that "deterrence . . . means nothing against shadowy terrorist networks with no nation or citizens to defend. Containment is not possible when unbalanced dictators with weapons of mass destruction can deliver those weapons on missiles or secretly provide them to terrorist allies."[69] Responding to these concerns, the national security strategy issued in September 2002 represented a shift in US national security policy. George W. Bush summarized his approach by saying, "We will defend the peace by fighting terrorists and tyrants. We will preserve the peace by building good relations among the great powers. We will extend the peace by encouraging free and open societies on every continent."[70]

An important element of this new approach was an effort to redefine the concept of *preemption*. Preemption, which has traditionally been seen as justified under international law, affirms the right of a state to defend itself by acting first in the face of an imminent danger. In effect, the Bush administration argued that the threshold of "imminence" should be lower when WMD are the threat of concern. As the administration stated in *The National Security Strategy of the United States*, "In an age where the enemies of civilization openly and actively seek the world's most destructive technologies, the United States cannot remain idle while dangers gather."[71] Critics responded by arguing that the Bush administration was really talking about preventive war in the classic sense: acting now to prevent a potential future threat. An American embrace of preventive war would be contrary to American traditions and set a bad precedent for countries around the world. In the eyes of these critics, the US-led invasion of Iraq in 2003 showed the risks of preventive war, as WMD were not found, and the invasion's aftermath proved more dangerous and complex than US planners had expected.

The debate on this element of the Bush national security strategy continues into the present day. Robert Jervis identifies three challenges to the Bush approach. First, it is inherently difficult to predict future threats. Second, important and relevant intelligence on past behavior and capabilities can be scarce and difficult to interpret. Third, it may be difficult to sustain both domestic support and international legitimacy when using force based on problematic information.[72] However, Gaddis argues that, although this doctrine is controversial, it may have been successful in thwarting subsequent terrorist attacks on US soil. Gaddis also agrees with the Bush administration's assessment that the traditional definitions of preemption and prevention are no longer relevant in the face of new threats.[73]

In addition to fighting terrorists and tyrants, the other two elements of the Bush national security strategy included building positive relationships with great powers and fostering democracy abroad. In practice, these aspects of the national security strategy proved difficult to implement consistently. The United States sought good relations with other great powers, but it resisted the inevitable constraints associated with seeking international consensus or support for its actions. Moreover, despite a desire to foster democratic development, the United States found itself working with many nondemocratic regimes in its struggle against terrorists. The tensions were classic ones. With regard to cooperation with other great powers, the freedom of unilateralism must be weighed against the advantages in capability and legitimacy provided by multilateralism. With regard to democracy promotion, US values must at times be weighed against material security interests. These challenges are likely to prove enduring.

The Wars in Afghanistan and Iraq. Over the long term, a strategy is likely to be judged by its perceived consequences. Evaluations of the national security policy of the Bush administration are likely to be most strongly defined by the wars in Afghanistan and Iraq. For this reason, a brief review of their origins and conduct is useful here.

Afghanistan. Within one month of the 9/11 attacks, US forces, with substantial assistance from CIA paramilitary operators, launched combat operations to invade Afghanistan. The purpose of the operation was to target the al Qaeda central leadership, including Osama bin Laden, and the Taliban regime in Afghanistan that had supported al Qaeda's operations. After several months of fighting, during which US conventional and special operations forces worked closely with the indigenous Northern Alliance militias, the Taliban were defeated.[74] The United Nations sponsored a series of meetings in Bonn, Germany, which eventually resulted in an interim government headed by a Pashtun leader, Hamid Karzai. Karzai became the first democratically elected president of Afghanistan on October 9, 2004.

After the initial defeat of the Taliban, military operations to support the newly formed Afghan government and to impede al Qaeda operations in the region continued throughout the presidency of George W. Bush. Consolidating national power in Afghanistan proved difficult, and al Qaeda operatives continued to work in remote areas of Afghanistan and the Federally Administered Tribal Areas of neighboring Pakistan. Beginning in August 2003, NATO initiated its first operation outside the Euro-Atlantic area, creating the International Security Assistance Force (ISAF) to "assist the government of Afghanistan and the international community in maintaining security."[75] US forces worked within and alongside ISAF, but the amount of US military power that could be committed to Afghanistan was constrained by the availability of forces, especially after operations began in Iraq.

Iraq. In response to Iraqi President Saddam Hussein's evasiveness regarding the enforcement of UN Security Council Resolutions relating to suspected WMD programs, and in line with the emphasis the Bush administration placed on the danger from "unbalanced dictators" with WMD in a world plagued by transnational terrorists, US forces led an invasion of Iraq in March 2003. In three weeks, the US-led coalition toppled Hussein's regime. Most Iraqi leaders fled and were eventually captured or killed; Saddam Hussein was captured in December 2003, eight months after the invasion and, after a trial, was executed in December 2006.

The political challenge of establishing a new representative government in place of an authoritarian regime proved to be much more difficult than the military operation required to defeat that regime. The United States established the Coalition Provisional Authority (CPA), led by Ambassador L. Paul Bremer, to administer Iraq until authority could be handed over to a new Iraqi government. The CPA worked toward the creation of representative government structures in a state where little tradition of democratic governance had ever existed.[76] Several US decisions, such as limiting the number of US forces deployed for stabilization operations, disbanding the Iraqi Army, and excluding senior members of Hussein's Ba'ath Party from government, were criticized as contributing to the postwar disorder and lawlessness that developed in many parts of Iraq.

After the US transfer of sovereignty back to Iraqi leaders on July 1, 2004, the situation did not improve. In fact, as the US military attempted to aid in the development of capable Iraqi army and police forces, attacks increased from insurgents who opposed the new government, and violence spread in many of Iraq's provinces. This violence received additional fuel from external forces, including al Qaeda and Iran, both of which saw in Iraq an opportunity to embroil the United States in a long-term conflict. After the bombing of the Golden Dome Mosque in Samarra in February 2006, the situation devolved into a sectarian civil war. In response to these developments, Congress appointed a bipartisan Iraqi Study Group to attempt to chart a new way forward.[77] By December 2006, US Ambassador to Iraq Zalmay Khalilzad and US Commander General George Casey concluded that the current strategy was not working and that "the coalition was failing to achieve its objectives."[78]

In January 2007, George W. Bush announced a new strategy, which included a "surge" of five brigades of the US Army and two Marine battalions, a concomitant surge of Iraqi forces (Iraqi military and policy forces increased by more than 100,000 in 2007), a focus on the Baghdad area, and additional diplomatic, political, and economic pressure. The surge was implemented by a new commander, General David Petraeus, who employed a counterinsurgency strategy that emphasized partnerships with Iraqi Security Forces and focused on protecting the Iraqi population. At the same time, political overtures toward moderate Sunni tribes took advantage of the extent to which al Qaeda in Iraq and other violent extremist groups had overplayed their hand and alienated the local population. As part of this "awakening" of the Sunni tribes, over 100,000 former insurgents joined organizations called "Sons of Iraq," which worked with coalition and Iraqi forces to provide local security. Though the Sons of Iraq had the desired positive impact on security conditions, the coalition also hoped that that this initiative would aid political reconciliation between the Sunni population in Iraq and the Shi'a-led government in Baghdad.

The situation in Iraq had improved by the end of Bush's presidency, but the cost and difficulty of the wars in both Afghanistan and Iraq exceeded initial estimates. Afghanistan and Iraq also revealed and perhaps widened the gap between the administration's strategy and the less flexible structure available to support that strategy.

Nuclear Weapons and Space Policy. Although it identified the limits of deterrence in the face of new threats, the Bush national security policy acknowledged the continued relevance of nuclear weapons for strategic deterrence against potential state adversaries. Its "new triad" of nuclear deterrence consisted of conventional and nuclear offensive strike systems, active and passive defenses that emphasized ballistic missile defense, and a responsive nuclear infrastructure.[79] Each of these elements relied heavily on the technological advantages the United States continued to hold over its competitors.

Although the United States had maintained a significant nuclear weapons capability since the end of the Cold War—despite the absence of a Soviet threat—the Bush administration saw concerns that competence had eroded. A 2008 task force appointed by the secretary of defense concluded that "there has been an unambiguous, dramatic, and unacceptable decline in the Air Force's commitment to perform the nuclear mission and, until very recently, little has been done to reverse it."[80] In response, DoD invested more in the means and tradecraft required to maintain US nuclear superiority safely.

The Bush administration also took a more activist policy toward space. Acknowledging the importance of using space for security and economic purposes, the national space policy asserted that "freedom of action in space is as important to the United States as air power and sea power."[81] The administration viewed US security as being dependent upon space, believed that this dependence would only grow, and aimed to retain US space primacy. Thus, to the disappointment of such states as China and Russia, the US was reluctant to support international agreements that could in any way threaten US preeminence beyond the Earth's atmosphere.

Defense Transformation. As the Bush administration sought to think beyond the traditional parameters of containment and deterrence in its national security policy, it emphasized transforming the military to respond to new threats. Even before the terrorist attacks of 9/11, Secretary of Defense Donald Rumsfeld focused on high-technology precision weapons and new ways of fighting enemies who would attempt to challenge American hegemony asymmetrically. During his tenure, from January 2001 to December 2006, Rumsfeld also sought to eliminate many military bases that had been established in Europe and East Asia during the Cold War. His goal was the creation of a lean and effective joint force that could deploy rapidly anywhere in the world on short notice.[82]

Many of these elements of transformation were prominent during the US campaign in Afghanistan in 2001–2002. Small land forces worked closely with coalition partners, utilizing unmanned aircraft. Their collaboration with US air assets from temporary bases in neighboring Uzbekistan and Kyrgyzstan seemed to epitomize the efficacy of transformation as well as the administration's success in rapidly changing the culture of a huge governmental institution. The strengths of transformation were again highlighted in the buildup and execution of the US overthrow of the Hussein regime in Iraq. Nevertheless, postconflict operations in Afghanistan and Iraq relied less on advanced technology and more on sustaining large, expensive ground forces, and the focus of transformation initiatives came to seem increasingly distant from current national security needs. Once again, strategy and structure began to appear out of alignment. Although the 2006 Quadrennial Defense Review (QDR) still highlighted the need to transform the military into a more agile and expeditionary force, it did not lay out a programmatic or budgetary path to the achievement of this objective.[83] The 2007 defense budget of $439 billion (up 7 percent from 2006 and 48 percent from 2001) highlighted more traditional goals of maintaining soldier readiness and procuring conventional and nuclear weapons systems.[84]

A final issue of national security structure that became more salient during the Bush administration relates to the interagency processes of the US government. Since the Goldwater-Nichols reforms of 1986, DoD has made significant strides in integrating the military services in order to improve their effectiveness in joint military operations. However, as the landscape changed in the early twenty-first century, it became clear that the United States would require more than effective armed forces to meet its security needs. It would need to integrate and bring to bear the expertise of multiple agencies and departments in the US government to deal effectively with new challenges. To take just one example, efforts to combat terrorist groups that operate across international borders may require diplomatic work done by the Department of State, efforts to impede terrorist financing done by the US Treasury, and military operations conducted by the Department of Defense, as well as collaboration among these entities and domestically focused organizations such as the Department of Homeland Security and the Federal Bureau of Investigation. Despite increasing calls for another landmark legislative reform along the lines of Goldwater-Nichols or the National Security Act of 1947, the challenges associated with making interagency collaboration more effective were not resolved then and drastic overhaul continues to appear unlikely in the near term.[85] (For more on this topic, see chapter 10.)

During the last year of George W. Bush's presidency, an economic crisis with origins in the US financial sector spread worldwide, sparking a deep economic recession at home and abroad. In addition, popular dissatisfaction with the costly wars in Afghanistan and Iraq had harmed the president's public approval ratings. Running for president in this environment, Senator Barack Obama campaigned on promises to expand government investment in domestic needs, to "finish the fight" against the Taliban and al Qaeda in Afghanistan, and to "end [the] war in Iraq responsibly."[86]

President Barack Obama, 2009–2017: Reassessing US Leadership in a Complex World

The priorities that would characterize the Obama administration were evident in its first national security strategy, published in 2010. First, the United States would focus on the domestic foundations of American power, with economic recovery being the highest priority. Second, the Obama administration would seek to restore the US reputation for moral leadership by ending certain practices, such as torture, that had characterized the fight against terror since 2001, and by reaffirming the rules-based international order and international institutions that the United States had helped to found in the wake of World War II. Third, the United States would engage actively with other countries around the world, strengthening alliances, ensuring robust dialogue with other major centers of power such as China and Russia, and negotiating with adversaries. Finally, the country would act using all instruments of power in an integrated fashion. While the US military was an important tool, it was not the best instrument for every situation; instead, the administration argued, the country would be most successful if it coordinated and integrated programs and policies across multiple areas: defense, diplomacy, economic development, homeland security, and intelligence.[87]

Iraq and Afghanistan. Following through on his campaign promise, in 2010 Obama announced the end of US combat operations in Iraq; by the end of 2011 the United States had withdrawn its combat forces from the country. Although initially viewed as a foreign policy success, this US withdrawal received greater criticism after a civil war broke out in Syria in 2013. The resulting lawlessness just beyond Iraq's western border provided an opportunity for a Sunni insurgent group called the Islamic State of Iraq. Established in Iraq in 2006, it had been largely defeated there by 2009, but it reconstituted as the Islamic State of Iraq and the Levant (ISIL) and gained control of wealth and territory across Syria and Iraq beginning in 2013.[88] Confronted by ISIL fighters, the Iraqi military suffered a number of significant defeats in northern and western Iraq in 2014.

Iraqi forces enjoyed some success against ISIL in late 2015 and early 2016, and by December 2017 Iraqi prime minister Haider al-Abadi declared victory over ISIL in Iraq.[89] However, worry about the influence of the ideology that enabled ISIL's initial victory persists, and debate about the US role in these developments is likely to continue.[90] Some blame US officials for inadequate attention to the Iraqi political process after the US withdrawal in 2011, while others argue that no amount of US involvement could have succeeded in causing then–Prime Minister Nouri al-Maliki to lead in the non-corrupt, non-sectarian manner necessary to enable the Iraqi government to attain legitimacy across its various communities.[91]

In Afghanistan, Obama also followed through on his campaign promise, committing an additional 17,000 military personnel to operations there within his first thirty days in office and then approving an additional surge of 30,000 forces in November 2009.[92] In a speech at West Point announcing the latter decision, Obama acknowledged the significance of cost as an issue shaping his decisions, reminding his audience that "the nation that I'm most interested in building is our own."[93] The Obama administration sought a strategy that, while avoiding excessive costs, would prevent Afghanistan from again becoming a haven for transnational terrorist groups. In October 2015, Obama announced the end of US combat operations in Afghanistan but also acknowledged that US national security interests would require that a small force remain in Afghanistan beyond the end of his administration. These residual forces would support counterterrorism missions and help Afghanistan build the military capacity it needs to provide for its own security.[94]

The Role of Technology: Cyber Capabilities and Drones. Advances in technology played several important roles in shaping the Obama administration's national security policies. In response to the rapid advance of information technologies and their significance to the US military, US Cyber Command was established in 2010 to unify efforts to operate and defend military cyberspace resources and to develop the capability to conduct offensive missions in cyberspace in support of joint force commanders. In addition to these missions, US Cyber Command was also given the mission to defend the country as a whole—not just the military's own cyberspace resources—in the cyber domain.[95] Although the clear priority in the early years of US Cyber Command's existence was on the defensive aspects of its mission, in early 2016 Secretary of Defense Ashton Carter revealed that the command's offensive capabilities were being used in US efforts to combat ISIL.[96]

A second example of the significance of advances in technology was the Obama administration's use of drones in counterterrorism missions. The use of drones to conduct targeted killings began under George W. Bush, but the number of strikes increased dramatically under Obama. The use of this technology was in part another reflection of Obama's concerns about cost, since the use of "drone strikes, special operations, and sophisticated surveillance" could be used to help the United States combat terrorist networks while avoiding expensive counterinsurgency or nation-building missions.[97] Although US drone strikes succeeded in eliminating some terrorist leaders, debates continue over their legality and effectiveness, as well as the potential for these strikes to spur foreign backlash, assist terrorist recruiters, or inspire attacks on US soil.[98] There is also a tension between the use of secret and deadly tools like drone strikes and Obama's desire to improve the image of the United States on the world stage.

The Obama administration also reduced the defense budget as part of its effort to tackle federal budget deficits. In FY 2016 constant dollars, total budget authority in the base budget (not including war-related supplemental funding) declined from approximately $769 million in FY 2008, before Obama took office, to just over $541 million in FY 2016.[99] The withdrawal of forces from Iraq and Afghanistan also permitted significant reductions in supplemental funding to support ongoing military operations. In testifying about the FY 2016 budget submission to Congress, Secretary of Defense Ashton Carter explained that the amount was sufficient to enable the US armed forces to "protect the homeland, build security globally, and project power and win decisively" at a manageable risk.[100]

As articulated in the 2014 QDR, the Obama administration's strategy required that DoD rebalance the joint force in order to respond to threats from across the spectrum of conflict; sustain its global posture while rebalancing to the Asia-Pacific region; improve modernization and readiness in a smaller force; and reduce overhead to deliver more combat power within existing funding limits.[101] Key capabilities that received special emphasis for continuing investment included cyber technology; missile defense; nuclear deterrence; capabilities to counter anti-access and area-denial strategies; precision strike; intelligence, surveillance, and reconnaissance; and special operations.[102]

Balancing Domestic Priorities and National Security Demands. Beyond Iraq and Afghanistan, a consistent theme in Obama's foreign and national security policy was the requirement to balance domestic needs and foreign policy demands. In his 2015 national security strategy, Obama affirmed his view that "American global leadership remains indispensable," but he also emphasized that this requires hard choices.[103] Those who view his policies as having been an overall success laud "his grasp of the big picture: his appreciation of the liberal international order that the United States has nurtured over the last seven decades, together with his recognition that the core of that order needed to be salvaged by pulling back from misguided adventures and feuds on the global periphery."[104] Important successes of the Obama administration, from this perspective, include withdrawal from Iraq, a reduction of the US commitment in Afghanistan, an agreement with Iran to limit its nuclear weapons capabilities, limited US involvement in the conflicts in Libya and Syria, a limited yet multilateral response to Russia's annexation of Crimea and involvement in Eastern Ukraine, and a strategic rebalancing to the Asia-Pacific region to reassure US allies in the face of China's growing power.

Critics of Obama's national security record list the failures of some of his early initiatives, including his aspirations to eliminate nuclear weapons worldwide, to make progress in Israeli-Palestinian peace talks, and to close the US detention facility at Guantánamo Bay, Cuba. They also question whether foreign policy activism was excessively limited in cases such as Syria in 2013 or in response to Russia's aggression in Ukraine in that same year. According to one critic, "It may be a truism that the country cannot be strong abroad unless it is strong at home, but it's also a fact that the country's economic prosperity depends on its security abroad—not only in the core of the liberal democratic world but often well beyond it."[105]

As one examines the record of the Obama administration in light of the brief history of US national security policy presented here, it is likely that the administration will be seen as having sought to rebalance national priorities in favor of domestic needs. As former government official Stephen Sestanovich points out, "Almost every important decision of Barack Obama's presidency has been shadowed by the issue of resource constraints."[106] These decisions included the administration's choice of policy instruments, as the Obama administration sought to leverage technology to pursue US interests at lower cost. Any assessment of the record would do well to include an evaluation of how well the Obama administration achieved this goal.

In addition to evaluating the Obama administration against its own stated objectives, future analysts and historians are also likely to judge the quality of specific choices pertaining to implementation. The Obama administration set out to improve the interagency process and to deploy instruments of US power in an integrated fashion. As explained further in chapter 10 of this volume, this is likely to be to be an enduring challenge.

Looking Ahead

This chapter began by suggesting that presidential administrations must grapple with international political and military developments, domestic political and economic influences, and technological change as they craft and implement US national security policy. US activism abroad since World War II has waxed and waned, but American presidents throughout this period have generally accepted that the United States would have to play a global leadership role as it navigated these demands. As of this writing, it is too soon to say whether the administration of President Donald Trump will continue to find it in the US interest to play a leadership role in addressing shared international security and economic challenges or will mark a fundamental departure from this trend. Trump campaigned on a theme of "America First" and has largely stood by this rhetoric during his first year in office. For example, the Trump administration announced the US withdrawal from the Trans-Pacific Partnership, expressed a desire to renegotiate the North American Free Trade Agreement, and has been less enthusiastic than previous presidents about American support for the Article 5 mutual aid clause of the NATO Treaty, indicating a willingness to move away from the constraints that come with multilateral forms of international cooperation.[107] In spite of these developments, however, the National Security Strategy of 2017, the first issued by the Trump administration, does offer support for traditional US allies and recognize the value of the postwar international order.[108]

From World War II until the end of the Cold War, the standoff between the United States and the Soviet Union led to a general consensus on containment as the overall strategic approach. However, the post–Cold War presidential administrations—those of George H. W. Bush, Bill Clinton, George W. Bush, Barack Obama, and Donald Trump—have faced a more diverse set of challenges. Future presidents will continue to confront the question of whether a US leadership role in global affairs best serves US interests as they navigate an increasingly dynamic, varied, and complex set of international political and military concerns.

Discussion Questions

1. What international and technological developments caused the United States to abandon its longstanding reliance on a policy of mobilization? How does a strategy based on deterrence differ from one based on mobilization?

2. The policy of containment was based on the perception of an aggressive, monolithic communist bloc of nations. What events of the late 1940s and early 1950s caused the United States to take this view of the communist threat? What impact did such an assessment have on US political and military policies?

3. How do domestic considerations make foreign and security policies different than they would be if they were formulated on the basis of international and strategic considerations alone?

4. How have technological innovations affected the evolution of US security policy since the end of World War II? To what extent can it be said that technology determines strategy?

5. Should the United States continue to invest in the maintenance of a substantial nuclear arsenal? What are the potential advantages and disadvantages of such a policy?

6. Given changes in technology as well as the rising importance of security threats posed by non-state actors, is there a meaningful distinction between *preemption* and *prevention* in the current strategic landscape? What are the national security implications of attacking threats before they are fully formed?

7. The 1986 Goldwater-Nichols Department of Defense Reorganization Act was a watershed reform effort that greatly influenced American national security policy. Given the increased complexity of today's challenges, does the United States need another major reform of the national security bureaucracy?

8. One of the enduring themes in the evolution of US national security policy is the tension between strategy and force structure. Does current policy achieve a successful reconciliation between these two?

9. Since 9/11, the United States has identified the spread of Islamic terrorism to be a threat to US national interests and global prosperity. Is this a long-term threat? How can the United States deal effectively with this problem?

10. Is it in America's national interest for the United States to continue to play a leadership role in global affairs? Why or why not?

Recommended Reading

Bolt, Paul J., Damon V. Coletta, and Collins G. Shackelford. *American Defense Policy.* Baltimore, MD: Johns Hopkins University Press, 2005.

Bush, George, and Brent Scowcroft. *A World Transformed.* New York: Random House, 1998.

Fukuyama, Francis. *America at the Crossroads: Democracy, Power, and the Neoconservative Legacy.* New Haven, CT: Yale University Press, 2006.

Gaddis, John Lewis. *Strategies of Containment: A Critical Appraisal of Postwar American National Security Policy.* Rev. and exp. ed. Oxford: Oxford University Press, 2005.

Gates, Robert M. *Duty: Memoirs of a Secretary at War.* New York: Alfred A. Knopf, 2014.

George, Alexander, and Smoke, Richard. *Deterrence in American Foreign Policy: Theory and Practice.* New York: Columbia University Press, 1974.

Greenstein, Fred I. *The Presidential Difference: Leadership Style from FDR to Barack Obama.* Princeton, NJ: Princeton University Press, 2009.

Halberstam, David. *War in a Time of Peace: Bush, Clinton, and the Generals.* New York: Scribner, 2001.

Ikenberry, G. John, and Peter Trubowitz. *American Foreign Policy: Theoretical Essays.* 7th ed. Oxford: Oxford University Press, 2014.

Isaacson, Walter, and Evan Thomas. *The Wise Men: Six Friends and the World They Made.* New York: Simon and Schuster, 1986.

Jervis, Robert. *American Foreign Policy in a New Era.* New York: Routledge, 2005.

Kennan, George. *American Diplomacy.* Chicago: University of Chicago Press, 1963.

Kernek, Sterling J., and Kenneth W. Thompson. *Foreign Policy in the Reagan Presidency: Nine Intimate Perspectives.* Lanham, MD: University Press of America, 1993.

Sestanovich, Stephen. *Maximalist: America in the World from Truman to Obama.* New York: Alfred A. Knopf, 2014.

Internet Resources

Documents in Law, History and Diplomacy, The Avalon Project at Yale Law School, http://avalon.law.yale.edu/default.asp

National Security Council, www.whitehouse.gov/nsc

US Department of Defense, www.defense.gov

Notes

1. Department of Defense, *Joint Publication 3-0: Joint Operations* (Washington, DC: Department of Defense, August 11, 2011), GL-16.

2. Department of Defense, *Joint Publication 1: Doctrine for the Armed Forces of the United States* (Washington, DC: Department of Defense, March 25, 2013), GL-8.

3. Department of Defense, *Joint Publication 1*, GL-9.

4. January 1, 1983, is given as the date of the "real-world birth of the Internet" in Mitch Waldrop, "DARPA and the Internet Revolution," Defense Advanced Research Projects Agency, 2009, 85, http://www.darpa.mil/about-us/timeline/modern-internet.

5. President Barack Obama, "Remarks by the President on Securing Our Nation's Cyber Infrastructure," May 29, 2009, http://www.whitehouse.gov/the-press-office/remarks-president-securing-our-nations-cyber-infrastructure.

6. Department of Defense, *Nuclear Posture Review Report* (Washington, DC: Department of Defense, April 2010).

7. Samuel P. Huntington, *The Common Defense* (New York: Columbia University Press, 1961), 3–4.

8. Office of the Historian, "Bretton Woods–GATT, 1941–1947," US Department of State, n.d., https://history.state.gov/milestones/1937-1945/bretton-woods.

9. Office of the Historian, "The Formation of the United Nations, 1945," US Department of State, https://history.state.gov/milestones/1937-1945/un.

10. Henry T. Nash, *American Foreign Policy: Response to a Sense of Threat* (Homewood, IL: Dorsey Press, 1973), 19.

11. Huntington, *Common Defense*, 41.

12. Nash, *American Foreign Policy*, 19.

13. "X" (George Kennan), "The Sources of Soviet Conduct," *Foreign Affairs* 25, no. 4 (1947): 575–76.

14. Walter Millis, ed., *The Forrestal Diaries* (New York: Viking Press, 1951), 350.

15. Huntington, *Common Defense*, 41.

16. Huntington, *Common Defense*, 43.

17. Huntington, *Common Defense*, 47.

18. President Harry S. Truman, address delivered to a joint session of Congress, March 12, 1947, reprinted in Joseph M. Jones, *The Fifteen Weeks* (New York: Harcourt, Brace & World, 1955), 272.

19. Nash, *American Foreign Policy*, 25.

20. Nash, *American Foreign Policy*, 29.

21. Warner Schilling, Paul Hammond, and Glenn Snyder, *Strategy, Politics, and the Defense Budget* (New York: Columbia University Press, 1962), 292.

22. James S. Lay Jr., "A Report to the National Security Council on United States Objectives and Programs for National Security (NSC 68)," April 14, 1950, 64, https://www.trumanlibrary.org/whistlestop/study_collections/coldwar/documents/pdf/10-1.pdf.

23. Huntington, *Common Defense*, 54.

24. For a discussion of US perceptions of communist intentions, see Morton Halperin, *Limited War in the Nuclear Age* (New York: John Wiley & Sons, 1963), chap. 3.

25. Huntington, *Common Defense*, 88.

26. Huntington, *Common Defense*, 56.

27. Huntington, *Common Defense*, 73–74.

28. Jerome Kahan, *Security in the Nuclear Age* (Washington, DC: Brookings Institution Press, 1975), 28.

29. “Text of Dulles’ Statement on Foreign Policy of Eisenhower Administration,” *New York Times*, January 13, 1954, 2.

30. John Foster Dulles, “The Evolution of Foreign Policy,” *Department of State Bulletin* 30 (January 25, 1954): 108.

31. David F. Rudgers, “The Origins of Covert Action,” *Journal of Contemporary History* 35, no. 2 (2000): 259.

32. Andrew Fraser, “Architecture of a Broken Dream: The CIA and Guatemala, 1952–54,” *Intelligence & National Security* 20, no. 3 (2005): 486–508; Andreas Etges, “All that Glitters Is Not Gold: The 1953 Coup against Mohammed Mossadegh in Iran,” *Intelligence & National Security* 26, no. 4 (2011): 495–508. See also Stephen Kinzer, *The Brothers: John Foster Dulles, Allen Dulles, and Their Secret World War* (New York: Time Books/Henry Holt and Company, 2013).

33. Michael Dunne, “Perfect Failure: The USA, Cuba and the Bay of Pigs, 1961,” *Political Quarterly* 82, no. 3 (2011): 454.

34. For a highly critical review, see Timothy Weiner, *Legacy of Ashes: The History of the CIA* (New York: Doubleday, 2007).

35. Huntington, *Common Defense*, 88.

36. Huntington, *Common Defense*, 92.

37. Huntington, *Common Defense*, 96–97.

38. Morton Halperin, *Defense Strategies for the Seventies* (Boston: Little, Brown, 1971), 46.

39. Huntington, *Common Defense*, 105.

40. John Foster Dulles, “Challenge and Response in U.S. Foreign Policy,” *Foreign Affairs* 36, no. 1 (1951): 31.

41. William W. Kaufmann, *The McNamara Strategy* (New York: Harper & Row, 1964), 29.

42. Alain C. Enthoven and K. Wayne Smith, *How Much Is Enough? Shaping the Defense Program, 1961–1969* (New York: Harper & Row, 1971), 21.

43. House Committee on Armed Services, *Hearings on Military Posture*, 85th Cong., 2nd sess., 1962, 3162.

44. What constituted “unacceptable” damage to an adversary could not be measured precisely. However, the planning figure accepted by US authorities was 25–33 percent of Soviet population and about 75 percent of Soviet industrial capacity. This judgment was influenced primarily by the demographics of Soviet population distribution and by the rapidly diminishing marginal returns beyond a certain level of retaliatory attack. For a more complete explanation of assured destruction criteria, see Enthoven and Smith, *How Much Is Enough?*, 207.

45. John F. Kennedy, Inaugural Address given in Washington DC, January 20, 1961, http://www.jfklibrary.org/Research/Research-Aids/Ready-Reference/JFK-Quotations/Inaugural-Address.aspx.

46. Edward R. Fried et al., *Setting National Priorities: The 1974 Budget* (Washington, DC: Brookings Institution Press, 1973), 292. For comparison, the roughly $78 billion spent at the height of the Vietnam War in 1968 is the equivalent of $601 billion in 2019 dollars after adjusting for inflation.

47. Halperin, *Defense Strategies for the Seventies*, 52.

48. Alton H. Quanbeck and Barry M. Blechman, *Strategic Forces: Issues for the Mid-Seventies* (Washington, DC: Brookings Institution Press, 1973), 6–7.

49. Quanbeck and Blechman, *Strategic Forces*, 9.

50. Halperin, *Defense Strategies for the Seventies*, 126.

51. Halperin, *Defense Strategies for the Seventies*, 126.

52. Bernard Brodie, "Technology, Politics, and Strategy," *Adelphi Papers* 9, no. 55 (London: International Institute for Strategic Studies, March 1969): 22.

53. Congressional Budget Office, *Future Budget Requirements for the 600-Ship Navy* (Washington, DC: Congressional Budget Office, September 1985), xi.

54. See John Lewis Gaddis, *How Relevant Was U.S. Strategy in Winning the Cold War?* (Carlisle Barracks, PA: Strategic Studies Institute, 1992), 14.

55. John G. Tower, Edmund S. Muskie, and Brent Scowcroft, *The Tower Commission Report: The Full Text of the President's Special Review Board* (New York: Bantam Books, 1987).

56. For an authoritative account of this legislation, see James R. Locher III, *Victory on the Potomac: The Goldwater-Nichols Act Unifies the Pentagon* (College Station: Texas A&M University Press, 2002).

57. See George Bush and Brent Scowcroft, *A World Transformed* (New York: Knopf, 1998).

58. H. W. Brands, "George Bush and the Gulf War of 1991," *Presidential Studies Quarterly* 34, no. 1 (2004): esp. 125–27.

59. See Don M. Snider, *The National Security Strategy: Documenting Strategic Vision* (Carlisle Barracks, PA: Strategic Studies Institute, 1992), 14.

60. See "Statement of the Secretary of Defense Dick Cheney before the Senate Budget Committee," February 3, 1992, https://www.c-span.org/video/?24135-1/defense-department-budget-proposal.

61. See *National Military Strategy of the United States* (Washington, DC: US Government Printing Office [GPO], January 1992), 6–10.

62. William J. Perry, "Defense in an Age of Hope," *Foreign Affairs* 75, no. 6 (1996): 64–79.

63. See, for example, Don M. Snider, "The Coming Defense Train Wreck," *Washington Quarterly* 19, no. 1 (1996): 89–102.

64. Michael O'Hanlon, "Clinton's Strong Defense Legacy," *Foreign Affairs* 82, no. 6 (2003): 126.

65. For a discussion reflecting campaign issues, see Lawrence Korb, Condoleezza Rice, and Robert B. Zoellick, "Money for Nothing: A Penny Saved, Not a Penny Earned, in the U.S. Military," *Foreign Affairs* 79, no. 2 (2000): 149–52.

66. Condoleezza Rice, "Promoting the National Interest," *Foreign Affairs* 79, no. 1 (2000): 51.

67. See Debate Transcript, *Commission on Presidential Debates*, October 11, 2000, http://www.debates.org/?page=october-11-2000-debate-transcript.

68. John Lewis Gaddis, "A Grand Strategy of Transformation," *Foreign Policy* 133 (November–December 2002): 50.

69. George W. Bush, "Address Delivered to the West Point Graduating Class," June 1, 2002, http://georgewbush-whitehouse.archives.gov/news/releases/2002/06/20020601-3.html.

70. The White House, *The National Security Strategy of the United States* (Washington, DC: The White House, September 2002), iv.

71. Ibid., 15.

72. Robert Jervis, *American Foreign Policy in a New Era* (New York: Routledge, 2005), 85.

73. See John Lewis Gaddis, "Grand Strategy in the Second Term," *Foreign Affairs* 84, no. 1 (2005): 2–15.

74. Stephen Biddle, *Afghanistan and the Future of Warfare: Implications for the Army and Defense Policy* (Carlisle Barracks, PA: US Army Strategic Studies Institute, November 2002).

75. North Atlantic Treaty Organization, "NATO and Afghanistan," November 10, 2017, http://www.nato.int/cps/en/natohq/topics_8189.htm.

76. L. Paul Bremer, *My Year in Iraq: The Struggle to Build a Future of Hope* (New York: Threshold Editions, 2006).

77. Iraq Study Group, *The Iraq Study Group Report* (Washington, DC: US Institute of Peace, 2006).

78. David H. Petraeus, "Report to Congress on the Situation in Iraq," September 2007, http://oai.dtic.mil/oai/oai?verb=getRecord&metadataPrefix=html&identifier=ADA473579.

79. The White House, *National Security Strategy of the United States* (Washington, DC: The White House, 2006), 22.

80. Secretary of Defense Task Force on DoD Nuclear Weapons Management, *Report of the Secretary of Defense Task Force on DoD Nuclear Weapons Management* (Washington, DC: Department of Defense, September 2008), 2.

81. As quoted by Marc Kaufman, "Bush Sets Defense as Space Priority," *Washington Post*, October 18, 2006, A01.

82. See Donald Rumsfeld, "Against the Unknown: Armed Forces Transformation for the 21st Century," *Hampton Roads International Security Quarterly* 2 (Autumn 2002): 6–15.

83. United States Department of Defense, *Quadrennial Defense Review Report* (Washington, DC: US GPO, February 6, 2006), v–vi.

84. *Budget of the United States Government, Fiscal Year 2007*, https://www.gpo.gov/fdsys/browse/collectionGPO.action?collectionCode=BUDGET.

85. See Clark A. Murdock, Michele A. Flournoy, Kurt M. Campbell, Pierre A. Chao, Julianne Smith, Anne A. Witkowsky, and Christine E. Wormuth, "Beyond Goldwater-Nichols: U.S. Government and Defense Reform for a New Strategic Era, Phase II Report" (Washington, DC: Center for Strategic and International Studies [CSIS], July 2005), http://csis.org/files/media/csis/pubs/bgn_ph2_report.pdf.

86. "Barack Obama's Acceptance Speech," *New York Times*, August 28, 2008, http://www.nytimes.com/2008/08/28/us/politics/28text-obama.html.

87. The White House, *National Security Strategy* (Washington, DC: The White House, May 2010), esp. 2–14.

88. Jessica Stern and J. M. Berger, *ISIS: The State of Terror* (New York: HarperCollins, 2015), 33–51.

89. Maher Chmaytelli and Ahmed Aboulenein, "Iraq Declares Final Victory Over Islamic State," *Reuters*, December 9, 2017, https://www.reuters.com/article/us-mideast-crisis-iraq-islamicstate/iraq-declares-final-victory-over-islamic-state-idUSKBN1E30B9.

90. United Nations, "ISIL 'Down but Not Out' in Iraq; UN Envoy Urges Efforts to Defeat Group's Extremist Ideology," *UN News*, November 22, 2017, https://news.un.org/en/story/2017/11/636992-isil-down-not-out-iraq-un-envoy-urges-efforts-defeat-groups-extremist-ideology.

91. For a critique of the US role, see Emma Sky, *The Unraveling: High Hopes and Missed Opportunities in Iraq* (Philadelphia: PublicAffairs, 2015), esp. 338, 341. For an alternative perspective, see Marc Lynch, "Obama and the Middle East: Rightsizing the U.S. Role," *Foreign Affairs* 94, no. 5 (2015): 19.

92. This decisionmaking process is the subject of Bob Woodward, *Obama's Wars* (New York: Simon & Schuster, 2010).

93. The White House, Office of the Press Secretary, "Remarks by the President in Address to the Nation on the Way Forward in Afghanistan and Pakistan," December 1, 2009, https://www.whitehouse.gov/the-press-office/remarks-president-address-nation-way-forward-afghanistan-and-pakistan.

94. The White House, Office of the Press Secretary, "Statement by the President on Afghanistan," October 15, 2015, https://www.whitehouse.gov/the-press-office/2015/10/15/statement-president-afghanistan.

95. Department of Defense, Quadrennial Defense Review Report, March 2014, 14–15, http://www.defense.gov/pubs/2014_Quadrennial_Defense_Review.pdf.

96. See, for example, US Department of Defense, "Department of Defense Press Briefing by Secretary Carter and Gen. Dunford in the Pentagon Briefing Room," February 29, 2016, http://www.defense.gov/News/News-Transcripts/Transcript-View/Article/682341/department-of-defense-press-briefing-by-secretary-carter-and-gen-dunford-in-the.

97. M. J. Boyle, "The Costs and Consequences of Drone Warfare," *International Affairs* 89, no. 1 (2013): 2.

98. Boyle, "The Costs and Consequences of Drone Warfare," 2; Jessica Stern, "Obama and Terrorism: Like It or Not, the War Goes On," *Foreign Affairs* 94, no. 5 (2015): 64–65. See also Micah Zenko, *Reforming U.S. Drone Strike Policies*, Council Special Report No. 65 (New York: Council on Foreign Relations, 2013).

99. Office of the Undersecretary of Defense (Comptroller), *National Defense Budget Estimates for FY 2016* (Washington, DC: Department of Defense, March 2015), 138–139.

100. US Department of Defense, "Submitted Statement—House Armed Services Committee (Budget Request)," as submitted by Secretary of Defense Ashton B. Carter, March 18, 2015, http://www.defense.gov/News/Speeches/Speech-View/Article/606654/submitted-statement-house-armed-services-committee-budget-request.

101. US Department of Defense, *Quadrennial Defense Review 2014* (Washington, DC: Department of Defense, 2014), v–xi.

102. US Department of Defense, *Quadrennial Defense Review 2014*, x–xi.

103. The White House, *National Security Strategy* (Washington, DC: The White House, February 2015), ii.

104. Gideon Rose, "What Obama Gets Right: Keep Calm and Carry the Liberal Order On," *Foreign Affairs* 94, no. 5 (2015): 2.

105. This sentence and the critiques listed in this paragraph draw on Bret Stephens, "What Obama Gets Wrong: No Retreat, No Surrender," *Foreign Affairs* 94, no. 5 (2015): 16.

106. Stephen Sestanovich, *Maximalist: America in the World from Truman to Obama* (New York: Alfred A. Knopf, 2014), 320.

107. Elizabeth Saunders, "Is Trump a Normal Foreign-Policy President? What We Know After One Year," *Foreign Affairs*, January 18, 2018, https://www.foreignaffairs.com/articles/united-states/2018-01-18/trump-normal-foreign-policy-president.

108. Peter Feaver, "Five Takeaways from Trump's National Security Strategy," *Foreign Policy*, December 17, 2017, http://foreignpolicy.com/2017/12/18/five-takeaways-from-trumps-national-security-strategy/.

II

National Security Policy Actors and Processes

4

Presidential Leadership and the Executive Branch

Alexander Hamilton described the crucial role of the president in national security affairs in Federalist No. 74: "The direction of war implies the direction of the common strength; and the power of directing and employing the common strength forms a usual and essential part in the definition of the executive authority."[1] While the founders of the United States appreciated the vital role of the executive in foreign policy, they were also determined to avoid investing in the president the "sole prerogative of making war and peace" as exercised by the British monarch.[2] As a result, the founders created a system in which the president and Congress have complementary—and at times conflicting—roles in the national security process.

The Presidency, the Constitution, and National Security

The authority and constraints on the president derive from the powers specified in the Constitution. To successfully implement initiatives in the national security arena, presidents need to make maximum use of their sources of authority while carefully managing constraints.[3]

The Executive and the Congress Share Power. The constitutional system of overlapping authority is evident in the formal powers granted to each institution. Broadly, the president is responsible for ensuring that the laws are faithfully executed, and he has been given the "executive power" to do so. Congress, however, is responsible for making "all laws which shall be necessary and proper for carrying into execution the foregoing powers vested by this Constitution in the Government of the United States." Under the Constitution, the president is the commander in chief of the army and navy, but has nothing to command unless Congress uses one of its enumerated powers to raise and support armies and to support and maintain a navy. The president has the authority to make treaties and to appoint ambassadors and other public ministers as well as the members of the national security team, which in modern times includes the secretaries of state, defense, and homeland security, the director of national intelligence, the chairman of the Joint Chiefs of Staff (JCS), and others. However, the power to make treaties and the power to appoint various officials are subject to the "advice and consent" of the Senate.

The Constitution gives the president substantial authority and initiative in foreign affairs. However, having given the president important powers to make and execute national security policy, the founders were deliberate in reserving to Congress the power to declare war. As a consequence of these built-in tensions, the Constitution presents to each president and each Congress an "invitation to struggle for the privilege of directing American foreign policy."[4]

A History of Increasing Presidential Prerogatives. With the Constitution as its starting framework, thc national security process grew out of the needs of the conduct of public affairs over time. In 1793, President George Washington asserted the prerogative of the president to act unilaterally in time of foreign crisis by issuing, without congressional consultation, a neutrality proclamation in the renewed Franco-British war. Succeeding administrations continued to struggle with questions of presidential versus congressional prerogative. In 1812, for example, President James Madison was unsuccessful in restraining congressional "war hawks" who helped precipitate war with England. In 1846, it was President James K. Polk who presented Congress with a fait accompli by placing American troops along the Rio Grande, where the resulting clash of arms quickly led Congress to vote for a declaration of war.

The presidential prerogative in foreign affairs, claimed first by Washington and then cultivated by his successors, was a generally established concept by the time of the Lincoln administration. Lincoln greatly expanded the potential range of presidential action by invoking the notion that "war powers" derived from the Constitution's designation of the president as commander in chief. The resulting growth of presidential power in the Civil War foreshadowed a trend in the relationship between national emergencies and executive power. Time and again, the executive branch would point to national self-preservation to justify the placement of extraordinary power in the hands of the president.[5]

President Franklin Delano Roosevelt's (FDR) carefully orchestrated policy of aiding Britain and its allies prior to World War II once again reflected the ability of a president to set national security policy unilaterally. Using executive agreements to avoid confronting an uncertain and isolationist Congress, FDR increasingly bound the United States to the Allied cause. The power of the executive further expanded after the attack on Pearl Harbor and the nation's subsequent entrance into World War II.

The Cold War Period. With the termination of World War II, a climate of peace was anticipated under the aegis of a powerful international organization, but this did not materialize. Instead, the postwar years ushered in a period of continuing confrontation that became known as the Cold War. Ideological conflict permeated the international environment, creating a war of nerves stretched taut by the possibility of nuclear war. In these circumstances, crisis again spurred the expansion of executive prerogatives. President Harry Truman led the United States into the Korean conflict in 1950 under the auspices of the United Nations without seeking a congressional declaration of war. Similarly, President John F. Kennedy escalated President Dwight D. Eisenhower's small commitment of less than 1,000 military advisors in Vietnam into a 16,000-man effort that included not only advisors but also helicopter transportation and other logistical capabilities.

By the mid-1960s, presidential initiative in foreign affairs had brought the United States into an extended conflict in Vietnam, and as the war dragged on, such presidential prerogative in foreign affairs came under vigorous attack. The "imperial president" became the subject of congressional and popular opposition, culminating in the July 1973 passage of the War Powers Act over President Richard M. Nixon's veto. This measure set a sixty-day limit on the president's power to wage an undeclared war.[6]

Despite its intent to limit presidential prerogative in foreign policy, the War Powers Act has thus far not proved a significant constraint on the president's power to take the country to war. Presidents have repeatedly refused to embrace this legislation; each since Nixon has taken the position that the act is an unconstitutional infringement on the president's authority.[7] Congress essentially played no role in President Ronald Reagan's decisions to put Marines in Lebanon or to invade Grenada in 1983, to place mines in Nicaraguan harbors in 1984, to bomb Libya in 1986, or to escort reflagged Kuwaiti ships in the Persian Gulf and to engage in battles with the Iranian Navy from mid-1987 through mid-1988. Nor did Congress play a meaningful part in President George H. W. Bush's decisions to invade Panama in 1989, liberate Kuwait in 1991, or intervene in Somalia in 1992. Similarly, President Bill Clinton did not get explicit congressional authorization before he ordered 20,000 US troops to enforce the Dayton Peace Accords in Bosnia in 1995, took the United States to war in Kosovo in 1999, or launched cruise missile attacks in Iraq in 1998 and in Afghanistan and Sudan in 1999.

This trend has continued into the twenty-first century. Although President George W. Bush received an authorization to use military force against the terrorists who attacked the United States on September 11, 2001, he did not cite this congressional action as being part of the basis of his authority for the US invasion of Afghanistan in October 2001.[8] George W. Bush also received a congressional resolution in 2002 that authorized him to use any means he deemed necessary to defend the United States against Iraq and enforce United Nations (UN) Security Council resolutions against the regime of Saddam Hussein, but "it would be incorrect to say that Congress decided on war. It decided only that President Bush should decide."[9] During the administration of President Barack Obama, the United States initiated military operations against Libya in 2011 without congressional authorization and President Donald Trump launched fifty-nine cruise missiles against Syria in 2017 without congressional authorization. If a president was determined to use military force, Congress would find it difficult to stop him.

The World after September 11. The primacy of the presidency over Congress in foreign affairs became more pronounced after the 2001 terrorist attacks in the United States. As mentioned above, within days of the attack, Congress passed a joint resolution authorizing the president "to use all necessary and appropriate force against those nations, organizations, or persons he determined planned, authorized, committed, or aided the terrorist attacks that occurred on September 11, 2001, or harbored such organizations or persons."[10] Just weeks later, Congress passed the USA PATRIOT Act, which expanded the government's ability to conduct surveillance on suspected terrorists. When George W. Bush made the announcement in October 2001 that the United States would use military force against Afghanistan to strike al Qaeda terrorist camps that were supported by the ruling Taliban regime, he did so with strong congressional and public support.[11] In the wake of the attacks, the need for strong executive leadership to fight terrorism seemed self-evident.

However, this view did not last long. The consensus on foreign policy deference to the presidency began to dissipate following the US invasion of Iraq in 2003. In addition to the Iraq Resolution that George W. Bush had secured from Congress in 2002, the United States obtained a UN Security Council resolution calling for "serious consequences" if Iraq did not comply with weapons inspections.[12] However, the Security Council could not reach agreement on a second resolution specifically authorizing military force, and the United States began war against Iraq in the spring of 2003 without explicit UN backing. While Congress and the public initially supported the president, critics became more vocal as the difficulty of constructing a new regime in Iraq became evident and as the facts found on the ground failed to support the most prominent justification for the war: that Iraq had weapons of mass destruction.[13] The Iraq conflict, in particular, raised many questions about whether the United States was witnessing a "new imperial presidency," with presidential power exceeding constitutional boundaries to a degree unprecedented since the Nixon-era abuses of power. An alternative interpretation attributed the expansion of presidential power less to executive usurpation than to congressional reluctance to challenge the president during foreign affairs crises.[14]

The American experience in Iraq prompted new calls for constraints on the president's power to take the country to war. Recognizing the ineffectiveness of the 1973 War Powers Act, a bipartisan group led by two former secretaries of state, James Baker and Warren Christopher, proposed a new law. The commission's proposal—the War Powers Consultation Act of 2009—sought to achieve a middle ground in the debate over war powers by requiring the president and Congress to engage in "meaningful consultation" before committing the nation to war.[15] The proposal also mandated that once Congress had been consulted, it would have to vote on the military action within thirty days. Such a measure would require Congress to take a position on the conflict, either reinforcing or publicly questioning the president's decision to use military force. However, despite calls for reform, this proposal never gained political traction.

While President George W. Bush had pushed the limits of executive authority in foreign affairs, President Barack Obama's administration sent mixed signals. On the one hand, his 2008 campaign emphasized ending the war in Iraq, "pragmatically" engaging with world leaders, and "enhancing the roles of diplomacy and multilateralism in American foreign policy."[16] In office, he staked out foreign policy positions that contrasted starkly with those of his predecessor, implying that George W. Bush's presidency illustrated the harmful effects of executive overreach. Obama pledged to work with Congress on matters of national security, and indeed, when considering a military response to Syria's use of chemical weapons in 2013, he asked for a congressional vote on the issue.[17] On the other hand, President Obama demonstrated a willingness to wield American military power without congressional approval. As mentioned above, in 2011 he deployed American military planes and ships as part of a North Atlantic Treaty Organization (NATO) air war in Libya to support forces that were opposed to Colonel Muammar Qaddafi. President Obama also dramatically expanded the use of drone attacks in the fight against al Qaeda and its affiliates and relied heavily on Special Operations Forces to carry out precision raids. As one commentator noted in 2012, "These new weapons dramatically expanded the president's ability to wage nonstop, low-level conflict, something just short of war, every day of the year."[18] The expansion of the potential battlefield through the development of new technologies further complicates debate over the scope of presidential war powers. Similarly, the Trump administration continued this trend toward exerting presidential authority with the aforementioned strike in Syria. Diplomatically, Trump exerted his authority by announcing that the U.S. Embassy in Israel would move from Tel Aviv to Jerusalem, and economically, he claimed a national security exception to impose tariffs on steel and aluminum. Many in Congress decried these actions but could not immediately block these presidential actions.

The Nature of Presidential Power. Expansion of presidential power in the realm of national security may now appear as a fait accompli. However, central to the Constitution's design is the concept that no branch of government should hold an unchallenged position of dominance in the conduct of public affairs. The resulting governmental framework of checks and balances fundamentally shapes the president's ability to influence the behavior of other political actors and institutions. Richard Neustadt insightfully described this as a system "not of separation of power but of separated institutions sharing powers."[19] The resulting setup allows the president to sit in a position where many actors require his help in achieving their objectives. By the same token, the president must depend on other actors to accomplish his own goals. This interactive process is seen in the ever-present dynamic tension between the president and Congress.

Given this array of institutions, much of presidential power is rooted in the informal power of persuasion rather than the formal powers provided in the Constitution. Noting the singular platform that it gave him to address the American public, President Theodore Roosevelt called the presidency a "bully pulpit"; FDR said it was a "place of moral leadership." More prosaically, Neustadt argued that presidential power rests in the ability to induce others to "believe that what [the president] wants of them is what their own appraisal of their own responsibilities requires them to do in their own interests, not his"; this, then becomes a matter of persuading others that furthering the president's goals is the best way to serve their own.

At the heart of the process of persuasion is bargaining. As Neustadt emphasizes, "Power is persuasion and persuasion becomes bargaining."[20] The president commands mass-media attention by virtue of his office. He enjoys the prestige of being chief of state, as well as the head of government. He has at his disposal a wide spectrum of rewards to confer and a significant number of penalties to impose. These potential points of concrete advantage in the bargaining process should not, however, be confused with presidential power, which requires the ability to wield these instruments to persuade other people that cooperation to support the president's goals will advance their own interests.

The Roles of the President. The president plays multiple roles in the execution of the office. He is the chief of state, commander in chief of the armed forces, chief diplomat, principal initiator of legislation, and chief executor of the laws. The president is also a party leader, national spokesperson, peacekeeper, manager of prosperity, and a world leader.[21] These roles tend to place the president at the center of national security policy making. In particular, in his role as chief of state, the president personifies the United States in its dealings with the world; due to his constitutional powers to appoint and receive ambassadors, the president is at the focal point of diplomatic activity. As commander in chief, he is at the apex of a large and elaborate security apparatus. None of these myriad roles is isolated from the others, and the president must satisfy the particular demands of each when confronting problems of national security. Moreover, as he plays these various roles, the president must deal with several distinct entities, each with their own interests.

Various trends have increased the significance of the president's national security roles. These trends include the increasing involvement of the United States in world affairs, which are marked by an atmosphere of constant danger; the development of a national contingency system around the president to enable an effective response to threats; advances in weapons technology that have increased the stakes in crisis management; and enhancements in communications technology that have accelerated the tempo of communication and response, and have also made it easier for a president to intervene more deeply into operational matters formerly left to military leaders. The national security process is increasingly saturated with information; the chief executive largely controls the organizations that are capable of assimilating large volumes of data, as well as the communication channels through which decisions based on that information can be relayed. Although vigorous presidents have always reached out to grasp the levers of government, recent trends have encouraged modern presidents to be especially activist.

Presidential National Security Functions. Within the complexity of the president's multiple roles, three major functions in the conduct of national security can be identified: resource allocation, policy planning, and coordinating and monitoring of operations.[22]

Resource Allocation. The maintenance of national security is expensive and requires a major commitment of resources in the president's budget each year. The budget is the main vehicle through which presidential priorities relating to resource use are communicated. The Office of Management and Budget (OMB), discussed briefly below, is the principal instrument the president uses in this allocation function.

Policy Planning. Policy planning involves the development of long-range designs. Examples include the Marshall Plan for the reconstruction of Europe after World War II, the expansion and evolution of NATO, and global coordination to address climate change. It also includes narrower and shorter-term plans to advance US interests and cope with emerging problems, such as the efforts of the Obama administration to cope with Iran's nuclear capabilities and development. Generally those engaged in policy planning seek to shape future events as well as prepare for contingencies. Historically, the focus of such planning has shifted among, or has been shared by, the Departments of State and Defense and the president's national security advisor, who heads the National Security Council (NSC) staff. This function is inherently challenging, and the need to coordinate with bureaucratic structures and procedures makes it all the more difficult.

Coordinating and Monitoring Operations. Coordination of operations requires overseeing the myriad day-to-day foreign and defense policy actions of government organizations and officials as they react to international circumstances and execute policy. The associated monitoring function is designed to provide feedback to the executive branch to ensure that government actions remain consistent with and advance American policy, as well as to ensure awareness of new data or changing conditions. In practice, the president tends to lean most on the national security advisor and NSC staff for coordination and monitoring tasks.

The Institutionalized Presidency and National Security Affairs

The complexity, scope, and magnitude of these three presidential national security functions gave rise to the institutionalized presidency in which individual efforts of the president are augmented by staff members who act in the president's name.

This apparatus, together with certain executive departments, forms the principal means of developing, directing, and coordinating national security policy. The key elements of this collective executive are the White House Office, the NSC and its staff, the State Department, the Department of Defense, the Department of Homeland Security, the Central Intelligence Agency, and the Office of Management and Budget (figure 4.1).

The White House Office. The organization and use of the White House staff tends to reflect a president's personal style, and the modern presidency has seen various arrangements as well as various levels of effectiveness. During FDR's tenure, staff operations tended to be chaotic: there was overlapping of assignments, lack of coordination, and often frustration on the part of the staff. However, the chaos was purposeful and served FDR well: receiving competing sources of information and analysis enabled him to develop alternatives and maintain options. World War II somewhat curtailed this approach, however, as the importance of secrecy increased and focus shifted to the operational concerns of global war.[23]

In the 1950s, President Eisenhower was at the opposite extreme. His staff was organized tightly around its chief of staff, initially Sherman Adams. Responsibilities were clearly defined, and there was a military style of hierarchy, neatness, and order. In the 1960s, the Kennedy and Johnson administrations utilized a less formal staffing system; a small staff concerned with national security had more direct and frequent access to the president. Under President Nixon (1969) and President Gerald Ford (1974), the White House staff was again organized along more structured lines. President Jimmy Carter (1977) endeavored to establish a more informal advisory system, initially operating without a chief of staff, but he soon found that the demands on the Oval Office necessitated some formal staffing procedures. President Ronald Reagan (1981) employed a hierarchical staffing system and relied heavily on delegating authority to a few close aides and empowering key cabinet officials. While President George H. W. Bush (1989) largely continued this model, he engaged more directly with his advisors in policy making, particularly in foreign affairs. In his first year in office, President Bill Clinton (1993) faced some organizational difficulties, which stemmed largely from his reluctance to delegate authority to his chief of staff and other advisors, but he ultimately developed a more structured White House operation, albeit one that was more informal than those of his immediate predecessors. The only chief executive to hold a master's degree in business administration, President George W. Bush (2001), adopted a structured and hierarchical White House staffing system consistent with a corporate management style. President Barack Obama (2009) preferred to be presented with competing alternatives in policy deliberations. This system of "multiple advocacy," however, appeared in a context of a powerful inner circle of political advisors.[24] President Donald Trump ran his staff much like he ran his business empire. Somewhat harkening to FDR's pre-war administration, Trump thrives off of competing inputs and many advisors using a less structured coordination process in comparison with that of most of his predecessors. After six months in of-

FIGURE 4.1 The Government of the United States

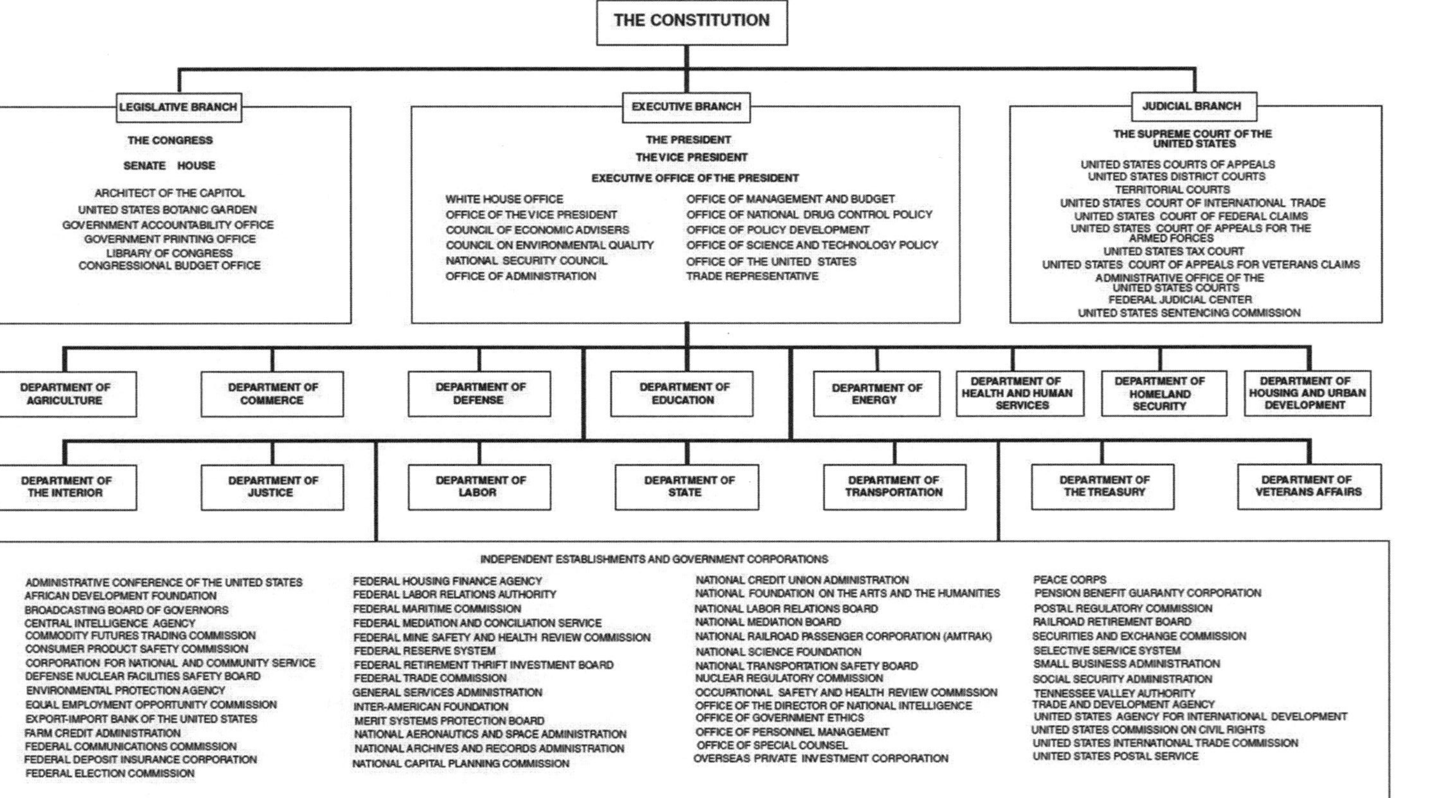

Source: US Government Manual, https://www.usgovernmentmanual.gov/

fice, in part to provide a more disciplined process in the White House, Trump replaced his first White House Chief of Staff, Reince Priebus, with his homeland security secretary, retired Marine Corps General John Kelly.

Despite similarities and differences in the functioning of the White House staff under different presidents, some pronounced trends appear over time. The most obvious is growth. The entire Hoover presidency (1929–1933) was staffed by three secretaries, a military aide and a naval aide, and twenty clerks. By 2016, approximately 460 people worked in the Obama White House, and another 100 to 150 were detailed there from other agencies on special assignments.[25] The growth in numbers is a symptom, and some would argue a cause, of increasing centralization of decision making. Such centralization can result in a significant divide between policy makers and the instruments of policy. A larger White House staff may also insulate the president more from the outside world. This becomes problematic if the perceptions of his internal staff do not adequately reflect external reality. As the NSC system has evolved and the position of the assistant directing its staff has strengthened, other White House staffs have played a diminishing role in national security matters.

The National Security Advisor. The position of assistant to the president for national security affairs, better known today as the "national security advisor," was created by Eisenhower in 1953. Eisenhower employed this special assistant primarily as a policy coordinator; since the 1960s, however, the position has also assumed an advocacy role and now has a significant policymaking role in the White House as well. In each administration, the role of the national security advisor is significantly shaped by his or her personal relationship with the president and how the president wishes the use the office. This role has also developed along with the evolution of the NSC staff, which the advisor heads.

National Security Council. The formalized coordination and policy planning functions of the presidency in national security matters are located in the National Security Council, created by the National Security Act of 1947. The NSC's statutory members include the president, the vice president, the secretary of state, and the secretary of defense. The director of national intelligence and the chairman of the JCS serve as statutory advisors. Additionally, the secretary of the treasury and the national security advisor regularly attend NSC meetings, and presidents often include the White House chief of staff, White House counsel, secretary of homeland security, and others as well (see chapter 10, especially table 10.2).[26]

Truman was instrumental in shaping the NSC to respond directly to the needs of the president rather than merely extending the interagency arrangements of the State-War-Navy Coordinating Committee, which had been created during World War II. The legislation that resulted in the 1947 National Security Act, which the Truman administration shepherded through Congress, provided for a separate staff to support the NSC. It did not rely, as before, on staff contributed from involved agencies. One scholar notes that Truman's "adroit maneuvers scotched the scheme of those who wanted to assure defense domination of the National Security Council by housing it in the Pentagon . . . and by designating the Secretary of Defense as Chairman in the President's absence."[27]

The NSC system was restructured during the Eisenhower administration to reflect both the new president's style and his assessment of global politics.[28] In keeping with his view of the importance of economic health to security, Eisenhower regularly invited his Treasury secretary and budget director to attend NSC meetings. He modeled the decisionmaking process on his experience as a commander in the military. He used the NSC apparatus regularly in the belief that, as he later wrote: "The secret of a sound, satisfactory decision made on an emergency basis has always been that the responsible official has been 'living with the problem' before it becomes acute. Failure to use, on a continuing basis, the NSC, or some similar advisory body, entails losing the capacity to make emergency decisions based on depth of understanding and perspective."[29]

The transition from the Eisenhower to the Kennedy administration involved a distinct change in presidential outlook and operating style.[30] Decision making involving national security became more ad hoc, with less reliance on the NSC. Critics charged that the Eisenhower system had impeded initiative and flexibility by subjecting proposals to overly formalized bureaucratic argument. Regarding the world as inherently dynamic, President Kennedy hoped to shape a national security system capable of coping with rapid change. Eschewing the previous focus on broad interagency input, Kennedy built a strong staff centralized in the White House. He relied on his special assistant for national security affairs for advice and for coordination of operations among the various agencies involved with national security.

Much more than his predecessor, Kennedy immersed himself in the details of selected aspects of policy. The Bay of Pigs, a failed military invasion of Cuba, in April 1961, shortly after Kennedy took office (discussed in chapter 3), was a lesson he did not soon forget. He had relied on the experts and judgments of the preceding administration and, as he remarked a year and a half later, "The advice of every member of the Executive Branch brought in to advise was unanimous—and the advice was wrong."[31] (His critics point out that his last-minute intervention, which canceled air support for the invasion force, also contributed to the fiasco.) Partly as a result, the president began to rely increasingly on his national security advisor to provide policy options. The full NSC met less frequently and tended to consider long-term questions concerning Laos, Berlin, the Nuclear Test Ban Treaty, and other problems of the early 1960s, which had already been extensively explored by ad hoc interagency task forces.

Although the NSC had been established to provide a coherent means of coping with the urgency of the atomic age, in practice it was not the locus of crisis management. As demonstrated during the Cuban Missile Crisis, Kennedy relied instead on a specially selected "Executive Committee" to bear the burden of deliberation and policy development. Consisting of the president's most trusted advisors, and unfettered by the statutory membership requirements of the NSC (though many of those advisors did participate), the "ExComm" reflected Kennedy's more individualized approach to national security policy making.

Lyndon Johnson was thrust into the presidency following the assassination of Kennedy in November 1963. Although he was a master of congressional politics, he had limited experience in international affairs. This lack of background, as well as his desire to bring a sense of continuity to his administration, resulted in few immediate changes to the Kennedy NSC system. The emergence of the Vietnam conflict in the mid-1960s became the central drama and tragedy of Johnson's foreign policy. Lacking the inclination to reach beyond his advisors to other key levers in the bureaucracy, Johnson further narrowed the process of deliberation and decision making to a small group. Many important national security decisions were made at informal and largely unstructured discussions at the president's periodic "Tuesday lunches," which generally included only members of the NSC and a few invited guests.[32]

In 1969, the Nixon administration departed from the largely ad hoc arrangements of the Kennedy-Johnson years, returning to a centralized system more akin to that of Eisenhower. Nixon placed the national security machinery firmly in the White House under the control of the president's national security advisor, Henry Kissinger. Kissinger adapted the interagency arrangements of the Johnson administration by assigning issues to Interdepartmental Groups chaired by assistant secretaries of state. These groups were responsible for studying specific problems, formulating policy choices, and assessing various alternatives. A Senior Review Group at the undersecretary level, chaired by Kissinger, dealt with Interdepartmental Group recommendations. Less important or contentious issues were decided at subordinate levels rather than being forwarded to the NSC. Although this approach allowed for the inclusion of the views of operating agencies, it lodged control squarely in the White House, where Nixon wanted it.

Nixon's NSC structure was further subdivided through the creation of various special groups subordinate to the NSC. For example, major issues centered on the Vietnam War were handled by a Vietnam Special Studies Group, while crisis planning was done by the Washington Special Actions Group. This evolution represented a further strengthening of the role of the national security advisor and the dominance of the NSC staff over the Department of State. It is noteworthy that, after he left government, Kissinger began to decry this trend, recommending instead that a president should make the secretary of state "his principal advisor and [should] 'use' the national security advisor primarily as a senior administrator and coordinator to make certain that each significant point of view is heard."[33]

President Carter's initial approach was to streamline his NSC staff while maintaining the same basic functions and powers as the Nixon-Ford staff. A number of NSC committees of the earlier era, which had been separate entities in name only, were merged into three basic committees: the Policy Review Committee, the Special Coordination Committee, and the preexisting assistant secretary–level Interdepartmental Groups.

The organizational arrangements of the NSC system in the Carter administration initially led to an increase in the power of the secretary of state, at the expense of the NSC advisor. Selected to chair many sessions of the Policy Review Committee, Secretary of State Cyrus Vance was able to shape policies of the Carter administration on issues including human rights and arms transfers. However, as the focus shifted from policy making to implementation, the power of National Security Advisor Zbigniew Brzezinski increased. Under Brzezinski's direction, the Special Coordination Committee dealt with issues concerning arms control, covert action, and crisis management. It was Brzezinski and the NSC staff who managed the Iranian hostage crisis, which dominated most of the last year of the Carter presidency.

Reagan came to office determined to downgrade the role of the NSC and the advisor to the president on national security affairs. His first national security advisor, Richard Allen, did not even report directly to him, and NSC management receded in visibility. After Allen's departure from office, the NSC was largely restored to a more significant policymaking role, and Allen's five successors reported directly to the president. In the Reagan administration, the secretaries of state and defense had significant authority in their respective areas of responsibility, with the NSC staff coordinating rather than independently advocating specific policies.[34]

Under George H. W. Bush, the NSC returned to the center of policy making. George H. W. Bush appointed as his national security advisor Brent Scowcroft, who had held the post briefly under Ford. Scowcroft made himself chairman of a Principals Committee at the cabinet level. His deputy was placed in charge of the senior subcabinet interagency forum—the Deputies Committee—which reviewed and monitored the work of the NSC interagency process and made recommendations on the development and implementation of policy.

George H. W. Bush held few formal NSC meetings, preferring to rely on the Principals Committee and the Deputies Committee to formulate and implement long-range strategy. For example, in April 1989, it was the Deputies Committee that drafted the document that spelled out the Bush administration's policy towards Iraq. By contrast, the president preferred to handle crisis situations in selected ad hoc groups or in one-on-one meetings. For example, key decisions relating to the Gulf War in 1990 were made by small groups of close advisors. Bush's NSC system resembled that of the Nixon era in formality, while his own personal decision-making style resembled the informality of Kennedy's.[35]

When he took office in 1993, President Clinton enlarged the membership of the NSC and included a much greater emphasis on economic issues in the formulation of national security policy. This was first and foremost evident in his creation of the National Economic Council (NEC), a body whose membership overlapped considerably with the NSC and whose chair, the national economic advisor, was added—along with the secretary of the treasury—as members of the NSC.[36] Still, the NSC retained its emphasis on traditional national security issues. Clinton's first national security advisor, W. Anthony Lake, played his role primarily behind the scenes until the need to explain Clinton's foreign policy better led him to begin to accept more public speaking engagements. Lake's successor in 1997, Samuel (Sandy) Berger played a more active role in communicating the president's foreign policy to the public as well as developing support for the president's policies in Congress.[37] One criticism of the Clinton administration's national security system was that it produced an ad hoc approach to national security policy, focused on crisis management but ineffective at overall planning.[38]

At the start of his first term in 2001, George W. Bush selected Condoleezza Rice to be his national security advisor. Rice was one of the president's closest foreign-policy advisors and a family friend. She was responsible for coordinating NSC meetings, but she faced competition for controlling foreign policy from several fronts, including Vice President Richard Cheney and Secretary of Defense Donald Rumsfeld.[39] When Rice became secretary of state in George W. Bush's second term, her successor as national security advisor, Stephen Hadley (previously her deputy), maintained a less public role. The structure of Bush's NSC system did not differ significantly from that of Clinton; most of the regional and functional bureaus remained essentially the same, even if some names changed slightly. George W. Bush did hold more frequent formal NSC meetings than his recent predecessors, often daily for a period after September 11, 2001, and weekly thereafter.

When President Obama took office in 2009, the expectation was that his administration's NSC would differ radically from that of his predecessor. Although some changes did occur (including merging the Homeland Security Council with the NSC), the administration retained many of the same structural and organizational processes as the previous three administrations.[40] At the start of his first term in 2009, President Obama selected James Jones, a retired marine general, as his national security advisor. Jones expected to be the primary conduit of national security information to the president, but others in the White House had Obama's ear, most notably Deputy National Security Advisor Thomas Donilon and Chief of Staff Rahm Emanuel. Jones was criticized as unable to manage the interagency process effectively.[41] After eighteen months on the job, Jones resigned. He was quickly replaced by Donilon, who had a stronger personal relationship with the president and who understood Obama's preference for a decisionmaking process that enabled the consideration of multiple alternatives.[42]

The NSC under President Trump had a tumultuous start when the president's first national security advisor, retired Lieutenant General Michael Flynn, resigned after just twenty-four days in office. Flynn resigned after misleading Vice President Michael Pence about his interactions with Russia's ambassador to the United States. In December 2017, Flynn pled guilty to one count of lying to the FBI during the special counsel investigation into potential Russian interference in the 2016 presidential election. Lieutenant General H. R. McMaster replaced Flynn as national security advisor in February 2017 and endeavored to provide structure and stability to the NSC.

The State Department. Since its creation in 1789 under its first secretary, Thomas Jefferson, the Department of State has been the customary operational arm of the US government in the conduct of foreign affairs. The department performs two basic functions: it represents the interests of the United States and its citizens in relations with foreign countries, and it serves as a principal source of advice to the president on all aspects of foreign affairs, including national security policy (figure 4.2).[43]

As a member of the cabinet, the secretary of state is traditionally the president's principal advisor on foreign policy, although this tradition has waned somewhat since the 1960s with the emergence of a succession of powerful national security advisors. In all cases, the secretary's role is shaped by his or her own talents and personal relationship with the president, as well as by the degree to which a president is involved in foreign policy. The more a president desires to become involved in foreign policy, the more difficult it is for the secretary of state to take initiatives and run the department. The relative strength of the secretary of state often reflects the president's intent more than the secretary's personal ability and assertiveness. President Nixon's choice in 1969 of William Rogers as secretary of state and his systematic bypassing, even humiliation, of the secretary is an eloquent example.[44] On the other hand, some presidents delegate authority for the foreign policy process and deemphasize the NSC; for example, Reagan appointed strong secretaries of state such as Alexander Haig, a former White House chief of staff and NATO commander, and George Shultz who, before Reagan made him secretary of state in 1983, had served earlier administrations as secretary of labor, secretary of the treasury, and director of the OMB.

A third approach was that of George H. W. Bush, who wanted to focus heavily on certain areas of foreign policy and appointed a close friend and confidant, James Baker, to handle others. Under this arrangement, Bush personally managed the Gulf War deployment and execution, while Baker followed up with a Mideast peace conference in Madrid in 1991. In some ways Bush was his own secretary of state, while Baker functioned as his close and powerful deputy.[45]

The combination of a secretary of state who is not assertive and a president who prefers to focus on the domestic agenda—such as Warren Christopher in Clinton's first term—can produce a foreign policy whose notable successes become associated with key subordinates. The Clinton administration was thus said to have several distinct foreign policy personalities, from Richard Holbrooke's negotiation of the Dayton Peace Accords, which helped resolve conflict in former Yugoslavian states of Bosnia and Herzegovina, to the predominant role of Special Envoy Dennis Ross in the Middle East peace process.

Under George W. Bush, the relative power of the secretary of state varied from his first to second terms, in large part due to his differing relationship with each incumbent. Bush's first secretary of state, Colin Powell, came to the office with a distinguished military record capped by service as the chairman of the JCS. Powell had also received special permission from Congress to serve, during his military career, as Reagan's national security advisor, and thus had expertise in the political realm as well. Yet Powell as secretary of state was repeatedly stymied by others in the administration, notably Vice President Cheney and Defense Secretary Rumsfeld. Powell was reportedly also frequently at odds with his White House counterpart, National Security Advisor Rice. To cite one example, Powell was unable to persuade the president to give more time for arms inspections before waging war against Iraq in 2003.[46] When Rice, a close confidant and friend of the

FIGURE 4.2 Department of State

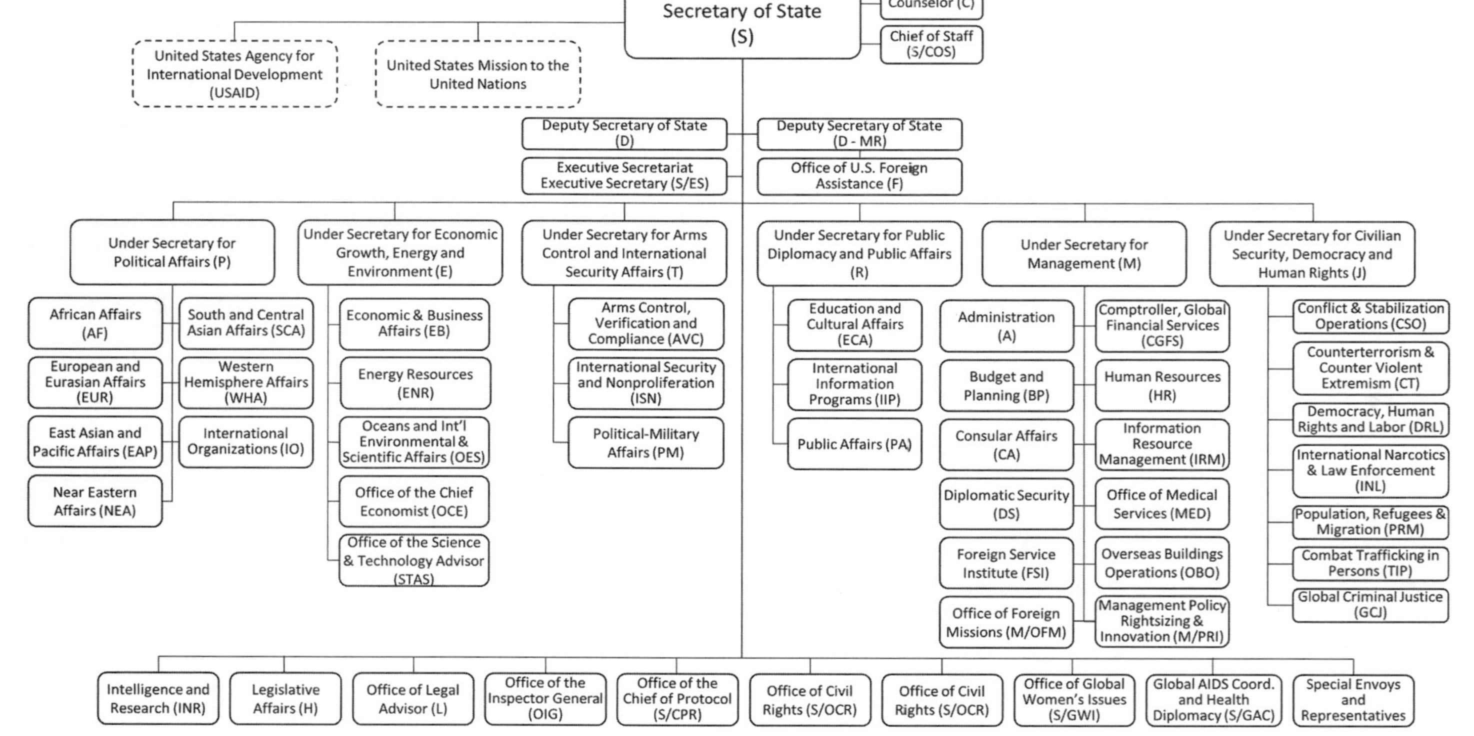

Source: State Department, https://www.state.gov/documents/organization/263637.pdf

president, became secretary of state in Bush's second term, she appeared to have greater influence than Powell in foreign policy.

Obama's relationships with his secretaries of state, unlike those of his predecessor, were shaped less by personal ties than by his general tendency to maintain White House control over national security policy. Thus, neither Hillary Clinton nor John Kerry were granted much autonomy during their respective tenures as secretary of state. The same can be said for Trump's first secretary of state, Rex Tillerson, who was granted little leeway to influence foreign policy, before President Trump replaced him after only fourteen months.

Personal dynamics with the president aside, the secretary of state faces a complex task in managing the internal workings of the bureaucracy. The State Department is broadly organized along two lines, geographic-regional responsibilities and functional responsibilities. With regard to geographic regions, special "desks" within the regional bureaus monitor the detailed actions and interactions of specific countries within the purview of a regional assistant secretary. The functional organizations, such as the Bureau of Political-Military Affairs, provide an alternative view of international dynamics. These functional bureaus present analyses that cut across geographic lines and sometimes across the analyses arising out of the regional desks as well.

For those observers of public affairs who long for quick and efficient solutions to difficult problems (and who may think that the world is more malleable than it is), the State Department is a source of constant frustration. Owing in part to the department's lack of a natural domestic constituency and in part to the public's belief that American interests and policies should and can always prevail, this frustration often results in vigorous and often mistaken criticism.[47]

Presidential displeasure with the Department of State, too, seems to be a recurring and bipartisan reaction. In general, presidential complaints about the State Department center on six issues: (1) quality of staff work in terms of analysis; (2) lack of speed in responses to requests and problems; (3) resistance to change and new approaches; (4) inadequacy in carrying out presidential decisions; (5) failure to lead in foreign affairs; and (6) the feeling that the leadership does not have control of its own department.[48] These misgivings about the State Department, although in many cases exaggerated, often impel activist presidents and activist secretaries to bypass the institution and instead to pursue largely individual initiatives in foreign affairs. For example, James Baker, who had served as undersecretary of commerce, White House chief of staff, and secretary of the treasury before becoming George H. W. Bush's secretary of state in 1989, brought in a group of outsiders who had relatively little foreign policy experience for most key positions, to the dismay of many career Foreign Service officers.

Determining the appropriate use of the Department of State in the national security process has long been a problem for presidents and secretaries. Operational demands ("putting out fires") and the inherent tension between useful specificity and diplomatic generality make the exercise of policy planning in the Department of State a perennial challenge. Attempts have been made to harness expertise for policy planning, such as Secretary of State George Marshall's creation in

1947 of the Policy Planning Staff with Ambassador George Kennan as its head.[49] The Policy Planning Staff was designed to focus planning on current issues and to anticipate future contingencies. Yet that staff and its successor organizations have invariably fallen short of expectations. Mid- and long-range planning for a complex and untidy world is intrinsically difficult, and it requires exceptionally talented people who are sensitive to the purposes and limits of policy, which must both pursue a long-term strategy and respond to immediate crises. Such talents, however, are always in short supply. Moreover, if the people who possess them are kept close to genuine issues so that their planning is relevant to the real world, then they are constantly drawn into short-range, operational planning and policy advice. In short, if the planners are talented and their subject timely, they tend to be diverted; if they are not, they tend to be ignored. As a result, much of the weight of policy planning has shifted to the NSC staff and the Department of Defense, though the same dynamics often degrade long-range planning in those entities.

There is one area in which the Department of State has largely maintained its hegemony: the daily conduct of American policy in foreign countries. President Eisenhower strongly reaffirmed the department's mandate to coordinate all American activities in foreign lands. The "country team" concept places the American ambassador in charge of all American programs within the country to which he or she is accredited. (The mandate does not extend to American military forces in the field, but it does apply to military assistance teams and to military officers assigned to embassies as attachés.) This approach attempts to unify the implementation of American national security policy within each foreign country.[50] Succeeding administrations have continued to endorse this concept, but there is a persistent tendency by departments and agencies other than State to fight it.

The Department of Defense. The Department of Defense is the president's principal arm in the execution of national defense policy. Composed of the three military departments (Army, Navy, and Air Force), the Joint Chiefs of Staff, nine regional and functional combatant commands (such as European Command or Special Operations Command), and numerous defense agencies with responsibility to provide services across the entire department (such as the Defense Intelligence Agency), the department constitutes the military instrument essential to credible policies (figure 4.3).

As created in 1947, the position of the secretary of defense was initially that of a weak coordinator. A series of defense reorganization acts, the latest of which was enacted in 1986, greatly strengthened the secretary's role, and the department has become more centralized to improve the efficiency and responsiveness of the military instrument. The essentials of the secretary's role were aptly described in 1971 and, despite reorganization and dramatic changes in the world, the description remains true today:

> Foreign policy, military strategy, defense budgets and the choice of major weapons and forces are all closely related matters of basic national security policy and the principal task of the Secretary of Defense is personally to grasp the strategic issues and provide

FIGURE 4.3 Department of Defense

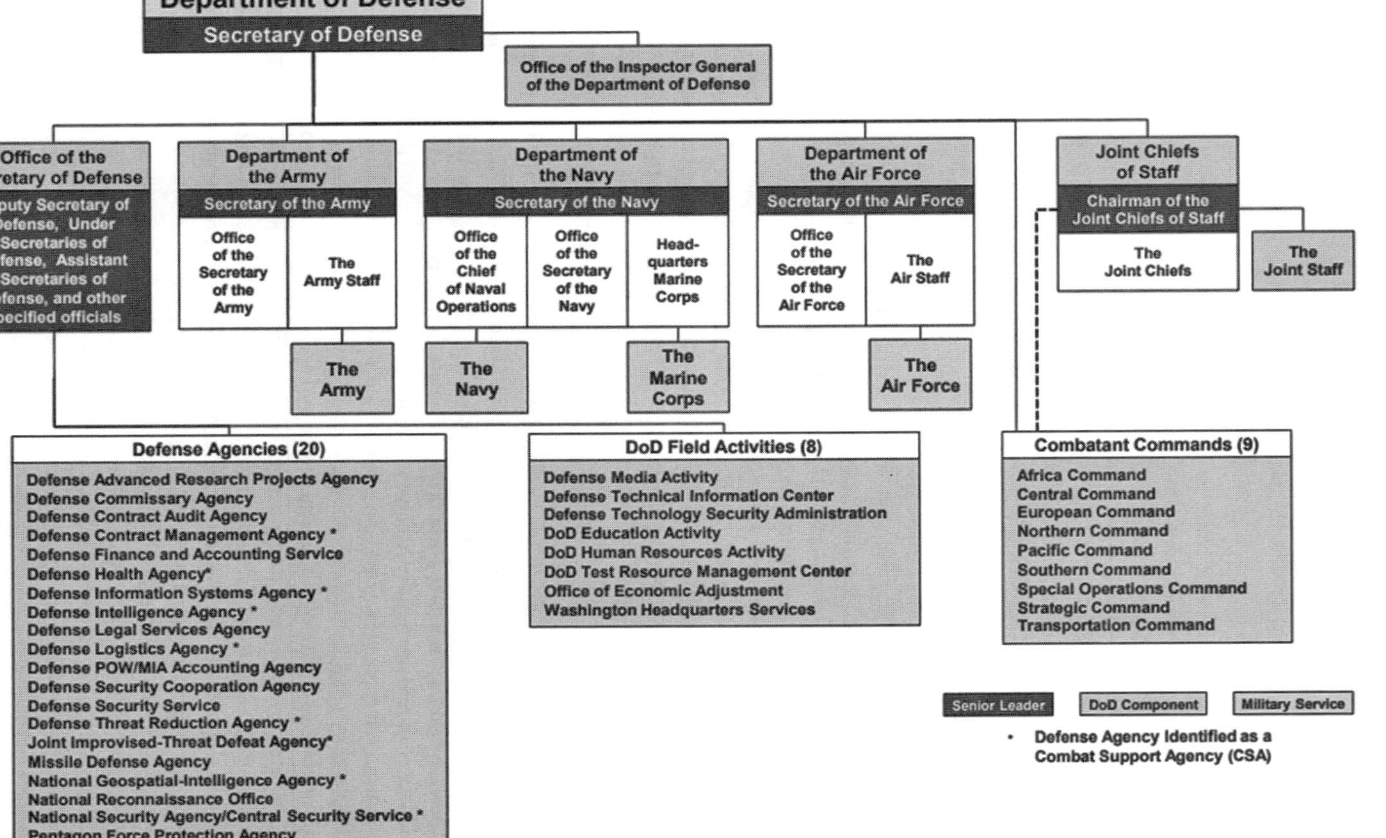

Source: DoD, http://dcmo.defense.gov/Portals/47/Documents/PDSD/201509_DoD_Organizational_Structure.pdf

> active leadership to develop a defense program that sensibly relates all these factors. In short, his main job is to shape the defense program in the national interest. In particular, it is his job to decide what forces are needed.[51]

Though the formal hierarchy is clear, the relative influence of the civilian leadership of the Pentagon and of its most senior uniformed leaders has varied over time. During the 1990s, some observers were concerned about what they saw as the inappropriate assertiveness of uniformed members of the military on policy issues. By contrast, President George W. Bush's first defense secretary, Donald Rumsfeld, was dominant in shaping the president's defense policies and was known for having a directive and demanding leadership style over military subordinates. Obama's relationship with the defense establishment was mixed. Obama had four different secretaries of defense, starting with Secretary of Defense Robert Gates, who was retained from the Bush administration. Many of them voiced frustration with excessive micromanagement from an increasingly intrusive NSC staff.[52] Obama had disagreements with his military leaders on the timing and size of troop surges and reductions, as well as conflicts over the appropriate size and budget priorities for the military. He generally relied on the NSC staff to impose his policy priorities on military issues.

In 2017, Trump appointed James (Jim) Mattis as the secretary of defense. A retired four-star marine general, Mattis was one of four current or retired generals to receive high appointments in the early Trump administration (the others were Flynn, McMaster, and Kelly). Early in his presidency, Trump revealed a strong desire for the presence of these military experts within his inner circle. However, significant national security policy decisions were still made largely within the White House.

The president exercises his constitutional authority as commander in chief of the armed forces directly through the secretary of defense to the commanders of the nine unified combatant commands. In strict legal terms, the chairman of the JCS and the JCS as a body are not in the chain of command; in practice, defense secretaries generally involve them in deliberations, drawing on their professional advice on policy and on appropriate and effective operational means to implement presidential directives. Although the normal flow of advice from the chiefs goes through the chairman and the secretary of defense, the 1986 Goldwater-Nichols legislation explicitly gives the individual members of the JCS a statutory right to go directly to the president. This provision was designed to assuage opponents of reorganization, who feared that independent military opinion would be stifled by a partisan secretary of defense or a dominant chairman.[53]

As the "hinge" between the highest civilian authorities and the uniformed military, the members of the JCS have two distinct roles in the Department of Defense. In their corporate role, they serve as the senior military advisors to the president, the NSC, and the secretary of defense. Individually, they serve as the leaders of their respective services. As a corporate body, the JCS includes the chairman and vice chairman of the JCS, the chief of staff of the Army, the chief of staff of the Air Force, the chief of naval operations, the commandant of the Marine

Corps, and the chief of the National Guard Bureau. The chairman or the vice chairman represents the JCS as a whole at meetings of the NSC and in other interagency forums. The president relies on the chiefs for military advice, but may also lean on them for supporting opinions, which are sometimes crucial to politically controversial foreign or national security policy initiatives. (A further discussion of the role of the uniformed military in the national security process can be found in chapter 8.)

The Central Intelligence Agency. The Central Intelligence Agency (CIA) was established under the National Security Act of 1947 with responsibility for the overall coordination and integration of the intelligence efforts of various governmental groups engaged in national security matters. Its director was named an advisor to the NSC. The CIA inherited many functions of the wartime Office of Strategic Services, in particular, gathering and analyzing information and conducting covert operations.

Prior to America's entry into World War II, the gathering of intelligence had not been institutionalized in any one agency but was incidental to the activities of several agencies, notably the State Department and the army and navy officers attached to embassies around the world. The climate of opinion was such that intelligence activities were seen as somewhat dishonorable; Henry Stimson, as secretary of state in the Hoover administration, dismissed the "spying" business with the maxim that "gentlemen do not read other gentlemen's mail."[54] However, the ravages of global war and the threat of communism had overcome the gentlemanly distinctions of an earlier age by 1947, and the CIA became a powerful force in American security policy.

Throughout the 1950s and 1960s, the CIA amassed considerable power within the government. As the dimensions and stakes of the Cold War expanded, so did the CIA. The agency also enjoyed unusual autonomy: from 1947 until 1977, the CIA was the only federal agency exempt from openly defending its budget and subjecting its activities to congressional oversight. Funds for the CIA were disguised in the defense budget, rendering outside assessment of program effectiveness impossible. The CIA was also strengthened by its primacy in intelligence gathering and analysis. As a result of long-term assignments to specific areas, the CIA's agents in the field, as well as its analysts at home, developed considerable expertise and produced relatively high-quality work.[55]

Since its inception, the CIA has also been involved in covert operations. In Iran in 1953 and in Guatemala in 1954, for example, the CIA supported coups that overthrew existing regimes. The CIA was the agent of the unsuccessful 1961 attempt at Cuba's Bay of Pigs to remove Castro from power. Such episodes of clandestine warfare, combined with CIA activity in Chile during the 1973 overthrow of President Salvador Allende and some improper actions by its personnel at home, convinced a number of critics that the CIA's scope and power should be curtailed. As the Cold War was eased by détente and American intervention was replaced by retrenchment in the early 1970s, these factors reinforced the tendency to rein in the CIA.

It later became apparent to many, however, that the downgrading of the CIA in the early 1970s went too far. The Carter administration, caught off guard in 1979 by the seizure of the American embassy in Teheran and the Soviet invasion of Afghanistan, began the process of revitalizing the CIA. During the Reagan administration, the CIA played a major role in American efforts to combat the spread of communism in the developing world. These activities, plus the agency's role in the Iran-Contra affair, again led to congressional and public criticism and a drop in public trust in the late 1980s.

With the end of the Cold War and the collapse of the Soviet Union, one principal purpose of the CIA evaporated. The agency attempted to deal with the new environment by adjusting its mission. For example, in the early 1990s the CIA began to intensify its economic intelligence activities, to coordinate US and foreign intelligence on global terrorism, and to integrate intelligence and law enforcement activities against narcotics producers and traffickers. However, its failure to predict major events such as the collapse of the Soviet Union, the Iraqi invasion of Kuwait, and the terrorist attacks of September 11, 2001, again damaged its credibility.

The role of the CIA was further complicated by the creation of the office of the director of national intelligence. Based on recommendations from the 9/11 Commission, Congress and George W. Bush approved the Intelligence Reform and Terrorist Prevention Act of 2004. This law authorized the creation of a director of national intelligence to coordinate the efforts of more than a dozen federal intelligence agencies, including the CIA, the National Security Agency, and the Defense Intelligence Agency.[56]

The Obama administration had a generally productive relationship with the intelligence community, despite the changing landscape. The relationship was particularly strong in the realm of counterterrorism and will be remembered for the cooperative work to capture and kill Osama bin Laden in Pakistan, where military teams operated under the CIA director. At the same time, however, the Obama administration struggled with high-profile intelligence leaks, the most prominent of which were the thousands of National Security Agency documents leaked by Edward Snowden in 2013. The relationship between the intelligence community and the Trump administration has been somewhat precarious given the president's questioning of intelligence findings on Russian interference in the 2016 presidential election. The status of this relationship will have an important impact on the direction of national security policy during Trump's tenure in office. (For more on the intelligence community, see chapter 7.)

Office of Management and Budget. The president uses the budget process to structure and implement national security priorities. The Office of Management and Budget (OMB) plays a crucial role in the creation of this budget and in the daily oversight of executive operations. Theodore Sorensen observed that "any President . . . must always be setting priorities and measuring costs. The official most often likely to loom largest in his thinking when he makes a key decision is not the Secretary of State or the Secretary of Defense but the Director of the Budget."[57]

The OMB has become an effective instrument of influence for presidents seeking to extend their control over an expanding bureaucracy. OMB personnel establish, under presidential guidance, the budget obligations and spending ceilings within which departments must plan. Budgets from the departments, including DoD and State, are routinely subjected to OMB review prior to presidential approval and submission to Congress to ensure that they accord with the president's priorities. This process helps restrain the special relationships that otherwise tend to proliferate between executive bureaus and congressional committees. In addition, as part of its management responsibilities, the OMB exercises a continuing oversight role over ongoing federal programs. This, too, enhances its position within the executive branch.[58]

Still, the ability of the OMB (and of the executive branch in general) to manage spending has long been at odds with congressional control of the purse strings, which includes members' prerogatives to consider the arguments of lobbyists or the interests of constituents in their home districts. These incentives shape the perennial conflict between the OMB and Congress over spending on national security. (The budget process is discussed in chapter 8.)

Constraints on Presidential Power

While the president has a myriad of tools at his disposal, presidential power is constantly challenged and tempered by other actors and institutions. The dynamic tension between the president and Congress is the most frequent and influential check on presidential action but many others exist as well. (This tension is further discussed in chapter 5 on the role of Congress.) Other countervailing forces include public opinion, the media, the courts, interest groups, the impact of past policies and programs, and the responsiveness of the executive bureaucracy, as well as the views, interests, and expected reactions of other countries.

Even with constitutional and political checks on executive power, presidents still wield greater influence in foreign and national security affairs than in domestic policy. In 1966, Aaron Wildavsky declared that the United States had "two presidencies," one with only limited constraints in national security and foreign affairs and the other with more active checks and balances from Congress, public opinion, and other actors, in domestic policy.[59] Wildavsky's thesis prompted many debates, particularly in the post–Cold War era, about the difficulty of measuring checks on presidential power as well as the challenge of separating foreign from domestic policy. Nevertheless, the expansion of presidential power in the aftermath of the 9/11 terrorist attacks suggests the continuing relevance of Wildavsky's analysis.

Public Opinion. The president can use the "bully pulpit" of the office to his advantage, as noted earlier in this chapter. However, public opinion can also be a constraint. Effective presidential leadership can tolerate short-term reverses in public acceptance, but over time a president's policies must have the support of a popular consensus. Though he got a lot done, Johnson was unable to carry out his

"Great Society" fully due to the burden of the unpopularity of the Vietnam War; the Iran-Contra scandal weakened the ability of Reagan to set budget priorities and establish trade policies; and George W. Bush could not fully pursue his domestic political agenda after support for the war in Iraq dwindled. These three examples also highlight the interconnectedness of foreign and domestic policy pursuits.

In the realm of national security affairs, the president maintains a substantial initial advantage in shaping public opinion. External crises tend to have a uniting effect on opinion. This "rally around the flag" effect provides an initial burst of public support for the president in times of war and other crises.[60] As events unfold, however, the public responds to new information coming from the combat zone. Casualties and the duration of the conflict, in particular, may result in diminishing support for the president's policies.[61] Some have argued that it is the public's perception of success that matters; the public will remain generally supportive of presidential wartime policies as long as they perceive that the United States is succeeding.[62] Because new information from the war zone affects public perception, the executive attempts to dominate channels of information to manage the message. This was vividly demonstrated in the Persian Gulf War in January and February of 1991. Unlike Vietnam, where reporters were allowed to roam freely, reporters were confined to escorted pools, and the Pentagon placed sharp restrictions on when and how they could talk to the troops. George H. W. Bush and his key advisors managed the flow of information in such a way that the execution of Operation Desert Storm by the president and the military appeared flawless.

The president's ability to control the message has become increasingly difficult since the early 1990s. During the wars in Afghanistan and Iraq, and in the face of criticism over its handling of the media in the Persian Gulf War, the Pentagon adopted an "embed" program, in which members of the media observed the military and its efforts from within. The spread of smart phones and social media has further democratized the dissemination of information from abroad. The use of Twitter, Facebook, Instagram, and other social media outlets during the Arab Spring highlighted the ability of individuals to use pictures and video to galvanize support for a cause. That groups such as the Islamic State of Syria and the Levant (ISIL) use the same platforms also points to the capacity of social media to have a profound influence.

However, in recent years, the balance may be shifting once again. Throughout his candidacy and into his presidency, Trump has used Twitter to bypass the traditional media filter on information. His ability to help determine and shape media coverage of particular topics indicates that, although social media may have democratizing potential, key traditional players still have the opportunity to dominate the media landscape and public agenda. This may be particularly true in national security because there are fewer players in the arena, and these actors are often used to doing their work out of the public eye.[63]

Public dissatisfaction with national security often manifests itself in the electoral process. In spite of growing national dissent, Johnson appeared to be surviving the Vietnam debate until "peace candidate" Eugene McCarthy's near-victory in the 1968 New Hampshire primary translated opinion into adverse votes. Similarly, Carter's perceived weaknesses in dealing with the Soviet invasion of Afghanistan and the taking of American hostages at the embassy in Iran, coupled with his delay in rebuilding America's military strength, proved to be fatal to his reelection. In addition to hampering a president's reelection prospects, public dissatisfaction with a war effort can shape subsequent elections as well. Frustration with, and a rejection of, the George W. Bush administration's war in Iraq contributed to then-Senator Obama's presidential victory in 2008.

Public opinion provides a barometer of popular feeling. A beleaguered president, however, more often needs a compass than a barometer. Public opinion polls report general reactions, but seldom provide a president with a clear policy direction. Moreover, public opinion generally lags behind the problem. FDR's struggle prior to World War II to awaken an indifferent and isolationist America to the dangers is a case in point. Both interpreting public opinion and influencing it have proven to be difficult yet essential presidential arts.

Interest Groups. Another form of public input, expressed in a more concerted manner, is the pressure exerted by organized interest groups. This has been especially true for ethnic interest groups, such as those representing Jewish, Greek, Armenian, Irish, Cuban, and East European communities.[64] All have influenced US foreign and security policy to varying degrees. Examples include the Irish American influence on US policies and actions with respect to Northern Ireland (and the adverse effects to US–United Kingdom relations during the first Clinton administration), and Americans of Eastern European descent concerned about Russian actions in Ukraine. The American Israel Public Affairs Committee (AIPAC) is often seen as highly influential in lobbying the president and Congress in support of strong ties with Israel.

Other types of interest groups also affect US national security policy and decision making by the president and Congress. Environmental groups significantly influenced the Obama administration to veto approval of the Keystone/XL Pipeline, which runs oil from Canada through the United States, and to support the Paris climate agreement to limit greenhouse gas emissions. Business interests continue to be vocal in their support of expanding trade opportunities around the world, including support of the Trans-Pacific Partnership trade agreement, despite opposition by an alliance of labor unions, environmentalists, and other interest groups. Reflective of the prominence of countervailing interest groups, President Trump reversed these policies by announcing that the United States would support the Keystone/XL Pipeline, withdraw from the Paris climate accords, and not become a party to the Trans-Pacific Partnership trade agreement.

Past Policies and Programs. As each president assumes office, the rhetoric of campaigning yields to a different perspective. The responsibilities of the presidency, including the continuation of programs and initiatives of a previous chief executive, now belong to the new officeholder. An example of this is the Obama administration's inheritance of the wars in Iraq and Afghanistan at the time of his inauguration. George W. Bush had ordered a "surge" of additional troops and resources to Iraq in 2007–2008, which was aimed at reducing the growing violence in the country. Because of the Iraq focus, however, the US effort in Afghanistan suffered from a shortage of resources. As the chairman of the JCS, Admiral Michael Mullen, stated in late 2007, "In Afghanistan we do what we can. In Iraq, we do what we must."[65] The Iraq "surge" effort had begun to show signs of success by late 2008, as then-Senator Obama was campaigning on the promise of quickly ending the war in Iraq and focusing attention on Afghanistan. He promised an expedited, sixteen-month timetable for complete withdrawal. Upon assuming office in early 2009, President Obama had the responsibility of consolidating gains achieved in Iraq, withdrawing US forces, and bringing the conflict to a successful resolution to enable a focus of effort on Afghanistan. Once off the campaign trail and confronted with the complexities of ending the war in Iraq, the administration modified its campaign promise to a more gradual pace, which generally coincided with the plans established by the previous administration.[66]

Policy is not created in a vacuum; rather, each new decision must be made within the context of already existing decisions and commitments. Powerful among these legacies are the budget decisions of previous administrations. This is especially true with regard to the development of weapons, because the military procurement process is characterized by long lead times. A new president is often unable to influence the types and amounts of weapons available to conduct military operations, and availability may shape overall strategy during his term of office. (See also chapter 3.)

Lack of Bureaucratic Responsiveness. Presidents' ability to execute or influence national security policy may be hampered by the necessity of relying on the bureaucracy for the implementation of policy decisions. The expansion of the executive bureaucracy has thus been, in many respects, a two-edged sword. From this expanded bureaucracy presidents derive greater access to and control over information, as well as the ability to develop and analyze a broader range of policy options. However, executive decisions must be implemented through the bureaucracy, and its growth widens the gap between policy making at the top and implementation at the grassroots level. As a result, presidential decisions may be delayed, amended, or even nullified.

The president is not the only actor hoping to control the bureaucracy. Congress has a number of means to empower or constrain executive departments and agencies, including control over the budget and confirmation of many executive appointments. Similarly, while senior agency officials are generally appointed by the president, the federal bureaucracy is staffed at middle and lower levels largely by career civil servants who may not fully share the president's perspectives on national security affairs. Furthermore, over time, cabinet secretaries themselves may grow to side with the civil servants with whom they work rather than with the president. Experienced bureaucrats often learn to influence the policymaking process by manipulating the number and range of policy options developed for consideration, by drafting implementation instructions that blunt the impact of a particular policy, or by delaying the implementation of a policy to the point that it becomes "overtaken by events." Bureaucratic "leaks" may be deployed to alert the media, and thereby the public, to particularly controversial policies under consideration before they can be implemented.

One need not always invoke mischievous motives, however, to explain how the executive bureaucracy can act as a constraint on presidential power. To receive careful analysis and consideration, major policy initiatives are circulated, or "staffed," among the various agencies that have interests in the ultimate policy outcome. Due to the increased size of the bureaucracy, this staff coordination can be a time-consuming process. Although presidents possess the means to bypass much of this process, one who attempts to short-circuit the full consideration of policy initiatives does so at the risk of an incomplete or inaccurate understanding of their implications. In short, presidents are often constrained in implementing major policies by the time required to study and analyze them, as well as to execute them.

Interests of Other Nations. Both in traditional foreign policy matters and also in what might initially appear to be domestic matters—such as environmental issues—the president must take into account the views of the leaders of other states around the world. As interdependence deepens in the years to come, this constraint on presidential freedom of action will clearly grow in importance. Examples of the interests of other countries are discussed in chapters 18 to 24, which deal with regional and transnational issues.

Looking Ahead

In many respects, the president's role in national security policy making is more fluid and unpredictable than that of any other major actor in the decisionmaking process. In both a constitutional and an institutional sense, the president is the focal point of the national security policy process. But more than most participants in that process, presidents have wide latitude in defining their role. Patterns of presidential involvement have varied in accordance with the style and experience of individual presidents. Always subject to important constraints, some presidents have chosen to become personally enmeshed in the details of policy making and implementation. Others have chosen a more passive role, delegating broad responsibilities to the cabinet and other senior officials. Given the nature of presidential authority and power, however, even the most passive chief executives of recent decades have occupied pivotal positions in the national security process.

Discussion Questions

1. How does the Constitution divide responsibility for foreign affairs between the president and Congress?

2. How has the War Powers Resolution of 1973 shaped presidential decision making regarding the employment of US military forces?

3. How have changes in technology influenced the scope of presidential prerogatives in national security policy?

4. The evolution of the national security policymaking process reflects a generally expanding role for the president's national security advisor. Is this good for American national security? What factors have contributed to this trend? Is this trend irreversible?

5. What factors tend to hinder the role of the Department of State in national security policy?

6. How have the entities created by the National Security Act of 1947—including the Central Intelligence Agency, the defense establishment, the Joint Chiefs of Staff, and the National Security Council—evolved since their inception?

7. Has the expansion of presidential power in the twenty-first century resulted in an "imperial presidency"? Why, or why not?

8. How have changes in traditional media and the creation of social media affected the ability of the president and other actors to influence national security policy?

9. What is the relationship, if any, between presidential campaigns and elections and the national security policy making process?

10. How did the wars in Iraq and Afghanistan affect presidential power in national security affairs?

Recommended Reading

Allison, Graham, and Philip Zelikow. *Essence of Decision: Explaining the Cuban Missile Crisis.* 2nd ed. New York: Longman, 1999.

Best, Richard A., Jr. *The National Security Council: An Organizational Assessment.* Washington, DC: Congressional Research Service, December 28, 2011.

Crabb, Cecil V., and Kevin V. Mulcahy. *Presidents and Foreign Policy Making: From FDR to Reagan.* Baton Rouge: Louisiana State University Press, 1986.

Fisher, Louis. *Presidential War Power.* 3rd rev. ed. Lawrence: University Press of Kansas, 2013.

Inderfurth, Karl F., and Loch K. Johnson. *Fateful Decisions: Inside the National Security Council.* New York: Oxford University Press, 2004.

Kissinger, Henry A. *The White House Years.* Boston: Little, Brown, 1979.

Lowi, Theodore J. *The Personal President: Power Invested, Promise Unfulfilled.* Ithaca, NY: Cornell University Press, 1986.

May, Ernest R., and Philip D. Zelikow. *The Kennedy Tapes: Inside the White House during the Cuban Missile Crisis.* Cambridge, MA: The Belknap Press of Harvard University Press, 1997.

Rothkopf, David J. *Running the World: The Inside Story of the National Security Council and the Architects of American Power.* New York: PublicAffairs, 2006.

Rudalevige, Andrew. *The New Imperial Presidency: Renewing Presidential Power after Watergate.* Ann Arbor: University of Michigan Press, 2006.

Recommended Internet Sources

The Center for the Study of the Presidency and Congress, www.thepresidency.org

The Department of Defense, www.defense.gov

The Department of State, www.state.gov
The National Security Council, www.whitehouse.gov/nsc
The Office of Management and Budget, www.whitehouse.gov/omb
The White House, www.whitehouse.gov/issues/foreign-policy

Notes

1. Alexander Hamilton, "The Command of the Military and Naval Forces, and the Pardoning Power of the Executive," Federalist No. 74, March 25, 1788, https://www.congress.gov/resources/display/content/The+Federalist+Papers#TheFederalistPapers-74.

2. Arthur M. Schlesinger Jr., *The Imperial Presidency* (Boston: Houghton Mifflin, 1973), 3.

3. The masculine pronoun "his" is used to refer to the president based on historical precedent, but this choice does not imply that the pronoun will apply to all future presidents.

4. Edwin S. Corwin, *The President: Office and Powers, 1787–1957* (New York: New York University Press, 1957), 171.

5. Schlesinger, *Imperial Presidency*, 291.

6. Robert A. Diamond and Patricia Ann O'Connor, eds., *Guide to Congress* (Washington, DC: Congressional Quarterly, 1976), 279.

7. Mathew C. Weed, *The War Powers Resolution: Concepts and Practice*, CRS Report R42699 (Washington, DC: Congressional Research Service, March 28, 2017), 6.

8. Louis Fisher, *Presidential War Power*, 3rd rev. ed. (Lawrence: University Press of Kansas, 2013), 207–9.

9. Fisher, *Presidential War Power*, 209.

10. US Congress, "Use of Force Resolution," September 14, 2001, 107th Cong., 1st Sess., https://www.congress.gov/bill/107th-congress/senate-joint-resolution/23.

11. The attacks against Afghanistan are discussed in Bob Woodward, *Bush at War* (New York: Simon & Schuster, 2002).

12. The text of UN Security Council Resolution 1441, November 8, 2002, available at http://www.un.org.

13. For an analysis of the pre-invasion planning for the war in Iraq as well as postwar reconstruction, see Bob Woodward, *Plan of Attack: The Definitive Account of the Decision to Invade Iraq* (New York: Simon & Schuster, 2004); and Bob Woodward, *State of Denial: Bush at War, Part III* (New York: Simon & Schuster, 2006).

14. For a thoughtful assessment of the expansion of presidential power in the George W. Bush administration after September 11, 2001, see Andrew Rudalevige, *The New Imperial Presidency: Renewing Presidential Power after Watergate* (Ann Arbor: University of Michigan Press, 2005).

15. James Baker III and Warren Christopher, Co-Chairs, *National War Powers Commission Report* (Charlottesville: University of Virginia Miller Center for Public Affairs, 2008).

16. Martin S. Indyk, Kenneth G. Lieberthal, and Michael E. O'Hanlon, *Bending History: Barack Obama's Foreign Policy* (Washington, DC: Brookings Institution Press, 2012), 5.

17. Ultimately, the decision whether to use force became a moot point when the Russian government brokered a diplomatic solution acceptable to the United States.

18. David Sanger, *Confront and Conceal: Obama's Secret Wars and Surprising Use of American Power* (New York: Crown Publishers, 2012), 244.

19. Richard E. Neustadt, *Presidential Power* (New York: New American Library, 1960), 42.

20. Neustadt, *Presidential Power*, 53, 47.

21. Clinton Rossiter, *The American Presidency* (New York: New American Library, 1960), 14–40.

22. Keith C. Clark and Laurence J. Legere, eds., *The President and the Management of National Security* (New York: Praeger, 1969), 19.

23. Clark and Legere, *The President*, 19.

24. James Pfiffner, "Decision-Making in the Obama White House," *Presidential Studies Quarterly* 41, no. 2 (2011): 244–47.

25. Discussion of the Hoover staffing arrangements is from Henry T. Nash, *American Foreign Policy: Response to a Sense of Threat* (Belmont, CA: Dorsey Press, 1973), 113. The Barack Obama White House figure is from the 2013 Annual Report to Congress on the White House Staff, available at http://www.whitehouse.gov/briefing-room/disclosures/annual-records/2013. Comments on the proliferation of presidential assistants are derived from Harold Seidman, *Politics, Position, and Power: The Dynamics of Federal Organization* (New York: Oxford University Press, 1970), 213.

26. Seidman, *Politics, Position, and Power*, 165. For current information on the NSC, see its website at www.whitehouse.gov/nsc.

27. Seidman, *Politics, Position, and Power*, 91.

28. Andrew J. Goodpaster, "Four Presidents and the Conduct of National Security Affairs: Impressions and Highlights," *Journal of International Relations* 2 (Spring 1977): 27–29.

29. Dwight D. Eisenhower, "The Central Role of the President in the Conduct of Security Affairs," in *Issues of National Security in the 1970s*, ed. Amos Jordan (New York: Praeger, 1967), 214.

30. For a discussion of the differences in national security policy making between Eisenhower and Kennedy, see Meena Bose, *Shaping and Signaling Presidential Policy: The National Security Decision Making of Eisenhower and Kennedy* (College Station: Texas A&M University Press, 1998).

31. John F. Kennedy, quoted in Clark and Legere, *President and Management of National Security*, 70.

32. David C. Humphrey, "NSC Meetings during the Johnson Presidency," *Diplomatic History* 18, no. 1 (1994): 29–45.

33. Henry A. Kissinger, *The White House Years* (Boston: Little, Brown, 1979), 30.

34. John G. Tower, Edmund S. Muskie, and Brent Scowcroft, *The Tower Commission Report: The Full Text of the President's Special Review Board* (New York: Bantam Books, 1987).

35. For Scowcroft's role, see John P. Burke, *Honest Broker? The National Security Advisor and Presidential Decision Making* (College Station: Texas A&M University Press, 2009), 151–97.

36. Chris J. Dolan and Jerel A. Rosati, "U.S. Foreign Economic Policy and the Significance of the National Economic Council," *International Studies Perspectives* 7, no. 2 (2006): 102–3.

37. Ivo H. Daalder and I. M. Destler, Moderators, "The Clinton Administration National Security Council," *The National Security Project: Oral History Roundtables* (Washington, DC: The Brookings Institution, September 27, 2000), especially 19–20.

38. Fred I. Greenstein and Richard H. Immerman, "Effective National Security Advising: Recovering the Eisenhower Legacy," *Political Science Quarterly* 115, no. 3 (2000): 335.

39. For illustrations of how Condoleezza Rice ran NSC staff meetings, see Woodward, *Bush at War*, 85–91, 242–46.

40. Alan G. Whittaker, Shannon A. Brown, Frederick C. Smith, and Elizabeth McKune, *The National Security Policy Process: The National Security Council and Interagency System*, Research Report, Annual Update (Washington, DC: Industrial College of the Armed Forces, National Defense University, US Department of Defense, August 15, 2011).

41. Bob Woodward, *Obama's Wars* (New York: Simon & Schuster), 2010.

42. Michael Gordon Jackson, "A Dramatically Different NSC? President Obama's Use of the National Security Council," paper presented at the Annual Meeting of the Western Political Science Association, March 2012, 11.

43. For a detailed history of the Department of State, see Elmer Plischke, *U.S. Department of State: A Reference History* (Westport, CT: Greenwood Press, 1999).

44. Kissinger, *White House Years*, 26–31.

45. Bob Woodward, *The Commanders* (New York: Simon & Schuster, 2002), and U.S. News and World Report, *Triumph without Victory* (New York: Warner Books, 1992), provide excellent descriptions of Bush's decisionmaking style.

46. Bob Woodward discusses Powell's role in the decision making leading to the 2003 war in Iraq in Woodward, *Plan of Attack*, 78–80.

47. Nash, *American Foreign Policy*, 71–72. See also Roger Hilsman, *The Politics of Policy Making in Defense and Foreign Affairs* (New York: Harper & Row, 1971), 47–48.

48. I. M. Destler, *Presidents, Bureaucrats, and Foreign Policy* (Princeton, NJ: Princeton University Press, 1972), 156–60.

49. Nash, *American Foreign Policy*, 91.

50. Nash, *American Foreign Policy*, 74.

51. Alain C. Enthoven and K. Wayne Smith, *How Much Is Enough?: Shaping the Defense Program, 1961–69* (New York: Harper & Row, 1971), 3.

52. See Robert M. Gates, *Duty* (New York: Alfred A. Knopf, 2014); Leon Panetta, *Worthy Fights: A Memoir of Leadership in War and Peace* (New York: Penguin, 2014); and Helen Cooper, "Hagel Resigns Under Pressure as Global Crises Test Pentagon," *New York Times*, November 24, 2014.

53. For example, see Staff Report to the Committee on Armed Services, *Defense Organization: The Need for Change*, US Senate, 99th Cong., 1st Sess., 1985, Senate Report 99-86, 422–23.

54. Henry Stimson, quoted in Miles Copeland, *Without Cloak or Dagger* (New York: Simon & Schuster, 1974), 36.

55. Nash, *American Foreign Policy*, 146–49. See also Marjorie Hunter, "Carter Won't Oppose CIA Cost Disclosure," *New York Times*, April 28, 1977, 17.

56. For information on Director of National Intelligence, see its website at www.dni.gov.

57. Theodore C. Sorensen, *Decision Making in the White House* (New York: Columbia University Press, 1963), 29–30.

58. For a detailed discussion of the origins of legislative central clearance, see Richard E. Neustadt, "Presidency and Legislation: The Growth of Central Clearance," *American Political Science Review* 48, no. 1 (1954): 641–71.

59. Aaron Wildavsky, "The Two Presidencies" [1966], in *Perspectives on the Presidency*, ed. Aaron Wildavsky (Boston: Little, Brown and Company, 1975).

60. John Mueller, "Presidential Popularity from Truman to Johnson," *American Political Science Review* 64, no. 1 (1970): 18–34.

61. John Mueller, *War, Presidents and Public Opinion* (New York: Wiley Press, 1973).

62. Christopher Gelpi, Peter D. Feaver, and Jason Reifler, "Success Matters: Casualty Sensitivity and the War in Iraq," *International Security* 30, no. 3 (2006): 7–46.

63. James Goldgeier and Elizabeth N. Saunders, "Good Foreign Policy Is Invisible" *Foreign Affairs*, February 28, 2017, https://www.foreignaffairs.com/articles/united-states/2017-02-28/good-foreign-policy-invisible.

64. James Schlesinger, "Fragmentation and Hubris: A Shaky Basis for American Leadership," *National Interest* 49 (Fall 1997): 3–9.

65. Julian E. Barnes, "U.S. Calls Iraq the Priority," *Los Angeles Times*, December 12, 2007, http://articles.latimes.com/2007/dec/12/world/fg-usafghan12.

66. Specifically, Obama drew forces down to 50,000 troops over nineteen months (rather than to zero troops in sixteen months), and then withdrew all remaining troops from Iraq in December 2011, which was the original Bush timeline. See Michael Gordon and Bernard Trainor, *Endgame: The Struggle for Iraq, from George W. Bush to Barack Obama* (New York: Random House, 2012), chap. 30.

5

Congress

In addressing the separation of powers, James Madison wrote in Federalist No. 51: "In republican government, the legislative authority predominates."[1] This may have been true in the realm of domestic politics at the time of the founding, but was less so as it pertained to foreign affairs. Alexander Hamilton stated in Federalist No. 70 that a key justification for a strong executive branch was "protection of the community against common attacks."[2] The executive branch tends to dominate security policy, although, on occasion, the legislative branch has blocked presidential national security initiatives. Moreover, Congress wields considerable control over some areas of national security, most notably budgets, through what is known as "the power of the purse." In addition, the potential for legislative involvement and the importance of congressional approval of executive action profoundly influence national security and foreign policy.

Congress and the Constitution

Congressional Powers. Article I, Section 8 of the Constitution provides the legislative branch with a formidable array of tools for participation in national security matters. Congress has the power to declare war; to raise and support armies; to provide and maintain a navy; to determine the rules and regulations governing the military; and to call forth the militia in times of crisis. Additionally, presidents must seek the "advice and consent" of the Senate for treaty ratification and for the appointment of senior governmental officials, including military officers. Moreover, Congress may react to and shape implementation of policy through its oversight role. Committee hearings and investigations can inform policy makers and highlight particular issues and areas of concern for the public. While these powers allow for input into foreign affairs and domestic security, a vital congressional influence over the executive derives from the power of the purse. With the ability "to lay and collect Taxes, Duties, Imposts and Excises, to pay the Debts and provide for the common Defense and general Welfare of the United States," Congress determines the appropriations levels for the entire executive branch, including the national security apparatus.[3] The Constitution specifies that the army should not receive appropriations for longer than a two-year term, so technically, unless each Congress reestablishes the army, it must demobilize. This provision reflects the founders' fear of standing armies, especially under a unitary executive serving as commander in chief.[4]

Mindful of its role to check a strong executive in foreign affairs, Congress has historically guarded its ability to use the power of the purse to shape foreign policy. In a 2012 speech about the role of defense in modern society, Representative Buck McKeon (R-CA), who was House Armed Services Committee chairman at the time, stated:

> The Founders did not impose caveats or limitations on the requirement that the federal government maintain the security of its people—only that the common defense of all states, and all territories, is provided for. They also empowered Congress to raise and support an Army and Navy. . . . The Air Force was a little before their time. Every year, the Armed Services Committee fulfills that two hundred year old obligation. The bill is the National Defense Authorization Act, which provides funding and sets Congressional policies for our military.[5]

The speech goes on to detail the areas in which McKeon planned to challenge the Obama administration's priorities in terms of army end strength, the industrial base, navy shipbuilding, and missile defense.

Despite having some potentially strong powers, it remains difficult for the legislative branch to proactively shape national security policy. Congress funds the military and can use this enumerated power to shape security policy. More often than not, however, congressional policy tends to react to presidential initiatives, largely as a result of institutional design. As a unitary actor, the president can act quickly and decisively, while a Congress of 535 members rarely holds uniform views or priorities on national security.

Aside from difficulty finding a single voice, Congress is slow to take the initiative on national security issues due to members' tendencies to act, as David Mayhew observed, as "single-minded seekers of re-election."[6] Richard Fenno suggests that legislators have three key motivations: reelection, influence within Congress, and good public policy. Reelection allows legislators to keep their jobs and, through increasing seniority, gain influence through more powerful committee assignments. Committee assignments can bring benefits to constituents, solidify reelection chances, and allow a focus on better public policy.[7] On the campaign trail, members of Congress rarely focus on foreign and national security policy because these are not usually issues that bring federal largesse to home districts and states, and they therefore do not help much with reelection. Good public policy may be a subsidiary concern of legislators. As former Senate Foreign Relations Committee

Chairman Richard Lugar (R-IN) observed, "There's almost no political sex appeal [in foreign policy]. . . . For those who get involved it's strictly a pro bono service."[8] In fact, public opinion generally lags behind the course of international events; consequently, congressional actions often respond to past developments.

Disadvantages Relative to the Executive Branch. As discussed in the previous chapter, the Constitution gives the president an array of powers in the national security and foreign policy realms. The design of the institution itself also offers some key comparative advantages over the legislative branch. In dealing with foreign powers, the executive enjoys the inherent advantage of unity of command. Hamilton wrote, "That unity is conducive to energy will not be disputed. Decision, activity, secrecy, and dispatch will generally characterize the proceedings of one man in a much more eminent degree than the proceeding of any greater number."[9] In periods of crises and particularly during armed conflict, centralized authority is required for swift and effective action, and presidential powers reach their pinnacle. The Constitution not only empowers the president as the commander in chief of the armed forces, but also makes him both head of state and head of government. Responding to emergencies, presidents have claimed implicit prerogatives not specifically mentioned in the Constitution. President Abraham Lincoln famously suspended the writ of habeas corpus during the Civil War without congressional approval; invoking a "doctrine of necessity," Lincoln claimed he had to break the Constitution in order to save it.[10] President George W. Bush similarly claimed that his powers as commander in chief extended to authorizing warrantless wiretapping and to establishing military commissions to try "unlawful combatants" during the Iraq and Afghanistan wars. President Barack Obama initiated and continued a bombing campaign in Libya (in conjunction with NATO) without prior congressional approval.[11]

In the establishment of national security policy, John Lehman writes, "It is the executive that proposes but the Congress that disposes."[12] Yet how Congress disposes is a complicated process in which members must placate various constituencies, moneyed interests, personal ideological considerations, and each other. To bring their policy ideas to fruition, legislators must generate legislative momentum through hearings, co-sponsorship, logrolling and trading of votes, and compromise. Two developments have recently made such political maneuvering more challenging. First, in 2011, Congress approved an "earmark moratorium," which limits the ability of legislators to marshal support for specific proposals through add-on provisions that are designed to help a particular district. While this may be a good way to limit unnecessary spending, it eliminates a tool that has often been used to get important legislation passed.[13] Second, ubiquitous media coverage, political polarization, and concern for how any type of concession, even if for the common good, might be portrayed has hindered the process of compromise.

In addition to its structural advantage, the executive branch also has an informational advantage over Congress. Lehman writes, "In terms of expertise, the disparity is enormous. In the executive departments, the richness and sophistication in scientific, technological, military, diplomatic, statistical, medical, educational, geological, fiscal, legal, and sociological skills are truly awesome. [In contrast,] Congressional staffs have a smattering of knowledge in all of these areas, but only a smattering."[14] When the president exerts executive authority, Congress faces a political choice: if it unites to counterbalance presidential declarations of power, it thereby assumes more responsibility for the outcome; if it accepts executive hegemony in national security affairs, it lets the president get the credit—or blame—for the policy.

Congressional Branch Passivity and Activism. Due to its lesser expertise, fractious nature, slow pace of decision making, and difficulty maintaining confidentiality, Congress has often been the minor partner in the national security process. Historical periods of congressional passivity in foreign affairs include President Thomas Jefferson's Louisiana Purchase, President Theodore Roosevelt's initiation of the Panama Canal project, President Franklin Delano Roosevelt's launch of the Lend-Lease Program, President Lyndon Johnson's response to the Gulf of Tonkin Resolution, and President Bill Clinton's bombing campaigns in Afghanistan, Iraq, and Sudan. After the September 11, 2001, terrorist attacks, Congress largely deferred to Presidents George W. Bush and Barack Obama and to their actions in Afghanistan, Iraq, Libya, Syria, and Yemen, against terror networks worldwide, and in negotiation of the Iranian nuclear agreement.

Still, Congress does sometimes become more active in the national security arena. Cecil V. Crabb and his colleagues identify three conditions leading to congressional activism in national security and foreign policy: (1) a clear public-opinion groundswell regarding America's international role; (2) tentative or weak presidential leadership; and (3) urgent domestic affairs that overpower foreign policy.[15] Historical events that reflect these conditions include congressional activity during and after the American Revolution; congressional hawks prior to the War of 1812; the Reconstruction Period following the Civil War; the Senate's refusal to ratify the Treaty of Versailles; the isolationist movement in Congress prior to World War II; and the War Powers Act and other moves to check unitary presidential action in response to the Vietnam War.

The role of Congress in national security is not confined to reacting to the executive branch: Congress can also partner with the president in setting priorities and policies. However, such occurrences are rare and tend to be short lived. The early Cold War era and the initial aftermath of 9/11 stand out as times when Congress and the president collaborated in efforts to create and maintain security policy.

Congressional Committees Covering National Security

When members of Congress become involved in security policy, their work begins through one or more committees. In 2016, twenty-one House and Senate committees had jurisdiction over national security and foreign policy.[16] Some of the most influential committees are discussed below.

Armed Services. The Senate Armed Services Committee (SASC) and House Armed Services Committee (HASC) are the authorizing committees for the Department of Defense (including the Departments of the Army, Navy, and Air Force); military research and development; the national security components of nuclear energy; the pay, promotion, benefits, and retirement system for members of the armed services; and strategic natural resources related to national security. These committees make substantive policy through legislation authorizing the terms and conditions of programs and activities related to defense. They also recommend appropriation levels for spending. Some members join these committees out of public-policy interest, while others are motivated more by the reelection incentive.

Consistent with the observation by former Speaker of the House Tip O'Neill (D-MA) that "all politics is local," geographical and economic constituencies surrounding military bases have disproportionate influence on these committees' policy decisions. These committees often discuss national security issues that have local effects, such as recommendations on closing defense bases and installations and the authorization of funding for procurement programs that result in jobs in the home district.

Appropriations. The Senate and House Appropriations Committees determine funding levels in defense and national security authorization bills through their Defense Subcommittees. No money is transferred in this process; rather, Congress grants budgetary authority to the specified agencies, activities, and programs. With budgetary authority, a federal entity can take on obligations requiring immediate or future expenditures, called *outlays*. Most national security spending comes primarily from three of the thirteen annual appropriations bills: defense, energy and water development, and military construction. The normal appropriations process supplies most defense-related funding, while continuing resolutions and supplemental appropriations measures historically provide for unanticipated needs (see chapter 8 for more details on the budget process).[17]

Foreign Affairs. The Senate Committee on Foreign Relations and House Foreign Affairs Committee are also important national security institutions within Congress. The Senate Committee on Foreign Relations assesses treaties with foreign governments and must approve all ambassadorial nominations. Given the Article II, Section 2 constitutional mandate that the Senate shall provide "advice and consent" on treaties, members of this committee see themselves as partners with the president in setting national security and foreign policy. Former Senator Jacob Javits (R-NY) wrote that the committee must "be a source of independent judgment and a potential check upon the actions of the executive branch on such fundamental matters as the use of military force, the conclusion of international commitments, the appointment of principal policy makers, and the financing of military and diplomatic programs."[18]

Television and media coverage of the Senate Committee on Foreign Relations can raise the public profile of its members, and the committee has been a traditional launching pad for future service. In 2008, for example, five presidential candidates—Senators Joe Biden (D-DE), Hillary Clinton (D-NY), John Kerry (D-MA), John McCain (R-AZ), and Barack Obama (D-IL)—served on the Committee on Foreign Relations. In 2016, two presidential hopefuls were on the Committee on Foreign Relations (Marco Rubio [R-FL] and Rand Paul [R-KY]). Lacking a similar constitutional mandate concerning treaties, the House Foreign Affairs Committee is less influential, though it still has the potential to shape foreign policy outcomes through the power of the purse when working in close concert with the House Budget Committee.

Other Committees with National Security Jurisdictions. A number of other committees affect national security policy. The House and Senate Select Committees on Intelligence deal with the intelligence community, including the Central Intelligence Agency and the National Security Agency. These committees focus on policy and procedural oversight, while the authorization and appropriation functions for most of the intelligence community are handled elsewhere in Congress. Both the House (in 2002) and the Senate (in 2003) empowered committees with specific jurisdiction over the function of homeland security. The prestige and power of these committees rest on their ability to exert jurisdiction over a broad governmental responsibility previously shared among many other committees.

Some other committees that may seem tangential to national security will, on occasion, have reason to provide input, such as the energy or veterans affairs committees. The competing claims of authority over national security highlight a key aspect of congressional policy making: the power bases are diffuse, and jurisdiction over national security policy is not definitively allocated among committees. Divergent constituency interests, opposing ideological considerations, and political maneuvering characterize the disjointed nature of congressional policy formulation and its national security institutions. Thus Congress has fewer opportunities and is less likely than the president to speak in a single, unified voice.

National Security Policy

Congressional involvement in national security policy comes mainly in three varieties: structural, strategic, and war powers. Structural policy relates to the allocation of resources. Strategic policy concerns the military, economic, and political posture and actions of the US government toward the accomplishment of nationally identified goals and objectives. War powers policy seeks to protect the nation from danger both at home and abroad.

Structural Policy. Structural policy involves the resource allocation of defense-related personnel and materiel. This includes weapons procurement, military base infrastructure, foreign arms sales, private contractor deals, and defense personnel policies. Because these activities provide legislators with the opportunity to steer important projects to their districts, thereby enhancing their reelection prospects, structural policy formulation receives the greatest congressional attention of the three policy areas.

Military Base Infrastructure. The Constitution grants Congress the authority to regulate property of the federal government, including military bases.[19] The placement of and activities within military bases around the nation can be a politically volatile topic, especially due to the economic dependence of neighboring communities. The elimination of obsolete military bases imposes particular pain on those states and districts in which those bases are located. As far back as the early 1900s, when frontier bases faced closure, members of Congress fought ferociously to keep them open. One story holds that when faced with the closure of the cavalry station in Brownsville, Texas, the young congressman John Nance Garner (later vice president of the United States) marched into the office of Secretary of War William Howard Taft (later president of the United States) to demand it remain open for economic reasons. Taft retorted, "What's the cavalry to do with economics?" Garner responded, "Mr. Secretary, it's this way. We raise a lot of hay in my district. We've got a lot of stores and we have the prettiest girls in the United States. The cavalry buys the hay for its horses, spends its pay in the stores, marries our girls, gets out of the army and helps us develop the country, and then more replacements come and do the same thing. It *is* economics. It *is* economics."[20] While the details may change, this relationship between members of Congress and their military-dependent constituencies remains largely the same today and is fraught with electoral risks and rewards.

That Congress engages in the process of determining which bases will remain open and which will close highlights how domestic politics can influence military and national security policy. Until the late twentieth century, the reelection interests of some members of Congress tended to overcome the diffuse national benefit that could be realized from the elimination of outdated installations. For example, starting in the 1950s, the military attempted to close a number of bases deemed unnecessary due to a 30 percent excess of military infrastructure capacity, but without success.[21] By the 1980s, it was evident that a new process was needed. Congress created the Defense Base Closure and Realignment Commission (BRAC), an extra-organizational body that provided congressional oversight while also insulating individual members of Congress from constituency backlash if bases were chosen for closure in their districts.

The process begins with the formation of an independent bipartisan BRAC whose members are nominated by the president and approved by Congress. The Pentagon submits a list of proposed closures and realignments to the commission, which then travels to various military bases on the list and holds hearings. These visits and hearings give members of Congress the opportunity to publicly defend their local bases and, incidentally, to publicly display their own powerlessness, as individual members, to stop or change the BRAC process. Based on these hearings and visits, the commission submits its final recommendations to the president. Following presidential approval, Congress has just forty-five days to disapprove the list in its entirety, or the list of base closures becomes law. With four closely spaced BRAC rounds in 1988, 1991, 1993, and 1995, and a more recent round in 2005, Congress successfully overcame the collective dilemma of base closures. Although this process generally insulates members from adverse political repercussions, Congress has been unwilling to initiate a new BRAC round since 2005. Even though the Department of Defense (DoD) included a BRAC plan as part of its 2015 budget request, that request was removed by the House Armed Services Committee.

Weapons Procurement. Congressional action on defense procurement follows the more traditional bipartisan distributive process of bringing federal dollars to constituents. Congress routinely spreads defense largesse around as widely as possible so that many constituencies benefit. It is not unusual for a weapon system to have multiple subcontractors spread across much of the United States. It is also common for members of Congress to override the Pentagon's program priorities with their own. For example, in 2013, the army planned a temporary shutdown of a tank plant in Lima, Ohio, due to a decreased need for M1 Abrams tanks. Lima's mayor responded that even temporarily shutting the plant would cause a loss of 1,100 jobs and would eventually lead to permanent closure.[22] Ohio's delegation to Congress, including Senator Rob Portman (R-OH) and Representative Jim Jordan (R-OH), argued that the tanks were important both for national security and for their constituencies. In 2013, Congress gave the Pentagon $436 million to improve the Abrams tank, and in doing so, kept the Lima plant from shutting down. According to Army Chief of Staff General Raymond Odierno, "If we had our choice, we would use that money in a different way."[23] Instead, the army was compelled to make unwanted improvements to a tank rather than pursuing other priorities.

The parochial interests of legislators can sustain weapons systems that are prone to lengthy development time, ballooning costs, and are of dubious strategic and tactical value. For example, in 2006, former Assistant Secretary of Defense Lawrence Korb described the F/A-22 Raptor fighter jet thus: "This plane, which is arguably the most unnecessary weapons system currently being built by the Pentagon, was originally designed to achieve superiority over Soviet fighter jets that were never built. Back in 1985 the Air Force claimed it could build 750 of these stealth fighter jets for $35 million each or at a total cost of $26 billion. . . . At the current time [2006], the Pentagon says it can buy 181 planes for $61 billion."[24] By 2011, the Pentagon had purchased a total of 196 F/A-22 Raptors for an average unit cost of $377 million per plane. This represents a 531 percent increase in costs, even after adjusting for inflation.[25] Despite high costs and lack of utility, legislators tend to be loath to relinquish projects like the F/A-22, for which there were over one thousand manufacturing contractors in forty-three states.[26]

Foreign Arms Sales. In 2011, the United States had arms sales agreements with developing nations worth $56.3 billion.[27] For Congress, foreign arms sale policy is a natural extension of the distributive politics of domestic military procurement. With the end of the Cold War in the early 1990s and the contraction of the US defense budget, the arms industry went through a series of consolidations and mergers. To maintain profit margins and sell off excess inventory, the industry sought revenues in the international arms export market. Citing the need to make American manufacturers more competitive in the crowded international market and to protect endangered defense industry jobs in various states and districts, Congress relaxed some of the constraints of the International Traffic in Arms Regulations, including a number of provisions of the Arms Export Control Act and the Foreign Assistance Act.[28]

In 1996, Congress enacted the Defense Export Loan Guarantee program. This law created essentially risk-free subsidies for sales by the US armament industry. Under this program, the Pentagon could guarantee up to $15 billion in private-sector loans to foreign countries for the purchase of US weapons. If the importing country were to default on the sale or lease payment, then the US government would cover 100 percent of the principal and interest of the loans. In the same year, Congress amended the Arms Export Control Act to allow the president to waive "recoupment fees" that foreign purchasers had previously been required to pay to offset US taxpayers' investment in weapons system research and development. The government could waive fees if it appeared that their inclusion in the price would result in loss of the sale.

These are two of many instances over the last decade in which Congress has used its power to help the defense industry. Between 1991 and 1999, US taxpayers paid $10 billion to finance arms exports between private American firms and foreign countries (this does not include, for example, the $2 billion provided to Saddam Hussein for the purchase of weapons technology prior to his 1990 invasion of Iraq).[29] Examinations of the underlying causes of these export policy decisions repeatedly reveal evidence that members of Congress have followed the familiar pattern of protecting constituency interests to enhance their reelection prospects.

Personnel Policy. Military personnel policy is a fourth major structural policy area that receives substantial congressional attention. Active duty, National Guard, and Reserve service members, their families, and military retirees constitute a formidable coalition of well-educated, organized citizens who vote in large numbers. Backed by powerful lobbying organizations, including the National Guard Association, the Navy League, the Air Force Association, the Association of the US Army, and the Military Officers Association of America, this vocal group has considerable sway on Capitol Hill. These military interest groups lobby Congress for increased military and retiree pay and benefits. Although no single factor accounts for specific trends, military pay has increased every year in the last fifty years, even in recent years when civilian government worker pay saw no annual increase.[30] Amid fiscal austerity imposed by sequestration, Congress significantly reformed military retirement beginning in 2018. The new "Blended Retirement System" reduces retirement pay for those who retire after twenty years of service by 20 percent, compared with those who retired under the pre-2018 retirement system. However, under the new system, all service members receive some funds for retirement, even if they stay in the military for as few as two years.

Military personnel policies that receive substantial national attention provide legislators the opportunity to take substantive policy stances that play to wider domestic audiences. These actions can be seen as a form of "position taking" for the benefit of constituents. David Mayhew defines position taking as a "public enunciation of a judgment statement on anything likely to be of interest to political actors. . . . The electoral requirement is not that [members] make pleasing things happen but that [they] make pleasing judgmental statements. The position itself is the political commodity."[31] In 2014, for example, Congress publicly investigated sexual harassment and assault throughout the military. These types of public hearings provided legislators the opportunity to voice their positions on political and cultural issues that were important to constituents back home. Despite such public declarations, however, congressional changes to personnel policy tend to be relatively minor; most personnel decisions are made by the Pentagon or the services.

Goldwater-Nichols and Congress as an Agent of Reform. The last time that Congress asserted itself in an area of significant structural policy was the landmark 1986 passage of the Goldwater-Nichols Department of Defense Reorganization Act. Glaring deficiencies in joint military service cooperation had contributed to a number of national security disasters in the late 1970s and early 1980s. These included the failed Desert One operation to rescue Americans held hostage by Iran in 1980, the suicide bombing of the marine barracks in Beirut in 1983, and the poorly coordinated invasion of the island of Grenada in 1983. For a number of influential legislators, including chairman of the Senate Armed Services Committee Senator Barry Goldwater (R-AZ), Representative William F. Nichols (D-AL), Senator Sam Nunn (D-GA), and Representative Les Aspin (D-WI), and key general officers, including Chairman of the Joint Chiefs General David Jones and Army Chief of Staff General Edward Meyer, these incidents solidified the belief that DoD was in need of reform. Despite the prominence of these leaders, structural reform was daunting due to the strong links between DoD and myriad congressional constituencies that benefited from the decentralized nature of the Pentagon, which allowed legislators to distribute federal dollars back to their home districts and states. As Amy Zegart writes, "Military duplication and inefficiency filled the trough of pork barrel politics."[32]

Goldwater-Nichols passed Congress, despite an uphill battle, because a number of key political factors aligned. First, the primary architect of the legislation, Barry Goldwater, was uniquely qualified to carry the bill forward. Goldwater was a staunch military advocate who had recently decided to retire from Congress. Freed from reelection concerns, he could push a bill that might otherwise have doomed his career, while his record of military support gave others political cover. Second, President Ronald Reagan stayed on the sidelines of the debate, and his lack of involvement weakened Pentagon resistance to the proposed reforms. With the benefit of these factors, congressional reformers fashioned a coalition of legislators to vote for the bill. It passed and, on October 1, 1986, Reagan signed Goldwater-Nichols into law.[33]

Goldwater-Nichols reformed DoD in three fundamental ways. First, the chairman of the Joint Chiefs as an individual replaced the corporate body of the Joint Chiefs as the principal military advisor to the president. Second, the law requires all military officers to serve in positions outside their service to qualify for promotion to general officer. And crucially, the law clarified the chain of command for combatant commanders. These commanders now respond directly to the secretary of defense and, ultimately, to the president for their orders and authority. The intent is to minimize service-chief interference in operational combatant commands and to reduce the parochialism of the individual services.

Many observers believe that Goldwater-Nichols was an important factor in the success of the American military in the 1990–1991 Persian Gulf War and the initial victories of the military in Afghanistan, Iraq, and Libya. The increase in joint operations and the elevated stature of combatant commanders relative to service chiefs are generally regarded as improvements in the execution of military policy.[34] Because of the gains in effectiveness as well as the efficiencies wrought by Goldwater-Nichols, many have called for similar reforms within or across other executive branch agencies.[35]

Strategic Policy. Strategic policy concerns the use of the power of the United States for the accomplishment of nationally identified political, economic, and military goals to enhance national security. As the head of both the government and the state, the president sets these goals with advice from the cabinet and other senior executive branch decision makers. These strategic goals orient the work of vast executive agencies, including the Departments of Defense, State, Treasury, Homeland Security, and Commerce. Many strategic goals, such as containment of communism during the Cold War, continue through multiple presidential administrations. To support its strategic objectives, the US government also relies upon agreements with other governments, international treaties, and membership in numerous international organizations such as the North Atlantic Treaty Organization (NATO), the World Trade Organization (WTO), and the United Nations (UN).

Budgetary Power. Congress's primary ability to shape strategic policy lies in its control over funding for government activities. The constitutional "power of the purse" allows Congress to allocate money among federal agencies to support its vision of the important aspects of strategic policy. The president sends a budgetary request to Capitol Hill on the first Monday of February every year. This request asks for the funds to support all government operations, including the president's national security strategy. Although Congress is not bound by the president's budget, this request serves as an opening position in negotiations between the executive and legislative branches over priorities. Since the president must ultimately sign any budget before it can be implemented, Congress must consider presidential preferences.

Following the president's submission, Congress sets forth its budget with the passage of the annual Concurrent Budget Resolution by April 15. This resolution controls the remainder of the annual budget process, which includes the approval of the thirteen different appropriations bills included in the overall budget. Most of the federal budget (71 percent) consists of mandatory spending, which includes interest on the national debt, Social Security, income security (such as disability insurance and tax rebates), and government health care (as in Medicare and Medicaid). The remaining 29 percent is discretionary spending, of which the largest single part is defense spending; it totaled $689 billion in the 2019 budget.[36] Although this is a significant amount, military spending as a proportion of gross domestic product is at relatively low levels in historical terms, as indicated in figure 5.1.

To guide strategic policy with respect to national security funding, Congress mandated in 1997 that DoD undertake a Quadrennial Defense Review (QDR).[37] Accordingly, the secretary of defense must conduct and oversee "a comprehensive examination of the national defense strategy, force structure, force modernization plans, infrastructure, budget plan, and other elements of defense programs and policies of the United States with a view toward determining and expressing the defense strategy of the United States and establishing a defense program for the next 20 years."[38] Congress intended the first QDR in 1997 to be a top-to-bottom review of the Clinton administration's national security strategy. The National Defense Panel, an independent, bipartisan committee of outside experts appointed by the House and Senate Armed Services Committees, was also created to provide Congress with a critique of administration policy as presented in the QDR. Legislators wanted to link long-term policies, programs, and procurement to the budget. The 1997 QDR was, however, a disappointment to many members of Congress. Leg-

FIGURE 5.1 National Defense Spending as a Percentage of Gross Domestic Product

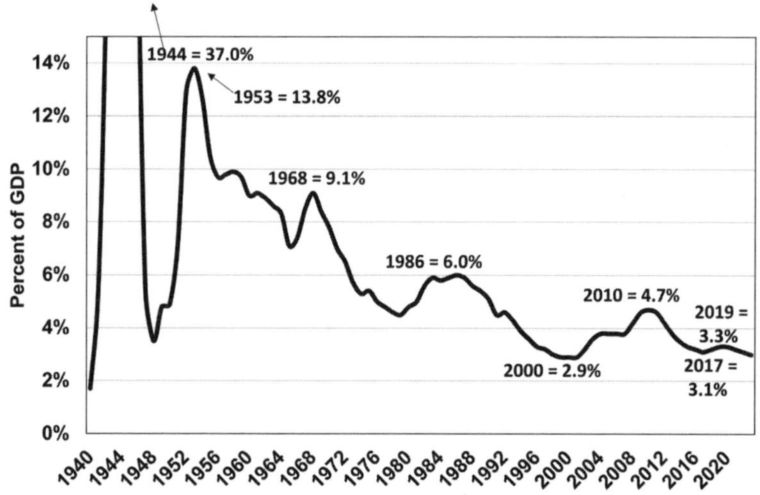

Source: Based on calculations from The White House, *Economic Report of the President, 2018*

islators had desired the QDR "to drive the defense debate to a strategy-based assessment of our future military requirements and capabilities," yet instead it became "a budget-driven incremental massage of the status quo."[39]

Even though the first QDR had failed to meet congressional intent, in 1999 Congress made the QDR mandatory every four years. The second QDR occurred in 2001. As it was mostly completed prior to the terrorist attacks of 9/11, its recommendations did not reflect the change in the nature of the threat facing the United States in their aftermath. The 2005–2006 QDR better reflected the original congressional intent, but responses to it were mixed. Those who praised this QDR pointed to its focus on national capability to meet emerging threats; critics emphasized a lack of consistency between statements of the strategic challenge and the programmatic responses offered by DoD. For critics, the statement of the national security problem facing the United States was fairly sound, but corresponding adjustments to the structure of the armed forces appeared to be lacking.[40] President Obama's DoD released two more QDRs, in 2010 and 2014. Both emphasized increased risk in the world, while acknowledging the budgetary realities of decreased available funding. The 2010 QDR was noted for its "pivot" to the Pacific, which aimed to rebalance forces and emphasize a change in the government's strategic focus.[41] Four years later, the focus of the next QDR remained in the Pacific, but also looked toward improving security in a time of fiscal austerity.[42]

Despite weaknesses in the process, the QDR does provide a means for members of Congress to work toward their individual and collective goals. Representatives and senators can hold public hearings on the QDR in an effort to influence the administration's strategic goals. Furthermore, the QDR helps legislators to link budgetary funding to policy goals. The State Department has followed this practice with a Quadrennial Diplomacy and Development Review (QDDR) in 2010 and 2015, which provides a similar assessment for foreign policy and development.[43] In conjunction with the power of the purse, Congress can be expected to continue to use the QDR, QDDR, or similar reviews to influence the president's overarching ability to set strategic policy.

Treaty Ratification. Relationships with foreign countries also shape the strategic policy of the United States. These relationships are often codified by formal treaty agreements between the United States and other members of the international community. As head of state, the president (or his or her delegates) negotiates the terms of these treaties, but the Constitution gives the Senate the power of treaty ratification. Two-thirds of the Senate must approve a treaty for it to go into effect.[44] To facilitate ratification, the president normally includes key legislators in discussions as treaties are developed. In rare cases, presidents have even requested that senior senators serve as active negotiators of treaties with foreign powers. The Senate has considered over fifteen hundred treaties, but only twenty-one have been rejected outright by the Senate; another forty-three never went into force because the Senate's modifications to the initial agreements were either so onerous that the foreign parties would not agree, or the modifications were unacceptable to the president.[45]

When it comes to treaty termination, the Constitution is silent. However, historical precedent treats the president as the sole authority to end American participation in a treaty. For example, in 2001 President George W. Bush withdrew the United States from the 1972 Anti–Ballistic Missile Treaty with Russia. The treaty was originally negotiated with the former Soviet Union at the height of the Cold War to bring some stability to the nuclear balance between the United States and the Soviet Union. The Bush administration withdrew from the treaty so that the United States could legally develop a limited anti–ballistic missile defense shield to protect against attacks by rogue states.

Treaty consideration highlights some of the ways the Senate can affect strategic policy. In December 2000, for example, President Clinton signed a treaty making the United States party to the International Criminal Court, but he did not submit it to the Senate for ratification. In May 2002, the George W. Bush administration announced that the United States would not become a party to the treaty. The primary concern of the Bush administration was that the International Criminal Court could assert legal jurisdiction over American soldiers and policy makers through trumped-up charges of war crimes based on legitimate uses of force during armed conflict and peacekeeping.[46] There was also concern that the court would assert jurisdiction over non-signatory nations, including the United States. As a result, Congress went further than President Bush, passing the American Service-Members' Protection Act in 2002. This law severed military assistance to any country that refused to agree not to extradite US citizens to the custody of the International Criminal Court if they were indicted.[47] In addition to President Bush's renunciation, these congressional actions concerned many of America's European allies, who were committed proponents of the new court. Many observers in both the United States and abroad believed that these congressional actions undercut the moral authority of the United States and its credibility in authoring future international law, bolstered an impression of US unilateralism, and hampered the ability of the United States to build coalitions in Iraq and Afghanistan.[48]

Congress may not have the ability to set strategic policy, but it can certainly complicate matters for a president attempting to do so. In addition to partisan differences, Congress as an institution often has different motivations to consider and different constituencies to represent than those that concern the president. The bicameral structure of the institution further impedes its ability to express a unified view or vision on security policy. Congress does not generally act with an international audience in mind; instead, it focuses on domestic constituencies. Presidents often attempt to sidestep the ratification process by entering into executive agreements rather than formal treaties. As discussed in chapter 17, the 2015 Iran nuclear deal is one of the more recent examples of the president's ability to work around congressional objections, notwithstanding the institution's formal power to ratify treaties.

War Powers Policy. When it comes to the ultimate strategic decision—the commitment of US forces to combat—Congress vies with the president over control of policy and decision making. US operations in Libya represent one of many instances of historical struggle between Congress and the president regarding war powers. In 2011, President Obama launched Operation Odyssey Dawn, a US operation, and decided that the United States would join in NATO's Operation Unified Protector to support Libyan rebels who opposed the regime of Colonel Muammar Qaddafi. The air campaign lasted six months, included 26,300 air sorties, expended 7,642 munitions, used over 113 US aircraft, and cost several billion dollars.[49] It was successful in assisting the rebels to topple Qaddafi from power. Although several administration officials briefed Congress, the administration argued that the requirement to notify the legislature under the War Powers Act did not apply because of the "limited nature, scope, and duration of the anticipated actions."[50] The House of Representatives passed a resolution that criticized the president for not seeking authorization, but rejected a more drastic resolution that would have required President Obama to stop US operations within fifteen days. The president continued the operation, without official notification to or approval by Congress, until Qaddafi was ousted from power and killed by the rebels.

The Origins of War Powers. War powers are a shared responsibility between the president and Congress. The Constitution grants Congress the power to declare war, along with the ability to raise and maintain both an army and a navy.[51] In contrast, the president's power stems from the constitutional role of commander in chief of the armed forces.[52] The president's role is far more than symbolic: it reflects a consensus among the Framers of the Constitution that unity of command was necessary to effective military action.

Notwithstanding numerous historical US military engagements, Congress has declared war only five times in over 225 years: the War of 1812, the Mexican-American War, the Spanish-American War, World War I, and World War II. On four of these occasions, a state of war existed prior to the formal declaration. On over three hundred separate occasions, US forces have been deployed abroad without a formal declaration of war.[53] Such cases range from short engagements that lasted for a matter of weeks, such as Grenada (1983), Panama (1989), and Libya (2011), to longer wars like those in Vietnam (1964–1975), Afghanistan (2001–present), and Iraq (2003–2011).

What is consistent in most of these cases is that it was the president who made the decision to enter the conflict, often with little or no prior consultation with Congress. Additionally, in each case Congress declined or was unable to garner enough support to attempt to block the president. In general, Congress defers to the president when it comes to protecting vital US interests abroad. Once the nation is committed, Congress finds it difficult to stop the president from acting, lest it invite political attack for not supporting the armed forces in conflict. For instance, during the 2008 presidential campaign, Senator Clinton, although critical of the Iraq War, said, "At this point, I am not ready to cut off funding for American troops. I am not going to do that."[54]

The War Powers Resolution and the Vietnam Era. The Vietnam War brought the issue of executive power to the forefront of political debate in the United States. Concerned that future presidents would overstep their constitutional authority as commander in chief by committing the United States to military actions, Congress passed the War Powers Resolution of 1973, which outlines a set of rules regarding the use of the military by the president. Under this resolution, "The President [must] submit a report to Congress within 48 hours after introducing U.S. armed forces in the absence of a declaration of war into hostilities or into areas of imminent involvement in hostilities. In the absence of congressional authorization of such activities, forces must be withdrawn within 60 days, with a possible extension of 30 days in cases of pending danger to forces during withdrawal."[55] The resolution was an attempt to strike a balance between the two competing branches of government. It recognizes that the president must have the ability to make decisions providing for the immediate defense of the nation in a time of crisis, but tries to prevent the president from having a "blank check" in this pursuit. Congress thought it necessary to compel presidential consultation once an immediate crisis had subsided. If not, this could give the president an unfettered ability to continue war actions indefinitely under the justification of the original crisis conditions.[56]

The War Powers Resolution was problematic from the outset. It was vague, and questions about its constitutionality spurred vigorous debate. When it first passed, many observers regarded it as evidence that Congress was once again willing to assert its constitutional role in the foreign policy process.[57] However, the War Powers Resolution can also be interpreted as giving the president the unilateral power to send a military force into conflict for sixty days.[58] By codifying executive powers that had previously been open to interpretation, the War Powers Resolution may have had the unintended consequence of strengthening the hand of the executive beyond the Framers' intent. Between 1973 and 2017, US presidents submitted 120 reports to Congress about US troop deployments abroad.[59] In some other circumstances, the action was so brief that no report was filed. Additionally, presidents have sometimes argued that certain actions did not invoke the War Powers Resolution, as there were no "imminent hostilities."

Challenges of the Post–Cold War Era. The fall of the Iron Curtain and the collapse of the Soviet Union occurred rapidly from late 1989 to 1991. In quick succession, the Warsaw Pact and the greater Soviet empire disintegrated into a number of smaller countries with serious economic problems stemming from years of neglect. The fall of the Soviet Union presented the United States and the rest of the world with many foreign policy and national security opportunities and challenges. While removing the one large threat that the United States had faced for nearly fifty years, the end of the Cold War destabilized many countries that no longer had financial support from a world superpower. This destabilization led to numerous small regional and ethnic conflicts that sometimes turned into civil war. The US Cold War military structure was not designed for a post-Soviet world and was slow to adapt to the new environment. Throughout the 1990s, the president and Congress competed for control in dealing with these crises.

In August 1990, Saddam Hussein dispatched Iraqi forces into Kuwait. The ease with which Iraqi forces took Kuwait alarmed many, who feared that Saudi Arabia and its rich oil fields might be the next target. President George H. W. Bush launched an aggressive diplomatic campaign to build an international consensus in opposition to Saddam Hussein. In addition to pushing for several UN resolutions condemning Iraq's actions, the administration secured pledges of financial and military support for a combined operation to drive Iraqi forces out of Kuwait.[60]

Despite the almost universal condemnation of Saddam Hussein's actions, many in the United States expressed significant concern over the potential outcome of the military operation against him. While initially rejecting a constitutional need for congressional support, President Bush did eventually ask for an Authorization for the Use of Military Force resolution. A vigorous debate ended on January 12, 1991, with a one-hundred vote margin in the House and a five-vote margin in the Senate in favor of the resolution. However, the close vote in the Senate did not reveal the true political situation. By the time of the vote, over 500,000 US troops were already in the region preparing for combat operations, which commenced on January 16, 1991. Under these circumstances, anything besides authorization was unlikely.[61]

One of the most demanding challenges of the early-to-mid 1990s was the disintegration of Yugoslavia and the resulting brutal ethnic conflict within Bosnia-Herzegovina. When the various warring groups agreed to end the conflict in 1995, it became clear that a large military force would be necessary to sustain the peace. The Clinton administration struggled to convince a Republican-controlled Congress of the necessity of committing US forces to this endeavor. Many legislators saw this as a European problem that Europeans should resolve.

In pushing for NATO and US commitment to the mission, President Clinton essentially involved the United States military by default. Only the US Army was large enough and powerful enough to maintain the fragile Dayton Peace Accords. Believing that the public would be unwilling to support a more substantial commitment, Congress and the president initially agreed to a one-year deployment.[62] After the US military was committed to peacekeeping in the Balkans, Congress reluctantly extended American involvement beyond the initial one-year mandate. Ultimately, American forces remained in Bosnia for more than a decade. This highlights an important point: once Congress gives authorization to commit US forces, it is the president who largely controls their deployment and mission timeline. The president, not Congress, is the one who declares "mission accomplished" and brings the troops home.

Congress and National Security after the Terrorist Attacks of September 11, 2001. The government's response to the 9/11 attacks demonstrates the inherent tension between the branches with regard to national security and foreign policy. Some interpreted the attacks as sufficient cause to allow the president to take immediate action both domestically and internationally without prior authorization by Congress. However, even in this situation, according to the War Powers Resolution, the president needed authorization to continue hostilities beyond the sixty-day limit. The brief negotiation with Congress following the attacks encapsulates many of the ambiguities with the War Powers Resolution in case of threats against domestic targets. President Bush desired a resolution that gave him broad authority not only to act against those deemed responsible for the attacks but also to act so as to deter and preempt future attacks. However, Congress, in the September 2001 Authorization for the Use of Military Force, gave the president only the authority to act against those responsible, out of concern that the extended authority he sought could be construed too broadly. Congress passed this joint resolution by a vote of 98–0 in the Senate and 420–1 in the House.[63]

Despite the margin of victory, this bipartisan show of unity did not last. Divisions erupted over the conduct of the "War on Terror" and raised questions as to the power of the president in relation to Congress. Given that the war was being waged against a tactic usually employed by non-state actors, what were the roles of the executive and the legislative branches? Jurisdiction was further muddied by the potential domestic nature of the security threat. In addition, which entities should take the lead in intelligence gathering also had to be determined.

While members of Congress overwhelmingly deferred to and supported the president's decision to invade Afghanistan to defeat the ruling Taliban regime and elements of al Qaeda, the legislative branch asserted itself more in moves to overhaul the domestic security apparatus. President Bush initially appointed a homeland security advisor and envisioned the position to have a similar function and role to that of the national security advisor. This appointment would remain within the White House and thus not be subject to congressional oversight. Congress opposed this approach and advocated for a separate agency to be responsible for securing the homeland. By elevating its leader to cabinet level, Congress would gain budgetary, oversight, and confirmation power over homeland security functions and personnel. The president initially rejected this approach, but ultimately acquiesced. The creation of the Department of Homeland Security enabled Congress to block future presidents from acting unilaterally on homeland security issues. Enhanced focus on domestic security also created a new distributive political opportunity for legislators to dispense additional federal contracts in their states and districts. (For more on homeland security, see chapter 6.)

A third significant action associated with the September 2001 attacks was the US decision to use force against Iraq. Shortly after the successful initial invasion of Afghanistan, President Bush and many of his advisors suggested that states such as Iraq were actively supporting terrorists and could supply them with weapons of mass destruction (WMD). A terrorist attack using WMD would be so catastrophic that the possibility justified the launch of preventive wars. Citing intelligence reports about Iraqi WMD, Congress authorized the use of force against Iraq in 2002; the US-led invasion of Iraq began in March 2003. The US military rapidly overthrew the government of President Saddam Hussein, but no WMD were found and many prior reports of WMD were discredited. The ensuing insurgency, sectarian strife, and significant loss of both Iraqi and American lives led many members of Congress to question their initial support. Riding a wave of public disenchantment with the war, Democrats recaptured Congress in 2006 after twelve years of Republican domination.[64]

Congress in the Obama Era. President Obama entered the White House in 2009 desiring to end the war in Iraq and to complete a successful mission in Afghanistan. After announcing a surge of 33,000 troops to Afghanistan in 2009, President Obama took control of much of his national security operations, relying on Congress only for funding approval.[65] At the outset of his administration, Obama sought to minimize the American footprint overseas by ending the combat mission in Iraq and shifting to more reliance on targeted drone strikes against terrorists. He also authorized the operation in Pakistan that killed Osama bin Laden, and the United States supported NATO operations in Libya. Throughout his tenure as president, Obama attempted to conduct operations through strategic partners and by promoting an agenda of democracy and human rights abroad. Most actions during this period were primarily executive-led. Obama took full advantage of executive powers, expanding the role of the National Security Agency and using drone strikes in Yemen, Somalia, Pakistan, and Iraq against al Qaeda, its affiliated terrorist groups, and ISIL. Congress attempted to conduct oversight and regain a foothold in the national security arena, but these efforts were somewhat limited in scope.

The Future of War Powers. When President Trump ordered a military strike in April 2017 that included fifty-nine Tomahawk cruise missiles against a Syrian airbase in response to a chemical weapons attack that killed dozens of Syrian civilians, he did not report this use of military force to Congress as the War Powers Resolution would seemingly require.[66] On the other hand, Congress did not challenge the Trump administration, likely due to the time-limited and generally successful nature of the attack. This is another example of how presidents have adapted to working around the War Powers Resolution. They are not eager to test its provisions in court for fear that their power could be restricted. Congress, facing the alternative of denying the executive freedom of action in a crisis, has generally given the authority the president sought. However, Congress has also moved to reassert its prerogatives when it perceives executive overreach. The executive and legislative branches are likely to continue to struggle over war powers policy.

Conclusion

The Framers gave Congress a distinct role in setting national security strategy. However, its inherent institutional weaknesses have at times hampered the legislative branch's ability to shape or counter presidential initiatives. Due to diffuse power bases, divergent member preferences, and slow decisionmaking processes, Congress is often a sideline player in setting national security policy. However, there are important exceptions to this generalization, and Congress has on occasion successfully altered executive branch initiatives and checked presidential power. Considered in terms of the three varieties of national security policy, Congress tends to be dominant in structural policy, where its members have the most at stake due to the distributive nature of national security policies. Uncoordinated and conflicting member preferences make Congress weaker when attempting to set strategic policy. Congress and the president actively wrestle for control of war powers policy, with the president historically holding the advantage. Subsequent chapters highlight specific tensions between Congress and the presidency concerning homeland security, intelligence, and budgeting policy, as well as periods and areas of agreement.

Given this examination of the impacts of Congress on national security policy in the past, it is useful to recognize that new dynamics may shape the future differently. It is unlikely that the Framers foresaw that the United States would become the sole global superpower or that they imagined that the US president would become one of the most influential political leaders in the world. These developments, which have been accompanied by significant new challenges for US security, tend to further strengthen the position of the president. Nevertheless, the view of the Framers that Congress provided the closest and most direct link to the American people remains valid. For this reason, the role of Congress in formulating and executing national security and foreign policy will remain important. Institutional capacity and the character of external challenges will continue to affect the extent to which Congress plays an effective role.

Discussion Questions

1. What are the constitutional powers of Congress in the national security arena?
2. What are the advantages of the president in the making of foreign and security policy?
3. What explains periods of relative congressional activism in national security affairs?
4. Which institutions within Congress have the greatest role in national security affairs? Why?
5. What are the three varieties of national security policy? In which policy area does Congress play the greatest role? Why?
6. To what extent do specific congressional interests influence structural policy with regard to military bases, weapons procurement, or foreign arms sales? What are the effects on military efficiency and effectiveness?
7. Is Congress well suited to playing the role of reformer within and among executive branch agencies? Why or why not?
8. What is the War Powers Resolution? Has it enhanced the role of Congress in national security affairs?
9. Should Authorizations for the Use of Military Force be time limited to prevent the executive branch from using them to engage in wars without end?
10. As the wars in Afghanistan, Iraq, and Syria continue to evolve, is Congress likely to play a greater or lesser role than the president in national security policy? Why?

Recommended Reading

Crabb, Cecil V., Glenn J. Antizzo, and Leila E. Sarieddine. *Congress and the Foreign Policy Process*. Baton Rouge: Louisiana State University Press, 2000.

Davidson, Roger H., Walter J. Oleszek, Frances E. Lee, and Eric Schickler. *Congress and Its Members*, 15th ed. Washington, DC: CQ Press, 2015.

Dodd, Lawrence C., and Bruce I. Oppenheimer, eds. *Congress Reconsidered*. 11th ed. Washington, DC: CQ Press, 2016.

Fisher, Louis. *Presidential War Power*. 3rd rev. ed. Lawrence: University Press of Kansas, 2013.

Hamilton, Lee H. *How Congress Works and Why You Should Care*. Bloomington: Indiana University Press, 2004.

King, Kay. *Congress and National Security*. Washington, DC: Council on Foreign Relations, November 2010.

Locher, James R. *Victory on the Potomac: The Goldwater-Nichols Act Unifies the Pentagon*. Rev. ed. College Station: Texas A&M Press, 2004.

Mann, Thomas E., and Norman J. Ornstein. *The Broken Branch: How Congress Is Failing America and How to Get It Back on Track*. New York: Oxford University Press, 2006.

Mayhew, David R. *Congress: The Electoral Connection*. New Haven, CT: Yale University Press, 1975.

Smith, Steven S., Jason M. Roberts, and Ryan J. Vander Wielen. *The American Congress*. 9th ed. Cambridge: Cambridge University Press, 2015.

Recommended Internet Resources

Constitution of the United States, National Archives, www.archives.gov
US Congress, www.congress.gov
US House of Representatives, www.house.gov
US Senate, www.senate.gov

Notes

1. James Madison, "The Structure of the Government Must Furnish the Proper Checks and Balances Between the Different Departments," Federalist No. 51, February 8, 1788, https://www.congress.gov/resources/display/content/The+Federalist+Papers#TheFederalistPapers-75.

2. Alexander Hamilton, "The Executive Department Further Considered," Federalist No. 70, March 18, 1788, https://www.congress.gov/resources/display/content/The+Federalist+Papers#TheFederalistPapers-70.

3. US Constitution, Article I, Section 8.

4. See, for example, "Brutus," "X: 24 January 1788," in *The Anti-Federalist Papers and the Constitutional Convention Debates*, ed. Ralph Ketcham (New York: Signet, 2003), 287–92.

5. Howard P. "Buck" McKeon, "The Common Defense: How Founding Principles Should Shape Our Armed Forces," remarks to the Hamilton Society (Washington, DC, April 25, 2012).

6. David Mayhew, *Congress: The Electoral Connection* (New Haven, CT: Yale University Press, 1974).

7. Richard F. Fenno, *Congressmen in Committees* (Boston: Little, Brown, 1973).

8. Roger H. Davidson and Walter J. Oleszek, *Congress and Its Members* (Washington, DC: CQ Press, 2006), 454.

9. Hamilton, "Federalist No. 70," para. 7.

10. Andrew Rudalevige, *The New Imperial Presidency* (Ann Arbor: University of Michigan Press, 2006), 30–32.

11. Harold Hongju Koh, *Libya and War Powers* (Washington, DC: US Department of State, June 28, 2011), http://www.state.gov/s/l/releases/remarks/167250.htm.

12. John Lehman, *Making War: The 200-Year-Old Battle between the President and Congress over How America Goes to War* (New York: Charles Scribner's Sons, 1992), 72.

13. Megan S. Lynch, *Earmark Disclosure Rules in the House: Member and Committee Requirements*, RS22866 (Washington, DC: Congressional Research Service, May 12, 2015).

14. Lehman, *Making War*, 66.

15. Cecil V. Crabb, Glenn J. Antizzo, and Leila E. Sarieddine, *Congress and the Foreign Policy Process* (Baton Rouge: Louisiana State University Press, 2000), 157–92.

16. Author's analysis based on "Congressional Committees" at https://www.govtrack.us/ on November 8, 2015.

17. Mary T. Tyszkiewicz and Stephen Daggett, *A Defense Budget Primer*, CRS Report RL30002 (Washington, DC: US Library of Congress, Congressional Research Service, 1998). For example, most of the funding for major combat operations in Iraq and Afghanistan from 2001 through 2010 was separate from the annual defense budget; this funding was requested and granted through supplemental or emergency appropriations. Although supplemental appropriations persist, the Obama administration incorporated funding for Iraq and Afghanistan into the annual budget.

18. Jacob B. Javits, "Congress and Foreign Relations: The Taiwan Relations Act," *Foreign Affairs* 60, no. 1 (1981): 54.

19. US Constitution, Article IV, Section 3.

20. Paul F. Boller, *Congressional Anecdotes* (New York: Oxford University Press, 1991), 287.

21. Kenneth R. Mayer, "Closing Military Bases (Finally): Solving Collective Dilemmas through Delegation," *Legislative Studies Quarterly* 20, no. 3 (1995): 393–416.

22. Loren Thompson, "Army Plan to Shut Only Tank Plant Faces Fierce Resistance," Forbes.com, May 7, 2012, http://www.forbes.com/sites/lorenthompson/2012/05/07/army-plan-to-shut-only-tank-plant-faces-fierce-resistance/.

23. David Francis, "Congress Keeps Approving Military Spending for Projects the Pentagon Doesn't Want," *Business Insider*, May 1, 2013, http://www.businessinsider.com/congress-approves-useless-military-spending-2013-5.

24. Lawrence Korb, "The Korb Report: A Realistic Defense for America," Business Leaders for Sensible Priorities, 2001, 7–8, http://www.cdi.org/.

25. David Axe, "Buyer's Remorse: How Much Has the F-22 Really Cost?" *Wired*, December 14, 2011, http://www.wired.com/2011/12/f-22-real-cost. Costs were adjusted for inflation using Total Obligational Authority procurement deflators found in Office of the Under Secretary of Defense (Comptroller), *National Defense Budget Estimates for FY 2016* (Washington, DC: Department of Defense, March 2015), table 5-5.

26. Dan Morgan, "Congress Backs Pentagon Budget Heavy on Future Weapons," *Washington Post*, June 11, 2004, A23.

27. Richard F. Grimmett and Paul K. Kerr, "Conventional Arms Transfers to Developing Nations, 2004–2011," CRS Report for Congress, R42678 (Washington, DC: Congressional Research Service, 2012).

28. Directorate of Defense Trade Controls, Bureau of Political-Military Affairs, US Department of State, *Defense Trade Controls Overview 2006*, 1, http://pmddtc.state.gov/reports/.

29. William D. Hartung, "Corporate Welfare for Weapons Makers: The Hidden Costs of Spending on Defense and Foreign Aid" (Washington, DC: CATO Institute in Policy Analysis, 1999), 5, http://www.cato.org/pubs/pas/pa350.pdf.

30. Military pay was increased 1.4 percent in 2011, 1.6 percent in 2012, and 1.7 percent in 2013, years when federal civilian workers had no pay increase. Costs were adjusted for inflation using Total Obligational Authority procurement deflators found in Office of the Under Secretary Of Defense (Comptroller), *National Defense Budget Estimates for FY 2016*, table 5-5.

31. David R. Mayhew, *Congress: The Electoral Connection* (New Haven, CT: Yale University Press, 1974), 61–62.

32. Amy B. Zegart, *Flawed by Design: The Evolution of the CIA, JCS, and NSC* (Stanford: Stanford University Press, 1999), 145.

33. For more, see Zegart, *Flawed by Design*; and James R. Locher, *Victory on the Potomac* (College Station: Texas A&M Press, 2002).

34. Michael Meese and Isaiah Wilson, "The Military: Forging a Joint Warrior Culture," in *The National Security Enterprise: Navigating the Labyrinth*, 2nd ed., ed. Roger Z. George and Harvey Rishikof (Washington, DC: Georgetown University Press, 2017), 142–61.

35. Sean M. Roche, "Is It Time for an Interagency Goldwater-Nichols Act?" *InterAgency Journal* 4, no. 1 (2013): 12–22.

36. The White House, *Economic Report of the President, 2018* (Washington, DC: White House, February 2018), table B-19.

37. National Defense Authorization Act for Fiscal Year 1997, PL 104-201 §923, September 23, 1996 (Washington, DC: GPO, 1996).

38. National Defense Authorization Act for Fiscal Year 2000, PL 106-65 §901, October 5, 1999 (Washington, DC: GPO, 1999).

39. Senator Joseph Lieberman, Remarks on the Senate Floor concerning the Quadrennial Defense Review, *Congressional Record*, May 19, 1997, S4673.

40. See, for example, Andrew Krepinevich, "The Quadrennial Defense Review," testimony before Congress, Center for Strategic and Budgetary Assessments, March 14, 2006, http://www.csbaonline.org/publications/.

41. US Department of Defense, *Quadrennial Defense Review 2010* (Washington, DC: US DoD, February 2010), 60.

42. US Department of Defense, *Quadrennial Defense Review 2014* (Washington, DC: US DoD, February 2014), iii–iv.

43. See US Department of State, *The Quadrennial Diplomacy and Development Review* (Washington, DC: US Department of State, 2015).

44. US Constitution, Article II, Section 2.

45. "Treaties," Senate History, United States Senate, March 2018, http://www.senate.gov/artandhistory/history/common/briefing/Treaties.htm.

46. Jennifer Elsea, *U.S. Policy Regarding the International Criminal Court*, CRS Report RL31495 (Washington, DC: US Library of Congress, Congressional Research Service, 2006), 7.

47. Colum Lynch, "Congress Seeks to Curb International Court," *Washington Post*, November 26, 2004, A02.

48. Eric S. Kraus and Mike O. Lacy, "Utilitarian vs. Humanitarian: The Battle over the Law of War," *Parameters* 32, no. 2 (2002): 83.

49. Karl P. Mueller, ed., *Precision and Purpose: Airpower in the Libyan Civil War* (Santa Monica, CA: RAND, 2015).

50. White House Report to Congress, "United States Activities in Libya," June 15, 2011, http://fas.org/man/eprint/wh-libya.pdf.

51. US Constitution, Article I, Section 8.

52. US Constitution, Article II.

53. Barbara Torreon, *Instances of Use of United States Armed Forces Abroad, 1798–2017*, CRS Report R42738 (Washington, DC: Congressional Research Service, October 12, 2017).

54. Roger Simon, "Feingold Ups the Ante on Iraq Funding," *CBS News*, January 30, 2007, http://www.cbsnews.com/stories/2007/01/30/politics/main2413236.shtml.

55. US Congress, War Powers Resolution, PL 93-148, 1973.

56. Louis Fisher and David Gray Adler, "The War Powers Resolution: Time to Say Goodbye," *Political Science Quarterly* 113, no. 1 (1998): 1–20.

57. Fisher and Adler, "The War Powers Resolution," 1–20.

58. Louis Fisher, "Congressional Checks on Military Initiatives," *Political Science Quarterly* 109, no. 5 (1994–1995): 749.

59. Torreon, *Instances of Use of United States Armed Forces Abroad, 1798–2017*.

60. Lawrence Freedman and Efraim Karsh, "How Kuwait Was Won: Strategy in the Gulf War," *International Security* 16, no. 2 (1991): 6–8.

61. Rudalevige, *The New Imperial Presidency*, 194–95.

62. Ryan C. Hendrickson, "War Powers, Bosnia, and the 104th Congress," *Political Science Quarterly* 113, no. 2 (1998): 241–58.

63. Davidson and Oleszek, *Congress and Its Members*, 346–47.

64. Nancy Pelosi, "Benchmarks without Deadlines Are Just Words: After Four Years, Words Are Not Enough," remarks on the House Floor, March 23, 2007, http://www.house.gov/pelosi/press/releases/March07/Supplemental.html.

65. Susan Cornwell, "Congress Approves Afghan Surge Funds," Reuters.com, July 27, 2010, http://www.reuters.com/article/2010/07/27/us-afghanistan-usa-funds-idUSTRE66Q6QZ20100727.

66. Andrew Rudalevige, "Trump's Missile Attack on Syria Might Be Satisfying. But It's Not Legal," *Washington Post*, April 7, 2017.

6

Homeland Security

Protecting the US homeland and its citizens against threats has been one of the foremost duties of government throughout the country's history. To this end, the Constitution empowers Congress to "raise and support Armies . . . provide and maintain a Navy," and "provide for calling forth the Militia to execute the Laws of the Union, suppress Insurrections and repel Invasions." The terrorist attacks of September 11, 2001, focused the nation on a dimension of this security challenge that had been receiving limited attention. The result was the most significant reorganization of the US government since 1947. Key to this reorganization was the creation of a new Department of Homeland Security. Additionally, Congress passed significant legislation designed to help prevent future attacks, and the Department of Defense formed a new combatant command to plan and implement the US military's actions to defend the homeland.

These efforts brought to light fundamental questions associated with providing homeland security in a liberal democracy with a federal system of government. The Tenth Amendment to the Constitution states that "The powers not delegated to the United States by the Constitution, nor prohibited by it to the States, are reserved to the States respectively, or to the people"; in doing so, it reinforces the American federal system of power-sharing among national, state, and local governments.[1] For example, although the federal government is responsible for ensuring the overall safety of its citizens from terrorist attacks, most American police power is controlled by state and local governments. Defining the respective roles and forging effective cooperation among the many organizations and federal, state, local, and tribal jurisdictions with stakes in various aspects of homeland security are important but difficult. The process of determining what to protect, how to protect it, and where to allocate resources is fraught with political and social consequences.

Moreover, liberty and security must be balanced in most major homeland security decisions, as demonstrated in debates over the limits of law enforcement authority, domestic intelligence operations, and the proper role of the military in the homeland. This chapter outlines the development of US homeland security efforts since 2001 and explores many of these issues.

The Search for a Definition

Prior to the terrorist attacks of 9/11, the term *homeland security* was rarely used in the United States. The activities now conducted under its umbrella were previously carried out by a variety of organizations at federal, state, and local levels in the name of law enforcement, national defense, border protection, customs, immigration, public health, and emergency management. The term *homeland security* was elevated into the public discourse in the immediate aftermath of the 9/11 attacks, most notably with the creation of the Office of Homeland Security on September 20, 2001.[2] Ever since the emergence of the term, however, there has been a debate about what activities should fall under homeland security. As with the long-running debate over the definition of terrorism, a number of different definitions of homeland security have been advanced, including differing definitions from different US government entities. Despite this lack of consensus, most proposed definitions fall within one of the following definitional categories:[3]

1. *Terrorism.* Homeland security is about preventing acts of terrorism and responding appropriately when the United States is attacked. This category is based on the foundational truth that this term is being discussed as a direct result of the 9/11 attacks, and future efforts under this rubric should focus on ensuring that similar events never occur again.
2. *All Hazards.* Homeland security is about preventing terrorism, protecting against manmade and natural hazards, and responding to and recovering from all types of catastrophic incidents. This category recognizes that much of the work currently being done under the homeland security umbrella has little to do with terrorism, and that many of the capabilities and skills developed in the name of homeland security are much more frequently used after natural disasters and manmade accidents than after terrorism events.
3. *Terrorism and Catastrophes.* Homeland security is about what the federal government, in particular the Department of Homeland Security (DHS), does to prevent, respond to, protect against, and recover from terrorist and catastrophic events. This definition suggests that the "all-hazards" category is excessively broad and incorporates too many smaller-scale activities that might distract from efforts to focus on the threats and hazards that were the impetus for the creation of the homeland security framework. Homeland security should then be seen as a special category for those incidents and activities that are of a significant enough scale to require the engagement and leadership of the federal government.
4. *Meta-hazards.* Homeland security is about any social trend or threat that can disrupt the long-term stability of the American way of life. This category

suggests a more literal interpretation of homeland security that focuses on those threats and hazards that truly threaten the survival of the US homeland. The vast majority of terrorist attacks do not present such a threat. Only truly existential hazards such as climate change, cyber security, energy scarcity, and decaying physical infrastructure rise to the level of existential threats to American society.

Each of these definitional categories has merits, flaws, biases, and varying degrees of utility. The prevalence of each one in public discourse has ebbed and flowed over time and in response to specific national incidents.[4] The US government's own definition of homeland security has shifted, and continues to shift, across these categories.

Origins of the Homeland Security Bureaucracy

Most government agencies now involved in homeland security existed prior to September 11, 2001. For example, the US Customs Service, which was incorporated into DHS in 2003, has been operating at US ports of entry since 1789. During most of the country's history, homeland security actions largely centered on defending borders and coastlines against external attack. This theme continued through the Cold War, with emphasis on civil defense activities and preparation for the possibility of a nuclear strike.[5] The threat of terrorism increasingly influenced the US homeland security agenda during the 1990s in response to the 1993 bombing of the World Trade Center, the 1995 bombing of the Murrah Federal Building in Oklahoma City, the 1996 Khobar Towers bombing in Saudi Arabia, the 1998 bombings of American embassies in Kenya and Tanzania, and the 2000 attack on USS *Cole* in Yemen.

As the twentieth century drew to a close, a growing realization that transnational terrorist networks and the proliferation of nuclear, biological, radiological, and chemical weapon technology posed a major threat to the US homeland led various government and academic groups to take a harder look at the country's ability to prevent or mitigate the effects of terrorist attacks. Well before 9/11, reports by the US Commission on National Security/21st Century (the Hart-Rudman Commission) and the Advisory Panel to Assess Domestic Response Capabilities for Terrorism Involving Weapons of Mass Destruction (the Gilmore Commission) recommended improvements in information sharing on terrorist threats, increased national preparedness for attacks, clarification of national priorities and objectives through strategic planning, and significant organizational changes in the executive branch.[6]

The events of 9/11 crystallized much of this thinking, and the government quickly embarked on an enormous reorganization designed to deal more effectively with the threat of future attacks. The key elements of this effort included the creation of the Department of Homeland Security (DHS), an extensive reorganization of the intelligence community, and passage of legislation, including the Uniting and Strengthening America by Providing Appropriate Tools Required to Intercept and Obstruct Terrorism (USA PATRIOT) Act of 2001, commonly referred to as the

Patriot Act. Additionally, the Department of Defense revised its command structure, establishing the US Northern Command, a new command focused on homeland security and defense issues.

The Department of Homeland Security. President George W. Bush announced the creation of the Office of Homeland Security (OHS) just nine days after 9/11, launching a whirlwind of action to centralize responsibility for most homeland security tasks in a single office. Despite an initial desire to limit bureaucratic expansion and to maintain White House control of homeland security, President Bush proposed the creation of a new Department of Homeland Security as a cabinet-level department in June 2002. This shift was largely prompted by Congress, which desired more oversight. President Bush's announcement, and the subsequent release of the first *National Strategy for Homeland Security*, articulated his administration's definition of homeland security as "a concerted national effort to prevent terrorist attacks within the United States, reduce America's vulnerability to terrorism, and minimize the damage and recover from attacks that do occur."[7] This definition put the administration squarely in the camp of those who argued that homeland security was about terrorism, with other activities being ancillary.

The new Department of Homeland Security subsumed the OHS and brought together all or parts of twenty-two new or existing organizations, including the Transportation Security Administration, the US Customs Service, the Immigration and Naturalization Service, the Federal Emergency Management Agency, the US Secret Service, and the US Coast Guard, each with wide-ranging duties and charters. With over 180,000 employees, DHS became the third-largest department in the US government (figure 6.1). Many states and local communities instituted similar organizational changes with the same goal of improving unity of effort in securing the homeland.

Despite general consensus on the need for change, criticism of the original Homeland Security Act reflects basic American tensions regarding the scope and purpose of federal government. Some charged that DHS did not have enough power to protect the homeland, while others argued that it had too much. For those in the first camp, DHS did not have the tools or integration necessary for its basic mission. In particular, DHS did not include the lead federal agency for domestic counterterrorism operations, the Federal Bureau of Investigation (FBI). DHS also lacked independent capabilities for intelligence gathering and analysis.[8] Moreover, because at its creation DHS was primarily focused on terrorism, rather than all hazards, it did not fully integrate organizations into a seamless disaster response system.

Those who felt that DHS was given too much power believed that bringing together multiple organizations under the department created the potential for abuse of power. Moreover, managing all of these organizations under one umbrella would be too difficult. Merging twenty-two different entities, each with its own history, bureaucratic processes, and priorities, was an enormous management challenge. Creation of a sense of common identity and purpose across the new

FIGURE 6.1 Department of Homeland Security

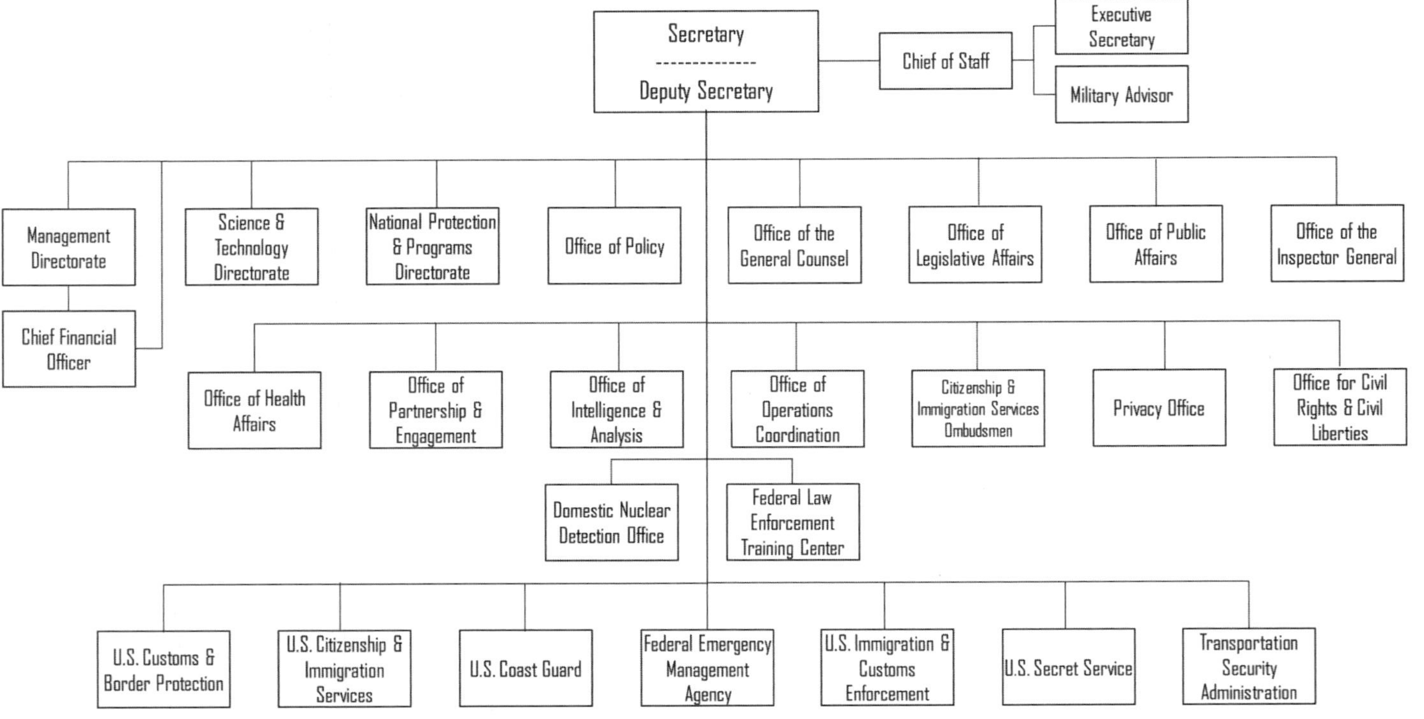

Source: DHS, http://www.dhs.gov/organizational-chart, as of August 26, 2016

department would be extremely difficult, as each unit brought its own missions and tasks, many of which had little to do with preventing terrorism. Despite assigning to DHS the prevention of terrorism as its primary mission, the Homeland Security Act also required that DHS "ensure that the functions of the agencies and subdivisions within the Department that are not related directly to securing the homeland are not diminished or neglected except by a specific explicit Act of Congress." Consequently, preventing terrorism was not a new mission that replaced previous missions; instead it was added to the existing array of activities and responsibilities.[9] The Coast Guard still had to conduct rescues; the Border Patrol still had to interdict drug traffickers; and the Federal Emergency Management Agency (FEMA) still had to react to hurricanes and earthquakes. Most DHS employees did not see defending against terrorism as their primary job on a daily basis; in fact, many saw it as a distraction from the other tasks that they believed should still be their priority.[10] In any case, the initial years of DHS operations were marked by the bureaucratic infighting, budget debates, and inefficiencies that could be expected to accompany any extensive governmental reorganization.[11] Congressional oversight was also problematic, as the committee structure in Congress was not reorganized to coincide with the reorganization taking place in the executive branch.

The Patriot Act. Passed during the same post-9/11 timeframe as several other major congressional initiatives and reauthorized in 2005, 2006, and 2011, the Patriot Act quickly became the most publicized and debated piece of homeland security legislation in the nation's history. The Patriot Act expanded government authority to fight terrorism by easing some restrictions on foreign intelligence gathering in the United States, facilitating information sharing between the intelligence and law enforcement communities, defining new crimes, and streamlining processes for prosecuting terror-related crimes. Not placated by the safeguards and congressional oversight requirement built into the act, opponents have charged that it does not do enough to protect individual privacy and that it leaves the door open for abuse of power.[12]

Provisions of the act have been challenged, with varying success, in the courts, and the debate continues over the appropriate role of government authority in combating terrorism. Controversy over aspects of the Patriot Act led to a failure to renew parts of the act on June 1, 2015. The next day, the Senate approved the Uniting and Strengthening America by Fulfilling Rights and Ensuring Effective Discipline over Monitoring Act, or *Freedom Act*, which renewed most parts of the original Patriot Act while changing some of its provisions. Under the Freedom Act, the FBI would have to make a more specific request, with approval of the Foreign Intelligence Surveillance Act (FISA) court, to obtain a call detail record from a telephone company. This stopped National Security Agency's practice of collecting bulk phone data.[13]

Taken as a whole, the enormous post-9/11 organizational, policy, and legislative reforms were designed with one purpose: facilitating effective action to protect the homeland. However, these choices are not made in a vacuum. Decisions on what specific actions to take and where to allocate scarce resources to maximize homeland security must consider many factors. These choices become even more difficult because they are made in a complex political environment.

Challenges in Homeland Security Planning and Execution

Protecting the US homeland is not an easy task practically or politically. It is an immense challenge to defend the nation's long borders (4,954 miles of sea borders, 5,923 miles of borders on land), process the remarkable volumes of people and goods crossing those borders at 326 ports of entry, protect the vast critical infrastructure of the nation (including, for example, 6,413 power plants, of which 104 are nuclear), and manage the inevitable variety of emergencies that occur. It requires effective coordination, risk management, and consideration and balancing of political and civil liberties.

Coordination. Given the scope of the problem and the variety of actors involved, homeland security ultimately depends upon effective coordination among government and nongovernment agencies at all levels. Cooperation is inherently difficult because government bureaucracies tend to follow a model that carefully delineates roles and responsibilities to ensure that each agency focuses on its specific mission; this enhances specialized expertise and reduces redundancy.[14] However, guarding against terrorist attacks requires coordination and cooperation among agencies at the federal, state, and local levels. Expertise existed prior to 9/11, but its fragmentation across agencies precluded the formation of a cohesive and comprehensive picture of the threat, which prevented government action that might have blocked the attacks.[15]

Adding to the challenge is that government agencies often have incentives not to cooperate with each other. Each agency has a strong self-interest to retain autonomy in its own functional areas and will tend to resist efforts to surrender authority over these particular areas. As Donald Kettl writes, "Every effort at cooperation inevitably requires each side to give a bit and, most important, to surrender a bit of the very autonomy that managers fight so hard to protect."[16] A study of the struggle of DHS to integrate its component agencies acknowledged that "core legacy organizations that migrated into DHS still generally set their own agendas."[17]

One method that has been used to address the coordination dilemma is the collocation of agencies in *fusion centers* to work on common issues, without necessarily surrendering any of their organizational authorities. At the highest federal level, this includes the National Counterterrorism Center (NCTC), which operates under the direction of the Director of National Intelligence (DNI) (and is described in more detail in chapter 7). It includes at least seventeen federal agencies that send individuals together to exchange information and work on common problems. At more local levels, the FBI has established 104 Joint Terrorism Task Forces (JTTF) throughout the United States in which over four thousand task force members from some five hundred state and local agencies and fifty-five federal agencies share intelligence and cooperate on common challenges.[18] DHS also supports fusion centers that, although operated by state and local governments, are supported with federal personnel, training, technical assistance, technology, and funding.[19] The key to the success of these fusion centers is that the infrastructure is provided by a lead agency (such as DNI for the NCTC, FBI for the JTTFs), and agencies can collocate members and cooperate to support common missions without surrendering any of their respective authority.

Risk Management. An open society, individual liberty, and a vibrant free market economy result in tremendous vulnerability. All levels of government must therefore make difficult choices regarding what to protect and how to protect it, how to allocate limited financial and personnel resources to deter or prevent attacks, and how to mitigate the effects of attacks or disasters when they occur. Securing the homeland requires risk management, and thus applying limited resources to an essentially unlimited list of potential tasks. Decisions at the federal level affect subsequent risk calculations at the state and local levels, and vice versa.

The risk management process is theoretically straightforward in its goals, but it is complex in its execution. The notion of prioritizing spending based on risk is common sense, but determining how to calculate that risk is both methodologically and politically complicated. In deciding what to protect, homeland security risk turns on three factors:

- *Threat*: the probability that a specific type of event—attack or disaster—will occur, as determined by intelligence or other indicators;
- *Vulnerability*: the probability that such an attack or disaster will succeed in causing damage; and
- *Consequences*: the costs of an attack or disaster.[20]

For example, the threat of a hurricane may be highest in major cities along the Gulf Coast or Atlantic seaboard; the threat of a terrorist attack may be higher in major metropolitan areas than in less densely populated rural locations. Vulnerability to threat and potential damage is a function of variables such as how physically "hardened" potential targets are, the likelihood that a threat against an area will be discovered before an attack or disaster occurs, and the anticipated response times and effectiveness of people and organizations that could respond to an event or attack. Consequences may include injuries or loss of life from an attack, direct and indirect financial losses, or psychological impacts.[21] Consequences may be increased by an absence of redundancy in key systems such as electrical grids, resulting in higher costs if a single critical node were destroyed.

Given the observed tendency of terrorist organizations like the Islamic State in Iraq and the Levant (ISIL) or al Qaeda to strike high-profile targets of symbolic value or locations where many people are gathered, such as mass transit systems in densely populated areas, a small shopping mall in suburban middle America could be characterized as having a low *threat* of terrorist attack. However, its lack of sizeable, well-trained security organizations and effective inspection procedures could make the same mall highly *vulnerable*; that is, an attack, if launched, would have a good chance of succeeding. The *consequences* of such an attack, in terms of potential loss of life and general panic, could be moderate to high. On the other hand, the threat to the Empire State Building may be high, as it fits the profile of desired terrorist targets, and the consequences of an effective attack would certainly be high, but it may be less vulnerable as a target due to significant existing security measures.

In practice, of course, it is difficult to assign numeric values to threat, vulnerability, and consequences so as to rank-order possible targets; the risk management methodologies often adopted by homeland security practitioners necessarily involve as much art as science. That said, the science does exist but is often poorly applied. One assessment of this challenge highlighted "probability neglect" as an explanation for why proper risk management tools had failed to materialize. Probability neglect results from several factors: focusing on worst-case scenarios (at the expense of preparing for higher probability events); adding, rather than multiplying, the probabilities (which violates risk assessment principles); assessing relative, rather than absolute, risk; inflating the importance of potential terrorist targets; and inflating terrorist capacities.[22] Because of these influences, initial formulas used by DHS to assess risk and assign funding were based more on arbitrary criteria or political calculations than on objective application of mathematically sound formulas.[23]

If one can overcome these challenges to complete a risk assessment and decide upon a rough priority of what ought to be protected, the next logical step, which adds a significant layer of complexity, is to determine how to provide protection. In other words, policy makers must then determine the most efficient and effective risk reduction measures and thus how to apportion resources among the following three tasks:

- *Deter threat:* credibly threaten, degrade, or disrupt terrorist networks that may be planning attacks, or alter the conditions to decrease the susceptibility of populations to radicalization and terrorist recruitment;
- *Mitigate vulnerabilities:* prevent or defeat attacks that are planned or attempted, through measures such as enhanced intelligence sharing, improved screening, enhanced physical security, and hardening of potential targets; and
- *Minimize consequences*: mitigate the effects of attacks, by improving coordination and capability of local first responders to assess damage and save lives.

Once potential risk reduction measures are determined and prioritized, finite resources may be allocated accordingly. Risk should be reduced in some areas and must, inevitably, be accepted in others. Evaluation of the effectiveness of risk reduction measures and continuous monitoring of any changes to previous assessments of threat, vulnerability, and consequences are then used to inform future decisions. Ideally, risk management for homeland security is conceptually a continuous, rational process, conducted by governments at the federal, state, and local levels.

Homeland Security and Politics. Regardless of the degree to which policy makers can accurately assess and manage risks, they must do so in a politicized decisionmaking environment. Politically, homeland security presents a classic collective-action dilemma.[24] While certain actions could be taken that enhance overall homeland security, their implementation may be prevented by the influence of individuals or groups—federal, state, or local politicians, private-sector entities, or public special-interest groups—for whom the actions impose a cost that they are unwilling to bear. This is often due to parochial concerns, because a group considers its own interests above those of the broader community (this would include the NIMBY, or "Not in My Back Yard," dynamic). For example, certain security measures that might improve border security could adversely affect individuals living near the border, perhaps due to construction near their property or economic impacts in their local community. Those who have to pay these costs, the local population, are far fewer in number than those who reap possible benefits—the rest of the nation as a whole—but the local population is more concentrated and motivated to get involved than the dispersed beneficiaries and may thus have disproportionate impact. Unwillingness to pay a short-term cost to achieve a long-term benefit can also complicate decision making. Legislators often have a short time horizon and are unwilling to pay the political price of decisions whose benefits will not be realized until after the next election cycle.[25]

Such collective action problems associated with local interests, a short-term focus, and other political considerations can lead to seemingly irrational decisions concerning the allocation of scarce resources. For example, if political leaders at all levels attempt to secure resources for their jurisdictions (of which there are some 87,000 in the United States) rather than support a "national interest" in homeland security (especially because this "national interest" is a difficult-to-define product of many subjective assessments, and therefore easy to dispute), the result is likely to be political bargaining and a pattern of resource allocation that differs greatly from what a rational risk management process would prescribe. Emergency responders across the nation, for example, will all want the most advanced equipment, regardless of the likelihood of their ever using it. Members of Congress will lobby for awarding homeland security–related contracts to firms in their own districts. Mayors will attempt to ensure that key facilities in their towns are included in lists of critical infrastructure that may receive additional funding or security. The combined result will inevitably be suboptimal from a national perspective.

This predicted dynamic has repeatedly been observed in the allocation of homeland security grants. In the wake of 9/11, Congress took several actions to provide money through states to local jurisdictions to reduce vulnerabilities and enhance the ability to prevent and to mitigate the effects of disasters and attacks. These included doubling funding for the Firefighter Investment and Response Enhancement (FIRE) Act and authorizing the State Homeland Security Grant Program and the Urban Area Security Initiative. Rational risk assessment did not appear to determine fund distribution for these programs. For example, Montana received $9.33 per capita in the initial FIRE grants, while California—a far more likely terrorist target—received only $0.86 per capita. FIRE grants were allocated when Republicans controlled Congress, and so Republican districts received more FIRE funding per capita than Democratic districts did. The State Homeland Security Grant Program funding included a "floor," which ensured that rural states benefited disproportionately. Even the Urban Area Security Initiative, intended to provide funding for America's high–population density cities facing the greatest threats without any minimum distribution requirement, included many grants that seemed out of proportion to risk. For example, New Haven, Connecticut, received $77.00 per capita, while New York City was granted just $5.84 per capita.[26] There have been numerous reports of this funding being spent on items whose utility in supporting homeland security is dubious, from expensive armored vehicles for small communities to snow cone machines as medical and/or recruitment tools.[27]

There is inherent tension between national power and local discretion in the US federal system. Unlike overseas military conflicts, where the president and the federal government have extensive powers, homeland security operates primarily within the domestic arena, where the president's powers are more limited than those of chief executives of most other countries. DHS may be able to identify a long list of key tasks to improve homeland security, but it has little authority over those in state and local governments who must carry out many of these tasks. State and local governments retain the authority to take actions they deem necessary to protect the interests of their communities, even if those interests might conflict with what the federal government determines to be the national interest. This is why the federal grant programs described above are significant and politically contentious: funding is one of the few tools that the federal government can use as leverage over the states.

Government allocation of resources for homeland security is crucial, but homeland security action is not limited to government. Public and private companies, nongovernmental organizations, and individual citizens are also involved. For example, the vast majority of critical infrastructure in the United States is owned by the private sector. There is much debate regarding the private sector's incentives to invest in security. Some argue that the private sector will not voluntarily secure itself, but will instead succumb to the lessons of the "tragedy of the commons": each entity will operate in its own self-interest, under-contributing to security, which results in long-term detriment to the industry or community. A company may be hesitant to spend on security, as it may affect short-term profits; it may rationally choose to accept the long-term risk of less security because, if something were to happen, the effect would likely affect its entire industry and not just that company. Some companies have resisted required vulnerability assessments, on the reasoning of increased legal liability if security deficiencies were documented but not addressed.[28]

The competing school of thought argues that owners and operators have a natural incentive to protect their businesses. Companies make money only when goods and services are flowing, so profits are maximized when they are operational as much of the time as possible. It costs less to take precautionary measures than it does to suffer a disaster and possibly go bankrupt. Despite its protestations, the private sector is already accustomed to the federal government imposing rules on industry, considering the vast amounts of federal regulation that apply to some industries.[29] Consequently, much private-sector action is already influenced by government or industry standards, which helps overcome the collective action problem. Each nongovernmental entity must make decisions about identifying and reducing risk. Preparedness efforts vary widely, just as they do among various state and local jurisdictions.

To summarize, leaders at all levels apply a risk management process, explicitly or implicitly, in a politically charged environment that includes many public and private players and interests. The overall result is a highly complex, potentially suboptimal, loosely integrated system for protecting the homeland.

Homeland Security and Civil Liberties. In addition to practical and political considerations, there is a significant normative aspect to homeland security choices. As demonstrated by the debate over provisions of the Patriot Act and then the Freedom Act, the United States must maintain a dynamic balance between two fundamental and sometimes conflicting imperatives: protecting the homeland and safeguarding the freedoms upon which the country was founded. The organizations, policies, and actions that may be most effective in preventing attacks on the homeland may threaten civil liberties and run counter to basic American values. Even so, American citizens may be willing to accept some reduction of liberty to increase their security. The result of this interplay tends to be a somewhat cyclical process in which institutions and policies are strengthened to increase security during times of perceived danger; then weakened, perhaps through enhanced congressional oversight, when liberty is unduly restricted or abuses take place, or when complacency sets in after long periods of perceived safety; and then strengthened again if the loosened security measures appear to be ineffective.[30]

This cycle was seen in practice as the events of 9/11 receded into the past, as public perception of threat decreased, and as some counterterrorism activities began to be perceived by the general public to violate civil liberties. Early concerns regarding protection of civil liberties in the post-9/11 environment emerged around the passage of the Patriot Act. These concerns grew as the public became more aware of controversies surrounding detention policy at Guantanamo Bay, extraordinary rendition, prisoner treatment at Abu Ghraib, and the use of "enhanced interrogation" methods. On the domestic front, much of the concern was related to treatment of the Muslim American community. While both the Bush and Obama administrations consistently stated that counterterrorism policies were not targeted at any one community or religion, members and representatives of Muslim American communities believed that they were being targeted for investigation based on their faith rather than on probable cause. These tensions have increased during the Trump administration due to anti-Muslim rhetoric during his campaign for the presidency as well as his 2017 executive order to bar many individuals from eight countries, six of which are predominantly Muslim (Iran, Libya, Syria, Yemen, Somalia, and Chad), from entering the United States. President Donald Trump grounded this action in concerns over homeland security. (The other two nations included in the immigration restriction were North Korea and Venezuela.)

Another significant controversy regarding civil liberties and homeland security surrounds the revelations by former National Security Agency contract employee Edward Snowden. Snowden came to international attention in June 2013 after he released to journalists thousands of classified documents revealing US intelligence collection and operations. His actions led to global debates over information privacy, civil liberties, and intelligence collection. These documents exposed a variety of surveillance programs that involved the collection of Internet usage data, metadata, account access to users of Google, Yahoo, and other major corporations, and numerous other forms of data. Most controversial from a domestic perspective were the accusations that the US government was inappropriately collecting communications metadata on US citizens. The technical nature of the material, and the fact that context was sometimes lacking from the released material, resulted in long-running disputes between the government and its critics regarding what precisely these programs allowed and what they were doing. Regardless, the episode laid bare the fundamental security-versus-liberty dilemma that all democracies face, as critics highlighted the perceived invasive nature of the programs, while the government responded that the programs were both legal and effective in combating terrorist threats. The question remains: How much invasiveness is the population willing to tolerate to achieve the desired level of security?

Much of the "liberty-versus-security" discussion hinges on expectations. What is an acceptable level of violence in the United States, and what financial and what nonmonetary cost is the public willing to pay to achieve this standard? The United States suffers over 40,000 fatalities due to automobile accidents and over 15,000 murders each year; the lack of greater efforts to reduce them suggests that these numbers are "acceptable" from a public interest perspective.[31] If the goal is that the country should never again experience a fatal terrorist attack, deterrence and prevention activities would logically demand great sacrifice in terms of resources and limitations on personal freedom. If the country is, instead, willing to live with low levels of terrorist violence and infrequent major attacks, the calculus changes significantly. Leaders thus face the difficult task of gauging the public's demand for security and its willingness to bear costs to achieve it. They must develop policies and allocate resources in accordance with this demand and attempt to ensure that public expectations are aligned with the realities of risk management. The apparent discrepancy between messages that seem to accept that "a future attack is inevitable," but that "we do not need to make radical changes to our daily lives" is understandable in this context. The dynamic American equilibrium between maintaining civil liberties and protecting the homeland is a permanent aspect of the political environment in which homeland security decisions are made.

The Quadrennial Homeland Security Review and Homeland Security Mission Areas

To address these and other challenges, Congress mandated that the Department of Homeland Security provide a comprehensive review of and approach to homeland security. DHS published the first *Quadrennial Homeland Security Review* (QHSR) in 2010 and conducted its second review in 2014. Unlike the *Quadrennial Defense Review*, which serves as a strategic planning document for the Department of Defense and its activities, the QHSR recognizes that much of the activity required to achieve the homeland security mission is not controlled by DHS.[32] Based on this reality, the document introduces the concept of the "homeland security enterprise," which it describes as "the Federal, State, local, tribal, territorial, nongovernmental, and private-sector entities, as well as individuals, families, and communities who share a common national interest in the safety and security of America and the American population."[33] Rather than a strategic plan for a federal department, the QHSR aims to be a strategic "framework" for the entire nation.

The QHSR acknowledges that because DHS is "a distributed system, no single entity is responsible for or directly manages all aspects of the enterprise."[34] The QHSR identified three categories of homeland security activities: those for which DHS possesses primary responsibility, such as border security and immigration; those for which DHS serves in a stewardship and coordination role while others execute, such as protection of critical infrastructure; and those for which other federal departments have lead responsibility, such as counterterrorism and defense. This third category once again highlights the difficult and unusual position of DHS: that is, the category over which it exerts the least control and influence is the one most directly tied to its highest priority under the Homeland Security Act of 2002: preventing acts of terrorism.

The QHSR addressed the definitional challenge by departing from the terrorism-focused definitions of homeland security used in the *National Strategy for Homeland Security* of both 2002 and 2007. The QHSR defines homeland security instead as "a concerted national effort to ensure a homeland that is safe, secure, and resilient against terrorism and other hazards where American interests, aspirations, and way of life can thrive."[35] This definition migrates from the terrorism-only definition to the all-hazards definition. In addition to the more traditional hazards of terrorism and natural disasters, it goes further to invoke the protection of American interests, aspirations, and way of life. The document identifies, as threats to these interests, economic instability, fossil-fuel dependence, global climate change, and other nations' failure to abide by international norms. More than any previous homeland security strategic document, the QHSR approached the "meta-hazards" definition articulated in the beginning of this chapter. The second QHSR, published in 2014, reaffirmed the 2010 definition.

One of the primary requirements set by Congress for the QHSR is that it outline the full range of critical homeland security mission areas for the country. The 2010 QHSR identified five missions, which were reaffirmed in the 2014 QHSR with minor edits to some of the component goals. These five missions are to prevent terrorism and enhance security; secure and manage US borders; enforce and administer US immigration laws; safeguard and secure cyberspace; and strengthen national preparedness and resilience.[36]

Prevent Terrorism and Enhance Security. This mission identifies three goals: first, prevent terrorist attacks by means of analyzing and sharing terrorism information, deterring and disrupting operations, strengthening transportation security, and countering violent extremism; second, prevent and protect against the acquisition or use of chemical, biological, radiological, or nuclear (CBRN) materials by anticipating such threats, identifying movement of such materials, and detecting and preventing CBRN use; and third, reduce the risk to the nation's critical infrastructure, key leadership, and events by enhancing security and protecting such assets. This is the most expansive of the five missions and probably the most challenging to coordinate due to the sheer number of entities involved, from the intelligence community and law enforcement entities that investigate terrorist threats to technical efforts to detect CBRN activity.

Secure and Manage US Borders. The goals identified for the border security mission are to secure US air, land, and sea borders to prevent illegal import, export, entry and exit; to safeguard and expedite lawful trade and travel by securing key nodes and pathways, managing risk, and ensuring compliance with US trade laws; and to disrupt and dismantle transnational criminal organizations by identifying and investigating such groups and disrupting their illicit pathways. Border security is seen as a key component of homeland security, even under the narrowest visions of the department's mission. While border security is an essential component of counterterrorism, the vast majority of this kind of DHS activity has little to do with terrorism. DHS staff involved in border security often see defense against terrorism as a distraction from their more pressing daily concerns of processing legal entry and exit, ensuring safety, identifying dangerous or illegal goods, and disrupting routine criminal activity. DHS employees are significantly challenged to identify possible terror threats while ensuring that their efforts in that area do not interfere with the efficient movement of legal people and goods.

Enforce and Administer US Immigration Laws. Similar to the border security mission, the immigration mission strives to strike a balance between combating illegal activity and ensuring that legal processes are effective and efficient. The goals are to strengthen and administer the immigration system via promoting lawful immigration, improving efficiency, and facilitating the integration of immigrants into American society; and to prevent unlawful immigration by preventing illegal entry, strengthening enforcement (including interior enforcement), reducing factors that drive unlawful immigration, and detaining or removing certain individuals identified as threats. As with border security, most challenges in this area have little to do with homeland security in the narrow terrorism-focused sense;

instead, they arise from broader political, social, and economic issues surrounding immigration policy.

Safeguard and Secure Cyberspace. Since 9/11, cyberspace has expanded to become a top priority for intelligence, law enforcement, and homeland security communities. Homeland security goals include strengthening the security and resilience of critical infrastructure; securing federal civilian cyber networks; advancing law enforcement reporting capabilities; and strengthening the overall cyber "ecosystem." The mission includes a broad effort to drive innovation, enhance security procedures, develop skilled cyber professionals, and boost public awareness.

Strengthen National Preparedness and Resilience. The "resilience" mission addresses the traditional elements of emergency management, including national preparedness, mitigation of hazards and vulnerabilities, emergency response, and recovery. The Obama administration introduced a focus on the concept of resilience, adopting this term for the QHSR and other strategic and structural changes. Based on the assumption that major accidents, disasters, and attacks will occur despite the best prevention and protection efforts, the focus is on building "the capacity of American society to be resilient in the face of disruptions, disasters, and other crises."[37] Hard lessons were learned from disasters like Hurricane Katrina and ongoing terrorist threats. While certain elements of the government had spent many years working on improving disaster response capabilities, the nation as a whole did not fully grasp the risks it faced, was not prepared to manage itself effectively in a crisis, could not withstand the disruptions disasters cause, and was not capable of recovering rapidly. The shift to resilience as the core operating principle required a corresponding shift away from reliance on top-down emergency management and instead toward engagement with stakeholders at all levels of government, the private sector, and even individuals and families.[38] Showing a continued commitment to this concept, the 2014 QHSR introduced the "Whole Community" approach, which focuses on understanding and meeting the needs of a community, engaging and empowering the local community, and strengthening what works well, which may vary from one place to another.[39]

The Military's Role in Homeland Security

The Department of Defense (DoD) has a long history of maintaining critical responsibilities and interests in almost all homeland security scenarios. Since the days of colonial militias, American military forces have played a prominent, continuous role in securing the homeland against state and non-state threats and in providing internal order when required. In addition to more "traditional" roles, such as fighting in the War of 1812 and the Civil War, conquering indigenous peoples, and providing coastal defense, military forces have been employed in the homeland to suppress rebellions and riots, explore the American West, put down strikes, enforce school desegregation, and respond to the full gamut of natural and manmade disasters. Despite American unease with using military forces, and especially regular forces in a domestic role, their manpower, resources, planning capability, and surge capacity ensure that they will always be considered an option when nonmilitary security and relief organizations appear inadequate.[40]

NORTHCOM. The national reaction to the 9/11 attacks led to a more focused debate on the desired role of the military in the homeland. This, in turn, led to rapid organizational change within DoD. In October 2002, the Pentagon created the US Northern Command (NORTHCOM), a combatant command with responsibility for a geographic area that includes the United States, Canada, Mexico, the Gulf of Mexico, and portions of the Atlantic and Pacific Oceans. NORTHCOM is charged with deterring, preventing, and defeating threats to US territory and US interests within this area and with providing assistance to other federal agencies as well as state and local governments (table 6.1). DoD identifies these missions as defending US territory from direct attack by state and non-state actors and defense support of civil authorities to distinguish the military's role from homeland security (while recognizing that there are significant overlaps between homeland defense and homeland security, which is within the purview of DHS).[41]

NORTHCOM conducts many of its homeland defense missions in close coordination with North American Aerospace Defense Command (NORAD), the

Table 6.1 Department of Defense Homeland Defense Missions, Objectives, and Capabilities

Missions	*Objectives*	*Core capabilities*
1. Defend US territory from direct attack by state and nonstate actors	**a. Counter air and maritime threats at a safe distance**	• Persistent air and maritime domain awareness • Capable, responsive air defense forces • Capable, responsive maritime forces
	b. Prevent terrorist attacks on the homeland through support to law enforcement	• Rapid and actionable intelligence on terrorist threats • Capabilities to counter IEDs • Capabilities to prevent terrorists' use of WMD in the homeland • Rapid acquisition, analysis, and dissemination of threat information • Programs to counter insider threats • Dual-effect military training
2. Provide Defense Support of Civil Authorities (DSCA)	**a. Maintain Defense preparedness for domestic CBRN**	• Postured, rapidly deployable CBRN response forces
	b. Develop plans and procedures to ensure DSCA during complex catastrophes	• Immediate response authority • Geographically proximate force sourcing • Ready access to non–National Guard Reserve forces

Source: Strategy for Homeland Defense and Defense Support of Civil Authorities, Department of Defense, February 2013

US-Canadian organization responsible for aerospace warning and aerospace control for North America. Indeed the NORTHCOM commander is "dual-hatted" as the commander of NORAD, having a Canadian deputy commander of NORAD. Other NORTHCOM responsibilities related to homeland defense include the designation of quick-reaction land forces to respond to threats; enhancing awareness of potential maritime threats through better information sharing; preparation to fire ground-based interceptors as part of the emerging ballistic missile defense system; and deployment of an integrated air defense system for the Washington, DC, area. NORTHCOM's civil support tasks have included providing security for high-profile national events such as presidential inaugurations, national political conventions, and the Super Bowl; supporting the National Interagency Fire Center in fighting wildfires; and providing detection and monitoring assistance to federal agencies interdicting drugs and other illicit traffic across US borders. Forces that may be necessary for NORTHCOM operations, both those permanently assigned as well as those assigned to it for specific missions, are kept at various stages of alert based on intelligence about potential threats.

Considerations Affecting Domestic Use of the Armed Forces. Refining the capability to conduct effective military operations in and near the homeland is part of a broader strategy of creating a layered defense of the United States. Ideally, the United States would seek to engage threats abroad, before they reach the homeland, but it may not be possible to detect or defeat all threats outside US territory, and some threats may not be apparent until an attack is imminent. In such cases, an appropriate response may require action by law enforcement organizations, DHS, the military, or a combination of these entities. When the employment of military forces is deemed necessary, their operating in the United States homeland presents several challenges, including legal and policy restrictions, interagency cooperation, and the need for unique capabilities.

Legal and Policy Restrictions. There are significant legal and policy restrictions on the domestic use of military forces, which are derived from historically based concerns that the US Army should not be used against US citizens. One prominent restriction arises from the Posse Comitatus Act of 1878, as amended: "Whoever, except in cases and under circumstances expressly authorized by the Constitution or Act of Congress, willfully uses any part of the Army or Air Force as a posse comitatus or otherwise to execute the laws shall be fined under this title or imprisoned not more than two years, or both."[42] Originally intended to prevent local sheriffs and US marshals from using federal troops to enforce the law in the post–Civil War South, the Posse Comitatus Act restricts use of active-duty military forces in a law enforcement capacity. There are important exceptions, however. Most notably, Congress long ago authorized the president, through the Insurrection Act of 1807, to use federal troops to restore public order in cases of "insurrection, domestic violence, unlawful combination, or conspiracy." Federal troops have more recently been authorized by law to assist civil authorities in some counterdrug operations and in the event of disasters involving weapons of mass destruction.

There are also legal and policy restrictions on the use of military assets for domestic intelligence collection or the retention of information on US persons. In general, domestic military intelligence activities are limited to analysis of information gathered by other sources to anticipate potential homeland defense threats. Even for actions unrelated to intelligence, government policy limits the ability of military commanders to employ forces domestically. Systems for authorizing movement of forces and engagement with threats in the US homeland generally are closely coordinated by NORTHCOM and the Pentagon. For civil support operations such as disaster relief, for example, authorization by the president or the secretary of defense is required before federal forces may act.

Interagency Cooperation. A second challenge for military operations in the homeland is that, to a much greater degree than for actions abroad, federal forces are unlikely to operate alone. Domestic missions will inevitably involve many other federal, state, and local organizations, and the military does not have lead responsibility in most cases. The Department of Homeland Security and law enforcement agencies are frequent partners; the National Guard is likely to be involved in any major domestic operation. In responding to emergencies or providing security for designated events, the National Guard generally acts under the control of state governors, in either State Active Duty or Title 32 status. State Active Duty is the authority under which governors may activate and deploy National Guard forces for state purposes and at state expense, usually in response to floods, earthquakes, wildfires, and other natural disasters, but also for manmade events such as riots, civil unrest, or terrorist attacks.[43] Under the authority of Title 32 (of the US Code), National Guard forces can be activated "in the service of the United States" for a primary federal purpose, but they remain under state command and control. For example, after 9/11, National Guard forces were deployed to airports at federal expense to assure airport security and compliance with federal aviation laws.[44] The federal government may mobilize and deploy National Guard forces under Title 10 for national defense purposes at home or around the world.[45] Such forces are said to be "federalized," as they are under the command and control of the president and the federal government, not the state. National Guard forces deployed to Iraq, Afghanistan, or other overseas contingencies have been activated under Title 10, as are Guard forces that have been deployed to the Canadian and Mexican borders to augment federal law enforcement agencies.

One advantage of State Active Duty or Title 32 status is that National Guard forces retain law enforcement authority when they are not federalized: Posse Comitatus Act restrictions apply only to federal (Title 10) forces. (Guard forces deployed to the border under Title 10 do not violate Posse Comitatus, however, because they only provide support to law enforcement officers and do not themselves enforce laws.) From the state's perspective, Title 32 is appealing because the federal government funds the operations while the governor commands the forces.

The fundamentally interconnected nature of homeland defense and civil support operations places a premium on effective interagency cooperation, but this is often difficult to achieve. Separate chains of command for state and federal forces, for example, make "unity of effort" more difficult. Realistic exercises involving all major players, the extensive use of liaisons, and frequent communication between military and civilian organizations can strengthen cooperation in deterring, preventing, defeating, or mitigating the effects of attacks and disasters.

The Need for Unique Capabilities. A third challenge is that the types of military operations likely to be needed in the homeland call for a somewhat different set of capabilities than combat operations abroad. If detected in time, the most likely terrorist threats could be defeated without placing a large strain on military capabilities. However, any use of military force for homeland defense would have to consider significant political sensitivities. Civilian casualties, abhorrent in any circumstance, are especially problematic for military operations in defense of the homeland.

Homeland defense operations are also likely to be extremely time sensitive. If threats are not detected until an attack is imminent or ongoing, an effective response capability would require that trained and ready forces are always on high alert. Military forces must be prepared and equipped to assist with a variety of consequence-management scenarios on US soil. If an attack with a weapon of mass destruction took place, elements of the US armed forces would undoubtedly be called on to help mitigate its effects. The types of military capabilities that might be required in the homeland include precision engagement, rapid response capacity, enhanced detection and tracking systems, and the ability to respond to chemical, biological, radiological, and nuclear attacks or disasters. These require the dedication of substantial resources, including organizations, personnel, funding, equipment, training, and other assets.

Case Study: Hurricane Katrina and Hurricane Sandy

The responses to Hurricane Katrina in 2006 and to Hurricane Sandy in 2012 provide a useful comparative illustration of the challenges of homeland security planning and execution and the extent to which the federal response described in this chapter has evolved.

Hurricane Katrina ravaged the city of New Orleans as well as large swaths of the Mississippi and Alabama coast on and after August 29, 2005. It was the costliest natural disaster in US history, resulting in well over $100 billion in property damage. Approximately 300,000 homes were destroyed or severely damaged. The hurricane caused over 1,200 deaths and displaced approximately 770,000 people. The disaster occurred when many reforms had recently been made: the Department of Homeland Security had been created; the National Incident Management System and National Response Plan were published in 2004; and NORTHCOM had been created to plan and execute military civil-support operations. Nevertheless, the government response to Katrina was widely criticized for ineffectiveness and inadequacy.

One key difficulty stemmed from the timing and sources of relief requests. Reflecting the US federal system, the National Response Plan had established a *bottom up* or *pull* model for disaster response. By design, local and state leaders request federal assistance when they deem their resources exhausted or overwhelmed. Federal assistance is provided through emergency support functions such as transportation, communications, and urban search and rescue, each led by the appropriate federal agency and coordinated by interagency centers at the local through the national level. Agencies request support from other federal organizations, including the Department of Defense, as required to implement their emergency support functions. A response system that relies on requests from local, state, and federal organizations requires that these requests be accurate and timely in order for the system to operate effectively and efficiently.

In the case of Katrina, the magnitude of the initial damage, and especially the flooding resulting from levee breaks in New Orleans, prevented a rapid, comprehensive assessment of needs. Breakdowns in the communication and power infrastructure exacerbated this problem. Thus, state and local government did not make timely requests for assistance. As a result, there were delays in relief reaching the affected areas, which led to additional suffering and increased civil disorder. There was a multi-day gap between the presidential disaster declaration for Louisiana on August 29 and the state's specific formal requests for federal assistance. Significant relief for the approximately 19,000 people who had sought shelter at the Morial Convention Center did not begin until September 2, days after Katrina struck New Orleans. Another reason for the delays was that the Federal Emergency Management Agency (FEMA), overwhelmed by the massive scale of Katrina, was unable to deploy adequate command and control capability or basic supplies such as food, water, and ice in a timely manner. According to most assessments, whether the lack was in staffing, planning, or leadership, FEMA was simply not up to the task of quickly coordinating the enormous relief effort.

As is normal for any large disaster, the military was called upon due to its comparative advantage in deployable manpower and large-scale logistical capability. More than 20,000 active troops and 50,000 National Guard troops became involved in the operation, primarily in Louisiana and Mississippi. They performed search and rescue missions in coordination with the US Coast Guard, provided medical care, established air traffic control for the area, and moved and distributed humanitarian relief supplies. Despite the magnitude of this effort, the speed and coordination of the military response were also criticized. Joint Task Force Katrina was activated on August 31, two days after the hurricane's landfall. Military leaders worked to "lean forward" by positioning supplies and equipment in the area without specific requests. However, many active-duty ground troops did not reach New Orleans until September 6. Just as some of the FEMA delay was due to the lack of clear requests from the affected states, a large part of the delay in employing military assets can be attributed to the absence of clear requests for assistance from FEMA.

The military response was also marked by inadequate coordination between active-duty federal forces and the National Guard, the latter operating under control of the state governors (in State Active Duty and later Title 32 status). There was only an ill-defined relationship of "coordination" between commanders of active-duty forces and the State Adjutant General, who commanded National Guard troops; nothing mandated how these distinct chains of command were to exchange information. Given the complexity and rush of the initial response, the efforts of active and National Guard troops were not always complementary. For example, search and rescue teams from both components reportedly sometimes went to the same locations, while elsewhere other citizens were left waiting for rescue. Lower-level leaders often did not have a clear picture of what other units were near them and what missions those others were performing. Separate chains of command create a coordination challenge, especially in a crisis situation, and coordination challenges are exacerbated if the ultimate commanders of the components—the president for Title 10 forces and the governors for Title 32 forces—do not agree on priorities for military action. Despite these difficulties, maintaining separate chains of command has advantages. Members of the National Guards in a Title 32 status retain some law enforcement authority, and the governor retains the ability to direct his or her state's troops, which may be politically important.

Katrina's Lessons Applied after Hurricane Sandy. After Hurricane Katrina, after-action reviews were conducted by groups and agencies at all levels of government. Decisions were made, legislation was passed, and reforms enacted to address deficiencies found in these evaluations. For example, the Post-Katrina Emergency Management Reform Act (PKEMRA) of 2006 strengthened FEMA's position within DHS, provided the FEMA administrator with a direct reporting relationship, under some circumstances, to the White House, and integrated preparedness activities into FEMA's existing response functions.[46] Under the National Response Framework of 2008, a revision of the National Response Plan, leaders in the homeland security enterprise could take the initiative in a crisis situation, rather than awaiting requests from state and local officials.[47] These reforms were tested when the nation encountered a real-world scenario that approached the scope and severity of Hurricane Katrina: the landfall of Hurricane Sandy on the East Coast of the United States in October 2012.[48] At the time, Hurricane Sandy was the second costliest storm in US history, causing $75 billion in damage, damaging or destroying nearly 400,000 homes, and killing over 125 people.

To remedy one of the core deficiencies found in the response to Katrina, many of the reforms had focused on ensuring a more proactive approach to disaster response. Thus, prior to Hurricane Sandy's landfall, FEMA worked closely with partners across the community to prepare for the storm, pre-positioning assets and deploying over nine hundred FEMA personnel. This proactive approach was championed by the White House, and President Obama directed all federal departments to "lean forward" and to minimize red tape. He also issued emergency declarations in advance of the landfall in eleven states to facilitate more rapid federal assistance.[49] Other key improvements enhanced FEMA ability to meet survivor needs through on-the-ground innovation and improved integration of response efforts with nongovernmental partners.[50] *The Hurricane Sandy FEMA After-Action*

Report concluded that, "the Sandy experience demonstrated significant progress achieved in recent years, but also confirmed that larger-scale incidents will stress the Agency's capacity for effective response and recovery."[51]

The military also endeavored to learn lessons from Hurricane Katrina, and it enacted reforms to improve future disaster response efforts. A key failure in 2005 had been the lack of coordination between active-duty forces and the National Guard. This led to the creation of the "dual-status commander": states and the Department of Defense can identify a single commander for an incident, usually a National Guard officer, to be given tactical control of both National Guard forces (State Active Duty and Title 32) and active-duty federal forces (Title 10). While this model had already been used in some previous smaller-scale events, Hurricane Sandy marked the first time a dual-status commander was used for a major multistate disaster.[52] Although some challenges remained, this setup mitigated the coordination problem.

The homeland security issues raised by Hurricane Katrina and Hurricane Sandy will continue to spur debate, especially given the federal nature of the United States. Assigning responsibility for disaster preparedness and response in a federal system, allocating resources, and defining the desired role of active-duty and state military forces will continue to be subject to on-going risk management and political considerations that influence all homeland security efforts.

Enduring Considerations

The specific issues and threats at the top of the homeland security agenda will vary over time, but the fundamental factors that make protecting the homeland such a difficult task will persist. First, vulnerabilities will always exceed homeland security capability in a free society. The number of potential targets in the United States and the amount of traffic entering the country by land, sea, and air make it impossible to defend the entirety of the homeland against every potential threat. Second, even in a political vacuum, risk management processes would be hard to apply in making homeland security choices. Even if threats, vulnerabilities, and consequences could be agreed upon, which is no easy task, resources could still be allocated in different ways, emphasizing different functions (deter, prevent, defeat, or mitigate the effects of attacks and disasters), different locations (the homeland, approaches to the homeland, or abroad), and different jurisdictions (local, state, federal, or international). There is considerable room for reasonable people to disagree on risk mitigation strategies. Third, political leaders making homeland security choices will often favor their constituencies rather than take a national perspective. Decisions on homeland security grants and other homeland security actions are subject to the same considerations of distributional politics that accompany all federal, state, and local governmental spending decisions. Fourth, homeland security requires action by a huge number of public and private organizations, each of which has its own organizational interests. The country's federal system of government ensures that preparation for and response to attacks and disasters inevitably involves many players at the local, state, and federal levels. Even if they agree in general terms on a common goal, effective cooperation among large bureaucratic organizations is difficult to achieve. Concerns over guarding autonomy, reducing uncertainty, and allocation of resources play a powerful role in shaping organizational behavior. Fifth, the optimal balance between securing the homeland and safeguarding civil liberties will remain contentious. Shifts in both directions will continue to occur, influenced by the level of threat the American public perceives and the amount of security it demands. Each shift will be hotly debated. In a democratic state, founded upon individual freedoms and confronted by new threats and challenges, this dynamic is both inevitable and appropriate. Finally, the military will always have a role within the homeland, and the country is likely to remain uneasy with its role. Unless resources spent on homeland security are radically increased, some problems—such as major natural disasters or attacks with nuclear, biological, chemical, or radiological weapons—will require capabilities possessed only by the US armed forces. Traditional US unease will persist, and any major action is likely to renew debates about the military's proper role.

These considerations define the environment in which homeland security choices are made and will be influenced by political and partisan dynamics. The security of the homeland is a fundamental and increasingly important responsibility of the federal government, which will continue to require thoughtful and careful planning, coordination, and execution to ensure that the United States is prepared to meet a wide variety of threats.

Discussion Questions

1. What factors determine the level of loss to terrorist attacks or natural disasters that is acceptable to the American people, and how have these factors changed over time?
2. How is the level of risk that is deemed acceptable affected by the US public's willingness to accept tradeoffs between liberty and security?
3. What principles should guide decisions about allocation of scarce resources for homeland security? Which functions (deter, prevent, defeat, mitigate), types of threat, and locations (local, state, federal) should be favored? Why?
4. What are the most significant challenges to the application of a rational risk management process to homeland security choices, and how can they best be addressed?
5. What lessons from the post-9/11 reorganization of government should guide similar reorganizations in the future?
6. Do law enforcement and intelligence agencies have adequate tools to counter threats to the homeland? How should their powers be limited to protect civil liberties?
7. In the realm of national security, why might decisions about homeland security be more likely to be influenced by domestic political considerations than foreign policy?
8. How much should response to disasters in the National Response Framework be a *pull* system based on request and how much should be *pushed* from the federal government? What determines this ratio?
9. What role should the US military—both active and Reserve Component forces, including the National Guard—play in homeland security? Should the military be given a more significant role following catastrophic incidents? Why, or why not?

10. How might recent experience in natural disaster relief affect the effectiveness and efficiency of national, state, and local responders in the wake of a domestic terrorist attack?

Recommended Reading

Department of Defense (DoD). *Strategy for Homeland Defense and Defense Support of Civil Authorities*. Washington, DC: DoD, February 2013.

Department of Homeland Security (DHS). *National Response Framework*. 2nd ed. Washington, DC: DHS, May 2013.

Howard, Russell D., James J. Forest, and Joanne C. Moore. *Homeland Security and Terrorism: Readings and Interpretations*. New York: McGraw-Hill, 2006.

Kettl, Donald F. *System under Stress: The Challenge to 21st Century Governance*. 3rd ed. Washington, DC: CQ Press, 2014.

Lewis, Ted G. *Critical Infrastructure Protection in Homeland Security: Defending a Networked Nation*. 2nd ed. Hoboken, NJ: John Wiley & Sons, 2015.

Martin, Gus. *Understanding Homeland Security*. Los Angeles: Sage, 2015.

Maxwell, Bruce. *Homeland Security: A Documentary History*. Washington, DC: CQ Press, 2004.

McGrane, Sean. "Katrina, Federalism, and Military Law Enforcement: A New Exception to the Posse Comitatus Act." *Michigan Law Review* 108, no. 7 (2010): 1309–40.

National Commission on Terrorist Attacks upon the United States. *The 9/11 Commission Report*. Washington, DC: US Government Printing Office, 2004.

Nicholson, William C., ed. *Homeland Security Law and Policy*. Springfield, IL: Charles C. Thomas, 2005.

Sauter, Mark A., and James J. Carafano. *Homeland Security: A Complete Guide to Understanding, Preventing, and Surviving Terrorism*. New York: McGraw-Hill, 2005.

White, Jonathan R. *Terrorism and Homeland Security*. Belmont, CA: Wadsworth, 2012.

Willis, Henry H., et al. *Estimating Terrorism Risk*. Santa Monica, CA: RAND Corporation, 2005.

Recommended Internet Resources

US Department of Homeland Security, www.dhs.gov

US Government Accountability Office (GAO), Homeland Security Reports, www.gao.gov/docsearch/featured/homelandsecurity.html

US Northern Command, www.northcom.mil

Notes

1. The United States Constitution, 1787.

2. Using *homeland security* in this context was a departure from the term more commonly used at the time, *homeland defense*. The official rationale was that homeland security was a broader term that encompassed more activities, including national defense, national preparedness, and intelligence and law enforcement activities. Some suggested at the time that this term was, in fact, selected so as to avoid any jurisdictional confusion between the Department of Defense and the new White House office. See William Safire, "The Way We Live Now: On Language: Homeland," *New York Times*, January 20, 2002.

3. These categories are drawn from the seven definitions of homeland security identified and described in Christopher Bellavita, "Changing Homeland Security: What Is Homeland Security?" *Homeland Security Affairs* 4, no. 2 (2008), http://hdl.handle.net/10945/25115.

4. The meta-hazards category is not as commonly cited as the other three, but elements of it repeatedly surface in various forums and even national policy documents.

5. Mark A. Sauter and James J. Carafano, *Homeland Security: A Complete Guide to Understanding, Preventing, and Surviving Terrorism* (New York: McGraw-Hill, 2005), 3–19, gives a brief overview of the history of US homeland security efforts.

6. United States Commission on National Security/21st Century, "New World Coming: American Security in the 21st Century" (September 1999), "Seeking a National Strategy: A Concept for Preserving Security and Promoting Freedom" (April 2000), and "Road Map for National Security: Imperative for Change" (February 2001); Advisory Panel to Assess Domestic Response Capabilities for Terrorism Involving Weapons of Mass Destruction, "Assessing the Threat" (December 1999), and "Toward a National Strategy for Combating Terrorism" (December 2000).

7. *The National Strategy for Homeland Security*, Office of Homeland Security, July 2002.

8. These deficiencies were not addressed until the December 2004 Intelligence Reform and Terrorism Prevention Act.

9. Donald F. Kettl, *System under Stress: The Challenge to 21st Century Governance*, 3rd ed. (Los Angeles: CQ Press, 2014), 51.

10. The focus on terrorism certainly had an impact on agencies' ability to abide by the Homeland Security Act's requirement that all preexisting activities not be diminished or neglected. For example, the Coast Guard spent 60 percent less time on drug interdiction in 2002 than it had in 1998. See Kettl, *System under Stress*, 51–52.

11. Michael Chertoff, Secretary of Homeland Security from 2005 to 2009, pointed out that it took the Department of Defense forty years to overcome its own growing pains and internal rivalries. While true, this of course does not mean that it is acceptable for DHS to take another twenty years to resolve its remaining issues. Paul C. Light, "The Homeland Security Hash," *Wilson Quarterly* 31 (Spring 2007): 38.

12. For an example of the debate over Patriot Act provisions, see Alice Fisher, "The PATRIOT Act Has Helped Prevent Terrorist Attacks," and Nancy Chang, "The PATRIOT Act Has Undermined Civil Liberties," both in *Homeland Security*, ed. James D. Torr (San Diego, CA: Greenhaven Press, 2004), 34–42 and 43–53.

13. The USA FREEDOM Act, June 2, 2015, https://www.congress.gov/bill/114th-congress/house-bill/2048.

14. Kettl, *System under Stress*, 57.

15. National Commission on Terrorist Attacks upon the United States, *The 9/11 Commission Report* (Washington, DC: US Government Printing Office, 2004).

16. Kettl, *System under Stress*, 50.

17. Cindy Williams, "Strengthening Homeland Security: Reforming Planning and Resource Allocation," 2008 Presidential Transition Series (Washington, DC: IBM Center for the Business of Government, 2008), 6; and James Carafano, "What Comes after Quadrennial Homeland Security Review?" testimony before the House Committee on Homeland Security, April 29, 2010.

18. Federal Bureau of Investigation (FBI), "Joint Terrorism Task Forces," n.d., https://www.fbi.gov/investigate/terrorism/joint-terrorism-task-forces.

19. "National Network of Fusion Centers Fact Sheet," August 21, 2015, http://www.dhs.gov/national-network-fusion-centers-fact-sheet.

20. Henry H. Willis et al., *Estimating Terrorism Risk* (Santa Monica, CA: RAND, 2005). The same logic is applicable to assessing risk from natural disasters.

21. See Government Accountability Office (GAO), "Review of Studies of the Economic Impact of the September 11, 2001, Terrorist Attacks on the World Trade Center," GAO-02-700R (Washington, DC: GAO, May 2002).

22. John Mueller and Mark G. Stewart, "Balancing the Risks, Benefits, and Costs of Homeland Security," *Homeland Security Affairs* 7, no. 16 (2011), https://www.hsaj.org/articles/43.

23. Ted Lewis and Rudy Darken, "Potholes and Detours in the Road to Critical Infrastructure Protection Policy," *Homeland Security Affairs Journal* 1, no. 2 (2005), https://www.hsaj.org/articles/177.

24. On collective action problems and "public goods" like homeland security, see Mancur Olson, *The Logic of Collective Action: Public Goods and the Theory of Groups* (Cambridge, CA: Harvard University Press, 1965). Olson argues that in most cases, groups of "rational, self-interested individuals will not act to achieve their common or group interests."

25. Michael Chertoff, *Homeland Security: Assessing the First Five Years* (Philadelphia: University of Pennsylvania Press, 2009), 68–79.

26. Information on grant programs from Peter Eisinger, "Imperfect Federalism: The Intergovernmental Partnership for Homeland Security," *Public Administration Review* 66, no. 4 (2006): 537–45.

27. Office of Senator Tom Coburn, "Safety at Any Price: Assessing the Impact of Homeland Security Spending in U.S. Cities," December 2012, https://www.hsdl.org/?view&did=726637.

28. Stephen Flynn, *America the Vulnerable: How Our Government Is Failing to Protect Us from Terrorism* (New York: HarperCollins, 2004).

29. Lewis and Darken, "Potholes and Detours"; Chertoff, *Homeland Security*, chap. 7.

30. Samuel P. Huntington, "American Ideals versus American Institutions," in *American Foreign Policy: Theoretical Essays*, ed. G. John Ikenberry, 2nd ed. (New York: HarperCollins College Publishers, 1996), 251–83. Huntington focuses on foreign policy institutions, but his discussion is applicable to homeland security as well.

31. Neal E. Boudette, "U.S. Traffic Deaths Rise for a Second Straight Year," *New York Times*, February 15, 2017, https://www.nytimes.com/2017/02/15/business/highway-traffic-safety.html?mcubz=0; FBI, "Latest Crime Statistics Released: Increase in Violent Crime, Decrease in Property Crime," September 26, 2016, https://www.fbi.gov/news/stories/latest-crime-statistics-released.

32. The Office of Management and Budget (OMB) estimates that the Department of Homeland Security (DHS) receives approximately 52 percent of annual homeland security funding. Thirty federal entities apart from DHS receive the other 48 percent of annual homeland security funding. The Department of Defense (DoD) receives approximately 26 percent of total federal homeland security funding. From Shawn Reese, "Defining Homeland Security: Analysis and Congressional Considerations," Congressional Research Service, January 8, 2013.

33. DHS, *Quadrennial Homeland Security Review Report: A Strategic Framework for a Secure Homeland* (Washington, DC: US Department of Homeland Security, February 2010), iii.

34. DHS, *Quadrennial Homeland Security Review*, 2010, 13.

35. DHS, *Quadrennial Homeland Security Review*, 2010, 13.

36. The missions and goals are articulated in the DHS 2014 *Quadrennial Homeland Security Review* (Washington, DC: US Department of Homeland Security, June 2014).

37. DHS, *Quadrennial Homeland Security Review*, 2010, 31.

38. DHS, *Quadrennial Homeland Security Review Report*, 2010, 31.

39. DHS, *Quadrennial Homeland Security Review*, 2014.

40. On concerns over broadening the military's domestic role, see Richard H. Kohn, "Using the Military at Home: Yesterday, Today, and Tomorrow," *Chicago Journal of International Law* 4, no. 1 (2003): 165–92.

41. Homeland defense is defined by the Department of Defense, *Strategy for Homeland Defense and Civil Support* (Washington, DC: US Department of Defense, June 2005) as "the protection of U.S. sovereignty, territory, domestic population, and critical defense infrastructure against external threats and aggression or other threats as directed by the President." This definition includes some overlap with homeland security, and the difference is not always distinct. For example, the case of interdicting a terrorist-operated ship intending to attack a port could be seen as both preventing a terrorist attack (homeland security) and protecting US territory and people against external threats and aggression (homeland defense). From a policy perspective, the critical challenge is determining whether the military or another agency (such as the Coast Guard, which is part of the Department of Homeland Security) will have the lead responsibility for particular types of actions in order to facilitate effective planning.

42. The Posse Comitatus Act is interpreted by Department of Defense policy to apply to the Department of the Navy (which includes the US Marine Corps) as well. No one has ever been prosecuted under the Posse Comitatus Act, but it figures in debates and decision making on these issues. On the history of the act and common misinterpretations, see John R. Brinkerhoff, "The Posse Comitatus Act and Homeland Security," *Journal of Homeland Security* 7 (February 2002), http://www.homelandsecurity.org/newjournal/articles/brinkerhoffpossecomitatus.htm.

43. Major General Timothy J. Lowenberg, "The Role of the National Guard in National Defense and Homeland Security," *National Guard* 59, no. 9 (2005): 97.

44. Lowenberg, "The Role of the National Guard."

45. Lowenberg, "The Role of the National Guard."

46. Daniel J. Kaniewski, "PKEMRA Implementation: An Examination of FEMA's Preparedness and Response Mission," statement by before the US House of Representatives Committee on Homeland Security, March 17, 2009.

47. FEMA, *National Response Framework*, January 2008, https://www.fema.gov/pdf/emergency/nrf/nrf-core.pdf.

48. Hurricane Sandy was a category 3 hurricane at its peak when it made landfall in Cuba. Its winds had subsided to 70 knots when it made landfall in New Jersey, just below the level at which a storm would be classified as a category 1 hurricane. Consequently, many media reports refer to the event as Superstorm Sandy. See Eric S. Blake et al., "Tropical Cyclone Report: Hurricane Sandy (AL182012), 22–29 October 2012," National Hurricane Center, http://www.nhc.noaa.gov/data/tcr/AL182012_Sandy.pdf.

49. FEMA, *Hurricane Sandy FEMA After-Action Report*, July 1, 2013, 9, https://www.fema.gov/media-library/assets/documents/33772. Although concern for US citizens was the priority, the fact that Hurricane Sandy struck ten days before a presidential election also provided a political incentive for a robust federal response.

50. FEMA, *Hurricane Sandy*, v.

51. FEMA, *Hurricane Sandy*, iii.

52. General Charles H. Jacoby and General Frank J. Grass, "Dual-Status, Single Purpose: A Unified Military Response to Hurricane Sandy," *Homeland Security Today*, March 9, 2013, https://www.hstoday.us/columns/guest-commentaries/exclusive-dual-status-single-purpose-a-unified-military-response-to-hurricane-sandy/.

7

Intelligence and National Security

In Federalist No. 75, Alexander Hamilton stated that the management of America's external relations would require "accurate and comprehensive knowledge of foreign politics."[1] John Jay declared that intelligence, managed prudently, was a useful and necessary capability for the infant republic.[2] Information about the outside world continues to be crucial to American national security policy, although the scope and methods of gathering information about other nations and actors, while protecting our own important information, have profoundly changed since America's founding. The challenges of the twenty-first century, including a complex international security environment and rapidly changing information technology, necessitate a robust and agile intelligence community.

The modern intelligence era in the United States began following the attack on Pearl Harbor with the creation of the Office of Strategic Services (OSS) in 1942. The OSS had two key responsibilities: to collect and analyze intelligence for the military and to conduct special operations not assigned to the military or other government entities. After the conclusion of World War II, the OSS was effectively dismantled as part of the military drawdown. However, the need for a lead office to manage, collect, evaluate, and disseminate foreign intelligence was recognized with the creation of the Central Intelligence Agency (CIA) in the National Security Act of 1947. That framework largely continued throughout the twentieth century, until the 2001 terrorist attacks resulted in a major post-9/11 reorganization of the US intelligence enterprise.

In more recent years, the reputation of the intelligence community has suffered because of the failure to accurately predict whether weapons of mass destruction (WMD) would be found in Iraq. As the *Final Report of the Commission on the*

Intelligence Capabilities of the United States Regarding Weapons of Mass Destruction concluded in 2005,

> On the brink of war, and in front of the whole world, the United States asserted that Saddam Hussein had reconstituted his nuclear weapons program, had biological weapons and mobile biological weapons production facilities, and had stockpiled and was producing chemical weapons. All of this was based on the assessments of the U.S. Intelligence Community. And not one bit of it could be confirmed when the war was over.[3]

The Weapons of Mass Destruction Commission, while acknowledging the difficulty of acquiring sound intelligence concerning WMD, blamed the failure on the intelligence community and its shortcomings in collection, analysis, and in the way that intelligence was provided to policy makers.[4]

Edward Snowden's 2013 leak of thousands of classified National Security Agency (NSA) documents further tarnished the reputation of the intelligence community on multiple fronts. The leak itself highlighted the NSA's inability to protect its own top secret information. Because the leaked documents revealed collection methods, other states, non-state actors, and private enterprises were able to take actions to impede US collection efforts. The substance of the leaks raised concerns about the conduct of domestic surveillance in the United States and reinvigorated debates over the balance between national security and civil liberties and privacy.

Despite these recent controversies, US intelligence remains the most technologically advanced, well-funded, and perhaps most successful intelligence operation in the world. This chapter explores the vast US intelligence apparatus and explains how members of the intelligence community and policy makers interact with one another to make national security decisions based on better and more complete information.

Information and Intelligence

Information is anything that can be known, while intelligence is a specific subset of "information relevant to a government's formulation and implementation of policy to further its national security interests and to deal with threats from actual or potential adversaries."[5] Although many associate the term primarily with military information, intelligence for the purposes of national security concerns more than armed capabilities. It may include political, economic, social, cultural, and technological information about an adversary.[6] Intelligence can be usefully categorized according to the time horizon in which it is expected to be used: strategic intelligence examines issues with long-term implications, such as political and economic trends, while tactical intelligence responds to immediate concerns to support near-term decisions about ongoing or imminent threats.[7]

Intelligence supports decision makers. Members of the intelligence community are ideally "seasoned and experienced advisors," who apply expert analysis to collected information.[8] Intelligence professionals attempt to envision what is possible or likely to occur in the future by analyzing and synthesizing current data; they provide decision makers with projections against which to measure policy alternatives. They may also develop policy options and provide an analytical basis for choosing among the options. President Barack Obama's decision to authorize Operation Neptune Spear to raid a compound suspected of being the home of al Qaeda leader Osama bin Laden in Abbottabad, Pakistan, was a direct use of intelligence. Satellites collected 387 images of the compound prior to the raid—intelligence that was "critical to prepare for the mission and [that] contributed to the decision to approve execution."[9] The success of this mission demonstrated the value of good intelligence. It is important to note that, while the best intelligence cannot guarantee sound policy, policy made with inadequate intelligence support may succeed only by accident.

The Intelligence Production Process

The work of intelligence can be understood as consisting of a five-part iterative cycle (figure 7.1) involving planning, collection, processing, analysis, and dissemination.[10] Although any specific intelligence operation may involve more complex and dynamic interactions, the conceptual clarity of the intelligence cycle is useful for understanding core intelligence functions. The five stages and the difficulties of each are discussed in turn below.

Planning. The planning stage begins when policy makers request specific information or reaffirm areas of continuing interest. Intelligence managers then review these requests, and, if ongoing efforts or existing databases are unable to satisfy them, the requests are approved as new intelligence requirements. Requirements are then tasked to agencies that have the operational capabilities necessary to collect the desired intelligence. Some of these projects are long term, requiring continuous attention, while others are discrete. Policy makers and their advisors are the key consumers of intelligence, and it is at the planning stage of the cycle that they are most active.[11]

FIGURE 7.1 The Intelligence Cycle

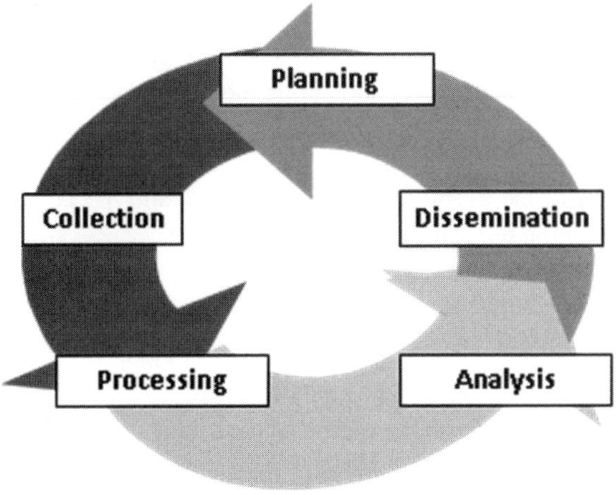

Problems in planning are usually related to unclear priorities or poor management.[12] National security policy may not be sufficiently clear with regard to needed content or priorities, thereby resulting in only vague or general guidance to intelligence planners. For example, the periodic national security strategy often contains a long list of concerns and goals but may not offer a means to figure out which problems take precedence over others. Consumers seldom articulate even their major continuing interests with a precision sufficient to inform the planning stage of the cycle adequately. As a result, intelligence managers frequently generate requirements to provide consumers with intelligence they appear to need but cannot or do not specifically request. Additionally, inadequate management, turf wars, and differing goals may cause various agencies within the intelligence community to work at cross purposes. For example, the CIA's focus on predicting future activity often leads to different needs and work than that of the Federal Bureau of Investigation (FBI), which can be more focused on criminal convictions based on past behavior. Different goals lead to different priorities, which can make it difficult to create a timely, consolidated intelligence picture.[13]

Collection. Once intelligence requirements are established, the collection stage begins. The six basic methods of collection are: open source, human intelligence, signals intelligence, imagery intelligence, measurement and signature intelligence, and geospatial intelligence.[14] All methods have value; the use of multiple methods facilitates the crosschecking of data, and each method has unique capabilities that can offset the limitations of the others.

Open Source Intelligence (OSINT). Open source intelligence is derived from print and broadcast news, academic studies, popular literature, the Internet, and other freely available media. Advances in information technology, the Internet, and other resources have resulted in an "explosion of information"; the challenge is now less one of scarcity of information than one of overabundance.[15] The difficulty is often to discern relevant information within the volumes of data that exist online and elsewhere.

Substantial intelligence increasingly comes from open source material. Terrorists, for example, use the Internet and public media to pass private messages or to incite others to act.[16] Because of the increasing use of social media platforms, open source information is essential for understanding the ideology and strategic plans of terrorist groups such as the Islamic State in Iraq and the Levant (ISIL) and al Qaeda.[17] Examination of social media allows intelligence operatives to learn about recruitment techniques, tactics, and events in real time on popular web sites such as YouTube, Twitter, and Facebook.

Human Intelligence (HUMINT). Human intelligence is information from a human source derived via overt or covert means and is usually collected by a government official or intelligence agent.[18] While some sources are friendly—such as "walk-ins" or refugees—others, such as detainees or prisoners of war, may be hostile. Although crucial, HUMINT receives only a small fraction of all the resources devoted to intelligence collection, largely because technological collection systems, such as imagery satellites, are more expensive. However, HUMINT may be the best method, and on occasion the only method, for gaining reliable information on the intentions of an adversary's leaders. Effective liaison with foreign intelligence services increases the potential utility of HUMINT. As the intelligence community increasingly focuses on non-state actors, HUMINT becomes more important for understanding current and future threats.[19]

There are many challenges to the production of quality HUMINT. First, conducting HUMINT operations involves obstacles ranging from language barriers to the difficulty associated with persuading people to engage in acts that their home countries may consider treasonous. Second, information gathered from human beings will only be as reliable and insightful as the sources themselves. Objectivity and accuracy may be hard to judge. Third, great time and patience, sometimes for years, may be required to cultivate important sources. Finally, HUMINT operations cannot be performed remotely: those involved may face personal danger and are vulnerable to adversary counterintelligence efforts.[20]

Signals Intelligence (SIGINT). Signals intelligence includes three areas: communications intelligence (COMINT), consisting of messages relayed between people; electronic intelligence (ELINT), which primarily involves the interception of radar signals; and foreign instrumentation signals intelligence (FISINT), which involves the interception of instrumentation signals such as radio command signals.[21] In only some cases will the analyst gain access to the "internals"—the content—of intercepted communications. Often a communications intercept analyst may gain access only to the "externals": data such as activity time, frequency, location, or similar characteristics. However, the technical signals and location information emitted by cell phones, computers, vehicles, radars, or missile silos can sometimes provide important clues about an adversary's disposition or future actions.

Although SIGINT is a tremendously productive collection method, it is also expensive in terms of money and human resources. The sheer volume of gathered information that must be analyzed is staggering. In addition, SIGINT relies on continuous technical innovation to keep pace with technological change and to stay ahead of new denial and deception techniques. Concerns over access, legality, and privacy may also impede data collection. A further challenge is that, as with all collection methods, the use of actionable intelligence from SIGINT may compromise the collection method and source.

Imagery Intelligence (IMINT). Imagery intelligence consists of representations of objects reproduced electronically or by optical means on film, electronic display devices, or other media. Collection efforts use photography and related imagery-producing techniques from "non–air breathers" (space-based satellites with surveillance equipment) and "air breathers" (manned or unmanned aircraft with surveillance equipment). IMINT products include electro-optical, multispectral, infrared, and radar imagery. IMINT allows for the study of areas that would otherwise be inaccessible. Although they are expensive, unmanned aerial collection platforms provide real-time intelligence while reducing the risk to human life. Imagery is also graphic and compelling; these qualities can make it especially valuable or persuasive.

IMINT does have limitations. Satellite orbits are predictable and adversaries can use this information to avoid detection. Air breathers are less predictable and can be directed almost instantly to a target, but they cannot stay in place for long periods of time.[22] Despite remarkable advances in technology, reconnaissance and surveillance systems cannot see everything, nor can they assure guaranteed accuracy in the interpretation of images, especially when those under observation use deception. The United States was reminded of this in the search for WMD in Iraq before and after the 2003 US-led invasion.[23]

Measurement and Signature Intelligence (MASINT). Measurement and signature intelligence involves the collection of optical, radio-frequency, thermal, acoustic, seismic, and material characteristics of targets. Examples of MASINT include information garnered from the noise of passing vehicles or the chemical composition of air and water samples.

Geospatial Intelligence (GEOINT). GEOINT is the analysis and visual representation of security-related activities on the earth. GEOINT productions rely on a combination of imagery, imagery intelligence, and geospatial information derived from satellites and GPS trackers.[24]

Processing. The third stage of the intelligence cycle takes raw information collected through the aforementioned methods and derives from it information relevant to policy makers. Prior to this stage, data is merely information without significance. For example, databanks of intercepted communications are of no utility until explored and understood by trained analysts. Intelligence processing can involve "exploiting imagery; decoding messages and translating broadcasts; reducing telemetry to meaningful measures; preparing information for computer processing; storage and retrieval; [and] placing human-source reports into a form and context to make them more understandable."[25] Processing, exploitation, and storage of data require considerable resources and are carried out across the entire intelligence community.

Analysis. In the fourth stage of the intelligence cycle, collected intelligence is further collated, assessed, related, integrated, and made understandable. Analysts may spot and highlight trends, assign probabilities to various outcomes, and illuminate choices available to policy makers. Ideally, intelligence analysts are experts in all aspects of their target—including the language and culture—and also adept at integrating volumes of data produced by a variety of collection methods into a comprehensive, coherent, and succinct portrayal.[26] For even the best analysts, however, fragmentary and uncertain information makes prediction difficult. This stage is critical to the effectiveness of the overall intelligence effort. Since a policy maker usually reads only a summary of available intelligence, the analytical quality, clarity, and brevity of intelligence reports profoundly influence the quality of national security decision making.

As with any project that involves selective filtering of information, the intelligence process is highly susceptible to bias. Analysts must act as a funnel and a filter as they condense and interpret large amounts of raw information to create succinct intelligence reports. During this process, personal knowledge and experience influence final products. Bias can manifest itself in several ways. In "projection" or "mirror-imaging," analysts may attribute their own characteristics, values, or thought processes to their subjects. This can result in flawed analyses because the subject may not, in fact, operate according to the analyst's expectations. Bias may stem from the conscious or unconscious incorporation of personal or organizational interests into assessments; for example, an analyst may overestimate military threat estimates to increase support for resources. Intelligence analysts may also be reluctant to challenge their agency's view or "party line." "Status quo bias" involves an expectation of continuity in a target. "Wishful thinking" relates to a tendency to avoid uncomfortable conclusions. "Premature closure" occurs when an analyst, having made a judgment, becomes resistant to future contradictory information.[27] Although efficiency and timeliness are important, some competition and duplication within the intelligence community can provide a healthy crosscheck to minimize the effects of potential sources of bias.

Another challenge at this stage is the potential for oversimplification of intelligence to create a parsimonious narrative. This may leave policy makers unaware of critical uncertainties or ambiguities. As with open source intelligence, an excess of information can sometimes be as much of a challenge as a lack of information; there is rarely enough funding or time to conduct all possible analyses. Intelligence managers must accept risk by deciding where to focus their limited resources and must attempt to communicate uncertainties accurately.[28]

Dissemination. In the final stage, intelligence products—usually written reports or briefings—are provided to consumers, including policy makers, the military, law enforcement agencies, or other interested agencies that can act on the information. Dissemination has its own challenges. The main difficulty in this stage is ensuring that the intelligence product is received in a timely manner by all who need it, including domestic and foreign consumers. Sometimes the classification of intelligence can make it unusable by or inaccessible to some who need it.[29] This can be particularly problematic with issues that require high levels of interagency coordination.

In the past, the sensitivity of intelligence sources and methods, as well as the content of intelligence reporting, led to the practice of limiting dissemination based on the "need to know": only policy makers and agencies with a specific need for highly classified information would gain access to it. The events of September 11, 2001, resulted in a shift toward a dissemination ethos of "a responsibility to provide." This change reflects the complexity of the current threat environment and the desire for extensive cooperation within and among government agencies across the federal system. Officials were expected to find ways to disseminate intelligence to all who may have a need for it.[30] However, since the 2013 Snowden breach, the pendulum on access has shifted again. Although they are conscious of their responsibility to provide intelligence, the agencies are more sensitive to threats originating from inside their organizations and are once again increasing restrictions on the dissemination of information.

The post-9/11 environment has been characterized by the need for "actionable" intelligence, particularly relating to future terrorist threats. Whether intelligence is actionable depends on a number of criteria: (1) specificity as to time, location, manner, and perpetrator; (2) credibility of sources; (3) corroboration of information by multiple sources; and (4) potential severity of consequences. Analysts use these criteria to evaluate whether information should go to key decision makers, and policy makers use them to decide whether or not they have sufficient basis to take action.

The five stages of the intelligence cycle may repeat if the original information needs are not satisfied or new questions emerge. This loop is continuous, and requests drive intelligence operations in all stages of the cycle.

The Importance of the Policy Maker in the Intelligence Production Process

As one career intelligence professional put it: "In Washington, there are only two possibilities: policy success and intelligence failure."[31] The intelligence community exists to meet the needs of the creators and implementers of national security policy. Those who understand both the expectations of policy makers and the capabilities of the intelligence community are best postured to help ensure that intelligence properly informs decision making. However, in practice, the role and influence of intelligence can vary considerably from one administration to another and sometimes even by issue area.[32] When the interagency process works effectively, a robust discussion of policy options and intelligence requirements contributes to close coordination between intelligence providers and policy makers. In contrast, "When that interagency process is more informal, kept within a small circle, or entirely hidden, [the intelligence community] is unable to understand what policy options are being considered and cannot produce timely and relevant intelligence."[33] Communication among intelligence officials and policy makers is therefore critical.

Policy makers must also understand the limitations of intelligence. For a variety of reasons, such as limited resources, time, and expertise, as well as adversaries' efforts at deception and denial, there is no way to know everything. If used properly, intelligence can "identify current developments and trends that will shape the future and affect U.S. interests" and give policy makers "a much better understanding of the situation they face."[34] However, even with all the resources of the intelligence community, intelligence cannot remove all risk from the decisionmaking process. For example, in April 2011, when intelligence analysts were asked about the likelihood of Osama bin Laden actually being at the Abbottabad compound, "The estimates ranged from 40 to 80 percent. . . . As the president said at one point, 'Look, it's a fifty-fifty proposition no matter how you look at it.'"[35] Although analyses that appear more definitive are more likely to be influential, intelligence professionals must remain accurate and not overstate their case. Decision makers need to receive intelligence with appropriate caveats and recognize that they themselves must ultimately weigh the risks. Decisions are nearly always based on less than perfect intelligence.

The potential to politicize intelligence can threaten the relationship between analysts and policy makers through the influence of partisan, bureaucratic, and personal politics in intelligence analysis. *Downward politicization* occurs when the policy maker influences analytical conclusions by openly expressing his or her desired conclusions or, more subtly, by dismissing or disregarding unwanted information or analyses. For example, in the analysis of the potential for WMD as a justification for the 2003 US invasion of Iraq, "Analysts and intelligence managers knew that any suggestion that Saddam's capabilities were limited would immediately draw hostile fire from their superiors. In this political climate it would have been hard for anyone to ask if the conventional wisdom about Saddam's WMD programs should be reexamined."[36] Similarly, members of the intelligence community, who have their own organizational, bureaucratic, and personal biases, might engage in *upward politicization*, providing intelligence that is influenced by those biases rather than reflecting an objective analysis of the data. Analysts "must be wary of digressing toward upward politicization, focusing on what the analyst personally believes to be important and then seeking out supporting facts and findings."[37] To avoid upward politicization, analysts must be self-conscious about their potential biases and must not approach the evidence with foregone conclusions in mind. Instead, they should base their findings on a rigorous, objective interpretation of the data. In either direction, politicization of intelligence undermines the relationship between policy makers and the intelligence community and reduces the quality of the intelligence product.

Covert Action

In addition to producing intelligence, portions of the intelligence community may act more directly as instruments of foreign policy through covert action. *Covert action* is activity of the US government to influence political, economic, or military conditions abroad in which the role of the US government is not apparent or is not acknowledged publicly.[38] At points throughout US history, especially during the Cold War, American leaders used the intelligence agencies as means of affecting or influencing events abroad in accordance with US foreign policy goals (see also the discussion of the Eisenhower administration in chapter 3). Some of these activities included subsidizing foreign newspapers and political parties, arming guerrilla forces, and providing logistical or paramilitary support for foreign military organizations or operations. More recently, the George W. Bush administration and the Barack Obama administration authorized the CIA to conduct covert strikes by unmanned aerial vehicles against terrorist targets in Pakistan, Yemen, and other states.[39]

Covert action is controversial within and outside of the intelligence community. Historically, it has been a significant foreign policy tool and can continue to provide policy makers with a way to execute selected policy decisions by means that are not within the authority or capability of other agencies. The CIA, for example, played an important role in the US invasion of Afghanistan to overthrow the Taliban regime in 2001.[40] The 2011 raid on Osama bin Laden's compound in Pakistan was conducted under CIA authority with military special operation forces detailed to work for the CIA.[41] After its success, the details were soon publically acknowledged (in more detail than many in the intelligence community and military would have desired), but if the operation had failed or been aborted, the United States might have been able to deny or limit public disclosure of the extent of the US action.

Despite its potential utility, there is a danger that an excessive focus on the covert activities of the intelligence community could skew popular understanding of the overall intelligence mission. Another difficulty in fostering understanding of these activities is that *covert action* is an imprecise and elastic term. It can apply as easily to a meeting between foreign agents as to elaborate, large-scale paramilitary operations over time spans measured in years. It is therefore hard to discuss this concept in a rational, meaningful way, especially in a public forum.

Covert activities have long been part of US statecraft, but they did not become subject to significant public scrutiny until the 1970s. When Congress created the CIA to perform certain intelligence coordination functions in 1947, it also directed the agency to undertake "other functions and duties related to intelligence affecting the national security as the National Security Council may from time to time direct." Since then, National Security Council (NSC) directives have given the CIA authority to conduct covert operations abroad consistent with American foreign and military policies.[42] Initially, these activities went unchecked by other branches of government. However, over time, Congress began to insist on oversight in this realm. An important step was the 1974 Hughes-Ryan Amendment requiring the president to report any planned covert action by the CIA to the appropriate committees of Congress "in a timely manner."

By the early 1980s, in the wake of public dissatisfaction over the inability to extricate US hostages from Iran during the Carter administration, development of the covert action function became more active. However, further development of covert action capabilities was severely weakened by the highly publicized Iran-Contra Affair in 1985 and 1986, which involved the diversion of funds from arms sales to Iran to anti-communist forces in Nicaragua. As a result of this episode, in 1991, Congress passed legislation requiring the president to give written approval for any covert action undertaken by any component of the US government and to notify Congress within forty-eight hours. In addition, the legislation mandates that the president must notify Congress when third countries or private citizens are to be used or take part in any significant way in covert US activity.[43]

Although covert operations survive in theory as an important vehicle for foreign policy implementation in special cases, they continue to be controversial. In addition to the challenge of preserving the secrecy necessary to their success, these operations are often risky in terms of lives as well as the costs their revelation can impose on the achievement of broader national security policy goals. For example, the existence and operation of secret CIA prisons stirred up great controversy during the administration of President George W. Bush. Critics questioned the need for a clandestine detention system, given the existence of legal and transparent detention and interrogation practices.[44] The significant expansion of covert drone strikes in the Obama administration was similarly controversial, especially after an American citizen, Anwar al-Awlaki, was killed by a lethal strike in Yemen in September 2011. This led to a major policy address in which Obama declassified information about the drone strike and committed to an increase in transparency and oversight of the drone program.[45] Policy makers must balance the need for covert operations to achieve policy goals against potential negative repercussions on domestic public support and on the US image abroad.

Counterintelligence

The goal of counterintelligence is to deny existing or potential adversaries the ability to collect information that could be used against the United States. Counterintelligence is one of the least understood and least appreciated functions of the intelligence community. It can be defined as "information gathered and activities conducted to identify, deceive, exploit, disrupt, or protect against espionage, other intelligence activities, sabotage, or assassinations conducted for or on behalf of foreign powers, organizations or persons, or their agents, or international terrorist organizations or activities."[46] Foreign intelligence agencies and other malign actors may seek to acquire classified technological data, business and economic secrets, and personal information belonging to the US government or to American companies or individuals. To combat this threat, US counterintelligence entities must be able to block foreign efforts to acquire sensitive information of all kinds. The 2015 theft from the US Office of Personnel Management of the results of background investigations for 21.5 million individuals was a significant breach of US security that reveals the importance of counterintelligence capabilities that can prevent such actions. In this case, Social Security numbers and other detailed personal information was stolen, which is not only embarrassing and costly for the federal government, but could also compromise the security of individuals who have access to sensitive information.

Like covert action, counterintelligence operations often spark controversy. There is general distrust of intelligence activities within the United States, yet this is precisely where counterintelligence officers must operate. This distrust increases when there are revelations of occasional agency overreach. For example, in 2007, Robert Mueller, the director of the FBI, was called before the Senate Judiciary Committee to explain failures on the part of the FBI to appropriately manage "national security letters"—instruments that enable the FBI to obtain communications and financial records without initial court oversight.[47] More broadly, since 9/11, "Civil liberties advocates have argued that the FBI's profiling of Muslim communities violates First and Fourteenth Amendment protections and that the sting operations on which many conspiracy terrorism convictions have been based often amount to entrapment."[48] While "no judge has yet dismissed charges on those grounds," even counterintelligence activities that are flawlessly managed can raise sensitive issues relating to potential infringement of the liberties of US citizens.[49]

Direction and Leadership of the Intelligence Community

The intelligence community consists of executive branch agencies and organizations that work both separately and in concert to conduct intelligence activities necessary for foreign relations and the protection of the national security of the United States. Some observers contend that the term *intelligence community* overstates the degree of cohesiveness in the American intelligence establishment. However, the term *community* hints at the difficulty of maintaining a central focus. There are formidable practical challenges associated with getting disparate entities to work together in harmony to develop the best possible intelligence products while avoiding excessive duplication of effort.

The National Security Council is the highest executive-branch entity that directs the national intelligence effort. The NSC works closely with the president on the national security strategy and on statements of national foreign intelligence objectives and priorities, which are then used to create specific guidance for the intelligence community. The NSC staff reviews all proposals for "special activities" (that is, covert actions) and makes recommendations to the president. It assesses proposals for sensitive intelligence collection operations and is informed of counterintelligence activities. The NSC also evaluates the quality of the intelligence product. The NSC staff, under the direction of the national security advisor or a lower-level interdepartmental group, accomplishes most of these missions. The members of the NSC themselves seldom provide specific direction to intelligence agencies.

Leadership of the Intelligence Community. The National Security Act of 1947 designated a director of central intelligence (DCI) to lead the intelligence community in responding to executive direction; it mandated that the head of the CIA would play that role. Management and coordination of the community was and continues to be quite difficult, despite efforts to strengthen the position. The DCI had supervisory responsibility, but did not have the authority to truly command any members of the community outside of the CIA. A particular challenge was that the

DCI did not control the majority of the resources dedicated to the intelligence function. These issues were addressed following the September 11, 2001, attacks.

The Intelligence Reform and Terrorism Prevention Act of 2004, the most significant legislative reform in the history of the US intelligence community, created a new position, the director of national intelligence (DNI), separate and distinct from the leadership of the CIA. In 2004, when George W. Bush signed the legislation into law, he said:

> [The DNI] will serve as the principal advisor to the President on intelligence matters. The DNI will have the authority to order the collection of new intelligence, to ensure the sharing of information among agencies and to establish common standards for the intelligence community's personnel. It will be the DNI's responsibility to determine the annual budgets for all national agencies and offices and to direct how these funds are spent.[50]

The DNI currently serves as the head of the intelligence community and acts as the principal advisor to the president and the NSC for intelligence matters related to national security. The Office of the DNI includes the National Intelligence Council, which was established in 1979 to act as a bridge between the intelligence and policy communities. This council provides the entire intelligence community with an independent analytical and estimative capability. It prepares National Intelligence Estimates (NIEs) drawing on all of the community's resources as well as nongovernmental experts. The DNI directs and oversees the creation of the National Intelligence Program; through this role, he or she has control over at least a portion of the budgets of the intelligence agencies, some of which also receive funding through different programs. The DNI also has authority over the personnel programs of the intelligence community. This authority enables the DNI to affect the career patterns and incentive structures of career intelligence officials in support of broad national goals.[51]

Although the role has more authority than its predecessor (the DCI), the job description of the DNI also contains some of the same difficulties. Most stem from the DNI's responsibility to "coordinate" across agencies while having little to no power to influence these agencies' decisions and activities. Senator Jay Rockefeller summarized such concerns during confirmation hearings for a new DNI in February 2007:

> We did not pull the technological collection agencies out of the Defense Department and we did not give the DNI direct authority over the main collection or analytical components of the community. We gave the DNI the authority to build the national intelligence budget, but we left the execution of the budget with the agencies. We gave the DNI tremendous responsibilities. The question is, did we give the position enough authority for him to exercise those responsibilities?[52]

Congress and the president continue to evaluate the relationship between the DNI and the larger intelligence community. While integration continues to improve, competition among intelligence agencies during a time of budget cutbacks ensures that old rivalries endure.

The Intelligence Reform and Terrorism Prevention Act of 2004 also codified the creation of the Terrorist Threat Integration Center, later renamed the National Counterterrorism Center (NCTC). The 2004 legislation placed the NCTC within the Office of the Director of National Intelligence (ODNI). Other centers, councils, and divisions that accomplish national intelligence integration are also part of the ODNI. The ODNI and its functions continue to evolve in anticipation of and reaction to changes in the national security environment.

Members of the Intelligence Community

The DNI oversees sixteen components, which together comprise the operating elements of the US intelligence community (figure 7.2). The CIA is the only component that is independent of a larger government agency or department. The other fifteen fall under the auspices of executive departments within the federal government: eight within the Department of Defense, two within the Department of Homeland Security, two within the Department of Justice, and three within other executive departments. Each of these entities is discussed below.

Central Intelligence Agency. The CIA collects information abroad and serves as the national manager for human-source collection (HUMINT). It is the agency within the community generally authorized to conduct covert activities, although the president can direct other agencies to be involved. Although its operations are conducted almost entirely outside the United States, it may participate in counterintelligence activities at home in support of the FBI, as well as in certain limited domestic activities that support overseas collection operations. For example, the CIA may contact an American citizen who has recently traveled abroad and had an experience or engagement that may aid in the collection of foreign intelligence.

Department of Defense. Half of all intelligence-related entities reside within DoD—a fact that demonstrates the importance of defense-related concerns to the entire intelligence enterprise. Unlike the CIA, which provides intelligence primarily to policy makers, DoD intelligence components serve both policy makers and military commanders. In 2003, the position of undersecretary of defense for intelligence was created, reflecting the increasing importance of intelligence. The undersecretary of defense for intelligence is responsible for coordinating efforts within DoD and serving as the focal point for interaction between the DNI and the larger intelligence community.[53]

Defense Intelligence Agency (DIA). Headquartered in the Pentagon, the DIA produces military and military-related intelligence for the Department of Defense. The director of the DIA serves as the principal advisor on substantive military intelligence matters to the secretary of defense and to the Joint Chiefs of Staff. The DIA also provides military input for national intelligence reports and supervises

FIGURE 7.2 The Intelligence Community

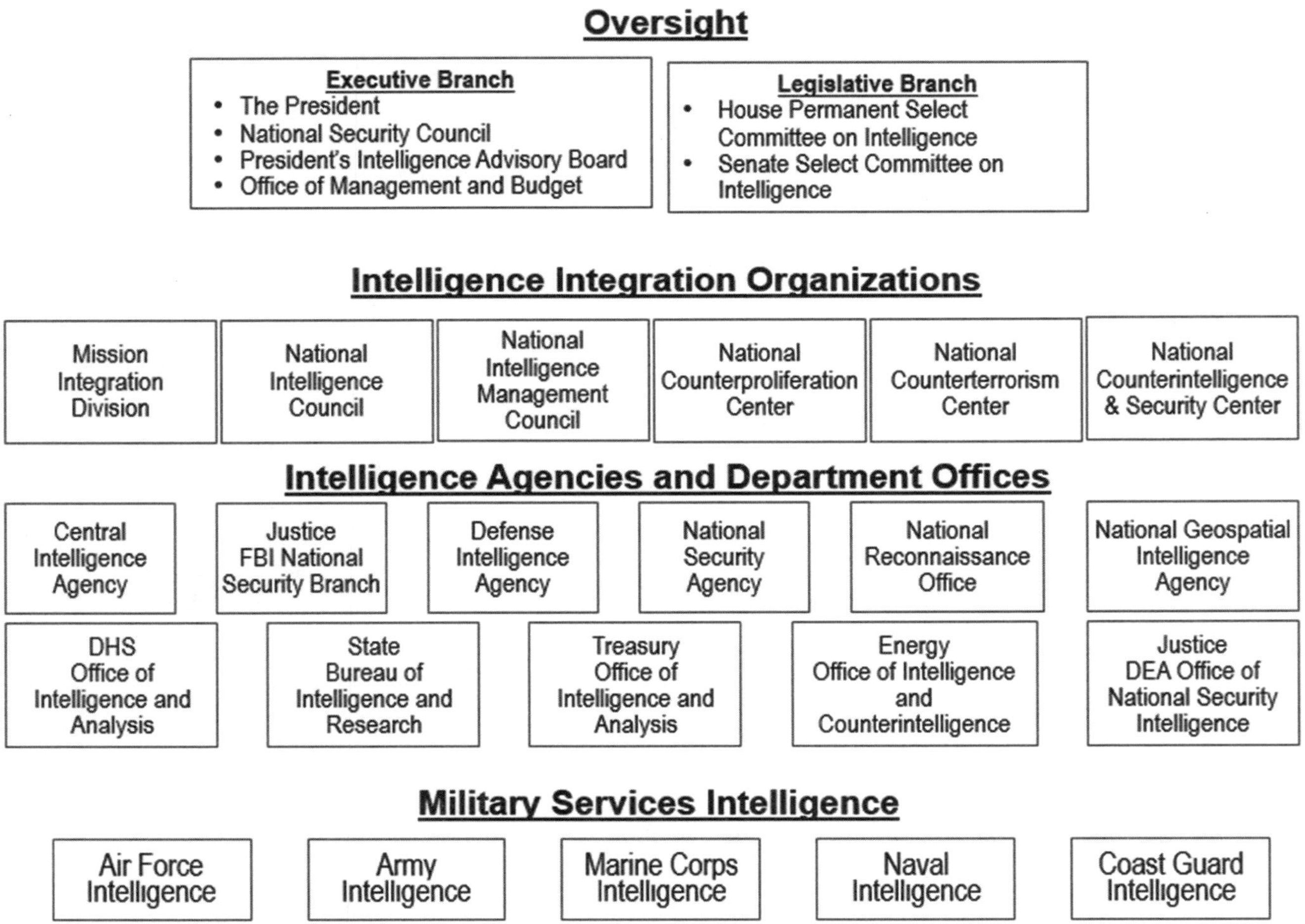

Oversight

Executive Branch
- The President
- National Security Council
- President's Intelligence Advisory Board
- Office of Management and Budget

Legislative Branch
- House Permanent Select Committee on Intelligence
- Senate Select Committee on Intelligence

Intelligence Integration Organizations

- Mission Integration Division
- National Intelligence Council
- National Intelligence Management Council
- National Counterproliferation Center
- National Counterterrorism Center
- National Counterintelligence & Security Center

Intelligence Agencies and Department Offices

- Central Intelligence Agency
- Justice FBI National Security Branch
- Defense Intelligence Agency
- National Security Agency
- National Reconnaissance Office
- National Geospatial Intelligence Agency
- DHS Office of Intelligence and Analysis
- State Bureau of Intelligence and Research
- Treasury Office of Intelligence and Analysis
- Energy Office of Intelligence and Counterintelligence
- Justice DEA Office of National Security Intelligence

Military Services Intelligence

- Air Force Intelligence
- Army Intelligence
- Marine Corps Intelligence
- Naval Intelligence
- Coast Guard Intelligence

the work of all military attachés abroad. The Central MASINT Organization, the focus for all national and DoD MASINT (measurement and signature intelligence) matters, is housed within the DIA.

National Security Agency (NSA). The NSA, headquartered at Fort Meade, Maryland, has three main strategic missions: to conduct signals intelligence, to provide information security, and to enable computer network operations by protecting them from attack. The NSA leads the government's cryptology and cyber efforts. It also works to block adversaries from accessing national security information. Because the NSA operates in the dynamic realm of information technology, it must constantly adapt to remain effective at its core missions. In recognition of the importance of offensive and defensive military operations in cyberspace that are beyond the intelligence function of the NSA, DoD created the US Cyber Command (USCYBERCOM) in 2009. USCYBERCOM is co-located with the NSA at Fort Meade; the director of the NSA is dual-hatted as the commander of USCYBERCOM.

Signals intelligence, information assurance, and computer network operations are becoming increasingly challenging as modes of information sharing expand ever more rapidly. For example, any number of mobile phone applications can be used to communicate, as can applications as seemingly farfetched as online video games. As methods proliferate, the NSA must work to keep up. Moreover, while traditional adversaries may have been state sponsored, in today's environment, myriad non-state actors seek classified information for all sorts of reasons, and the NSA must work to protect information from them. Hackers from inside and outside attempt to breach private and government databases with increasing frequency. Edward Snowden's data breach from inside the NSA highlighted the crucial importance of protecting the government from insider threats.

National Reconnaissance Office (NRO). The NRO has acted as "the nation's eyes and ears in space" since 1961.[54] Due to the sensitivity of its responsibilities, the existence and functions of the NRO were declassified only in 1992. The NRO is jointly managed by the secretary of defense and the DNI; the DNI establishes the office's requirements and collection priorities.[55]

National Geospatial-Intelligence Agency (NGA). The national manager for classified and unclassified imagery products from satellites and other sources, the NGA replaced the National Intelligence Mapping Agency in 2003. The NGA is also responsible for providing timely, relevant, and accurate collection and analysis of geospatial intelligence in support of military forces and national requirements.

Army, Air Force, Navy, and Marine Corps Intelligence. Each of the services has its own intelligence and counterintelligence capabilities. These service component entities provide support to decision makers at tactical, operational, and strategic levels.

Department of Homeland Security (DHS). DHS houses two components of the intelligence community. The first is the Office of Intelligence and Analysis, responsible for overseeing and integrating all of the intelligence elements of the department (see chapter 6 for the organizational structure of DHS). The Office of Intelligence Analysis is the federal government's lead for sharing intelligence information with state and local governments and with the private sector. The second component of the intelligence community within DHS is Coast Guard Intelligence, which was transferred from the Department of Transportation along with the rest of the Coast Guard when DHS was created.

Department of Justice (DOJ). DOJ contains two components of the intelligence community. The first of these is the FBI. Although primarily a domestic investigative and law enforcement agency, the FBI has extensive domestic counterintelligence and security responsibilities. After the September 11, 2001, terrorist attacks, the "overriding priority" of the FBI became "protecting America by preventing future attacks."[56] In 2005, President George W. Bush directed the creation of a National Security Branch of the FBI to oversee its counterterrorism, counterintelligence, and intelligence functions. The director of this branch also coordinates FBI national security efforts with the rest of the intelligence community. The FBI has fifty-six field offices in major US cities, over 380 resident offices in smaller communities, and numerous legal attachés located in embassies worldwide.[57]

The second component of the intelligence community within the Department of Justice is the Drug Enforcement Agency (DEA). The DEA's Office of National Security Intelligence "is responsible for providing drug-related information responsive to [intelligence community] requirements."[58] The DEA has experience operating in foreign environments and, with ninety-one offices in seventy countries, is the largest US law enforcement agency presence abroad.[59]

Department of State. Diplomatic reporting is a valuable form of information gathering. State Department representatives stationed overseas regularly report on developments relevant to US foreign policy, including information about political, sociological, economic, and scientific trends and events in other nations. For the rest of the community as well as for the secretary of state, the State Department's Bureau of Intelligence and Research (INR) generates intelligence products pertinent to US foreign policy. The secretary of state works closely with the DNI, and the State Department with the CIA, to ensure that intelligence activities are useful and appropriate to American foreign policy.

Department of the Treasury. The Treasury Department's Office of Intelligence and Analysis was established in 2004. Led by an assistant secretary and residing within the Office of Terrorism and Financial Intelligence, this office focuses on issues related to flows of monetary support for threats to national security, including financing in support of terrorism and nuclear proliferation.[60]

Department of Energy. The Department of Energy works with the State Department to collect information on foreign energy matters, particularly nuclear energy, and other intelligence as needed. The Office of Intelligence and Counterintelligence within the Department of Energy provides technical expertise to the broader intelligence community to help evaluate and counter nuclear proliferation and other specific threats related to the nation's energy infrastructure.

Intelligence Oversight

Although gathering intelligence about a nation's adversaries was a common government practice long before the existence of the United States, the Constitution does not mention this function nor does it specifically authorize intelligence operations. Because the goal of intelligence is to aid in national defense and foreign affairs, authority often tends to follow similar lines. The tensions between Congress and the president in other areas of national security policy are echoed in debates over control of the intelligence process and organizations. Both branches view access to relevant information and control of intelligence policy as vital to informed decision making.

Congressional Perspective and Actions. The National Security Act of 1947 reflected a broad consensus at the time that the president should generally have unfettered control of the intelligence community. This consensus began to erode in the early 1970s, due to concerns over the risk of an "imperial presidency" as the Watergate scandal unfolded and amid allegations concerning CIA involvement in the 1970 Chilean presidential elections and subsequent coup. In response to these developments, in 1974 Congress passed the Hughes-Ryan Amendment to the Foreign Assistance Act; it required that, prior to the expenditure of appropriated funds for non-collection intelligence activities in foreign countries, the president must issue a "finding" that declares the activity to be "important to the national security" of the United States and must report this finding to appropriate congressional committees.

Around the same time as this amendment, both the House and Senate launched investigations into CIA misconduct. The two committees operated concurrently, but the Senate committee (known as the Church Committee after its chairman, Senator Frank Church, a Democrat representing Idaho) took the lead. Its investigatory charter was broad and open ended, instructing the committee to measure intelligence activities against standards of both legality and propriety. After examining records, listening to witnesses, and deliberating at length, the committee determined that the United States had been involved in several political assassination plots. Operational authorization procedures within the intelligence community seemed so deliberately compartmentalized and secretive that a plan to kill a foreign leader could be generated without explicit presidential approval.

The Church Committee's final report called for adherence to "fair play" ideals. The committee believed that the looseness of operational rules and discretion had sometimes led to US intelligence operations that were characteristic of those that might be conducted by a totalitarian regime. Remedies suggested by the committee included clear legislative delineation of the scope of permissible activities (via a statutory charter for the intelligence community) and better procedures for supervising intelligence agency operations (including more congressional oversight).

After the investigations concluded, Congress undertook two self-imposed tasks: to organize its oversight machinery and to pass legislative charters setting forth authorizations and restrictions for the intelligence community. Congress created the Senate Select Committee on Intelligence (SSCI) in 1976 and the House Permanent Select Committee on Intelligence (HPSCI) in 1977. The SSCI stated that its intent was to serve congressional and constitutional interests by obtaining information relevant to foreign policy decisions; to use the budget process as a mechanism to control intelligence activities; to control the intelligence community by investigation; and to review proposals for covert operations.

The 1978 Foreign Intelligence Surveillance Act (FISA) further strengthened congressional scrutiny of intelligence operations. This act requires judicial warrants for electronic surveillance used in intelligence or counterintelligence operations within the United States whenever communications of "United States persons" might be intercepted. This act also created the Foreign Intelligence Surveillance Court (FISC), which is staffed with judges whose security clearances are sufficient to enable them to make decisions about the appropriateness of issuing FISA warrants.

After the September 11, 2001, terrorist attacks Congress, together with the president, created and chartered the 9/11 Commission to "to investigate facts and circumstances relating to the terrorist attacks of September 11, 2001," including those that were related to the intelligence community.[61] One of the significant problems identified by the commission was inadequate communication between law enforcement and intelligence agencies and among the various entities of the intelligence community.

Responding to commission recommendations, the Intelligence Reform and Terrorism Prevention Act of 2004, in addition to establishing the office of the director for national intelligence and the NCTC, created an independent Privacy and Civil Liberties Board, whose members are appointed by the president and confirmed by the Senate, to protect the civil liberties of American citizens and ensure they are not infringed upon by laws, policies, or decisions of the executive branch.[62]

After 9/11, congressional activism in the oversight of intelligence gradually intensified in response to perceived intelligence community overreach and failures. For example, the SSCI hearings on the NSA following the Snowden leaks in 2013 contained sharp criticism of the intelligence community. Senator Ron Wyden (D-OR) referred to "reckless reliance on secret interpretations of the law" and charged that "misleading and deceptive statements" were made to the public by senior leaders in the intelligence community.[63] In 2014, the SSCI published portions of its report on CIA policies regarding torture as a means of intelligence gathering. This report, too, was critical; it declared that "pressure, fear, and expectation of further terrorist plots do not justify, temper, or excuse improper actions taken . . . in the name of national security."[64] While its immediate response to 9/11 was to expand the authorities of the intelligence community, it rapidly became clear that Congress intended to preserve its strong oversight role.

Executive Oversight. The executive branch also has the ability to conduct oversight of the intelligence community. For example, the President's Intelligence Advisory Board (PIAB) provides the president with an assessment of the quality of intelligence products and management. Established in 1956 by President Eisenhower as the President's Board of Consultants on Foreign Intelligence Activities, the PIAB has had varying degrees of influence since its founding. The PIAB is an advisory board that can make recommendations to the president through its semiannual report, but it does not have any policy authority.

Other procedures to preclude unauthorized activities were instituted after allegations of intelligence community abuses—both domestic and abroad—generated considerable concern in the United States in the 1970s. The Intelligence Oversight Board (IOB), a panel of private citizens appointed by the president, reviews and reports to the president on the intelligence community's internal procedures and operational activities. The task of the IOB, now a standing committee within the PIAB, is to oversee the intelligence community's compliance with the Constitution, laws, and other presidential directives.

As with congressional oversight, executive oversight of the intelligence community has varied in intensity and effectiveness over time. The executive branch directs the intelligence community but it also seeks to make use of independent mechanisms for ensuring oversight, which can be difficult. Partisan politics, the priorities of a given presidential administration, and the continuously changing national security environment prompt continual reassessment and adjustments for intelligence oversight by all branches of government.

Judicial Oversight. Historically there has been little judicial oversight of the intelligence community, largely because most intelligence activities take place overseas and are directed against foreign nationals or nations. Judicial involvement on the domestic front tends to be concerned with potential violations of individual liberties, especially the Constitution's Fourth Amendment protections against unreasonable searches and seizures, or those that are not supported by a proper warrant. A substantial curb by the judiciary on the intelligence community arose from the US Supreme Court's 1967 decision in *Katz v. United States*, in which the Court extended Fourth Amendment protections to areas in which a person has "a reasonable expectation of privacy."[65]

The aftermath of the Watergate scandal and its revelations of the recording of personal communications without warrants fueled the public's concern that all warrants must be governed by a legal process. The 1978 FISA legislation discussed above "authorized the Chief Justice of the United States to designate seven federal district court judges to review applications for warrants related to national security investigations" within a Foreign Intelligence Surveillance Court.[66]

FISA also requires that a court order or warrant be obtained from this court, now usually known as the FISA court, for all electronic surveillance for intelligence purposes within the United States.[67] Warrant applications under FISA are drafted by attorneys in the General Counsel's Office at the NSA, at the request of an officer of one of the federal intelligence agencies. Each application must contain the attorney general's certification that the target of the proposed surveillance is a "foreign power" or "the agent of a foreign power" and that, if the target is a US citizen or resident alien, the target may be involved in the commission of a crime.[68]

The FISA court system remained largely unchanged from its creation until the passage of the Patriot Act in 2001. The act sought to enhance the ease of cooperation between the intelligence community and law enforcement by lowering the threshold for obtaining a surveillance warrant, expanding the ability of the FBI to gather information without a warrant, and expanding surveillance on the Internet. In addition, the Patriot Act expanded the time periods for which the FISA court could authorize surveillance and increased the number of judges serving the court from seven to eleven.[69]

Judicial oversight is limited to the realm of legal interpretation and reaction to past behaviors by the intelligence community, in sharp contrast to Congress, which has the ability to subpoena, to address policy issues, and to control funding affecting future actions by the intelligence community.[70] However, the role of the judiciary is likely to continue to grow over time as transnational threats to US national security and the interconnectedness created by advances in information and other technologies increasingly blur distinctions between foreign and domestic national security concerns.

Current and Future Challenges

As is evident from this chapter, today's intelligence community operates in a challenging and dynamic environment. Its mission is made more difficult by the imperative that it cover an increasingly diverse array of malign actors with the capability to harm US interests, even as it continues to weather a series of controversies. An apparent decision by President Donald Trump to downplay or reject the conclusions of the intelligence community regarding Russian interference in the US presidential election of 2016 is only the most recent instance in which the integrity and judgment of key members of the intelligence community have been called into question.[71] As long as the intelligence function remains important to US national security, the capabilities, competence, and credibility of the US intelligence community will remain an important national security concern. Congressional, executive, and judicial oversight will remain important in ensuring that the operations of the intelligence community advance US national interests while continuing to protect the privacy and civil liberties of individual Americans.

Discussion Questions

1. What is intelligence, and what contribution does the intelligence community make to the national security decisionmaking process?

2. How does the intelligence production cycle work? What drives its operations?

3. What are the characteristics, challenges, and role of Human Intelligence (HUMINT) as part of intelligence collection?

4. How is the intelligence community structured? Who leads the intelligence community?

5. How did the events of September 11, 2001, shape the current structure?

6. What resources are used in Open Source Intelligence (OSINT)? How is OSINT important to the US intelligence effort?

7. In what ways can bias influence analysis? How can policy makers and the intelligence community guard against the effects of bias?

8. How has oversight of the intelligence community changed since World War II? Which branches of government provide the most oversight today, and how?

9. Given an increased focus on non-state actors in the current international security environment, what types of intelligence collection and analysis will become most important in the coming years?

10. Should covert action remain an important instrument of US national security policy? What are the strengths and weaknesses of this policy tool?

Recommended Reading

Andrew, Christopher. *For the President's Eyes Only: Secret Intelligence and the American Presidency from Washington to Bush*. New York: Harper Perennial, 1996.

Cilluffo, Frank J., Ronald A. Marks, and George C. Salmoiraghi. "The Use and Limits of U.S. Intelligence." *Washington Quarterly* 25, no. 1 (2002): 61–74.

Clark, Robert M. *Intelligence Analysis: A Target-Centric Approach*. 2nd ed. Washington, DC: CQ Press, 2007.

Dupont, Alan. "Intelligence for the Twenty-First Century." *Intelligence and National Security* 18, no. 4 (2003): 15–39.

George, Roger Z., and Robert D. Kline. *Intelligence and the National Security Strategist: Enduring Issues and Challenges*. Washington, DC: National Defense University Press, 2004.

Lowenthal, Mark M. *Intelligence: From Secrets to Policy*. 3rd ed. Washington, DC: CQ Press, 2006.

National Commission on Terrorist Attacks. *The 9/11 Commission Report*. New York: W. W. Norton, 2004. Also available at www.9-11commission.gov/report/.

Odom, William E. *Fixing Intelligence: For a More Secure America*. New Haven, CT: Yale University Press, 2003.

Scott, Len, and Peter Jackson. "The Study of Intelligence in Theory and Practice." *Intelligence and National Security* 19, no. 2 (2004): 139–69.

Shulsky, Abram N., and Gary L. Schmitt. *Silent Warfare: Understanding the World of Intelligence*. 3rd ed. Washington, DC: Brassey's, 2002.

Stiefler, Todd. "CIA's Leadership and Major Covert Operations: Rogue Elephants or Risk-Averse Bureaucrats?" *Intelligence and National Security* 19, no. 4 (2004): 632–54.

Taylor, Stan, and David Goldman. "Intelligence Reform: Will More Agencies, Money, and Personnel Help?" *Intelligence and National Security* 19, no. 3 (2004): 416–35.

Recommended Internet Sources

Central Intelligence Agency Center for the Study of Intelligence, www.cia.gov/library/center-for-the-study-of-intelligence

Office of the Director of National Intelligence, www.odni.gov

The United States Intelligence Community, www.intelligencecareers.gov

US House of Representatives Permanent Select Committee on Intelligence, http://intelligence.house.gov

US Senate Select Committee on Intelligence, http://intelligence.senate.gov

Notes

1. Alexander Hamilton, "The Treaty Making Power of the Executive," Federalist No. 75, March 26, 1788, https://www.congress.gov/resources/display/content/The+Federalist+Papers#TheFederalistPapers-75.

2. John Jay, "The Powers of the Senate," Federalist No. 64, March 7, 1788, https://www.congress.gov/resources/display/content/The+Federalist+Papers#TheFederalistPapers-64.

3. *Final Report of the Commission on the Intelligence Capabilities of the United States Regarding Weapons of Mass Destruction,* March 31, 2005, 3, http://govinfo.library.unt.edu/wmd/report/wmd_report.pdf. See also "Report of the U.S. Senate Select Committee on Intelligence on the U.S. Intelligence Community's Prewar Intelligence Assessments on Iraq," July 7, 2004, http://www.gpo.gov/fdsys/granule/CRPT-108srpt301/CRPT-108srpt301/content-detail.html.

4. Richard A. Best Jr., "U.S. Intelligence and Policymaking: The Iraq Experience," CRS Report for Congress (Washington, DC: Congressional Research Service, December 2, 2005). One effort that does examine the role of policy makers in pre–Iraq War intelligence is Office of the Inspector General, "Review of Pre-Iraqi War Activities of the Office of the Undersecretary of Defense for Policy," Report No. 07-INTEL-04 (Washington, DC: Department of Defense, February 9, 2007).

5. Abram N. Shulsky and Gary L. Schmitt, *Silent Warfare: Understanding the World of Intelligence*, 3rd ed. (Washington, DC: Brassey's, 2002), 1.

6. Mark M. Lowenthal, *Intelligence: From Secrets to Policy*, 3rd ed. (Washington, DC: CQ Press, 2006), 6.

7. Melanie M.H. Gutjahr, ed., *The Intelligence Archipelago: The Community's Struggle to Reform in the Globalized Era* (Washington DC: Center for Strategic Intelligence Research, 2005), 8.

8. Lowenthal, *Intelligence*, 7.

9. Greg Whitlock and Barton Gellman, "To Hunt Osama bin Laden, Satellites Watched Over Abbottabad, Pakistan, and Navy SEALs," *Washington Post*, August 29, 2013.

10. Much of the discussion of the intelligence production cycle is based on basic information found on the United States Intelligence Community web site, https://www.intelligencecareers.gov/.

11. Lowenthal, *Intelligence*, 2.

12. Russell E. Travers, "Failures, Fallacies and Fixes: Posturing Intelligence for the Challenges of Globalization," in *The Intelligence Archipelago: The Community's Struggle to Reform in the Globalized Era*, ed. Melanie M. H. Gutjahr (Washington, DC: Center for Strategic Intelligence Research, 2005), xiii.

13. Travers, "Failures, Fallacies and Fixes," xiii.

14. US Intelligence Community, *How Intelligence Works*, n.d., https://www.intelligence careers.gov/icintelligence.html.

15. Joseph S. Nye Jr., *Soft Power: The Means to Success in World Politics* (New York: PublicAffairs, 2004), 105–6.

16. Cilluffo, Marks, and Salmoiraghi, "The Use and Limits of U.S. Intelligence," 68.

17. See for example, Jarrett M. Brachman and William McCants, *Stealing Al-Qa'ida's Playbook*, Combating Terrorism Center Report (West Point, NY: US Military Academy, February 2006).

18. Dan Elkins, *Managing Intelligence Resources* (Alexandria, VA: DWE Press, 2004), 1–2.

19. Cilluffo, Marks, and Salmoiraghi, "The Use and Limits of U.S. Intelligence," 68.

20. See Bob Drogin, *Curveball: Spies, Lies, and the Con Man Who Caused a War* (New York: Random House, 2007) for a lively account of the pitfalls of HUMINT concerning WMD in the lead-up to the Iraq War.

21. Elkins, *Managing Intelligence Resources*, 1–2.

22. Cilluffo, Marks, and Salmoiraghi, "The Use and Limits of U.S. Intelligence," 68.

23. See Central Intelligence Agency, *Iraq's Weapons of Mass Destruction Programs* (Washington, DC: CIA, October 2002).

24. US Intelligence Community, *How Intelligence Works*.

25. US Intelligence Community, *Processing*, n.d., https://www.intelligencecareers.gov /icintelligence.html.

26. Cilluffo, Marks, and Salmoiraghi, "The Use and Limits of U.S. Intelligence," 70.

27. Robert M. Clark, *Analysis: A Target-Centric Approach*, 2nd ed. (Washington, DC: CQ Press, 2007), 3–4.

28. Clark, *Analysis*, 3–4.

29. Cilluffo, Marks, and Salmoiraghi, "The Use and Limits of U.S. Intelligence," 70.

30. Michael McConnell, "Nomination of Mike McConnell to be Director of National Intelligence," Hearing Before the Select Committee on Intelligence, United States Senate, February 1, 2007, 10, https://www.intelligence.senate.gov/sites/default/files/hearings/110225 .pdf.

31. Thomas Finger, "Office of the Director of National Intelligence: From Pariah and Pinata to Managing Partner," in *The National Security Enterprise*, ed. Roger Z. George and Harvey Rishikof, 2nd ed. (Washington, DC: Georgetown University Press, 2017), 187.

32. Lowenthal, *Intelligence*, 177.

33. Roger Z. George, "Central Intelligence Agency: The President's Own," in *The National Security Enterprise*, ed. Roger Z. George and Harvey Rishikof, 2nd ed. (Washington, DC: Georgetown University Press, 2017), 219.

34. Martin Petersen, "The Challenge for the Political Analyst," in *Intelligence and the National Security Strategist: Enduring Issues and Challenges*, ed. Roger Z. George and Robert D. Kline (Washington, DC: National Defense University Press, 2004), 427.

35. Robert M. Gates, *Duty: Memoirs of a Secretary at War* (New York: Knopf, 2014), 540.

36. Robert Jervis, "Reports, Politics, and Intelligence Failures: The Case of Iraq," *Journal of Strategic Studies* 29, no. 1 (2006): 36.

37. Amanda J. Gookins, "The Role of Intelligence in Policy," *SAIS Review* 28, no. 1 (2008): 71.

38. See Frederic F. Manget, "Intelligence and the Rise of Judicial Intervention: Another System of Oversight," *Studies in Intelligence* 39, no. 5 (1996), https://www.cia.gov/library

/center-for-the-study-of-intelligence/csi-publications/csi-studies/studies/96unclass/manget.htm.

39. See Maritza Ryan, "A Game of Drones—Unmanned Aerial Vehicles (UAVs) and Unsettled Legal Questions," in *The Fundamentals of Counterterrorism Law*, ed. Lynne Zusman (Chicago: American Bar Association, 2014), 185–211.

40. For a first-hand account, see Gary C. Schroen, *First In: An Insider's Account of How the CIA Spearheaded the War on Terror in Afghanistan* (New York: Presidio Press, 2005).

41. Secretary of Defense Robert Gates explained that "if [the raid] was carried out under Defense Department authority, the U.S. government could not deny our involvement; CIA, on the other hand, could." Gates, *Duty*, 542.

42. See David F. Rudgers, "The Origins of Covert Action," *Journal of Contemporary History* 35, no. 2 (2000): 249–62.

43. George Lardner, "Restrictions Approved on Covert Action," *Washington Post*, August 16, 1991, 22.

44. Benjamin Banner, "Secret Prisons under Scrutiny," *Associated Press*, March 26, 2007.

45. Barack Obama, "Obama's Speech on Drone Policy," *New York Times*, May 23, 2013, http://www.nytimes.com/2013/05/24/us/politics/transcript-of-obamas-speech-on-drone-policy.html.

46. Center for Development of Security Excellence, "Counterintelligence Awareness Glossary," n.d., https://www.cdse.edu/documents/toolkits-fsos/ci-definitions.pdf.

47. Richard B. Schmitt, "FBI Has Some Explaining to Do; Senators Question the Bureau's Director about Abuses of Power," *Los Angeles Times*, March 28, 2007, A-12.

48. Zachary Laub, "The FBI's Role in National Security," June 21, 2017, https://www.cfr.org/backgrounder/fbis-role-national-security.

49. Laub, "The FBI's Role in National Security."

50. George W. Bush, "President Signs Intelligence Reform and Terrorism Prevention Act," White House, Office of the Press Secretary, December 17, 2004, http://georgewbush-whitehouse.archives.gov/news/releases/2004/12/20041217-1.html.

51. See for example the DNI's "joint duty" initiative, found in Office of the Director of National Intelligence, *United States Intelligence Community 100 Day Plan for Integration and Collaboration*, April 2007, 3, https://www.dni.gov/files/documents/Newsroom/Reports%20and%20Pubs/100_Day_Plan.pdf.

52. Senator John D. Rockefeller, "Hearing of the Senate Select Committee on Intelligence: The Nomination of Mike McConnell to be Director of National Intelligence," February 1, 2007, 3.

53. Department of Defense Directive 5143.01, SUBJECT: Undersecretary of Defense for Intelligence (USD[I]), October 24, 2014, http://dtic.mil/whs/directives/corres/pdf/514301p.pdf.

54. Office of the Director of National Intelligence (ODNI), *An Overview of the United States Intelligence Community*, 2007, 19, http://oai.dtic.mil/oai/oai?verb=getRecord&metadataPrefix=html&identifier=ADA500311.

55. Elkins, *Managing Intelligence Resources*, 2–4.

56. ODNI, *An Overview of the United States Intelligence Community*, 2007, 15.

57. FBI, "Field Offices," n.d., https://www.fbi.gov/contact-us/field-offices; and FBI, "Overseas Offices," n.d., https://www.fbi.gov/contact-us/legal-attache-offices.

58. ODNI, *An Overview of the United States Intelligence Community*, 2007, 14.

59. Drug Enforcement Association (DEA), "Office Locations," March 9, 2018, http://www.dea.gov/about/Domesticoffices.shtml.

60. ODNI, *An Overview of the United States Intelligence Community*, 2007, 13.

61. National Commission on Terrorist Attacks, *The 9/11 Commission Report* (New York: W. W. Norton, 2004), also available at www.9-11commission.gov/report/.

62. The Privacy and Civil Liberties Oversight Board, "History and Mission," n.d., https://www.pclob.gov/about/.

63. Hearing before the Senate Select Committee on Intelligence, January 29, 2014, http://www.intelligence.senate.gov/hearings/open-hearing-current-and-projected-national-security-threats-against-united-states#.

64. Report of the Senate Select Committee on Intelligence, Study of the Central Intelligence Agency's Detention and Interrogation Program, December 9, 2014, https://www.gpo.gov/fdsys/pkg/CRPT-113srpt288/pdf/CRPT-113srpt288.pdf.

65. *Katz v United States*, 389 US 347 (1967), https://supreme.justia.com/cases/federal/us/389/347/case.html.

66. Federal Judicial Center, "Foreign Intelligence Surveillance Court and Court of Review, 1978–Present," n.d., https://www.fjc.gov/history/courts/foreign-intelligence-surveillance-court-and-court-review-1978-present.

67. James S. Van Wagenen, "A Review of Congressional Oversight: Critics and Defenders," *Studies in Intelligence*, Semiannual Edition, no. 1 (1997), https://www.cia.gov/library/center-for-the-study-of-intelligence/csi-publications/csi-studies/studies/97unclass/wagenen.html.

68. Federal Judicial Center, "Foreign Intelligence Surveillance Court and Court of Review, 1978–Present."

69. Federal Judicial Center, "Foreign Intelligence Surveillance Court and Court of Review, 1978–Present."

70. Manget, "Intelligence and the Rise of Judicial Intervention."

71. Sara Murry and Jeremy Herb, "Trump Still Unconvinced Russia Meddled in 2016 Election," February 14, 2018, https://www.cnn.com/2018/02/13/politics/trump-unconvinced-russia-meddled-election/index.html.

8

The Role of the Military in the Policy Process

The role of the military in US national security policy is unique and crucial for several reasons. First, the military's coercive capabilities make democratic civilian political control a matter of central importance. This concern shaped the drafting of the US Constitution, which establishes the basic legal framework that continues to govern military affairs to this day. Second, especially since the 1950s, the US military has received a large share of national resources. The Department of Defense (DoD) is in effect America's largest company, spending over $689 billion each year, and it has over 2.9 million active-duty, reserve, and civilian employees who work in more than 160 countries.[1] Military spending constitutes the single largest category of discretionary spending in the US federal budget (see chapter 9). The importance of the military instrument to US national security policy makes the effectiveness of America's military institutions a matter of great consequence (see chapters 13 through 17). While other chapters discuss how military power is used, this chapter concentrates on the ways in which military leaders and institutions engage in national security policy making.

The American Historical Experience

Early American History and the US Constitution. America's wariness of standing armies is rooted in the colonial experience (as discussed in chapter 2). The founders had experienced the negative effects of a powerful and often oppressive British army, and they also recognized the unfortunate consequences of militarism in the countries of Europe.

After the Revolutionary War, the American army was essentially disbanded. The national government had the task of governing under the Articles of Confederation, which gave it very little power to maintain an army or even to raise one for national emergencies. After several violent domestic uprisings (most notably an uprising of farmers against crushing debt and higher taxes in 1786 and 1787, known as Shays' Rebellion), and with increasing border threats, the founders convened a constitutional convention in 1787 to improve a government that was decidedly weak in many facets of national security.

The Framers of the US Constitution found it challenging to agree on a formulation that would provide for physical security from foreign and domestic threats while simultaneously protecting the state and society from the potential dangers of a standing army.[2] Douglas Johnson and Steven Metz explain: "Amid intense debate and calls to ban a standing army altogether, the Framers of the Constitution crafted a compromise between military effectiveness and political control. They trusted balance, the diffusion of power, and shared responsibility—all basic elements of the new political system—to control the military."[3] These elements were codified in the final document and the Bill of Rights through several provisions designed to "provide for the common defense."[4]

- Article I, Section 8 of the Constitution gives control over the military to the legislative branch by granting it specific powers such as "to declare war," "to raise and support Armies," and "to provide and maintain a Navy." The Constitution grants the states the explicit authority to maintain militias. These provisions were intended to preclude the executive branch from making war without the consent of the legislature and to balance state and federal power.
- Article II, Section 2 of the Constitution gives the roles of both chief executive and commander in chief to the president. This ensures civilian supremacy by placing the chief executive at the top of the military chain of command, and aids military effectiveness by providing for unity of command in the employment of military forces.
- The Second Amendment emphasizes the role of the citizen-soldier by providing for "the right of the people to keep and bear Arms." Like the militia clause, this provision keeps the federal government from having a monopoly on the means of war.
- The Third Amendment protects US citizens from the pre-Revolutionary British custom of quartering soldiers in private homes "without the consent of the Owner."

The intricate system of checks and balances was meant to enable the establishment and employment of an effective military while ensuring it could never become a danger to the society it was created to protect. This formulation also ensured the involvement of both the president and Congress in the making of military policy (see chapters 4 and 5).

Influence of the Military on National Policy Is Historically Rare. Prior to World War II, the military had significant influence on the formulation of national policy only in exceptional cases, mostly linked directly to wartime. For example,

General Winfield Scott, commander in Mexico in 1846, established occupation policies in the territory that he conquered. During the Civil War, the commanding general of the Union army exerted great influence upon the secretary of war, the president, and Congress, especially in the latter years when Ulysses S. Grant held that command. Perhaps the most direct instance of military policy making in that conflict occurred with the reestablishment of state and local governments in the South; President Abraham Lincoln adopted the programs instituted by military commanders for such governance as national policy in 1863. Military influence in policy formulation was also evident during the occupation of the Philippines beginning in 1902, immediately after the Spanish-American War. Later, during World War I, General John J. Pershing had wide discretion in dealing directly with Allies and in imposing requirements on the national government at home. Shortly after World War I, General Pershing and General Peyton C. March proposed plans to Congress for maintaining an army substantially stronger than the pre–World War I establishment. Congress seriously considered these plans but ultimately rejected them, primarily due to budget limitations.[5]

The examples above typify the generally accepted rule prior to World War II that the military should play little role in the formulation of national security policy except during wartime, when the armed forces were responsible for executing such policy. The general absence of any major threats to the nation's existence, apart from the Civil War, left the military services in times of peace with only the tasks of continental defense, suppression of indigenous peoples, internal development (especially of rivers and railroads), protection of trade, contingency planning, and passive support of a largely isolationist foreign policy. Neither the structure of government nor the necessity of military missions compelled sustained involvement of the military in national policy.

World War II and the National Security Act of 1947. World War II and the immediate postwar years marked a significant break with the past. The clear wartime need for interdepartmental coordination of political-military affairs led to the establishment of the State-War-Navy Coordinating Committee in late 1944, consisting of senior civilian officials from each department and supported by a system of interdepartmental subcommittees, which included senior military participants. This committee structure marked the beginning of institutionalized military influence at the highest levels of the national security bureaucracy.

The demands of World War II also led to other important changes in the role of the military in the national security policy-making process. First, the uniformed chiefs of the services began to meet regularly as the Joint Chiefs of Staff (JCS) and to maintain direct liaison with the president.[6] Second, the services played the leading role in developing war-termination and postwar occupation policies, due to factors that included the relative detachment of the State Department from military operations and the national goal of "total victory." The key political decision of whether the US Army would take Berlin, for example, was not made in Washington but was left to the discretion of the military commander in Europe, General

Dwight D. Eisenhower.[7] After the war ended, officials of the military government made critical decisions in occupied areas, including Berlin. For example, senior War Department officials determined the number and ideological composition of the political parties permitted in postwar allied-occupied Germany.[8] In Japan, General Douglas MacArthur ruled over the occupation with enormous autonomy. Third, superior organization and resources enabled the military to play an expanded role in all areas of national security policy formulation. The Operations Division of the War Department's general staff, which formed the core of US wartime and immediate postwar political-military planning efforts, was particularly effective.[9]

In the postwar years, civilian elements gradually began to reassert their traditional roles in foreign policy.[10] State Department leadership in postwar European recovery, symbolized by the Marshall Plan, and the central role of the State Department in postwar political and economic planning shifted the initiative in policy making away from the military establishment. The military's advantage in organizational terms began to shrink, and so did its resources. Military appropriations dropped sharply, and army strength contracted from over 12 million active duty personnel in 1945 to less than 1.6 million two years later.[11]

Nevertheless, policy makers and military personnel retained the lessons of political-military coordination learned during World War II. The National Security Act of 1947 formalized many of the joint and interdepartmental committees and advisory groups that had been formed during the war, creating a structure to facilitate civil-military coordination. In addition to establishing the National Security Council (NSC) and a secretary of defense (see chapters 3, 4, and 10), the act created a "national military establishment," consisting of the three service departments (Army, Navy, and Air Force) linked together by a series of joint committees and coordinated by the chiefs of the three services sitting collectively as the JCS. The members of the JCS, who were authorized to have staffs to assist in their roles, became the principal military advisors to the president and secretary of defense. The act also provided the legal basis for the creation of US military unified and specified commands worldwide.

The Key West Agreement of 1948 designated the JCS to be the executive agent for unified and specified commands.[12] The JCS would be responsible for day-to-day communications and supervision of operational forces, as well as coordination among the services to define the roles and missions of each. Legislation in 1949 strengthened the secretary of defense by creating a unified DoD with authority over the services. It also removed the service secretaries from the president's cabinet and from the NSC, increased the size of the joint staff, and added a chairman to preside over the JCS.

The gradual centralization of a national military establishment during and after World War II, first codified in the 1947 National Security Act, dramatically changed the power relationships between and among the services, Congress, and other executive branch departments.[13] With America deeply involved in global affairs after its overwhelming victory, how each institution or organization influenced national security policy in relation to the others became a dynamic issue that continues to challenge policy makers to this day.

The Cold War. By 1949, the Communist Party's victory in China's civil war, Soviet initiatives in Greece, the Middle East, Berlin, and Eastern Europe, and the Soviet acquisition of nuclear weapons prompted a series of Western countermeasures, which together constituted the policy of containment (discussed in chapter 3). Recognition of the urgent necessity for allied cooperation led to significant US military assistance to friendly states.[14] Military expertise was also relied upon in the development of the North Atlantic Treaty Organization (NATO) and to secure allied agreement for the rearmament and participation of Germany in the build-up of NATO.[15] Military officers charged with overseeing occupied areas after the war, such as General MacArthur in Japan and General Lucius Clay in Germany, as well as distinguished World War II leaders, such as Generals George C. Marshall, Dwight D. Eisenhower, and Omar Bradley, continued to serve in national positions of great responsibility and influence.

With the beginning of the Korean War in 1950, a major reallocation of national resources again took place; this time the change was more enduring. In a period of four years (1950–1954), the share of the gross national product (GNP) devoted to national defense rose from 5.2 percent to 13.5 percent, and military expenditures nearly quadrupled from $13 billion in FY 1950 to $50.4 billion in FY 1953.[16] The hostilities in Korea expanded and complicated the military's role in the formulation and execution of policy. One of the first lessons of the Korean War was that the World War II concept of autonomy for the theater commander in the prosecution of the war would have to be curtailed significantly. MacArthur was relieved of command in the Far East by President Harry Truman after a long series of attempts by MacArthur to shape US policy in his theater independent of consideration of events in Europe or of overall national policy.[17] At a time when concern about war with the Soviets in Europe was high, a local commander could no longer be allowed to make policy without regard for worldwide ramifications. The JCS and their civilian superiors feared that the communist attack in Korea was a feint and a prelude to a full-scale assault in Europe. As the nation moved through the uncharted waters of a war fought for limited objectives that did not require total national mobilization, military leaders had to assess how to use military means to support political objectives in ways that differed strikingly from the "unconditional surrender" and "total victory" formulations of World War II.

Despite the enlargement of the military establishment after the Korean War and the increased US projection of military influence abroad, strong interservice rivalries tended to weaken the military's voice within the national security establishment. These rivalries had certain strategic and political advantages. The conflict of ideas and doctrines generated rival solutions to strategic and technological problems; for example, the Army and the Air Force each developed its own intermediate-range ballistic missiles (known as Jupiter and Thor, respectively).[18] Some potential conflicts between civil and military institutions were deflected into competition among military groups, whose resolution required civilian judgment; civilian control was thus enhanced. Civilian political leaders were able to find military support for different strategic concepts, and interservice rivalry gave them convenient political cover. Interservice rivalry provided an easy target to place blame for "deficiencies in the military establishment for which just possibly they [political leaders] might be held responsible."[19]

Yet the drawbacks of these rivalries were also evident. Cost-effective management of DoD proved inordinately difficult, as the uniformed services sometimes appealed departmental—or even presidential—decisions to congressional allies for support. The JCS was seldom able to agree upon an overall defense program within budgetary ceilings. In turn, the public spectacle of disagreement and dissension eroded confidence in the efficacy of military judgment, which had been so high in the early years after World War II. More serious were fears that the defense organization was simply ineffective, relying on logrolling and compromise, without effective planning or real control by anyone.[20]

In the years that followed the National Security Act of 1947, efforts at DoD reorganization repeatedly sought to increase civilian control over the military while reducing the harmful tendency to allocate resources and develop policies on a bargaining-for-shares-of-the-pie basis. Controversies over weapons systems procurement and service missions also prompted efforts toward centralization of control. In 1958, Congress amended the National Security Act to give the secretary of defense greater authority, more influence in strategic planning, and greater control over the JCS. The military departments were further downgraded administratively, and the functions of the military were revised to take away control over unified and specified commands and give it to the secretary of defense.

The reforms of the 1950s empowered the secretary of defense to exercise greater control over the department and the services. The tools of cost accounting and systems analysis developed under Secretary Robert McNamara in the 1960s enhanced this control. Supported by a host of talented "whiz kids," McNamara used the new techniques to preempt military influence in both procurement and strategy.[21] In part, this greater centralization was a logical outcome of the development of new budgetary and analytical techniques. More fundamentally, however, it grew out of persistent service disagreements, expansion of civilian staff, and increased public demand for civilian control over the military. (See chapter 9 for more discussion of McNamara's effect on defense management.)

Although centralization was necessary for both strategic and economic reasons, it posed a severe dilemma for the military, especially for the JCS. The chairman of the JCS directed the joint staff, but was not empowered to provide a unified military opinion unless all of the service chiefs agreed. Unanimous agreements among the chiefs could be obtained, but often required suboptimal compromises. Split decisions, where the chiefs were not unanimous, were even worse from the perspective of the military because they placed the final decisions on military matters in civilian hands without benefit of a military recommendation. The loyalties of the individual chiefs to their own services were, of course, sometimes a factor in disagreements, but continued rivalry also reflected fundamental differences over strategy and sometimes the relative capabilities of the various military staffs. The 1958 DoD reorganization expanded the joint staff and directed the joint chiefs to concentrate on their joint responsibilities and to delegate the running of their respective services to their vice chiefs. However, service staffs remained larger and more prominent than the joint staff and promoted parochial service interests in the joint arena. The tension between independent service perspectives and the need for a joint military approach continued throughout most of the Cold War.

The Goldwater-Nichols Act of 1986. It took nearly three more decades and several episodes of poor performance by the military (including the failed hostage rescue attempt in Iran in 1980 and the poorly coordinated invasion of Grenada in 1983) before Congress again addressed military effectiveness and civilian control. The Department of Defense Reorganization Act of 1986, commonly known as Goldwater-Nichols, was the most far-reaching legislation to address military organization since the National Security Act of 1947 (see also chapter 5).

Goldwater-Nichols had several key features intended to promote "jointness" among the services. First, the authority of the chairman of the JCS was strengthened. The chairman was designated the principal military advisor to the president, the NSC, and the secretary of defense; no longer required to report only JCS consensus positions, the chairman was authorized to offer his best professional military advice. Second, the new position of JCS vice chairman was created, with the expectation that this officer would act in the interest of the military establishment as a whole with a focus on integrating the separate research, development, and procurement activities of the services. Third, legislation created a "joint specialty" within service personnel systems and required the services to send their best officers to both the joint staff in Washington and to the unified commands in the field. Goldwater-Nichols required that officers with joint service receive their fair share of promotions and specified that no officers could be promoted to general or admiral without joint service experience. The authority of commanders of unified and specified commands was also strengthened through the establishment of a chain of command that ran directly from the president to the secretary of defense to these commanders. Increased jointness and interservice operational cooperation were the underlying purposes and end result of the 1986 Act.

Post–Cold War Policy Making in the 1990s. There have been no significant structural changes in the formal role of military advisors and their advice on national security matters since the passage of Goldwater-Nichols in 1986. Instead, it is the nature of the personal relationships between senior military leaders and senior civilian leaders, including the president and secretary of defense, that has dominated discussions of the role of the military in the policy-making process. Soon after the end of the Cold War, US armed forces were deployed to the Persian Gulf after Saddam Hussein's Iraqi Army seized Kuwait in August 1990. In those military operations, President George H. W. Bush gave JCS Chairman Colin Powell the forces he requested and allowed Powell and the theater commander to conduct the campaign without detailed political oversight. As an example of his influence, Powell reportedly influenced the president to stop the ground war after one hundred hours.[22] The war resulted in a lopsided military victory for the

US-led coalition. As one observer later noted, "In less than six weeks, 795,000 Coalition troops destroyed a defending army of hundreds of thousands, losing only 240 attackers."[23] Despite the military success, however, failures in planning for war termination and shortcomings in US political achievements were soon apparent.[24] Consequently, the lessons for US civil-military relations were mixed. Some praised the high degree of professional military autonomy in the design and conduct of the military campaign, while others argued that greater political involvement—especially in planning for war termination—might have led to a better political outcome for the United States.[25]

As the 1990s progressed, the US military experienced a post–Cold War drawdown even as the armed forces were increasingly used for stabilization operations. The number of active-duty service members decreased from 2.1 million in 1990 to 1.4 million in 2000; this smaller military was deployed to crises in Somalia, Haiti, Bosnia, Kosovo, and elsewhere (see chapter 3).[26] The election of Bill Clinton, who was president from 1993 through the end of the decade, created a further important dynamic because he was the first president since World War II without military service. Many senior members of his administration had little or no military experience, and the president himself had a reputation for a general lack of interest in military affairs as well as a perceived personal lack of regard for the military.[27] Anecdotal evidence indicating that the professional military lacked appropriate respect for Clinton as commander in chief, as well as the apparent influence of powerful JCS chairmen, particularly Powell, led some observers to claim that threats to adequate civilian control over the military constituted a "crisis" in US civil-military relations.[28]

Some observers attributed these perceptions of a crisis to timing: an administration that seemed to lack credibility in military affairs came into office at the same time that the JCS had a particularly popular and activist chairman in the person of Powell. Others emphasized structural factors, such as a concern that Goldwater-Nichols had centralized too much power in the chairman and the JCS.[29] A third potential source of friction was the nature of the stabilization missions assigned to the military in the 1990s. These services tended to see these operations, in which decisive victory could not be the goal, as undesirable distractions from preferred core tasks.[30] However, most analysts agreed that claims of a crisis were exaggerated.[31] Even during the Clinton administration, at least one observer saw the balance being restored during the tenures of successive JCS chairmen.[32]

Policy Making after September 11, 2001. In contrast to concerns during the 1990s about excessive military influence, after 9/11 there were concerns that the balance had tipped too far in the opposite direction.[33] When Donald Rumsfeld, who had served previously as secretary of defense under President Gerald Ford, reassumed that office under President George W. Bush in January 2001, he had a definite agenda. His priorities included the transformation of the military and the assertion, or reassertion, of stronger control by the Office of the Secretary of Defense (OSD) over the services, as well as stronger civilian control over the military. Rumsfeld's transformation agenda drew upon considerable thinking in the US defense community about a "Revolution in Military Affairs" based on high-technology, precision stand-off weapon systems, and information dominance (see chapter 3).

The need to reestablish civilian control seemed to arise from the belief that the military "had become too independent and risk-averse during eight years under President Bill Clinton."[34] Rumsfeld pursued his agenda with a high degree of personal self-confidence and aggressiveness. Although JCS Chairman Richard Myers praised him as having healthy relationships with senior officers and the joint staff, many others described Rumsfeld as "frequently abusive and indecisive, trusting only a tiny circle of close advisers, seemingly eager to slap down officers with decades of distinguished service."[35]

Rumsfeld's tenure as Secretary of Defense got off to a rough start, but his reputation rebounded after the 9/11 attacks. One of Rumsfeld's first tasks was the Quadrennial Defense Review of 2001. This process generated such tension between Rumsfeld and the services, as well as between Rumsfeld and Congress, that there was speculation that Rumsfeld could be the first member of George W. Bush's cabinet to depart.[36] The terrorist attacks on September 11, 2001, and the apparent success of the subsequent invasion of Afghanistan transformed this dynamic. The US and coalition campaign appeared to validate both Rumsfeld's intensely hands-on management style and his goal of transformation to a more high-tech form of warfare.[37]

Despite vast budget increases in the wake of 9/11, however, relations between Rumsfeld and senior military leaders continued to deteriorate during the planning for the war in Iraq and especially after the 2003 invasion. These tensions were made public with the testimony given by Army Chief of Staff Eric Shinseki before the Senate Armed Services Committee in February 2003. When Senator Carl Levin asked Shinseki for his estimate of the forces that would be required to stabilize Iraq after an invasion, Shinseki's answer of "several hundred thousand" drew official and public rebuke from Rumsfeld, Deputy Secretary of Defense Paul Wolfowitz, and Vice President Dick Cheney.[38] This episode implied that the war-planning process for Iraq did not include broad and open consultations with senior military leaders.

The failures in planning and adaptability that led to serious US difficulties in post-invasion Iraq were partly a function of ineffective coordination and cooperation among military and civilian leaders.[39] The 2006 Iraq Study Group report documented the importance of effective civil-military relations and the specific challenges of that time:

> The U.S. military has a long tradition of strong partnership between the civilian leadership of the Department of Defense and the uniformed services. Both have long benefited from a relationship in which the civilian leadership exercises control with the advantage of fully candid professional advice, and the military serves loyally with the understanding that its advice has been heard and valued. That tradition has been frayed, and civil-military relations need to be repaired.[40]

The report went on to recommend that "the new Secretary of Defense should make every effort to build healthy civil-military relations, by creating an environment in which the senior military feel free to offer independent military advice not only to the civilian leadership in the Pentagon but also to the President and the National Security Council, as envisioned in the Goldwater-Nichols legislation."[41]

Soon after the Iraq Study Group issued its report, DoD gained new leadership: Robert Gates became secretary of defense in December 2006 and General David Petraeus became the commander of forces in Iraq in February 2007. Direct communication of senior military with civilian leaders increased, including a weekly video teleconference among Petraeus, Gates, George W. Bush, and other NSC members.[42] Petraeus shaped the doctrine and strategy that would provide the foundation for the 2007 troop surge, and many viewed him as the public face of the administration's policy. Petraeus adeptly built coalitions among academics, military leaders, and political leaders that enabled the adoption of US counterinsurgency policies in Iraq.[43]

After the election of President Barack Obama, debates about troop levels and counterinsurgency policy continued, although the focus shifted from Iraq to Afghanistan. The prominence of senior military leaders in those debates was not always welcome in the White House. In September 2009, a classified assessment by General Stanley McChrystal, the US commander in Afghanistan, was leaked. This assessment included McChrystal's observation that the US military required both a change in strategy and increased resources to avoid failure in Afghanistan.[44] One month later, Ambassador Karl Eikenberry, a retired three-star general who had commanded US and international forces in Afghanistan, sent a series of classified cables expressing his concern that increased troop levels without Afghan political reform would be costly and counterproductive. These, too, became public. The release of both these documents coincided with a major review of the administration's Afghanistan policy and gave the impression that military leaders were inappropriately trying to force the president into a specific decision. In early December 2009, Obama announced that the United States would send an additional 30,000 troops to Afghanistan.[45]

It appears that there was a vigorous debate prior to the president's announcement of this "surge," but several commentators suggested that civil-military interactions under Obama were characterized by conflict rather than cooperation. Author Bob Woodward alleged that senior military leaders—including JCS Chairman Michael Mullen, McChrystal, and then US Central Command (CENTCOM) commander Petraeus—had blocked the development of a counterterrorism option that the president had requested.[46] Such accusations contributed to a growing perception of civil-military conflict at the highest levels. This was reinforced by McChrystal's resignation after the publication of a damaging article in *Rolling Stone* magazine.[47] Although the article did not offer explicit evidence that McChrystal had undermined the administration's goals, it portrayed his staff officers as irreverent, unprofessional, and disrespectful of senior administration officials.[48] Both incidents contributed to perceptions that senior military officers were attempting to assert more influence over policy than they had during Rumsfeld's tenure.

In recent years, it has become increasingly evident that the military's role in the policymaking process is not limited to the executive branch. Congress plays an important role in lawmaking, appropriations, and military appointments, and members of Congress can call military leaders to testify before congressional committees across a range of issues (see chapters 5 and 10). As American commitments in the wars in Iraq and Afghanistan waned and as budgets tightened, Congress began to take a larger role in personnel policies, including the repeal of the "Don't Ask, Don't Tell" policy concerning homosexuals in the military and in the budget decisions under sequestration imposed by the Budget Control Act of 2011. Members of Congress have become more involved in attempting to influence decisions to use military force in places like Libya and Syria.[49] The committee system provides members of Congress with the means to influence national security policy, but it also can draw media attention and thus provide military leaders with a public platform for their professional opinions. Unlike private conversations in the White House, such testimony is public. In 2013, confrontations between military and civilian leaders over the use of military force, transgender policy, and the defense budget prompted at least one commentator to decry the state of civil-military relations.[50] More recently, however, the Trump administration's increases in the fiscal year 2019 defense budget request ameliorated some of the causes for tension between civilian and military leaders.

The Role of the Military Today. Since World War II, there have been a number of trends concerning the role of the military in the national security process. First, military power has remained a central means through which the United States pursues its security. Although defense spending has declined as a proportion of the economy and the federal budget, it remains the largest single part of discretionary spending (see chapter 9) and enables the United States to maintain global presence and influence. Concurrently, the formal decisionmaking structure supporting the president and the NSC evolved and grew to meet the policy coordination needs of a global superpower with large standing military forces (see chapter 10). With resources and combatant commands that cover the entire world, military leaders are usually a part of any foreign policy discussion, even if there is only minimal military involvement.

Second, expanding overseas defense commitments have increased military involvement in policy making and ensured that such involvement is not always limited to purely military issues. Beginning with Eisenhower's unique position as the first supreme allied commander in Europe at the outset of the Cold War, combatant commanders have increasingly expanded their role and influence. Regional commanders "have evolved into the modern-day equivalent of the Roman Empire's proconsuls—well-funded, semi-autonomous, unconventional centers of US foreign policy."[51] The vast resources wielded by DoD give military personnel a distinct advantage, especially compared with their counterparts from State, the US Agency for International Development, and other agencies.

Third, individual members of the military have sometimes been selected to serve in personal advisory roles at senior levels while still on active duty. During the Kennedy years, for example, General Maxwell Taylor was recalled to active duty to serve as military representative to the president before being appointed JCS chairman. During the Nixon administration, General Alexander Haig was deputy national security advisor and later White House chief of staff, before becoming NATO commander. The placement of military officers in senior national policy positions was criticized in 1987 after Marine Lieutenant Colonel Oliver North, working as an NSC staff member, diverted funds from arms sales to Iran to provide illegal support to anti-communist "Contra" rebels in Nicaragua. These activities were undertaken with the approval of Vice Admiral John Poindexter, the national security advisor. Ultimately, the North-Poindexter episode came to be seen as an isolated incident, and it did not preclude President Ronald Reagan from appointing then–Lieutenant General Colin Powell as his national security advisor, a position normally occupied by a civilian. During the George H. W. Bush administration, General Michael Hayden was principal deputy director of national intelligence and later CIA director, both while still on active duty. Similarly, Lieutenant General Doug Lute served as deputy national security advisor for both the George W. Bush and Barack Obama administrations while still on active duty. President Trump appointed Lieutenant General H. R. McMaster to serve as national security advisor while still on active duty after retired Lieutenant General Michael Flynn resigned in 2017.

Another trend, partly the result of those previously discussed, is that military officers have become both increasingly capable of operating at higher levels of the US government and increasingly influential in national security policy matters. Goldwater-Nichols created additional billets in which officers serve at the political-military nexus, and the resulting career incentives encouraged some of the most promising military officers to pursue joint opportunities that broadened their perspectives early in their careers.[52] Greater experience was complemented by a military education system that began to produce more officers with advanced civilian university degrees. These advanced degrees became increasingly important to military promotions. In 1965, no members of the JCS had advanced degrees; by 1981, they all did.[53] In addition, senior professional schools such as the services' war colleges (where colonels spend a year of study to be eligible for promotion to general or admiral) have added study of the nonmilitary aspects of national security to their programs. Most senior service colleges are accredited to award masters degrees to their students.

The role of the military in the national security process has continued to grow and to become more complex in the post-9/11 world. Debate over whether the military has exercised an appropriate level of influence in the appropriate venues of national security policy is ongoing; achieving a stable equilibrium will continue to be a challenge.

The Civil-Military Gap and Civil-Military Relations

An additional challenge to finding a stable equilibrium in US civil-military relations may stem from a gap between the values of long-serving members of the military and the society they swear to protect and to serve. Following the Cold War, scholars began to examine these differences, asking whether "a 'gap' in values between the armed forces and civilian society [had] widened to the point of threatening the effectiveness of the military and impeding civil-military cooperation."[54] Research confirmed that, over the preceding generation, the proportion of officers who self-identified as Republican had increased from 33 percent to 64 percent, and found other important differences between officers as a group and civilians on a range of political and cultural issues.[55] A particular source of concern was that a sample of successful mid-grade officers believed that they should "insist" (rather than merely advise) on issues relating to engagement in military conflicts.[56] While scholars and practitioners did not see a crisis, they argued that indicators of a gap were worthy of more attention by senior civilian and military leaders responsible for the relationship.

A recent theory posits that there is not a single civil-military gap, but rather four overlapping ones: a cultural gap, a demographic gap, a policy-preference gap, and an institutional gap.[57] The cultural gap exists because military training and war create distinct experiences. The demographic gap stems from a combination of factors, including the establishment of an all-volunteer force (AVF) and the regional differences in base locations and recruiting. Both of these gaps are likely to influence the policy preferences and political affiliations of those in the military, thereby contributing to the so-called policy-preference gap. Since the 1990s, conservatism and Republican identification among senior officers have remained significantly higher than among the general population, although some evidence suggests that enlisted soldiers are more representative of society than are the officer corps.[58] The institutional gap stems from the way in which differences in the resources and capacity of the military, on the one hand, and civilian governmental agencies, on the other, may result in excessive influence by the military on policy decisions. Despite evidence of the existence of these gaps, there is significant disagreement about whether and how the differences between civilians and those in the military affect the formulation of national security policy.[59]

The "Right" Amount of Civilian Control. Although there are many points of debate in American civil-military relations, there is fundamental agreement on one point: in the United States, civilian control—or more precisely democratic political control—is a central guiding principle. The US military is and should be subordinate to the president and to certain designated officials in the executive branch, as well as to elected political leaders in Congress. According to the US Constitution, the executive and the legislative branches of the federal government share authority and responsibility for military affairs.

Despite a broad consensus on this issue, there is nevertheless plenty of room for disagreement on more subtle points, as illustrated in previous examples from the Clinton, George W. Bush, and Obama administrations. Although there is no serious concern over a military coup or military revolt in the United States, not all important issues in American civil-military relations are settled. Those that are still debated include whether there should be limits to civilian involvement in the formulation and execution of military policy, strategy, and operations; the appropriate role and relative influence of Congress in military policy and strategy; and the appropriate extent and exercise of military influence during the formulation of national security policy. The optimal pattern of US civil-military relations would ensure democratic political control while also facilitating sound strategic decision making and the creation of effective military institutions.[60]

The "Purist" versus "Fusionist" Schools of Thought. The American military is far from monolithic in character or in outlook. One of the recurring debates since World War II has been over its appropriate role in the formulation and execution of national security policy. General Matthew Ridgway, Army chief of staff in 1955, expressed the traditional "military purist" perspective: "The military advisor . . . should give his competent professional advice based on the military aspects of the programs referred to him, based on his fearless, honest, objective estimate of the national interest, and regardless of administration policy at any particular time. He should confine his advice to the essential military aspects."[61] The purist case does not deny the complexity of national security issues—they are recognized to be a blend of economic, political, and military components—but they are to be determined by civilian policy makers. The professional officer is an expert only on the military component. In providing advice to policy makers, therefore, professional officers should confine themselves to purely military considerations. In this view, officers are not competent to provide economic or political judgments or opinions, and they should not be asked to do so.

An alternate view, the "fusionist" approach, maintains that in the changed environment of national security policy in the post–World War II environment, "purely military" considerations do not exist.[62] Moreover, in a world of global terrorism and proliferating weapons of mass destruction, in which the military consumes significant economic resources and in which the use of force may have tremendous political implications, military decisions inevitably have considerable economic and political consequences and vice versa. Therefore, in giving their advice, professional officers should incorporate political and economic considerations along with military factors.

Many civilian and military leaders tend to be fusionists. President John Kennedy implicitly expressed the fusionist thesis in a speech to graduating West Point cadets when, after stressing future military command responsibilities, he added: "The non-military problems which you will face will also be the most demanding—diplomatic, political, economic. You will need to know and understand not only the foreign policy of the United States, but the foreign policy of all countries scattered around the world. You will need to understand the importance of military power and also the limits of military power. You will have an obligation to deter war as well as to fight it."[63] Maxwell Taylor, former chairman of the JCS and military representative to the president, warned that "nothing is so likely to repel the civilian decision-makers as a military argument which omits obvious considerations which the president cannot omit. . . . If they [the Joint Chiefs] want to persuade the President, they had better look at the totality of his problem and try to give maximum help."[64]

This debate between fusionists and purists occurred among scholars as well as practitioners. Perhaps the foremost critic of "fusionism" was Samuel P. Huntington, who warned in 1957, in *The Soldier and the State*, that if the military "broadened" its professional worldview to incorporate civilian-defined "political realities," it might gain access to the highest levels of the policy process, but it could no longer speak on strategic matters from an adequately military perspective. The country and the national security process would be better served by a military that cultivated its autonomous ethic in a politically neutral, professional institution. In return, the state would gain a "politically sterile and neutral" professional officer corps "ready to carry out the wishes of any civilian group which secures legitimate authority within the state."[65]

A leading advocate of fusionism was Morris Janowitz, who laid out his perspective in *The Professional Soldier* (1960).[66] In contrast to Huntington's emphasis on professional autonomy and a degree of separation, Janowitz believed that it would be unrealistic to rely on an apolitical and relatively detached military: "In the United States, where political leadership is diffuse, civilian politicians have come to assume that the military will be an active ingredient in decision-making about national security."[67] To be effective during the Cold War, he argued, the US military must be aware of the international political consequences of military action and must understand the primacy of political objectives and the occasional need for limits on the application of force.[68]

In practice, both the purist and the fusionist perspectives have shortcomings. The purist perspective tends to posit a degree of separation between political and military affairs that simply does not and cannot exist. As military theorist Carl von Clausewitz argued in *On War*, at the highest level of decision making the idea of a "purely military" opinion makes no sense, since "no major proposal for war can be worked out in ignorance of political factors." He goes on to argue, "To bring a war, or one of its campaigns, to a successful close requires a thorough grasp of national policy. On that level strategy and policy coalesce."[69] It is unhelpful for officers to expect that there will a bright line between political and military issues. A second problem is that a purist perspective may tend to foster a conception of military expertise that is inadequately narrow. For example, an army that focuses primarily on fighting and winning major conventional wars may have difficulty achieving military and political objectives in other environments that demand a broader array of skills.[70]

The fusionist perspective may lead to the opposite problem: a vanishing professional ethos and loss of clarity with regard to core military tasks. The military's functional expertise as prioritized by the purists, and the military's political sophistication and responsiveness as emphasized by the fusionists, are complementary values that are always in tension. Within that tension, a circumscribed sphere of professional autonomy within which the military can develop its ethos and practical expertise is necessary to ensure the military's functional effectiveness as an instrument of national security policy.

Guiding the Partners' Behavior in Civil-Military Relations. An understanding of the military's role in the national security policy process must be grounded on one fact: the American military lacks the charter, the inclination, and the opportunity to play the primary role in the establishment of strategic ends. Nevertheless, the military can be influential, albeit largely indirectly, at the most senior levels. As one scholar observes, "The potential impact of the chiefs' views on the public and the Congress can never be ignored by a president or a secretary of defense. . . . The chiefs no doubt retain power to influence national decisions to some degree on some security issues, and to add legitimacy to one view or another."[71] Recent research confirms that statements by senior military leaders do influence public opinion about whether or not to use military force.[72]

The preceding discussion underscores the challenges associated with having a professional officer corps deeply involved in planning and executing national security policy. In this context, Richard Kohn raises an important question about the civil-military relationship: "What behaviors on both sides might lead to the kind of cooperative partnership that would produce both civilian control and wise, effective decision making?"[73] One answer is to establish a guiding set of principles, or norms, that govern the behavior of both military and civilian leaders in the formulation and execution of national security policy. According to one analyst, "The military profession's first obligation is to do no harm to the state's democratic institutions and the democratic policy-making processes they establish. The civilian political leadership sets political objectives that the military supports in good faith. The military leadership should apply its expertise without 'shirking' or taking actions that, in effect, have a self-interested effect on policy outcomes."[74]

Keeping these guidelines in mind, three norms should guide military leaders' engagement in policy discussions:

- Military leaders should always represent the uniquely military perspective in all policy deliberations and discussions, both public and private;
- When asked for their professional opinions and advice, military leaders must render such advice forthrightly and apolitically;
- Once national-level policy has been formulated and announced, whether it is a budget, a strategy, or an operational concept, it is the responsibility of military leaders to follow and implement that policy to the best of their ability.

Establishing and gaining adherence to norms to govern civilian behavior presents different challenges. Competitively selected military officers stay on continuous active duty for thirty-five years or more, practicing their military arts daily whether in peace or war, advancing through several levels of professional military education, and constantly adapting new professional knowledge to their experiences. On the civilian side, however, new leaders are elected or appointed only episodically. Few serve a full career in the national security arena, and often the senior civilian leadership changes entirely after a presidential election. Although this is by design under the US constitutional system, it also has significant drawbacks.

One difficulty is the general lack of familiarity among civilian leaders with national security affairs at the beginning of each new presidential administration.[75] Civilian political leaders may enter the policymaking arena essentially "cold" on the issues and without the extensive personal networks required to support the creation of an effective global security policy. While this deficiency is usually overcome within a year or so, for a significant period, military advisors tend to be far more knowledgeable than their civilian leaders. Civilian and military leaders must rapidly develop personal relationships of trust and comity that promote mutual exploration of policy and learning so that they can develop, review, and implement policy effectively.

Although the civil-military dialogue will always be "unequal" in the sense that civilians have the last word, it is possible to conceive of norms for civilian behavior in the civil-military relationship that would facilitate effective policy making. One scholar articulated the principal norm for civilian leaders as "equal dialogue, unequal authority."[76] Civilian leaders ultimately responsible for critical national security decisions are more likely to be successful if they are aware of the full range of military views on a particular issue. An "equal dialogue" should be employed to support the civilian decision makers' "unequal authority." Not all administrations have followed this approach: military voices carried more weight during the Clinton years, while Rumsfeld dominated the dialogue during the early years of the George W. Bush administration. Intentional preparation of civilians for leadership within the national military establishment would facilitate a more equal dialogue. For example, more civilians from the intelligence, diplomatic and, congressional staff communities could attend military senior service schools.

The Political Activities of Military Officers. One enduring issue that stems from the 1990s civil-military crisis debate concerns the political activities of serving or retired members of the military. For example, despite the fact that JCS Chairman General Colin Powell had approval from his civilian superiors in 1992 to publish his views on intervention in the Balkans in the *New York Times* and on the use of military power in *Foreign Affairs*, analysts continue to debate the appropriateness of his doing so.[77] In critiquing the concept of limited intervention one month before a presidential election, the first of these articles had the potential to constrain the next president's freedom of action on an important foreign policy issue.

Other forms of potentially problematic political activity include the increasingly public and occasionally partisan political roles played by retired flag officers. For example, retired Admiral William Crowe, who had been JCS chairman, endorsed candidate Clinton in the 1992 presidential campaign. General Tommy Franks, previously commander of US Central Command during the Afghanistan and Iraq invasions, endorsed George W. Bush's reelection in 2004. In 2006, several retired officers precipitated the "Revolt of the Generals," publicly criticizing current US military policies in Iraq and expressing opposition to civilian leaders, Rumsfeld in particular, who were most responsible for these policies.[78] In the 2016 presidential campaign, teams of retired flag officers were led by retired Marine General

John Allen for Hillary Clinton and by retired Army Lieutenant General Michael Flynn for Donald Trump. In each case, candidates highlighted these endorsements, implying that they were indicative of broad military support. Additionally, increasing numbers of retired senior officers are participating as media analysts and endorsing candidates for political office.[79]

Some believe that such statements by retired flag officers serve an important function in better informing Congress and the American public, who may benefit from another source of military expertise. However, others argue that the continued association of these senior officers with the active military makes their public critiques of policy and civilian policy makers inappropriate and dangerous for civil-military relations.[80] In some cases, such activities raise serious conflicts of interest, as many admirals and generals have taken lucrative post-retirement jobs in the defense industry.[81] The political activities discussed here raise concerns about an erosion of the tradition of military neutrality and abstention from politics.[82]

The Current Structure of the National Military Establishment

The Goldwater-Nichols legislation is generally viewed as having been very successful in improving "the areas that the original sponsors of the Goldwater-Nichols Act considered most pressing—military advice, the unified commanders, contingency planning, joint officer management, and military operations."[83] Such success is due in part to an organizational structure that places a premium on achieving military effectiveness through efficient planning and coordination. (See chapter 4.)

Six combatant commands have responsibility for specified regions of the globe (figure 8.1), while three other combatant commands have worldwide functional responsibilities not bounded by geography: US Special Operations Command, US Strategic Command, and US Transportation Command. The regional combatant commanders seek to address a wide variety of security-related needs whose nature varies, depending on the region. Meeting these demands requires extensive coordination within the US government as well as the maintenance of a direct line of communication along their chain of command, which includes the secretary of defense and the president, with communications generally flowing through the JCS.

Although the combatant commanders have broad responsibility, their success hinges upon close interaction and coordination with the individual services: the Army, Navy, Air Force, and Marine Corps. The services themselves are responsible for training, equipping, maintaining, and providing the forces that are or may be assigned to the unified commands, and then supporting them for the duration of their deployments. The services have little direct influence in decisions guiding the conduct of operations, but they do play a crucial role in providing and then supporting operationally deployed forces.

The JCS—the chairman, vice chairman, service chiefs, and the chief of the National Guard Bureau—play a preeminent role in coordinating actions among the individual services and the unified combatant commands. Because the service chiefs also sit as members of the JCS and have the statutory authority to provide

FIGURE 8.1 Global Combatant Command Areas of Responsibility

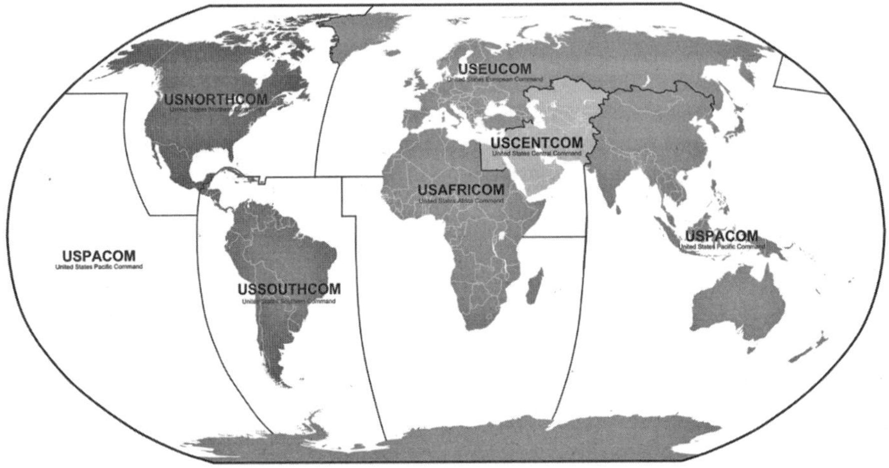

Source: https://www.defense.gov/About/Military-Departments/Unified-Combatant-Commands/

expert advice, they are the natural link between the individual services and the combatant commands. The JCS is also a critical nexus of interaction between civilian policy makers and the uniformed military.

Within DoD, the Office of the Secretary of Defense (OSD) plays a prominent role in defining and overseeing national security and military policy. Internal DoD directives mandate that "in providing immediate staff assistance and advice to the secretary of defense, the OSD and the JCS, though separately identified and organized, function in full coordination and cooperation."[84] This requirement is intended to enhance civilian control as well to ensure that the secretary of defense receives the best possible staff support and advice. The OSD is supported by a number of exceptionally qualified military officers, as well as talented civilians.

Looking Ahead

The role of the uniformed military in the national security process will continue to evolve with changes in civilian leadership and changes in the use of the military as an instrument of foreign policy. Because the United States is likely to remain a world power that is deeply involved in the international political system, it is highly unlikely that the influence of the US military will ever again be as insignificant as it was prior to Pearl Harbor. Ensuring that the future military role in the national security process is both effective and appropriate will be a continuing challenge.

Discussion Questions

1. How and why did military influence in the policy process increase significantly immediately prior to and throughout World War II?

2. How did changes in US foreign policy following World War II influence the restructuring of the national security establishment?

3. How do organizational structure and statutory guidance influence the military's participation in the policy process?

4. How did the Goldwater-Nichols Act of 1986 alter the role of the military in the policy process?

5. Should a military officer limit professional advice strictly to military matters or should she provide a full evaluation, including consideration of diplomatic, political, economic, and other factors? Why?

6. Is there an "unequal dialogue" between military and civilian leaders in the policy-making process? What are the responsibilities of both parties to this dialogue?

7. Are there "gaps" between the military and civil society? If so, how much of a problem are these gaps? What, if anything, should be done to address them?

8. Do you believe that US civil-military relations are healthy? Why or why not?

9. What is the proper role of the military in the policy process? Are problems with national security policy more likely to result from too much military influence or too little?

10. What are the responsibilities of the military departments and the combatant commands? What is the role of the JCS and of its chairman in the relationships among these entities?

Recommended Reading

Cohen, Eliot A. *Supreme Command: Soldiers, Statesmen, and Leadership in Wartime.* New York: The Free Press, 2002.

Dempsey, Jason K. *Our Army: Soldiers, Politics and American Civil-Military Relations.* Princeton, NJ: Princeton University Press, 2009.

Feaver, Peter D., and Christopher Gelpi. *Choosing Your Battles: American Civil-Military Relations and the Use of Force.* Princeton, NJ: Princeton University Press, 2004.

Feaver, Peter D., and Richard H. Kohn, eds. *Soldiers and Civilians: The Civil-Military Gap and American National Security.* Cambridge, MA: MIT Press, 2001.

Herspring, Dale R. *The Pentagon and the Presidency: Civil-Military Relations from FDR to George W. Bush.* Lawrence: University Press of Kansas, 2005.

Huntington, Samuel P. *The Common Defense: Strategic Problems in National Politics.* New York: Columbia University Press, 1961.

———. *The Soldier and the State.* Cambridge, MA: The Belknap Press of Harvard University Press, 1957.

Janowitz, Morris. *The Professional Soldier* [1960]. New York: The Free Press, 1964.

Kohn, Richard H., ed. *The United States Military under the Constitution of the United States, 1789–1989.* New York: New York University Press, 1991.

Locher, James R. *Victory on the Potomac: The Goldwater-Nichols Act Unifies the Pentagon.* College Station: Texas A&M University Press, 2004.

McMaster, H. R. *Dereliction of Duty: Lyndon Johnson, Robert McNamara, the Joint Chiefs of Staff, and the Lies that Led to Vietnam.* New York: HarperCollins, 1997.

Nielsen, Suzanne C., and Don M. Snider, eds. *American Civil-Military Relations: The Soldier and the State in a New Era.* Baltimore, MD: Johns Hopkins University Press, 2009.

Stevenson, Charles A. *Warriors and Politicians: U.S. Civil-Military Relations under Stress.* New York: Routledge, 2006.

Recommended Internet Sources

The Department of Defense, www.defense.gov
The Joint Chiefs of Staff, www.jcs.mil
The National Security Council, www.whitehouse.gov/nsc
Unified Command Plan, www.defense.gov/Sites/Unified-Combatant-Commands

Notes

1. Office of the Under Secretary of Defense (Comptroller), "Defense Budget Overview, Fiscal Year 2019 Budget Request," US Department of Defense, http://comptroller.defense.gov/Portals/45/Documents/defbudget/fy2019/FY2019_Budget_Request_Overview_Book.pdf.

2. For a thorough discussion of the Framers' views and their intense debate over the issue of standing armies, see Richard H. Kohn, "The Constitution and National Security: The Intent of the Framers," in *The United States Military under the Constitution of the United States, 1789–1989*, ed. Richard H. Kohn (New York: New York University Press, 1991), 61–94.

3. Douglas Johnson and Steven Metz, *American Civil-Military Relations: New Issues, Enduring Problems* (Carlisle Barracks, PA: Strategic Studies Institute, 1995), http://www.strategicstudiesinstitute.army.mil/pdffiles/PUB287.pdf.

4. Adapted from David F. Trask, "Democracy and Defense: Civilian Control of the Military in the United States," *Issues of Democracy* 2, no. 3 (July 1997): 9–13.

5. See Urs Schwarz, *American Strategy: A New Perspective* (New York: Doubleday, 1966), 48.

6. Walter Millis, *Arms and the State* (New York: Twentieth-Century Fund, 1958), 124–32.

7. John C. Ries, *The Management of Defense* (Baltimore, MD: Johns Hopkins University Press, 1964), 26–30.

8. Gerhard Loewenberg, "The Remaking of the German Party System," in *European Politics: A Reader*, ed. Mattei Dugan and Richard Rose (Boston: Little, Brown, 1971), 259–80.

9. Cordell Hull, *The Memoirs of Cordell Hull* (New York: Macmillan, 1948), 2:1625–1713.

10. Secretary of State Hull opted out of political-military planning even before direct American involvement in World War II. During the war he devoted a large part of his own and his department's energy and talents to planning the fledgling United Nations Organization.

11. Office of the Under Secretary of Defense (Comptroller), *National Defense Budget Estimates for 2016* (Washington, DC: Department of Defense, March 2015), 258.

12. The Key West Agreement was based on meetings of the service chiefs in Key West, Florida, in March 1948 and was later memorialized in a memorandum from Secretary of Defense James Forrestal, "Functions of the Armed Forces and the Joint Chiefs of Staff," April 21, 1948, http://cgsc.cdmhost.com/utils/getfile/collection/p4013coll11/id/729/filename/730.pdf.

13. Amy B. Zegart, *Flawed By Design: The Evolution of the CIA, JCS, and NSC* (Stanford, CA: Stanford University Press, 1999), 109–48.

14. See Burton M. Sapin and Richard C. Snyder, *The Role of the Military in American Foreign Policy* (New York: Doubleday, 1954).

15. Lawrence M. Martin, "The American Decision to Rearm Germany," in *American Civil Military Decisions*, ed. Harold Stein (Birmingham: University of Alabama Press, 1963), 652–60.

16. Samuel P. Huntington, *The Common Defense: Strategic Problems in National Politics* (New York: Columbia University Press, 1961), 54.

17. An excellent discussion of the MacArthur case can be found in Millis, *Arms and the State*, 259–332.

18. Michael H. Armacost, *The Politics of Weapons Innovation: The Thor-Jupiter Controversy* (New York: Columbia University Press, 1969).

19. Huntington, *The Common Defense*, 380.

20. For a good discussion of the postwar problems of interservice rivalry, see Ries, *Management of Defense*, 129–92. Huntington, *The Common Defense,* 123–96, explores why defense issues frequently are resolved by political bargaining.

21. See Alain C. Enthoven and K. Wayne Smith, *How Much Is Enough? Shaping the Defense Program, 1961–1969* (New York: Harper & Row, 1971).

22. See Bob Woodward, *The Commanders* (New York: Simon & Schuster, 1991); and U.S. News and World Report, *Triumph Without Victory* (New York: Warner Books, 1992).

23. Stephen Biddle, "Victory Misunderstood: What the Gulf War Tells Us about the Future of Conflict," *International Security* 21, no. 2 (1996): 142.

24. See Mark Garrard, "War Termination in the Persian Gulf: Problems and Prospects," *Aerospace Power Journal* 15, no. 3 (2001): 42–50.

25. Eliot Cohen, "Supreme Command in the 21st Century," *Joint Force Quarterly* 31 (Summer 2002): 53–54.

26. Michael O'Hanlon, "Clinton's Strong Defense Legacy," *Foreign Affairs* 82, no. 6 (2003): 126–34.

27. Richard H. Kohn, "The Erosion of Civilian Control of the Military in the United States Today," *Naval War College Review* 55, no. 3 (2002): 10.

28. See Richard H. Kohn, "Out of Control: The Crisis in Civil-Military Relations," *National Interest* 35 (Spring 1994): 3–17; Russell F. Weigley, "The American Military and the Principle of Civilian Control from McClellan to Powell," *Journal of Military History* 57, no. 5 (1993): 27–58; and Eliot A. Cohen, "Playing Powell Politics," *Foreign Affairs* 74, no. 6 (1995): 102–10. This discussion of the 1990s "crisis" draws on Suzanne C. Nielsen, "Civil-Military Relations Theory and Military Effectiveness," *Public Administration and Management* 10, no. 2 (2005): 5.

29. Edward N. Luttwak, "Washington's Biggest Scandal," *Commentary* 97, no. 5 (1994): 29–33.

30. Deborah D. Avant, "Are the Reluctant Warriors Out of Control? Why the U.S. Military Is Averse to Responding to Post–Cold War Low-Level Threats," *Security Studies* 6, no. 2 (1996/1997): 51–90.

31. Deborah D. Avant, "Conflicting Indicators of 'Crisis' in American Civil-Military Relations," *Armed Forces and Society* 24, no. 3 (1998): 375–88; James Burk, "The Logic of Crisis and Civil-Military Relations Theory: A Comment on Desch, Feaver, and Dauber," *Armed Forces and Society* 24, no. 3 (1998): 455–62; Kohn, "The Erosion of Civilian Control," 9.

32. Lyle J. Goldstein, "General John Shalikashvili and the Civil-Military Relations of Peacekeeping," *Armed Forces and Society* 26, no. 3 (2000): 387–411.

33. See, for example, Michael C. Desch, "Bush and the Generals," *Foreign Affairs* 86, no. 3 (2007): 97–108. See also the responses: Richard B. Myers, Richard H. Kohn, and

Mackubin T. Owens, "Salute and Disobey? The Civil-Military Balance, before Iraq and After," *Foreign Affairs* 86, no. 5 (2007): 147–56.

34. Vernon Loeb and Thomas E. Ricks, "Rumsfeld's Style, Goals Strain Ties in Pentagon: 'Transformation' Effort Spawns Issues of Control," *Washington Post*, October 16, 2002, A01.

35. Loeb and Ricks, "Rumsfeld's Style," A01.

36. Al Kamen, "Donny, We Hardly Knew Ye," *Washington Post*, September 7, 2001, A-27.

37. See Donald H. Rumsfeld, "Transforming the Military," *Foreign Affairs* 81, no. 3 (2002): 20–32.

38. For an authoritative account of this episode, see Matthew Moten, *Presidents and Their Generals: An American History of Command in War* (Cambridge, MA: The Belknap Press of Harvard University Press, 2017), 362–65.

39. For accounts of the postwar planning effort, see Michael Gordon and Bernard Trainor, *Cobra II: The Inside Story of the Invasion and Occupation of Iraq* (New York: Pantheon, 2006); and Thomas Ricks, *Fiasco: The American Military Adventure in Iraq* (New York: Penguin, 2006).

40. James A. Baker III and Lee H. Hamilton, co-chairs, *The Iraq Study Group Report*, December 2006, 52, http://bakerinstitute.org/Pubs/iraqstudygroup_findings.pdf.

41. Baker and Hamilton, *The Iraq Study Group Report.*

42. Michael R. Gordon and Bernard E. Trainor, *The Endgame: The Inside Story of the Struggle for Iraq, from George W. Bush to Barack Obama* (New York: Pantheon Books, 2012).

43. Fred Kaplan, *The Insurgents: David Petraeus and the Plot to Change the American Way of War* (New York: Simon and Schuster, 2013).

44. There is no evidence that McChrystal or his staff leaked the report. It was published twenty-two days after it was sent to Secretary of Defense Gates. See in Bob Woodward, "More Forces or 'Mission Failure,'" *Washington Post*, September 21, 2009.

45. "Remarks by the President in Address to the Nation on the Way Forward in Afghanistan and Pakistan," United States Military Academy at West Point, December 1, 2009, http://www.whitehouse.gov/the-press-office/remarks-president-address-nation-way-forward-afghanistan-and-pakistan.

46. Bob Woodward, *Obama's Wars* (New York: Simon and Schuster, 2010).

47. Michael Hastings, "The Runaway General," *Rolling Stone*, June 22, 2010, http://www.rollingstone.com/politics/news/the-runaway-general-20100622.

48. Marybeth Ulrich, "The General Stanley McChrystal Affair: A Case-Study in Civil-Military Relations," *Parameters* 41 (Spring 2011): 86–100.

49. Jim Michaels, "General Dempsey Grilled about U.S. Policy in Syria," *USA Today*, July 18, 2013, http://www.usatoday.com/story/news/politics/2013/07/18/dempsey-senate-armed-services-confirmation/2551037/.

50. Micah Zenko, "The Soldier and the State Go Public: Civil-Military Relations Haven't Been This Bad in Decades," *Foreign Policy Online*, September 25, 2013, http://www.foreignpolicy.com/articles/2013/09/25/the_soldier_and_the_state_go_public.

51. Dana Priest, "A Four-Star Foreign Policy?" *Washington Post*, September 28, 2000, A1. See also Dana Priest, *Waging War and Keeping Peace with America's Military* (New York: Norton, 2003).

52. Christopher P. Gibson and Don M. Snider, "Civil-Military Relations and the Potential to Influence: A Look at the National Security Decision-Making Process," *Armed Forces and Society* 25, no. 2 (1999): 196.

53. Gibson and Snider, "Civil-Military Relations and the Potential to Influence," 207.

54. Peter D. Feaver and Richard H. Kohn, "The Gap: Soldiers, Civilians, and Their Mutual Misunderstandings," *National Interest* 61 (Fall 2000): 29.

55. Feaver and Kohn, "The Gap," 31–32.

56. Feaver and Kohn, "The Gap," 44.

57. Jon Rahbek-Clemmensen, Emerald M. Archer, John Barr, Aaron Belkin, Mario Guerrero, Cameron Hall, and Katie E. O. Swain, "Conceptualizing the Civil-Military Gap: A Research Note," *Armed Forces & Society* 38 (October 2012): 669–78.

58. Heidi Urben, "Civil Military Relations in a Time of War: Party, Politics and the Profession of Arms," PhD dissertation, Georgetown University, 2010; see also Jason K. Dempsey, *Our Army: Soldiers, Politics and American Civil-Military Relations* (Princeton, NJ: Princeton University Press, 2009).

59. Pew Research, Social and Demographic Trends, "The Military-Civilian Gap," October 2011, http://www.pewsocialtrends.org/series/the-military-civilian-gap/.

60. These concerns are central to Samuel P. Huntington, *The Soldier and the State* (Cambridge, MA: The Belknap Press of Harvard University Press, 1957), esp. 2–3.

61. Matthew Ridgway's "Farewell Letter" to Secretary of Defense Charles E. Wilson, June 27, 1955 in Matthew B. Ridgway, *Soldier: The Memoirs of Matthew B. Ridgway* (New York: Harper Brothers, 1956), 323–32.

62. For a short summary and critique of the fusionist theory, see Huntington, *Common Defense*, 350–54.

63. John F. Kennedy, Commencement address, delivered at West Point, June 1962, http://www.presidency.ucsb.edu/ws/?pid=8695.

64. Maxwell D. Taylor, unpublished address given at West Point, February 18, 1969.

65. Huntington, *The Soldier and the State*, 83–85.

66. Morris Janowitz, *The Professional Soldier* [1960] (New York: The Free Press, 1964).

67. Janowitz, *The Professional Soldier*, 342.

68. Janowitz, *The Professional Soldier*, 342, 257–79.

69. Carl von Clausewitz, *On War*, ed. Michael Howard and Peter Paret (Princeton, NJ: Princeton University Press, 1976), 111.

70. See Thomas L. McNaugher, "The Army and Operations Other than War: Expanding Professional Jurisdiction," in *The Future of the Army Profession*, ed. Don M. Snider and Gayle L. Watkins (Boston: McGraw-Hill, 2002), 155–78.

71. John G. Kester, "The Future of the Joint Chiefs of Staff," *AEI Foreign Policy and Defense Review* 2, no. 1 (1980): 11.

72. James T. Golby, Kyle Dropp, and Peter Feaver, "Listening to the Generals: How Military Advice Affects Public Support for the Use of Force," *Center for a New American Security*, April 2013, https://www.cnas.org/publications/reports/listening-to-the-generals-how-military-advice-affects-public-support-for-the-use-of-force.

73. Richard H. Kohn, "Building Trust: Civil-Military Behaviors for Effective National Security," in *American Civil-Military Relations: The Soldier and the State in a New Era*, ed. Suzanne C. Nielsen and Don M. Snider (Baltimore, MD: Johns Hopkins University Press, 2009), 274.

74. Marybeth Peterson Ulrich, "Infusing Normative Civil-Military Relations Principles in the Officer Corps," in *The Future of the Army Profession*, 2nd ed., ed. Don M. Snider and Lloyd J. Matthews (Boston: McGraw-Hill, 2005), 663.

75. Gibson and Snider, "Civil-Military Relations," 193–218.

76. Richard K. Betts, "Are Civil-Military Relations Still a Problem?" in *American Civil-Military Relations: The Soldier and the State in a New Era*, ed. Suzanne C. Nielsen and Don M. Snider (Baltimore, MD: Johns Hopkins University Press, 2009), 29–36.

77. Colin L. Powell, "Why Generals Get Nervous," *New York Times*, October 8, 1992, 35; Colin L. Powell, "U.S. Forces: Challenges Ahead," *Foreign Affairs* 71, no. 5 (1992): 3–41.

78. Martin L. Cook, "Revolt of the Generals: A Case Study in Professional Ethics," *Parameters* 38 (Spring 2008): 4–15.

79. David Barstow, "One Man's Military-Industrial-Media Complex," *New York Times*, November 29, 2008, http://www.nytimes.com/2008/11/30/washington/30general.html. See also James Golby, Kyle Dropp, and Peter Feaver, "Military Campaigns: Veterans' Endorsements and Presidential Elections," *Center for a New American Security*, October 2012, https://www.cnas.org/publications/reports/military-campaigns-veterans-endorsements-and-presidential-elections.

80. Mackubin Thomas Owens, "Rumsfeld, the Generals, and the State of U.S. Civil-Military Relations," *Naval War College Review* 59, no. 4 (2006): 79.

81. Citizens for Responsibility and Ethics in Washington, "Strategic Maneuvers," October 2012, http://www.citizensforethics.org/pages/strategic-maneuvers-generals-defense-department-revolving-door.

82. See Risa A. Brooks, "Militaries and Political Activities in Democracies," in *American Civil-Military Relations: The Soldier and the State in a New Era*, ed. Suzanne C. Nielsen and Don M. Snider (Baltimore, MD: Johns Hopkins University Press, 2009), 229–36.

83. James R. Locher III, "Has It Worked? The Goldwater-Nichols Reorganization Act," *Naval War College Review* 54, no. 4 (2001): 112.

84. Department of Defense Directive Number 5100.1, "SUBJECT: Functions of the Department of Defense and Its Major Components," December 21, 2010, 2, http://dtic.mil/whs/directives/corres/pdf/510001p.pdf.

9

Planning, Budgeting, and Management

The United States produces and consumes millions of ordinary private goods every day—automobiles, blue jeans, pencils, and so on—but nobody ever asks, "How many pencils does the United States need?" or, "How will those pencils be produced?" Instead, multiple institutions comprise a market that provides signals—through prices—to individual producers and consumers. The producers and consumers make decentralized decisions to produce, sell, buy, and consume pencils. No grand conductor orchestrates, plans, budgets, or manages pencils. There is no US national pencil agency, no secretary of pencils, no congressional committee on pencils, and no book chapter on planning, budgeting, and management of pencils. Nevertheless, the right number of pencils seems to be produced by this self-emergent order, which results in what economists call a market equilibrium.

The Economic Nature of National Security

If the market for private goods like pencils can determine how many to produce and how to produce them, why does a massive, centralized infrastructure seem necessary to answer those same questions for national security? The difference is inherent in the very nature of the product itself: national security. As a public good, national security has two distinctive characteristics that affect the way that society must manage the allocation of relevant resources.

The first distinction between national security and the pencil has to do with the ability to establish, maintain, and transfer an exclusive property right over the product. For the pencil, possessing and using it establishes the exclusive property right. In the economics literature, this ease of establishing a property right is called "excludability." A pencil is an easily excludable good, but once a unit of national security is produced, it is generally available to all: the producer cannot decide who can and who cannot benefit from national security. It is therefore considered non-excludable in provision.

The second distinction between national security and the pencil is a difference in whether the product can be consumed simultaneously by multiple users. If someone is currently using a pencil, others must wait their turn. A pencil is thus deemed "rival" in consumption: only one person can consume or use it at any given time. When a unit of national security is produced, each individual in the society consumes that unit simultaneously. When others join this society, they also gain security with little or no degradation to the security enjoyed by those who are already there. National security is therefore considered non-rival in consumption.

These two characteristics—being non-excludable in provision and non-rival in consumption—are reflected in the characterization of national security as a public good. While decentralized markets can produce, provide, and allocate private goods, they are unable to produce, provide, or allocate, efficiently and effectively, goods and services that are non-excludable and non-rival—that is, public goods.[1] No private person or firm would produce something that they could not possess, nor pay for something that, once produced, could be consumed freely by all. Therefore, as Adam Smith observed in 1776, it is the government that must provide national security:

> According to the system of natural liberty, the sovereign has only three duties to attend to; three duties of great importance, indeed, but plain and intelligible to common understandings: first, the duty of protecting the society from the violence and invasion of other independent societies; secondly, the duty of protecting, as far as possible, every member of the society from the injustice or oppression of every other member of it, or the duty of establishing an exact administration of justice; and, thirdly, the duty of erecting and maintaining certain public works and certain public institutions which it can never be for the interest of any individual, or small number of individuals, to erect and maintain; because the profit could never repay the expense to any individual, or small number of individuals, though it may frequently do much more than repay it to a great society.[2]

Thus, the burden of production, provision, and distribution of national security falls to the sovereign, or in the case of the United States, to the people as a whole or their representatives.

Since society as a whole is responsible for production, provision, and distribution of national security, the next question is: How much national security should be produced? In theory, there should be just enough national security to make society as well-off as possible. That is, the productive resources available to society—labor, physical capital, and natural resources—should be allocated among various private goods and public goods, including national security, to maximize overall social welfare. This is achieved when society could not increase its own well-being by releasing resources from the production of national security (reduce the production of national security by one unit) and making those resources available to other production processes (increase the production of pencils or blue jeans).[3]

When some productive resources are transferred to the government to meet national security objectives, an "opportunity cost" is imposed on society: this is the lost opportunity of producing other goods and services with those same resources to meet private consumption or other social goals. The concept of the opportunity cost of additional national security was explained by President Dwight Eisenhower in 1953: "The cost of one modern heavy bomber is this: a modern brick school in more than 30 cities. It is two electric power plants, each serving a town of 60,000 population. It is two fine, fully equipped hospitals. It is some 50 miles of concrete highway. We pay for a single fighter plane with a half million bushels of wheat. We pay for a single destroyer with new homes that could have housed more than 8,000 people."[4] Even for President Eisenhower, whose background and personal experience might suggest that he would favor military expenditures, the contentious issue of "how much is enough," as well as precisely what national security capabilities the nation should develop, were major concerns. For these reasons, the system of planning, budgeting, and managing national security spending necessarily involves Congress and the president. They must decide the allocation of resources among national security, other government functions, and private goods. If political leaders' decisions conflict with the views of the citizens they represent, then citizens can express their preferences for alternate allocations of resources through political participation, ultimately by voting for officials who better reflect their preferences.

Given competing demand for scarce resources, one objective of national security policy must be to obtain the most security possible for each dollar of expenditure. This process is not perfect. Even if a system could be designed to achieve the greatest possible efficiency in one sector of national security—say cyber security—it would be impossible to meet all national security goals in other sectors, such as protection of American seaports. Resource constraints mold ideal goals into less-than-ideal objectives. National security objectives are not absolutes, but instead result from evaluation of the available options. The realistic options facing society are not bankruptcy with perfect security, on the one hand, versus prosperity while risking national-security disaster, on the other. Rather, society must confront the far more difficult questions of how much expenditure for national security is required and how much risk it is willing to accept, so that adequate resources remain available for other government programs, private consumption, and investment.

The Challenge for Strategic Planners

In addition to economic trade-offs, Eisenhower noted the uncomfortable balance between a free society and a centralized infrastructure making choices on behalf of society's overall welfare. In his farewell address, he expressed concern over domination by any one part of society over national security decision making and resource allocation, lest it undermine, instead of contribute to, social well-being:

> In the councils of government, we must guard against the acquisition of unwarranted influence, whether sought or unsought, by the military-industrial complex. The poten-

tial for the disastrous rise of misplaced power exists and will persist. We must never let the weight of this combination endanger our liberties or democratic processes. We should take nothing for granted. Only an alert and knowledgeable citizenry can compel the proper meshing of the huge industrial and military machinery of defense with our peaceful methods and goals, so that security and liberty may prosper together.[5]

With this warning in mind, national security planners must consider the following: What are society's national security objectives, and how can productive resources and the instruments of national security best be used to meet these objectives effectively? Not only must national security policy makers agree on objectives and the instruments that will be used to pursue them, but they must also grapple with how much of each instrument should be used. In a broad sense, this means agreeing on the right approach to national security—how specific combinations of force, diplomacy, and economic power should be used—and how to allocate scarce resources to create the required capabilities.

The National Security Council (NSC) is responsible for coordinating national security policies among many agencies, but it possesses no statutory power to control the actions of these agencies. Moreover, lawmakers do not annually debate a single national security budget proposal; rather they are compelled to analyze the proposed achievement of security objectives piece by piece. Multiple agencies compete for shares of national security dollars and for roles in shaping and executing national security policy.

Previous chapters have identified a wide range of actors who play key roles in the national security process. A distinct subgroup of these actors plays the dominant role in providing federal funds to execute the national security strategy. Broadly speaking, national security planning, budgeting, and management is limited to three distinct governmental arenas: defense, homeland security, and international affairs (diplomacy). Within these three broad arenas of security are more specific security-related activities, such as intelligence, law enforcement, and economic instruments of power.

In terms of resources, defense is clearly predominant. This is not surprising, nor is it anomalous historically or when compared to security planning and budgeting in many other countries. The resources required to sustain defense are typically tremendous; in the United States, defense spending constitutes the single largest discretionary government expenditure. Because of its significant role and tremendous weight within the security policy process, the Department of Defense (DoD) is the primary focus of this chapter. An evaluation of DoD's role in national security planning and budgeting also offers insight into the problems and tensions that exist throughout the national security community.

The Federal Budget

The crafting of the federal budget is a contentious political process, characterized by repeating cycles of conflict and resolution. Conflict stems from the fact that the budget process is not simply a matter of allocating huge sums of dollars, but also one of setting national priorities. The political nature of such an endeavor naturally leads to conflict among a wide range of powerful actors including Congress, its individual members, the president, his or her staff, a huge federal bureaucracy, the military services, states, lobbyists, citizens, and sometimes even international actors. The stakes are high because resources are limited: pursuit of one actor's specific objectives will likely be challenged by another's. Despite this intense conflict, budgets must be resolved. Customary budgetary procedures regulate conflict by parceling out tasks and roles, establishing expectations and deadlines for action, and limiting the scope of issues that are considered. Conflict is dampened by the fact that these repetitive tasks are completed with little or no change, year after year, and by the routinized behavior of individuals involved.[6]

Key budget actors include the president, the Office of Management and Budget (OMB), federal departments and agencies, congressional tax and budget committees, the Congressional Budget Office (CBO), congressional authorization committees (the committees with jurisdiction over certain governmental programs, such as the Senate Committee on Armed Services), the congressional appropriations committees and their subcommittees, and the Government Accountability Office (GAO). Budgeting involves thousands of participants, but very often their roles in the process are prescribed by the iterative budget process.

By law, the president must submit a budget to Congress by the first Monday in February for the following fiscal year. The US government fiscal year starts on October 1 and concludes on the next September 30 (designated by the year corresponding to January 1). In February 2019, for example, the president submits the Fiscal Year (FY) 2020 budget, which covers October 1, 2019, to September 30, 2020. Although the president's budget submission officially begins the annual budget cycle, federal agencies will have started the annual process much earlier. During the spring a year prior to the budget submission, budget policy is developed, following the budget formulation process outlined in table 9.1.[7]

After the president submits the budget in February, the action moves to Capitol Hill. As specified in the Constitution, Congress must authorize all federal appropriations. It does so in a statutory process reflected in table 9.2.[8] There are several key steps in the process. First is the adoption of a budget resolution; this is an agreement between the House and Senate on the overall size of the budget and its general composition in terms of functional categories such as national defense, international affairs, and so forth. The amounts in these functional categories are then allocated to each congressional committee with jurisdiction over spending; subsequent legislation considered in the House and Senate must be consistent with these allocations, as well as the agreed aggregate levels of spending and revenues. In some years, the budget resolution may also contain reconciliation instructions. These instructions identify committees that must recommend changes in laws affecting revenues or direct spending programs within their jurisdiction in order to implement specific priorities agreed to in the budget resolution. All committees receiving such instructions must submit recommended legislative proposals to their respective (House or Senate) budget committee. Reconciliation bills are then considered, and sometimes amended, by the full House and Senate.

Table 9.1 Executive Branch Budget Timetable (FY 2020)

Date	*Action to be completed*
Spring 2018	OMB issues spring planning guidance to executive branch agencies.
Spring and Summer 2018	OMB and the executive branch agencies: • identify major issues for the upcoming budget; • develop and analyze options for the upcoming fall review; • plan for the analysis of issues for future decisions.
July 2018	OMB issues detailed instructions for budget data (officially known as OMB Circular A-11).
September 2018	Executive branch agencies make budget submissions.
October–November 2018	OMB staff analyzes agency budget proposals in light of presidential priorities, program performance, and budget constraints.
Late November 2018	OMB director recommends a complete set of budget proposals to the president.
Late November 2018	OMB informs all executive branch agencies about the decisions on their budget requests.
December 2018	Executive branch agencies may appeal decisions to OMB and the president.
January 2019	Agencies prepare and OMB reviews congressional budget justification materials.
First Monday in February 2019	President must transmit the FY 2020 budget to Congress.

Source: Office of Management and Budget

Congressional approval of each year's spending is divided into thirteen separate appropriations bills that cover broad categories of spending. These appropriations bills are prepared by the House and Senate Appropriations Committees and their subcommittees, which review the requests of particular agencies or groups of related functions. During committee and subcommittee hearings, agency representatives answer questions and defend their requests. In addition to government officials, lobbyists and other witnesses may also testify. Although the appropriations committees have broad discretion in allocating funds, they must stay within the totals set forth in the budget resolution.

When examining the interaction between the federal bureaucracy and Congress, it is important to note the difference between authorization and appropriation legislation. Authorization legislation is an act of Congress that establishes a government program and defines the amount of money it can spend. For defense, this is normally done by the House and Senate Armed Services Committees. An authorization bill, however, does not provide any money: only an appropriations act can do this. Appropriations for spending on the military originate in the House and Senate appropriations committees' subcommittees on defense. The process for developing a defense budget within the overall federal budget is discussed later in this chapter.

Table 9.2 Congressional Budget Process Timetable (FY 2020)

Date	*Action to be completed*
First Monday in February 2019	President submits FY 2020 budget to Congress.
February 15, 2019	CBO submits report on economic and budget outlook to budget committees.
Six weeks after president's budget is submitted	Committees submit reports on views and estimates to respective budget committee.
April 1, 2019	Senate Budget Committee reports budget resolution.
April 15, 2019	Congress completes action on budget resolution.
June 10, 2019	House Appropriations Committee reports last regular appropriations bill.
June 30, 2019	House completes action on regular appropriations bills and any required reconciliation legislation.
July 15, 2019	President submits mid-session review of budget to Congress.
October 1, 2019	Fiscal year 2020 begins; ends September 30, 2020.

Source: Congressional Research Service

Spending for National Security

The Department of Defense dominates the national security budget, but national security spending is not just for military forces; spending for homeland security, diplomacy, and foreign affairs also come under the national security umbrella. Of course, the vast and disparate bureaucracies involved—in terms of personnel, funds, and missions—create an ongoing puzzle for national security planning. How do these individual organizations overcome bureaucratic barriers to join in an effective, unified approach to achieving national security objectives? How can scarce resources be effectively allocated among multiple agencies and departments, given that these separate entities are typically in competition with one another?

Figure 9.1 illustrates spending for Fiscal Year 2019. The pie chart represents the entire federal budget, including mandatory and discretionary spending. *Mandatory* spending includes interest payments on the existing debt and entitlements, including Social Security, income security (such as unemployment, food stamps, supplemental security income, some veterans benefits, and housing assistance), and health care (including Medicare and Medicaid). Entitlement spending programs "give eligible recipients a legal right to payments from the government and as such, the government is obligated to make such payments even if the budget and appropriation acts do not provide sufficient funds."[9] Many entitlements, such as Social Security and Medicare, are funded in part from individuals' prior contributions (via taxes) designated for those programs. The only way to reduce mandatory spending is to change the timing of or eligibility for benefits, which is extremely difficult. Politicians and the public are typically unwilling to cut entitlement spending because of the importance of these programs in society and the belief, by law and policy, that government has the obligation to provide these promised payments to

FIGURE 9.1 US Federal Spending, FY 2019

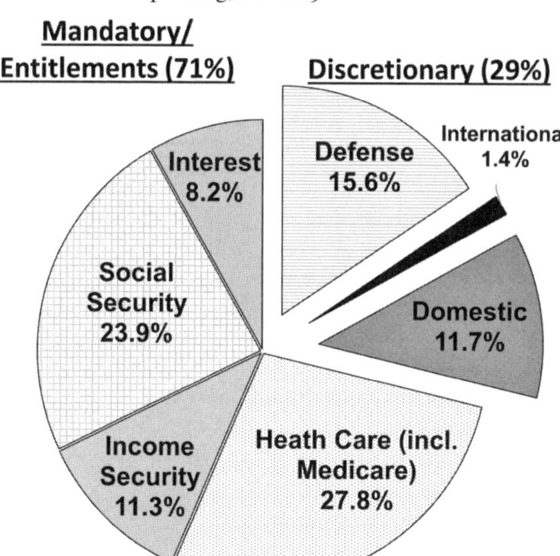

Source: Economic Report of the President, February 2018

eligible individuals. These programs provide the "social safety net" that most Americans are not willing to forego even when there are clear trade-offs, including with national security spending.

The *discretionary* portion of the federal budget provides significant opportunity for conflict and debate over the proper allocation of scarce resources. Discretionary funding proposals must be renewed by departments and the president each year, and must also survive the authorization and appropriation processes in Congress. A discretionary program can be "killed" at several decision points throughout this process, which lends itself to a great deal of jockeying and compromise.

Since World War II, mandatory spending has increased so much that it now dominates the federal budget. In 1946, the share of the budget committed to mandatory spending was only 12 percent.[10] By 1960 it had grown to 29 percent. In the past sixty years, mandatory spending has increased to include 71 percent of federal expenditures (see figure 9.2).[11] This is due to many factors, most importantly the creation and expansion of entitlements over the past century, such as Social Security in 1935, Medicare in 1965, and Medicare Part D in 2006. Another important cause is changing demographics. The retirement of the baby boomer generation, coupled with increased health care costs and longer life expectancy, is driving up the cost of entitlements. As mandatory spending increases, either overall spending must increase or discretionary spending must decrease to offset it. To pay for any overall increases, the government must increase taxes or it must borrow funds and thereby raise the national debt. Fortunately, low interest rates in recent

FIGURE 9.2 Changes in Federal Spending, 1960–2019

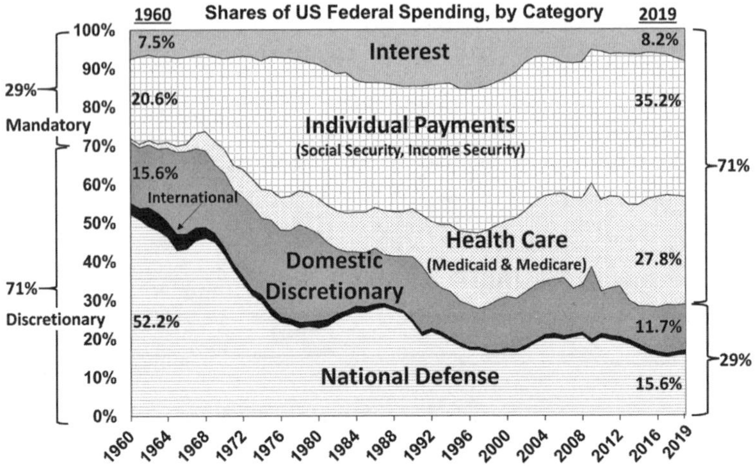

Source: Economic Report of the President, February 2018

years have limited the cost of interest on the national debt. As interest rates increase, the cost of interest payments on an increasingly large debt will also increase the cost of mandatory spending.

During the first half of the twentieth century, the president had a tremendous amount of power over federal budgeting. In the 1960s, however, a variety of factors motivated Congress to reassert its institutional prerogatives. This trend came to a head in the early 1970s when Congress fought with President Richard Nixon over budget priorities and procedures. The result was the Congressional Budget and Impoundment Control Act of 1974. Although this act did not alter the formal role of the president in the budget process, it created budget committees in each house and the Congressional Budget Office, and made other statutory changes to enhance Congress's role in fiscal decisions. The result was a system with more conflict between the executive and legislative branches. Discretionary funding proposals, in particular, became the primary battleground on which each branch fought for its vision of national priorities. As the discretionary funding proportion decreased, these battles became more intense.

As shown in figure 9.1, discretionary spending constituted about 29 percent of budget outlays in FY 2019. Defense dominated discretionary spending: at 15.6 percent of the overall budget, it was 57.2 percent of all discretionary spending. The other components of discretionary security spending—homeland security (at 4.4 percent) and international affairs (at 3.4 percent) combined to equal an additional 7.8 percent of discretionary spending.[12] What stands out most in this analysis is the enormous share of funds allocated to the military, compared with other instruments of national security policy. One reason for this imbalance is simply that large, high-quality, all-volunteer armed forces and their associated equipment are expensive.

Developing a balanced national security program and translating it into budgets acceptable to the Congress, the public, and other executive agencies is an extraordinarily demanding public policy effort. Accomplishing it requires articulation of national security goals and objectives, identification of the departmental and agency strategies and specific capabilities required to meet the defined objectives, and setting priorities that apportion risks (given that no amount of spending will address all the possible security concerns that strategists and planners identify). What follows describes these challenges, and how the DoD seeks to overcome them through its Planning, Programming, Budgeting, and Execution (PPBE) system.

Evolution of Defense Budgeting

Ideally, a budgetary process assists an organization to perform three essential functions: planning, management, and control. The planning process, which translates the goals of an organization into specific objectives, must provide some mechanism for adjusting objectives and resource allocations to total levels of expenditure. The management function involves the establishment and execution of projects or activities to meet the approved objectives. Finally, the control process monitors the results of various activities measured against the objectives and ensures that expenditures fall within specified limits. DoD needed a system to enable the secretary of defense to plan, manage, and control defense resources effectively.

Prior to the creation of the Department of Defense, the Department of the Navy and the Department of War (which included the Army and the Army Air Corps) would submit their budget proposals separately. These budget proposals would be approved by the president and then considered by two separate authorizing committees in each house of Congress. After the National Security Act of 1947, DoD submitted a consolidated, centralized budget. This centralization provided the Office of the Secretary of Defense (OSD) with additional authority to make tradeoffs among defense programs to shape national security strategy more coherently and more effectively.

Although subsequent defense reorganizations, including amendments to the National Security Act of 1947 in 1949, 1953, and 1958, brought the secretary of defense increasing authority, budgetary process reform occurred slowly. Secretary of Defense Robert McNamara, who took office with the Kennedy administration in 1961, was the first person in that position to shape defense policy actively. In doing so, he developed the budgeting process that largely remains today. Instead of merely reviewing plans and budgets prepared by the services, McNamara had a presidential mandate to evaluate and balance alternative methods of accomplishing the nation's security objectives. For example, several strategic nuclear weapons systems—such as Minuteman missiles, strategic bombers, and Polaris missile submarines—contributed to the same objective of deterring nuclear attack. In deciding how much of the defense budget to allocate to each system, the cost and effectiveness of all three systems needed to be compared. This was virtually impossible under the system that McNamara inherited because it was arrayed in terms of service inputs, including personnel, operations, maintenance, and military construction, rather than in terms of end products or missions. While forces and weapons were normally considered "horizontally" across services in the planning process, expenditures were portrayed "vertically" within each service by accounting category. The integration of military planning, which was the domain of the Joint Chiefs of Staff (JCS), with budgeting, the domain of the civilian secretaries and comptroller organization, required a link between mission objectives and expenditures.

McNamara's solution was "program budgeting," under which all military forces and weapons systems were grouped into mission-oriented defense programs according to their principal military purpose, regardless of traditional service boundaries. Programs were then subdivided into program elements. For example, the General Purpose Forces Program included as program elements both Marine and Army forces, such as brigades and divisions. With expenditure data arrayed by program, a decision maker could readily observe how funds were distributed over mission-related outputs and how those funds were allocated among different forces and weapons systems within each program.

The Planning, Programming, and Budgeting System (PPBS) that McNamara instituted made it possible to link expenditures more closely to the national security objectives to which they were directed, to compare the relative value of various expenditures, and to apply the resultant decisions to force structure and weapons procurement. PPBS improved the ability of DoD to analyze defense decisions and coordinate interrelated activities. In practice, it also centralized power in the hands of McNamara and the OSD. It did so by providing a systematic methodology for identifying key issues, focusing the attention of the senior leadership on them, organizing the sequence of and participation in the decision process, recording decisions, and shaping the defense program and budget to reflect them.

Although PPBS has often been criticized, it has been retained as the basic structure for defense strategy, program, and budget development through successive presidential administrations. In fact, as a result of numerous government-wide management initiatives over the last twenty-five years, other departments and agencies have essentially adopted the PPBS approach. Although DoD changed PPBS in 2003 to Planning, Programming, Budgeting, and Execution (PPBE) to increase emphasis on budget execution, most of the components remain the same.

The Planning, Programming, Budgeting, and Execution (PPBE) Process

In the PPBE process, the secretary of defense establishes policies, strategy, goal priorities, and fiscal constraints for the department, which are used to guide resource allocation decisions. The PPBE process consists of four distinct but overlapping phases: planning, programming, budgeting, and execution.

Planning. The *planning* phase of PPBE is a collaborative effort by OSD and the joint staff that begins with an annual articulation of national defense policies and military strategy, known as the Strategic Planning Guidance.[13] The Strategic Planning Guidance incorporates the latest National Security Strategy, National Defense Strategy, Quadrennial Defense Review guidance, and other strategic directives. The PPBE planning process results in fiscally constrained guidance and priorities for the development of programs (such as for military forces, modernization, readiness, sustainability, and supporting business processes and infrastructure activities). The results of this planning effort are then articulated in a document known as the Joint Programming Guidance. The Joint Programming Guidance is the link between planning and programming. It provides guidance to each DoD component—military departments and defense agencies—for the development of a program proposal by each, known as the Program Objective Memorandum (POM).

Programming. The programming phase begins with the development by each DoD component of a POM that responds to the guidance and priorities of the Joint Programming Guidance within fiscal constraints. Normally completed in the summer before the submission of the president's budget the following February, the POM provides a fairly detailed and comprehensive description of the proposed programs, including a time-phased allocation of resources by program projected six years into the future. In addition, each DoD component may identify important programs not fully funded (or not funded at all) in the POM and assess the risks associated with the funding shortfalls. The senior leadership in the OSD and the joint staff review each POM to help integrate the various DoD component POMs into a coherent overall defense program. In addition, the OSD staff and the joint staff can raise issues with selected portions of any POM, or any funding shortfalls in the POM, and propose alternatives. Issues not resolved at lower levels are forwarded to the secretary of defense for decisions, and the resulting decisions are documented in a Program Decision Memorandum.

Budgeting. The budgeting phase of PPBE overlaps with the programming phase.[14] Its purpose is to convert the programmatic view into a format appropriate to the congressional appropriations structure, along with supporting budget justification documents. The budget projects resources only two years into the future, but with considerably more financial detail than the POM. Upon submission, each budget estimate is reviewed by analysts from the Office of the Undersecretary of Defense (Comptroller) and the Office of Management and Budget. Their review seeks to ensure that programs are funded in accordance with current financial policies and that they are properly and reasonably priced. The review also ensures that the budget documentation is adequate to justify the programs that will be presented to Congress. If budget staffs cannot resolve issues during the review, they are forwarded to the deputy secretary of defense for decisions. These decisions are incorporated into an updated budget submission provided to the OMB. Then, the overall DoD budget is provided as part of the president's budget request to Congress.

Execution. The execution review occurs simultaneously with the program and budget reviews. The purpose of the execution review is to provide feedback to senior leadership concerning the effectiveness of current and prior resource allocations. To the extent that performance goals of an existing program are not being met, the execution review may lead to recommendations to adjust resources or restructure programs to achieve desired performance goals.[15] The execution analysis supports DoD in its development of the Annual Performance Report, a submission required as part of the Government Performance Results Act of 1993.

Timing. The PPBE process is complex and detailed for a single fiscal year. Complexity is multiplied because, at any given time, at least four different budgets are being prepared. In the summer of 2019, for example, DoD was:

- Executing the FY 2019 budget, which lasted from October 1, 2018, to September 30, 2019;
- Defending the FY 2020 budget, submitted to Congress in February 2019;
- Preparing the POM submission for the FY 2021 budget; and
- Conducting planning for the FY 2022 submission.

If an unforeseen event takes place—from a public health crisis like the 2014 outbreak of Ebola to a military intervention such as the 1991 Gulf War—all of these budgets may be affected, requiring complex and cascading readjustments of priorities.

Budgeting during Crisis

In addition to the standard PPBE process, two features of federal budgeting have dominated much of defense planning, budgeting, and management in the past two decades. The first issue has been finding a way to provide funding for ongoing wars, and the second has been attempting to constrain overall spending for the purpose of controlling the US fiscal deficit.

Supplemental Appropriations. In addition to the formal budget process, Congress has the ability to appropriate funds to cover unexpected outlays. One of the most important advantages of such supplemental appropriations is that they allow the government to react quickly to unexpected events, such as natural disasters or unforeseen military operations. While the regular appropriation process lasts around nine months, supplemental requests are normally approved within four months.[16] During the 1990s, such supplemental appropriations were used for the 1991 Gulf War and for peacekeeping missions in Somalia, Haiti, and the Balkans. Congress has also used supplemental appropriations for relief after hurricanes, flooding, and other domestic disasters. After 9/11, supplemental appropriations were used for Afghanistan, Iraq, and homeland security measures. Over time, more of the budget requirements for war could be anticipated, and thus, rather than permitting the president to have a flexible "shadow budget" for operations, Congress and DoD established a separate category of budget requests called *overseas contingency operations* (OCO). These OCO funds are in addition to the basic defense budget, and they provide funding that is intended only for support of wartime operations. The use of the OCO designation is intended to keep wartime spending separate from routine budgets.

Constraining Spending. Budgeting reflects a classic economic problem of unlimited wants and limited resources. Although each specific request for spending may seem, on its face, completely justified, the total of all justified requests exceeds the amount of funding available. In response, Congress and the president have approved legislation that limits federal spending. This includes the Graham-Rudman-Hollings Act of 1985, the Budget Enforcement Act of 1990, the Budget Enforcement Act of 1997, the Pay-As-You-Go Act of 2010, and the Budget Control Act of 2011.[17] The problem is that the circumstances confronting the federal government in any given year will be different from those that existed when discipline-forcing budget acts were approved: the economy may be less robust than predicted, wars may be longer or more expensive, a hurricane's devastation may require emergency spending, or political conditions may have changed. So the strict limits in the acts are also subject to the ability of Congress—if pushed by a crisis (real or contrived)—to grant a temporary reprieve from constraints that were deemed necessary for long-term fiscal stability.

In August 2011, the United States was only days away from exceeding the federal debt limit (also referred to as the *debt ceiling*); absent congressional action, it might have failed to meet its obligations to pay entitlement recipients, federal workers, holders of US debt, and federal contractors. As a result, the Standard and Poors rating agency reduced the US bond credit rating from AAA to AA+. A last-minute compromise was reached in which Congress raised the debt ceiling and passed the 2011 Budget Control Act (BCA). That Act specified that if Congress did not limit future spending to specified amounts, dramatic and severe reductions of discretionary spending would be automatically implemented in a process known as *sequestration*.[18] An automatic order would permanently cancel budget resources to achieve required savings in outlays.

In 2013, sequestration was imposed. It slashed $109 billion from discretionary spending, with half coming from defense spending and half coming from nondefense spending (entitlement spending was exempt). The president exempted military salaries from the reductions, but every other defense and nondefense account was reduced across the board. The result was involuntary furlough of government workers, curtailment of contracts, and other unplanned reductions in government programs. The automatic sequestration undermined the otherwise rational PPBE process.

With the sequestration threat reemerging in 2016, the official DoD Quadrennial Defense Review concluded that "the return of sequestration-level cuts in FY2016 would significantly reduce the Department's ability to fully implement our strategy . . . [and] risks associated with conducting military operations would rise substantially. Our military would be unbalanced and eventually too small and insufficiently modern to meet the needs of our strategy, leading to greater risk of longer wars with higher casualties. . . . Ultimately, continued sequestration-level cuts would likely embolden our adversaries and undermine the confidence of our allies."[19] This conclusion is extraordinary because it states that following the law, which is the obligation of all federal departments, would lead to devastating consequences for the country. In the 2016 defense authorization signed in November 2015, Congress and the president agreed to count some regular defense spending as OCO and to permit a similar increase in domestic spending, suspending sequestration constraints until after the 2016 election. In February 2018, Congress approved and the president signed the Bipartisan Budget Act of 2018, which adjusted the sequestration caps for another two years, but did not remove them entirely. This continued to postpone the time at which the federal government must find a solution to significant deficit spending. It is likely that the challenges of managing supplemental appropriations and confronting sequestration or similar budgetary constraints will continue to dominate defense planning, budgeting, and management in the future.

The Outlook for Planning, Budgeting, and Management

Ideally, the distribution of scarce government resources into security expenditures would perfectly reflect the government's foreign and security policies and explicit trade-offs between investments in security and in other social values. In practice, this is difficult to accomplish because of the fragmented nature of the US national security apparatus and the fact that national security is a public good. Planning for and funding ongoing operations as well as wartime spending continue to be difficult challenges. Moreover, as the largest component of discretionary spending, defense spending will likely continue to face increasing budgetary constraints in the future.

The US government as a whole struggles with determining how much and what types of national security are needed. This struggle affects its ability to determine how much to spend on national security and to evaluate defense with respect to other types of expenditures. Given that national security goals are essentially unlimited, while national resources to achieve them are scarce, how can the national security process be effectively managed? The answer is elusive. The president can use the NSC to coordinate the actions of several agencies, but there is no unified national security apparatus with the capability to plan, manage, and control all national security–related spending. In addition, the checks and balances built into the US system of government inevitably lead to tensions and cross purposes in the process. It is difficult for the president and Congress to agree on national security priorities; even when there is general agreement over objectives, there will still be disagreements over what instruments of power to use and the relative emphasis appropriate to each. The structure and processes currently in place, although better than those of the past, do not lend themselves to efficient unified decisions.

Discussion Questions

1. What is it about the fundamental properties of national security that makes it hard to produce and allocate through competitive markets? What problems do governments face in producing and allocating national security?
2. Is it inherently impossible to achieve all of the country's ideal national security goals? Why or why not?
3. Should the United States seek to create a more unified national security apparatus? If so, what should it look like? What political factors would make the formation of such an organization difficult?
4. What agencies and organizations play a central role in the federal budget process? Are some agencies more powerful than others? Why?
5. What factors limit the ability of the president and Congress to reshape the federal budget radically?
6. What is the difference between mandatory spending and discretionary spending? Why are these categories significant to national security?
7. Why has discretionary spending decreased steadily as a proportion of the federal budget in recent decades? What factors affect discretionary spending priorities?
8. What is program budgeting and how is it different from previous budgeting practices?
9. Describe the overall PPBE cycle. What are the roles of the president, DoD, and Congress in this process?
10. How do various crises affect the budget cycle? What effect do supplemental appropriations and sequestration have on the process?

Recommended Readings

Enthoven, Alain C., and K. Wayne Smith. *How Much Is Enough? Shaping the Defense Program, 1961–1969*. New York: Harper & Row, 1971.

McCaffery, Jerry L., and L. R. Jones. *Budgeting and Financial Management for National Defense*. Greenwich, CT: Information Age Publishing, 2004.

McNaugher, Thomas. *New Weapons, Old Politics: America's Military Procurement Muddle*. Washington, DC: Brookings Institution Press, 1989.

O'Hanlon, Michael E. *Budgeting for Hard Power: Defense and Security Spending under Barack Obama*. Washington, DC: Brookings Institution Press, 2009.

———. *Healing the Wounded Giant: Maintaining Military Preeminence while Cutting the Defense Budget*. Washington, DC: Brookings Institution Press, 2013.

Rubin, Irene S. *The Politics of Public Budgeting: Getting and Spending, Borrowing and Balancing*. Washington, DC: CQ Press, 2010.

Schick, Allen. *The Federal Budget: Politics, Policy, Process*. Washington, DC: Brookings Institution Press, 2000.

Wilson, George C. *This War Really Matters: Inside the Fight for Defense Dollars*. Washington, DC: CQ Press, 2000.

Recommended Internet Sources

The Center for Strategic and Budgetary Assessments, www.csbaonline.org
The Office of Management and Budget (OMB), www.whitehouse.gov/omb

The Office of the Under Secretary of Defense, Comptroller, www.defenselink.mil/comptroller
The RAND Corporation, www.rand.org

Notes

1. Paul A. Samuelson, "The Pure Theory of Public Expenditure," *Review of Economics and Statistics* 36, no. 4 (1954): 387–89.

2. Adam Smith, *An Inquiry into the Nature and Causes of the Wealth of Nations*, ed. C. J. Bullock (New York: PF Collier and Son, 1906), 4:466–67.

3. Abram Burk, "A Reformulation of Certain Aspects of Welfare Economics," *Quarterly Journal of Economics* 52, no. 2 (1938): 310–34.

4. See Dwight D. Eisenhower, "The Chance for Peace," address delivered to the American Society of Newspaper Editors, April 16, 1953, contained in "Public Papers of the Presidents," The American Presidency Project, http://www.presidency.ucsb.edu/ws/.

5. Dwight D. Eisenhower, "Military-Industrial Complex Speech," Public Papers of the Presidents of the United States, Dwight D. Eisenhower, 1959: Containing the Public Messages, Speeches, and Statements of the President, January 1 to December 31, 1959, General Services Administration, National Archives and Records Service, Office of the Federal Register, 1035–40.

6. Allen Schick, *The Federal Budget: Politics, Policy, Process*, 3rd ed. (Washington, DC: Brookings Institution Press, 2007).

7. Office of Management and Budget, *Preparation, Submission, and Execution of the Budget*, Circular No. A-11 (Washington, DC: Office of Management and Budget, June 2015), section 10, 3–4.

8. James V. Saturno et al., *Introduction to the Federal Budget Process*, Report 98-721 (Washington, DC: Congressional Research Service, December 3, 2012).

9. George C. Edwards III, Martin P. Wattenberg, and Robert L. Lineberry, *Government in America: People, Politics, and Policy*, 12th ed. (New York: Pearson Longman, 2006), 453–60.

10. Calculations based on Bureau of the Census, "Outlays of the Federal Government 1789 to 1970," in *Historical Statistics of the United States, Colonial Times to 1970* (Washington, DC: Department of Commerce, 1975), 1114.

11. Figures 9.1 and 9.2 are based on data from Council of Economic Advisors, *Economic Report of the President* (Washington, DC: Government Printing Office, February 2018).

12. "Fiscal Year 2017 Historical Tables: Budget of the U.S. Government—Tables 5.5." (Washington, DC: Office of Management and Budget, February 2017), https://www.whitehouse.gov/wp-content/uploads/2018/02/hist05z5-fy2019.xlsx. "International Affairs" includes funding for the Department of State, the US Agency for International Development, foreign aid, and US funding of multilateral organizations, such as the United Nations.

13. This document has sometimes been referred to as the Defense Planning and Programming Guidance, or Defense Planning Guidance. See "Planning, Programming, Budgeting and Execution Process (PPBE)," September 29, 2017, https://dap.dau.mil/acquipedia/Pages/Default.aspx.

14. Prior to 2015, budget submissions were simultaneous with POM submissions. Starting with the FY 2017 budget, DoD returned to a staggered submission in which budget documents were prepared after POM submission; this allowed DoD to produce better, more

defensible budget submissions. See "Planning, Programming, Budgeting & Execution Process (PPBE)."

15. See Defense Acquisition University, "Planning, Programming, Budgeting, and Execution Process," *Defense Acquisition Guidebook*, December 5, 2017, chap. 1, https://dag.dau.mil/Pages/Default.aspx.

16. Jerry L. McCaffery and L. R. Jones, *Budgeting and Financial Management for National Defense* (Greenwich, CT: Information Age Publishing, 2004), 189.

17. Saturno et al., *Introduction to the Federal Budget Process.*

18. Technically, the 2011 Budget Control Act (BCA) appointed a bipartisan Joint Committee on Deficit Reduction (the so-called Super Committee) to solve the budget impasse. However, the Super Committee failed to achieve a compromise, and it was that failure in November 2011 that precipitated sequestration.

19. Department of Defense, *Quadrennial Defense Review 2014* (Washington, DC: Department of Defense, March 4, 2014), 53.

10

Putting the Pieces Together

National Security Decision Making

National security decision making is complex and fascinating because it occurs at the nexus of two worlds. As Samuel Huntington explains: "One [world] is international politics, the world of balance of power, wars and alliances, the subtle and brutal uses of force and diplomacy to influence the behavior of other states. The other world is domestic politics, the world of interest groups, political parties, social classes with their conflicting interests and goals."[1] National security affairs influence and are influenced by both the domestic and international worlds, for national security involves the application of resources at home and abroad in an attempt to make the domestic society more secure.

The institutional arrangements developed to advise and assist the president in security matters are often referred to as the *national security decisionmaking process*. It is an interagency process because it necessarily involves multiple governmental organizations across a range of issue areas, some of which are not traditionally associated with national security (for example, commerce and the environment). When trying to understand American foreign and national security policy and actions, factors such as international affairs or domestic politics tell only part of the story. The process of how decisions are made can be at least as important: understanding the national security decisionmaking process is essential.

The national security decisionmaking process is a system of formal and informal coordination within the executive branch to ensure that senior leaders identify national interests and objectives clearly; that issues requiring presidential attention are identified and raised in a timely manner; and that viable options, costs, benefits, and risks are thoroughly considered. Occasionally, this includes coordination with Congress (see chapter 5). The process encompasses the full breadth of national security decisions, from developing national strategy to determining the content of particular presidential speeches. The national security decisionmaking process is also a management system that helps the president carry out his responsibilities as head of the executive branch by enabling the president's staff to adjudicate and coordinate issues that fall within the responsibilities of more than one department or agency.

The president's staff—specifically the National Security Council (NSC) staff, in concert with others in the Executive Office of the President—actively administers this process. The backbone of the formal process is a constant churn of interagency meetings, commonly referred to as the *NSC system*, supported by formally prepared and staffed memoranda, intelligence estimates, and other papers. At the top, meetings include the president, the president's senior advisors, and the heads of departments and agencies, known as the *principals*. Below this level, presidents are supported by a structure of subordinate councils and working groups. Most of the activity occurs in these subordinate meetings, without the direct participation of the president or the principals. Around this formal apparatus, a set of informal arrangements continually evolves in response to the needs of the president.

The national security decisionmaking process is aligned with the annual budget process (described in chapter 9). A wide range of internal department and agency systems feed into both of these processes. These internal systems are augmented by a growing number of lateral agency-to-agency coordination mechanisms, and increasingly by interagency centers, such as the National Counterterrorism Center (NCTC, discussed in chapter 7), which integrate elements of various agencies into a single organization with a specific mission. The national security decisionmaking process is actually a system of processes that extends from the White House into a variety of executive branch entities.

It is tempting to assume that the interagency process operates in a regularized way according to rules and timelines. Sometimes it does; more often, it does not. For every rule governing how the interagency process is supposed to function (such as "this committee handles that issue"), there are exceptions. Indeed, there is no real manual or rulebook, although documents that purport to be such abound.[2] The processes used to support major decisions differ significantly from one administration to the next and even within an administration, depending on the issues.

Factors that Shape Decision Making

Several institutional dynamics affect the national security decisionmaking process. This section surveys the most important of these factors.

The Presidency. The president's job is unique. In the words of Richard Neustadt: "No one else sits where he sits or sees quite as he sees; no one else feels the full weight of his obligations."[3] The president, unlike many of his foreign counterparts, is both head of state—the country's symbolic leader—and head of government—the chief executive. Broad executive power is vested in the president directly by the Constitution, not granted by Congress. The president's national security powers are formidable and, as discussed in chapter 4, continue to expand over time. As a result, the president's attention is often stretched thin.[4] Moreover, domestic and international publics have high expectations of the most powerful leader in the world. In addition to these demands, foreign and national security policies also present the president's best opportunity for a legacy. The national security decisionmaking process belongs to the president and is responsive to these imperatives.

Separation of Powers, Pluralism, and Federalism. The national security decisionmaking process reflects the basic characteristics of the US political system.[5] For the purposes of this chapter, two features stand out. The first—the subject of chapters 4 and 5—is the US system of separated powers, or more accurately, of separate institutions that share power.[6] The second is political and social pluralism: the more pluralist the society—that is, the more numerous and distinct are its ethnic, cultural, religious, or other disparate groups—the greater the number of entities that interact with the decisionmaking process and structure, and the more difficult it becomes to develop coherent national strategy and policy.[7]

While pluralism is the defining characteristic of the American domestic policy realm, the foreign policy realm is different. There are fewer interest groups, and most do not have the political clout of domestic policy groups. Apart from the mass media, whose influence in both spheres is comparable, the most influential voices in foreign policy debates emanate from a small population of national security elites, from a few public policy think tanks, and from America's top academic institutions. While the number of influential actors continues to rise, the foreign policy arena is less crowded than the domestic policy arena.

In 1966, Aaron Wildavsky argued that two presidencies exist: one for domestic affairs and one for foreign affairs. Wildavsky's thesis is no longer quite as accurate in some areas (for example, international trade), but it remains useful in the national security realm. Says Wildavsky: "The President's normal problem with domestic policy is to get congressional support for the programs he prefers. In foreign affairs, in contrast, he can almost always get support for policies that he believes will protect the nation—but his problem is to find a viable policy."[8]

Until relatively recently, the "two presidencies" thesis meant good news for the president in national security affairs. Presidents have been able to act without the express approval of Congress far more often in foreign affairs than on domestic issues. However, the political reality of two presidencies now cuts both ways. The importance of domestic security concerns to the president's national security responsibilities began to grow in the early 1990s with the first World Trade Center attack in 1993 and the 1995 Oklahoma City bombing, and then dramatically increased in the wake of the September 11, 2001, terrorist attacks (see chapter 6). Further domestic terrorist threats in the last decade, including the Boston Marathon bombings in 2013 and the San Bernardino and Orlando shootings in 2015 and 2016, respectively, increased the linkages between foreign policy and domestic security. Moreover, recent high-profile mass shootings, to include Sandy Hook in 2012, Charleston in 2015, Las Vegas in 2017, and Parkland in 2018, further blur the lines between domestic and security policy. Protecting the country now requires, in the words of the 9/11 Commission, "unity of effort across the foreign-domestic divide."[9]

From the average American's perspective, the conceptual distinction between national security and homeland security may be largely meaningless. However, the distinction has practical significance. First, the domestic implications of homeland security policy mean that the president must share power with Congress on such issues. As Wildavsky observes, "It takes great crises . . . for Presidents to succeed in controlling domestic policy," and a president's domestic policy proposals succeed only half as often as his national security proposals.[10] The events of 9/11 triggered such a crisis, but President George W. Bush's ability to pass domestic legislation eroded more quickly than his ability to enact foreign policy initiatives. For example, Bush's proposal to provide first responders with smallpox inoculations failed, but three months later he was able to take the country into war with Iraq. President Barack Obama was able to enact several important foreign policy initiatives, including withdrawal of US military forces from Iraq, deploying forces back to Iraq to confront the Islamic State in Iraq and the Levant (ISIL), and negotiating a nuclear deal with Iran, despite vocal challenges to his foreign policy endeavors. Obama's domestic policy agenda faced stiffer opposition and met with less success; a notable example was his inability to secure substantive gun control legislation in the wake of the 2012 Sandy Hook school shooting tragedy and other mass shootings.

Second, the vigorous engagement of interest groups with Congress and the bureaucracy impinges on the president's power in homeland security matters. Because homeland security policies touch the daily lives of Americans and frequently collide with competing domestic priorities, interest groups and private sector firms become involved. These may include organizations ranging from the National Rifle Association and Lockheed Martin to Facebook and Google.

Third, the president shares power with the states, and governors are frequently uncooperative: the president has his interests, and they have theirs. For example, with regard to immigration policy—an issue that affects both foreign policy and domestic concerns—seventeen state governors sued the Obama administration over its immigration policy in 2015 and four state governors sued the Trump administration over its refugee and travel ban in 2017. Both policies were implemented by presidential executive orders and both were challenged in the courts. For all of these reasons, since 9/11, the president's national security predominance simply no longer exists across a critical range of security policies.[11]

The effect of the distinction between national security and homeland security on national security decision making is threefold. First, even as expectations that the president will protect the country have risen since 9/11, the heightened relevance of domestic issues to security has meant that the president's power has diminished. Second, the development and implementation of coherent national security policy has become more challenging due to the involvement of more domestic agencies and policy instruments that were previously outside of the realm of national security policy. The durable relationships among interest groups, relevant executive branch agencies, and corresponding congressional committees—sometimes known as *iron triangles*—mean that policy making takes longer, involves more compromise, and is incremental. Third, the center of gravity for many security issues has shifted from the Senate to the House of Representatives, whose members' votes more often reflect how policy affects their districts rather than the nation as a whole. As a result, security policy today is increasingly influenced by public opinion. For example, the tension between local and federal priorities is seen in communities concerned about the regional economic impact of the Department of Defense (DoD)'s Base Realignment and Closure (BRAC) proposals. While the closure of excess infrastructure may enable DoD to produce more military capability for the nation for a lower cost in taxpayer dollars, the economic impact of the loss of a military installation can be significant to a specific local community.

Domestic Politics. During the Truman administration, the Republican chair of the Foreign Relations Committee, Senator Arthur H. Vandenberg from Michigan, famously claimed that "partisan politics stops at the water's edge." Now, though, this view is harder to sustain. While domestic politics do not necessarily preclude desirable courses of action, they do make some presidential decisions tougher or more costly. Domestic politics can narrow or influence options (that President John Kennedy had talked tough on Cuba during the 1960 presidential election surely influenced his decision to approve the Bay of Pigs operation), put new options on the table (it was Richard Nixon, the ardent anticommunist president, who could open up relations with Communist China), or simply roil the waters (an example was the 2015 speech by Israel's prime minister to a Joint Session of Congress just when the Obama administration was negotiating a nuclear deal with Iran). Domestic politics can also remove some presidential options completely, albeit rarely, and usually through a conflict over the formal powers of the president and Congress; an example was congressional opposition to Obama's military strike on Syria in 2014, or to his executive order in 2009 to close the US detention facility at the US Naval Station at Guantánamo Bay, Cuba.[12] Similarly, domestic politics can lead to specific foreign policy actions, such as when Congress overwhelmingly approved significant sanctions on Russia over President Trump's objections in 2017.[13]

Perhaps the most important domestic political factor affecting many of the president's power calculations is the electoral cycle. In a first term, a president's prospects for reelection constrain choices; in a second term, the president may have more freedom to act, but less influence with Congress. In either case, foreign leaders may use their understanding of the US political and electoral systems to enhance their own bargaining positions.[14]

The impact of domestic politics does not always happen at the margins, nor is it new. Ernest May argues that the Monroe Doctrine, which opposed European colonialism in the Americas and became the bedrock of American strategy toward Latin America for nearly a century, is best understood in terms of domestic politics.[15] The geopolitical situation mattered to President James Monroe, but it mattered most in terms of what it spelled for the domestic political fortunes of his party. John Quincy Adams, who helped formulate the doctrine as Monroe's secretary of state, was elected to succeed Monroe at least in part because of the domestic popularity of this international policy. Domestic politics is a critical variable—sometimes the most important variable—in the national security decisionmaking process. This need not be cause for cynicism; in a democracy, good policy is policy that gets enacted, and politics is how it gets enacted; good strategy is strategy that can be maintained. To be effective, a policy maker must be a pragmatist, not a perfectionist.

Ever-Increasing Complexity in National Security Affairs. No realm of affairs has grown more complex more quickly than national security, which must integrate political, diplomatic, military, economic, technological, cultural, and psychological dimensions.[16] Each new challenge creates a policy demand. Government adds a function, agencies specialize, and jurisdictions overlap. Integrating national security policy becomes simultaneously more important and more difficult. The burden on the president becomes greater.

As complexity rises, so does the interrelatedness of issues. The most familiar example is the connection between security and international economic policy, but interrelatedness is growing in many specific policy areas (for instance, counterterrorism intelligence) and individual programs. Fewer problems fall solely within the purview of a specific agency, and it is increasingly unlikely that an individual department or agency is cognizant of all the ways in which its policies and programs relate and interact to those of others.[17] At a minimum, agencies differ in their priorities. For example, although both the Department of Justice and DoD had legal authorization to investigate the disclosure by WikiLeaks of top-secret documents related to Afghanistan, the departments' internal priorities differed. Ultimately, DoD took the lead on the investigation, with the Justice Department in a supporting role.[18]

For most of the last sixty years, this phenomenon of interrelatedness affected domestic and economic policy more than national security policy. The Department of State, DoD, and the Central Intelligence Agency (CIA) were granted distinct, even exclusive statutory authorities for most of what they do. This is no longer the case. The 9/11 Commission report observed that, even when national security professionals are committed to collaboration, it is difficult to force cooperation. The NSC system must increasingly and deliberately foster these interconnections to forge coherent policies.

With respect to each new challenge of interrelatedness, the president has three choices: (1) assume a new coordination burden, (2) decide that a particular issue is not a sufficiently high priority to warrant presidential attention, or (3) provide guidance or impose requirements on the agencies to effect lateral coordination on their own. The first option has the cost of increasing the size and diffusing the focus of the president's staff. The second runs the risk of miscalculation, as a seemingly low-priority issue may surface later as a major problem. The third option is problematic at best: presidential commands are "but a method of persuasion . . . and not a method suitable for everyday employment."[19]

Growth of the Federal Government. As policy needs expand, government tends to expand as well. The number of executive agencies with national security interests continues to grow in order to address new demands; so does the number of specialized bureaus, offices, and centers.[20] Meanwhile, Congress creates new committees and subcommittees. In 2003, for example, George W. Bush created the position of the undersecretary of defense for intelligence, one of five new undersecretaries added between 1998 and 2004. This political appointee is responsible for the coordination of DoD-wide intelligence activities. While this is an important function, it adds to the number of actors involved in the interagency process. Similarly, the NSC staff "has become bigger, roughly doubling since 1992 to about 400 people" by the end of the Obama administration in 2016.[21] The Trump administration has said that its NSC staff will be smaller and less operational, but it is unclear whether this will remain true as the administration confronts the myriad demands of national security decision making.

Departmentalism, Parochialism, and Turf. Many civil servants stay in the same department for their entire careers, allowing agencies to develop expertise and provide continuity to changing administrations. The executives at the tops of government organizations must develop support within their bureaucracies to get things done, even when their means of doing so may not exactly align with the president's priorities.[22] The views of government employees within particular departments and agencies and the views, over time, of their politically appointed leaders, are naturally more parochial than the president's. Cabinet secretaries become defenders of their departments' functions and constituencies; they seek to stake out and to defend their "turf."[23] Elliot Richardson, who held four cabinet positions, stated that "cabinet members are forced by the very nature of their institutional responsibilities to be advocates of their departmental programs."[24] Since cabinet members respond to more than just the president's agenda, the president has an incentive to centralize decision making in the White House and to use the national security decisionmaking process to assert control.

The National Security Act of 1947 and the National Security Council

Both the president and the agencies involved need an agreed upon process for national security decision making. As interrelatedness increases and as the president's coordination burden rises, so does that of the agencies. The result is an increase in conflicts that only the president can adjudicate. Describing Kennedy's cabinet during the Cuban Missile Crisis, Graham Allison and Richard Neustadt wrote: "What top officials needed from the President [was] . . . a forum for discussion, a referee for arguments, assurance of a hearing, and a judgment on disputes. Their jurisdictions were at once divided and entangled. . . . None could act alone."[25] As the Tower Commission, which was formed in the wake of the Iran-Contra scandal in 1986, stated: "The NSC system will not work unless the president makes it work."[26]

The National Security Act of 1947 established the fundamental institutional architecture for the formal national security decisionmaking process. After World War II ended, the wartime structure of ad hoc relationships and temporary committees dissolved, but the nation's security interests could not be pursued effectively by agencies acting independently. With an appreciation for this challenge, President Harry Truman gave a speech in December 1945 that called for a unified defense establishment.[27] Supporting his call for unification were the Army and War Departments. The Navy, which opposed this proposal, favored decentralization; it persisted in this stance through various reorganizations, including Goldwater-Nichols in 1986 (which is described in chapter 8).

The National Security Act that emerged in July 1947 was a compromise. The act created a secretary of defense (but not yet a unified defense department), the Joint Chiefs of Staff (JCS), the Air Force, the CIA, and several other entities. It also created the NSC to "advise the President with respect to the integration of domestic, foreign, and military policies relating to the national security so as to enable the military services and the other departments and agencies of the Government to cooperate more effectively in matters involving the national security."[28] The NSC was authorized to have a staff, managed by an executive secretary. As flaws of the initial plan became apparent, Congress amended the act in 1949, creating a DoD with full authority over the military services, removing the service representatives from the cabinet and the NSC, and creating a chairman of the JCS who would serve as the military advisor to the NSC. Additional adjustments occurred in 1958, 1986 and in 2004 (table 10.1).

Table 10.1 The National Security Council (NSC) as Established by the National Security Act of 1947, as Amended

Chair:	**President**
Members:	**Vice President** (added 1949)
	Secretary of State
	Secretary of Defense (Secretaries of Army, Navy, and Air Force removed in 1949) Secretaries and under secretaries of other executive departments and of the military departments, when appointed by the president with advice and consent of the Senate
Statutory Advisors:	**Chairman, Joint Chiefs of Staff** (added 1949), or vice chairman in chairman's absence (added 1986)
	Director of National Intelligence (added 2004, replacing director of Central Intelligence)

Source: US Code, Title 50, Chapter 15, Subchapter 1, Section 402, as amended by the National Security Act Amendments of 1949, the Defense Reorganization Act of 1958, the Goldwater-Nichols Act of 1986, and the Intelligence Reform and Terrorism Prevention Act of 2004.

The National Security Council in Practice. By the end of the Truman administration, the current basic structure was in place: the statutory NSC with an executive secretary responsible for facilitating meetings, communicating with the president, and overseeing a supporting staff. The staff was given responsibility for coordinating interagency committees and managing the preparation of policy papers.[29] The position of national security advisor was created in 1953 (see also chapter 4).

The National Security Act authorized the president to appoint other cabinet secretaries and undersecretaries to the NSC, with Senate approval. No president has sought such approval, although every president has added participants. Table 10.2 compares how each of the recent administrations has tailored the NSC to its needs. After the Eisenhower administration and before 9/11, formal meetings of the NSC were generally infrequent—on average slightly more often than once a month. George W. Bush convened the NSC more frequently: every day for a period following 9/11, and once or twice a week thereafter (often by secure video teleconference [VTC]).[30] As with the George W. Bush administration, in the Obama and Trump administrations, crises typically generate a flurry of formal NSC meetings; between crises, meetings occur less frequently.[31]

Formal meetings occur less often than lower-level meetings for a number of reasons. First, the president does not need a formal meeting to confer with his national security team. Decisions can be made any time the president gathers the right people or the right advice. Second, much of the value of the NSC system is created in meetings that occur below the principals' level without the president. These meetings improve the decisionmaking process by coordinating policy, crafting distinct options, clarifying differences, and minimizing the issues that require the president's attention.

The NSC Staff. The NSC staff has three enduring purposes: to advise the president; to coordinate the development of policy across the executive branch; and to monitor the implementation of presidential decisions, policies, and guidance.[32] The most important staff position is the national security advisor, supported by one or more deputy national security advisors. Each president and national security advisor customizes the structure of the NSC staff based on the needs of the president, the challenges at hand, and the capabilities of the individuals on the NSC staff. Colin Powell, President Ronald Reagan's national security advisor, said that "at the end of the day, the duty of the National Security Council staff and the assistant is to mold themselves to the personality of the president."[33]

Clinton added to the NSC staff a second deputy, for international economic affairs, who also reported to the director of the National Economic Council (NEC). The NSC under George W. Bush grew to include six deputies for key policy functions; the number was reduced to four deputies under President Obama and this continued at least through the early years of the Trump administration, albeit with some slight differences in responsibilities.[34] The rationale for additional deputies is to attract a sufficiently senior person to the position and to ensure that he or she has appropriate status within the White House and with the departments and agen-

Table 10.2 The National Security Council (NSC) as Augmented and Organized by Recent Presidents, 1989–2018

	George H. W. Bush	*William J. Clinton*	*George W. Bush*	*Barack Obama*	*Donald J. Trump*
Nonstatutory members or regular attendees added by the president (in addition to statutory members listed in table 10.1)	Secretary of the Treasury (unless asked not to attend) National Security Advisor Chief of Staff to the President	Secretary of the Treasury National Security Advisor Chief of Staff to the President US Representative to the UN Assistant to the President for Economic Policy	Secretary of the Treasury National Security Advisor	Secretary of the Treasury National Security Advisor Secretary of Homeland Security US Representative to the UN	Secretary of the Treasury National Security Advisor Secretary of Homeland Security Attorney General Secretary of Energy US Representative to the UN Homeland Security Advisor CIA Director
May attend all meetings			Chief of Staff to the President Assistant to the President for Economic Policy Counsel to the President	Chief of Staff to the President Assistant to the President for Economic Policy Counsel to the President	Chief of Staff to the President Counsel to the President Deputy Counsel to the President for National Security OMB Director
May attend when invited	Attorney General Department and agency heads Other senior officials NSC special statutory advisers	Attorney General Department and agency heads Other senior officials NSC special statutory advisers	Attorney General OMB Director Department and agency heads Other senior officials	Attorney General OMB Director Department and agency heads Other senior officials	Secretary of Commerce US Trade Representative Assistant to President for Economic Policy

cies. Below the deputies on the NSC staff are senior directors responsible for key geographic and functional policy areas; each senior director typically oversees three to eight directors, who are the "action officers" of the NSC staff. Directors are a mix of policy generalists and subject-matter experts, each with a specific portfolio. They range from very senior officials with long-time policy experience to talented up-and-comers. A director's influence is only partially determined by seniority; it is mostly determined by policy acumen, political skill, relationships, and results. The White House is an entrepreneurial place—results earn relevance—and there is no shortage of strong individuals seeking to engage in the policy process. Tactful and effective directors can earn access, while some senior directors and even deputies may find themselves marginalized.[35]

Members of the NSC staff come from a variety of backgrounds: government, academia, the private sector, and think tanks. Many individuals' careers cross sectors, offering multiple vantage points on security issues. Military officers in every rank from captain to four-star general have served in positions on the NSC staff, from director to national security advisor. They have essential military knowledge and experience, understand how to organize and run staffs, are nonpartisan, and may offer critical continuity during changes of administration. Common challenges for military officers are adapting to the unfamiliar fluidity of the White House and walking a careful line between policy and politics in a place where partisanship can profoundly shape the policy process.

The specific policy demands facing an administration shape the staff structure. If the NSC staff and agencies begin to have routine meetings on a particular topic, then it becomes practical to designate an NSC official of appropriate rank, supported by a handful of NSC directors, to manage that portfolio. For example, the George W. Bush administration created the Iraq and Afghanistan directorate, the Combating Terrorism directorate, and the Strategic Communications and Global Outreach directorate.[36] Later, signaling shifts in focus, the Obama administration eliminated the posts of deputy national security advisors for Iraq and Afghanistan and for global outreach.

The Interagency Process

Although details and titles have varied across administrations, the national security decisionmaking architecture has been relatively stable since 1989. It comprises a principals committee (PC), a deputies committee (DC), and subordinate interagency policy coordination committees (PCCs).

Principals Committee. A principals committee meeting is an NSC meeting without the president. The PC's main functions are to advise the president and to coordinate and resolve interagency policy issues at the national strategic level. The frequency of PC meetings increases to meet demands. The core participants are the NSC members and advisors and the national security advisor. The vice president and the White House chief of staff also attend some PC meetings, and others may attend from time to time. The national security advisor convenes and chairs the meeting and ensures that the necessary documents (usually three-to-six page memos called "PC papers") are prepared and disseminated in advance. The PC may meet daily or even twice a day during crises and often handles rapidly unfolding or time-sensitive issues.

Deputies Committee. The deputies committee, which has been called "the engine of policy," is particularly useful.[37] The DC resolves those interagency issues that can be handled without engaging the principals; it elevates critical or contentious issues that require the attention of the principals or the president; and it presents issues to the principals in a manner that sets a foundation for deliberation. While it makes few truly strategic decisions, there are many important policy decisions that may require dissemination and action more than confidentiality. Essential White House and departmental staffers regularly attend DC meetings, which are less formal than NSC or PC meetings. The DC supervises the work of the subordinate committees, where most policy issues are introduced and some are settled. Occasionally, for high-priority initiatives or during crises, important issues begin at the DC level rather than in the subordinate committees.

The NSC DC is generally chaired by the deputy national security advisor; it includes the deputy secretaries of state, treasury, energy, homeland security, and defense; the deputy attorney general; the deputy director of the Office of Management and Budget (OMB); the deputy to the US representative to the United Nations; the deputy director of national intelligence (DNI); the vice chairman of the JCS; and the assistant to the vice president for national security affairs. If the issue concerns a particular area (such as Iraq or Afghanistan), the relevant ambassadors and commanders (or their deputies) may participate (by secure VTC).[38] The deputy national security advisor generally convenes and chairs the meeting; the deputy national security advisor for international economic affairs chairs meetings that concern economic issues and have a slightly augmented membership. As with the PC, the NSC staff typically prepares and circulates a DC paper before the meeting. During crises, DC meetings often parallel PC meetings to prepare for or follow up on the principals' decisions and to ensure clear communication and coordination. This rhythm can drive an intense cascade of recurring meetings in the agencies to support both policy formulation and implementation.

Policy Coordination Committees. Policy coordination committees (PCCs) are organized around specific geographic or functional policy areas. PCCs accomplish the bulk of the work of integrating policy, adjudicating conflicts, and framing issues for the deputies and principals. Sometimes the PCC elevates an issue to the DC for resolution; sometimes the DC makes a policy decision and sends it to the PCC to work out the details. The number and composition of PCCs vary over time.

The scope, membership, rank of participants, frequency, and authority of an PCC depend on the issues the PCC handles and the level of responsibility given to it. Members typically include political appointees at the level of deputy assistant secretary or occasionally assistant secretary, senior agency officials, senior military officers from the Office of the Secretary of Defense and the Joint Staff, and other experts. Membership is a mix of political and career officials. Although attendance is controlled, the roster is relatively flexible: agencies will send representatives they feel should be involved, and White House staff will attend as circumstances and their portfolios require. An NSC senior director usually chairs the PCC to coordinate the actions of the departments and agencies and to ensure that they are consistent with the administration's overall policy.

A properly led PCC cultivates a sense of teamwork, encouraging collaboration and communication outside of scheduled meetings. Membership and working relationships often endure from one administration to the next, so few issues are truly new to PCCs. Since PCC chairs have no formal authority to override any one agency, a single agency can be obstructionist and prevent consensus. In response, the PCC has three choices: compromise to achieve consensus, continue to search for common ground, or elevate disputes to the DC. Because PCCs must be selective about what they elevate, there is strong pressure to achieve consensus, which can quash bold or innovative policies.[39]

PCCs often establish subordinate groups (sub-PCCs) for high-priority initiatives or to coordinate certain activities. Some of these groups endure as standing bodies, but many are short term. Occasionally, the DC may establish an ad hoc working group, or the national security advisor may direct a member of the NSC staff to form a focused interagency working group on a policy initiative with the intent of introducing that initiative at the DC or PC level. The operations of the NSC, PC, DC, PCCs, and sub-PCCs are depicted in figure 10.1.

Substantive Products. Some presidential decisions are not written down but are conveyed orally, directly to the president's advisors and cabinet secretaries. However, most decisions are communicated in writing, either as overarching statements of policy (such as the *National Security Strategy* [NSS]), guidance to the executive branch (as in a presidential directive on human trafficking), or statements to meet legal requirements. Some of these are common and important enough to warrant description.

Strategies. Important articulations of national strategy occur in presidential speeches, which reflect the president's thoughts and the essence of policy. Recent presidents have also found value in articulating policy in the form of national strategy documents; some of these are required by law. The 1986 Goldwater-Nichols Act, for example, requires the president to submit an annual NSS to Congress. Producing such documents can become a major task of PCCs, the NSC staff, and relevant agencies. The Trump administration was the first administration to have published its NSS before the end of the administration's first year in office.[40]

While the Pentagon has a formal system of generating strategic documents, the process within the White House and the interagency system does not follow a similarly cyclical or systematic sequence. The lack of a rigorous long-term strategy

FIGURE 10.1 Machinery of the National Security Council System

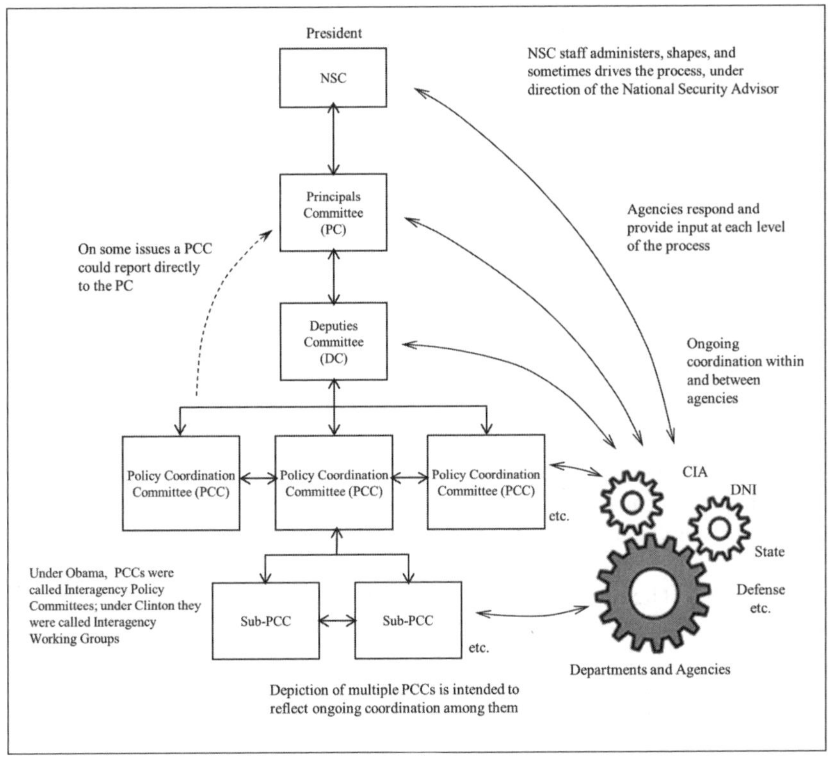

and planning function within the national security decisionmaking process has long been criticized.

Presidential Directives. Presidential directives are legally binding instruments for communicating presidential decisions about the national security policies of the United States. Most presidential directives include language intended to articulate an overarching approach or strategy that must be interpreted, implemented, and regularly reassessed. Because of their broad nature, the degree to which they remain legally binding from one presidential administration to the next is open to interpretation.

Executive Orders. Executive orders are generally narrower in nature than presidential directives. They address issues by giving specific and unambiguous direction. Executive orders are legally binding orders issued to federal agencies under the president's constitutional authority to "take care that the Laws be faithfully executed." Most executive orders are issued to carry out laws passed by Congress or rulings by the courts. Some executive orders set new policy.

As of 2018, presidents had issued more than 13,800 numbered executive orders. Franklin Delano Roosevelt issued the most: 3,721 executive orders during his more than three terms in office. In their two terms of office each, Bill Clinton, George W. Bush, and Barack Obama issued 364, 291, and 276 executive orders, respectively. A handful of Obama's earliest executive orders, including changes to interrogation practices in intelligence collection and the directive to close the Guantánamo Bay Naval Base Detention facility, signaled his intentions to alter some national security policies established by his predecessor. Donald Trump issued fifty-eight orders in his first year in office. Several of those orders affected national security policy, including banning immigration of foreign nationals from specific countries, imposing sanctions on Venezuela, and expanding sanctions on North Korea.[41]

Assessing the Value of the Formal Interagency Process. Sometimes the formal process does exactly as intended: it ensures that the key details of important policy decisions are fully developed and coordinated by agency experts and are endorsed by the principals, enhancing the likelihood of a significant and lasting national security or foreign policy success. As former Secretary of State Henry Kissinger recognized, "A foreign policy achievement to be truly significant must at some point be institutionalized."[42] The formal process adds value by establishing the setting. The routines of the formal process create an essential foundation of coordination and foster relationships that are helpful when nonroutine situations arise.

The formal process is particularly useful for coordinating the details of policy implementation once the president has made a decision. It helps ensure that information is not distorted as it moves upward to or downward from the president. It also helps reveal unexamined assumptions, minimizes the chance of overlooking viable alternatives, and provides an opportunity for the full airing of costs, benefits, and risks. A solid body of scholarly research strongly suggests that such practices improve presidential decision making.[43] The process also provides a foundation for department and agency "ownership" of decisions: organizations that have had the opportunity to have their views considered by policy makers are more likely to support the resulting decision.

Shortcomings of the Formal Process. The formal process also has flaws. This section briefly reviews some of the shortcomings that are most often cited by presidents or their advisors.

Lack of Presidential Control of the Bureaucracy. The formal process can help the president rein in the bureaucracy, but it can also be a hindrance. Sometimes it is the president who is reined in. In the words of Senator Henry M. Jackson (D-WA) in 1965, the president "has been left in an unenviable position. He has found it necessary to undertake an endless round of negotiations with his own department heads."[44]

Lack of Accountability. The formal process, with cumbersome and dense interagency procedures and committees, may result in an overemphasis on coordination and end up diluting responsibility for policy planning and implementation. On the other hand, pulling decision making out of departments and agencies and into the White House can undermine responsibility and accountability within the president's cabinet.

Inflexibility, Lack of Creativity, and Over-Cautiousness. Formal meetings of bureaucrats sitting in their usual seats—with their agendas, position papers, and enumerations of second-order effects—may not generate fresh thinking or innovative policy. A powerful example is seen in the result of a formal interagency policy review on the question of German unification in early 1989—just months before the fall of the Berlin wall. National Security Review-5 (NSR-5) concluded that "it serves no U.S. interests for us to take the initiative to raise" the question of German unification.[45] George H. W. Bush thereafter decided to "create action-forcing events, including [two] presidential trips [to Europe] and speeches that would oblige the [US] government . . . to deploy ideas about the direction of policy."[46] Approximately eighteen months after the formal interagency review and its pessimistic assessment, a treaty reunifying Germany as a full member of NATO was signed. The formal national security decisionmaking process did not assist, and may in fact have impeded, a major foreign policy success at the end of the Cold War.

Inability to Keep Pace. The world, the White House, and the bureaucracy move at different speeds. As exemplified by the rapid political change across North Africa and the Middle East that began in 2011—commonly known as the "Arab Spring"—international events occasionally move at a very rapid pace. When this occurs, the formal process can be hard pressed to keep up. Opportunities must be seized; nuance must be understood and accommodated. It is often the march of events, not the methodical deliberation of White House and agency policy makers, that forces the broadest strokes of American policy to emerge.

The president's best chance for a legacy is in the foreign policy arena, and the president must assume that only four years will be available to accomplish it. But the formal process, in particular the PCC-level forums that survive in one form or another for successive administrations, does not ordinarily respond to the electoral cycle.

"Death by a Thousand Cuts." The formal system is geared toward consensus. The deputies, the principals, and the president cannot be called on to settle what a former NSC senior director described as "extended interagency disputes too small to be seen without the aid of a magnifying glass."[47] Accommodation requires compromise; as a result, specific and prescriptive words are often replaced with broad, noncommittal language in PCC and DC meetings. Presidential advisors have no

authority to act as tiebreakers; if they were to do so without the explicit acquiescence of the group, they would corrupt the integrity of the process. Even when a conflict reaches the president, consensus usually rules.

Lack of Confidentiality. The creation of security policy, especially concerning negotiations with other nations, often requires secrecy at one point or another. This becomes increasingly difficult to maintain with the involvement of more personnel across the bureaucracy.

Lack of Strategic Coherence. A major criticism of the NSC system and the NSC staff is its inability to do long-range planning. The NSC staff is uniquely positioned to administer such a function, but it tends to be drawn into the short-term world of deadlines and immediate political needs. President Dwight Eisenhower established a formal planning board to conduct strategic (if not grand-strategic) planning, but that architecture was dismantled in the Kennedy administration, and nothing similar has yet been resurrected.[48]

Role of the National Security Advisor

Power in the executive branch is often determined by proximity to the president, and few are more proximate than the national security advisor. That one person sits at the crux of the formal process and the unique needs of the president. Debate about the proper role of the national security advisor revolves around the degree to which he or she should be a policy-neutral honest broker, a policy advocate, or some combination of the two. Within the boundaries of the law, the national security advisor serves the president's needs, and the president largely determines the role that he or she plays.

Honest Broker. There is broad consensus that the national security advisor and the NSC staff must be the custodians of the formal interagency process. This involves exercising quality control, conveying (and by necessity filtering) information, ensuring that relevant information and intelligence are available, conveying the president's views when authorized and appropriate, ensuring that a full range of options has been developed and considered, ensuring that agency heads have an opportunity to express their views, accurately presenting those views to the president, guaranteeing the confidentiality of advice, accurately communicating decisions, and monitoring implementation of presidential decisions and policies.[49]

Policy Advocate. Because national security advisors who act as advocates risk alienating the principals, policy advocacy is often seen as undermining the honest-broker role. However, even effective "brokers" have an obligation to express their views to the president within appropriate boundaries. For example, the president may need to hear an under-represented point of view.[50] Sometimes national security advisors faced with intransigent agencies and an unresponsive process have resorted to advocacy to move policy forward.[51]

Other Roles of the National Security Advisor. Although the role of policy advocate in some circumstances is now an accepted one for the national security advisor, extensions of this behavior are more controversial. Policy design, public communication, diplomacy, and implementation tend to associate the advisor with specific policies. Such additional roles could also serve as a source of tension with principals. For example, if the national security advisor represents the president's policies in the media, this may compete with the traditional role of the secretary of state as the principal voice on foreign affairs.

What the President Needs: The Importance of Informal Process

Every president must balance the need for high-quality decisions with the need for consensus and the prudent use of time and other policymaking resources. The president also has limited windows of opportunity when circumstances and political forces align to make certain choices possible. Presidents need to be able to make decisions at different speeds and with different levels of effort.[52] For these reasons, every president has from time to time stepped outside of the formal process to seek counsel.

Smaller, informal meetings foster essential collegiality, are more confidential and candid, and can be more productive. Principals devote their energy and time preparing for such meetings in a way that they do not for formal committees.[53] In such meetings, principals may bargain with one another, breaking the logjams produced by the formal process. Informal and one-on-one consultations may also allow the president to draw on input from others without yielding any power in the process.[54] Because they have greater freedom to brainstorm and engage ideas, informal groups can be more conducive to creativity.

Small, informal groups become particularly important to presidents during crises. During such situations, the factors affecting presidential decision making become more acute and the constraints more formidable. The best-known example occurred during the Cuban Missile Crisis. President Kennedy's ad hoc advisory executive committee arrived at a course of action that was a successful result of the informal process. Neustadt and Allison argue that the improvised procedures of this group gave Kennedy's advisors "the very things they needed, under circumstances bound to minimize parochialism, strengthening their sense of common service to the top."[55]

However, small informal groups are prone to some of the same flaws common to many decisionmaking processes. "Groupthink" may lead to excessive optimism and risk taking, discounting warnings, ignoring ethical and moral consequences, stereotyping adversaries, pressuring group members who express strong dissenting arguments, self-censorship of doubts and counterarguments, shared illusion of unanimity concerning judgments, or self-appointed "mind guards" who shelter the group from adverse information that would challenge the group's thinking.[56] Another problem with small groups is that they shut out of the process officials in the departments and agencies who need access and guidance. Departments and agencies across the government need the interagency process as much as the president does. Moreover, there is reason to be concerned that small groups might have difficulty managing multiple crises at once.

Looking Ahead

The president's job is unique and uniquely demanding with impossibly broad responsibility, high expectations, and a relatively weak management hand in practice. Domestic politics frame every choice, even if the president decides to disregard or minimize their significance. The challenges will continue to multiply as the problem of homeland security further blurs distinctions between the traditional realms of national security and domestic policy. The complexity of national security policy has increased, resulting in more specialized functions, greater interrelatedness among issues, and a larger bureaucracy, while congressional committees remain as dispersed and distinct as ever. The DNI and interagency centers represent attempts to improve coordination in key functional areas, but they also complicate decision making.

As a result, the incentive will continue for future presidents to centralize national security policy in the White House even further. Presidents' use of informal process and confidential advice will continue to rise, as will the role of the national security advisor more as an advocate than as an honest broker. Large White House national security policy staffs are likely to remain the norm, and a hierarchical, multilayered interagency committee architecture is likely to endure. Even as the formal national security decisionmaking process becomes more important to facilitate interagency coordination, its value as an advisory system may decline.

Can the institution of the presidency realistically handle the full burden of national security policy development and coordination throughout the executive branch? Constitutionally, of course, the president alone bears the responsibility. Practically, someone with a manageable scope of responsibility is needed to coordinate the efforts of the departments and agencies. In addition to the three options noted earlier in this chapter for a president faced with any coordination challenge (coordinate it, leave it alone, or tell the agencies to coordinate with each other), there is a fourth option. The president may delegate sufficient authority to someone else, such as the DNI. The role of the DNI may become a model for further reforms in the national security decisionmaking process in the coming years.

Future adjustments to national security decisionmaking may well involve changes in the management of the personnel involved in the process. There continue to be calls for legislation to require national security personnel to receive some form of interagency education, or to serve in agencies other than their "home agency" as a prerequisite to career advancement (similar to the joint service requirements for military officers created by the Goldwater-Nichols Act of 1986, as discussed in chapter 5). Whether the Goldwater-Nichols Act can serve as a useful precedent for the broader national security community remains to be seen.

Discussion Questions

1. If you had just joined the policy staff of the NSC, what issues from chapters 4 through 10 would you most keep in mind?

2. How does the nature of the US political system affect the national security decisionmaking process? How has this changed over time?

3. Why does the power of the president in foreign policy differ from that in domestic policy? To what extent is that changing?

4. Given the importance of career civil servants, should Congress require that national security professionals rotate through various agencies throughout their careers?

5. How have the coordination challenges facing the NSC and its staff grown more complex since 9/11?

6. Is it possible to move some of the growing interagency coordination burden outside of the White House? How? What would the president gain or lose as a result?

7. Can the formal interagency process be improved? What changes might be appropriate, and what would be their advantages and disadvantages?

8. How could the national security decisionmaking process be modified to emphasize development of long-range strategy, instead of being reactive to urgent crises?

9. What are the appropriate roles for the national security advisor? Why? How might those roles evolve? What would happen to decision making as a result?

10. If you were the president of the United States, what management style for national security would you adopt, and why? How would you structure the formal and informal processes to get information and to make decisions most effectively?

Recommended Reading

Allison, Graham T., and Philip Zelikow. *Essence of Decision: Explaining the Cuban Missile Crisis*. 2nd ed. New York: Longman, 1999.

Burke, John P. *Honest Broker? The National Security Advisor and Presidential Decision Making*. College Station: Texas A&M University Press, 2009.

Burke, John P., and Fred I. Greenstein. *How Presidents Test Reality: Decisions on Vietnam, 1954 and 1967*. New York: Russell Sage Foundation, 1989.

George, Roger Z., and Harvey Rishikof, eds. *The National Security Enterprise: Navigating the Labyrinth*. 2nd ed. Washington, DC: Georgetown University Press, 2017.

Haney, Patrick J. *Organizing for Foreign Policy Crises: Presidents, Advisors, and the Management of Decision Making*. Ann Arbor: University of Michigan Press, 1997.

Janis, Irving L. *Groupthink: Psychological Studies of Policy Decisions and Fiascoes*. Boston: Houghton Mifflin, 1982.

Neustadt, Richard E. *Presidential Power and the Modern Presidents*. 3rd ed. New York: The Free Press, 1990.

Rothkopf, David J. *Running the World: The Inside Story of the National Security Council and the Architects of American Power.* New York: PublicAffairs, 2005.

Sarkesian, Sam C., John Allen Williams, and Stephen J. Cimbala. *US National Security: Policymakers, Processes, and Politics*. 5th ed. Boulder, CO: Lynne Rienner, 2012.

Recommended Internet Sources

The 9/11 Commission Report, www.9-11commission.gov/report/911Report.pdf
The National Security Council, www.whitehouse.gov/administration/eop/nsc

Notes

1. Samuel P. Huntington, *The Common Defense* (New York: Columbia University Press, 1961), 1.

2. See, for example, Alan G. Whittaker, Frederick C. Smith, and Elizabeth McKune, *The National Security Policy Process: The National Security Council and Interagency System* (Washington, DC: National Defense University, 2005).

3. Richard E. Neustadt, *Presidential Power and the Modern Presidents*, 3rd ed. (New York: The Free Press, 1990), 8.

4. Neustadt, *Presidential Power and the Modern Presidents*, 8.

5. Robert L. Pfaltzgraff and Uri Ra'anan, *National Security Policy: The Decision-Making Process* (Hamden, CT: Archon Books, 1984), 291.

6. Neustadt, *Presidential Power and the Modern Presidents*, 29.

7. Pfaltzgraff and Ra'anan, *National Security Policy*, 291.

8. Aaron Wildavsky, ed., *Perspectives on the Presidency* (Boston: Little, Brown, 1975), 448.

9. National Commission on Terrorist Attacks upon the United States, *9/11 Commission Report* (New York: Barnes and Noble, 2004), 400.

10. Wildavsky, *Perspectives on the Presidency*, 448–49.

11. See Chris Hornbarger, "National Strategy: Building Capability for the Long Haul," in *Homeland Security and Terrorism: Readings and Interpretations*, ed. Russell Howard, James Forest, and Joanne Moore (New York: McGraw-Hill, 2005), 272–322.

12. Susan Davis, "Senate Delays Syria Vote as Obama Loses Momentum," *USA Today*, September 10, 2013.

13. Peter Baker and Sophia Kishkovsky, "Trump Signs Russia Sanctions into Law, With Caveats," *New York Times*, August 2, 2017.

14. Henry Kissinger, *Years of Upheaval* (Boston: Little, Brown, 1982), 368.

15. Ernest R. May, *The Making of the Monroe Doctrine* (Cambridge, MA: Harvard University Press, 1975).

16. Pfaltzgraff and Ra'anan, *National Security Policy*, 292.

17. Roger B. Porter, *Presidential Decision Making: The Economic Policy Board* (Cambridge: Cambridge University Press, 1980), 10.

18. Pete Yost, "AP Source: DOJ supports DOD in WikiLeaks probe," *Boston Globe*, July 27, 2010, http://www.boston.com/news/nation/washington/articles/2010/07/27/ap_source_doj_supports_dod_in_wikileaks_probe/.

19. Neustadt, *Presidential Power and the Modern Presidents*, 28.

20. Porter, *Presidential Decision Making*, 7.

21. Derik Chollet, "What's Wrong with Obama's National Security Council?" *Defense One*, April 16, 2016, http://www.defenseone.com/ideas/2016/04/whats-wrong-obamas-national-security-council/127802/.

22. I. M. Destler, *Presidents, Bureaucrats, and Foreign Policy* (Princeton, NJ: Princeton University Press, 1972), 56–57.

23. The best discussion of this is James Q. Wilson, *Bureaucracy: What Government Agencies Do and Why They Do It* (New York: Basic Books, 1989), esp. 179–95.

24. Elliot Richardson, *The Creative Balance* (New York: Holt, Rinehart and Winston, 1976), 76.

25. Richard E. Neustadt and Graham T. Allison, Afterword, in Robert F. Kennedy, *Thirteen Days: A Memoir of the Cuban Missile Crisis* (New York: W. W. Norton, 1999), 133.

26. John Tower, Edmund Muskie, and Brent Scowcroft, *The Tower Commission Report: The Full Text of the President's Special Review Board* (New York: Times Books, 1987), 79.

27. This section draws heavily on David Aidekman, "The National Security Act of 1947: Background, History, and Politics," unpublished memorandum of the Harvard-Stanford Preventive Defense Project, October 26, 1999.

28. National Security Act of 1947, U.S. Code, Title 50, Chapter 15, Subchapter 1, §402.

29. John E. Endicott, "The National Security Council: Formalized Coordination and Policy Planning," in *National Security Policy: The Decision-Making Process*, ed. Robert L. Pfaltzgraff and Uri Ra'anan (Hamden, CT: Archon Books, 1984), 185.

30. Whittaker, Smith, and McKune, *The National Security Policy Process*, 11.

31. See John P. Burke, *Becoming President: The Bush Transition, 2000–2003* (Boulder, CO: Lynne Rienner, 2004), 165.

32. While it is common convention to refer to the staff as "the NSC," this chapter uses the terms "NSC" to refer to the formal council and "NSC staff" for the White House staff that supports it.

33. Colin Powell, as quoted in David Auerswald, "The Evolution of the NSC Process," in *The National Security Enterprise: Navigating the Labyrinth*, 2nd ed., ed. Roger Z. George and Harvey Rishikof (Washington, DC: Georgetown University Press, 2017), 37.

34. In the Trump administration, in addition to the national security advisor, four officials involved in the NSC staff have the rank of "assistant to the president." Those included the deputy national security advisor, the deputy national security advisor for strategy, the homeland security advisor, and the NSC executive secretary.

35. Porter, *Presidential Decision Making*, 213.

36. Brookings Institution, *Organizational Charts of the NSC*, June 2016, https://www.brookings.edu/wp-content/uploads/2016/07/Organizational_Charts_of_the_NSC.pdf.

37. David J. Rothkopf, *Running the World: The Inside Story of the National Security Council and the Architects of American Power* (New York: PublicAffairs, 2005), 267.

38. Presidential Policy Directive 1 (PPD-1), "Organization of the National Security Council System," The White House, issued February 13, 2009, https://www.hsdl.org/?view&did=34560.

39. Samuel Berger, in Ivo H. Daalder and I. M. Destler, moderators, "The Role of the National Security Advisor," transcript of the Brookings Institution National Security Council Project: Oral History Roundtable, October 25, 1999, 79.

40. *National Security Strategy of the United States of American* (Washington, DC: The White House, December 2017), https://www.whitehouse.gov/wp-content/uploads/2017/12/NSS-Final-12-18-2017-0905.pdf.

41. Federal Register, *Executive Orders Disposition Tables Index*, March 4, 2018, https://www.federalregister.gov/executive-orders.

42. Kissinger, *Years of Upheaval*, 434.

43. See John P. Burke, "The Neutral/Honest Broker Role in Foreign-Policy Decision Making: A Reassessment," *Presidential Studies Quarterly* 35, no. 2 (2005): 233–35.

44. Senator Henry M. Jackson, *The National Security Council: Jackson Subcommittee Papers on Policy-Making at the Presidential Level* (New York: Praeger: 1965), 19.

45. Philip Zelikow and Condoleezza Rice, *Germany Unified and Europe Transformed: A Study in Statecraft* (Cambridge, MA: Harvard University Press, 1997), 26–27.

46. Zelikow and Rice, *Germany Unified and Europe Transformed*, 25.

47. Zelikow and Rice, *Germany Unified and Europe Transformed*, 159–60.

48. See Daalder and Destler, "Role of the National Security Advisor," 19–21.

49. See also Tower, Muskie, and Scowcroft, *The Tower Commission Report*, 90.

50. Burke, "The Neutral/Honest Broker Role in Foreign-Policy Decision Making," 242.

51. Rothkopf, *Running the World*, 367, writes that Clinton National Security Advisor Anthony Lake abandoned the "honest broker" role to pursue a solution in Bosnia in 1995.

52. William W. Newmann, *Managing National Security Policy: The President and the Process* (Pittsburgh: University of Pittsburgh Press, 2003), 208. Newmann cites John W. Kingdon, *Agendas, Alternatives, and Public Policies* (Boston: Little, Brown, 1984), but no particular page number.

53. Porter, *Presidential Decision Making*, 27.

54. Patrick J. Haney, *Organizing for Foreign Policy Crises: Presidents, Advisers, and the Management of Decision Making* (Ann Arbor: University of Michigan Press, 1997), 128.

55. Neustadt and Allison, Afterword, 131.

56. Irving L. Janis, *Groupthink: Psychological Studies of Policy Decisions and Fiascoes* (Boston: Houghton Mifflin, 1972), 197–98.

III

Ways and Means of National Strategy

11

Diplomacy and Information

Dean Acheson, secretary of state from 1949 to 1953, once said, "The purpose for which we carry on relations with foreign states is to preserve and foster an environment in which free societies may exist and flourish. Our policies and actions must be tested by whether they contribute to or detract from achievement of this end."[1] Shaping the environment in an increasingly complicated world is a continuing major challenge requiring all the instruments of national power, including diplomatic, information, military, economic, and other tools.[2]

The United States has historically been able to induce other nations to act as it desires through its capacity to wield carrots and sticks, but in addition it has been a powerful magnet, attracting other countries to align with US policy. This capacity to attract—to get others to identify with a state's objectives and to cooperate with its policies—has become known as *soft power*, in contrast to the *hard power* of coercion using military force or other material capabilities.[3] Soft power arises from the attractiveness of a country's culture, political ideals, and policies. Many of the soft power tools of the United States are wielded not by the government, but by the private sector. Private foundations, religious entities, nongovernmental organizations, and other civic institutions have enormous capacities to serve US interests abroad as well as at home. The Department of State's 2015 *Quadrennial Diplomacy and Development Review* (QDDR), explained that "America's contributions and influence are not limited to formal cooperation with governments and international and regional organizations. In an era of diffuse and networked power, and with federal funding constrained, our diplomats and development professionals must focus on strengthening partnerships with civil society, citizen movements, faith leaders, entrepreneurs, innovators, and others who share our interests and values."[4] Enlisting private-sector leaders, organizations, and activities in a common effort to shape the international environment in ways that foster and protect free societies requires deliberate, ongoing effort by the government, as well as a measure of trust on all sides.

Other instruments, including diplomacy, foreign aid, trade assistance (or denial), partnerships, alliances, leadership roles in international organizations, humanitarian activities, international public health operations, cultural and educational exchanges, public diplomacy, military posture, and international mediation can be used to influence the actions of foreign states. Several of these instruments of power are discussed in this chapter; economic instruments are discussed in chapter 12.

Diplomacy

Diplomacy is usually the first instrument in the state's foreign policy tool kit to be used. It is "the art and practice of conducting negotiations between representatives of groups or states . . . through professional diplomats with regard to issues of treaties, trade, war and peace, economics, and culture."[5] The goal of American diplomacy is to advance and secure national interests as much as possible without provoking conflict or resentment. As former Secretary of Defense Chuck Hagel explained, "Diplomacy is . . . an essential tool in world affairs [to be used] where possible to ratchet down the pressure of conflict and increase the leverage of strength."[6] Despite a historic American distrust of diplomacy, as noted in chapter 2, it is an essential instrument of the country's power.

American diplomacy is primarily the responsibility of the Department of State (as discussed in chapter 4). Under the first secretary of state, Thomas Jefferson, the diplomatic service conducted political relations with foreign countries, while the consular service dealt with commercial matters and the needs of American citizens abroad. Jefferson used diplomats to execute formal instructions transmitted to them from the secretary of state, and he directed them to report "such political and commercial intelligence as you may think interesting to the United States . . . [including] information of all military preparations and other indications of war."[7] Although the State Department has expanded its roles and functions significantly since 1789, US ambassadors overseas continue to bear most of the responsibility for ensuring the diplomatic coordination of foreign assistance and foreign policy in their appointed countries. Each ambassador serves as the president's personal representative to the foreign government. Additionally, as the chief of mission (COM), they are responsible for the coordination of the country team, which includes representatives of US agencies present within that country to accomplish various US policy objectives. With the exception of some military forces, who are under the authority of combatant commanders, all US government personnel officially working in a foreign country are subject to the authority of the COM.

Types of International Diplomacy. Diplomacy is rarely used in isolation; rather it is often a precursor or a complement to other foreign policy tools. Given the complexity of the challenges and threats that the United States faces, America pursues diplomacy through many methods. Among the most significant are: exchanging envoys on specific issues, creating or adapting international institutions, participating in international meetings, establishing alliances, and signing treaties. These methods are pursued in different arrangements, including bilateral, multilateral, regional, and supranational relationships.

Bilateral Diplomacy. Bilateral diplomacy, conducted between two states, is a common form of international diplomacy. Types of bilateral diplomacy include treaties, military and cultural exchanges, and bilateral agreements. Of the 193 member states of the United Nations (UN), the United States maintains diplomatic relations with all but three. (The exceptions are Iran, North Korea, and Bhutan, though the United States maintains warm, but not formalized, relations with Bhutan.[8]) Although the strengths of these bilateral relationships differ, all adhere to a set of mutually recognized minimum standards set forth in the 1961 Vienna Convention on Diplomatic Relations. The Department of State maintains an extensive database on the nature and scope of the US bilateral relationship with each state.[9]

The bilateral relationship between the United States and Canada may be the best example of a close and enduring diplomatic success. Between the United States and Canada is the world's longest shared international boundary and their bilateral relationship is one of the closest in the world. Over $1.7 billion in goods and 400,000 people cross between the countries each day.[10] In defense, law enforcement, environmental protection, and free trade, the two countries work closely on multiple levels. American defense arrangements with Canada are more extensive than with any other country. The binational Permanent Joint Board on Defense provides policy-level consultation on bilateral defense matters. Canadian and US military forces cooperate on continental defense within the framework of the binational North American Aerospace Defense Command (NORAD).[11]

The United States and Canada work together to resolve and manage transboundary issues. Given their geographic proximity, the two countries cooperate on a range of bilateral boundary waters adjudications, environmental and fisheries issues, and international high seas governance initiatives. Both countries are founding members of the Arctic Council, which was created in 1996. In 2009, they formed the bilateral Clean Energy Dialogue to expand research to build a more efficient electricity grid based on clean and renewable energy. This partial list highlights the mutual benefits that can be derived on a range of issues through bilateral diplomatic ties.

Multilateral Diplomacy. This includes treaties, exchanges, and agreements conducted among three or more countries. Multilateral diplomacy is also practiced through US membership in international institutions and organizations as well as participation in international forums. In 2010, the State Department's first QDDR put the case for multilateralism:

> The United States cannot and should not shoulder the burden of the range of transnational threats and challenges facing the international community alone. It is imperative

> that we partner with other countries, enlist their support, and expect that they shoulder their share of the burden. That burden-sharing is facilitated by a strong relationship with states that share our interests, U.S. leadership in global institutions like the United Nations, and a pragmatic approach to scores of multilateral institutions and agreements.[12]

Multilateral arrangements can increase cooperation, reduce burdens to individual states, and achieve mutual interests.

Multilateral diplomacy is more complex than bilateral diplomacy but potentially more powerful. Securing and advancing US interests in large organizations is difficult, but when achieved, it can generally produce stronger and more resilient policies. Although the international system lacks a world government, generally accepted rules provide some order to multilateral activities. For example, UN membership is granted to governments demonstrating sovereign control over historically recognized geographic boundaries, regardless of the popular support for that government. UN membership obligates members to assume the commitments of previous governments, acknowledge established borders, and commit to noninterference in the domestic affairs of other states.[13]

An individual state's influence in multilateral diplomatic forums depends on the rules of the forum itself. For example, UN rules grant extra influence in the form of veto power to the five permanent members of the Security Council, which are the United States, Great Britain, France, Russia, and China. In contrast, the World Trade Organization (WTO) grants one vote to each member state regardless of its size or influence. Other organizations, such as the International Monetary Fund (IMF), grant influence and voting rights based on a country's financial contribution. Because the United States is the IMF's largest financial supporter, it generally has more influence than any other single country in the organization.[14]

The increasing interdependence fostered by globalization makes the pursuit of American interests through multilateral diplomacy even more useful. For example, agreements among many states are necessary to manage increases in tourism and commerce brought about by developments in transportation and information technology. Multilateral cooperation is also important in addressing less positive consequences of globalization, such as the increased salience of transnational threats, including environmental destruction, terrorism, and crime. Countering these threats requires more than unilateral or bilateral activity; multilateral agreements and cooperation are necessary for transnational coordination.

In addition to forging formal multilateral relationships, governments are increasingly turning to less formal forums, especially with regard to economic issues. In the mid-1970s, a small group of countries with advanced economies formed the core of what became known as the Group of Seven (G7) (from 1998 to 2014, when Russia was temporarily a member, this organization was known as the G8). This informal group, which meets annually, continues to act as an important global forum for promoting international economic cooperation. In 1999, looking to expand the number of participants in global economic governance, nineteen countries with major developed or emerging-market economies, plus the European Union (EU), formed the Group of Twenty (G20). The G20 rose to prominence during the global financial crisis of 2008–2009 and has become an additional important forum for international economic cooperation. The G20 leaders usually meet annually. Although their main concerns center on financial and economic policies, they also discuss related issues including food security, development aid, migration, and the environment.

Proponents argue that the G20 provides an effective forum for advancing multilateral diplomatic efforts for three reasons. First, the G20 includes all of the major economic players, which together represent two-thirds of the world's population, 90 percent of the world's GDP, and 80 percent of the world's trade. Second, the fact that the forums nearly always involve national heads of state, as opposed to their representatives, facilitates commitments in major policy areas. Third, as the range of issues discussed by G20 leaders expands, the forum enables more potential trade-offs among major concerns—climate change and trade, for example—that are not possible in issue-specific gatherings; this, in turn, increases the opportunities for cooperation.[15] Many of the criticisms of the G20, which are similar to those of other multilateral organizations, stem from concerns over which countries are able to join and which are excluded. In addition, despite its prominence during the 2008–2009 financial crisis, the larger size of the G20 raises concerns that divergent interests will impede cooperation. While every tool has its strengths as well as its limitations, multilateral diplomacy through formal institutions such as the United Nations, or informal forums such as the G20, will continue to be an important tool of American foreign policy.

Regional Diplomacy. Conducted by states in a specific geographic area, this is a common form of multilateral diplomacy. These relationships are important because neighboring states have greater stakes in their area's economic, security, and environmental issues. States often choose regional solutions because of the greater ease of negotiation and implementation among countries with similar interests.

Regional diplomacy often takes place through geographically based international organizations. These vary in structure, which depends largely on their history. For example, the Organization of American States (OAS) started as a regional diplomatic conference in 1890; it is the world's oldest regional organization. The OAS supports the full range of interests of its thirty-five member states through political dialogue, cooperation and, in some cases, international treaties. The North Atlantic Treaty Organization (NATO), founded in 1949, is a highly structured regional security institution aimed at safeguarding the freedom and security of its members through political and military means. The Association of Southeast Asian Nations (ASEAN) was formed in 1967 as an informal venue to support economic growth, social progress, and cultural development initiatives. Some regional organizations focus on economic and development cooperation; these are especially prominent in Africa.

The regional institutions mentioned here represent only a few examples of ongoing venues for regional diplomacy. These and other regional associations are shown

FIGURE 11.1 Select Regional Organizations and Agreements

in figure 11.1. Many such groups have produced transformational effects for member countries in economics, security, labor, the environment, and other areas.

Supranational Political Developments. These represent a relatively new category of international diplomacy in which nation-states attempt to form a common external policy and governing body to which each cedes some sovereign control. The European Union is the only actor currently fitting this description; other regional organizations, such as the African Union, may eventually move toward such a structure.[16] In many ways, the European Union operates as a single entity: institutions and processes of collective supranational governance in which EU ministries take a leading role now supersede some aspects of bilateral diplomatic relations between EU member states. The European Union itself has diplomatic relations with non-member countries, such as the United States and Russia, and it behaves as a single member in the G20 and some other multilateral organizations, as explained further in chapter 23.

US Diplomatic Efforts. Given the US position as a superpower, American diplomatic efforts can be highly influential, especially when they involve simultaneous diplomacy in multiple forms. The US handling of Iran's pursuit of nuclear technology, with which it could threaten other countries in its region, provides an example: the United States promoted multilateral sanctions (discussed in chapter 12), which eventually led to negotiations between Iran, the EU, and the "P5 + 1" countries (the five permanent members of the UN Security Council, plus Germany). The United States chose multilateral diplomacy to capitalize on interests that were shared by traditional allies such as France, Germany, and the United Kingdom, as well as to enlist the influence of other powerful states, including China and Russia. Multilateral diplomacy sustains US engagement while bringing to bear the influence of other powers that have common interests. Deciding whether to engage

in multilateral diplomacy involves weighing the potential value of multilateral solutions against the complexity of securing their adoption. The diplomatic effort towards Iran was successful diplomatically: all parties approved the Joint Comprehensive Plan of Action in July 2015.

Diplomatic efforts, although potentially powerful, are subject to several limitations. First, compromises are frequently required to achieve diplomatic solutions. Critics of the Iranian nuclear deal argue that the United States compromised too much in an effort to reach an agreement; the Obama administration defended it as the best deal that could be reached under the circumstances.[17] Second, significant patience is often required because diplomatic solutions are slow to be reached and then implemented, as evidenced repeatedly in the Arab-Israeli peace process. Third, the relatively small size of the State Department as the chief agency for diplomacy—especially in comparison with US investment in the military instrument of power—limits the institutional capacity of the US government to pursue diplomatic initiatives. For example, the 2019 federal budget authority for the State Department was only $42 billion, which includes foreign aid (roughly two-thirds of the total) and provides for only about 30,000 personnel. The same year, the Department of Defense (DoD) budget was $689 billion, and the defense workforce included approximately 2.9 million personnel.[18]

Domestic political conditions can significantly affect a national leader's flexibility in diplomacy. International negotiations, whether they are bilateral, multilateral, or regional, generally reflect a "two-level game."[19] At the international level, policy makers may be constrained in how flexibly they can negotiate by their particular domestic political situation. For example, President Woodrow Wilson sought to bring the United States into the League of Nations after World War I, but his weak domestic position resulted in rejection of this proposal by the US Senate.[20] Sometimes, in contrast, domestic political dominance or a particular reputation at home can permit greater flexibility abroad. President Richard Nixon's reputation as a staunch anticommunist enhanced his flexibility in altering the US relationship with the People's Republic of China from confrontation to détente in the 1970s. Finally, the need to seek an international agreement can be used by a national leader to advance a particular domestic agenda. For example, international agreements might enable the leaders of developing countries to pursue otherwise unpopular policies of fiscal restraint when these policies are linked to continuing favorable international loans or trade arrangements.

During the past century, the focus of American diplomacy has undergone considerable change. Early in the twentieth century, the United States followed a doctrine of dollar diplomacy: diplomatic efforts designed to advance economic interests abroad were primarily focused on economic issue areas. Prior to entering the war in 1917, the United States relied on diplomacy to assist in the pursuit of Allied victory in World War I. Following World War I, the United States tried again to withdraw from the world beyond the Western Hemisphere, as discussed in chapter 2. To the extent America remained engaged abroad, its diplomacy focused on disarmament and occurred largely through international conferences that attempted, unsuccessfully, to find ways to limit the risk and the severity of war.[21]

Following World War II, the US approach toward diplomacy was transformed to make more effective use of US global leadership (also discussed in chapter 2). The United States became more explicitly activist in pursuit of multilateral solutions to a range of international issues. It was a key player in the construction of post-war international institutions designed to support an open international economic order as well as cooperation in international peace and security. US foreign policy during this time was conducted in a bipolar context due to the threat posed by the Soviet Union. The dominant focus was on containment and deterrence of communism. During the 1970s and 1980s, US diplomacy centered on the prevention of nuclear war through bilateral and multilateral treaties: the Nuclear Non-Proliferation Treaty (NPT), the Strategic Arms Limitation Treaties (SALT), the Anti–Ballistic Missile (ABM) Treaty, and the Intermediate-Range Nuclear Forces (INF) Treaty. After the fall of the Soviet Union in 1990–1991, US diplomacy shifted to focus on the economic and political development of the former communist states and their integration into the West, on nonproliferation and counterproliferation efforts aimed at securing the nuclear weapons and materials of former Soviet states, and on securing support for peacekeeping and stability operations in regional and ethnic conflicts.

After the terrorist attacks of September 11, 2001, US diplomatic efforts became centered on building and maintaining support for combating international terrorism while continuing to promote regional stability and American economic interests. The United States expended significant effort to secure international support for US operations in Iraq and Afghanistan. At the peak of the war in Afghanistan in 2011, one-third of the 145,397 foreign forces that composed the International Security Assistance Force deployed to Afghanistan came from the forty-nine other states in the coalition supporting the operation.[22] The Obama administration sought diplomatic solutions to a myriad of other international crises in addition to Iraq and Afghanistan, including the nuclear deal with Iran and reestablishing diplomatic relations with Cuba after sixty years of diplomatic isolation. The administration similarly used diplomatic efforts in attempts to prevent and mitigate conflict and violent extremism in ongoing crises in Somalia, Libya, Yemen, Syria, and elsewhere in the Middle East. The Obama administration also increased diplomatic efforts to address the global challenge of climate change. As a reflection of the centrality of the president to diplomacy, Trump rolled back some aspects of Obama's diplomatic initiatives, particularly with regard to climate change and Cuba. However, the Trump administration used diplomacy, along with economic and military power, to address the issue of North Korean nuclear weapons.

The Information Element of Power

Information resources such as print media, radio, television, and the Internet can be used to collect, control, and disseminate information to influence the perceptions and behaviors of international audiences; thus they constitute another potentially powerful tool to achieve US security goals. Joseph Nye points out that governments can exert influence through threats, inducements, or attraction.[23] He argues that attraction, which relies primarily on others' perceptions, is generally the most cost-effective way to influence the long-term behavior of others. The information instrument of national power directly affects perceptions and attitudes, which, in turn, can influence other countries' behavior.

The ongoing information revolution has had mixed effects on the ability of the state to wield information as a tool. As the capabilities of states have increased, access to this tool has broadened to a host of other users; as a result, the spread of particular information has become more difficult to manage and nearly impossible to control. Information technology enables corporations, individuals, and other non-state actors to create and rapidly disseminate information for a wide variety of purposes. Singer and songwriter Paul Hewson (known by his stage name of "Bono") can use Twitter to raise awareness about HIV/AIDS in Africa; members of the Islamic State of Iraq and the Levant can use the same platform to spread gruesome images to recruit supporters and instill fear in others. Within this complex environment, governments must deal in various ways with information as a complement to diplomatic, military, economic, and other elements of power.

The use of information as an instrument of power is problematic for the US government for several important reasons. First, the notion of government control of information raises the specter of propaganda that could undermine democratic institutions, impede a free press, and contravene cherished American liberties. Consequently, facilitating government control of information is fraught with difficulty. Second, the information provided to an international audience can only be as effective as the policy that it is attempting to promote. If a particular US policy is unfriendly or hostile toward another country or region, no amount of salesmanship is likely to make that policy palatable.[24] Finally, in a reflection of US ambivalence toward government control of information, no one agency or department has control of strategic communications, and different government agencies use different terminology—both of which are impediments to the creation of a unified US message.

The use of information as an element of power is often referred to as *strategic communications*; the term implies the use of messaging to achieve specific national objectives. Strategic communications encompasses four areas of government operations: public diplomacy, public affairs, international broadcasting, and information operations. These concepts are discussed in turn below.

Public Diplomacy. This consists of efforts by a national government to engage, inform, and influence the population of a foreign state through direct or indirect communication. Public diplomacy is different from traditional diplomacy, described in the first section of this chapter, in that, where the object of traditional diplomacy is the government of a foreign state, the target of public diplomacy is the foreign population. Public diplomacy includes efforts to interact directly with citizens, community and civic leaders, journalists, and other opinion leaders of another country to influence a foreign population's attitudes and actions so that they will align more closely with US policies and be more supportive of US national interests. Indirect forms of public diplomacy include student exchanges, cultural activities, economic engagement, the Internet, social media, and other means by which foreign populations are exposed to Americans, their ideas, and their culture. Public diplomacy requires a long-term perspective to build enduring relationships and promote understanding of the United States and its culture, values, and policies.

During World War II, the Office of War Information ran "the largest propaganda operation in the world." Immediately after the war, it was virtually shut down and relegated to a small office in the State Department amid concerns that the state might be tempted to reinvigorate a large government-run propaganda operation.[25] In 1953, however, as the Cold War progressed, the Eisenhower administration created the United States Information Agency (USIA) to counter the Soviet ideological threat with information. Although an independent agency, USIA worked closely with the State Department to operate offices that provided libraries, books, and publications in hundreds of foreign cities worldwide. In 1999, following the end of the Cold War, USIA merged with (and was submerged within) the State Department. Public diplomacy continues to be most directly associated with the State Department, but its sponsorship and activities are much wider. The administrations of George W. Bush and Barack Obama increased the budget and bureaucratic profile of public diplomacy, although its status continued to pale in comparison to the emphasis placed on public diplomacy throughout the Cold War. The Trump administration reversed the course set by its immediate predecessors, reducing public diplomacy spending that supports information dissemination, cultural exchanges, speaking engagements, and other related activities from $1.2 billion in 2017 to $736 million in the 2019 budget.[26]

International Broadcasting Services. Funded by the US government, these transmit news, information, public affairs programs, and entertainment programs to foreign audiences through radio, television, and web-based systems. During the Cold War, Radio Liberty and Radio Free Europe were part of USIA and extended the mission of public diplomacy onto the airwaves. This has continued with Radio Free Asia, Radio and TV Martí directed at Cuba, and the Al Hurra radio and television stations that broadcast in the Arab world. These broadcasts compete with other media as they attempt to reach their target audiences. During the Cold War, the challenge was technological: USIA broadcasts sought to reach as deep as possible behind the Iron Curtain, but most information media within the Soviet Union were controlled. Currently, the main challenge comes from competition with multiple radio, television, and Internet information sources, many of which have approaches that do not favor US policy. Broadcasters must first attract audiences through entertaining or informative programming before news and information can reach them.

Public Affairs. All government agencies seek to provide Americans with accurate information about what their government is doing. The target audience for public affairs is domestic, which is what distinguishes public affairs from public diplomacy. The practical significance of this distinction has diminished significantly in light of advancements in information technology and the compression of news cycles. The government has much less ability to "narrowcast" specific messages for specific audiences; almost everything that is broadcast can be seen everywhere. For example, a press conference at the White House is instantaneously beamed around the world; it frequently includes content that is designed to influence foreign as well as domestic audiences. Similarly, a press statement made by a US official in Baghdad or Beijing may be intended primarily for a foreign audience, but will be reported and seen by the domestic US audience as well. Despite the seeming conflation of public diplomacy and public affairs, US government agencies maintain organizational distinctions between the two because of the sensitivity of appearing to "propagandize" domestic audiences.

Information Operations. The U.S military describes its role in the information element of power as information operations. During military operations, DoD employs information-related capabilities, integrated with "other lines of operation to influence, disrupt, corrupt, or usurp the decision making of adversaries and potential adversaries while protecting our own."[27] This definition expands beyond merely providing messages to inform and influence target audiences; it includes military operations that target an adversary's physical and information infrastructure. A brief review of several major components of information operations illuminates this distinction.

Military Information Support Operations (MISO) convey selected information to foreign audiences to influence the emotions, perceptions, and ultimate behavior of foreign populations, military organizations, or decision makers. Examples of MISO include the use of broadcast and print media, advertising, or leaflet drops. Formerly known as *psychological operations*, MISO is distinguished from public diplomacy because MISO is conducted or directed by military organizations in support of a military campaign.[28]

Other information capabilities are also components of military operations, but because of their impact on the control, processing, and dissemination of information, DoD includes them in the broad discussion of information-related capabilities. *Military deception* consists of actions taken to mislead the enemy to help accomplish the military mission. *Operations security* protects information about US or allied military operations so that enemy forces cannot use that information to their advantage. *Electromagnetic spectrum operations* uses offensive electronic measures such as jamming to attack enemy systems, and defensive measures such as encryption to protect the capability of friendly forces to communicate using electronic systems. *Cyberspace operations* expand electronic warfare to include the capability to attack, defend, and exploit computer systems and networks as part of military operations. Finally, *key leader engagements* are planned meetings with foreign military and civilian leaders in a conflict area to understand their circumstances and influence their actions. The extent to which each of these information-related capabilities may be used depends upon the specific type of military campaign being supported.

Although information operations have the potential to aid a military campaign significantly, concerns remain that a military-controlled propaganda machine could exercise excessive power. For example, DoD established the Office of Strategic Influence soon after 9/11 with the intent of "developing a full spectrum influence strategy that would result in greater foreign support of US goals and repudiation of terrorists and their methods." Even though this may have been an appropriate objective, it raised the specter of military officials manipulating information, peddling propaganda, or deliberately providing misleading or incorrect information in foreign media, which led to a significant backlash among public affairs officials, the media, and others. The secretary of defense closed the office less than six months after it had been created.[29]

The US government continues to struggle to create an organizational structure to manage information successfully. The Department of State, which created the post of undersecretary for public diplomacy and public affairs in 1999, maintains organizational primacy in issues of strategic communications. President Obama signed Executive Order 13584 in 2011 to create the Center for Strategic Counterterrorism Communications (CSCC), which reports to the undersecretary of state for public diplomacy and public affairs.[30] The CSCC was established to coordinate government-wide foreign communications activities targeted against violent extremism. Even with the mission and interagency authority to coordinate public diplomacy, international broadcasting, and information operations, the management of strategic communications is extremely difficult. Moreover, nongovernmental actors that influence the populations of other countries can undermine government-coordinated information. For example, when the pastor of a small church in Florida burned a copy of the Koran in 2011, the international attention undermined American messaging in the Muslim world and resulted in riots in Afghanistan and protests elsewhere.[31] The information element of power is important, but will remain one of the most difficult to manage and execute.

Other Instruments of Statecraft

Diplomacy and information are essential components of US policy toward any country, but many other instruments are also used to further national security goals. Economic instruments, including trade, development assistance, sanctions, and financial controls are discussed in chapter 12. Formal military alliances are discussed in chapter 13. Two other aspects of national security policy are important: military posture and global health initiatives.

Military Posture. This consists of the basing, deployment, and exercises of military forces during peacetime, and can include the size, equipment, readiness, positioning, and activities of military units and strategic assets. Military posture can have strategic effects on the international environment. A strong military presence can reassure allies, deter enemies, and dissuade potential future adversaries from engaging in bellicose behavior or competitive military buildups.

During the Cold War, the United States stationed hundreds of thousands of forces in Europe, as part of NATO, to deter a Soviet attack. These US forces routinely trained with the armed forces of NATO allies, and US commanders assumed primary leadership roles in NATO. The United States maintained a large military presence on the Korean peninsula and in Japan after the 1953 armistice ended fighting in the Korean War. The United States negotiated basing rights and used naval forces in joint exercises and port calls to show the flag in areas important to US national security. A forward military presence in strategically critical areas reinforced diplomatic efforts to contain communism and promote US and allied interests in stability and prosperity.

After the Cold War, US forces in Europe and Korea were reduced, but the headquarters, units, and facilities that remain can have a significant influence, especially in response to international crises. Military officials have stressed that Europe is "an ocean closer" to many areas of concern, such as when US forces deployed to the Balkans in the 1990s, to Afghanistan and Iraq in the 2000s, and to Eastern Europe in 2015 after Russia annexed the Crimean peninsula.[32] Navy carrier battle groups make port calls and conduct operations in support of US policy, and the US Army has developed a similar concept of *Regionally Aligned Forces*: these are army units that provide specifically trained and culturally attuned military forces ready to deploy to specific countries. These deployments can be combined with the use of information and diplomacy to reinforce US commitments and strengthen enduring relationships.

Global Health Initiatives. These are a specific means through which the United States can exert significant influence as it seeks to improve the well-being of foreign populations. Throughout the developing world, capacity to meet basic health needs is severely limited. There is an estimated global shortage of more than 4 million health-care workers; hospitals, clinics, training centers, and other forms of infrastructure are badly needed. The 2015 QDDR observed that "the return on investments in global health is greater than previously understood: for every dollar invested in health today, there is a projected benefit to GDP of $9–$20 by 2035."[33] Some efforts in this realm are reactive in nature; American leadership in stemming the Ebola epidemic in West Africa that began in 2014 is one example. Other initiatives entail long-term investments. The largest such program is the President's Emergency Plan for AIDS Relief (PEPFAR). Created during the George W. Bush administration, PEPFAR entails a US government commitment of more than $70 billion to prevent and treat HIV/AIDS, tuberculosis, and malaria in countries throughout the world.[34]

Given the intrinsic importance of health and the glaring inadequacies of current global care, health initiatives are a significant way that the United States can shape the international environment in favorable ways. The United States has substantial assets to deploy in this area and, in the FY 2019 budget, it committed $6.3

billion to support global health programs.[35] A focused, continued effort to address global health needs, which complements numerous effective private initiatives, can assist other countries while promoting international peace and stability.

Shaping the International Environment

The United States has an array of tools, including diplomacy, information, and other instruments of power, to achieve its national security policy goals. These capabilities can be integrated with the economic instrument (discussed in chapter 12) and the military instrument (discussed in chapters 13–17) to shape the international environment. The use of all these instruments of power in an integrated manner can enable policy makers to leverage the strengths and mitigate the weaknesses of each to maximum advantage for the United States.

Discussion Questions

1. What is the purpose of diplomacy, and what policy instruments can be used in US diplomatic efforts?
2. Compare and contrast multilateral diplomacy with bilateral diplomacy. When might each be most useful?
3. Can the strengths of the bilateral diplomatic relationship between the United States and Canada be replicated elsewhere, or are there factors that make this cooperation unique?
4. How important are multilateral institutions and their programs to the United States, and what should the US role be in those organizations?
5. Identify some of the limitations of diplomatic efforts. How might these limitations be overcome?
6. Has the US use of the information element of power adapted to keep up with changes in information technology?
7. What would improve strategic communications most: improved organization and coordination, more resources, or something else?
8. What are the ethical considerations associated with the US government's use of the information instrument of power?
9. How are the lines becoming blurred between public diplomacy and public affairs? What are some potential unintended consequences?
10. What diplomatic and information measures are appropriate complements to US changes in military posture or efforts to promote global health?

Recommended Reading

Berridge, G. R. *Diplomacy, Theory and Practice.* New York: Palgrave Macmillan, 2010.

Cooper, Andrew F., Jorge Heine, and Ramesh Thakur, eds. *The Oxford Handbook of Modern Diplomacy.* Oxford: Oxford University Press, 2013.

Cox, Michael, and Doug Stokes. *US Foreign Policy.* New York: Oxford University Press, 2012.

Gilpin, Robert. *The Political Economy of International Relations.* Princeton, NJ: Princeton University Press, 1987.

Herring, George C. *From Colony to Superpower: U.S. Foreign Relations since 1776.* New York: Oxford University Press, 2011.

Kissinger, Henry. *Diplomacy.* New York: Simon & Schuster, 1994.
Mead, Walter Russell. *Special Providence: American Foreign Policy and How It Changed the World.* New York: Knopf, 2001.
Nye, Joseph S., Jr. *The Future of Power.* New York: PublicAffairs, 2011.
———. *Soft Power: The Means to Succeed in World Politics.* New York: PublicAffairs, 2004.
Pigman, Geoffrey Allen. *Contemporary Diplomacy, Representation and Communication in a Globalized World.* Cambridge, UK: Polity Press, 2010.
Pinker, Steven. *The Better Angels of Our Nature: Why Violence Has Declined.* New York: Penguin, 2012.

Internet Resources

American Diplomacy, www.unc.edu/depts/diplomat
Public Diplomacy Alumni Association (PDAA), http://pdaa.publicdiplomacy.org
United Nations, www.un.org/english
University of Southern California Center on Public Diplomacy, http://uscpublicdiplomacy.org/
US Department of State, www.state.gov

Notes

1. Dean Acheson as quoted in "Ends & Means," *Time*, December 18, 1964, 38.

2. Scholars and national security policy makers so often refer to the four elements of power—diplomatic, information, military, and economic—that they are known as the "DIME" model. Especially since 9/11, other elements of power have occasionally been added, most often law enforcement, intelligence, and financial elements of power, discussed in chapters 6, 7, and 12, respectively.

3. Although all of these instruments of power have been used in international relations throughout history, the distinctions between soft power and hard power were explicitly articulated in Joseph S. Nye Jr., *Soft Power: The Means to Success in World Politics* (Cambridge, MA: PublicAffairs, 2004).

4. Department of State, *Enduring Leadership in a Dynamic World: Quadrennial Diplomacy and Development Review, 2015* (Washington, DC: Department of State, 2015), 9.

5. Kennon H. Nakamura and Susan B. Epstein, *Diplomacy for the 21st Century: Transformational Diplomacy*, RL 34141 (Washington, DC: Congressional Research Service, 2007), 1.

6. Chuck Hagel, "Speech on Iraq/Middle East at Johns Hopkins School for Advanced International Studies (SAIS)," December 7, 2006, cited in Nakamura and Epstein, *Diplomacy for the 21st Century*, 2.

7. Department of State, Office of the Historian, *A Short History of the Department of State: A Diplomatic Tradition*, n.d., http://history.state.gov/departmenthistory/short-history/diplomatictradition.

8. See US Department of State, "Bureau of Intelligence and Research Fact Sheet—Independent States in the World," April 20, 2016, http://www.state.gov/s/inr/rls/4250.htm. The United States and the Kingdom of Bhutan have not established formal diplomatic relations; however, the two governments have cordial informal relations.

9. See US Department of State, "U.S. Bilateral Relations Fact Sheets," March 2018, http://www.state.gov/r/pa/ei/bgn/index.htm.

10. See Bureau of Western Hemisphere Affairs Fact Sheet, U.S. Relations with Canada, February 2018, http://www.state.gov/r/pa/ei/bgn/2089.htm.

11. See Government of Canada, "National Defence and the Canadian Armed Forces: The Canada-U.S. Defence Relationship," BG 13.055, December 4, 2014, http://www.forces.gc.ca/en/news/article.page?doc=the-canada-u-s-defence-relationship/hob7hd8s. See also www.norad.mil.

12. *The First Quadrennial Diplomacy and Development Review* (Washington, DC: Department of State, 2010), 55.

13. "Chapter I: Purposes and Principles," *Charter of the United Nations*, June 26, 1945, http://www.un-documents.net/ch-01.htm.

14. International Monetary Fund, "IMF Executive Directors and Voting Power," March 2018, www.imf.org/external/np/sec/memdir/eds.htm.

15. Arvind Panagariya, "The G20 Summit and Global Trade: Restore Credit and Resist Protectionism," Brookings Institution, March 14, 2009, http://www.brookings.edu/research/opinions/2009/03/14-g20-trade-panagariya.

16. Geoffrey Pigman, *Contemporary Diplomacy* (Cambridge, UK: Polity Press, 2010), 54.

17. See Philip Gordon, "Assessing the Nuclear Deal with Iran," testimony before the Senate Armed Services Committee, August 5, 2015, http://www.cfr.org/iran/assessing-nuclear-deal-iran/p36878.

18. See Office of Management and Budget, *Budget of the United States, FY 2019* (Washington, DC: US Government Printing Office, 2018), table 5.1.

19. See Robert D. Putnam, "Diplomacy and Domestic Politics: The Logic of Two-Level Games," *International Organization* 42, no. 3 (1988): 427–60.

20. Lloyd E. Ambrosius, "Woodrow Wilson, Alliances, and the League of Nations," *Journal of the Gilded Age and Progressive Era* 5, no. 2 (2006): 139–65.

21. International conferences in which the United States participated included the Washington Naval Conference, the London Conference, and the "Pact of Paris."

22. See International Security Assistance Force (ISAF), "Troop Contributing Nations," March 4, 2011, available at http://www.nato.int/isaf/placemats_archive/2011-03-04-ISAF-Placemat.pdf.

23. See Nye, *Soft Power.*

24. See Torie Clark, *Lipstick on a Pig* (New York: Free Press, 2006).

25. See Wilson Dizard Jr., "Remembering USIA," *Foreign Service Journal* 80 (July/August 2003): 57.

26. Department of State, *Congressional Budget Justification FY 2019* (Washington, DC: Department of State, 2018), 16.

27. The Joint Staff, *Information Operations*, Joint Publication 3-13 (Washington, DC: Joint Staff, November 20, 2014), ix.

28. In June 2010, DoD replaced the term "psychological operations" (PSYOPS) with Military Information Support Operations (MISO). See Arturo Munoz, "U.S. Military Information Operations in Afghanistan" (Santa Monica, CA: RAND, 2012).

29. Defense Science Board Task Force on Strategic Communication, *Final Report* (Washington, DC: Department of Defense, September 2004), 24–25.

30. The White House, "Executive Order 13584—Developing an Integrated Strategic Counterterrorism Communications Initiative" (Washington, DC: The White House, September 9, 2011).

31. See Kevin Sieff, "Florida Pastor Terry Jones's Koran Burning has Far-Reaching Effect," *Washington Post*, April 2, 2011.

32. See Testimony of Wesley K. Clark, House Committee on Armed Services, 106th Cong., 1st sess., March 17, 1999, with regard to the Balkans. See Statement of General Philip Breedlove, House Committee on Armed Services, 114th Cong., 1st sess., February 25, 2015, with regard to Eastern Europe.

33. Department of State, *Quadrennial Diplomacy and Development Review, 2015.*

34. The President's Emergency Plan for AIDS Relief, "Funding and Results," July 2016, http://www.pepfar.gov/funding/index.htm.

35. Department of State, *Congressional Budget Justification FY 2019*, 135–38.

12

Economics

Economic power has always been a vital component of national security affairs. "To watch vigilantly on the military front must never mean to be blind on the domestic front," President Dwight D. Eisenhower said. "In our present world . . . a crippled industry or a demoralized working force could be the equivalent of a lost battle. Prolonged inflation could be as destructive of a truly free economy as could a chemical attack against an Army in the field."[1] From the economic collapse of the Soviet Union at the end of the Cold War to widespread political and social unrest following a severe global recession in the late 2000s, history often reminds world leaders of the importance of economic prosperity in securing a stable peace.

The singular nature of American economic capacity affords US policy makers extraordinary global reach and crucial leverage. In 2016, the median household income in the United States reached $72,707, and the US gross domestic product (GDP) exceeded $18.6 trillion.[2] Americans take such numbers for granted, but they are extraordinary in a historical sense. Before 1973, only the United States had exceeded $1 trillion in annual GDP; even today, only fourteen other countries have joined that elite group. US economic production is nearly as much as that of the next three largest economies combined (China at $11.2 trillion, Japan with $4.9 trillion, and Germany with $3.5 trillion); the US economy is tens of thousands of times larger than many of the world's smallest economies.[3] As an example of comparative US wealth, a single US corporation, Apple, had approximately $206 billion in cash on hand in September 2015, which was greater than the 2015 GDP of New Zealand—an advanced, industrialized country.[4]

When considering the mechanisms through which economic well-being affects national security, the most obvious connection is simply that a wealthy country can afford to spend more on defense. A country with deeper coffers can pay for more

troops, invest in better technologies and equipment, and train its personnel more intensively. In this sense, the connection between economic power and military power is quite direct: greater economic capacity can provide greater military capacity. For example, US defense spending in the 2019 budget request was $689 billion, more than a third of total military expenditures worldwide and over four times that of the next largest military budget (China's). As a fraction of GDP, however, US military spending ranked twentieth in the world, with just 3.3 percent of national income devoted to defense.[5]

The connection between economic power and national power can also be more subtle. Independent of its military hardware and personnel, a state can use its economic strength to influence the decisions of other states. The United States frequently imposes economic sanctions on countries that pursue policies antithetical to US values or interests. For example, after Russian forces entered the Ukraine in March 2014, the United States and the European Union imposed multilateral sanctions on the Russian economy and on thirty-two senior Russian officials.[6] Similarly, economic sanctions imposed on Iran by the United States and the international community induced Iran to negotiate an agreement to limit its nuclear program, which was concluded in 2015. The United States also offers economic rewards to countries that support its policy goals or to encourage policies that the United States would like to see adopted. Perhaps the most effective and influential example of the US exercise of its economic power to influence the international security environment is the Marshall Plan in post–World War II Europe. In rebuilding European economies with US aid, the plan also dampened the spread of communism and resulted in widespread liberalization of trade policy.

The challenge of developing economic power as a component of national security is twofold: a state must build its economic capacity, and it must develop its ability to effectively wield the associated power. Moreover, this challenge is complicated by the increasingly interdependent nature of international economic relationships. The total value of world trade rose from $143 billion in 1962, as reported by the World Trade Organization (WTO), to over $18.9 trillion in 2014, a 132-fold increase in fifty-two years.[7] This trade occurs under numerous bilateral and multilateral trade agreements, which connect the world through a robust web of economic interdependence. Every hour of the day, over $210 billion flows through foreign exchange markets as payments for international trade and as short-term and long-term investments.[8]

Economic globalization adds a layer of complexity to the projection of US national power abroad. One has only to look at the rapid expansion of US-China economic ties over the past decade to see a striking example of how globalization can make for strange and uneasy bedfellows. China has grown rapidly, in large part through the strength of its exports, with its economy more than doubling in size over the past decade. The United States has become China's largest single export market. The United States has enjoyed a new source of foreign borrowing in China, which has purchased significant amounts of US government securities in the past five years. In 2018, China held $1.17 trillion in US treasuries, representing over one-third of China's total foreign currency holdings of $3.15 trillion.[9] This relationship has allowed China to grow and the United States to keep interest rates relatively low, but its increasingly unbalanced nature has also given rise to concerns regarding the future of the US manufacturing base, the level of US indebtedness to China, and the relative strength of the yuan.

This chapter examines the connection between US economic power and US national security. Although there are countless connections between economics and national security, this chapter focuses primarily on those stemming from global interdependence. Building from a description of the sources of economic power and complexities arising from globalization, the discussion focuses on the form and implementation of the economic instruments of US national security and on potential security vulnerabilities attributable to the US economy.

Building Economic Power

Leaders have long recognized the importance of economic prosperity to national power and military strength, but their understanding of the sources of economic power has evolved over time. In the seventeenth century, most governments sought to maximize balance-of-payments surpluses by ensuring that exports exceeded imports, which allowed countries to accumulate reserves of gold and precious metals. Under *mercantilism*, as this system was known, trade partners primarily sought to out-produce one another. As a result, this system fomented beggar-thy-neighbor policies, as all countries worked to increase exports while restricting imports through tariffs and other trade regulation. England, for example, deliberately restricted the development of manufacturing in its colonies in an effort to keep colonial markets dependent on English exports and to maintain a robust flow of gold and silver from the colonies to the British treasury.

Beginning in the mid-eighteenth century, economists Adam Smith and David Ricardo challenged the mercantilist paradigm, arguing that specialization by individuals, firms, and nations could increase productivity and that unrestricted trade at both the individual and national levels would achieve the greatest possible outcome. Smith argued that if individuals pursued their self-interest, specializing in the task at which they were relatively most efficient, they would maximize economic welfare as if guided by an "invisible hand." Ricardo developed the concept of *comparative advantage*, demonstrating that all nations would be better off if each specialized in the production of goods at which it was relatively more productive. Ricardo's model displaced the mercantilist approach and informs the system of international trade underpinning today's global economy.

Modern economic theory has further developed and transformed the ideas of Smith and Ricardo to accommodate the scale and complexity of the contemporary economy. Formal macroeconomic models now rest on the notion that production is central to economic growth because overall welfare and quality of life depend on income and output, rather than on amassing stores of gold in government vaults. Firms generate income by employing the various factors of production—raw materials, labor, physical capital, land, entrepreneurial ability—and compensate the owners of these factors according to the value that each adds. States achieve long-run economic growth either by increasing the available factors of production or by improving the productivity of the existing factors. Short-term policy variations, such as changes in the money supply, transitory tax breaks, or large government expenditures, may produce short-run fluctuations in output but will not typically affect the fundamental drivers of long-term economic growth.

History, geography, and culture have mixed in complex ways to create a diverse set of economic outcomes around the globe (figure 12.1). Since direct governmental seizure of land, labor, or capital has serious international consequences in the modern world and the age of terrestrial exploration has ended, governments now generally rely on "pro-growth" economic policies to increase national output through greater factor mobilization or productivity increases. To raise labor output, for example, a government might seek to increase the number of workers by providing work incentives for specific segments of the population (such as women, younger, or older workers), relaxing immigration policies, or expanding the number of hours worked. Labor productivity also depends on workers' skills, so a government may expand education and training programs or otherwise incentivize investments in human capital.

As an alternative, a country may choose to focus on the productivity of its physical capital stock. Regardless of the training, health, and motivation of a country's workforce, its economic output can be constrained by crumbling infrastructure, obsolete machinery, or an inadequate communications network. A country unable to alter its physical capital stock will eventually encounter the law of diminishing marginal returns as it attempts to add more labor to an overburdened supply of

FIGURE 12.1 Size of Nation by Global Economic Production

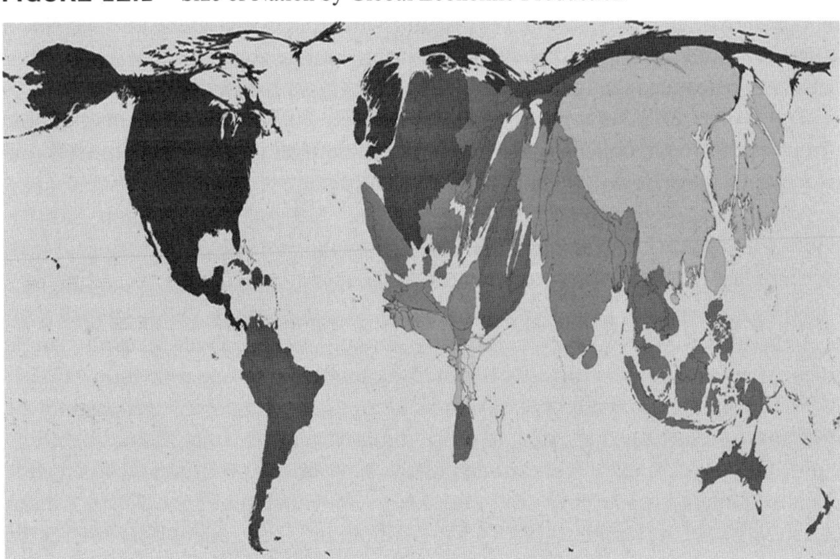

Source: Worldmapper, February 2018, http://www.worldmapper.org/

equipment and production facilities. To raise the levels of physical capital, governments establish legal regimes to define and enforce property rights, assure adequate infrastructure, and manage public resources in a sustainable manner. Additionally, governments create incentives to increase household and business savings, for example by driving down interest rates so that firms are able to borrow money more cheaply. Responsible fiscal policy is also vital to sustaining optimal levels of physical capital, since high levels of government borrowing can lead to higher interest rates, making it harder for private companies to borrow funds for capital projects. This phenomenon is known as the "crowding out" of private capital formation through government expenditures and borrowing.

Economists generally agree that productivity-enhancing technologies offer a country the greatest potential for long-term economic growth. Government policies that provide incentives for technological growth, such as strong intellectual property laws, funding of basic research and development, and reducing the regulatory burden for opening new businesses, generally enhance economic power. By the same logic, burdensome regulation or weak enforcement of intellectual property law can hinder productivity and diminish economic performance.[10]

In one of the rare examples of a macro-level natural experiment, two nations with similar initial allocations of natural resources and labor, combined with a shared geography and history, have experienced drastically different macroeconomic outcomes. International decision makers artificially created the countries of North Korea and South Korea along the 38th parallel following the surrender of Japan in World War II. In contrast to South Korea's extensive involvement in the international economy, North Korea has restricted engagement with much of the world, repressed its labor force, and diverted enormous national resources into a massive military build-up. One economic result is that the average South Korean's income of $39,400 is more than twenty times larger than that of the average North Korean.[11] Figure 12.2 dramatically illustrates another result, showing the contrast between states that pursue diametrically opposing economic policies.

The American economic experience illustrates the economic gains possible through pro-growth policies and legislation. Economists typically laud the strength of American legal and financial institutions as important contributors to the country's long-run economic success. For example, American corporations are encouraged to pursue research and development by the promise of capturing, at least temporarily, the full return on innovative products or concepts, a protection provided by a strong US patent system. The US banking system's unparalleled ability to match investors with potential entrepreneurs and to deliver financial capital to existing corporations further promotes the process of productive innovation.

While the marginal effect of any particular pro-growth policy decision may be difficult to isolate, the net effect of these initiatives in the United States is hardly debatable. For example, liberal trade policies have opened US markets to cheaper resources and a broader array of goods. After the much maligned North American Free Trade Agreement (NAFTA) was finalized, US trade within the region grew from $290 billion in 1993 to $1.1 trillion in 2012.[12] The need for constant technological change has also become recognized in postwar American business.

FIGURE 12.2 Nighttime Lights on the Korean Peninsula

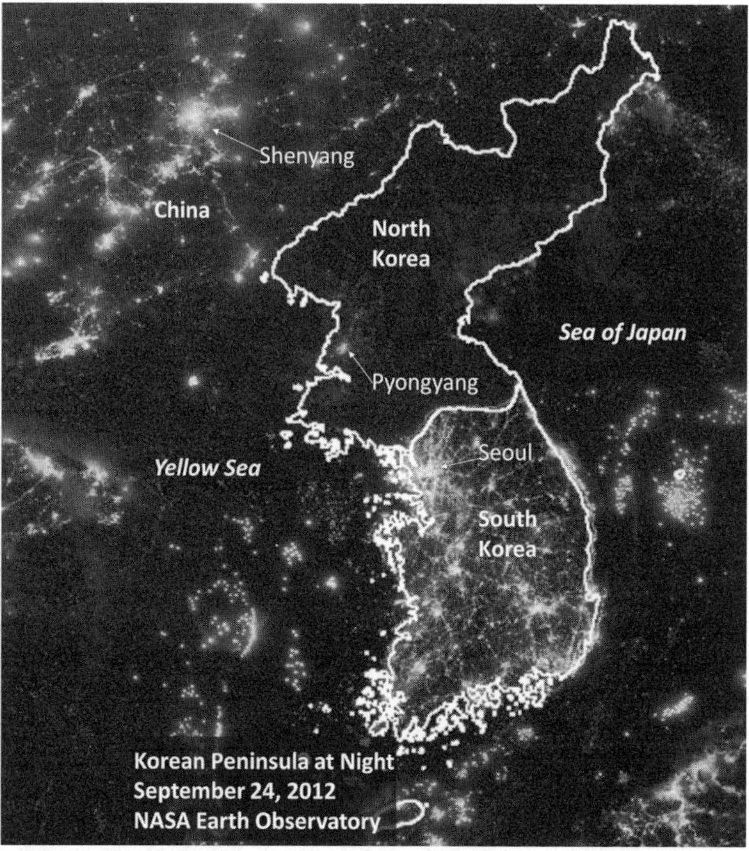

Source: National Aeronautics and Space Administration, September 24, 2012, https://earthobservatory.nasa.gov/NaturalHazards/view.php?id=79796

Large corporations allocate substantial amounts of funding to research and development; many partner with universities conducting research that may have business applications. The US government sought to bolster this relationship between the private sector and academia by establishing the National Science Foundation in 1950 to "to promote the progress of science; advance the national health, prosperity, and welfare; to secure the national defense."[13] This independent federal agency, with a $7.5 billion budget in 2017, is a major source of federal research funding for mathematics, social sciences, computer sciences, and other critical areas of research.

In addition to deriving benefits from a stable domestic financial industry, the United States occupies a distinct role in global financial markets. Following the instability and devastation of the interwar period and World War II, the United States used its relative position of power and prosperity to influence the design of the Bretton Woods international monetary system. The US dollar became the centerpiece of an international exchange rate agreement, which secured its status as the international reserve currency. Although the currency convertibility system created by the Bretton Woods agreements came to a formal end in 1971, prior adherence to the system and the size of the US economy have ensured that international financial markets still implicitly place the dollar above all other currencies as a medium of economic exchange.[14] Even amid the financial crisis of 2008–2009, the US dollar continued to be the currency of choice, as a "rush to quality" by investors reinforced continued reliance on the dollar and linkages with the US economy. Many foreign nations continue to finance government expenditures via dollar-denominated debt, helping to ensure that the United States continues to occupy a unique position in global finance and enabling it to employ the tools described later in this chapter.

War and Economic Growth. Although defense policy is not commonly mentioned in discussions of long-run economic growth, defense expenditure decisions can drastically influence a country's course of development.[15] On the one hand, some level of physical security is a prerequisite for any economic activity. In a war-torn country, just going to work or to a market can be risky, with high potential costs. Such uncertainty and risk reduce the incentive to make longer-term investments. In US efforts at nation building in Iraq and Afghanistan, basic security was proven to be a prerequisite for successful economic growth and development. Oil production in Iraq came to a halt around 2003 and only recovered to prewar levels in 2007.[16] The major problem facing reconstitution of this industry, vital to both Iraq and the United States, was the futility of spending on infrastructure projects while sectarian strife persisted. As one observer noted, "Money is a weak carrot and a weak stick when people are shooting at each other."[17]

In addition to threatening the physical acts of economic exchange, war often alters or destroys productive capacities. It may damage vital buildings and equipment, disrupt daily routines and supply chains, divert resources from investment, and reduce the skilled labor pool through death, conscription, or displacement.[18] For example, by November 2007, when the war in Iraq was at its height, more than one million Iraqis, most of whom were well educated, including 31 percent educated at the university level, had fled to Syriya.[19] Several years later, in the midst of the 2015 Syrian refugee crisis, many Iraqi refugees returned home to Iraq, while over four million Syrian refugees, many of whom could have contributed productively to the Syrian economy, fled to neighboring countries. This displacement of well-educated citizens undermines economic growth. Even in the absence of open warfare, high levels of military spending can diminish an economy's long-run growth potential by drawing labor and capital away from nondefense industries, as reflected in the North Korean economy.[20]

Ultimately, defense expenditure decisions represent a balance of two competing demands: the genuine need for security and the economic consequences of over-spending. During the Cold War, the Soviet Union allocated an estimated

20–25 percent of its GDP to defense spending in an attempt to match the West in military capabilities. This massive military commitment drew labor, capital, and technology away from sectors where additional production might have led to greater economic growth. The United States generally devoted a substantially smaller fraction of its economy to defense during the Cold War. Although there were many factors in the Soviet defeat in the Cold War, the "imperial overstretch" of the Soviets, as Paul Kennedy describes it, was certainly a major contributor.[21]

The net result of US economic and defense policy is that the United States is uniquely positioned to influence global security matters. America's economic capacity and reach contribute immensely to US influence abroad. However, increasing economic interdependence between the United States and the rest of the world continuously alters the nature of this influence and the resulting effectiveness of economic instruments as tools of US national security policy.

National Security in an Era of Globalization

Interdependence is a defining feature of today's global system, and this development is relatively new. Thomas Friedman, in *The World Is Flat* (2005), gives many colorful and persuasive examples of the ways in which far-flung regions and peoples now share unexpected connections. Many of these connections are of an economic nature, occurring through markets, and the macroeconomic statistics bear out Friedman's anecdotal evidence. Between 1950 and 2014, the volume of world merchandise trade increased dramatically (figure 12.3). Trade in manufactured goods grew more than eight times faster than the growth of global GDP.

FIGURE 12.3 World Merchandise Trade by Major Product Group, 1950–2014

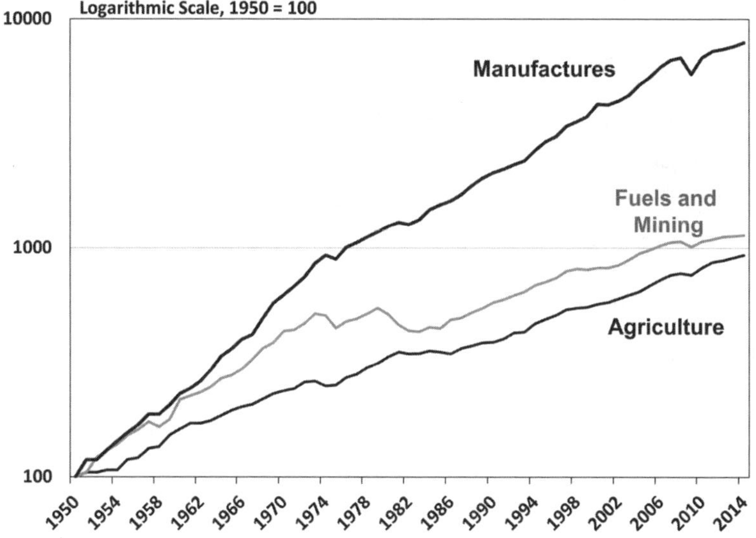

Source: World Trade Organization, *International Trade Statistics*, 2014, https://www.wto.org/

markets + trade → interdependence

Because of the size of its domestic economy, the United States is less dependent on world trade than many other countries. The combined value of US exports and imports in 2017 was 27 percent of US GDP; by contrast, China's trade represented 40 percent of its GDP.[22] However, the vast size of the US economy also means that its trading volumes are uniquely large. According to the WTO, the United States accounted for 13.9 percent of all world merchandise imports in 2016, making it the world's leading importer in terms of sheer volume, and it accounted for 9.1 percent of all world merchandise exports, making it the second leading exporter behind China.[23] The direction of US trade flows is also instructive: Asia, then North America, then Europe are the country's primary trading partners (figure 12.4).[24]

Although public attention has focused on the growth of world trade and its implications for US domestic industries and national incomes, the world's largest single market is not a product market at all: it is a global market for foreign exchange. The WTO estimates that total world merchandise exports exceeded $16 trillion in 2016; the Bank for International Settlements reported that *daily* global turnover in foreign exchange had reached $5.1 trillion in 2016.[25] This means that less than four days of trading in the foreign exchange market is roughly the monetary equivalent of an entire year of world merchandise exports. Moreover, this trade has grown rapidly: it has quadrupled from 2001 to 2016, controlling for exchange rate fluctuations.[26]

International portfolio investment—the cross-border flow of funds into foreign financial assets such as stocks, mutual funds, and debt securities—has also grown

FIGURE 12.4 Percentage of Total US Trade by Trading Partner

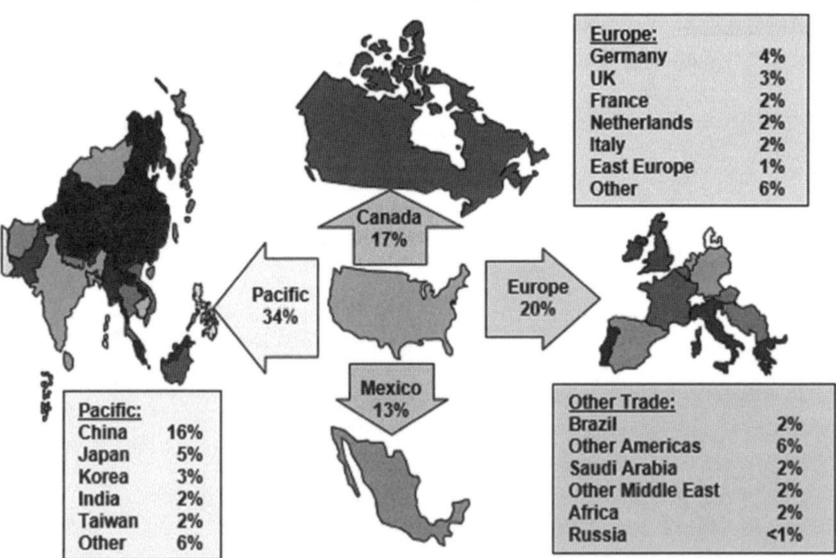

Source: International Monetary Fund, *Direction of Trade Statistics*, December 13, 2015, http: data .imf.org

rapidly. Researchers at the McKinsey Global Institute estimate that foreign investment assets reached $96 trillion in 2010.[27] More interdependence of financial markets typically provides better access to capital and improved efficiency. By contrast, foreign direct investment—the foreign ownership of domestic business operations, real estate, or other valuable assets—tends to be lopsided with investors from developed countries holding 87 percent of global foreign investment assets.[28] While the United States is the world's largest direct investor in other countries, the $15.3 trillion in US holdings of foreign assets is exceeded by its $18.4 trillion in foreign debt.[29]

Economic Instruments of US National Security

The unique role and capability of the United States in maintaining both domestic and international security stem directly from its extraordinary economic capacity. Operating through the Departments of State, Treasury, and Defense, US leaders are able to utilize many economic instruments to achieve national security objectives. These include "sticks" such as trade sanctions and financial controls, as well as "carrots" such as economic and military assistance.

Wielding economic power in pursuit of national security objectives requires careful calculation of the associated costs and benefits to the domestic economy. In many situations, the level of interdependence in the current global economy prevents the United States from making use of its economic policy tools without causing some degree of harm to the US economy. Nonetheless, the US government retains and sometimes utilizes these tools to pursue a multitude of security objectives.

Trade Sanctions. Conventional economic sanctions seek to achieve political goals by imposing economic costs on the target country, either by denying benefits from international trade or by limiting access to international financial markets. Trade sanctions are attractive to policy makers because they have more bite than diplomacy alone but lower costs and risks than the use of military force. The key question is whether economic coercion can achieve desired policy objectives in a particular situation.

The logic is based on a straightforward cost-benefit analysis. If the costs inflicted on the target country through economic sanctions are greater than the benefit of its problematic politics, then a rational target state will choose to concede on the issue, all else being equal. By this logic, sanctions may force concessions. In some situations, even the credible threat of sanctions may serve as a deterrent for undesirable behavior. Ideally, this threat would lead to the best possible scenario, in which the target's undesirable actions are effectively discouraged and the imposition of the sanctions is avoided.

In reality, trade sanctions have rarely been a foreign policy panacea. Research to measure the effectiveness of sanctions does not paint an encouraging picture. Studies evaluating 204 sanctions episodes during 1914–2000 yield results ranging from an optimistic 34 percent success rate[30] to a more pessimistic 5 percent success rate.[31] Other influential work examining myriad Russian sanctions on former Soviet satellite states show a success rate of 38 percent in the 1990s,[32] dwindling to a success rate of only 14 percent in the 2000s[33] as the newly independent states developed economic ties with the European Union. By their nature, trade embargos are double-edged swords, imposing costs on both the target and the coercing state. In 1995, for example, US participation in sanctions against twenty-six countries reduced US merchandise exports by an estimated $15–19 billion and cost approximately 200,000 jobs in the relatively lucrative export sector.[34] Coercing states may incur significant domestic economic costs for unsuccessful sanctions that are not offset by the value of political concessions by the target state.

The United States has increasingly turned to economic sanctions since the 1970s in spite of a growing body of research that suggests sanctions are relatively crude and ineffective foreign policy tools. Three rational explanations support this seemingly contradictory behavior. First, in spite of a mixed track record, in certain instances sanctions do succeed or contribute to success, sometimes in combination with diplomatic or military pressure. For example, sanctions likely played a contributing role in Libya's decision to take public responsibility for the Pan-Am Flight 103 terrorist bombing, pay reparations to victims' families, and formally abandon its weapons of mass destruction program in 2003.[35] In 2014, Iran agreed to return to the bargaining table, and eventually agreed to limitations on its nuclear development program, after years of increasingly stringent globally coordinated sanctions contributed to Iran's negative real GDP growth rate (–1.5 percent) and inflation of 42.3 percent in 2013.[36] The costs imposed by the sanctions increased US bargaining power and dampened Iran's desire to defy international pressure to negotiate.

Second, the credible threat of sanctions, which attempts to force compliance from target states before sanctions are actually imposed, may represent most of the overall value of trade sanctions. If this is true, then the majority of cases in which actual sanctions are observed would be cases in which the prior threat of sanctions had already failed. This creates a "sanctions paradox" whereby sanctions are most likely to be imposed when they are least likely to succeed.[37] This would explain why a majority of observed sanctions do not achieve meaningful policy goals. Even so, the ineffective sanctions must be implemented to reinforce the credibility of future threats.

Third, to either domestic or international audiences, a sanction may possess some symbolic value that is an end in itself, regardless of its ability to change the target's behavior. The act of sanctioning the target state may be intended to assuage domestic political pressure, rally support for an issue, or reinforce other diplomatic actions. Imposing sanctions may be a way of appearing to do something when in reality no effective options are available. Sanctions may also communicate resolve to the international community, demonstrating US commitment to the principles surrounding a dispute. These signals are ends in and of themselves, independent of the effectiveness of the sanctions in altering the target nation's behavior.

When the United States does impose trade sanctions, it is generally to achieve one or more of four possible outcomes: compliance, subversion, deterrence, and symbolism.[38] *Compliance* seeks to force some type of behavioral change or concessions from the target state. Policy makers usually publically announce compliance as the goal of a sanctions episode when, in reality, they may be pursuing other primary goals. *Subversion* seeks to remove the ruling party, destabilize the country, or overthrow the regime. It is relatively easy to assess these goals, since the outcome would be a substantial and visible change. *Deterrence* seeks to discourage the target state from taking an undesirable action. Assessing this outcome is quite difficult, given that it is difficult to determine whether the target state was actually deterred by the sanctions or decided not to take the undesirable action for some other reason. *Symbolism* is meant to send messages to domestic or international audiences as an end in itself.

Trade sanctions fail to achieve concessions from target states for one of two general reasons: the sanctions are relatively ineffective, or the sanctions are relatively effective but the target still does not comply. A primary reason for ineffective sanctions in the current global economy is the relative ease with which target states may circumvent them by adjusting production, consumption, or trade partnerships to account for the lost trade with the coercing state. This ease of substitution in the modern international trade environment often renders unilateral sanctions ineffective. For example, US efforts to sanction Soviet Russia in response to its invasion of Afghanistan in 1979 were fruitless, as the Soviet Union increased its grain imports from Argentina. In contrast, multilateral sanctions are generally more effective due to the larger economic costs of trade substitution for the target state.[39] However, even multilateral sanctions that enjoy broad support can suffer from potential leakage problems as it is extremely difficult to seal off borders between countries to eliminate smuggling. This was illustrated during UN sanctions against Yugoslavia in 1992 in response to Serbia's role in Bosnian ethnic cleansing. Even though Serbia was surrounded by countries that were abiding by the sanctions, significant and widespread smuggling along Serbia's borders allowed most critical supplies to continue flowing into the country. Participating border states, including Albania, Bulgaria, and Romania, were ill-equipped or unwilling to stop the smuggling, and some government officials skimmed off large profits associated with the evasion of the sanctions.[40]

In other cases, while sanctions are relatively effective in achieving economic outcomes, they still do not produce the desired political results. Some trade sanctions are designed to lower the standard of living of the population so as to generate sufficient internal pressure on the ruling elites to force political concessions or regime change. North Korea is an example of a country that, though crippled by decades of international sanctions, still adamantly defies international norms. Resilience to international pressure is generally bolstered by a heightened sense of nationalism in the face of external coercion, or by the target government's indifference to human suffering. For example, a 2013 Gallup poll shows that 47 percent of Iranians surveyed blamed the United States for hardships imposed by economic sanctions, while only 10 percent placed blame on the Iranian government.[41] Former UN Secretary General Boutros Boutros-Ghali has stated that "sanctions . . . are a blunt instrument. They raise the ethical question of whether suffering inflicted on vulnerable groups . . . is a legitimate means of exerting pressure on political leaders whose behaviour is unlikely to be affected by the plight of their subjects. Sanctions also always have unintended or unwanted effects."[42]

The mechanisms through which sanctions succeed or fail are relatively complex, but they are reflected in a few guiding principles. Trade sanctions that quickly impose heavy costs and have broad, multilateral support tend to be more effective than those that are easy to circumvent, ramp up slowly, or are imposed unilaterally. Sanctions that pursue modest goals are more likely to succeed than those that seek concessions linked to the target state's identity, long-term interests, or regime change. Sanctions work best on target countries that are democracies, share a history of economic ties, and enjoy relatively friendly relations with the country or countries imposing the sanctions.

Financial Controls. In addition to using sanctions, the United States protects its security interests by exerting economic power through global capital markets. The US Treasury exercises wide-ranging authority to target the financial assets of individuals, groups, or countries that pose security threats. These threats may be directed at the US financial system and could involve activity related to terrorism, money laundering, drug trafficking, and the like. The Treasury first exercised its financial control powers following the German invasion of Norway in 1940 to prevent Nazi repatriation and confiscation of the Norwegian gold, foreign exchange, and securities held outside of Norway. Recent US financial controls targeting North Korea, Iran, Syria, Sudan, and Libya have involved coordination with allied governments in compliance with UN and other international mandates.[43]

In adapting to the evolving threats from nonstate as well as state actors, Congress greatly expanded the Treasury Department's financial control powers after 9/11. Section 311 of the USA PATRIOT Act of 2001 authorized Treasury to designate a foreign jurisdiction or financial institution as being "of primary money laundering concern," leading to the imposition of cumbersome information-gathering and record-keeping requirements on US financial institutions that deal with these foreign entities. These broad third-party sanctions limit the ability of financial enablers of rogue actors to participate in the global financial system by increasing their costs and putting at risk their financial reputations and their ability to conduct legitimate business.

The Treasury Department has, as of mid-2016, effectively employed Section 311 sanctions against four foreign countries and thirteen financial institutions.[44] For instance, the United States cut off the second largest state-owned commercial bank in Iran from access to the US financial system on the grounds that it had financed terrorist groups. European and Asian banks with activities in the United States also cut off the Iranian bank from operations in other currencies.[45] Because the Iranian bank's inability to issue letters of credit in dollars severely undermined its bank deposits, Iran protested to the International Monetary Fund (IMF).

Implementation of such "smart financial power" can be difficult. First, for optimal effect, financial sanctions undertaken multilaterally (rather than bilaterally) require a level of international coordination that can be hard to achieve. Second, the forces of supply and demand in global economic warfare are more than a two-way street. For instance, consider that Russia supplies energy to Europe and receives German manufactured goods in return. If the United States were to impose stringent financial sanctions on Russia in response to its military threats in Ukraine, it would be imposing a cost on Russia but also potentially on its European allies; even if the Europeans found an alternative to Russian energy, Russia might retaliate by boycotting German manufactured goods. This could potentially trigger a European recession. Given this scenario, it is unlikely that the United States could achieve broad multilateral support for its actions.

Even in the event of a successful multilateral agreement on financial controls, decision makers must determine how to coordinate these controls with other measures.[46] For example, just when it appeared that the scope and cumulative effect of two years of financial isolation measures and trade sanctions were materially undermining Iran's economy, the Treasury backed off its sanctions in late 2013 in support of a Department of State–led diplomatic initiative to freeze Iran's nuclear program.[47] Some argue that if the financial isolation had been continued, it might have achieved a nuclear agreement on terms more favorable for the United States.[48]

The policies of the Treasury Department and the State Department exhibited similar conflict during the administration of George W. Bush with the on-again, off-again timing of economic sanctions to encourage North Korea to join South Korea, Japan, China, Russia, and the United States in the Six-Party Talks to address North Korean nuclear weapons. For the ensuing ten years, from 2006 to 2016, the United States maintained trade sanctions against North Korea, but no financial sanctions per se. After additional nuclear weapons and ballistic missile tests in 2017, the Trump administration significantly expanded trade sanctions and imposed financial sanctions on North Korea.[49] While some experts believed that financial controls could encourage establishment of alternative mechanisms, such as a shadow or criminal banking system outside of the control of international monitoring and regulation, others felt that the controls could have a significant effect on the regime of North Korea's leader Kim Jong-un.[50]

Foreign Economic Assistance. Foreign economic assistance is often used to promote a donor country's interests by helping to stabilize or develop a recipient state's economy or otherwise to influence its social, political, or military actions. Foreign economic assistance is the flow of money, goods, or services to a recipient state specifically to promote its economic development, social welfare, governance, and security.[51] The Marshall Plan to rebuild Europe after World War II offers the archetypal example of the use of foreign assistance as a long-term instrument of economic power to further national interests. The billions of dollars in economic assistance provided to war-torn Europe under the Marshall Plan helped to alleviate human suffering while also diminishing the appeal of local communist parties, helping to rebuild allies against potential Soviet expansion, and bolstering trading partners in the international economy.

As a symbol of support, the US government often extends foreign economic assistance in quick response to international incidents and in combination with other policies. In 2014, the decision of Ukrainian President Viktor Yanukovych to break off negotiations with the European Economic Union (EU), in favor of Russia's offer of $15 billion in economic assistance, triggered street unrest in Kiev that led to the toppling of his presidency. Congress reacted by approving $1 billion in emergency loan guarantees to help ensure Ukraine's financial soundness and to support its right to self-determination.[52] After Russia's subsequent military invasion and annexation of the Crimean Peninsula, the United States also imposed travel sanctions and financial controls against senior Russian government officials in order to impose costs on Russia for its behavior and to discourage Russia from further military escalation.[53]

In some instances, the United States has offered assistance in return for a recipient state's cooperation on specific national security goals. This has had mixed results. Pakistan joined the effort to combat terrorism after the 9/11 attacks and received an increase of US economic assistance, from $91 million in 2001 to $1.15 billion in 2002, supplemented by billions more in subsequent years and reimbursement for Pakistani support to US security operations.[54] However, in 2003, the Turkish government declined to allow US ground forces to traverse Turkey for operations in Iraq, despite the US offer of a $6 billion assistance package and $24 billion in loan guarantees.[55]

US officials face difficult questions in determining recipients and appropriate levels of aid: Which populations are in the greatest need? Which can best utilize the assistance? Which aid best supports strategic interests? The top recipients of US non-military economic assistance in 2016 were Afghanistan ($1.17 billion), Ethiopia ($1.10 billion), Kenya ($1.03 billion), Syria ($916 million), Uganda ($729 million), Nigeria ($713 million), Ghana ($709 million), Jordan ($689 million), and South Sudan ($671 million).[56] Regionally, Sub-Saharan Africa received the largest share of total US economic assistance in 2016, at 36 percent of the US total.

The problems of underdevelopment and the resulting failures of states have gained increased prominence as national security issues since al Qaeda organized the terrorist attacks of September 11, 2001, from the mountains of Afghanistan. America has used economic power much more in the post-9/11 world as a supplement to its military might: aggregate US economic assistance to Afghanistan, Iraq, and Syria in 2016 was twenty-one times the level of aid for those states in 2001. Aid tends to follow the focus of US military operations: Iraq was the top recipient of combined US economic and military assistance from 2003 to 2007 (with a high of $11.4 billion of total assistance in 2006), Afghanistan was the top recipient from 2008 to 2015 (with a high of $14.5 billion in 2011), and by 2016 assistance to each country was nearly equal with $5.3 billion for Iraq and $5.1 billion for Afghanistan—as the US continued to support military operations in each country.[57]

Important actors in foreign economic assistance provided by the United States include the United States Agency for International Development (USAID), the Department of State, and the Department of the Treasury. The world has evolved since President Kennedy established USAID in 1961, and so too has the significance of economic power in furthering national security interests. The 2010 US

National Security Strategy captures the importance of development in national security policy: "Through an aggressive and affirmative development agenda and commensurate resources, we can strengthen the regional partners we need to help us stop conflicts and counter global criminal networks; build a stable, inclusive global economy with new sources of prosperity; advance democracy and human rights; and ultimately position ourselves to better address key global challenges by growing the ranks of prosperous, capable, and democratic states that can be our partners in the decades ahead."[58] The 2017 *National Security Strategy* continued to include development, albeit with a tighter focus on US gains: "targeted use of foreign assistance, and modernized development finance tools can promote stability, prosperity, and political reform, and build new partnerships based on the principle of reciprocity."[59] American economic assistance in 2016 totaled $34.8 billion.[60] The uses of US assistance are illustrated in figure 12.5.

In addition to aid delivered by the State Department and USAID, the Department of the Treasury also plays a pivotal role in foreign economic assistance: it manages the US role in the International Monetary Fund (IMF) and the World Bank, the multilateral institutions established by the Bretton Woods Agreement of 1944. The IMF, an organization with 189 member countries, oversees a $524 billion fund and serves as a lender of last resort to help stabilize a recipient state's monetary position, currency, and balance of payments.[61] The World Bank, the IMF's sister institution, provides subsidized loans or loan guarantees for critical development projects related to infrastructure, health, and education.[62]

FIGURE 12.5 US Economic Assistance, by Category, FY 2014 ($ billions)

Source: USAID, *U.S. Overseas Loans and Grants* (Washington, DC: USAID, 2014)

The IMF and the World Bank have their critics, including those who are suspicious of the institutions as tools of Western power. Although the United States, as the largest contributor and shareholder of both Washington-headquartered institutions, possesses both the biggest board vote (about 17 percent) and the only veto power of any member state, evidence demonstrates that America's control of these institutions is limited. For instance, despite US opposition, World Bank lending to Iran resumed in 2000 after a seven-year hiatus.[63] While the IMF and the World Bank have shortcomings, each plays an important role in stabilizing fragile states and enabling trade.

Two lines of academic debate have developed over the effectiveness of foreign assistance in furthering economic development and in aligning the policies of recipient states more with US national interests and preferences. Milton Friedman has argued that foreign economic assistance pumps up government bureaucracies, subsidizes inefficient governance practices, lines the pockets of government officials, and generally fails to reach those in true need.[64] Conversely, Jeffrey Sachs and Joseph Stiglitz, among others, have argued that while economic assistance may not always be successful, it has indeed spurred poverty reduction and economic development in many recipient states.[65] In countries such as Afghanistan or Iraq, where performance to US standards has yet to be demonstrated but needs remain critical, the cessation of economic assistance would arguably put at risk US national security interests. While some US aid is given to support long-term economic development and its merits should be judged accordingly, much of US aid is given to support other US policy goals.

Second, debate exists as to which "strings," or conditions, ought to be attached to economic assistance to maximize its positive effect on the donor state. To receive assistance, states might be required to exercise fiscal discipline, accept certain public expenditure priorities, engage in tax reform, embrace market-based interest rates and exchange rates, undertake trade liberalization, permit foreign direct investment, privatize state enterprises, deregulate, or enforce intellectual property rights. Such conditions, and others, have been incorporated into guidelines for assistance to be granted under the IMF and World Bank.

The United States remains the world's largest bilateral donor, disbursing almost $21 billion in economic assistance in 2016 to 184 countries, a dollar total that is 40 percent more than the total of military assistance (described below) that it disbursed to 158 countries in the same year.[66] On the one hand, this significant amount of money facilitates a multitude of meritorious foreign initiatives. On the other hand, this use of taxpayer funds to pursue foreign initiatives is performed at the opportunity cost of foregoing other perhaps equally or even more meritorious domestic initiatives (such as to bail out failing US cities or repair aging infrastructure). While there is debate surrounding the value of foreign aid in achieving US global policy goals, the resources expended on foreign aid remain relatively small in comparison to overall macroeconomic activity and government expenditure: total economic *and* military assistance represents only 0.27 percent of US GDP, about 1.5 percent of total US government expenditures, and 7 percent of the amount spent on national defense.[67]

Foreign Military Sales and Assistance. The world's military arms trade is big business, and the United States is by far the world's largest supplier. By way of illustration, the value of all global arms sales in 2015 totaled $79.9 billion; arms sales by the United States accounted for $40.2 billion or over half of every dollar spent in this market.[68] France ranked a distant second with $15.3 billion and Russia was third with $11.1 billion.[69]

Under the Arms Export Control Act of 1976, the United States operates with two distinct systems for the export of weapons: defense commercial sales (DCS) and foreign military sales (FMS). In DCS, US suppliers of articles, services, and technology obtain a commercial arms export license from the Department of State to permit the export of military goods to a specific country. In FMS, the sale of military equipment from the US government to a foreign government is approved by the Department of State and is executed by DoD's Defense Security Cooperation Agency. In the example of arms sales in 2015, cited above, of the $40.2 billion in US arms sales, approximately $23.2 billion were DCS and $17.0 billion were FMS.[70]

The geographic distribution of FMS reflects both geopolitical developments and US national security interests. Qatar is the largest purchaser in the US FMS program, paying $8.8 billion in FY 2014. Behind Qatar, the next five largest buyers are Saudi Arabia at $3.8 billion, Iraq at $3.2 billion, Kuwait at $2.0 billion, and Japan and South Korea at $1.9 billion each. Next in line are India and Israel at $1.0 billion each, with the United Kingdom ($934 million) and Australia ($801 million) rounding out the top ten countries.[71] In the years 2008–2011, through just the FMS program, United States firms delivered a total of 944 surface-to-air missiles, 348 tanks and self-propelled guns, 234 armored personnel carriers, 53 supersonic combat aircraft, 57 helicopters, and 5 major naval surface combatants to countries around the world.[72] In just one recent quarter, the FMS program was coordinating sales of Sidewinder missiles to Korea, a C-130 fleet upgrade to Pakistan, equipment in support of F-16 aircraft to the United Arab Emirates, Apache Longbow Helicopters and Hellfire missiles to Iraq, and V-22B Block C aircraft to Israel.[73]

In addition to authorizing allies to make FMS purchases, the United States also extends assistance, in selected circumstances, to finance those purchases. For example, during the war in Afghanistan, the United States extended over $10 billion annually in military assistance in support of Afghan defense and security forces through specific legislation and appropriations. To support its allies in scenarios where US forces are not directly involved, the United States may offer military assistance to foreign countries through non-repayable grants or direct loans under the Foreign Military Financing program, which, like FMS, is administered by DoD. Under this program, Israel, Jordan, Pakistan, and Somalia received a combined total of nearly $4 billion in military assistance in 2014.[74] Foreign military assistance, whether in the form of military sales or financing, is an instrument of economic power that allows the United States to pursue its security objectives by enabling its allies to gain military strength.

Security Implications of Economic Vulnerabilities

While the US economy is the source of many advantages, there are several distinct areas in which economic realities constitute potential sources of concern. This section focuses in detail on two of these areas: the national debt and foreign direct investment.

National Debt. In 2018, the US national debt stood at $21.5 trillion, surpassing the country's GDP of $20.0 trillion.[75] From 2008 to 2018, the national debt more than doubled, increasing by $11.5 trillion, accelerated by spending on stimulus packages designed to lift the economy out of the 2008–2009 recession, increasing entitlement spending, and the financing of military operations in Iraq and Afghanistan. Forecasts for the coming decade project that the debt will continue to grow, both numerically and as a proportion of GDP. The Congressional Budget Office (CBO) estimates that, under current law, the total debt will grow by another $10.1 trillion between 2018 and 2027.[76] As of 2018, approximately 41 percent of US government debt was held by the federal government and the Federal Reserve Bank. Foreign countries held another 31 percent, led by China and Japan with $1.2 trillion and $1.1 trillion, respectively. The remaining portion, approximately 28 percent or $5.8 trillion, was held by banks, pension funds, and private investors.[77]

Former Chairman of the Joint Chiefs of Staff Admiral Mike Mullen, among others, has stated that "the single biggest threat to national security is our debt."[78] The national debt could threaten American national security in two possible ways. First, foreign owners of large amounts of US debt might be able to influence American foreign policy or manipulate the US economy as part of an "economic attack" on the state. Second, the amount of money spent on interest or on paying down the principal of the national debt could divert resources, resulting in reductions in military capabilities or decreased US flexibility to respond to unexpected events such as recessions or wars.

Foreign ownership of US debt raises fears that a country like China could eventually have the power to influence American policy. These same fears existed in the 1980s with the rise of Japan as an economic power.[79] One oft-repeated concern is that if China were to sell off US debt rapidly, this could devalue the dollar and throw the US economy into a recession. If this were possible, China would have leverage over the United States and could use this power to influence US policy.

However, these fears are generally unfounded. Macroeconomic theory, observed evidence, and a close examination of Chinese motives indicate that China does not purchase US Treasury securities to gain political or economic leverage. Rather, these purchases are a byproduct of China's export-driven growth strategy, which results in it maintaining a persistent trade surplus with the United States. Withholding dollars from the currency exchange market allows China to keep the renminbi weak against the dollar and keep Chinese exports competitively priced for US consumers. Since China exports more value than it imports, the result is an accumulation of dollar cash reserves in the Bank of China. To earn interest on these dollars, China chooses to purchase US debt because it is a safe investment with a comparatively attractive yield.

If China did wish to harm the US economy, it might attempt to liquidate significant amounts of US debt rapidly in an attempt to devalue the dollar and drive up interest rates. Many analysts agree, however, that it is unlikely that such a move would have any significant long-term effects on the US economy.[80] Any effects would be limited and short term, and could be addressed through monetary policy by the US Federal Reserve. While the possibility remains that Chinese actions could devalue the dollar in the short term, this would also have serious consequences for the Chinese economy.[81] A weak dollar and weak US economy would decrease demand for Chinese exports and reduce the value of China's remaining security holdings. The economic interdependence of the US and Chinese economies thus ensures that any coercive economic policy attempted by one against the other would be a double-edged sword. At least one study of Chinese attempts to influence US policy reveals that China could gain little leverage from its creditor status with the United States.[82]

While foreign ownership of national debt poses little risk, the debt and its rapid growth do have potentially severe national security implications (see also chapter 9). As the debt increases, government payments of interest on this debt also increase. This amount becomes a nonnegotiable requirement for government expenditure, because a failure to pay would result in default and catastrophic economic consequences. In 2018, payments of interest on the national debt represented just over 7 percent of all federal spending.[83] As the size of the debt increases or as interest rates rise, this percentage will also increase, leaving less money available for other government spending, including national defense. Forced reductions in defense spending could have grave national security implications in the long run. Furthermore, as the debt increases, the government's ability to finance a future war becomes more complicated. It is more difficult, both economically and politically, to finance a war through additional taxes than through borrowing. If the ability to raise money is limited by the impact of accumulated debt, the resulting reduction in the ability to finance military action could also adversely affect the ability to issue a credible threat of force. Ultimately, this sequence of events could weaken the US position in negotiations and the credibility of its threats to use military force.

Foreign Direct Investment. America's public policy towards inbound foreign direct investment (FDI) has historically been highly permissive, as is consistent with a free and open society. US policy has been predicated on the belief that unimpeded inward-bound flows of investment help enhance the level and technological quality of the state's capital stock with many benefits for GDP growth, employment, productivity, innovation, and overall US economic competitiveness. Under this laissez-faire approach, the United States has come to enjoy the world's largest annual inflows of FDI, valued at over $225 billion in 2011 alone. The aggregate value of FDI within US borders is estimated to be approximately $3.5 trillion.[84]

However, the United States has two prominent exceptions to its open FDI policy; both arose following 9/11 to address potential economic vulnerabilities for national security reasons. First, US laws restrict foreign ownership or control of American enterprises that operate in "critical industries," defined as representing "systems and assets, whether physical or virtual, so vital to the United States that the incapacity or destruction of such systems and assets would have a debilitating impact on security, national economic security, national public health or safety, or any combination of those matters."[85] Critical industries include telecommunications, transport, energy (including nuclear), water, banking, emergency services, government contracting, and cyber and physical infrastructure.

Second, the president is empowered with broad discretionary authority to suspend or prohibit foreign acquisitions of, or mergers with, existing domestic commercial interests, if deemed a threat to US national security. The Committee on Foreign Investment in the United States (CFIUS), an interagency body led by the Treasury Department, actively reviews the national security implications of business transactions that could result in significant influence or control of US business enterprises by foreign persons or entities, including potential US adversaries or enemies.

A high-profile test of the CFIUS's review procedures came in 2006, when Dubai Ports World, one of the world's largest commercial port operators owned by the government of Dubai, attempted to acquire British-owned P&O Ports, which held the leases to operate six major US seaports including New York harbor. Although President George W. Bush supported the Dubai acquisition as being consistent with a free and competitive economy, congressional leaders eventually prevailed in their objection to the acquisition, based primarily on the grounds that America's ports should remain free of foreign control that might otherwise undermine national security, particularly with regard to nefarious inbound freight shipments.[86]

How best to strike a balance between economic efficiency and national security is continually evolving and remains an unsettled area of national security policy. Members of Congress recently inquired about the rise of FDI originating from the $6 trillion in global assets of state-owned investment funds known as sovereign wealth funds. While the CFIUS selectively restricts inbound FDI, in 2013 the Obama administration launched SelectUSA, an initiative to make attracting foreign direct investment in the United States as important a part of US foreign policy as promoting exports abroad.[87] A balanced pursuit of the country's dual but conflicting goals of promoting economic efficiency while preserving US security interests has grown only more complex over time.

What the Future Holds

Through actions such as its withdrawal from the Trans-Pacific Partnership trade agreement, renegotiation of the North American Free Trade Agreement, and imposition of tariffs, the administration of President Donald Trump has reflected skepticism about the value of free trade to the US economy. While political dynamics could well be decisive, the processes of globalization, to include the continued growth of world trade, a deepening of world capital markets, and the increased global diffusion of technology, are likely to continue. These trends will lead to gradual shifts in patterns of economic activity and the global distribution of power, with many implications for US national security policy. If current growth trends persist, for example, the national security advantage that the United States enjoys due to its relative economic size will decrease as countries with high growth rates, such as China and India, continue to develop.

For all its promise of raising global wealth and efficiency, globalization also brings challenges that stem from uneven gains, both internationally and domestically. In a more globally competitive world, the United States, along with other developed countries, will have to work to extend the benefits of globalization to states, particularly in Africa and the Middle East, that are challenged by economic stagnation and political instability. Constructive integration into the global economy promises mutual gain, as economic growth provides a useful foundation for gains in domestic governance and international peace and security. Countries will also have to manage the tension between macroeconomic policies intended to promote GDP growth and those that aim to reduce the income gap or address other distributional concerns. This effort will be exacerbated by aging populations in most of the industrialized world, which will leave governments facing ever-larger retired populations (and electorates) in need of benefits, alongside smaller pools of workers to generate the required tax revenue. Debates over the fiscal crises that will result from this imbalance have been at the center of US politics since the 2008–2009 recession, as mandatory spending programs increasingly dominate the federal budget and leave little room for expenditures on foreign policy initiatives. Should this debate continue unresolved, slower growth in the developed world will adversely affect the world economy and reduce the ability of these countries to serve as partners to one another in foreign assistance and military alliances.

The United States will continue to use economic power to further its own economic, security, and political interests, while simultaneously seeking to maintain an economic base sufficient to support a strong military. The perennial debate over how to allocate national resources between defense and other vital programs will continue, complicated by the undeniable synergies between economic strength and security policy. Tensions will inevitably arise between the security agenda, where the ideals of self-sufficiency and isolationism beckon, and the economic agenda, dominated by arguments favoring interdependence and more open flows of goods, information, and capital.

Success in meeting these challenges will depend on many factors, only some of which will remain under US control. For both its own sake and the health of the international system, the United States must pursue sound economic policies at home: budget reform and fiscal discipline, a tax code that encourages savings and productive investments, and a legal and regulatory regime that promotes innovation and productivity. Simultaneously, it must devote appropriate attention and resources to the defense base so that military forces can be prepared to intervene in a persistently dangerous world. Even as he emphasized free market economics,

Adam Smith made the essential point succinctly: "Defense is of much more importance than opulence."[88]

Discussion Questions

1. What does the vast economic power of the United States imply for national security policy?
2. What basic conditions determine the long-run economic prosperity of a country? Which matters more in determining prosperity—a country's resources or its policies?
3. How can the United States not only accumulate economic power—the possession of which is a necessary condition for military strength—but also exercise such power effectively and intelligently in an increasingly complex world?
4. How do US sources of economic power shape the availability of its economic instruments of national security?
5. Which image better describes the increasingly globalized economy: a house of cards that can collapse with a single failure or a spider web, which is resilient in the face of shock or shifts? How does a decision maker's image of the economy affect policy?
6. What might be "best practices" for applying US economic power to further US foreign policy aims? How has the array of economic instruments of US national security evolved since 9/11 and the rise of nonstate security threats?
7. Why have efforts at economic coercion not been more successful? Explain the challenges associated with the use of sanctions and financial controls.
8. How effective a tool is foreign aid? Should it be expanded or reduced as a tool of US national security policy?
9. How does US borrowing from abroad affect national security? To what extent does US foreign debt limit US leverage within global capital markets or otherwise constrain US foreign policy?
10. How credible is the potential economic threat posed by China's significant holdings of US government debt?

Recommended Reading

Bhagwati, Jagdish. *In Defense of Globalization*. New York: Oxford University Press, 2007.

Collier, Paul. *The Bottom Billion: Why the Poorest Countries Are Failing and What Can Be Done about It*. New York: Oxford University Press, 2007.

De Soto, Hernando. *The Mystery of Capital: Why Capitalism Triumphs in the West and Fails Everywhere Else*. New York: Basic Books, 2000.

Easterly, William. *The Elusive Quest for Growth: Economists' Adventures and Misadventures in the Tropics*. Cambridge, MA: MIT Press, 2001.

Eichengreen, Barry. *Globalizing Capital: A History of the International Monetary System*. Princeton, NJ: Princeton University Press, 2008.

Friedman, Thomas L. *The World Is Flat: A Brief History of the Twenty-First Century*. New York: Farrar, Strauss and Giroux, 2005.

Kennedy, Paul. *The Rise and Fall of the Great Powers*. New York: Random House, 1987.

Maddison, Angus. *Contours of the World Economy, 1–2030 A.D.* New York: Oxford University Press, 2007.

Stiglitz, Joseph. *The Great Divide: Unequal Societies and What We Can Do about Them*. New York: W. W. Norton, 2015.

US National Intelligence Council. *Global Trend: Paradox of Progress.* Washington, DC: National Intelligence Council, January 2017.

Zarate, Juan. *Treasury's War: The Unleashing of a New Era of Financial Warfare.* New York: PublicAffairs, 2013.

Recommended Internet Resources

Bureau of Economic Analysis, www.bea.gov
Council of Economic Advisors, www.whitehouse.gov/cea
Federal Reserve Economic Data, https://research.stlouisfed.org/fred2/
Foreign Assistance Data, www.foreignassistance.gov
International Monetary Fund, www.imf.org
UN Economic and Social Development, www.un.org/development/desa/en
US Agency for International Development, www.usaid.gov
World Bank, www.worldbank.org
World Trade Organization, www.wto.org

Notes

1. Dwight D. Eisenhower, "Radio Address to the American People on the National Security and Its Costs," May 19, 1953, *The American Presidency Project, Online*, ed. Gerhard Peters and John T. Woolley, http://www.presidency.ucsb.edu/ws/?pid=9854.

2. Council of Economic Advisors, *Economic Report of the President 2018* (Washington, DC: US Government Printing Office, 2018), table B-2 and B-9.

3. See International Monetary Fund, World Economic Outlook, October 2017, http://www.imf.org/external/datamapper/datasets/WEO.

4. Evan Niu, "How Much Cash Does Apple Have?" *Motley Fool*, November 15, 2015, https://www.fool.com/investing/general/2015/11/15/apple-cash.aspx. New Zealand GDP is from International Monetary Fund, World Economic Outlook, October 2017. GDP is a measure of the output produced in a year, not the entire value of all productive assets in the economy.

5. Total military expenditures information taken from the International Institute for Strategic Studies (IISS), "Chapter 10: Country Comparisons and Defence Data," *The Military Balance 2017* (London: International Institute for Strategic Studies, February 2017). For military expenditures as a percentage of GDP by country (calculated on an exchange-rate basis), see World Bank, World Development Indicators, February 2018, http://data.worldbank.org/indicator/MS.MIL.XPND.GD.ZS.

6. "Sanctions: What Could Be the Next Move?" BBC News, March 21, 2014, http://www.bbc.co.uk/news/business-26612848.

7. World Trade Organization (Press Release), "Modest Trade Recovery to Continue in 2015 and 2016 Following Three Years of Weak Expansion, April 14, 2015, https://www.wto.org/english/news_e/pres15_e/pr739_e.htm. World trade is measured in total merchandise exports (current US dollars).

8. Trading in foreign exchange markets averaged $5.1 trillion per day in April 2016. See Bank for International Settlements, *Triennial Central Bank Survey: Foreign Exchange Turnover in April 2016:* (Basel: Bank for International Settlements, September 2016), 3, http://www.bis.org/publ/rpfx16fx.pdf.

9. US Treasury Department, "Major Foreign Holders of Treasury Securities," March 15, 2018, http://ticdata.treasury.gov/Publish/mfh.txt.

10. This chapter focuses primarily on the proximate determinants of economic growth: labor, capital, technology, and other inputs. A large and growing body of literature addresses the deeper determinants of growth, including geography and institutions. The geography thesis is well articulated in Jeffrey D. Sachs, "Institutions Don't Rule: Direct Effects of Geography on Per Capita Income," NBER Working Paper No. 9490 (Cambridge, MA: National Bureau of Economic Research, 2003). The institutions thesis is supported by several authors, among them Hernando de Soto, *The Mystery of Capital: Why Capitalism Triumphs in the West and Fails Everywhere Else* (New York: Basic Books, 2000).

11. Figures for income per capita are from the CIA, *World Factbook*, March 2018, https://www.cia.gov/library/publications/the-world-factbook/, using purchasing power parity conversions and 2017 data.

12. Mohammed Aly Sergie, "NAFTA's Economic Impact," Council on Foreign Relations, February 14, 2014, http://www.cfr.org/trade/naftas-economic-impact/p15790#p2.

13. National Science Foundation, "About the National Science Foundation," March 2018, www.nsf.gov.

14. See Barry Eichengreen, *Globalizing Capital: A History of the International Monetary System*, 2nd ed. (Princeton, NJ: Princeton University Press, 2008).

15. Defense spending has been linked with technological innovations that may enhance long-run growth. See Vernon W. Ruttan, *Is War Necessary for Economic Growth? Military Procurement and Technology Development* (New York: Oxford University Press, 2006).

16. Lee Hudson Teslik, "Iraq, Afghanistan, and the U.S. Economy," Council on Foreign Relations, March 11, 2008, http://www.cfr.org/afghanistan/iraq-afghanistan-us-economy/p15404#p5.

17. Greg Bruno, "Rebuilding Iraq," Council on Foreign Relations, January 17, 2008, http://www.cfr.org/iraq/rebuilding-iraq/p15019#p3.

18. See Paul Collier, *Breaking the Conflict Trap: Civil War and Development Policy* (Washington, DC: The International Bank for Reconstruction and Development/World Bank, 2003); and Paul Collier and Anke Haeffler, "Greed and Grievance in Civil War," *Oxford Economic Papers* 56, no. 4 (2004): 563–95.

19. Andrew Harper, "Iraq's Refugees: Ignored and Unwanted," *International Review of the Red Cross* 90, no. 869 (2008): 170, 173.

20. "Crowding out" of private capital formation is known to become a particular risk during wartime. For example, Jeffrey Williamson suggests that crowding out during the Napoleonic Wars with France created a drag on the British industrial revolution; Jeffrey Williamson "Why Was British Growth So Slow during the Industrial Revolution?" *Journal of Economic History* 44, no. 3 (1984): 687–712. In the United States, spending on the Vietnam War concurrently with President Lyndon Johnson's Great Society programs created strong inflationary pressures and high interest rates.

21. See Paul Kennedy, *The Rise and Fall of the Great Powers* (New York: Random House, 1987).

22. WTO, *International Trade Statistics* (Geneva: World Trade Organization, 2017), http://stat.wto.org/.

23. WTO, *International Trade Statistics.*

24. Data on US trading partners are based on calculations of total combined imports and exports for 2014, as stated in International Monetary Fund, "Direction of Trade Statistics," *eLibrary*, 2016, http://data.imf.org/.

25. Bank for International Settlements, *Triennial Central Bank Survey: Foreign Exchange Turnover in April 2016* (Basel: Bank for International Settlements, December 2016), 3, http://www.bis.org/publ/rpfx16fx.pdf.

26. Bank for International Settlements, *Triennial Central Bank Survey*, 9, table 1.

27. Charles Roxburgh, Susan Lund, and John Piotrowski, "Mapping Global Capital Markets 2011" (San Francisco: McKinsey Global Institute, 2011), 2, http://www.mckinsey.com/insights/global_capital_markets/mapping_global_capital_markets_2011.

28. Roxburgh, Lund, and Piotrowski, "Mapping Global Capital Markets 2011," 34.

29. Roxburgh, Lund, and Piotrowski, "Mapping Global Capital Markets 2011," 8.

30. This estimate is presented in Gary C. Hufbauer, Jeffrey J. Schott, and Kimberly A. Elliot, *Economic Sanctions Reconsidered: History and Current Policy*, 3rd ed. (Washington, DC: Institute for International Economics, 2009). An episode is considered successful if sanctions contribute to even partial achievement of foreign policy goals. However, the criticism is that this criterion is too loose.

31. Robert A. Pape "Why Economic Sanctions Still Do Not Work," *International Security* 23, no. 1 (1998): 66–77, uses a stricter criterion for success in order to isolate the coercive effect of economic sanctions as a stand-alone alternative to military force. Pape asserts that of the forty cases deemed a success, eighteen were actually determined by force, not economic sanctions; eight were failures, in which the target state never conceded to the coercer's demands; six were trade disputes, not instances of economic sanctions; and three were indeterminate. This leaves only five successful coercions under Pape's stricter criteria of success.

32. Daniel Drezner, *The Sanctions Paradox: Economic Statecraft and International Relations* (Cambridge: Cambridge University Press, 1999).

33. Evan Hillebrand and Jeremy Bervoets, "Economic Sanctions and the Sanctions Paradox: A Post-Sample Validation of Daniel Drezner's Conflict Expectations Model," *Munich Personal RePEc Archive*, May 2013, https://mpra.ub.uni-muenchen.de/50954/.

34. Gary C. Hufbauer, Jeffrey J. Schott, and Kimberly A. Elliot, *U.S. Economic Sanctions: Their Impact on Trade, Jobs, and Wages*, Working Paper (Washington, DC: Peterson Institute for International Economics, 1997).

35. Eben Kaplan, "How Libya Got off the List," Council on Foreign Relations, October 16, 2007, http://www.cfr.org/libya/libya-got-off-list/p10855#p4.

36. See CIA *World Factbook*, March 2018, for estimates of inflation.

37. Dean Lacy and Emerson M. S. Niou, "A Theory of Economic Sanctions and Issue Linkage: The Roles of Preferences, Information, and Threats," *Journal of Politics* 66, no. 1 (2004): 25–42.

38. James M. Lindsay, "Trade Sanctions as Policy Instruments," *International Studies Quarterly* 30, no. 2 (1986): 153.

39. Some research suggests that ad hoc coalitions are actually counterproductive because the coercer generally pays significant economic or political costs to build the coalition, which will suffer from problems negotiating the conditions of the sanctions and lack the necessary enforcement mechanisms to ensure success. Such problems are generally mitigated when the coalition is formed through an existing international organization. For more, see Daniel W. Drezner, "Bargaining, Enforcement, and Multilateral Sanctions: When Is Cooperation Counterproductive?" *International Organization* 54, no. 1 (2000): 73–102.

40. Thinly veiled smuggling practices were tolerated. For instance, Yugoslav airliners would fly into Romania with no passengers, fuel up, return to Yugoslavia, offload the fuel, and repeat the trip. Raymond Bonner, "How Sanctions Bit: Serbia's Neighbors," *New York Times*, November 19, 1995.

41. Mohamed Younis, "Iranians Feel Bite of Sanctions, Blame U.S., Not Own Leaders," *Gallup World*, February 7, 2013.

42. Secretary General of the United Nations, *Report of the Secretary-General on the Work of the Organization* (New York: United Nations, 1995).

43. For a list of the Treasury Department's financial sanctions, see Office of Foreign Assets Control, "Sanctions Programs and Information," March 2018, http://www.treasury.gov/resource-center/sanctions/Pages/default.aspx.

44. Office of Foreign Assets Control, "Sanctions Programs and Information."

45. International Monetary Fund, "Islamic Republic of Iran: 2006 Article IV Consultation," *IMF Country Report Number 07/100* (Washington, DC: International Monetary Fund, March 2007), 17.

46. For a Treasury insider's perspective on the evolution and limits of financial controls as an instrument of economic power after 9/11, see Juan Zarate, *Treasury's War: The Unleashing of a New Era of Financial Warfare* (New York: PublicAffairs, 2013).

47. See Michael R. Gordon, "Accord Reached with Iran to Halt Nuclear Program," *New York Times*, November 23, 2013.

48. See Kathleen Hunter and Indira A. R. Lakshmanan, "Iran Sanctions Would Be Expanded under U.S. Senate Bill," *Bloomberg News*, December 19, 2013, http://www.bloomberg.com/news/2013-12-19/senators-introduce-measure-to-add-standby-iran-sanctions.html.

49. President Donald J. Trump, "Imposing Additional Sanctions with Respect to North Korea," Executive Order 13810, September 20, 2017, *Federal Register* (82) no. 184, 44705–44709, https://www.treasury.gov/resource-center/sanctions/Programs/Documents/13810.pdf.

50. See, for example, Joshua Stanton and Sung-Yoon Lee, "Financial Sanctions Could Force Reforms in North Korea," *Washington Post*, February 20, 2014, http://www.washingtonpost.com/opinions/financial-sanctions-could-force-reforms-in-north-korea/2014/02/20/61d1a3a4-99ab-11e3-b931-0204122c514b_story.html.

51. As used in this discussion, economic assistance includes all types of economic foreign aid, which a state provides to other countries. It does not include military aid (which is discussed in a separate section) or aid funded by commercial firms, charities, or other nongovernmental organizations.

52. Jonathan Weisman and David S. Joachim, "Congress Approves Aid of $1 Billion for Ukraine," *New York Times*, March 27, 2014, http://www.nytimes.com/2014/03/28/world/europe/senate-approves-1-billion-in-aid-for-ukraine.html.

53. "Obama's Statement on New Sanctions against Russia," *New York Times*, March 17, 2014, http://www.nytimes.com/2014/03/18/world/europe/obamas-statement-on-new-sanctions-against-russia.html.

54. K. Alan Kronstadt, *Pakistan-U.S. Relations*, IB94014 (Washington, DC: Congressional Research Service, March 6, 2006), 16.

55. Carol Migdalovitz, *Iraq: Turkey, the Deployment of U.S. Forces, and Related Issues*, RL31794 (Washington, DC: Congressional Research Service, 2003).

56. Figures include all aid provided, except that from DoD, and are compiled from USAID, *U.S. Overseas Loans and Grants: Obligations and Loan Authorizations, July 1 1945–September 30, 2016* (also known and hereafter referred to as "the *USAID Greenbook*"), https://explorer.usaid.gov/reports-greenbook.html.

57. Figures compiled from the *USAID Greenbook 2016*. All figures are in 2016 inflation-adjusted dollars.

58. President Barack Obama, *National Security Strategy* (Washington, DC: US GPO, May 2010), 15.

59. President Donald Trump, *National Security Strategy* (Washington, DC: US GPO, December 2017), 34.

60. *USAID Greenbook 2016.* Also note that State and USAID have collaborated on a unified data display known as the "Foreign Assistance Dashboard" to make all US government foreign assistance investments available in an accessible format. The data and figures are available at: http://www.foreignassistance.gov/.

61. International Monetary Fund, *IMF Annual Report 2017* (Washington, DC: International Monetary Fund, 2017), http://www.imf.org/external/pubs/ft/ar/2017/eng/index.htm.

62. Treasury also leads US engagement in regional multilateral development banks (MDBs), which include the Asian Development Bank, the African Development Bank, and the European Bank for Reconstruction and Development.

63. "World Bank Lending to Iran," Subcommittee on Domestic and International Monetary Policy, Committee on Financial Services, US House of Representatives (Washington, DC, October 29, 2003).

64. Milton Friedman, "Foreign Economic Aid," *Yale Review* 47, no. 4 (1958): 501–16.

65. See Jeffrey Sachs et al., "Ending Africa's Poverty Trap," *Brookings Papers on Economic Activity*, no. 1 (2004): 117–240; Joseph Stiglitz, "Overseas Aid Is Money Well Spent," *Financial Times*, April 14, 2002.

66. *USAID Greenbook 2016.*

67. Authors' calculations. The agencies in the US government responsible for fostering economic and political development abroad have also been characterized as "less developed" than those charged with ensuring US military security. See Francis Fukuyama, *America at the Crossroads* (New Haven, CT: Yale University Press, 2006), especially 149–54.

68. See Richard F. Grimmett and Paul K. Kerr, *Conventional Arms Transfers to Developing Nations, 2004–2011*, R42678 (Washington, DC: Congressional Research Service, August 24, 2012), 3.

69. Catherine A. Theohary, *Conventional Arms Transfers to Developing Nations, 2008–2015*, R44716 (Washington, DC: Congressional Research Service, December 2016), 21. For each year 2008–2014, Russia had been second to the US in arms sales; 2015 was the first year in which France over took Russia.

70. Data on FMS and FMF are from Defense Security Cooperation Agency (DSCA), Department of Defense, "Foreign Military Sales, Foreign Military Construction Sales, and Other Security Cooperation Historical Facts as of September 30, 2016," http://www.dsca.mil/sites/default/files/fiscal_year_series_30_september_2016.pdf. The DCS is the difference between the total sales from Shanker, op. cit., and the FMS sales.

71. DSCA, "Foreign Military Sales."

72. Grimmett and Kerr, *Conventional Arms Transfers*, 64.

73. See Defense Security Cooperation Agency, "Major Arms Sales," April 2014, http://www.dsca.mil/major-arms-sales.

74. See DSCA, "Foreign Military Sales."

75. *Economic Report of the President 2018*, table B-17.

76. Congressional Budget Office, *An Update to the Budget and Economic Outlook: 2017 to 2027* (Washington, DC: Congressional Budget Office, June 2017), 13.

77. Department of Treasury, *Treasury Bulletin: Ownership of Federal Securities*, March 2018. Federal government debt includes borrowing against funds required to pay a future obligation (such as Social Security) and debt held by the Federal Reserve as a portion of its overall asset portfolio. See also Department of the Treasury, "Major Foreign Holders of Treasury Securities."

78. Geoff Colvin, "Adm. Mike Mullen: Debt Is Still Biggest Threat to U.S. Security," *Fortune*, May 10, 2012.

79. Eduardo Porter, "O.K., Japan Isn't Taking Over the World. But China . . . ," *New York Times*, July 3, 2005.

80. See Wayne M. Morrison, *China-U.S. Trade Issues*, RL33536 (Washington, DC: Congressional Research Service, March 17, 2015).

81. If China sells Treasury securities, it accumulates dollar cash reserves. If it spends these dollars on US goods, it will drive up the value of its currency and harm its export market, while the US export market will grow. If it sells the currency to a third party, then the new owner of the dollars must either spend them in the United States or buy US treasury securities, thus negating the adverse effects of the sell-off on the US economy. Alternatively, the third party could hold on to the dollar cash reserves until the dollar returns to its long-run value and would earn a profit from changing value of the dollar.

82. Daniel W. Drezner, "Bad Debts: Assessing China's Financial Influence in Great Power Politics," *International Security* 34, no. 2 (2009): 7–45.

83. *Economic Report of the President 2018*, table B-19.

84. James K. Jackson, *Foreign Investment and National Security: Economic Considerations*, RL34561 (Washington, DC: Congressional Research Service, December 11, 2013), 4–5.

85. PL 107-56, Title X, Sec. 1014, October 26, 2001, and 42 U.S.C. Sec. 5195c(e), as summarized by James K. Jackson, *The Exon-Florio National Security Test for Foreign Investment*, RL33312 (Washington, DC: Congressional Research Service, March 29, 2013), 15.

86. Guidance on CFIUS national security considerations was published in December 2008. For background details on CFIUS, see http://www.treasury.gov/resource-center/international/Pages/Committee-on-Foreign-Investment-in-US.aspx.

87. Vinai Thummalapally, "Day One at the SelectUSA 2013 Investment Summit," Department of Commerce International Trade Administration (ITA) blog, October 31, 2013, http://blog.trade.gov/2013/10/31/day-one-at-the-selectusa-2013-investment-summit/.

88. Adam Smith, *An Inquiry into the Nature and Causes of the Wealth of Nations* (New York: Bantam, 2003), chap. 2.

13

Military Power

While the diplomatic, information, and economic instruments of national power are important—particularly the economic one because it supports all the others—the military instrument of power has the greatest potential to be decisive in the execution of American national security policy. Because the use of military force always brings associated and sometimes significant costs, however, the resort to force should always be a weighty decision, subject to very careful consideration by national security policy makers. As many policy makers have learned to their sorrow, it is often much easier to go to war than to disengage from one on satisfactory terms. Further, it is important to recognize that even when military power is employed, the likelihood of an acceptable and enduring outcome will usually be increased through the simultaneous, coordinated application of other US instruments of power.

This is the first of five chapters that explore the military instrument of power in detail. This chapter discusses how strategic logic informs the use of force, assessments of military strength, the functions of force, military alliances, constraints on the military instrument, and traditional US perspectives, as well as recent history that can be expected to influence future American uses of the military instrument of power. Building upon this basis, the next four chapters cover specific military challenges: conventional war; asymmetric conflicts, terrorism, and violent extremist organizations; counterterrorism and counterinsurgency; and nuclear policy.

Strategic Logic: The Use of Force for the Purposes of the State

When considering the use of force, a number of basic propositions from classic works in military theory have lasting value. This section draws in particular on two of those classics, Sun Tzu's *The Art of War* and Carl von Clausewitz's *On War*. Because of the enduring nature of their contributions and the power of their insights, it is useful to quote these authors on key points. Both theorists note that the decision to go to war has significant consequences. From Sun Tzu: "War is a matter of vital importance to the State; the province of life or death; the road to survival or ruin."[1] Similarly, Clausewitz writes that war is "no place for irresponsible enthusiasts" but rather "a serious means to a serious end."[2] These cautionary notes are the best place to start when thinking about using military power.

Clausewitz's famous statement that "war is merely the continuation of policy by other means" has significant implications for those who must make decisions relating to the use of force.[3] It is clear from the context of this observation that Clausewitz is challenging a contemporary view that holds that when war begins, the role of politics and political leaders recedes and perhaps even vanishes until peace is once again achieved. Clausewitz finds this dichotomous view of peace and war to be "thoroughly mistaken."[4] Politics and diplomacy do not cease when states resort to force; instead, political leaders have just added one more instrument of power to the means that they are applying to achieve their purposes.

Clausewitz argues that war is a unique human activity, inevitably shaped by danger, chance, uncertainty, and such human elements as physical courage, moral courage, and endurance.[5] Its unpredictability also stems from interaction with a living adversary. To Clausewitz, war is neither an art nor a science; rather, it is a complex human endeavor that is, like commerce or politics, shaped by the interaction of its participants.[6] Although war takes place in a unique environment, it is also completely subordinate to the political purposes that give it meaning. In Clausewitz's metaphor, war has its own grammar but not its own logic. When those who think about war seek to separate it from political factors, they are "left with something pointless and devoid of sense."[7]

These insights provide a powerful basis for strategic thinking. First, they clarify that the political end being sought—the politically desired outcome to follow any use of force—must govern all planning. As Clausewitz says, "No one starts a war—or rather, no one in his senses ought to do so—without first being clear in his mind what he intends to achieve by that war and how he intends to conduct it."[8] This way of approaching potential uses of force requires careful consideration and specification of the desired end state. Clarity about political purposes will make it more likely that appropriate means (military and other instruments of power) and ways (concepts for the application of those means) will be employed: "The political object is the goal, war is the means of reaching it, and means can never be considered in isolation from their purpose."[9]

In some cases, means and ways will have implications for the ends being sought. Clausewitz argues that, although political purposes must govern, they must not "be a tyrant."[10] The strategic planning process may reveal costs and risks that political leaders find unacceptable, making the pursuit of a particular political goal or a particular course of action infeasible. For example, President John F. Kennedy decided not to seek the destruction of Soviet missiles in Cuba in 1962 after he learned of the scale of required air strikes and of the uncertainty as to their results. In such circumstances, the most rational approach may be to modify the goals themselves. To support strategic decision making, senior military leaders must be able to understand political purposes while bringing to bear their expertise in the grammar of war: "On the one hand, he [the general] is aware of the entire political situation; on the other, he knows exactly how much he can achieve with the means at his disposal."[11] The senior general or admiral in charge of a theater of operations "is simultaneously a statesman."[12]

According to Clausewitz, the nature of war depends on the characteristics of a particular era, characteristics of involved states and peoples, relations among the belligerents, and the scale of the political purposes at stake. Given the importance of strategic interaction, the political purposes of all involved must be considered.[13] One side in a conflict may, for example, have limited interests at stake and therefore may devote only limited means, while its opponent may view the conflict as a struggle for existence: "The first, the supreme, the most far-reaching act of judgment that the statesman and commander have to make is to establish . . . the kind of war on which they are embarking; neither mistaking it for, nor trying to turn it into, something that is alien to its nature. This is the first of all strategic questions and the most comprehensive."[14] Recognizing that the history of warfare includes conflicts of all degrees of intensity, Clausewitz posits that the future of conflict will see similarly diverse wars. They will likely vary along a spectrum, ranging from armed stand-offs to extremely intense struggles for national survival. If a very limited application of force is most in line with a government's limited political purposes in a particular situation, the military commander's "main concern will be to make sure the delicate balance is not suddenly upset in the enemy's favor and the half-hearted war does not become a real war after all."[15]

The emphasis of Clausewitz and Sun Tzu on careful planning and calculation is tempered by their recognition of the uncertainty that pervades war.[16] Sun Tzu emphasizes the fluidity of war and the importance of being able to act with boldness according to the situation. Clausewitz recognizes that political purposes can change during the course of a war due to new diplomatic, political, economic, or military developments. For Clausewitz, this means that close and constant communication between political leaders and generals is required. The influence of policy must be pervasive: "Policy, then, will permeate all military operations, and, in so far as their violent nature will admit, it will have a continuous influence on them."[17]

Due to the uncertainty of war, military planners may seek to apply maximum military means, even if the political purposes are strictly limited, but this would disregard costs. Book II of Sun Tzu's classic focuses on the human and material expense of war; it argues for swift rather than prolonged operations to manage costs.[18] Clausewitz describes a timeless basis for estimating required resources:

> To discover how much of our resources must be mobilized for war, we must first examine our own political aim and that of the enemy. We must gauge the character and ability of its government and people and do the same with regard to our own. Finally, we must evaluate the political sympathies of other states and the effect the war may have on them. To assess these things in all their ramifications and diversity is plainly a colossal task.[19]

Estimating costs, although difficult, is necessary. To apply unlimited means regardless of these calculations "would often result in strength being wasted, which is contrary to other principles of statecraft," and would also be likely to cause domestic political problems, because the means would be disproportionate to the ends being pursued.[20] A population is less likely to support an expensive war for a cause it does not deem worthy of such sacrifice. Public protest as the US war in Vietnam continued in the 1970s, or the perception of "war-weariness" when the United States military withdrew from Iraq in 2011, illustrate this point.

Given that wars have varying degrees of importance and intensity, Clausewitz observes that some wars may appear more political than others. In a relatively unlimited war, such as World War II, where the goal was national survival or the complete overthrow of the enemy, the political end and military objectives aligned relatively naturally, and the requirement for detailed political guidance may be lessened. On the other hand, when political leaders seek to use force to achieve specific and limited purposes, extensive political involvement may be more necessary, as the political impact of each military action must be carefully calibrated. US participation in the Korean War in 1950 or the air war in Libya in 2011 offer examples of this point.

In some cases, it may be difficult to find an appropriate military objective to support a particular political goal, and so a proxy will be sought. In many such cases, the "substitute must be a good deal more important" to cause an opponent to yield.[21] For example, when the United States sought to prevent Serbian President Slobodan Milošević from continuing the ethnic cleansing of Albanians in Kosovo in 1999, it did so by threatening the survival of his regime. In any event, "While policy is apparently effaced in the one kind of war and yet is strongly evident in the other, both kinds are equally political."[22] The meaning of either sort of war lies in the political purposes it serves.

Speaking of the potential consequences of the use of force, Sun Tzu warns: "If not in the interests of the state, do not act. If you cannot succeed, do not use troops. If you are not in danger, do not fight. A sovereign cannot raise an army because he is enraged, nor can a general fight because he is resentful. For while an angered man may again be happy, and a resentful man again be pleased, a state that has perished cannot be restored, nor can the dead be brought back to life."[23] Strategic planners should keep in mind the ends pursued, the significance of strategic interaction, the prevalence of uncertainty, and the costs associated with even limited uses of force.

The military instrument of power is obviously a key tool for US national security policy makers. Simply due to its sheer size and claim on national resources, the military instrument of national power is of great significance. As discussed in chapter 8, the US Department of Defense (DoD) is America's largest corporation, and military spending accounts for more than half of all discretionary spending in the US federal budget (see chapter 9). Prospects for its successful use are undoubtedly enhanced when key decision makers engage in rigorous strategic thinking, carefully reconciling ends, ways, and means, to leverage all instruments of power relevant to a particular situation.

The military theory discussed in this section also has implications for the patterns of US civil-military relations that are discussed in chapter 8. In the twentieth century, the US military went from peacetime noninvolvement in national security policy making to extensive and continuous involvement during the Cold War and beyond. The pattern of civil-military interaction in wartime has also changed over time. In World War II, for example, US military leaders often enjoyed tremendous autonomy. Later, potential difficulties with this degree of autonomy in a more limited conflict were revealed: during the Korean War, President Harry Truman found it necessary to relieve his theater commander, General Douglas MacArthur, for failure to adhere to Truman's policies. At the other end of the spectrum, many in the US military thought that political leaders granted their military commanders too little autonomy during the Vietnam War, as these leaders engaged in detailed management such as selecting specific targets for strategic bombing. More recently, when Secretary of Defense Donald Rumsfeld decided to remove specific units from the roster of forces to be deployed for the Iraq campaign before the Iraq War in 2003, this was widely criticized as inappropriate meddling in the specific expertise of military leaders (see chapter 8). Neither political leaders' noninvolvement nor their micromanagement is desirable. Prospects for strategic success are generally enhanced when the political leaders of a government retain overall direction and remain involved, and when their interactions with their military commanders are characterized by vigorous dialogue and an open, two-way exchange of information regarding relevant diplomatic, political, economic, and military developments.

Assessing Military Power

Chapter 1 argues that power is one of the most important concepts in international politics, yet it is also difficult to define power precisely for a variety of reasons. To enable comparisons of relative power, some scholars, such as international relations theorist Kenneth Waltz, focus on measurable capabilities. Waltz's concept includes seven elements: size of population, territory, resource endowment, economic capability, military strength, political stability, and competence.[24] Of these, military strength may be the most obvious, yet it is also one of the most difficult to estimate accurately.

The basic rationale for military power is its contribution to a state's national security and the attainment of a state's political purposes. Practically every major sovereign state has sought military strength. Indeed, until Japan became an exception by minimizing its military forces after World War II, the significance of a country on the world scene had tended to be correlated directly with its armed might. In the words of one scholar, "No 'great power' in the present or past has failed to maintain a large military establishment, and those states which aspire to great power status allocate a large portion of their resources to developing an impressive military machine."[25]

Despite its intrinsic importance, the link between armed forces and foreign policy objectives is not the only motivation for building military forces. A military establishment has always been one of the trappings of sovereignty, and heads of state may feel compelled to maintain one as a status symbol. For some developing nations, the maintenance of a military establishment to influence external political relations may appear to be an irrational allocation of scarce resources that could otherwise be devoted to internal development.[26] In other less-developed countries, however, the military has been instrumental in preserving internal political order and in fostering economic development.[27]

The Nature of Military Power. It is a fundamental error to characterize military power in the abstract. To observe that the United States is the most militarily powerful state in the world means that, compared to every other country, the United States has the strongest military forces. But that statement is misleading; in certain situations the United States might be powerless to achieve specific objectives despite its significant military capabilities. Barry Posen, for one, has observed that the US military in the early twenty-first century enjoys tremendous military advantages in the "global commons"—in space, in the air above thirty thousand feet, and at sea beyond the littoral regions—but does not enjoy comparable advantages in "contested zones" such as littoral and urban areas.[28] It is dangerous to jump from general characterizations of military capabilities to estimates of the prospects for success in any particular application of military power. As former Council on Foreign Relations President Les Gelb noted, "The United States is probably the most powerful nation in history, yet far more often than not, it can't get its way."[29]

An assessment of the military challenge posed by an adversary requires analyzing both capabilities and intentions, although sometimes politicians and analysts focus solely on one or the other. An adversary's intentions can be especially difficult to ascertain, because they can change rapidly for a number of reasons, and because adversaries often have strong incentives to mislead others about what goals they intend to pursue. Military capability analysis that provides estimates of other states' military forces is more concrete, yet it also involves significant uncertainty. This is so because, as in the case of national power discussed in chapter 1, the factors involved are dynamic—susceptible to constant and sometimes dramatic change—and they are situational, varying not only over time but also with the particularities of situation and geography. All factors considered in capability analysis are not absolute but relative to other states' capacities to employ military means directed to the same or related objectives.

The dynamic, situational, and relative nature of military capability is seen in the Korean War. At the outbreak of that conflict in the summer of 1950, the United

States enjoyed a virtual monopoly of nuclear weapons. Consequently, American military capability seemed almost unlimited. If two atomic bombs dropped on Hiroshima and Nagasaki could end World War II with such finality, why not in Korea?

The reason is that the two cases were drastically different. First, the nature of the threat had changed. By 1945 the United States and its allies had defeated all other enemies except Japan. In 1950, however, the Soviet Union—an ally of North Korea—was becoming an increasingly threatening Cold War adversary. It maintained powerful conventional forces and had its own fledgling atomic force. In fact, the US Joint Chiefs of Staff (JCS) felt that the Korean War might well be a Soviet diversion and that the United States needed to save its small arsenal of nuclear weapons for the possibility of a main Soviet attack in Europe. Second, nuclear weapons were not particularly appropriate for the Korean War, where the targets inside North Korea were essentially bridges and troop concentrations, rather than cities like Nagasaki, where nuclear weapons would be more effective. Leveling Chinese cities after China's "volunteers" intervened massively in Korea would have generated all-out war with the People's Republic of China and perhaps with the Soviet Union as well. Third, America's allies, especially the British, and many Americans themselves strongly opposed the use of nuclear weapons.[30] In 1950, the United States did not have the same freedom to use nuclear weapons that it had in 1945; military capability in this case changed because the overall situation was fundamentally different.

Capabilities assessment is complex, typically requiring multivariate analysis. Consideration must be given to the following factors (illustrated very generally):

- *Force Size and Structure*. How large are one's own, one's allies', and one's adversaries' military establishments in terms of forces-in-being and trained reserves? How many people under arms are at the disposal of the various US services (Army, Navy, Air Force, Marines)? In how many active and reserve units are they deployed, and how are the units structured and equipped? How well do the branches of each military service, and the different land, air, and sea services that make up a country's armed forces, operate together?
- *Weapons Systems*. How many and what types of weapons systems are at the disposal of one's own and the opposing forces? What is the potential of these weapons in terms of range, accuracy, lethality, survivability, and reliability?
- *Mobility*. What are the locations of both sides' units and weapons systems? How quickly and by what means could they be moved to strategically and tactically important locations? How much airlift and sealift are available for overseas operations?
- *Logistics (Supply)*. Given the fact that military units can carry only so much equipment with them and must be resupplied if they are to remain in action for more than a few days, how efficient and vulnerable are systems of resupply?
- *Strategic, Operational, and Tactical Doctrines*. What are the nature and the quality of the doctrines of force deployment and military engagement that fundamentally guide the employment of military units?

- *Training.* What is the level of training of both forces-in-being and reserve units? How proficient are soldiers in employing their weapons under varying conditions? How skilled are forces in combined arms operations?
- *Military Leadership.* How effective are the officers and noncommissioned officers in the chain of command through which orders are issued and carried out?
- *Morale.* Morale is a function of many variables and is absolutely vital to success in combat. Hence, what are the levels of unit morale? Especially important for the armed forces of democratic nations, what would be the level of popular support for the employment of force in various contexts?
- *Industry.* What is the industrial capacity of a given state to produce military equipment of the types and in the amounts likely to be required for sustained long-term combat? How quickly could the country switch from production of civilian goods to war materiel?
- *Technology.* What is the level of technological capability and integration of weapons systems and command, control, communications, computers, and intelligence (C4I) systems? What is the status of new technology development for weapons and C4I in a nation's military research, development, test, and evaluation processes?
- *Intelligence.* How effective are one's own and other nations' technical and human intelligence-gathering means? What is the level of competence and speed in analyzing raw intelligence data to produce and disseminate estimates useful to decision makers?
- *Popular Will.* How prepared would the population be to sustain the domestic deprivations such as conscription or rationing that could result from sustained, large-scale wartime activities? How involved would the population be in the event of a long war?
- *National Leadership.* What are the levels of resolve and skill of a nation's leaders? How effective will the leadership be in maintaining national unity and ensuring coordination between military strategy, operations, and political purposes? How effective is the national leadership at applying national resources toward wartime needs?[31]
- *Alliances and Coalitions.* What is the status of alliances and potential coalitions, which could change opposing force ratios significantly? What is the quality of alliance and coalition commitments under various conditions, in terms of military units, weapons systems, bases, and supplies likely to be made available?

Taken together, weighed and blended, these factors can produce a reasonable assessment of military capability. The assessment process must be continuous, for there is insufficient time available in times of crisis to gather anew all required data. Ideally, such capability analysis results in a series of cost/risk calculations, which, coupled with a political assessment of an adversary's intentions, can form the basis for decisions about the preparation and use of the military instrument. Major policy choices confronting decision makers inevitably involve costs—

material and nonmaterial, domestic and international—arising from the impacts of those choices. Risk, in terms of the probabilities of success or failure, is also inherent in virtually all major policy decisions. Military capability analysis aids the policy maker in judging what costs and risks are likely, relative to the value of the objective sought: the more important the objective, the higher the costs and risks the policy maker is likely to accept.

The Functions of Force. In the international system as it exists today, states retain the ultimate right and capacity to resort to military force. As one scholar notes, "The legitimacy of force as an instrument of foreign policy, although often denounced by philosophers, historians, and reformers, has rarely been questioned by those responsible for foreign policy decisions of their nations."[32] What, then, are the purposes for which military force might be used?

Robert Art sets forth a valuable framework for thinking about these questions using what he labels the four functions of military force. The first of these is the use of military power in a *defensive* role. Defense "is the deployment of military power so as to be able to do two things—to ward off an attack and to minimize damage to oneself if attacked."[33] Art argues that states will choose to develop the capability to defend themselves when possible, because a capacity for self-defense is the most reliable way to ensure one's security. Within the definition of defense, Art includes the passive development of military capability as well as active uses of force, such as preemptive strikes that would weaken or destroy part of an enemy force.

Second, nuclear and conventional military forces can be employed in a *deterrent* role. Art defines deterrence as "the deployment of military power so as to be able to prevent an adversary from doing something that one does not want him to do and that he might otherwise be tempted to do by threatening him with unacceptable punishment if he does it."[34] At base, deterrence is a psychological phenomenon; its objective is to manage the expectations of one's actual or potential opponent. Yet deterrence must also rest on credibility: the undoubted will and ability to perform the threatened act if deterrence fails. The success of a deterrent approach depends on a state's ability to convince its adversary that an attempt to gain an objective would cost more than it is worth, and that the cost to the state of applying the punishment would be less than the cost of conceding the objective.[35]

Deterrence assumes a rational, informed opponent. An irrational (or ill-informed) opponent who will accept destruction or disproportionate loss as a consequence of a selected course of action cannot be deterred. Deterrence must also be considered in relation to the nature of the states, alliances, or groups that are to be deterred and the particular action that is to be deterred. For example, a threat of massive nuclear retaliation would be unlikely to deter a terrorist group from planting bombs on aircraft or in crowded city centers. In addition to lacking credibility because of its disproportionate nature, deterrence is problematic against an adversary who is difficult to communicate with, to identify, and to locate. To be able to deter an adversary by threatening unacceptable punishment, one must be able to hold something at risk that is valued by said adversary.

A third function of military force is *compellence*. Compellence, writes Art, is "the deployment of military power so as to be able either to stop an adversary from doing something that he has already undertaken or to get him to do something that he has not yet undertaken."[36] The means of compellence is the direct application, or the threat of application, of military force. The objective of compellence is to cause an adversary to decide that further pursuit of its course of action would incur increasing costs incommensurate with any possible gain. If the message being sent is not compelling, however, as was the case with the gradual and limited application of US force in Vietnam, or it is not received as intended, then the adversary may not respond in the desired fashion.

A fourth function is *swaggering*, which Art describes as "a residual category" in which "force is not aimed directly at dissuading another state from attacking, at repelling attacks, nor at compelling it to do something specific."[37] This category serves as a reminder that military capabilities may not always be developed or used for purposes rationally connected to a country's national security but instead can, at times, be pursued in the interest of international or domestic prestige of a particular regime or individual leader.

A fifth function, not clearly subsumed in any of the above categories, is *acquisitive*. Historically, military force has been an important tool for states seeking to seize the territory or resources of others for exploitation. Although there are a number of constraints on states seeking to employ force for this purpose, perhaps most profoundly demonstrated by the refusal of the United States and other countries to let Saddam Hussein retain Kuwait after his successful invasion of that country in 1990, there are conditions under which military conquest has indeed redounded to the material benefit of the conquering state.[38] In addition, other goals may be sought. For example, Russia's military seizure of Crimea in the summer of 2014 appears to have resulted in at least domestic political gains for the Russian regime.

Given the security challenges of globalization, transnational threats, and weak or failing states, it is useful to think about a sixth possible function of force: *providing order*. Such a function recognizes that military logistics and quasi-policing capabilities—even those developed primarily for other purposes—may help create a secure environment in an area as a precondition for political stability and economic activity. The United States and other countries are likely to continue to turn to the military instrument of power to enable immediate responses to human rights catastrophes or other humanitarian disasters at home or abroad, such as the situation in Somalia in the early 1990s or the outbreak of the Ebola virus in West Africa in 2014. However, as Art recognized, "Force can easily be used to maim and kill, but only with greater difficulty and with great expenditure of effort, to rule and pacify."[39] The employment of military force to fulfill all of the functions listed above will almost always be made more effective when combined or supported by other instruments of national power. In the case of intervention within the territory of another state, military force alone will almost certainly be inadequate to the creation of a sustainable solution. (See chapter 16 for more on military intervention.)

Louis XIV called military force "the last argument of kings" and so inscribed his cannons. The situations in which military force remains a final arbiter have been somewhat circumscribed in the nuclear era, at least among nuclear powers and their allies. Accordingly, the employment of "gunboat diplomacy"—shows of force as a coercive instrument—has dwindled in frequency. Still, the capabilities of opposing military forces do serve to limit and regulate claims among states with competing interests.[40]

Alliances and Military Power

The numerous American alliances, treaties of guarantee, and military base agreements around the world constitute a complex alliance structure that is, cumulatively, a response to the various perceived threats to US foreign policy objectives that have arisen since World War II. In 1947 the United States signed the Rio Pact, breaking a 150-year tradition of avoiding foreign entanglement. The North Atlantic Treaty Organization (NATO) was created in 1949 as a direct response to the growing Soviet threat in Europe. With the outbreak of the Korean War in 1950, the United States began adding Asian allies. In relatively quick order, several alliances were formed: US-Japan (1951), US-Philippines (1951), Australia–New Zealand–US Security Treaty (ANZUS, 1951), US–South Korea (1953), Southeast Asia Treaty Organization (SEATO, 1954), and US–Republic of China (1954), followed by limited US participation in the Central Treaty Organization (CENTO, 1956). Further bilateral defense treaties were signed with Iran, Pakistan, and Turkey in 1959. In support of these and subsequent commitments, the United States currently facilitates over $40.2 billion in arms sales to allied governments, disburses over $15 billion in military aid to 158 countries around the world, and has hundreds of thousands of military personnel members deployed overseas.[41]

Why Do States Join Alliances? An alliance is a contract that, like other contracts, bestows rights and advantages but also places obligations and restrictions on the contracting parties. Unlike contracts in domestic law, however, there is no higher authority to which states can appeal when there is a breach of contract. The primary consideration of national leaders contemplating an alliance is that the benefits of the prospective alliance outweigh the loss of flexibility incurred by becoming dependent upon acts of omission or commission by other states in the alliance. Hans Morgenthau writes, "A nation will shun alliances if it believes that it is strong enough to hold its own unaided or that the burden of commitment resulting from an alliance is likely to outweigh the advantages to be expected."[42]

In an international system that can be described as "semi-organized anarchy," states seek various forms of cooperative behavior designed to enhance strength and reduce risk. They attempt to produce the type and degree of international order that best ensures their own interests. On issues of international peace and security, where power tends to be the common currency, "The question as to whose values or ends will prevail . . . is determined finally by the relative power positions of the [opposing] parties."[43] Stephen Walt has stressed that alliances most often emerge not just in response to imbalances of power but more specifically in response to the perception of a hostile threat from an aggressive power.[44]

Three motives for alliances spring from a focus on power, and all of them relate to a state's attempts to meet its security needs. First, a state may join or create an alliance to amass the capabilities necessary to achieve a foreign policy goal (wherein the state's own means are insufficient for its ends). Second, a state may enter into an alliance to favorably shape security developments, such as a state joining NATO in an effort to shape the alliance's response to global and regional threats.[45] Third, a state may join an alliance to reduce costs. This may be true if a state is seeking multiple objectives and does not want to commit all or an excessive part of its capabilities to any one specific end. A second variant of this cost-reduction motive relates to defense economy. A good example of this is the establishment of the European Defense Agency as a subordinate organization of the European Union in July 2004. Its specific goals are to enhance Europe's military capabilities and strengthen European defense industries while creating better value for European taxpayers by reducing the redundancy created by separate national defense programs.[46]

In addition to increasing power, as Robert Osgood notes, alliances may serve the functions of preserving the internal security of members, restraining allies, or creating a degree of international order.[47] The first of these functions, the preservation of internal security, may prove increasingly important in the future, as states confront growing threats from international terrorism, drug trafficking, weapons proliferation, and cross-border refugee flows. The second purpose, restraining allies' behavior, is common throughout history and is practiced by both the larger, more powerful actors and the weaker, subordinate actors in an alliance. Finally, alliance structures can create predictable, regulated patterns of interaction that reduce sources of friction and conflict and enhance international order.

Alliances and US National Security Policy. When thinking about the role of alliances in US national security policy, recognizing the costs is as important as considering the benefits. As discussed in the preceding section, alliances entail commitments that reduce flexibility, and alliance structures sometimes restrain as well as support alliance members. Even when restraint is not the goal, the very existence of an alliance—as well as its decisionmaking procedures—can have that effect. For example, the existence of the 1991 Gulf War coalition shaped George H. W. Bush's decision not to topple Hussein's regime after expelling Iraq from Kuwait. Whether this was a wise strategic decision is debatable; that it was shaped by incentives created by the existence of a multinational coalition seems certain. On the other hand, NATO led the 2011 air war against Libya; it is not likely that any one NATO member would have taken unilateral action to support the rebels that toppled Colonel Muammar Qaddafi, but the alliance structure with its ready-made military operational procedures facilitated that intervention.[48]

The power contributions of states within alliances are not simply additive. Even within the well-developed and mature structure of NATO, the pace of US technological advancement enabled by significant investment has created problems of interoperability between US forces and those of its NATO allies (see chapter 23). In addition, although operating in the context of an alliance may offer diplomatic and domestic political benefits, "Alliance operations [also] pose significant problems at the tactical, operational, and even the strategic level, which often make them less integrated, skillful, and responsive compared to unilateral operations."[49]

In the context of a superpower competition with the Soviet Union, it may have been relatively easy for US policy makers to decide that the benefits associated with membership in formal alliances outweighed the costs. However, the end of the Cold War gave rise to a debate over whether temporary ad hoc "coalitions of the willing" or even unilateral approaches might sometimes be superior. Indeed, the George W. Bush administration chose to use these approaches during Operation Enduring Freedom and Operation Iraqi Freedom, and the Obama administration attempted to build a "coalition of the willing" to support Operation Infinite Resolve in Iraq and Syria. Although a unilateral operation may lose many of the benefits of an alliance, such as burden sharing and military interoperability, many of the constraints associated with alliances also can be reduced. Where one comes down on this debate is likely to be shaped by the importance one ascribes to the perceived legitimacy of US action abroad and the extent to which the support of allies in other, similar operations is likely to be needed in the future.

Building Partner Capacity. Constrained defense budgets and the proliferation of diverse threats around the globe have added a new dynamic to American debates about coalitions: the necessity of building partner capacity. Because of limited resources, American defense leaders have increasingly articulated the need for stronger security partnerships and encouraged partner nations to contribute more toward their own defense, the security of their regions, and overall collective security. Local and regional actors almost always understand their culture, politics, and security challenges better than US policy makers do. Consequently, successful efforts could "leverage these countries' unique skills and knowledge" to enhance prospects for national and international stability and security.[50]

Critics of this approach focus on two potential downsides to building partner capacity. First, they point out that building professional military forces that are both effective and responsive to legitimate political authorities is extremely difficult, time-consuming, and costly. For example, despite an American investment of billions of dollars over almost a decade, large formations of the Iraqi Security Forces simply collapsed in the face of attacks by the Islamic State in Iraq and the Levant (ISIL) during 2014. Second, even if American training and equipping efforts can produce competent military forces that are accountable to a legitimate political authority, there is no guarantee that the countries involved will share American interests or that they will pursue goals consistent with US national security policy over the longer term. Ultimately, US decisions about whether or not to invest in a partner state's military capacity should be informed by assessments of whether the state involved has an effective political governing structure and by the prospects for an enduring productive relationship between the target state and the United States.

Constraints on the Military Instrument

The use of military force historically has been a "prerogative power," reserved for state sovereigns to decide. Since the rise of European mass nationalist movements in the Napoleonic era, however, the authority of heads of state has rested increasingly upon the support of the populace from which the personnel and resources of mass warfare are drawn. Prior to the nineteenth century, battlefields were usually relatively restricted, and battles, for the most part, touched only the lives of those directly involved in combat. The virtually total wars of the nineteenth and twentieth centuries—that is, the Napoleonic Wars, the American Civil War, and the two World Wars—changed this situation, bringing the carnage and anguish of war into the lives and homes of entire populations.

The communications and information revolutions have further enhanced the involvement of the general population in warfare, leading to increased public scrutiny of the use of military force. World opinion (or, more accurately, opinion in the leading democratic states) has for some time expressed abhorrence of unrestricted warfare. It should be noted that although the force of international opinion can be a constraint, it can also serve as an impetus for action in cases of egregious human rights abuses or humanitarian disaster.[51] In other cases, an international perception of a war's legitimacy may actually contribute to greater domestic support for intervention.[52]

In addition to popular opinion, international law and institutions can constrain the use of force. The League of Nations and later the United Nations (UN) drew on just war theory and existing laws of war as they attempted to distinguish between legitimate and illegitimate uses of military force. In international law, *aggression* is outlawed, and only the use of military force for defense against aggression is deemed to be *just*. The categories associated with the justice of going to war, or *jus ad bellum*, are just cause, competent authority, right intention, last resort, and reasonable chance of success; the standards within a war, or *jus in bello*, are discrimination between combatants and noncombatants and the proportionality of each military action. These have become important international law criteria in evaluating military action.[53] Although international law and institutions are plagued by uncertain enforcement, they can nevertheless create perceptions of legitimacy and establish procedures that aid states in cooperating to counter threats to international peace and security.

Other constraints on the use of force flow from advances in technology and from changes in the distribution of power within the international system. Nuclear weapons, for example, may have deterrent and prestige value, but many analysts argue that they are and should be unusable for any other purposes, including compellence and support for diplomacy.[54] Further, although the United States may enjoy enhanced freedom of action in a world in which it is the only superpower, this distribution of power constrains others. No other state can make a credible direct military threat against the United States or one of its allies as long as the United States maintains a powerful nuclear arsenal, significant conventional power projection capability, strong alliances, and sufficient national will.

A final international constraint lies in the repercussions of the use of force for a country's other national interests. In day-to-day diplomacy, international consensus against an act of military aggression usually represents more sound than fury. However, the longer-term impact may be quite different. As Klaus Knorr has pointed out:

> If a state flagrantly flouts an internationally sanctioned restraint on military aggression, it may, in the event of success, gain the object of aggression and in addition perhaps inspire increased respect for its military prowess; but it may also tarnish its nonmilitary reputation and provoke attitudes of suspicion and hostility that, over the longer run if not immediately, will become organized politically, and perhaps militarily as well. This amounts to saying that the respect a nation enjoys—respect for acting properly, with sensitivity to internationally widespread moral standards, and with sobriety and restraint in resorting to military power—is a precious asset in foreign affairs. It is an asset that assists in holding and gaining allies, and generally in promoting a favorable reception for its diplomatic initiatives.[55]

One might argue that the widely respected status of Germany and Japan today disproves the thesis of adverse long-term effects of aggression. Yet Germany and Japan are still watched especially carefully by neighboring states, and Japan has rejected all but self-defense forces since World War II. Moreover, neither state now has—nor is likely to acquire in the near future—a military nuclear capability.[56]

In addition to international constraints on the use of force, there are also domestic constraints. Two of the most important of these are domestic public opinion and cost. In the United States, public opinion is often initially supportive of decisive actions by the president in the area of national security—the "rally around the flag" effect.[57] Over time the degree of public support is likely to be influenced by a variety of factors, including perceptions of the stakes involved, costs in terms of lives and resources, prospects for success or failure, and even international approbation or disapproval. What world opinion cannot accomplish by direct impact upon the leadership of a democratic state, it may over time be able to effect indirectly by influencing public attitudes and national legislatures. Foreign opposition and criticism, for instance, had some impact upon American public attitudes during the US involvement in Vietnam from 1965 to 1975 and even more impact during the US war in Iraq after 2003. Domestic public opposition to the Vietnam conflict resulted in a congressional cutoff of military supplies to the South Vietnamese government. Domestic concerns about the length and efficacy of the Iraq War contributed to the 2011 American troop withdrawal from Iraq.

A second important domestic constraint on the use of force is cost, particularly for the more industrialized nations with advanced weapons. Technological sophistication has increased the costs of weapons systems enormously. Costs associated with personnel have also skyrocketed in the industrial democracies, particularly in the United States after the introduction of the all-volunteer force in 1973. In the last two decades, the United States has deployed relatively fewer troops but provided more infrastructure to protect, support, and enhance the capacity of each of those deployed. For example, at the height of the surge in Iraq in 2007, the United States deployed 170,300 troops, approximately one-third as many as the 543,000 deployed to Vietnam in 1968 or the 509,129 deployed to Desert Storm in 1991. The incremental cost in 2007 was about $470,000 per troop deployed, costing the United States over $6.6 billion per month at the height of the surge.[58] These funds went mostly for equipment, transportation, base support infrastructure, security, and training of partner forces. Much of this work was accomplished by contractors; indeed, since 2007 contractors have usually outnumbered the US troops deployed. For example, for every ten uniformed military deployed in the Balkans, Afghanistan, and Iraq, on average there were ten to twelve contractors. The comparable number in Vietnam, World War I, and World War II, was fewer than two.[59] Increased use of contractors has limited the number of troops required, but with a concomitant increase in costs.

All these constraints have the potential to influence US national security policy, but their weight varies over time. For example, President George H. W. Bush seemed highly sensitive to international constraints in advance of the 1991 Desert Storm offensive against the Iraqi invasion of Kuwait; he began building a UN consensus to support the action even before taking the case to Congress. In contrast, President Bill Clinton with regard to Kosovo in 1999 and President George W. Bush with regard to Iraq in 2003 made it clear that their actions would not depend on obtaining advance approval from the United Nations. At times, President Obama seemed sensitive to congressional support. For example, he reversed his decision to launch airstrikes in Syria in 2013 after significant congressional opposition.[60] President Trump demonstrated little concern for international or congressional approval in his April 2017 cruise missile strikes against Syria. Although the constraints listed here may not necessarily determine outcomes, they can be relevant considerations as policy makers decide whether or not and how to use force.

An American Perspective on the Use of Force

Decisions about when and how to use US military force continue to be hotly contested, often around the tenets of what has come to be known as the "Weinberger Doctrine." In 1985, in what was widely seen as a response to the lessons of the Vietnam War, Secretary of Defense Caspar Weinberger presented six major tests to be applied before employing US combat forces:

1. The United States should not commit forces to combat overseas unless the particular engagement or occasion is vital to US national interests or those of US allies.
2. If the United States decides it is necessary to employ combat troops, it should do so wholeheartedly and with the clear intention of winning. If the country is unwilling to commit the forces or resources necessary to achieve its objectives, it should not commit them at all. Of course, if the particular situ-

ation requires only limited force to win its objectives, forces should be sized appropriately.

3. If the United States decides to commit forces to combat overseas, it should have clearly defined political and military objectives, it should know precisely how its forces can accomplish those clearly defined objectives, and it should have and send the forces needed to do just that.
4. The relationship between US objectives and the forces committed—their size, composition and disposition—must be continually reassessed and adjusted if necessary. When conditions and objectives change during the course of a conflict, US combat requirements must also change.
5. Before the United States commits combat forces abroad, there must be some reasonable assurance it will have the support of the American people and their elected representatives in Congress. This support cannot be achieved unless US leaders are candid in making clear the threats the country faces; the support cannot be sustained without continuing and close consultation.
6. The commitment of US forces to combat should be a last resort.[61]

Later, Chairman of the JCS Colin Powell enunciated a more concise but similar standard for the employment of US forces. Powell stressed the importance of clear political objectives and adequately sized and decisive means.[62] Like Weinberger's six tests, the Powell Doctrine aimed at keeping US troops out of wars to which the country was not fully committed.

These propositions share much of the strategic logic set forth by Clausewitz. Like Clausewitz, Weinberger emphasized clear political objectives and the need to reconcile ends, ways, and means carefully and continuously. However, Weinberger exceeded Clausewitz's prescriptions in his effort to restrict the use of force to instances in which vital interests are at stake, force can be committed "wholeheartedly," public support is assured in advance, and force is used as a last resort. Many commented on his doctrine, but Weinberger's most prominent antagonist in this debate was then Secretary of State George Shultz. Stressing that "force and diplomacy must always go together," Shultz rejected Weinberger's vital interest, last resort, and public support criteria, which he called "the Vietnam syndrome in spades . . . and a complete abdication of the duties of leadership."[63]

Despite its critics, the Weinberger Doctrine has long influenced debates over US national security policy and the use of force. It is associated, by many, with the US success in the Persian Gulf War of 1990–1991 (see chapter 20), as well as with what some see as a beneficial reluctance by the US military to engage in limited military operations in the 1990s, including in Somalia, Haiti, Bosnia, and Rwanda (see chapter 8).[64] The Weinberger and Powell Doctrines also appear to have been buttressed by the difficulties faced by the United States in Iraq after the successful 2003 invasion. To some extent, the initial Iraq campaign plan was informed by a concept called "rapid dominance," which was meant to succeed by creating "shock and awe" rather than physically overwhelming the adversary. This concept was initially set out in 1996 in deliberate opposition to what analysts saw as the Weinberger-Powell "decisive force" approach then prevailing in the Pentagon.[65] To the extent that this new approach resulted in an inadequate US resourcing of the requirements of post-invasion Iraq, the example appears to strengthen the "decisive force" approach of Weinberger and Powell.

Still, criticisms of the Weinberger Doctrine by Secretary Shultz and others have merit. As discussed below, political leaders are likely to continue to face an international environment in which they find utility in actual or potential uses of force for less-than-vital interests, when public support is not guaranteed, and before it is a matter of last resort. Seeking limited purposes, political leaders will seek to employ limited ways and means. Many military leaders, on the other hand, can be expected to continue to adhere to Powell's emphasis on decisive force and to want to use overwhelming means when force is applied.[66] This situation is likely to result in persistent tensions in US decision making about the use of force.

American Military Power Today

The United States faces a complex and uncertain international strategic environment. The US position is characterized by important strengths. The United States has at its disposal an unrivaled concentration of political, economic, and military power and is able to pursue its national interests in an environment characterized by relative peace among great powers. Many of the most economically developed major powers in the international system—such as the United Kingdom, Germany, France, and Japan—are also democracies and US allies. The prospect of war among these countries appears inconceivable at this point in history. This prevalence of peace among the most advanced states is still an unusual situation in the history of international politics.[67]

Nevertheless, powerful states have begun to reassert themselves on the world stage, and nonstate actors pose significant security concerns. The 2004 National Military Strategy and the 2006 Quadrennial Defense Review (QDR) created a framework that portrays a range of contemporary threats to US national security. Although the figures were not repeated in subsequent QDR publications, the concepts remain relevant and the terms continue to be used in national security policy analysis.

Threats can be described as traditional, disruptive, irregular, or catastrophic (as depicted in figure 13.1).[68] After observing US conventional war-fighting superiority for more than two decades, other states seem less likely to pose a *traditional threat* that directly challenges American military superiority head-to-head. To increase prospects of success when seeking to oppose the United States, adversaries are instead developing the capability to present *disruptive threats* via information warfare, directed energy weapons, biotechnology, and anti-access, area-denial, or anti-space systems. At the same time, the United States must deal with potential *irregular threats*, not easily addressed with conventional military strength, posed by entities outside the traditional state-based framework, such as terrorist groups, insurgencies, and violent extremist organizations. In Iraq and Afghanistan, US forces worked with host nation forces to confront such irregular threats. In the

FIGURE 13.1 Challenges in the US Security Environment

Traditional Threats	Disruptive Threats
State-based challenges to US power using recognized military capabilities, uniformed militaries, and legacy nuclear forces in well-understood forms of competition and conflict	Breakthrough, asymmetric counters to US strengths; examples include cyberwar and anti-access, area-denial strategies and capabilities
Irregular Threats Unconventional methods; often used to counter a stronger state's traditional advantages; terrorism, violent extremist organizations, insurgency, ethnic conflict, civil war, guerrilla war	**Catastrophic Threats** Weapons of mass destruction (WMD) or "WMD-like" attacks on US interests or the US homeland by state or nonstate actors

extreme, some transnational terrorist groups, such as al Qaeda and ISIL, pursue the advances in communication and transportation that have underpinned globalization, as well as advances in weapons technology, including weapons of mass destruction, and as a result could pose a *catastrophic threat* to US national interests. The ability of North Korea, Iran, or other states to attack the United States with weapons of mass destruction (WMD) is also a catastrophic threat. As stated in the 2017 *National Security Strategy*, the United States will continue to counter catastrophic threats by taking efforts "to detect nuclear, chemical, radiological, and biological agents and keep them from being used. [And] augment measures to secure, eliminate, and prevent the spread of WMD and related materials, their delivery systems, technologies, and knowledge to reduce the chance that they might fall into the hands of hostile actors. [And] direct counterterrorism operations against terrorist WMD specialists, financiers, administrators, and facilitators."[69] These four threats—traditional, disruptive, irregular, and catastrophic—provide a way to think about the challenges that American military forces face today.

Enduring Issues. Three central issues are likely to be of enduring importance in US defense policy. The first of these is adapting to and implementing change. The 2018 *National Defense Strategy* "acknowledges an increasingly complex global security environment, characterized by overt challenges to the free and open international order and the re-emergence of long-term, strategic competition between nations. These changes require a clear-eyed appraisal of the threats we face, acknowledgement of the changing character of warfare, and a transformation of how the Department conducts business."[70] Any organization the size of the Department of Defense with ongoing current national security responsibilities requires a concerted effort to change military structures to best support the evolving strategy.

A look at the historical relationship between strategy and structure in US national security policy, such as that provided in chapter 3, suggests that a mismatch between the two is not uncommon. Overcoming it will require supportive domestic political developments as well as a concerted effort to change large government bureaucracies, including those in DoD. In this case, changing military organizations is particularly challenging because diverse capabilities will be required to confront the full range of traditional, disruptive, irregular, and catastrophic threats.

A second important issue is the specific nature of today's security threats and the cooperative approaches necessary to address them. To take just one example, the irregular threat of terrorism is not solely—or even primarily—a military problem: a successful strategy is likely to require diplomatic, informational, economic, financial, intelligence, and law-enforcement actions. The *National Defense Strategy* captures this succinctly: "Effectively expanding the competitive space requires combined actions with the U.S. interagency to employ all dimensions of national power."[71] As noted in chapter 10, coordination across organizational lines does not come easily to government bureaucracies and can also be difficult internationally among different governments. Making the already complex US interagency process function more effectively is likely to require determined and sustained effort. Similarly concentrated effort is needed to enable US departments and agencies to work more effectively with partners abroad.

A final enduring issue relates to planning and budgeting. The United States will never be perfectly secure; defense planners will always face the challenge of apportioning limited means to manage rather than eliminate risks. The challenge is even greater when all the instruments of national power, discussed in chapter 9, are taken into account. The United States lacks a national security apparatus that can plan, manage, and control all national security-related spending. Even more difficult will be creating and managing the interagency and international partnerships so important to succeeding against many current and emerging national security challenges.

The next four chapters discuss various uses of military power in security policy. Chapter 14 examines the use of conventional forces against the traditional and potentially disruptive threats posed by the military forces of other states. Chapter 15 addresses irregular and potentially catastrophic threats such as asymmetric challenges, terrorism, and violent extremist organizations. Chapter 16 complements chapter 15 by discussing the types of counterterrorism, counterinsurgency, and other military operations that concentrate primarily on irregular or asymmetric threats. Chapter 17 explains nuclear policy, which addresses the catastrophic threat of nuclear weapons, whether they are controlled by a state or a nonstate actor.

Discussion Questions

1. What did Clausewitz mean by "War is merely the continuation of policy by other means"?

2. What would Clausewitz argue is the appropriate relationship between a political leader and a military commander in making decisions about the use of force?

3. How does Clausewitz describe the nature of war? How is this helpful in thinking about the use of force?
4. What are the challenges associated with assessing military capability? What factors should be considered when making an assessment?
5. What are the functions of military force? What is deterrence, and what factors affect its success or failure?
6. Why do states join alliances? In addition to aggregating power, what purposes can alliance membership serve?
7. What are important international and domestic constraints on the use of force in the current era? Under what conditions might these constraints be more or less powerful?
8. Should the United States today work only within formal alliances, or is it better to assemble "coalitions of the willing"?
9. Is the Weinberger Doctrine a useful guide to US thinking about the use of force? What are its strengths and weaknesses?
10. What challenges in the international security environment do US defense policy makers see as requiring the actual or potential application of US force? As US military capabilities must evolve in the next twenty years, in what areas do they need to become more capable?

Recommended Readings

Art, Robert J., and Kenneth N. Waltz. *Military Power and International Politics.* 6th ed. Lanham, MD: Rowman & Littlefield, 2004.

Baylis, John, James J. Wirtz, Eliot A. Cohen, and Colin S. Gray, eds. *Strategy in the Contemporary World: An Introduction to Strategic Studies.* 2nd ed. Oxford: Oxford University Press, 2007.

Biddle, Stephen D. *Military Power: Explaining Victory and Defeat in Modern Battle.* Princeton, NJ: Princeton University Press, 2004.

Brooks, Risa A., and Elizabeth A. Stanley. *Creating Military Power: The Sources of Military Effectiveness.* Stanford, CA: Stanford University Press, 2007.

Clausewitz, Carl von. *On War.* Translated and edited by Michael Howard and Peter Paret. Princeton, NJ: Princeton University Press, 1976.

Paret, Peter, Gordon A. Craig, and Felix Gilbert. *Makers of Modern Strategy from Machiavelli to the Nuclear Age.* Princeton, NJ: Princeton University Press, 1986.

Posen, Barry R. *Restraint: A New Foundation for U.S. Grand Strategy.* Ithaca, NY: Cornell University Press, 2014.

Sun Tzu. *The Art of War.* Translated and edited by Samuel B. Griffith. Oxford: Oxford University Press Paperback, 1971.

Walzer, Michael. *Just and Unjust Wars: A Moral Argument with Historical Illustrations.* 5th ed. New York: Basic Books, 2015.

Weigley, Russell F. *The American Way of War: A History of United States Military Policy and Strategy.* Bloomington: Indiana University Press, 1977.

Recommended Internet Resources

Department of Defense, *Quadrennial Defense Review Report*, March 4, 2014, http://www.defense.gov/Portals/1/features/defenseReviews/QDR/2014_Quadrennial_Defense_Review.pdf

Department of Defense, *Summary of the 2018 National Defense Strategy of the United States of America* (Washington, DC: Department of Defense, January 2018), https://www.defense.gov/Portals/1/Documents/pubs/2018-National-Defense-Strategy-Summary.pdf

Notes

1. Sun Tzu, *The Art of War*, trans. and ed. Samuel B. Griffith (Oxford: Oxford University Press Paperback, 1971), 63. It was originally written in the fifth century B.C.

2. Carl von Clausewitz, *On War*, trans. and ed. Michael Howard and Peter Paret (Princeton, NJ: Princeton University Press, 1976), 86. It was originally published in 1832. For a more thorough discussion of this point, see Suzanne C. Nielsen, *Political Control over the Use of Force* (Carlisle, PA: Strategic Studies Institute, May 2001).

3. Clausewitz, *On War*, 87.

4. Clausewitz, *On War*, 87; see also 605–7.

5. Clausewitz, *On War*, 104.

6. Clausewitz, *On War*, 149.

7. Clausewitz, *On War*, 605.

8. Clausewitz, *On War*, 579.

9. Clausewitz, *On War*, 87.

10. Clausewitz, *On War*, 579.

11. Clausewitz, *On War*, 112.

12. Clausewitz, *On War*, 111.

13. Clausewitz, *On War*, 585.

14. Clausewitz, *On War*, 88–89.

15. Clausewitz, *On War*, 604.

16. See Sun Tzu, *The Art of War*, 71, on the importance of making extensive calculations prior to deciding to go to war.

17. Clausewitz, *On War*, 87.

18. Sun Tzu, *The Art of War*, 72–76.

19. Clausewitz, *On War*, 585–86.

20. Clausewitz, *On War*, 78, 585.

21. Clausewitz, *On War*, 81.

22. Clausewitz, *On War*, 88.

23. Sun Tzu, *The Art of War*, 143.

24. Kenneth N. Waltz, *Theory of International Politics* (New York: McGraw-Hill, 1979), 131.

25. K. J. Holsti, *International Politics: A Framework for Analysis*, 2nd ed. (Englewood Cliffs, NJ: Prentice-Hall, 1972), 77.

26. Martha Finnemore, "Norms, Culture, and World Politics: Insights from Sociology's Institutionalism," *International Organization* 50 (Spring 1996): 325–47.

27. Henry Bienen, *The Military and Modernization* (New York: Aldine Atherton, 1971), 11–14.

28. See Barry R. Posen, "Command of the Commons: The Military Foundation of U.S. Hegemony," *International Security* 28, no. 1 (2003): 5–46.

29. Leslie H. Gelb, *Power Rules: How Common Sense Can Rescue American Foreign Policy* (New York: HarperCollins, 2009), 3.

30. See Bernard Brodie, *Strategy in the Missile Age* (Princeton, NJ: Princeton University Press, 1959), 319–21.

31. See Risa A. Brooks and Elizabeth A. Stanley, *Creating Military Power: The Sources of Military Effectiveness* (Stanford, CA: Stanford University Press, 2007), 17–20.

32. Holsti, *International Politics*, 305.

33. Robert J. Art, "To What Ends Military Power?" *International Security* 4, no. 4 (Spring 1980): 5.

34. Art, "To What Ends Military Power?," 6.

35. Jerome D. Frank, *Sanity and Survival: Psychological Aspects of War and Peace* (New York: Random House, 1967), 139.

36. Art, "To What Ends Military Power?," 7. See also Thomas C. Schelling, *Arms and Influence* (New Haven, CT: Yale University Press, 1966), 69–86.

37. Art, "To What Ends Military Power?," 10.

38. See Peter Liberman, *Does Conquest Pay? The Exploitation of Occupied Industrial Societies* (Princeton, NJ: Princeton University Press, 1996).

39. Art, "To What Ends Military Power?," 25.

40. See J. I. Coffey, *Strategic Power and National Security* (Pittsburgh, PA: University of Pittsburgh Press, 1971), 72–73.

41. Catherine A. Theohary, *Conventional Arms Transfers to Developing Nations, 2008–2015*, R44716 (Washington, DC: Congressional Research Service, December 2016), 21, and USAID, *U.S. Overseas Loans and Grants: Obligations and Loan Authorizations, July 1 1945–September 30, 2016* (also known as "the *USAID Greenbook*"), https://explorer.usaid.gov/reports-greenbook.html.

42. Hans J. Morgenthau, *Politics among Nations: The Struggle for Power and Peace*, 5th ed. (New York: Knopf, 1973), 181.

43. Norman J. Padelford and George A. Lincoln, *The Dynamics of International Politics*, 2nd ed. (New York: Macmillan, 1967), 5.

44. Stephen M. Walt, *The Origins of Alliances* (Ithaca, NY: Cornell University Press, 1987).

45. This discussion of alliance motives is adapted from Raymond F. Hopkins and Richard W. Mansbach, *Structure and Process in International Politics* (New York: Harper & Row, 1973), 306–8.

46. European Defence Agency: *Building Capabilities for a Secure Europe*, March 2018, https://www.eda.europa.eu/docs/documents/EDA_Brochure.

47. Robert Endicott Osgood, *Alliances and American Foreign Policy* (Baltimore, MD: Johns Hopkins University Press, 1968), 21–22.

48. Karl P. Mueller, ed., *Precision and Purpose: Airpower and the Libyan Civil War* (Santa Monica, CA: RAND, 2015).

49. Nora Bensahel, "International Alliances and Military Effectiveness," in *Creating Military Power: The Sources of Military Effectiveness*, ed. Risa A. Brooks and Elizabeth A. Stanley (Stanford, CA: Stanford University Press, 2007), 200.

50. Martin Dempsey, "The Bend of Power," *Foreign Policy* online, July 25, 2014, http://foreignpolicy.com/2014/07/25/the-bend-of-power/.

51. See Stanley Hoffmann, *The Ethics and Politics of Humanitarian Intervention* (Notre Dame, IN: University of Notre Dame Press, 1996).

52. Joseph Grieco, Christopher Gelpi, Jason Reifler, and Peter Feaver, "Let's Get a Second Opinion: International Institutions and American Public Support for War," *International Studies Quarterly* 55, no. 2 (2011): 563–83.

53. See Roger W. Barnett, "Legal Constraints," 117–25, and Michael Walzer, "The Triumph of Just War Theory (and the Dangers of Success)," 24–30, both in *American Defense Policy*, 8th ed., ed. Paul J. Bolt, Damon V. Coletta, and Collins G. Shackleford Jr. (Baltimore, MD: Johns Hopkins University Press, 2005).

54. See David C. Gompert et al., *Nuclear Weapons and World Politics: Alternatives for the Future* (New York: McGraw-Hill, 1977), 83–88.

55. Klaus Knorr, *On the Uses of Military Power in the Nuclear Age* (Princeton, NJ: Princeton University Press, 1966), 67–68.

56. See Stanley Hoffman, *Gulliver's Troubles, or the Setting of American Foreign Policy* (New York: McGraw-Hill, 1968), 418–21; and Hanson W. Baldwin, *Strategy for Tomorrow* (New York: Harper & Row, 1970), 237–46. However, rearmament again became an issue of political debate in Japan in the early twenty-first century (see chapter 18).

57. William M. Darley, "War Policy, Public Support, and the Media," *Parameters* 35, no. 2 (2005): 121–34.

58. Calculations based on Amy Belasco, *The Costs of Iraq, Afghanistan, and Other Global War on Terror Operations Since 9/11*, Report RL33110 (Washington, DC: Congressional Research Service, March 29, 2011).

59. Defense Science Board, *Task Force on Contractor Logistics in Support of Contingency Operations* (Washington, DC: Department of Defense, June 2014), 10.

60. Susan Davis, "Senate Delays Syria Vote as Obama Loses Momentum," *USA Today*, September 10, 2013, http://www.usatoday.com/story/news/politics/2013/09/09/obama-congress-syria-vote-in-doubt/2788597/.

61. Caspar W. Weinberger, "The Uses of Military Power," *Defense '85* (Arlington, VA: American Forces Information Service, January 1985), 2–11.

62. Colin L. Powell, "U.S. Forces: Challenges Ahead," *Foreign Affairs* 71, no. 5 (1992): 32–45.

63. George Shultz, *Turmoil and Triumph* (New York: Charles Scribner's Sons, 1993), 650. A more thorough discussion of this debate can be found in Suzanne C. Nielsen, "Rules of the Game? The Weinberger Doctrine and the American Use of Force," in *The Future of the Army Profession*, project dir. Don M. Snider and Gayle L. Watkins, ed. Lloyd J. Matthews (Boston: McGraw-Hill, 2002), 212–14.

64. Kenneth J. Campbell, "Once Burned, Twice Cautious: Explaining the Weinberger-Powell Doctrine," *Armed Forces & Society* 24, no. 3 (1998): 357–74.

65. Harlan Ullman and James Wade Jr., *Shock and Awe: Achieving Rapid Dominance* (Washington, DC: National Defense University, Institute for National Strategic Studies, 1996), xxviii–xxix.

66. Richard K. Betts, "Are Civil-Military Relations Still a Problem?," in *American Civil-Military Relations: The Soldier and the State in a New Era*, ed. Suzanne C. Nielsen and Don M. Snider (Baltimore, MD: Johns Hopkins University Press, 2009), 14.

67. Robert Jervis, *American Foreign Policy in a New Era* (New York: Routledge, 2005), 12.

68. Figure 13.1 and the ensuing discussion are based on *The National Military Strategy of the United States of America* (Washington, DC: Joint Chiefs of Staff, 2004); *Quadrennial Defense Review Report* (Washington, DC: Department of Defense, 6 February 2006).

69. The White House, *National Security Strategy of the United States of America* (Washington, DC: The White House, December 2017), 8.

70. Department of Defense, *Summary of the 2018 National Defense Strategy of the United States of America* (Washington, DC: Department of Defense, January 2018), 2 (hereafter *National Defense Strategy*).

71. *National Defense Strategy*, 5.

14

Conventional War

The American experience during the past quarter century could cause one to question the continued relevance of conventional military capabilities. As the Cold War ended and the "unipolar moment" of outsized US power began, it was reasonable to ask what kind of conventional, state-on-state conflicts Americans might find themselves fighting.[1] Following the terrorist attacks of September 11, 2001, and given apparent US superiority over other countries' conventional forces, including the Iraqi Army in 1991 and 2003, some questioned whether the United States would ever again fight a conventional military opponent, arguing that the military should instead shift significant resources toward confronting unconventional and asymmetric threats.[2] Further impetus for this shift was the idea that American forces might be best prepared for the scenario that was least likely: a conventional military confrontation against the traditional threat of an opposing military force.

Nevertheless, recent Chinese military actions in the South China Sea, Russian military action in Georgia and Ukraine, and continuing tensions on the Korean peninsula highlight the importance of conventional war planning and its enduring relevance to American national security policy. According to the 2018 *National Defense Strategy*, "the central challenge to U.S. prosperity and security is the *re-emergence of long-term, strategic competition* by what the National Security Strategy classifies as revisionist powers. It is increasingly clear that China and Russia want to shape a world consistent with their authoritarian model—gaining veto authority over other countries' economic, diplomatic, and security decisions."[3] States will continue to be the primary actors in the international arena and any that might ignore the potential of military conflict, including conventional war, will do so at their own peril.[4] While a conventional war may be less likely, it is among the most dangerous threats that the United States faces. An American military unable to win a force-on-force engagement with another country's armed forces could find itself unable to defend important US national interests.

Conventional war includes traditional threats and disruptive threats (shown in the upper two boxes of the chart on challenges to US national security in figure 13.1 in chapter 13). *Traditional threats* are the force-on-force military operations that occur in a conventional war. Adversaries seek to defeat one another's military forces to accomplish their political aims. After discussing traditional threats and distinguishing between general war and limited war, this chapter goes on to discuss the *domains of warfare*, including the land, air, sea, space, and cyber domains. To understand the nature of *disruptive threats*—technological or operational advances that enable a potential adversary to challenge US interests in the future—this chapter highlights the importance of technology as an element of national security strategy and explores the role of innovation. The chapter concludes by discussing the potential for conventional war in various regions of the world and the issues that will continue to confront US policy makers regarding conventional war.

Traditional Threats

Military planning and resource allocation around the world remain heavily focused on the development of armed forces to combat other military forces. How a nation confronts traditional threats of opposing military forces varies based the state's degree of commitment to the military operation and the political objectives involved.

General War. General conventional war means that the resources of a state are mobilized on a massive scale to fight for "total victory" over a clear and defined enemy, whether it be a single state or a coalition. The two world wars in the last century are commonly regarded as general conventional wars: the resources of opposing coalitions of belligerent states were mobilized on a massive scale in a war fought for "victory," defined as requiring a relatively unconditional surrender by the vanquished enemy.[5] In these wars, progress toward victory was measured by the geographical movement of battle lines established by mass military formations and by the destruction or capture of enemy units. Victory was the result of destroying the enemy's economic or military capacity to continue to fight, or its political will to do so. Such victories are affirmed by a formal exchange of signatures on a document of surrender or a treaty that ends the war.

Some theorists believe that the advent of nuclear weapons may preclude any future general conventional war along the lines of World War II.[6] Nevertheless, the Soviet Union (with the Warsaw Pact) and the United States (with the North Atlantic Treaty Organization [NATO]) deployed several hundred thousand troops opposite each other in Europe during the Cold War (1945–1989), in preparation for what both sides expected could have been a general war. In addition, general conventional war is still possible among non-nuclear states fighting for objectives not centrally involving important interests of the nuclear powers; the Iran-Iraq War of 1980–1988 is one example. Theoretically, limited wars could occur even among nuclear states, as long as the states restrict the conflict to the use of conventional forces, with the threat of nuclear retaliation deterring both states from escalating the conflict. The concept of *mutually assured destruction* (MAD), discussed in more detail in chapter 17, implies that no rational head of state would invite nuclear self-destruction by the first use of nuclear weapons against a similarly equipped nuclear weapons state; therefore traditional conventional military strategy and tactics remain applicable and possible even among nuclear opponents. Although the logic of these propositions seems compelling, they have never been tested in the nuclear era. Indeed, there has never been a general conventional conflict between nuclear powers.[7]

Limited War. *Limited conventional war* is one in which at least one side fights with constrained resources, in a constrained geographic area, or for only limited and specific objectives. Limited war "reflects an attempt to *affect* the opponent's will, not *crush* it, to make the conditions to be imposed seem more attractive than continued resistance, to strive for limited specific goals and not for complete annihilation."[8]

Limited war is hardly novel: historically, few wars have resulted in the utter physical or political demise of a contending state. Rome's total destruction of Carthage occupies a special place in history in large part because it was so unusual an event; the term "Carthaginian peace" is sometimes used to describe the consequences of total war. In contrast, throughout much of Western history, the means, scope, objectives, and consequences of war were curtailed by the limits of states' military power and of their ability to project that power beyond their own borders. Together, such constraints tended to restrict the objectives for which states went to war and their expectations about what might be achieved.

While the concept of limited war is familiar to historians and military theorists, it does not fit well with traditional American perspectives toward war. As discussed in chapter 2, Americans historically have approached war in moralistic terms; the United States should fight only "just" wars and should not wage war simply for narrow self-interest. Although the Korean conflict (1950–1953) was fought as a limited war, it did not make limited war doctrines popular.[9] The most common reaction to it among Americans was "never again." Secretary of State John Foster Dulles formulated the doctrine of "massive retaliation" with nuclear weapons with the intent of deterring future limited wars similar to Korea; it was still widely viewed as a viable policy into the late 1950s.[10]

Contemporary limited war doctrine grew out of Western fears of nuclear war sparked by Cold War developments, including: Soviet explosion of an atomic bomb in 1949 and subsequent demonstration of a thermonuclear capability in the 1950s; Russia's launch of Sputnik in 1957, which set off an arms competition in space; domestic fears of bomber and missile "gaps" between the United States and the Soviet Union; and general fears of an unfavorable balance of power, which became known in the nuclear era as the "balance of terror." Limited alternatives to massive retaliation had to be found when nuclear retaliation in response to nonnuclear threats risked the nuclear devastation of one's own country. Massive retaliation seemed particularly inappropriate to containing the perceived threat of communist subversion in so-called wars of national liberation in the developing world during the 1950s and 1960s.

American military involvement in Vietnam was shaped in its early years by various doctrines of counterinsurgency warfare. After the US troop buildup in 1965, these doctrines were supplemented by limited-war and controlled-escalation strategies, which guided the application of conventional military force. Important US objectives—principally, the security of an independent, noncommunist government in South Vietnam—were clear and limited at the outset of the conflict, in contrast to North Vietnam's unlimited war against South Vietnam. They proved, however, difficult to achieve. Few could have estimated the effect of the restraints on American strategy, tactics, and resources. As limits on US means and actions grew—motivated by mounting casualties, escalating monetary costs, concern about direct Chinese involvement, and international and domestic public sentiment against the war—objectives became still more limited, with the United States willing to settle for any kind of government in South Vietnam as long as it was freely elected and secure from North Vietnamese military aggression. By 1975, the United States had become unwilling to dedicate resources even to this limited objective.[11]

The outcome of the American experience with limited war in Vietnam was stated succinctly: "The war is over, the cost enormous, and the side which the United States backed lost."[12] Partly as a consequence, the practice and even the study of limited war as a strategic policy and counterinsurgency as doctrine were eschewed after Vietnam. The strategy, tactics, and determination to apply decisive force that brought a quick, decisive victory to the United States in the first Gulf War of 1990–1991 were, in large part, due to lessons learned from limitations in Vietnam.

After the terrorist attacks on September 11, 2001, the United States initiated limited wars against al Qaeda and its affiliates in Afghanistan and later against Saddam Hussein's regime in Iraq. These wars were limited by their objectives, which initially emphasized "regime change" in Afghanistan and Iraq and targeted strikes wherever al Qaeda leaders could be found. The US military rapidly achieved these limited objectives by toppling the Taliban government in Kabul in 2001 and the Ba'athist government in Baghdad in 2003. Each operation only took a matter of weeks. However, after the end of major combat operations and the defeat of the conventional military forces in each case, the United States had significant difficulty "winning the peace" in support of the governments that replaced those that had been deposed. Each war evolved from a limited war against a conventional military adversary to a protracted counterinsurgency against an irregular threat. The military forces that effectively defeated the traditional conventional threat had difficulty adapting rapidly to conducting counterinsurgency in support of stability operations. (Counterinsurgency warfare and other nonconventional military operations are discussed in chapter 16.)

Domains of Warfare

Recognizing the various domains in which conventional warfare takes place is critical to the analysis of national security policy. Historically, military forces have engaged in war on the ground, in the air, and at sea. More recent domains of potential conflict include space and cyberspace.

Most conventional war in the last century was considered generally symmetrical, with forces in each domain fighting each other. In World War II, for example, most battles were concentrated in a specific domain—on the ground, in the air, or at sea. The outcome of battle was largely a function of combat between similar formations—infantry or armor battalions against each other, or aircraft against aircraft, or navy ships against one another. Support from one domain to the other was relatively limited: for example, air forces might provide reconnaissance and bombing in support of ground operations; ground forces could seize ports in support of naval operations; naval forces could attack enemy air defenses in support of airpower.

During the Cold War, however, the concepts of force-on-force battles changed, especially in US doctrine. As the Soviet Union built up its massive conventional military power and the United States implemented the all-volunteer force in 1973, it became increasingly important for the US military to substitute technological capability, joint force integration, and improved quality of forces for a larger and less well-trained conscription-based military. The Department of Defense (DoD) placed a premium on forces in all domains of war working jointly with each other to provide asymmetric advantages that could capitalize on technological sophistication and integration of networked forces to confront opposing conventional forces. In the 1991 Gulf War, for example, the US military led a coalition that destroyed the Iraqi Army, which was, at the time, battle-hardened from eight years of combat with Iran. The fourth largest army in the world, the Iraqi Army consisted of 900,000 men; 63 combat divisions, 8 of which were elite Republican Guard divisions; 5,747 tanks, 1,072 of which were Soviet T-72s; 3,500 artillery cannons, 330 of them self-propelled; and 1,127 combat aircraft.[13] The US force was less than half the size of the Iraqi Army and required logistics support in the austere Saudi desert six thousand miles away from its home base. A conventional force-on-force comparison using traditional force estimates might have shown that the advantage was with the Iraqis, and certainly would not have predicted a rapid and decisive US victory. However, US forces significantly enhanced their capability through the integrated use of air, naval, intelligence, and other assets to produce a combined effect that was greater than the sum of the individual parts. Six US Navy carrier battle groups and hundreds of aircraft executed thirty-eight days of air strikes prior to the commencement of ground operations. When the ground war began, the US-led coalition's lopsided conventional victory over Iraq's numerically superior force demonstrated the value of integrated joint operations, superior equipment, effective training, quality personnel, and experienced leadership. The synergy possible with joint operations among three domains of warfare—ground, air, and sea—had become an integral component of American conventional war capabilities and provided a significant advantage in combat. In addition, the ability of the US-led coalition to draw on assets in space—especially the Global Positioning System (GPS) as it navigated an expansive and relatively featureless desert—was essential to its overwhelming victory.

Space. The importance of GPS and other space-based resources may have been made evident by the 1991 war, but the recognition that space-based assets had important military and nonmilitary purposes dates back to the early Cold War. On October 4, 1957, the Soviet Union launched Sputnik, the first satellite in space, illustrating the potential for intelligence gathering, communications, and other strategically significant uses of space. The ensuing "space race" between the United States and the Soviet Union led to significant technological developments including, most notably, landing men on the moon, as well as the deployment of myriad satellites for both military and commercial use. Throughout much of the Cold War, both superpowers used space for intelligence, surveillance, and reconnaissance (ISR), as well as communications, rather than for weapons. Both states generally permitted unfettered access to space and did not interfere in each other's space programs. The Outer Space Treaty, approved by the United States, the Soviet Union, and the United Kingdom in 1967, and later signed by eighty-eight other nations, bars placement of nuclear weapons or other weapons of mass destruction in space, and it prohibits any military activities on the moon.[14]

After the 1991 Gulf War, both the commercial and military uses of space expanded significantly. The US military and the rest of the world became dependent on space-based communications, so much so that the US DoD now maintains the constellation of GPS satellites, originally deployed for targeting purposes, as a public good that is available to all users free of charge.[15] Even as space has become more crowded with both commercial and military satellites, technology to target objects in space continues to be developed. In an October 1997 test, the Army fired its Mid-Infrared Advanced Chemical Laser (MIRACL) at an orbiting US satellite. While DoD characterized the test as defensive, in that it was intended to test the vulnerabilities of satellites, others, including the Russians, described it as the offensive development of an antisatellite weapon. In 1998, the DoD *Annual Report* declared that "space power has become as important to the nation as land, sea, and air power. . . . DoD is committed to utilizing and, if required, controlling space to assist in the successful execution of the National Security Strategy."[16] Space will remain an area in which relatively unfettered US access is a critical national security requirement into the foreseeable future.

There are two dominant approaches to providing access to space; one emphasizes military control and the second emphasizes cooperative diplomacy.[17] The first approach involves the United States developing a military capability to secure vital interests in space. DoD has given US Strategic Command (STRATCOM) the responsibility to "plan and conduct space force enhancement, space support, defensive space control, space situational awareness, and as directed, offensive cyberspace operations and space force application," which includes providing "unity of command and unity of effort in the unimpeded delivery of joint space capabilities to supported commanders and, when directed, to deny the benefits of space to adversaries."[18] Although all services contribute, the US Air Force, and specifically the Fourteenth Air Force headquartered in California at Vandenberg Air Force Base, provides the joint command of space operations for the United States.

The cooperative diplomacy approach has been conducted in parallel with the military effort and includes arms control and other cooperative measures involving both government and commercial space organizations to facilitate access and minimize the need for the militarization of space. States have generally cooperated with regard to space access and exploration. However, it is technically difficult to develop a space control regime that could verifiably limit antisatellite weapons without encroaching on legitimate uses of space. For example, the US Space Shuttle had the maneuverability to dock with and to snatch or destroy satellites, but it was not generally considered an offensive weapon. Since the United States has the greatest presence in space for both commercial and military uses, any arms control in space would likely place the greatest burden on US space operations.

Other countries have also determined that they need the capability to operate in space as a component of their national strategies. In the past decade, China has developed and tested antisatellite weapons of increasing sophistication. In 2007, China launched an antisatellite weapon, based on the DongFeng-21C road-mobile intermediate range ballistic missile (IRBM); it destroyed the Chinese FY-1C weather satellite at an altitude of 534 miles, creating more than 3,000 pieces of trackable space debris.[19] In 2013, in a second Chinese test, the rocket passed through a much higher orbit, reaching an altitude of 18,600 miles, near the altitude of satellites in geosynchronous earth orbit. This test demonstrated China's capability to reach the orbit that includes "the most valuable real estate in space," where the United States and other nations keep their most important and sensitive satellites.[20] In September 2014, Russia launched a satellite that it later maneuvered to a position directly between two US commercial communications satellites operated by Intelsat, at some points moving to within five to ten kilometers of the satellites.[21]

These incidents prompted US officials to increase their efforts concerning both military and diplomatic approaches to protecting US interests in space. To develop military capability, the Pentagon added $5 billion to the $22 billion already allocated for space programs to protect US assets and control space. General John Hyten, commander of US Air Force Space Command, explained that his personnel need to think of themselves differently: "They are warriors. . . . And they need to recognize that they are war fighters."[22] Assistant Secretary of State for Arms Control Frank Rose said that the United States "is committed to preventing conflict from extending into space, and our diplomatic strategy supports this goal. The possibility of conflict in space is in no one's interest."[23] Managing control of space on behalf of the United States while developing cooperation and arms control to provide free access to space will be an ongoing challenge for national security policy.

Cyberspace. Cyberspace is the most important new domain for both military and non-military activity. The cyber domain comprises the use of computers, information technology, and information networks. It affects communications, critical infrastructure, effective governance, military security, finance, and many other aspects of everyday life in most countries around the world. As with the space domain, the United States disproportionally benefits from cyber activities, and if, somehow, cyberspace could be made secure with unfettered access for all, the United States would benefit tremendously. Secretary of Defense Chuck Hagel said in 2014, "The United States does not seek to militarize cyberspace. Instead, our government is promoting the very qualities of the Internet in integrity, reliability, and openness that have made it a catalyst for freedom and prosperity in the United States and around the world."[24]

It is unlikely, however, that access to cyberspace could ever be fully secure. Threats in cyberspace are ubiquitous and complex. They are propagated by amateur hackers, sophisticated criminals, nefarious businesses, and numerous state actors in concert with their intelligence organizations, military forces, and state-supported proxies. In the United States, individuals, private businesses, information technology providers, and governments at all levels of the US federal system have responsibilities to protect their cyber activities and thereby contribute to overall cyber security.

Although addressing cyber threats is not exclusively or even primarily a military mission, the military has an important role to play.[25] The DoD Cyber Strategy outlines three primary missions for US military involvement in cyberspace: "First, DoD must defend its own networks, systems, and information. . . . [Second], DoD must be prepared to defend the United States and its interests against cyberattacks of significant consequence. Third, if directed by the President or the Secretary of Defense, DoD must be able to provide integrated cyber capabilities to support military operations and contingency plans."[26] These three missions provide a useful structure for thinking about American national security policy and conflict in the cyber domain.

Defense of DoD Information Networks. In 1969, DoD's Advanced Research Projects Agency developed ARPAnet, which was the precursor to the Internet, to transfer information efficiently among multiple computers at different locations. Today, the Department of Defense Information Network (DoDIN) is a vital resource for DoD. In 2011, DoD declared cyberspace to be an operational domain for the purpose of organizing, training, and equipping military forces.[27]

US military capabilities depend on assured access to secure cyber resources, but providing this vital access is particularly difficult because the DoDIN is one of the most frequently targeted networks in the world. A watershed moment occurred in 2008 when the DoD "suffered a significant compromise of its classified military computer networks. It began when an infected flash drive was inserted into a US military laptop."[28] That flash drive contained malicious computer code developed by a foreign intelligence agency; the code spread to both unclassified and classified systems and provided a "digital beachhead" that could deliver data to servers under foreign control. This penetration, and the steps required to counter it worldwide, showcased why coordinated cyber operations had become necessary.

To coordinate all of the missions identified in the DoD Cyber Strategy, DoD established the US Cyber Command (USCYBERCOM) in 2009. Its commander is also "dual-hatted" as the director of the National Security Agency, the US government's lead intelligence agency for signals intelligence, information assurance, and support for computer network operations (see chapter 7). The Defense Information Systems Agency (DISA) operates the DoDIN. The DISA commander is also the commander of the Joint Force Headquarters–Department of Defense Information Networks (JFHQ-DoDIN), which reports to USCYBERCOM and conducts many of the operational-level missions required to defend DoD networks.[29] Together, these military organizations provide strategic direction, policy, planning, technical capability, and operational teams to defend US military networks worldwide. The lessons learned from defending military networks can assist government and critical infrastructure to defend against attacks in the civilian domain as well.

Defense against Significant Cyberattacks. Defense against cyberattacks is primarily the responsibility of individuals, businesses, and civilian government agencies; the military engages only in limited circumstances of specific national importance or in those in which military capabilities can significantly contribute. The use of US military capability to defend against attacks aimed at government or other civilian targets presents challenging political and policy choices.

An analogy may be helpful in illustrating this particular policy challenge. To prevent bank robberies that steal physical wealth, bank employees must securely lock the vault, a bank must hire appropriate private security guards and install burglar alarms, and the local and state police must work with private firms to protect the area; when a bank is robbed, local police and the Federal Bureau of Investigation (FBI) respond. Although stationing an army squad to guard the bank or using assault helicopters to pursue bank robbers could be helpful, those are not missions deemed appropriate for the military. Similarly, to prevent cyberattacks that could steal or destroy wealth in cyberspace, bank employees must secure their computers; the bank must purchase and implement appropriate information security systems; and local, state, and federal officials must work with private firms to protect cyberspace; when a bank suffers a cyberattack, police and the FBI investigate. Just as the military does not try to stop bank robbers, it would be neither appropriate nor possible for DoD to defend all government and civilian cyber networks.

Nevertheless, there is a role for DoD to play in this arena. For the US government, the Department of Homeland Security (DHS) is the lead agency responsible for the information security of government information systems; the FBI is the lead agency responsible for investigating cyberattacks. When they are requested to do so, USCYBERCOM and other DoD organizations may support DHS and the FBI to improve the defense of government and private-sector cyber resources.

In some cases, the attacks could be so massive or damaging that it would be appropriate for DoD to respond. For example, in 2014, North Korea hacked Sony

Pictures, purportedly to protest a film called *The Interview*, which depicted a fictional assassination plot against North Korean President Kim Jong-un. The direct cost of that attack was estimated to be $100 million including investigation, computer repair and replacement, lost productivity, and the cost to protect those whose personal data was stolen.[30] It does not include the inestimable cost of the loss of trade secrets and the damage to Sony's reputation from the attack. The size of this attack and the fact that its target was freedom of expression led the president to order DoD's involvement. This might seem surprising; however, consider that if North Korea launched a missile attack that destroyed $100 million in property with the objective of stopping the public showing of a movie, then military involvement would almost certainly have been seen as warranted. As USCYBERCOM Commander Admiral Michael Rogers said, "I never thought . . . [that] I would be dealing with the aftermath of a major penetration and destructive act directed against a motion picture company. But that is exactly what happened in the case of the destructive hack of Sony."[31]

Support to Military Operations. Cyber activities can also be used in military operations in support of national objectives. For example, Stuxnet, a software virus, surreptitiously penetrated the uranium enrichment centrifuges at Iran's Natanz nuclear facility, causing the programmable logic controllers to manipulate the speed of the centrifuges, which caused their failure. Hundreds of centrifuges were destroyed for reasons that were not evident to Iran's engineers; this set back the Iranian nuclear program significantly. Without confirming details of or responsibility for the attack, Michael Hayden explained that "previous cyberattacks had effects limited to other computers. . . . This is the first attack of a major nature in which a cyberattack was used to effect physical destruction. . . . I think destroying a cascade of Iranian centrifuges is an unalloyed good—you can't help but describe it as an attack on critical infrastructure."[32] Although the Stuxnet virus appears to have been narrowly targeted to work only against Iranian nuclear centrifuges, other attacks on critical infrastructure may not be so discriminating and could have unintended or unanticipated effects far beyond the intended target. That is among the reasons that the offensive use of cyber capabilities must be carefully controlled.

In addition to attacking critical infrastructure, military forces could use cyberattacks in conjunction with ground, air, sea, and space operations to achieve effects that degrade, defeat, or destroy a conventional enemy. Each of the US military services—the Army, Navy, Air Force, and Marines—has created its own cyber forces, which operate as service component commands of USCYBERCOM. Those commands include 6,000 people organized into 133 cyber teams, each of which contributes to a specific part of the DoD Cyber Strategy. Of those teams, 50 operate to protect their services, combatant commands, or the DoDIN; 18 teams focus on national cyber protection; and the remaining 65 teams focus on national or combat missions.[33] These teams collectively constitute the Cyber Mission Force, which provides capability in the cyber domain to complement military capabilities in other domains.

The use of cyber capabilities is in its infancy. Governments, industry, and military forces throughout the world are developing roles, missions, legislation, and authorities to engage effectively in the cyber domain. There will likely be more cyberattacks, greater integration of cyber defense, and more uses of offensive cyber operations in the future. Development of an effective policy and national security capabilities in the cyber realm will be a key concern for policy makers in the years ahead.

Disruptive Threats: Rise of a Peer Competitor

A peer competitor is a state that could compete militarily, head-to-head, with the United States. To achieve that status, one of the things another country would have to do would be to achieve major advances in technology, operational art, or some combination of the two with which to counter decades of US investment in high-technology weapons. If these activities did not seek to replicate US capabilities, but rather counter them through asymmetric means, they would constitute disruptive threats.

Although technology and the ability to use military systems effectively are important—and often the former is of little usefulness without the latter—the prospect of "leap-ahead" technologies concerns many defense analysts. As Secretary of Defense Chuck Hagel explained:

> Disruptive technologies and destructive weapons, once solely possessed by only advanced nations, have proliferated widely, and are being sought or acquired by unsophisticated militaries and terrorist groups. Meanwhile, China and Russia have been trying to close the technology gap by pursuing and funding long-term, comprehensive military modernization programs. They are also developing anti-ship, anti-air, counter-space, cyber, electronic warfare, and special operations capabilities that appear designed to counter traditional U.S. military advantages—in particular, our ability to project power to any region across the globe by surging aircraft, ships, troops, and supplies.[34]

Because of the high cost and length of time required to develop and procure a new weapon system, it is difficult, once a state has committed to developing a particular system, to halt that production cycle in favor of a newer, more potent one. While one country is developing a weapon system that was the most technologically advanced at the time the program was initiated, another country could "leap ahead" with even more advanced technology by starting at a later date when the technology is more advanced. As a result, disruptive threats could emerge.

Research and Development. The establishment and maintenance of a strong technology base and leadership in scientific investigation are principal determinants of a state's future technological capability. Military research and development (R&D) capability is an important indicator of the future military power of a state. Modes of conventional war fighting and war prevention have become inextricably linked to the technological and scientific sophistication of weapons systems.

If investment in progress in technological fields is inadequate, the military component of national power will erode as competitors making technological advances are able to pass it by. Such a state might then instead become dependent on importing sophisticated defense systems, which could constrain its policy options. States therefore view the technological potential and capabilities of opponents as major factors in capability assessments.[35]

Rapid advances in technology can significantly affect national security in at least three distinct ways. First, a successful technological breakthrough can have a considerable impact on the quality and capability of conventional forces. For example, GPS, which is now commonly used in daily life for such purposes as automobile navigation, was first used in combat in Operation Desert Storm in 1991. Prior to the relatively specific technological breakthrough of GPS, maneuvering several divisions of thousands of vehicles over a desert with few terrain features would have been extraordinarily difficult. However, deployment and training with GPS just months before the war provided a technology that "revolutionized combat operations on the ground and in the air during Operation Desert Storm and was—as one Allied commander noted—one of two particular pieces of equipment that were potential war winners."[36] If China, Russia, or some other conceivable peer competitor could develop a technological breakthrough of similar significance, it would have the potential to disrupt American military advantages in a major aspect of combat operations.

A second significant aspect of technology's contribution stems from the uncertainty inherent in newness and change. A sizable R&D program, even if it is unsuccessful in achieving major breakthroughs, creates the possibility of associated successes or surprise advances. This introduces a degree of uncertainty into a potential adversary's calculations, intensifying its sense of risk over particular policy alternatives. Another concern generated by unknowable risks is that an adversary's technological breakthrough could render much of a nation's standing military force obsolete. Even if such a breakthrough did not immediately result in military defeat, the cost of adapting or rebuilding a force could be prohibitive. A breakthrough could affect the quality of a state's existing military and, consequently, its calculations of relative power. Quickly changing calculations of relative power and balance of power could lead to conventional conflict. In the absence of other options, the losing state in the R&D competition might feel compelled to initiate conflict with the winner preemptively to avoid certain future defeat because of its new technological inferiority.

The implications of a true breakthrough pose a dilemma. Given the often lengthy lead time from concept to application and the high rate of technological change in the world, planners of the first state to discover a concept will be reluctant to concede the initiative to the second discoverer, yet the first state might err by locking itself into the development, procurement, and deployment of the earliest operational prototype, a first-generation system. An opponent, in response, could concentrate instead on the development of more advanced second-generation applications and might be able to balance the first state's capability with a more advanced system in almost the same time frame. Historically, this case is illustrated by the "missile gap" of 1958–1962. The Soviet Union, by launching Sputnik, demonstrated its technological capability to build an intercontinental ballistic missile (ICBM). Immediately thereafter, Soviet leaders began implying that the Soviets were deploying first-generation ICBMs (although, in fact, they were not).[37] The United States, uncertain about the truth of Soviet statements, rushed missile programs to completion and deployed first-generation ICBMs to counter the supposed threat. The problem of uncertainty and the fear of technological breakthrough contributed to the US reaction. In retrospect, the outcome of this situation was counterproductive for both sides: the Soviet Union suddenly found itself on the inferior side of the strategic balance, faced with a larger US missile force than previously anticipated. The United States found itself with a costly and obsolete first-generation missile force, which soon had to be phased out and replaced.

Today, to balance the need to adopt advanced technology while attempting to avoid the deleterious impact of locking in first-generation technology, many military acquisition programs use spiral development. *Spiral development* is a form of evolutionary acquisition in which the end-state technology is not specified when a program starts; instead, the military requirements are refined incrementally as the technology is developed based on feedback from users and new technological advances. As the rate of technological change increases in the information age, it is critically important for research, development, and acquisition systems to be able to adapt.[38]

The third way that rapid technological change can affect national security is, ironically, the possibility of overreliance on technological breakthroughs, which may appear to provide a significantly advanced capability but instead may be less effective or otherwise easily countered. For example, in conducting the air war against ground units in Kosovo, many US military leaders believed that the technological advances and increased sophistication of intelligence, aircraft, and precision munitions (described below as the "second offset strategy") would have a significant effect on the Serbian military. After the war, however, detailed bomb damage assessments indicated that the bombings had at best a "modest effect" on targets because the Serbian military countered the advanced technology through relatively inexpensive camouflage and deception.[39]

In the worst case, fascination with technology can distract national security decision makers from the nature and ultimate purpose of warfare. As Fred Kagan observes, "The U.S. strategic community in the 1990s was in general so caught up with the minutiae of technology that it lost sight of the larger purpose of war, and therefore missed the emergence of a challenge even more important than that of technology—the challenge of designing military operations to achieve particular political objectives."[40] Although technological breakthroughs can have a significant, even decisive, effect on military competition, overestimating technology's ability to ameliorate the inherent uncertainty and friction of warfare can risk failures in national security policy.

Defense Innovation and Offset. The United States can prevent a potentially disruptive power from developing technology with a strategic military advantage by developing systems that counter adversaries' potential advantages. The term *offset* is used because the strategy does not attempt to match an adversary: "tank for tank, plane for plane, person for person. [That] is just not economical. And it's not right for democracies to have [the] large standing forces that you might need to deter a potential enemy."[41] Leveraging joint action among the domains of warfare discussed above, the United States uses technology, operational concepts, and organizational constructs to counter or offset potential advantages of other states. Currently, DoD is conducting the "third offset strategy."

To understand the current offset strategy, a brief review of previous DoD innovations is useful. The first offset strategy was employed in the 1950s to counter the Soviet Union's growing conventional military power. Articulated in NSC 162/2, the "New Look" defense strategy emphasized investment in nuclear weapons, as well as sea, land, and air-based delivery systems for conventional deterrence (see chapter 3).[42] The massive capability of nuclear weapons was an effective deterrent, at least until the Soviet Union appeared to reach strategic nuclear parity and the threatened use of nuclear weapons was no longer credible.

The second offset strategy of the 1970s and 1980s featured the development of ISR, precision-strike weapons, stealth technology, enhanced battle management, and increased use of space. These advances proliferated in multiple systems including the F-117A stealth fighter, the B-2 stealth bomber, the Airborne Warning and Control System (AWACS), the Joint Surveillance and Target Attack Radar System (JSTARS), GPS, the Army Tactical Missile System (ATACMS), and numerous other precision-guided munitions. What was even more important than any individual system, however, was the ability to integrate all of these systems through "jam-resistant tactical data-links and 'packet communication' networks pioneered with ARPAnet."[43] This second offset could credibly counter Soviet numerical superiority; Operation Desert Storm in 1991 was a robust validation of its effectiveness.

The United States considered the transformative and decisive results of the second offset strategy in Operation Desert Storm to be a "Revolution in Military Affairs" (RMA).[44] During his time in the George W. Bush administration in 2001, Secretary of Defense Donald Rumsfeld vigorously pursued the RMA, using the term "defense transformation," creating an Office of Force Transformation, and publishing Transformation Planning Guidance to manage the changes.[45] Many believed that increasingly lethal and precise weapons, coupled with information dominance, would facilitate decisive military operations without the need for mobilizing large land forces. Thus, defense transformation focused on increasing reconnaissance and intelligence capabilities, standoff munitions, and computers to integrate all components of an increasingly complex and fast-paced battlefield. The defeat of the Taliban in Afghanistan and the overthrow of Saddam Hussein's regime in Iraq seemed initially to validate this approach. As demonstrated by continued operations in Iraq and Afghanistan, however, such conventional capabilities do not necessarily translate to victory when fighting an adversary that purposely avoids such strengths using asymmetric warfare.

China, Russia, and other countries have also studied the results of the second offset strategy and have developed their own similar capabilities in ISR, stealth, precision-guided weapons, command systems, and other technologies. These technologies combine to provide potential adversaries with anti-access/area denial (A2/AD) capabilities that could challenge US regional access and freedom of action. Anti-access strategies prevent the entry of US forces into a theater of operations, and area denial operations prevent freedom of action in the area under an adversary's direct control.[46] A2/AD strategies constitute a disruptive threat to US national security, because they asymmetrically counter US conventional superiority and preclude the United States from intervening in support of its national objectives.

Beginning in late 2014, the US military undertook the implementation of a third offset strategy to counter A2/AD strategies and prepare for future disruptive threats from great powers. The specific components and outcomes of the third offset strategy will depend on the scope, pace, and nature of technological and organizational developments. Deputy Defense Secretary Robert Work explained in 2015 that the third offset strategy is "focused on the operational level of war, or the campaign. . . . The big idea really is about . . . human-machine collaboration and combat teaming."[47] Like previous innovations, this strategy may take ten to fifteen years to yield results, but new technologies will likely leverage US advantages in unmanned operations, extended-range air operations, undersea warfare, stealth, and complex system integration.[48]

Although the focus of R&D is often on the technology, other important aspects are common to all three offset strategies. First, the organizational and conceptual change may be as important as technological change in creating a new military capability that is effective on the battlefield. GPS was a significant technological breakthrough, but it did not have great military utility until commanders used it to allow units to operate more independently across featureless desert sands. Second, a key consideration of any offset strategy is that it must also be affordable (see chapter 9): if the United States could afford to build a large enough military to overcome any disruptive threats from the Soviet Union previously, or Russia or China today, then the adversaries' capabilities would not need to be "offset." Finally, although technological innovations can change the conduct of war, no matter how significant those innovations are, they cannot change the fundamental political nature of warfare (described in chapter 13), eliminate the uncertainty and friction inherent in warfare, or obviate the need for conventional forces.

Potential for Conventional Conflicts. A short list of potentially hostile regional powers includes North Korea and China in East Asia, Russia in Central Asia and Eastern Europe, and Iran in the Middle East. In other areas of the world, such as South Asia, longstanding rivalries could rupture into open conflict. The 2017 *National Security Strategy* states that "China and Russia aspire to project power worldwide, but they interact most with their neighbors. North Korea and Iran also pose the greatest menace to those closest to them. But, as destructive weapons proliferate and regions become more interconnected, threats become more difficult to contain. And regional balances that shift against the United States could combine to threaten our security."[49] Whether these or other regional powers are or will become hostile to US strategic interests depends largely on two factors: first, the historical relationship that the country has had with the United States; and second, the extent to which specific foreign policy goals of the two sides diverge or conflict. In the short term, the United States can do little regarding history, but it has significant influence over foreign policy goals. Through positive interactions with a potentially hostile regional power, the United States may be able to overcome challenges emerging from problematic historical relationships.

The US approach to Japan and Germany after World War II is an example of the productive integration of potentially disruptive powers. Both countries have sophisticated military forces and R&D capacities, and both are capable of developing technologies that could threaten US interests. This has not happened. Instead, American engagement with these states over more than seventy years has helped to make them US allies. Although they may compete economically and sometimes differ diplomatically, it is inconceivable that these countries and the United States would threaten one another militarily.

At first glance, it might appear that the United States could simply act multilaterally to discourage regional powers from becoming hostile to US interests, and otherwise generally act in a manner to reduce suspicion about American intentions. The strategic challenge for the United States in this approach would be to pursue its fundamental security interests, including its interest in combating terrorism worldwide, without inducing great-power competition or the rise of hostile regional hegemons. However, aggressively combating terror could continue to require the United States to act unilaterally in some cases, with the unintended effect of provoking hostility. Unilateral US action could cause other states to strengthen themselves militarily or to form alliances to be better postured to oppose—or defend themselves against—the United States.

Many countries in the world have interests that could precipitate conventional conflict in which the United States could become involved. Part IV of this volume provides a more detailed analysis of regional issues confronting the United States and potential state-on-state conflicts and crises that might occur. Here, a quick overview of some of the potential contingencies in the international security environment today reveals several possibilities for conventional wars.

The Korean Peninsula will be a major source of friction for the foreseeable future. A great divide exists between North and South Korea, and, political rhetoric and diplomatic overtures notwithstanding, no major actor in the region supports near-term unification of the peninsula. North Korea has tested both nuclear weapons and ballistic missiles, in continued defiance of international sanctions and suasion. Additionally, it maintains a military with more than one million service members, potentially armed with chemical, nuclear, and even biological weapons. These forces, most of which are positioned in relatively close proximity to the demilitarized zone separating the two Koreas, pose a constant danger of surprise attack or unintended military incidents. North Korean forces would eventually lose in a conventional war against the US–South Korean Combined Forces Command, which consists of approximately 20,000 US and 625,000 South Korean uniformed personnel. Nevertheless, North Korea's possession of nuclear weapons has dramatically increased the risks associated with such a conflict. Even absent the use of nuclear weapons, North Korea could wreak destruction in the greater Seoul metropolitan area, where almost a third of South Koreans reside.

China continues to undergo a transition from a centrally planned state-led economy to a more open market economy. The robust economic expansion of the last three decades has slowed, and the future rate of Chinese economic growth and political reforms may not be sufficient to satisfy its population, the largest in the world.[50] Should Chinese leaders attempt to shore up domestic support by resorting to hyper-nationalism through a confrontation with the United States in the South China Sea or by attempting to regain control of Taiwan (as some feared in 1996 when China tested missiles in the Taiwan Straits), the consequences would be severe. Japan and other Asian powers would be gravely concerned by such Chinese bellicosity, and regional economic and political relations would be seriously affected.

Russia continues to have economic, demographic, and political problems within its own borders, but that has not constrained—and perhaps it has encouraged—its increased international military activities. Russia's annexation of Crimea from Ukraine in 2014 and the implicit threat to other countries in Eastern Europe led the United States in 2015 to deploy military forces to reassure NATO members about the US commitment to their defense. Operation Atlantic Resolve included military exercises, a rotational presence across Europe, and increases in the responsiveness of forces, especially in Eastern European NATO countries, through enhancing logistics facilities and prepositioning of equipment.[51] Further actions by Russia that threaten NATO states could precipitate increased deployment of US and other NATO forces.

The Middle East will likely be the most pressing area of regional instability to concern American strategists for years to come. The threat from the Islamic State in Iraq and the Levant (ISIL) and al Qaeda, continued instability in Syria and Libya, and the struggling governments in Iraq and Afghanistan will all require continued US engagement in the region. Threats to Israel, the question of Palestine, the Iranian threat, and instability in other nations could precipitate increased US engagement in Middle East conflicts.

The dispute between India and Pakistan, both nuclear powers, over Kashmir will be a strategic concern for the United States for the foreseeable future. The tense situation in Kashmir has repeatedly led to conventional conflict; the United States does not want to see tensions there result in a full-scale conventional conflict that might escalate into nuclear war. Because both countries are integral players in the US effort to combat terrorism worldwide, it is conceivable—although unlikely—that the United States would directly intervene with conventional forces as part of an international effort to bring any conflict over Kashmir to an early resolution.[52]

Future Challenges in Conventional War

Responding to these and other regional instabilities and conflicts will pose challenges similar to the limited-war concerns that prevailed during the Cold War. At issue will be US interests, objectives, means, and constraints. Each of these four factors will affect the American approach to future conventional wars.

The US *interests* involved will largely determine the extent to which future conflicts will be limited. The more significant the interests, the more general, widespread, and intense the war might be. World War II, in which two great powers threatened the United States in different regions of the world, required an all-out US response, in contrast to the localized challenge later posed by North Korea. The nature of the US interests involved will affect limitations in the actual waging of any war. In the 1991 Gulf War, for example, the George H. W. Bush administration determined that Saudi Arabia's security and the preservation of international access to Middle East oil were vital US interests and worth a major, if still limited, effort.

Defining and pursuing interests became more challenging at the end of the Cold War. The extent to which international politics was a zero-sum game seemed to diminish, as it was no longer the case that every gain for Moscow was perceived as a loss for Washington. In the twenty-first century, it is sometimes difficult to determine which US interests are at risk in the developing world and what level of military action is justified to protect them. The George W. Bush administration decided that the possibility that the Saddam Hussein regime possessed weapons of mass destruction posed an unacceptable risk to the United States and that military conflict was necessary to remove that putative risk. There remains well-known disagreement within the United States and in the international community over this decision.

In terms of *objectives*, architects of US conventional-war strategies face practical difficulties in efforts to distinguish between limited and general war. Regional conflicts may threaten only limited US interests and demand only a limited US military effort, but it might appear much closer to a general war to the target country, which may suffer significant damage. The focus on regional conflicts also leads to confusion, if not outright conflict, between political and military objectives, arising from the tension between the aims of a limited war and the intense fighting that may be required to achieve them. For example, in 2014 President Obama announced that US troops would deploy to Iraq to work with allies with the objective to "degrade and ultimately destroy the terrorist group known as ISIL." In articulating the means, he declared, "These American forces will not have a combat mission—we will not get dragged into another ground war in Iraq."[53] However, after some of those troops were killed in combat, both the public and policy analysts questioned whether the Obama administration had chosen a realistic role for the military, given American objectives.

The *means* used to pursue conventional war have become somewhat different in an era that includes a persistent threat of global terrorism. Policymakers accept that all international conflicts have important social, economic, and political foundations and cannot be treated solely as military phenomena. In the Gulf War (1990–1991), Afghanistan (2001), and Iraq (2003 and 2014), diplomacy was needed to assemble an international coalition, secure the support (or at least the eventual acquiescence) of the United Nations, obtain basing rights, and contribute to myriad other tasks. The withdrawal of US forces, which contributed to ISIL's defeat of the Iraqi Army in Mosul, Fallujah, and Ramadi three years later, may be attributable to the diplomatic failure to achieve a status of forces agreement that would have allowed US forces to remain in Iraq after 2011. Economic actions may be required, such as seizing and otherwise limiting the assets of an enemy, stabilizing the economy during a war, and contributing to economic growth after a conflict has ended. Ubiquitous communications from war zones require robust public information efforts to shape the narrative describing military actions. While fighting conventional wars will still be primarily a military responsibility, contributions from the "whole of government" will be required in any future conflict.

One of the most powerful *constraints* on US action will continue to be public opinion. At the outset of the wars in Afghanistan and Iraq, public reactions to the 9/11 attacks fueled public support for American involvement in these conflicts. Despite the paucity of international support for military action in 2003 (which had been critical in the First Gulf War), the president made the case to the American public that removing Saddam Hussein from power was a vital national objective that justified military intervention. The wars in Afghanistan and Iraq embroiled US forces for much longer than had been expected, leading to public war-weariness. The American public may now be unwilling to support additional prolonged military deployments. For example, public opinion did not favor military action in Syria in 2013, even after the Assad regime had crossed the "red line" of using chemical weapons.[54] Opposition from the public and eventually from Congress led President Obama to decide not to take military action against Syria. He subsequently added troops only cautiously and incrementally to the counter-ISIL mission in Iraq. The costs of war in casualties, time, and spending, as well as the outcome of the current conflicts in Afghanistan and against ISIL, are likely to place significant constraints on decisions by future presidents to engage in conventional wars. Although President Trump continued and expanded US military operations in Iraq and Syria, he did so without seeking explicit support from Congress and without significant public debate (see chapter 5).

Looking Ahead

The United States will encounter formidable challenges in the conduct of conventional conflicts in the coming decades. Although traditional military force-on-force conflicts seem less likely, they are still possible and most US military forces remain oriented toward preparing for conventional conflict. Achieving synergies from combined forces in all domains of war—ground, air, sea, space, and cyber—is increasingly important to conventional war and is a particular strength of US forces. To the extent that there may be a disruptive threat from China, Russia, or another power, the adversary's use of technology to develop A2/AD or other capabilities could cause significant problems for US forces. DoD has therefore engaged in the third offset strategy to encourage innovations that will create additional US military capability. Even in an era of counterterrorism and counterinsurgency operations (discussed in chapter 16), the United States must continue to be ready for conventional war. Policy makers and citizens must understand how best to think about the interests, objectives, means, and constraints involved.

Discussion Questions

1. What is limited conventional war and how does it contrast with general conventional war?
2. To what extent is the concept of general war relevant to the United States as a policy option? Is it more relevant to other states? Why?
3. Were the Arab-Israeli wars of 1967 and 1973 and the Gulf War of 1990–1991 limited wars? Was the Iran-Iraq War limited or general? The 2003 Iraq War? By what standard? From whose perspective?
4. How important is capability in one of the domains of war—land, air, sea, space, or cyber—in comparison to the joint relationship of capabilities across the domains of war?
5. How has the advent of space and cyberspace as domains of war changed the way that nations fight conventional wars?
6. What effect can a nation's R&D programs have on a potential enemy's perception of its military capability? What effect could the third offset strategy have on the US ability to wage conventional war?
7. Do the current rapid advances in technology make it more likely that a peer competitor might present a disruptive threat to the United States? How should the United States respond to such a competitor?
8. If the United States had compelling national interests in a specific region in the world, could a regional conflict there escalate into a general conventional war? From whose perspective?
9. How should US interests affect the objectives and the means that the United States employs in a conventional war?
10. What are the most likely conventional wars that the United States will face in the next ten years? Who would the most likely opponents be? Why?

Recommended Reading

Brown, John S. *Kevlar Legions: The Transformation of the U.S. Army, 1989–2005*. Washington, DC: Center of Military History, 2011.

Dougherty, Kevin. *The United States Military in Limited War: Case Studies in Success and Failure, 1945–1999*. Jefferson, NC: McFarland & Co., 2012.

Fontenot, Gregory, E. J. Degen, and David Tohn. *On Point: The U.S. Army in Operation Iraqi Freedom*. Fort Leavenworth, KS: Combat Studies Institute Press, 2004.

Haass, Richard N. *Intervention: The Use of American Military Force in the Post–Cold War World*. Washington, DC: Carnegie Endowment for International Peace, 1994.

Kagan, Frederick W. *Finding the Target: The Transformation of American Military Policy*. New York: Encounter Books, 2006.

Klotz, Frank G. *Space, Commerce, and National Security*. New York: Council on Foreign Relations, January 1999.

Martinage, Robert. *Toward a New Offset Strategy: Exploiting U.S. Long-Term Advantages to Restore U.S. Global Power Projection Capability.* Washington, DC: Center for Strategic and Budgetary Assessments, 2014.

O'Hanlon, Michael E. *Healing the Wounded Giant: Maintaining Military Preeminence while Cutting the Defense Budget.* Washington, DC: Brookings Institution Press, 2013.

US Department of Defense. *The DoD Cyber Strategy.* Washington, DC: Department of Defense, 2015.

———. *Quadrennial Defense Review 2014.* Washington, DC: Department of Defense, March 4, 2014.

Walt, Stephen. *Taming American Power: The Global Response to U.S. Primacy.* New York: W. W. Norton, 2005.

Internet Resources

Center for Strategic and Budgetary Assessments, http://csbaonline.org/
The Institute for the Study of War, www.understandingwar.org
The Project on Defense Alternatives, "The RMA Debate," www.comw.org/rma

Notes

1. See Charles Krauthammer, "The Unipolar Moment," *Foreign Affairs* 70, no. 1 (1991): 23–33.

2. For an argument that wars in the future will not primarily be competitions between military forces, see Thomas X. Hammes, "War Evolves into the Fourth Generation," *Contemporary Security Policy* 26, no. 2 (2005): 189–221.

3. Secretary of Defense Jim Mattis, *Summary of the 2018 National Defense Strategy of the United States of America* (Washington, DC: Department of Defense, January 2018), 2 (emphasis in the original).

4. See John J. Mearsheimer, *The Tragedy of Great Power Politics* (New York: W. W. Norton, 2003).

5. For the United States, even the world wars were "limited" in the sense that not all of its material resources were mobilized. See Henry A. Kissinger, "The Problems of Limited War," in *The Use of Force*, ed. Robert J. Art and Kenneth N. Waltz (Boston: Little, Brown, 1971), 102.

6. Andre Beaufre, *An Introduction to Strategy, with Particular Reference to Problems of Defense, Politics, Economics, and Diplomacy in the Nuclear Age*, trans by R. H. Barry, with a preface by B. H. Liddell Hart (New York: Praeger, 1965), 85.

7. While there has been no direct general conventional war, there have been at least two historical cases of limited conventional war between two countries possessing nuclear weapons. First, in the Korean War, American and Soviet pilots engaged in air-to-air combat. Second, between May and July of 1999, Pakistan and India fought the Kargil conflict in Kashmir (see chapter 19).

8. Kissinger, "The Problems of Limited War," 104.

9. The fact that the Korean War remained a limited war was due as much to chance as to design—the option of using nuclear weapons was never completely off the table—whereas in subsequent Cold War conflicts, nuclear weapons were never seriously considered.

10. See Samuel P. Huntington, *The Common Defense* (New York: Columbia University Press, 1961), 342–43.

11. Bruce Palmer Jr., *The 25-Year War: America's Military Role in Vietnam* (New York: Simon & Schuster, 1984), 151.

12. W. Scott Thompson and Donaldson D. Frizzell, eds., *The Lessons of Vietnam* (New York: Crane, Russak, 1977), 279.

13. General Norman Schwarzkopf's description of the size of Iraqi forces, as cited in Bob Woodward, *The Commanders* (New York: Simon & Schuster, 1991), 248–49.

14. Bureau of Arms Control, Verification, and Compliance, *Treaty on Principles Governing the Activities of States in the Exploration and Use of Outer Space, including the Moon and Other Celestial Bodies* (Washington, DC: Department of State, January 27, 1967), http://www.state.gov/t/isn/5181.htm.

15. The cost of GPS borne by the defense budget and US taxpayers was $1.1 billion per year in 2018. See "The Global Positioning System," March 2018, www.gps.gov.

16. William S. Cohen, *Annual Report to the President and the Congress* (Washington, DC: Department of Defense, 1998), 67.

17. An excellent study that captures the perspective on space is Frank G. Klotz, *Space, Commerce, and National Security* (New York: Council on Foreign Relations, January 1999).

18. Joint Chiefs of Staff, *Joint Publication 3-14 Space Operations* (Washington, DC: Joint Chiefs of Staff, May 29, 2013). The accomplishment of many of these tasks are delegated to the Joint Functional Component Command for Space.

19. Brian Weeden, "Through a Glass, Darkly: Chinese, American, and Russian Anti-Satellite Testing in Space," March 17, 2014, 9, Secure World Foundation, http://www.thespacereview.com/article/2473/1.

20. The "most valuable real estate in space" quotation is from Air Force General John Hyten, commander of US Air Force Space Command. See Christian Davenport, "Fearing Hostilities in Space, Pentagon Fortifies Satellites," *Washington Post*, May 10, 2016, A1.

21. Mike Gruss, "Russian Satellite Maneuvers, Silence Worry Intelsat," *Spacenews*, October 9, 2015. Since a satellite in geosynchronous orbit moves at about 27,700 km per hour, another object within 5 or 10 kilometers can be dangerously close.

22. Hyten, quoted in Davenport, "Fearing Hostilities in Space."

23. Rose, quoted in Davenport, "Fearing Hostilities in Space."

24. Chuck Hagel, "Retirement Ceremony for General Keith Alexander" (Washington, DC: Department of Defense, March 28, 2014), http://archive.defense.gov/Speeches/Speech.aspx?SpeechID=1837.

25. For a more detailed discussion of the cyber domain, see Suzanne C. Nielsen, "The Role of the U.S. Military in Cyberspace," *Journal of Information Warfare* 15, no. 2 (2016): 27–38.

26. Department of Defense, *The Department of Defense Cyber Strategy* (Washington, DC: Department of Defense, April 2015), 4–5.

27. Department of Defense, *The Department of Defense Cyber Strategy*, 4–5.

28. William J. Lynn, "Defending a New Domain: The Pentagon's Cyberstrategy," *Foreign Affairs* 89, no. 5 (2010): 97–108.

29. Sydney J. Freedberg, "DISA, CYBERCOM Stand Up New Cyber HQ," *Breaking Defense*, January 12, 2015, http://breakingdefense.com/2015/01/disa-cybercom-stand-up-new-cyber-defense-hq/.

30. Lisa Richwine, "The $100 Million Cost of the Sony Cyber Attack," *Fiscal Times*, December 10, 2014, http://www.thefiscaltimes.com/2014/12/10/100-Million-Cost-Sony-Cyber-Attack.

31. "An Interview with Michael S. Rogers," *Joint Force Quarterly* 80 (1st Quarter 2016): 79.

32. Michael Hayden, as quoted in David Sanger, *Confront and Conceal: Obama's Secret Wars and Surprising Use of American Power* (New York: Crown, 2012), 200. Sanger attributes the Stuxnet attack to American and Israeli intelligence, but the source of the cyberattack has never been officially confirmed.

33. The missions of the various Cyber Mission Force Teams are specified in Department of Defense, *Quadrennial Defense Review 2014* (Washington, DC: Department of Defense, March 2014), 41. The total of six thousand personnel is from Cheryl Pellerin, "Rogers: CYBERCOM Defending Networks, Nation," *DoD News*, August 18, 2014, http://www.defense.gov/news/newsarticle.aspx?id=122949.

34. Chuck Hagel, "Defense Innovation Days," opening keynote speech, Southeastern New England Defense Industry Alliance (Washington, DC: Department of Defense, September 3, 2014).

35. For a theoretical treatment of this point, see Klaus Knorr, *Military Power and Potential* (Lexington, MA: Heath, 1970), 73–90.

36. Scott Pace, Gerald P. Frost, Irving Lachow, David R. Frelinger, Donna Fossum, Don Wassem, and Monica M. Pinto, *The Global Positioning System: Assessing National Policies* (Santa Monica, CA: RAND, 1995), 245. The authors identified the other decisive "war-winning" equipment as night-vision devices.

37. For details of this campaign, see Arnold L. Horelick and Myron Rush, *Strategic Power and Soviet Foreign Policy* (Chicago: University of Chicago Press, 1965), 58–70.

38. See Michèle A. Flournoy and Robert P. Lyons III, "Sustaining and Enhancing the U.S. Military's Technological Edge," *Strategic Studies Quarterly* 10, no. 2 (2016): 3–13.

39. See Bruce R. Nardulli et al., *Disjointed War: Military Operations in Kosovo* (Santa Monica, CA: RAND, 1999).

40. Frederick W. Kagan, *Finding the Target: The Transformation of American Military Policy* (New York: Encounter Books, 2006), 253.

41. Robert Work, "Remarks by Deputy Secretary Work on Third Offset Strategy" (Washington, DC: Department of Defense, April 28, 2016).

42. NSC 162/2 was the Eisenhower administration's decision memorandum that articulated the New Look strategy. See Robert Martinage, *Toward a New Offset Strategy: Exploiting U.S. Long-Term Advantages To Restore U.S. Global Power Projection Capability* (Washington, DC: Center for Strategic and Budgetary Assessments, 2014).

43. Martinage, *Toward a New Offset Strategy*, 14.

44. The term "Revolution in Military Affairs" is most commonly attributed to the Soviet Marshal Nikolai V. Ogarkov, who wrote about a "Military Technical Revolution" in the 1970s. See Steven Metz and James Kievit, *Strategy and the Revolution in Military Affairs: From Theory to Policy* (Carlisle Barracks, PA: Strategic Studies Institute, US Army War College, June 27, 1995).

45. Department of Defense, *Transformation Planning Guidance* (Washington, DC: Department of Defense, April 2003).

46. Although the emphasis on A2/AD is new, some defense experts have highlighted the issue for over a decade. See Andrew Krepinevich, Barry Watts, and Robert Work, *Meeting the Anti-Access and Area-Denial Challenge* (Washington, DC: Center for Strategic and Budgetary Assessments, 2003).

47. Robert Work, "Reagan Defense Forum: The Third Offset Strategy" (Washington, DC: Department of Defense, November 7, 2015).

48. Martinage, *Toward a New Offset Strategy*, 39–45.

49. The White House, *National Security Strategy of the United States of America* (Washington, DC: The White House, December 2017), 45.

50. Youwei, "The End of Reform in China: Authoritarian Adaptation Hits a Wall," *Foreign Affairs* 94, no. 3 (2015): 2–7; and Hu Angang, "Embracing China's 'New Normal': Why the Economy Is Still on Track," *Foreign Affairs* 94, no. 3 (2015): 8–12.

51. US European Command, "Operation Atlantic Resolve" (Stuttgart, Germany: USEUCOM, December 31, 2015), http://www.defense.gov/Portals/1/features/2014/0514_atlantic resolve/docs/Operation_Atlantic_Resolve_Fact_Sheet_31_DEC_2015.pdf.

52. C. Raja Mohan, "India and the Balance of Power," *Foreign Affairs* 85, no. 4 (2006): 19.

53. Barack Obama, "Statement by the President on ISIL" (Washington, DC: The White House, September 10, 2014).

54. Charles M. Blow, "War-Weariness," *New York Times*, August 30, 2013.

15

Irregular Threats

Terrorism, Insurgencies, and Violent Extremist Organizations

America's fight against irregular threats resembles Hercules's battle with the Hydra: when the United States acts to defeat one manifestation of the threat, another form emerges. Immediately following the terrorist attacks of September 11, 2001, the United States declared war on terrorism, struggled to improve its understanding of terrorists and asymmetric warfare, invested in a variety of counterterrorism weapons, including drones and Special Operations Forces (SOF), and created new legal authorities to combat the threat.[1] To deny a safe haven to the perpetrators of the September 11 attacks, the United States led an invasion of Afghanistan to overthrow the Taliban government. The sense of threat created by the terror attacks on US soil, and the possible nexus between a rogue regime with weapons of mass destruction and terrorist networks with global reach, also led the United States to invade Iraq.

After the initial success of the invasions of Afghanistan in 2001 and Iraq in 2003, the United States increasingly found itself battling insurgents as well as terrorist networks. Although US goals in Afghanistan and Iraq shifted in the years following the initial interventions, a common challenge was to facilitate the establishment of Afghan and Iraqi institutions that would be able to govern these two countries and avert the development of new threats to international peace and security after the withdrawal of foreign forces. As the United States and its allies and coalition partners sought to establish conditions for stable and, ideally, representative self-governance, the threats posed by insurgents as well as terrorists led the United States to develop capabilities for counterinsurgency (COIN) and stability operations.

Later, as the United States and its partners began to reduce their troop presence in Afghanistan and Iraq, violent extremist organizations (VEOs) emerged that not only threatened portions of Iraq and Syria, but also have expanded attacks against civilian targets in Europe and the United States. The ability of VEOs to inspire homegrown extremists to conduct "lone wolf" attacks makes individual acts of terrorism exceptionally difficult to prevent. To respond to the VEO threat, the United States invested in programs to counter violent extremism, which included strengthening domestic surveillance, using of social media, and enhancing information campaigns.

As the United States continues to face irregular threats that use asymmetric warfare against states and their conventional military forces, it is worth asking whether a more systematic analysis could guide a better American response. This chapter concentrates on explaining irregular threats (shown in the lower left box, figure 13.1 in chapter 13), especially three primary manifestations of the threat: terrorist groups, insurgencies, and violent extremist organizations.

The increasing importance of irregular threats to US national security is the product of several broad trends in the international environment. First, the incidence of failing and failed states around the world has contributed to a lack of governance and the growth of organizations that benefit from instability. Second, the forces of globalization have increased the interconnectedness of states and peoples around the world, but have not necessarily contributed to the emergence of a homogenous global society. Third, the proliferation of global communication and weapons of mass destruction (WMD) technologies can make the threat from hostile groups and individuals too costly to ignore. Fourth, the relative influence of the United States and other great powers has declined since the end of the Cold War. Finally, American strengths in conventional warfare provide incentives for hostile actors to challenge the United States in asymmetric and nontraditional ways.

This chapter outlines irregular threat actors and their activities, such as improvised explosive device (IED) attacks, publicized beheadings, and "lone wolf" attacks on soft civilian targets. It explains how these differ from conventional threats such as battles between organized military forces, major naval engagements, and air-to-air combat, and it points out why this distinction matters. This chapter begins with a definition of irregular threats and their use of technological and organizational asymmetry to achieve their objectives. Then it provides a brief overview of the US understanding of asymmetric warfare and US policy toward irregular threats. The chapter then describes and distinguishes among terrorist groups, insurgencies, and VEOs. (Potential responses to these irregular threats, including the use of counterterrorism and counterinsurgency, are the focus of chapter 16.)

Defining Irregular Threats

The terms used to describe threats have evolved over time. In 2005, for example, the national defense strategy use the term *irregular challenges* to refer to threats created by "those employing 'unconventional' methods to counter the *traditional* advantages of stronger opponents."[2] By 2008, the US defense guidance specified that "we must display a mastery of irregular warfare comparable to that which we possess in conventional combat."[3] The need to "build and sustain tailored capabilities appropriate for counter terrorism and irregular warfare" continued to be an emphasis in the 2012 Defense Strategic Guidance, which made this imperative the first of ten primary military missions.[4] By 2015, the National Military Strategy did not use the term "irregular," but instead described the threat of "transregional networks of sub-state groups" and discussed US "efforts to disrupt, degrade, and defeat VEOs," that is, violent extremist organizations.[5] Similarly, the 2018 *National Defense Strategy* explained that "*non-state actors* also threaten the security environment with increasingly sophisticated capabilities. Terrorists, trans-national criminal organizations, cyber hackers and other malicious non-state actors have transformed global affairs with increased capabilities of mass disruption."[6] Although terminology has evolved, the definitions given in this chapter represent the most common use of the terms in the context of US national security policy.

Irregular threats are individuals or groups that are not an acknowledged part of another state's military or security forces, that tend to pursue some ideological or political objective, and that use asymmetric warfare to achieve their objectives. The first part of the definition refers to the legal and political status of the belligerents. Although some may operate with the support of a state (such as state-sponsored terrorist groups or proxies) and may operate transnationally across borders, the term *irregular threats* refers to nonstate actors. Such a group may seek to hold territory and even to defeat an existing government and thereby gain the status of a state, but to the extent that a group conducts governmental functions in only a limited region, or not at all, it is considered an irregular threat.

The second part of the definition—that irregular threats pursue some ideological or political objective—distinguishes irregular threats from common banditry, crime, hooliganism, smuggling, or piracy. Although some irregular threat groups may work with transnational criminals to instigate state instability or profit from it, such groups are termed an irregular threat only if they pursue some larger ideological or political objective. "When combating an irregular enemy, [a state] cannot help being in competition with that big idea. . . . The irregular foe will be striving with imagination and perhaps some competence to make [the state's] claims for better governance look like lies."[7] Combating irregular threats is different from conducting law enforcement activities against criminal organizations, because it requires not only attacking the group itself but also countering or delegitimizing the political purpose or the ideology that is motivating the group and its followers.

The final part of the definition of irregular threats is the means or mode of conflict. Groups posing irregular threats could be defeated handily if they concentrated their efforts on symmetric attacks against conventional military targets. Instead, they employ asymmetric tactics, such as terrorism, hijacking, insurgency, radicalization, bombings, kidnapping, cyberattacks, and propaganda, against specific weaknesses of their adversaries. The specific form of an irregular threat could vary indefinitely; the definition encompasses any mode of force employment that responds asymmetrically to an adversary's conventional military strengths. Because the use of asymmetric warfare is so important to understanding irregular threats, the next section describes it in detail.

Asymmetric Warfare

The Chinese strategist Sun Tzu observed that "an army may be likened to water, for just as flowing water avoids the heights and hastens to the lowlands, so an army avoids strengths and strikes weaknesses."[8] If a combatant's attempt to strike at an enemy's weaknesses was enough to classify the conflict as asymmetric, however, then the definition would describe almost all conflicts. Few generals would deliberately choose to attack where the enemy has the greatest potential to defeat the attack. The definition of asymmetry is more nuanced than simply the strategy of avoiding strong points and targeting weaknesses.

Asymmetric warfare means that a belligerent is using a technological or organizational capacity that the other side does not have or cannot effectively use to degrade military capabilities or to achieve political objectives directly. Although any military force can and will use technological or organizational asymmetry to gain an advantage in warfare, this chapter describes it in detail because it is a defining characteristic of irregular threats. For example, the Islamic State of Iraq and the Levant (ISIL) has used both technological capacity, such as publicizing such actions as beheadings, death by burning, and bombings on social media and thereby amplifying their impact, and organizational capacity, such as encouraging "lone wolf" actors, using non-uniformed combatants, recruiting foreign fighters, and decentralizing operations, to degrade Syrian and Iraqi military capabilities and to achieve political objectives. In most cases, law, policy, or custom constrains the United States and other states from employing similar technological and organizational capabilities.

It can be useful to distinguish between technological asymmetry and organizational asymmetry, although the boundary between these can blur, and both forms might be present in one conflict.

Technological Asymmetry. In a conflict characterized by *technological asymmetry* a belligerent chooses to employ specific weapons or resources that others are not using to strike at its enemy's weaknesses. For example, a sophisticated weapon system, such as an unmanned aerial vehicle, is a technological asymmetry if the adversary lacks this weaponry, or cannot employ it due, for example, to social norms or legal constraints. Technological asymmetry does not necessarily imply high technology: the box cutters used by the 9/11 hijackers are a tragic example of the lethality of low-tech weaponry employed asymmetrically. Technological asymmetry may be used to degrade a belligerent's military capability. For example, improvised explosive devices (IEDs) deployed against US vehicles during the war in Iraq decreased the US forces' freedom of movement. Technological asymmetry can sometimes achieve political objectives directly. For example, in the 1983 Beirut barracks bombing, a terrorist organization used vehicle-borne IEDs to strike at a military barracks. The attack eventually resulted in the withdrawal of American and French forces and the dissolution of the Multinational Force in Lebanon.

The US national security community recognizes the danger of technological asymmetry, appreciating that low-tech weaponry is often seen by adversaries as an attractive and inexpensive alternative to US technological superiority derived from decades of research and development. Weapons of mass destruction (WMD) may be the most feared manifestation of technological asymmetry. WMD represent an asymmetric technology because only a few states have WMD, and they could be most devastating against civilian populations and similar "soft" or unprotected targets. Although the United States and some of its allies have nuclear weapons, legal, operational, and policy constraints could preclude their use in defense or retaliation, even against an adversary that used WMD. In addition, the United States and other states have foresworn the possession and use of biological and chemical weapons by becoming signatories to international bans.

Organizational Asymmetry. *Organizational asymmetry* refers to the ways in which a belligerent arranges forces and resources, including command and control methods, hierarchy, and doctrine. An irregular threat organization might attack a state in ways that are difficult for a state to counter because of the latter's hierarchical force structure or existing doctrine. For example, an insurgent group could circumvent the conventional military strength of a state through the creation of a loosely affiliated citizen-soldier structure that is difficult to detect and disrupt as its members hide among the civilian population. In terms of doctrine, insurgents may take an approach to targeting that emphasizes strikes on poorly defended areas, such as critical infrastructure and civilian targets, or against targets of symbolic value.

Cyber capabilities are a technological asymmetry, but they could also assist in developing organizational asymmetry (as discussed in chapter 14). Cyber attacks are an example of technological asymmetry because states may be constrained from overtly employing offensive cyber capabilities by a desire to avoid conflict escalation in cyberspace or because they want to prevent collateral damage. Cyber capabilities can support organizational asymmetry by facilitating a diffuse command and control system. Social media, the "deep web," encrypted applications, and other communication tools have allowed groups that pose irregular threats to establish horizontal networks that can avoid detection by intelligence agencies or targeting by security forces. These technologies may also facilitate recruiting, enable the training of "self-radicalized" individuals, motivate "lone wolf" actors, and promote extremist propaganda.

Advantages of Asymmetry. Asymmetry, whether technological or organizational, may produce three primary advantages: surprise, evasion, and deniability. Asymmetric warfare may offer the advantage of surprise. It is designed to allow a weaker enemy to attack a critical target without being interdicted or detected beforehand by a stronger enemy. By using decentralized forces and technology to avoid detection, irregular forces could strike targets in any number of locations with little or no warning.

Evasion and impunity may be advantages of asymmetric techniques; they make it more difficult for an adversary to find, track, and punish those responsible for committing violent acts. In insurgencies, this may involve hit-and-run attacks, ambushes, or the use of remotely detonated weapons. While those willing to become martyrs may commit suicide attacks, those organizing or supporting such operations tend to do so in a way that facilitates their own impunity and self-preservation.

Deniability is a potential advantage of asymmetric tactics. Attackers will often deny, mask, or obscure their own involvement (however, many groups may claim credit for a successful attack to aid in notoriety and recruitment). A quick attack followed by escape prevents the target force from accurately identifying the specific individuals who organized and executed the attack and then responding to those individuals with overwhelming force.

Terrorist groups, insurgencies, and VEOs can pose both technological and organizational asymmetric threats. They may use low-tech weapons such as remotely detonated devices to avoid detection, or more high-tech weapons, such as WMD or malware attacks against critical infrastructure, to affect large populations. Such groups might also employ organizational asymmetry, such as using hidden networks or inciting "lone wolf actors" to exploit the weaknesses of conventional militaries that are constrained by hierarchy and doctrine. Such asymmetric capabilities could be used to degrade conventional military capabilities, as Boko Haram did against the Nigerian military.[9] Asymmetric capabilities could aim to achieve political objectives directly, such as with the Provisional Irish Republican Army's use of terrorism to force a British withdrawal from Northern Ireland.

Asymmetric Warfare, Irregular Threats, and US Policy. In the 1990s, after the collapse of the Soviet Union ended the relatively symmetric standoff of the Cold War between the United States and the Soviet Union, US national security policy makers began to focus more intensively on asymmetric threats, and on actions to address such threats. The 1997 Quadrennial Defense Review (QDR) noted that US conventional superiority deterred adversaries from seeking direct military confrontation; instead, adversaries were likely to use "means such as terrorism, WMD threats, information warfare, or environmental sabotage to achieve [their] goals."[10] In many ways, this tendency toward asymmetry on the part of US adversaries was the natural outgrowth of decades of US policy that had sought conventional superiority.

American policy makers remained concerned about the proliferation of WMD throughout the 1990s, but expanded their focus beyond states to concerns about nonstate actors. The desire to ensure that nuclear weapon stockpiles and capabilities in the former Soviet Union would not fall into the wrong hands led to the creation of the Nunn-Lugar Cooperative Threat Reduction Program in 1991. The concern to limit proliferation of WMD also led to the creation of the Defense Threat Reduction Agency in 1998. Other efforts in the 1990s included initiatives to improve infrastructure security and the employment of diplomatic and economic means to secure, reduce, and monitor nuclear weapons–related capabilities.

While the WMD threat was obvious, the threat posed by shadowy organizations that lacked tanks or planes proved more difficult to grasp or to articulate. Prior to 9/11, the United States crafted few policy responses to organizational asymmetry. After the 9/11 attacks, however, the United States broadened its threat analysis and began to take seriously the threats arising from groups wielding organizational asymmetries; it also sought to develop its own capabilities to counter such threats. Post-9/11 efforts to combat transnational terrorist networks included doctrinal developments and paradigm shifts like the F3EAD (Find, Fix, Finish, Exploit, Analyze, and Disseminate) targeting cycle, the publication of *Field Manual 3-24: Counterinsurgency*, and the establishment of the Asymmetric Warfare Group (described further in chapter 16).[11]

This broadened threat analysis also affected how the US military trained and developed its leaders. In 2008, Secretary of Defense Robert Gates called for officers and noncommissioned officers with "uncommon agility, resourcefulness, and imagination, leaders willing and able to think and act creatively and decisively in a different kind of world and a different kind of conflict than we have prepared for over the last six decades."[12] Innovations that would give the military greater flexibility in its ability to recruit and retain talent, such as the Department of Defense's "Force of the Future" initiatives, are examples of how recognition of irregular threats led to "new thinking on the qualities" that would be needed in the country's military officers.[13]

The United States also increased investment in Special Operations Forces (SOF), after recognizing that SOF's organizational form, such as its flatter organizational structure made up of small units, would facilitate more rapid responses to battlefield developments.[14] The specific missions of SOF, including the precise targeting of individuals and the conduct of special warfare, were also in greater demand. During the 2014 reduction of US forces in Afghanistan, senior Defense officials emphasized an even greater future role for SOF, primarily in conducting operations that extend beyond the military's traditional purview. These would include "empowering host nation forces, providing appropriate assistance to humanitarian agencies, and engaging key populations. These long-term efforts increase partner capabilities to generate sufficient security and rule of law, address local needs, and advance ideas that discredit and defeat the appeal of violent extremism."[15] Through such operations (described in more detail in chapter 16), the United States has enhanced its capabilities to counter the increased global threat of groups posing irregular threats.

During the wars in Iraq and Afghanistan, the United States found that organizational asymmetry dramatically changed the dynamics of conflict. When a terrorist group deploys its forces in an unconventional manner, for example, the organization is by choice and by definition not bound by traditional military constraints that are codified in international laws such as the Geneva Conventions. This decoupling of belligerents from traditional, state-based military structures and legal constraints also has implications for their recruitment of fighters. International organizations can be "networked, adaptable, and empowered by cyberspace to find new ways to recruit, train, finance, and operate" beyond a domestic pool of recruits.[16] The rise of ISIL, in particular, brought widespread attention to the implications and challenges of international recruitment.

Perhaps the most significant impact of asymmetry in the post–9/11 era is the increasing dominance of political impact over military success. In conventional warfare, the outcome of a conflict is heavily dependent on the match-up of physical strength, including control of terrain, troop strengths, and quality of materiel available to both sides. Of course, all warfare is in part a psychological contest of wills between two adversaries, but in conventional war, the advantage is generally with the side that has the larger force, and military victories tend to foster political success. However, this may not be true in asymmetric warfare. Insurgents may, for example, be able to disconnect their desired political outcome from the military reality: "In asymmetric conflicts, insurgents may gain political victory from a situation of military stalemate or even defeat."[17]

The United States and its allies and partners initially approached the war in Iraq—and the war in Afghanistan after the initial invasion—through the lens of conventional warfare. They used metrics of success that were drawn from the physical realm, such as counting the number of insurgents killed and the frequency of incidents of violence against coalition troops. Conventional militaries considered "the conflict's outcome according to the military verdict of the battlefield between the sides actually fighting."[18] This approach, which was the predominant model until around 2007, overlooked the fact that in asymmetric warfare, the outcome may depend upon more than merely defeating a traditional enemy. Factors such as public perception and government legitimacy may be more significant than the number of enemy forces killed. According to this broader conception of war, "The military outcome does not provide a stable basis upon which to define the conflict's outcome."[19] When fighting an irregular threat, the conflict's center of gravity is frequently the population, rather than the terrain or the enemy as it might be in a conventional conflict.

After the drawdown of the majority of US forces from Afghanistan and Iraq, the United States encountered a brief lull in irregular threats; some even questioned whether the end of asymmetric warfare had finally arrived. This question was largely answered by the subsequent emergence of VEOs and the continued threat posed by terrorist groups and insurgencies. Reflecting the seriousness with which the United States considers the asymmetric threat posed by VEOs, the 2015 *National Military Strategy* stated that the two primary US military objectives are to defeat potential state adversaries, and to lead multiple coalition efforts to disrupt, degrade, and defeat VEOs. That VEOs were placed on par with state-based security threats signifies their importance to US national security. A significant focus on asymmetric warfare appears to be here to stay.

Terrorist Groups

Just as there are differences in terminology with regard to irregular threats, there are also differences in the terms used to describe the groups that pose them. Regardless of the term used, all are nonstate actors, all are driven by some kind of ideological or political aim, and all use asymmetric warfare to achieve their ends.

The three major groupings of concern to policy makers today are terrorists, insurgencies, and VEOs.

Terrorism has long been seen as an effective form of asymmetric warfare because it is a tactic available to states, organizations, and individuals who lack the conventional military capability they would need to compete symmetrically. Terrorists can attack much stronger enemies by organizing their own forces to evade detection, operating flexibly, concentrating on soft targets, and exploiting security vulnerabilities. Because terrorists use both organizational and technological asymmetries to their advantage, even the strongest states have found terrorist organizations to be formidable and persistent threats. After considering the definition of terrorism, this section provides a history of terrorism and then examines several ways that terrorists are distinct from conventional military combatants.

Defining Terrorism. The term *terrorist* is used frequently, but not always carefully: "Most people have a vague idea or impression of what terrorism is, but lack a more precise, concrete and truly explanatory definition of the word."[20] The term's negative moral connotation exacerbate the definitional challenge of terrorism: "If one party can successfully attach the label *terrorist* to its opponent, then it has indirectly persuaded others to adopt its moral viewpoint."[21]

There are two main approaches to defining terrorism. The first takes the motivations behind the act into consideration. It does not apply the term *terrorist* to groups seeking to promote social change or to end political repression, because oppressed groups may have no methods of recourse other than violence. This argument is loosely captured by the cliché "one man's terrorist is another man's freedom fighter." Despite its potential romantic appeal, this manner of defining terrorism has limited utility because of the obvious difficulty of reaching agreement on which motivations would or should justify violence.

The alternative approach defines terrorism "by the nature of the act, not by the identity of the perpetrators or the nature of their cause."[22] According to this argument, terrorism is a crime according to domestic law, and in a declared war, acts of terrorism would be war crimes. Bruce Jenkins has defined terrorism with reference to the nature of the act: "The violence is directed mainly against civilian targets. The motives are political. The actions are generally carried out in a way that will achieve maximum publicity. The perpetrators are usually members of an organized group, and unlike other criminals, they often claim credit for the act. And finally, the act is intended to produce effects beyond the immediate physical damage."[23] Jenkins' definition is similar to that commonly cited by the US Federal Bureau of Investigation (FBI), which defines terrorism as violent acts "intended to intimidate or coerce a civilian population, influence the policy of a government, or affect the conduct of a government."[24] In both definitions, it is the fact that an attack is intended to produce a political effect beyond its direct impact, rather than the motivations behind it, that distinguishes an act of terrorism.

A Brief History of Terrorism. Even a brief historical survey demonstrates that terrorism has taken many forms and has not always appeared as it does now. While terrorism is currently associated with revolutionary goals, such as overthrowing a regime or ending foreign presence in a country, the term was first popularized during the French Revolution of the late eighteenth century. At that time, terrorist tactics were used by the new revolutionary state, which sought to maintain order by terrorizing those who advocated a return to monarchy.[25] Later, however, terrorism was adopted by revolutionary groups. For example, revolutionaries employed terrorism against the ruling regimes of the Russian, Ottoman, and Hapsburg Empires. With the rise of fascism and nazism in the 1930s, terrorism again became associated with the actions of states: terrorist tactics were among the tools of the "repression employed by totalitarian states and their dictatorial leaders against their own citizens."[26]

The connotation of terrorism shifted again after World War II, when it became associated with anticolonialist movements in Asia, Africa, and the Middle East. Following these movements, terrorism remained primarily connected to revolutionaries and employed by an even more diverse group of nationalists, ethnic separatists, and ideologically motivated groups. For example, the late twentieth century witnessed the rise of single-issue terrorism, such as eco-terrorism.[27] These historical manifestations of terrorism are all united by the characteristics of terrorist acts—namely, that extrajudicial violence is employed in pursuit of political change.

While the different periods in terrorism's history are easy to distinguish in retrospect, researchers struggle to articulate the defining characteristics of late twentieth-and early twenty-first century terrorism. Some argue that this period is best described as an era of radical Islamic terrorism. These observers cite a history that includes the Islamic Revolution of 1979 in Iran, the First and Second Palestinian Intifadas in Israel, and attacks on American targets such as the U.S.S. *Cole*, the World Trade Center, US embassies abroad, and the Pentagon. A certain fundamentalist interpretation of Islam helped to motivate attacks on civilian transportation, culture, and entertainment in Madrid, London, Paris, and Brussels in the twenty-first century. Many of the "lone-wolf" attackers in the United States and Europe were apparently radicalized by those adhering to extreme interpretations of Islam. Critics of the label "radical Islamic terrorism," on the other hand, point out that the majority of the victims of such groups as al Qaeda and ISIL have been Muslims. Critics also argue that the use of the term "radical Islamic terrorism" plays into the terrorists' hands by associating all of the world's Muslims with the actions of a very small and unrepresentative minority.

Elements of Terrorism. Based on their motivations and self-image, terrorists are distinct from other groups, such as soldiers, revolutionaries, and criminals. They see themselves "as reluctant warriors, driven by desperation—and lacking any viable alternative—" to fight an otherwise intransigent source of oppression. A revolutionary, for example, may readily admit to being a revolutionary, but a terrorist "will *never* acknowledge that he is a terrorist and moreover will go to great lengths to evade and obscure any such inference or connection."[28] Instead, terrorists will insist that the real terrorists are corrupt regimes or capitalistic systems.

In addition to being primarily nonstate actors who would deny the charge of terrorism, terrorists also share what is, perhaps, an unexpected characteristic: they tend to be more educated and more socially connected than their peers in the general population.[29] Prior to the emergence of quantitative study of characteristics of terrorists, many thought terrorism was linked to extreme poverty and disenfranchisement. Yet the majority of post-9/11 quantitative research on terrorism, developed from an extensive database, has not found any correlation between poverty and terrorism at either the individual or the state level: terrorists are not poorer than their compatriots, and poor countries are not more likely to export terrorists than wealthier ones.

Robert Pape argues that suicide bombers, a distinct subset of terrorists, are motivated not by poverty or by a psychological disorder, but by their desire to "coerce modern liberal democracies to make significant territorial concessions."[30] When considered in this sense, terrorists are using terrorism to pursue "politics by other means," which is the essence of warfare as Clausewitz described it (see chapter 13). Yet describing terrorism as similar to other tactics is highly controversial; many officials argue that there is a "fundamental qualitative difference" between terrorism and traditional warfare. Warfare is governed by rules, such as the Geneva and Hague Conventions, even if those rules are not always fully effective in practice. States have prohibited certain types of weapons, targets, and tactics, such as hostage taking. While states have certainly been guilty of infractions, these transgressions are deemed war crimes, and they precipitate legal and normative reprisals. As Bruce Hoffman notes, the same is not true of terrorists, of whom a defining characteristic is "a refusal to be bound by such rules of warfare and codes of conduct."[31] It is both less controversial and more analytically correct to state that what distinguishes terrorism from other tactics of warfare is that terrorism uses technological and organizational asymmetric capabilities that its targets cannot effectively use.

Insurgencies

The term *insurgency* is not as contentious as the term *terrorism*, although its definition also invites controversy. Most organizations define insurgency as a rebellion against a recognized authority, such as a sovereign government. For example, the US military defines insurgency as "the organized use of subversion and violence to seize, nullify, or challenge political control of a region."[32] When thinking about the actions and purposes of both sides in such a conflict, it is important to keep in mind that an insurgency is fundamentally the result of a "political legitimacy crisis of some kind."[33] Insurgents contest their target's status as a recognized authority, and the resulting conflict is fueled by this disputed legitimacy.

Like terrorists, insurgents use both technological and organizational asymmetric capabilities that the established authority does not have or cannot effectively use. A terrorist group that initially had only the capacity to conduct attacks against soft civilian targets may, by gaining weapons, support, and personnel, grow into an insurgency that can degrade its target's military capabilities or directly threaten the legitimacy of the government. In contrast to terrorists, insurgents have some military capacity to challenge conventional military forces, and they frequently use military weapons to achieve their goals. For example, as the insurgency was developing in Iraq in 2003 to 2006, insurgents used raids, ambushes, mortars and other indirect fire, and other attacks against Iraqi, American, and other coalition military forces. The insurgents also used terrorism as a tactic by attacking civilian targets. In some cases, they combined tactics in complex attacks in which, for example, a car bomb would destroy a marketplace and then insurgents would attack military forces who were responding to the car bomb. Insurgents have historically relied on tactics and weapons systems that would interfere with the mobility of adversaries, who, although conventionally stronger, were often burdened by complex logistics. Some examples include the Tamil Tigers' use of suicide belts during their insurgency in Sri Lanka, and the Mahdi Army's use of explosively formed penetrators, designed to destroy US armored vehicles, in Iraq.

Insurgencies have also used organizational asymmetric capabilities, which are especially effective against government forces that are constrained by hierarchy and by engrained doctrine that is slow to change. For example, during the Malayan Emergency of 1948–1960, the Malayan National Liberation Army insurgents employed unconventional force structures, including training camps across the Thai border, which allowed the insurgent fighters to conceal themselves among civilians. Insurgents may be able to adapt their doctrine rapidly, fielding new tactics, assessing their efficacy, and then sharing these lessons throughout their flat organizations. For example, after the Tamil Tigers recognized the utility of female fighters and suicide bombers, they rapidly integrated women into their ranks, to devastating effect.

Because insurgents use their organizational and technological asymmetric capabilities to strike at conventional militaries in ways that government forces cannot easily match, a conventional military may need to develop its own asymmetric capabilities to wage a successful counterinsurgency campaign. Conventional militaries that rely solely on conventional capabilities, such as firepower, may find these capabilities ineffective. In insurgencies, the battlefield is greater than just the physical terrain, and a count of those killed or captured is usually a poor metric of performance. As Thomas Ricks explained, "A raid that captures a known insurgent or terrorist may seem like a sure victory for the coalition. . . . The potential second- and third-order effects, however, can turn it into a long-term defeat if [such] actions humiliate the family, needlessly destroy property, or alienate the local population."[34] Combating insurgency requires a much different approach than engaging in conventional conflicts.

A Brief History of Insurgency. Most military historians find the birth of the modern concept of insurgency in the activities of Spanish irregulars against occupying French forces between 1808 and 1814. The United States, at the end of the nineteenth century, became embroiled in a counterinsurgency campaign of its own in the Philippines. In this operation, which began as part of the Spanish-American War, US forces fought for fifteen years before defeating the insurrection. As exemplified by both these cases, prior to the twentieth century insurgencies or guerrilla wars were most often efforts by indigenous populations to preserve existing political, social, or cultural governance arrangements in the face of foreign conquest or intervention.

Prior to World War II, insurgencies were still most often motivated by a desire to end foreign rule. Western imperial powers, even while acknowledging the principle of national self-determination in some contexts, continued to engage in both regular and irregular warfare in defense of their empires. During the Cold War, and particularly after extensive European decolonization in the 1950s, insurgencies often took on a more ideological character.[35] The United States and the Soviet Union selectively supported insurgent forces or incumbent governments. For example, the United States provided training and logistical support to rebels in Afghanistan during the 1980s against the Afghan government and its Soviet patron.

US interest in insurgency naturally grew during the Vietnam War. The national security community relied on scholarship from David Galula and others to develop "pacification" and other programs such as the Civil Operations and Revolutionary Development Support (CORDS). After the Vietnam War, however, the United States largely eschewed insurgency-related scholarship and reverted to its historical norm of prioritizing preparation against conventional threats.[36] It was not until the post-9/11 era that the United States revived its interest in insurgencies and in developing capabilities to wage counterinsurgency campaigns. The importance of insurgencies and related irregular threats was codified in 2005, when the Department of Defense recognized stability operations as a "core military mission" for the first time.[37] The term *stability operations* referred to operations that were not purely offensive or defensive, but instead involved diverse components such as law enforcement, political and sectarian reconciliation, reconstruction, and the provision of essential services. (Chapter 16 discusses counterinsurgency in detail.)

Insurgencies in the first decade after the Cold War and the early twenty-first century have much in common with insurgencies in previous periods, but also manifest some potentially significant differences. An element of continuity is that most insurgencies involve contests over political legitimacy. They are also more likely to occur in situations in which social and economic stratification in society is particularly high.[38] The uneven effects of globalization have aggravated perceptions of relative deprivation, as those supporting insurgencies are increasingly aware of the differences in living standards both in their region and in the world.

Contemporary Insurgencies. While there are elements of continuity with the past, many insurgencies in the current era display some new characteristics.[39] One relates to the underlying circumstances out of which insurgencies grow. US military doctrine states that post–Cold War insurgencies "typically emerged from civil wars or the collapse of states no longer propped up by Cold War rivalries. . . . Similar conditions exist when regimes are changed by force or circumstances."[40] When insurgencies flow from conditions of state collapse, state failure, or forcible regime change, a counterinsurgency faces a greater challenge: to build, and not just restore, "political order and legitimacy where these conditions may no longer exist."[41]

A second issue relates to the goals of insurgent forces. Since the end of the Cold War, "ideologies based on extremist forms of religious or ethnic identities have replaced ideologies based on secular revolutionary ideals. These new forms of old, strongly held beliefs define the identities of the most dangerous combatants in these new internal wars. These conflicts resemble the wars of religion in Europe before and after the Reformation of the 16th century. People have replaced nonfunctioning national identities with traditional sources of unity and identity."[42] To the extent that insurgent groups are organized around fundamental aspects of identity and religion, compromise and ultimate political reconciliation may be more difficult.[43]

A third noteworthy characteristic of contemporary insurgencies is their transnational nature. The international dimension of insurgencies during the Cold War often consisted of the external involvement of the superpowers or their allies in internal conflicts, which had an ideological dimension. Transnational connections have become more complex and extensive over time, enabled by communication technologies and driven by many of the same processes that constitute globalization. Insurgents still generally direct their attacks against specific local governments, but some groups have leveraged technological asymmetries, through use of the Internet and social media, to gain members, supporters, and funding globally.

Violent Extremist Organizations

The term *violent extremist organization* (VEO) is relatively new and reflects a desire to come to a deeper understanding of the nature of groups posing an irregular threat to the United States. *Violent extremists* are "individuals who support or commit ideologically-motivated violence to further political goals."[44] While this definition overlaps with that of other irregular threats, members of VEOs are more loosely affiliated than members of terrorist cells or insurgent groups. They represent a spectrum of followers, from core leaders of the VEO to isolated kindred spirits who follow, fund, or support it. In many cases, individuals who are in the core leadership of a VEO could also be called terrorists or insurgents, because these core leaders are specifically identified with the group and are active in its direction.

Two attacks in the United States illustrate why policy makers have begun to use the term *violent extremist organization* to describe irregular threats. In November 2009, Major Nidal Hassan killed thirteen people and wounded thirty-two others at Fort Hood, Texas. Although not a member of or formally directed by any terrorist group, he was in regular email contact with al Qaeda in the Arabian Peninsula (AQAP) operative Anwar al-Awlaki, based in Yemen. Hassan shared violent extremist views, self-identified with AQAP, and then developed his own operation to support the VEO apparently without direct guidance to do so.[45] Second, in April 2013, Tamerlan Tsarnaev and Dzhokhar Tsarnaev set off bombs at the

Boston Marathon, killing three and injuring nearly three hundred others. There is no evidence that they had contact with a terrorist group, but they had become radicalized, in part, by listening to online sermons from al Qaeda leaders, and they used al Qaeda's publications, including the *Inspire* online magazine to learn how to build bombs.[46] The ability to leverage technology to communicate, radicalize, motivate, and instruct loosely affiliated followers like Hassan and the Tsarnaev brothers is what makes VEOs and the individuals motivated by them so dangerous.

The 2015 *National Military Strategy* argues that the combined technological and organizational asymmetric capabilities used by VEOs "pose an immediate threat to transregional security by coupling readily available technologies with extremist ideologies." VEOs employ technological asymmetric capabilities "to propagate destructive ideologies, recruit and incite violence, and amplify the perceived power of their movements. . . . [VEOs] use improvised explosive devices (IEDs), suicide vests, and tailored cyber tools to spread terror while seeking ever more sophisticated capabilities, including WMD."[47] The organizational asymmetric capabilities employed by VEOs include international recruitment, which is accomplished by calling on individuals to act on behalf of the organization without specific guidance from higher headquarters (such as "lone wolf" actors), and social media tools that enable VEOs to obtain financial and other support from sympathetic individuals.

Labeling a particular irregular threat, such as al Qaeda or ISIL, as a terrorist group, an insurgency, or a VEO might seem to involve a merely semantic distinction, but it has significant implications for threat response. When a threat is labeled a terrorist or insurgent group, the tools considered will generally include the military instrument of power. To the extent that a group is identified as a VEO, the more appropriate response is to counter the ideas that lead to violent extremism and the susceptibility of individuals to recruitment; this prioritizes nonmilitary instruments of power.[48]

The United States has called together many parts of the government in an attempt to counter VEOs. Internationally, the effort to counter violent extremism with information resources is coordinated by the State Department (discussed in chapter 11). Domestically, the Department of Homeland Security provides "resources to communities to build and sustain local prevention efforts and promote the use of counter-narratives to confront violent extremist messaging online."[49] In 2016, this program included $10 million in grants "to help states and local communities prepare for, prevent, and respond to emergent threats from violent extremism."[50] These efforts reflect an understanding that countering the long-term influence of a VEO will require addressing the factors that enable the VEO to recruit individuals to its cause.

Looking Ahead

When combating irregular threats employing asymmetric warfare, the role of the state is often reactive. The state's hierarchical organizations and the complex legal and normative restrictions within which policy makers operate means that the state must play catch-up to terrorists, insurgents, and VEOs, whose flatter organizations and disregard of constraints allow them to innovate rapidly. In some respects, however, the response of the state to an irregular threat is similar to the state's response to a traditional threat in a conventional conflict: the state uses its own power to amass a range of weapons, including asymmetric ones, to employ against enemies. Technological responses include improving intelligence, amassing vast quantities of data, conducting real-time analysis, responding with weaponized drones, and other measures. Organizational responses may include creating additional interagency operations/intelligence centers (known as *fusion cells*), expanding special operations forces, integrating special operations and conventional forces, empowering local governments, modifying legal authorities, and revising military doctrine. For example, the administration of President George W. Bush sought to redefine preemptive war, which is permissible under international law, so that the term would encompass expanded use of military force to protect against irregular threats.

The dramatic terrorist attacks on American soil on September 11, 2001, and the US military interventions in Afghanistan and Iraq that followed have motivated academics to engage in new research and policy makers to develop new doctrine, programs, and systems. The dialogue between research and policy has been strong and productive, but the United States continues to struggle in its efforts to combat irregular threats. As new scholarship emerges on the motivations of terrorists, the lessons from Iraq and Afghanistan, and the efficacy of different techniques to counter violent extremism, that scholarship can assist policy makers in planning, resourcing, and executing policy to counter terrorism, insurgencies, and violent extremist organizations.

In addition to developing new policies and doctrines, US policy makers may need to alter the way they think about the problem. While the United States often seems to consider irregular threats as challenges to be overcome, it may be more appropriate to see them as endemic problems, like crime and piracy, which may be addressed more or less effectively but will never be eliminated fully. Without this paradigm shift, the United States may engage in shortsighted efforts that defeat particular heads of the Hydra but do not result in any significant, long-term gains to American national security.

Discussion Questions

1. Does the global proliferation of irregular threats suggest an end to the era of conventional conflicts, or do current conflicts involving irregular threats constitute a historical aberration?
2. Compare the threat to national security from an irregular threat, a traditional conventional threat, and a criminal gang: Which is more difficult to combat? Which should policy makers worry about most?
3. How important is the particular ideology of a group posing an irregular threat?
4. Why are asymmetric capabilities important to terrorists, insurgencies, and VEOs?

5. What policies can the United States adopt to minimize its vulnerability to asymmetric attacks?

6. Some argue that the terrorist groups of today constitute a completely new type of threat that demands a new policy response. Is this proposition correct, or can previous defense strategies be adapted to face this threat?

7. What are the most important distinctions among terrorist groups, insurgencies, and VEOs?

8. How would you compare the relative military and political strengths of terrorists, insurgencies, and violent extremist organizations? Against what types of targets could each group have a greater advantage than the others?

9. How are twenty-first century insurgencies different from those in the past? Why have they changed and what are the implications for US national security policy?

10. How can or should the United States counter the ability of violent extremist organizations to radicalize individuals remotely?

Recommended Readings

Boot, Max. *Invisible Armies: An Epic History of Guerrilla Warfare from Ancient Times to the Present*. New York: Liveright, 2012.

Department of the Army. *Field Manual 3-24: Counterinsurgency (FM 3-24/MCWP 3-33.5)*. Washington, DC: Department of the Army, 2006.

Galula, David. *Counterinsurgency Warfare: Theory and Practice*. New York: Praeger, 1964.

Hoffman, Bruce. *Inside Terrorism*. Rev. and exp. ed. New York: Columbia University Press, 2006.

Krueger, Alan. *What Makes a Terrorist: Economics and the Roots of Terrorism*. Princeton, NJ: Princeton University Press, 2008.

Mack, Andrew. "Why Big Nations Lose Small Wars: The Politics of Asymmetric Conflict." *World Politics* 27, no. 2 (1975): 175–200.

Pape, Robert. *Dying to Win: The Strategic Logic of Suicide Terrorism*. New York: Random House, 2006.

Simpson, Emile. *War from the Ground Up*. Oxford: Oxford University Press, 2012.

Sun Tzu. *The Art of War*. Translated and edited by Samuel B. Griffith. Oxford: Oxford University Press, 1971.

Wright, Lawrence. *The Looming Tower: Al-Qaeda and the Road to 9/11*. New York: Vintage, 2007.

Internet Resources

Combating Terrorism Center at West Point, www.ctc.usma.edu
The Long War Journal, www.longwarjournal.org

Notes

1. See Andrew Silke, "Research on Terrorism," in *Terrorism Informatics*, ed. H. Chen et al. (New York: Springer, 2008), 27–50.

2. Department of Defense, *The National Defense Strategy of the United States* (Washington, DC: US Government Printing Office, March 2005), 2 (emphasis in the original).

3. Department of Defense, *National Defense Strategy* (Washington, DC: Department of Defense, June 2008), 4.

4. Department of Defense, *Sustaining U.S. Global Leadership: Priorities for 21st Century Defense* (Washington, DC: Department of Defense, January 2012), 4.

5. Joint Chiefs of Staff, *The National Military Strategy of the United States of America 2015* (Washington, DC: Joint Chiefs of Staff, June 2015), i, 3.

6. Secretary of Defense Jim Mattis, *Summary of the 2018 National Defense Strategy of the United States of America* (Washington, DC: Department of Defense, January 2018), 3 (emphasis in the original).

7. This definition is informed by Colin S. Gray, "Irregular Warfare: One Nature, Many Characters," *Strategic Studies Quarterly* 1, no. 2 (2007): 35–57; quotation with regard to ideology at 44.

8. Sun Tzu, *The Art of War*, trans. and ed. Samuel B. Griffith (Oxford: Oxford University Press, 1971), 101

9. Boko Haram is an Islamist militant group that has attacked Nigeria's police and army, as well as civilian targets, since 2009. See Mohammed Aly Sergie and Toni Johnson, "Boko Haram," Council on Foreign Relations Backgrounders, March 5, 2015, http://www.cfr.org/nigeria/boko-haram/p25739.

10. Secretary of Defense, *Quadrennial Defense Review, 1997* (Washington, DC: Department of Defense, 1997), section 2, http://www.dod.mil/pubs/qdr/.

11. See Liam S. Collins, "Military Innovation in War: The Criticality of the Senior Military Leader," PhD dissertation (Woodrow Wilson School, Princeton University, June 2014).

12. Robert Gates, "The West Point Evening Lecture," Address to the United States Military Academy, West Point, New York, April 22, 2008.

13. Ann S. Tyson, "Army's Next Crop of Generals Forged in Counterinsurgency," *Washington Post*, May 15, 2008. For details on DoD's "Force of the Future," see Ashton Carter, "Memorandum, SUBJECT: Forging Two New Links to the Force of the Future," November 1, 2016, https://www.defense.gov/News/Special-Reports/0315_Force-of-the-Future.

14. The Special Operations Forces budget increased from $2.3 billion in 2001 to $10.5 billion in 2012. Linda Robinson, "The Future of Special Operations," *Foreign Affairs* 91, no. 9 (2012): 110–22.

15. William McRaven, "Posture Statement," 112th Congress, testimony before Senate Armed Services Committee, March 6, 2012, 6, https://fas.org/irp/congress/2012_hr/030612mcraven.pdf.

16. McRaven, "Posture Statement," 5.

17. Andrew Mack, "Why Big Nations Lose Small Wars: The Politics of Asymmetric Conflict," *World Politics* 27, no. 1 (1975): 177.

18. Emile Simpson, *War from the Ground Up* (Oxford: Oxford University Press, 2012), 4.

19. Simpson, *War from the Ground Up*, 4.

20. Bruce Hoffman, *Inside Terrorism* (New York: Columbia University Press, 2006), 1.

21. Bruce M. Jenkins, *The Study of Terrorism: Definitional Problems* (Santa Monica, CA: RAND, December 1980), 1.

22. Jenkins, *The Study of Terrorism*, 2–3.

23. Jenkins, *The Study of Terrorism*, 3.

24. Dale L. Watson, Testimony before the Senate Select Committee on Intelligence, February 6, 2002, https://archives.fbi.gov/archives/news/testimony/the-terrorist-threat-confronting-the-united-states.

25. Hoffman, *Inside Terrorism*, 3.

26. Hoffman, *Inside Terrorism*, 14.

27. Between 1980 and 2000, the Federal Bureau of Investigation recorded 335 incidents of suspected terrorism in the United States. Of these, 247 were attributed to domestic terrorists, while 88 were determined to be international. Watson, Testimony.

28. All quotations in this paragraph are from Hoffman, *Inside Terrorism*, 22 (emphasis in the original).

29. See Robert A. Pape and James K. Feldman, *Cutting the Fuse: The Explosion of Global Suicide Terrorism and How to Stop It* (Chicago: University of Chicago Press, 2010); and Alan B. Krueger, *What Makes a Terrorist?* (Princeton: Princeton University Press, 2007).

30. Robert A. Pape, "The Strategic Logic of Suicide Terrorism," *American Political Science Review* 97, no. 3 (2003): 343.

31. Hoffman, *Inside Terrorism*, 28.

32. Joint Chiefs of Staff, *Joint Publication 1-02, Dictionary of Military and Associated Terms* (Washington, DC: Department of Defense, February 15, 2016), 142.

33. Bard E. O'Neill, *Insurgency and Terrorism* (Washington, DC: Brassey's, 1990), 17.

34. Thomas Ricks, *Fiasco: The American Military Adventure in Iraq* (New York: Penguin, 2006), 418.

35. Ian F. W. Beckett, *Modern Insurgencies and Counterinsurgencies: Guerrillas and Their Opponents since 1750* (New York: Routledge, 2001).

36. David Petraeus, "The American Military and the Lessons from Vietnam," PhD dissertation (Woodrow Wilson School, Princeton University, 1987).

37. This codification of the importance of stability operations was specified in Undersecretary of Defense for Policy, *Department of Defense Directive Number 3000.05* (Washington, DC: Department of Defense, November 28, 2005), 2.

38. Robert Taber, *The War of the Flea: Guerrilla Warfare in Theory and Practice* (New York: Lyle Stuart, 1965), 180.

39. Beckett, *Modern Insurgencies and Counterinsurgencies*, viii.

40. Department of the Army, *Field Manual 3-24: Counterinsurgency (FM 3-24/MCWP 3-33.5)* (Washington, DC: Department of the Army, 2006), 1–4.

41. Department of the Army, *Field Manual 3-24*, 1–4.

42. Department of the Army, *Field Manual 3-24*, 1–4.

43. See Donald L. Horowitz, "A Harvest of Hostility: Ethnic Conflict and Self Determination after the Cold War," *Defense Intelligence Journal* 1, no. 2 (1992): 137–63; and Chaim Kaufmann, "Possible and Impossible Solutions to Ethnic Civil Wars," *International Security* 20, no. 4 (1996): 136–75.

44. The White House, "Empowering Local Partners to Prevent Violent Extremism in the United States," August 2011, 1, https://obamawhitehouse.archives.gov/sites/default/files/empowering_local_partners.pdf.

45. Bruce Hoffman, Edwin Meese, and Timothy Romer, *The FBI: Protecting the Homeland in the 21st Century* (Washington, DC: Federal Bureau of Investigation, March 2015), 39.

46. Hoffman, Meese, and Romer, *The FBI*, 39.

47. Joint Chiefs of Staff, *The National Military Strategy*, 4.

48. Joby Warrick, "How a U.S. Team Uses Facebook, Guerilla Marketing to Peel Off Potential ISIS Recruits," *Washington Post*, February 6, 2017.

49. Department of Homeland Security, "Countering Violent Extremism," January 19, 2017, https://www.dhs.gov/countering-violent-extremism.

50. Department of Homeland Security, "FY 2016 Countering Violent Extremism (CVE) Grant Program," https://www.dhs.gov/cvegrants.

16

Counterterrorism, Counterinsurgency, and Stability Operations

The irregular threats of terrorist groups, insurgents, and violent extremist organizations (VEOs) present difficult policy challenges. As described in chapter 15, groups that pose irregular threats use asymmetric warfare to attack the weaknesses and negate the conventional military strengths of their adversaries. With regard to the United States, these groups may argue that any successful attacks on US forces demonstrate the group's ability to fight and win against a superpower. From the coordinated terrorist attacks on September 11, 2001, to the "lone wolf" attack in an Orlando night club for which terrorists claimed credit in 2016, such attacks not only cause direct harm and destruction, but also expose vulnerabilities and exacerbate fear in US society. Irregular threat groups also seek to take advantage of any missteps by US forces. When a US military weapon that is intended to attack a terrorist mistakenly strikes a hospital, wedding party, or other civilian target, these groups portray the US action as a deliberate act of barbarism rather than as a tragic outcome of the fog and friction inherent in war.

In spite of these difficulties, there are specific concepts, techniques, and lessons that guide US national security policy to address irregular threats. This chapter provides an overview of military intervention against irregular threats and then discusses in detail counterterrorism, counterinsurgency, and stability operations.

The Nature of Military Intervention

There are two conceptual issues to consider with regard to military intervention. First, the overall decision to intervene is intrinsically difficult because of the uncertain outcomes of such a decision. Second, the way in which the US military regards operations other than conventional war has changed in the years since 9/11.

Decision to Intervene. In most cases, irregular threats may not immediately threaten a vital national interest or pose an existential threat to the United States. However, inaction against these threats may not be prudent because, over time, irregular threat groups could foment instability, create humanitarian crises, undermine international commerce, threaten US allies, or otherwise harm US interests. On the other hand, there are also potential downsides to military intervention against an irregular threat: it could bolster support for the group, increase its local and global notoriety, and exacerbate the threat. In addition, US action will incur costs in lives and resources and may have undesirable second- and third-order political and diplomatic effects. Policy makers assess the decision to intervene militarily in a particular situation based on the goals of US national security policy, the interests of the countries in the region, the capability of US and other coalition forces, and the likelihood of success. Chapter 13 details the strategic logic of the use of force, and the same logic applies to irregular threats.

Even with the benefit of hindsight, it can be difficult to determine whether military action to counter an irregular threat was the right decision, especially after considering the total costs and effects of each decision to intervene or not intervene. Consider, for example, the differing US responses to attacks by al Qaeda separated by two decades. After al Qaeda attacked the US embassies in Kenya and Tanzania in 1998, the military developed several counterterrorism options to attack al Qaeda and its leader, Osama bin Laden. Those operations were never approved because of a lack of "actionable intelligence" and the belief that a "tactical operation, if it did not go well, could turn out to be an international embarrassment for the United States."[1] In contrast, after the 9/11 attacks, the United States intervened militarily in Afghanistan to defeat the Taliban regime that had supported al Qaeda and to prevent al Qaeda from having a base of operations from which it could launch further attacks against the United States. Although the latter decision to intervene received domestic and international support, subsequent US and coalition operations in Afghanistan proved more extended and costly than anticipated.

Decisions about whether or not to intervene in support of allies can be similarly challenging. Examples include Vietnam in the 1950s and 1960s, Iraq from 2003 to 2011, and Libya in 2011. In 1954, the government of France asked President Dwight D. Eisenhower to support French forces then under siege at Dien Bien Phu in Vietnam; Eisenhower decided not to intervene.[2] However, after the United States had provided advisors to Vietnam in 1961 and after the 1964 Gulf of Tonkin resolution, President Lyndon Johnson decided to introduce US combat units into Vietnam to defeat the North Vietnamese Army and the insurgents that threatened the Republic of Vietnam (South Vietnam). The ensuing war proved to be extremely costly to the United States and Vietnam. US efforts to preserve the independence of South Vietnam ultimately proved unsuccessful, and it fell to North Vietnam in 1975.

The Iraq and Libya examples reveal some of the challenges associated with decisions to engage in counterinsurgency and postconflict stability operations. After US-led military operations to topple Saddam Hussein's regime, the United States supported the new Iraqi government with a counterinsurgency campaign from

2003 to 2011. By contrast, after US involvement in an air campaign that contributed to the fall of Muammar Gaddafi in Libya in 2011, the United States did not participate in postconflict stability operations in support of organizations such as the Libyan National Transitional Council, which sought to establish a successor government. Both of these choices resulted in strategic outcomes that were problematic for the United States. In Iraq, the war vastly exceeded initial cost estimates and did not ultimately prevent instability, as centrifugal forces reemerged after the US military withdrawal in 2011. On the other hand, the failure of the United States and other countries to invest in Libya after the overthrow of Gaddafi may have allowed the growth of violence, instability, and transnational terrorist groups there.

The rest of this chapter presents accumulated knowledge about the circumstances under which counterterrorism, counterinsurgency, or stability operations are more or less likely to succeed. However, there are no guarantees. The difficulty of adequately estimating all of the dynamics that will affect the success of a military operation, especially those involving irregular threats, means that even if the best military doctrine, training, and judgment are applied, success cannot be assured. The strategic decisions of belligerents, the reactions of populations involved, and the inherent uncertainties of warfare combine to make any prediction of the outcome of military operations difficult. It is also difficult to predict the outcome of a decision not to intervene. This chapter does not provide arguments for or against intervention in any particular circumstance; rather, it articulates the dynamics and considerations that should inform that choice.

The Question of Lesser Included Cases. Throughout the Cold War, the US military's major emphasis was on conventional, and possibly nuclear, conflict with the Soviet Union. Military units, training, equipment, and doctrine concentrated on conventional conflict; other operations, such as peacekeeping or other actions against irregular threats, were considered "lesser included cases." The assumption was that military forces that were prepared for a regular conflict against a conventional adversary would also be able to respond adequately to irregular threats.

After the end of the Cold War, some US military deployments did not conform to the conventional force-on-force missions for which the armed forces had prepared. These deployments were part of several operations: Provide Comfort in Northern Iraq, 1991–1996; Restore Hope in Somalia, 1992–1993; Uphold Democracy in Haiti, 1994–1995; Joint Endeavor in Bosnia, 1995–1996; and Allied Force in Kosovo, 1999. In each case, the official doctrinal term for these operations was *Military Operations Other Than War* (MOOTW). As General John Shalikashvili, then chairman of the Joint Chiefs of Staff, explained in the military's 1995 doctrinal publication on the subject, "While we have historically focused on warfighting, our military profession is increasingly changing its focus to a complex array of military operations—other than war," including counterterrorism, counterinsurgency, humanitarian assistance, and peacekeeping.[3] The military's perspective during the 1990s with regard to confronting irregular threats is captured in the following excerpt from the joint doctrine:

> *MOOTW include a wide range of challenging operations for which U.S. forces need to be prepared.* . . . However, commanders must remember that their *primary mission will always be to prepare for, fight, and win America's wars.* This is the U.S. military's most rigorous task and requires nothing less than top priority when training and equipping our forces.[4]

The clear implication is that counterterrorism, counterinsurgency, and other operations against irregular threats would be secondary tasks when compared to "real warfighting" against conventional threats.

Because MOOTW were seen as "lesser included cases," there was very little institutional preparation for how to address irregular threats. Although Special Operations Forces had counterterrorism as a specific mission, there was limited preparation or training for counterinsurgency, peacekeeping, or other operations confronting irregular threats. The services did not create specialized units; MOOTW training was mostly limited to the specific preparations made by individual units immediately before they deployed. The assumption was that a well-trained conventional unit could conduct a peacekeeping or counterinsurgency operation with only a modest level of additional training.

After the initial US-led invasion in October 2001 led to a sustained US presence in Afghanistan, and as US forces faced a growing insurgency in Iraq in 2003–2006, the US military revised its approach to irregular threats in general and to counterinsurgency in particular. In November 2005, the Department of Defense (DoD) issued DoD Directive 3000.05, which specified that "stability operations are a core U.S. military mission that the Department of Defense shall be prepared to conduct and support. They shall be given *priority comparable to combat operations* and be explicitly addressed and integrated across all DoD activities including doctrine, organizations, training, education, exercises, materiel, leadership, personnel, facilities, and planning. . . . U.S. military forces shall be prepared to perform all tasks necessary to establish or maintain order when civilians cannot do so."[5] Under this directive, stability operations encompassed the activities that would be needed to establish or maintain order in states and regions. This included efforts to rebuild security forces; operate correctional facilities and judicial systems; revive economic activity; and develop representative governmental institutions. This DoD directive made explicit what many commanders in Iraq and Afghanistan had come to recognize through firsthand experience: conducting counterinsurgency operations was a mission as important as conventional warfare, with its own complexities and requirements. It was not merely a "lesser included case," but rather a responsibility that would require specialized doctrine, leader development, training, and equipment.

Counterterrorism

Combating terrorism requires a concerted, long-term, multifaceted strategy involving all elements of government as well as important actors from within the broader society. Counterterrorism had been a specific mission of the US Special

Operations Command since its creation in 1986, but emphasis on counterterrorism significantly increased after 9/11. While the national strategy for counterterrorism has been revised over time, it has concentrated on four key goals:

- Defend US citizens and interests at home and abroad;
- Defeat terrorists and their organizations;
- Deny sponsorship, support, and sanctuary to terrorist organizations; and
- Diminish the underlying causes of terrorism.[6]

Since 9/11, combating terrorism has been a national priority that has received increased means to accomplish the goals listed above. This function intrinsically requires contributions from—and coordination among—multiple departments and agencies of the US government. The sections below describe key policy considerations with respect to each goal.

Defend US Citizens and Interests. Protecting Americans at home and abroad in an age of terrorism has required government structures to adapt. Rather than react to terrorist attacks, the government has sought to move to the "left of the boom"—the part of the timeline before the explosion—to anticipate, prevent, or preempt terrorist attacks. Significantly increased intelligence efforts, including enhanced coordination and sharing across federal, state, and local governments, have been accompanied by the creation of entirely new agencies, including the Department of Homeland Security and the National Counterterrorism Center (described in chapters 6 and 7, respectively).

The increased intelligence gathering necessary to defend the homeland has sometimes raised questions about the proper balance between the individual's right to privacy and the government's need for information. The Obama administration's *National Strategy for Counterterrorism* explicitly stated that privacy rights, civil liberties, and civil rights were core values of the strategy, and recognized a need to balance security with transparency. These values are important because the preservation of "rights and liberties is essential to maintain the support of the American people for our [counterterrorism] efforts."[7] A police state that significantly restricted individual rights might be better able to defend against terrorism, but this would undermine the very principles that provide the foundation for the American system of government. Striking a balance between security and privacy will continue to be a challenge for policy makers striving to defend the homeland.

Defeat Terrorists and Their Organizations. Policy makers often choose the military instrument of power as they seek to disrupt, degrade, dismantle, and defeat terrorists and their affiliates. In specific war zones, such as Iraq or Afghanistan, direct military action against terrorist organizations to kill or capture terrorists is one component of a comprehensive stabilization strategy. Military forces also conduct operations outside of those areas, such as in Pakistan, Yemen, or Syria, to kill or capture terrorists. In some cases, when US policy makers find it necessary or desirable to conceal or deny US involvement, they may place military forces under the temporary authority of a US intelligence agency. For example, elements of the Joint Special Operations Command were administratively attached to the director of the Central Intelligence Agency (CIA) for the 2011 raid on Osama bin Laden's compound in Abbottabad, Pakistan. The rationale for this was that if the raid had been "carried out under Defense Department authority, the US government could not deny our involvement; CIA, on the other hand, could."[8] The operation was a success and was well publicized, but had it failed or been aborted, the fact that it had been conducted under the authority of the CIA might have made it more likely that the operation could be kept secret.

In addition to such direct-action raids, both the intelligence community and military forces have used unmanned aerial vehicles (UAVs), commonly known as drones, to collect intelligence and then attacked specific targets with precision-guided missiles. Drones "are the keys to a 'light-footprint strategy'" to accomplish specific counterterrorism objectives with lower costs and lower risks to US special operations or conventional military forces.[9] On the other hand, the use of drones is controversial for many reasons. Armed drones might be used to conduct a targeted strike against a specific individual in a foreign country (which some could consider assassination) or, in some cases, without the specific authorization of the state involved (which some could consider a military attack). In addition, these strikes are sometimes undertaken without due process of law (even if the target is an American), and they risk error or collateral damage (which may not be proportional to the objective desired).[10]

President George W. Bush was the first president to permit the use of armed drones to attack terrorist targets in foreign countries, and he authorized forty-seven drone strikes while he was president. President Barack Obama significantly expanded this practice throughout his administration. Between 2004 and 2016, the United States conducted 392 strikes in Pakistan; between 2002 and 2017, the United States conducted 172 drone strikes in Yemen.[11] President Obama provided a lengthy defense of targeted drone strikes, noting that they are part of: "a just war—a war waged proportionally, in last resort, and in self-defense. . . . The use of drones is heavily constrained. . . . We act against terrorists who pose a continuing and imminent threat to the American people and when there are no other governments capable of effectively addressing the threat. . . . To do nothing in the face of terrorist networks would invite far more civilian casualties."[12]

As with any new technology, answers to the moral, legal, organizational, and procedural questions raised by the use of drones use are still evolving. The United States has made the greatest use of drones for both intelligence and targeted killings and thereby established precedent for their use as legitimate weapons of war. As other nations and even terrorist groups develop similar technologies, it will be important to establish international norms and laws to govern their use. The fact that the United States relies heavily on the use of drones is certain to make the procedures and the restrictions on their use a critical aspect of American national security policy.

Deny Sponsorship, Support, and Sanctuary to Terrorist Organizations. Terrorism is risky, and it is not normally a financially profitable endeavor. Terrorist organizations require significant ongoing support, protection, funding, and bases. While states may find it difficult to capture or kill specific terrorists, they can coordinate to restrict the areas in which terrorist organizations can freely operate. A critical aspect of the US approach has been to expand from military-focused counterterrorism operations to the pursuit of "a 'Whole-of-Government Effort' . . . [that] integrates the capabilities and authorities of each department and agency, ensuring that the right tools are applied at the right time to the right situation in a manner that is consistent with US laws."[13] Today, many different agencies of the US government contribute to efforts to undermine support for terrorist groups.

As discussed in chapter 12, one critical effort has been coordination by the US Department of the Treasury of the use of financial tools in support of counterterrorism. Leveraging financial tools can be helpful for many reasons.[14] First, terrorist groups must rely on external sources of funds for their operations. Intelligence agencies can often "follow the money" to understand the reach and scope of terrorist organizations. Second, the US Treasury Department and its foreign counterparts can designate an organization, individual, or foreign financial entity as being involved in supporting terrorism. Such a designation restricts that actor from engaging in the global financial system and makes all of its financial transactions significantly more difficult. Third, although there may not be international agreement about whether a specific individual or organization is involved in terrorism, most states recognize similar financial crimes. Many foreign countries are more willing to cooperate with the United States to prosecute individuals or impose sanctions for money laundering or fraud than they might be to agree to a terrorism prosecution. Concerted actions against the financial and economic activities of terrorist groups can limit the resources available to them and divert their leaders' focus toward protecting their finances, thus degrading their ability to plan, supply, and coordinate complex acts of terrorism.

Denying sanctuary is one of the ways in which counterinsurgency contributes to counterterrorism strategy. Terrorist groups need places from which to operate, and often seek to establish safe havens in poorly governed countries that lack the capacity to control movement within their territories. Both the State Department and the Defense Department work with foreign countries to help build their capacity to control and eliminate the operations of terrorist organizations in their midst. Improvements in border security, intelligence, economic development, political participation, police effectiveness, and military capability are among the efforts that can limit terrorist groups' access to physical sanctuary. For example, the Combined Joint Task Force–Horn of Africa (CJTF-HOA) conducts stability operations using approximately two thousand troops stationed in Djibouti. CJTF-HOA trains security forces in several countries in East Africa in counterterrorism, professionalization, peace operations, humanitarian assistance efforts, and other operations aimed at enhancing the long-term stability of the region.[15] Supporting a partner country in its counterinsurgency campaign can be an effective means to deny terrorist organizations access to safe havens.

Terrorist groups, as strategic actors, seek to develop alliances with other organizations that have similar objectives and interests. Al Qaeda, which is based in Pakistan, has affiliations with organizations in other locations such as Yemen, East Africa, the Arabian Peninsula, the Maghreb, and Southeast Asia. Affiliate groups from many different countries have pledged allegiance to the Islamic State in Iraq and the Levant (ISIL).

The degree of allegiance and centralized control varies significantly, however, and can be a strategic vulnerability: an effective counterterrorism strategy can exploit fissures among groups and use a group's actions to discredit it among its followers. For example, a comprehensive study of Arabic primary sources indicated that, at the height of al Qaeda's attacks in 2004–2008, most of its victims (over 85 percent) were Muslims, not Westerners.[16] Publication of the facts from this study by Arab newspapers led to a backlash against al Qaeda and accusations by leaders of different groups, each blaming the other for the violence and the bad publicity.

A critical aspect of denying support for terrorist groups is to keep them from developing, acquiring, or using weapons of mass destruction (WMD). This unquestionably requires a whole-of-government approach: intelligence, diplomacy, law enforcement, control of nuclear materials, arms control, border security, foreign military cooperation, and international coordination are all essential to prevent terrorists from acquiring WMD capability. Nuclear nonproliferation, Cooperative Threat Reduction, and the Proliferation Security Initiative (discussed in chapter 17) all contribute to efforts to prevent terrorists from gaining access to the world's most dangerous weapons.

Diminish the Underlying Causes of Terrorism. Eliminating the underlying causes of terrorism is exceptionally difficult, whether they are based on generations-old grievances, lack of legitimacy, exclusion from the political process, lack of opportunity, or other factors. Some efforts have addressed those causes directly by encouraging states to expand individual rights, improve economic development, and address underlying grievances. Much of the US effort has concentrated on addressing the ideology and terrorist propaganda that persuade individuals to support terrorist or extremist organizations.

Efforts to counter the underlying causes of terrorism must begin with an understanding of terrorist organizations and their motivations. Without using the information from terrorists themselves to explain their motivation, it is easy to make erroneous assumptions about what motivates terrorists. However, terrorist leaders often communicate with their widely dispersed followers and potential followers through the Internet. Intelligence agencies and policy makers can read, analyze, understand, and exploit these communications, although it takes a concentrated effort to do so. Organizations such as the CIA's Open Source Center and the Combating Terrorism Center at West Point specialize in analyzing publicly available information about terrorists and other organizations.[17] These organizations, along with scholars around the world who conduct research in this area, have made significant contributions in helping policy makers understand the narratives and ideologies that shape terrorist groups.

The US Countering Violent Extremism (CVE) initiative is a comprehensive approach to combating extremist ideologies that radicalize, recruit, or incite individuals to violence. Under CVE, state and local government officials develop plans "tailored to addressing the root causes and community needs" at the local level, with pilot programs established in Boston, Los Angeles, and Minneapolis-St. Paul.[18] At the federal level, both the Department of Homeland Security and the FBI have CVE programs to diminish the appeal of terrorist and extremist groups. To influence audiences overseas, the State Department has the Center for Strategic Counterterrorism Communications (see chapter 11). As part of the overall public diplomacy effort, the United States tries to counter the terrorist narrative by discrediting it and by supporting a counternarrative that is specifically tailored for each region.

The four goals discussed above are mutually reinforcing. As the government better defends the homeland and succeeds in thwarting terrorist attacks, the image of al Qaeda or ISIL as successful becomes increasingly difficult for terrorist leaders to sustain. The elimination of terrorist leaders, the denial of territory, and the interruption of financial support further undermine the success of terrorist groups. These material losses may undercut terrorist claims to effectiveness and legitimacy. As a result, individuals who might otherwise be susceptible to recruitment or to providing funding may turn away from terrorist groups instead of supporting them.

Counterinsurgency

Counterinsurgency differs from counterterrorism because of the nature of the group posing the irregular threat. In contrast to many terrorist groups, insurgents are fighting for political legitimacy and control of a particular region or state (see chapter 15). They tend to have greater localized strength, which they may use to confront and threaten government, police, and military forces in a specific area.

The recent renaissance of counterinsurgency doctrine within the US armed forces developed from necessity. After rapidly defeating the Iraqi military in the 2003 invasion, US forces struggled to respond to the escalating sectarian conflict that followed. Different units in Iraq pursued different approaches toward insurgency, with varying degrees of success. In 2005, one influential critic writing in the military's professional journal observed that while the US "Army is indisputably the master of conventional warfighting, it is notably less proficient in . . . Operations Other Than War."[19] This observation was contemporaneous with the military's own study of the history of counterinsurgency warfare and the contemporary American experience in Iraq; the result was a completely new doctrinal manual for the US Army and US Marine Corps. Its preface notes that "counterinsurgency operations have been neglected in broader American military doctrine and national security policies since the end of the Vietnam War over 30 years ago."[20]

The objective of doctrine is to provide a consistent approach to warfare, which commanders adapt to the specific local situation that they confront. In counterinsurgency doctrine, the focus is not on the military defeat of an adversary, as it is during conventional war; instead, the focus is on population security and the fostering of "effective governance by a legitimate government."[21] Figure 16.1 shows the insurgent (on the left of the diagram) competing for influence with the government that is countering the insurgency. Between the insurgents and those who support the government lies the neutral or passive population, which includes people who are concerned primarily with their own welfare. Counterinsurgency involves providing security to this large, uncommitted portion of the population to convince its members to support the government. Ways to do so include conducting combat operations, building up host-nation forces, providing essential services, supporting governance, and increasing economic development—efforts shown in figure 16.1 as arrows moving from left to right. All of this requires concurrent information operations efforts—the larger arrow—aimed at ensuring that local people understand the actions taken to defeat the insurgency, so they will be more likely to support the government.

A common misperception is that counterinsurgency is similar to peacekeeping operations and consists primarily of stability operations (the bottom three arrows in the middle of figure 16.1). In reality, effective counterinsurgency operations involve much more than "winning hearts and minds." In addition to stability operations, they must include offensive operations and defensive operations. Offensive

FIGURE 16.1 Counterinsurgency Lines of Operations

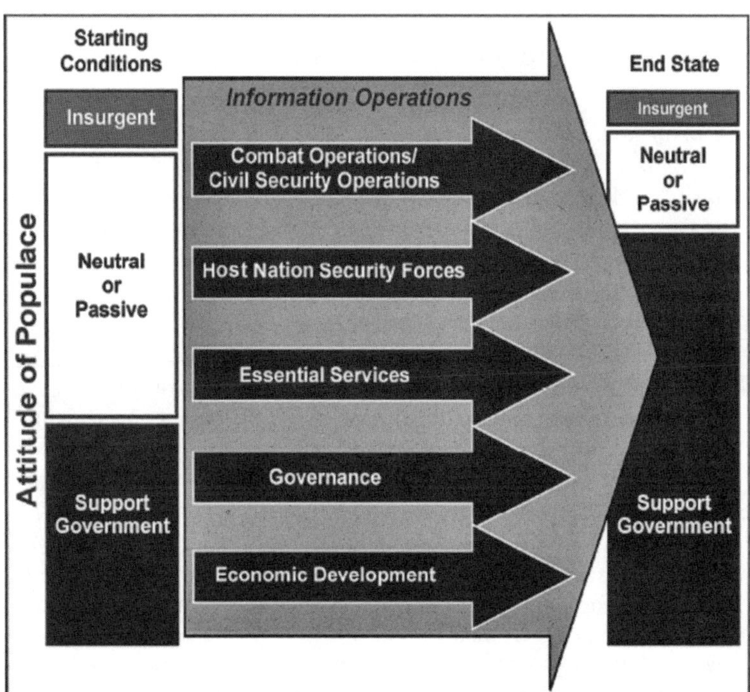

operations concentrate on killing or capturing the insurgents who are the "irreconcilable" portion of the population. It is essential that counterinsurgent forces conduct such offensive operations in a discriminating way so that their actions do not inspire more insurgents than they kill. Defensive operations protect friendly forces and minimize casualties. Since the purpose is to enhance the legitimacy of the host government, foreign military forces that are operating in support of the government must partner effectively with the host nation and its security forces.

During the early years of the Iraq War, there may have been too much emphasis on defensive operations. In 2005, President George W. Bush said, "Our strategy can be summed up this way: As the Iraqis stand up, we will stand down."[22] Consequently, many American units consolidated on large forward operating bases and concentrated on training Iraqi forces, rather than partnering with Iraqi forces in operations to protect the population at the local level.[23] This approach proved to be inadequate and was reversed as part of the surge of US forces to Iraq in 2007. Orchestrating all three aspects of counterinsurgency—offense, defense, and stability operations—is extremely complex and must be done by combatants at all levels.

In counterinsurgency, the same unit will often be responsible for "providing relief in one part of a city, keeping the peace in a second, and fighting intensively against a determined foe in a third."[24] Marine General Charles Krulak described this challenge as the *three-block war*, in which soldiers and marines may be "confronted by the entire spectrum of tactical challenges in the span of a few hours and within the space of three contiguous city blocks."[25] One of the most challenging parts of counterinsurgency is the need to understand the environment and to adapt operations so as to enhance the population's support for the government.

Counterinsurgency Principles. It is very difficult to prescribe how unit leaders should adapt to any and all situations, so instead, military doctrine articulates principles to guide leaders as they conduct counterinsurgency operations. Every insurgency is likely to have a few unique characteristics, some of which are at least partially "determined by specific historical and cultural circumstances."[26] US military doctrine reflects historical experience that has revealed some principles of general utility.[27]

- *Legitimacy is the main objective.* The primary purpose of counterinsurgency operations is to buttress the legitimacy of the supported government. What constitutes political legitimacy may depend on social, political, and historical context, but all actions must be informed by this primary purpose.
- *Unity of effort is essential.* Counterinsurgency is not solely a military operation. Civilian and military counterinsurgency resources should be under a common authority where possible, but complete unity of command is unlikely. Therefore, military commanders at all levels must coordinate extensively with other government agencies, host-nation forces and agencies, intergovernmental organizations, and even nongovernmental organizations to integrate and coordinate counterinsurgency efforts.

- *Political factors are primary.* Since the main goal of counterinsurgency forces is to establish or buttress the legitimacy of the supported government, political factors must receive foremost consideration in the conduct of operations. This is because "military actions conducted without proper analysis of their political effects will at best be ineffective and at worst aid the enemy."[28]
- *Counterinsurgents must understand the environment.* The goal of counterinsurgency operations and the complex environment in which they take place make it necessary for counterinsurgent forces to have deep understanding of the cultural, social, and political characteristics of their environment, as well as an understanding of important actors and groups, and of who exercises power and how.
- *Intelligence must drive operations*. The actions of counterinsurgents operating at all levels must be informed by reliable, timely, and detailed intelligence reporting. Stated another way, "with good intelligence, a counterinsurgent is like a surgeon cutting out the cancers while keeping the vital organs intact."[29]
- *Insurgents must be isolated from their cause and support.* To succeed over the long term, counterinsurgent forces must isolate insurgents from material or ideological sources of support from local and international sources. To do this, counterinsurgents may use physical, information, diplomatic, or legal means.
- *Security under the rule of law is essential.* The security of the population is essential to the legitimacy of the supported government. Counterinsurgent forces should seek to transition from combat operations to police enforcement as rapidly as possible, and to ensure that the actions of forces supporting the government are consistent with the rule of law.
- *Counterinsurgents should prepare for long-term commitment.* Insurgencies have typically been protracted forms of conflict. Because the population is more likely to give their allegiance to the government when they have a high expectation of the determination and staying power of counterinsurgent forces and of their prospects for success, a long-term commitment is often needed.

US military doctrine also recognizes a number of other imperatives for US forces. They must manage information and expectations, use the appropriate level of force, learn and adapt, empower leaders at the lowest levels of command, and support the host nation.[30] These principles and imperatives have significant implications for military forces participating in counterinsurgency operations, demanding restraint, intellectual agility, and good judgment at all levels of leadership.

The Relationship between Counterterrorism and Counterinsurgency. In some US theaters of war, such as in Iraq or Afghanistan, coordinated counterterrorism operations are an essential component of an effective counterinsurgency. In these contexts, counterterrorism generally refers to the offensive part of a counterinsurgency campaign: the kinetic military actions aimed at capturing or killing terrorists or insurgents. Conventional military units, which are responsible for a particular area on the ground, sometimes conduct such operations. Special Operations units, which have specialized intelligence, training, equipment, and personnel, also conduct these offensive operations, ideally in close cooperation with conventional forces in the local area. In either case, the success of broader counterinsurgency efforts has a significant impact on the success of counterterrorism operations and vice versa. The elimination of terrorists or irreconcilable insurgents is likely to improve security for the local population. To the extent that the population feels more secure, its members are more likely to provide critical intelligence and improved situational awareness, informing both counterterrorism operations and subsequent actions by counterinsurgent forces to capitalize on success.

When viewed at a global level, the relationship is reversed: counterinsurgency can be seen as part of global counterterrorism strategy. Counterterrorism includes taking actions to influence global and regional environments so that they are inhospitable to terrorist networks. Counterinsurgency operations seek to strengthen a particular state's ability to control its own territory and thereby oppose terrorist networks. When policy makers discuss a "CT-only" strategy, they generally mean special operations or other targeting of terrorists without a complementary counterinsurgency campaign that would support partner countries and their security forces in order to enhance their legitimacy and their ability to exercise control over their territories. Although a "CT-only" strategy may entail fewer forces, costs, and risks to US and allied forces, it may often be less effective: the concentration on offensive operations could exacerbate tensions with local populations and thus fail to make the environment more forbidding to terrorists over the longer term.

Counterinsurgency Challenges. Historical as well as contemporary examples of US involvement in counterinsurgency reveal a number of challenges. Some of these challenges are not just characteristic of counterinsurgency operations, but are likely to be evident in other forms of military intervention in response to irregular challenges. Such issues include the appropriateness and the adequacy of the capabilities and capacities of individual US government organizations and agencies; the need for effective, extensive interagency cooperation; the costs of the operations; the requirement for domestic support; and the need to plan for conflict termination.

US Government Agency Capability and Capacity and the Interagency Process. A recurring theme in current US military doctrine is that, while military force may be successful in responding to many irregular challenges to American national security, the United States must also integrate diplomatic, information, and economic instruments of power to succeed in counterinsurgency.

To play their needed role, organizations and agencies across the US government must have both the *capability* to deploy and the *capacity* to perform these functions at the required scale. As one study states: "While the US military is unmatched in terms of its effectiveness, capabilities, and reach, the US government lacks a standing, deployable capacity for stability operations in non-DoD agencies."[31] The study notes that "recent changes in US interventions—increased operational tempo, rapid success on the battlefield, and an ever-expanding list of post-conflict objectives—have dramatically increased the need for rapid civilian deployments."[32] In the absence of civilian agency capability, military units might undertake a broad array of tasks relating to economic, social, and political development at which they are not expert, and which may stretch military resources.

This dynamic helps to explain why US military and defense analysts often champion the development of civilian capabilities and capacity.[33] In a November 2007 speech, Secretary of Defense Robert Gates said:

> My message is that if we are to meet the myriad challenges around the world in the coming decades, the country must strengthen other important elements of national power both institutionally and financially, and create the capability to integrate and apply all the elements of national power to problems and challenges abroad. . . . One of the most important lessons of the wars in Afghanistan and Iraq is that military success is not sufficient to win: economic development, institution-building and the rule of law, promoting internal reconciliation, good governance, providing basic services to the people, training and equipping indigenous military and police forces, strategic communications, and more—these, along with security, are essential ingredients for long-term success.[34]

Gates pointed out that in the absence of civilian partners, the US military had sought to meet many of these challenges, and he argued that much of the resulting organizational learning on the part of the military should be retained and institutionalized. Nevertheless, he said, these efforts were "no replacement for the real thing—civilian involvement and expertise."[35] Although the State Department responded positively to Gates's ideas and increased the number of diplomats assigned to partner with military commanders, there has not been significant organizational change to increase civilian capacity.[36]

Interagency Cooperation. Beyond organizational capability and capacity, the effectiveness of the interagency process is also essential. Whether in response to crises or in the management of ongoing operations, interagency cooperation is still largely ad hoc. As discussed in chapter 9, there is no single, unified national security apparatus with the capability to plan, manage, and control all national security-related spending. The interagency process has continued to expand and grow more complex over time as new functions and entities have been added to the US government to respond to new national security needs (see chapter 10). Recommendations for improving US government effectiveness in interagency cooperation have included proposals to institutionalize strategic planning, clarify presidential national security guidance, specify interagency roles and responsibilities, and develop more robust mechanisms to strengthen connections among "policy, resource allocation, and execution."[37] These recommendations have much to commend them, but obstacles to their implementation remain great.

Costs of the Operations. As discussed above, counterinsurgency operations may require the commitment of significant resources for several years. US funding

Table 16.1 Deaths from Wars in Iraq and Afghanistan, 2001–2015

	Iraq	*Afghanistan*	*Total*
US servicemembers	4,483	2,353	6,837
DoD civilians	13	5	18
US government civilians (non-DoD)	6–12	10–15	16–27
US contractors	1,620	1,592	3,212
Journalists	221	25	246
NGO workers	62	331	393

Source: Sara Thannhauser and Christoff Luehrs, "The Human and Financial Costs of Operations in Afghanistan and Iraq," in *Lessons Encountered: Learning from the Long War*, ed. Richard D. Hooker Jr. and Joseph J. Collins (Washington, DC: National Defense University Press, 2015), 421–30.

totaled $815 billion for the war in Iraq and $686 billion for the war in Afghanistan through fiscal year 2014.[38] As of 2015, over 10,000 US military, civilian, and contractor personnel had been killed in Iraq and Afghanistan (table 16.1). Over 31,951 service members have been wounded in Iraq and 20,069 in Afghanistan.[39] Among these wounded are many who have suffered life-changing injuries and who face long-term disability.

Even these budgetary and casualty figures do not capture the full range of costs that may be associated with a large-scale American military intervention. Additional important categories of costs include diplomatic costs, especially if a US military intervention lacks strong multilateral support; opportunity costs, as the demands of intervention make it difficult to address other national security priorities; loss of confidence in government leaders and institutions if interventions falter or fail; stress created by war on the constitutional balance between government institutions; the effect of a US intervention on international or regional peace and stability; and the physical destruction and loss of life in the target country. Such costs cannot be predicted with certainty. On the other hand, inaction can bring its own costs and risks, while a successful intervention could enhance the influence of US leaders at home and abroad. The potential balance of these costs and benefits is worthy of evaluation as national security policy makers assess various courses of action.

Public Support. One of the principles of counterinsurgency operations discussed above is the need for a long-term commitment. Ambassador Ryan Crocker reaffirmed this general principle in September 2007 testimony to Congress with regard to the US intervention in Iraq. He argued that while the United States might achieve its goal of a "secure, stable democratic Iraq at peace with its neighbors," the "process will not be quick, it will be uneven, punctuated by setbacks as well as achievements, and it will require substantial US resolve and commitment."[40] The link between domestic public opinion and US government policy is not simple or direct. Nevertheless, national security policy makers face the challenge of sustaining a US commitment in an environment in which a majority of Americans many not support such a commitment.

Americans have traditionally approached national security affairs with a degree of impatience, as chapter 2 described; protracted limited wars do not fit this temperament. The US historical experience provides some interesting precedents for thinking about the potential for sustaining protracted military interventions abroad. Declining US public support was a major factor in the US military withdrawal from Vietnam in 1973, from Somalia in 1994, and from Iraq in 2011. On the other hand, the United States sustained a military commitment in Bosnia for ten years beginning in 1995 with little public attention or opposition, even though policy makers had claimed that the operation would last for only one year. Similarly, even after an extended US intervention in Afghanistan that began in 2001, a majority of Americans in 2015 still supported keeping US troops in Afghanistan into 2017 and the Trump administration continued US troop commitments to Afghanistan.[41] This brief survey suggests that while sustained US public support should not be taken for granted, it may be achievable depending on the circumstances. In any event, the need to sustain public support is one of the considerations US policy makers should keep in mind as they consider military intervention.

Conflict Termination. A final challenge, related to many of those above, is conflict termination. Like the challenges previously discussed, this one applies to a broad range of military operations as well as to counterinsurgencies. Conflict termination is critical because the best way to judge the success of a military operation is by considering the peace that comes after the war has ended. Tactical and operational victories alone may not achieve the country's political purposes; adequate planning and resources for actions necessary to bring a particular intervention to a successful conclusion are also critical.[42] The continuing instability and governance challenges that followed the initial success of the US-led invasions of Afghanistan in 2001 and Iraq in 2003 are examples in which the inadequacy of plans for the requirements of war termination have had costly consequences.

Stability Operations

Stability operations are a component of counterinsurgency operations, along with offensive and defensive operations. Military forces may also conduct stability operations outside of a counterinsurgency environment. In many circumstances, it may be appropriate to use military forces to conduct operations that shape the environment in support of US policy and to prevent war. Chairman of the Joint Chiefs General Colin Powell recalled that he almost had "an aneurysm" when, in 1993, Secretary of State Madeline Albright challenged him to answer the question: "What's the point of having this superb military you're always talking about if we can't use it?"[43] The purpose of stability operations is to use the capacity of the US military in pursuit of foreign policy objectives, even in circumstances that do not necessarily involve vital national interests or require combat operations. As discussed above, in 2005 the Department of Defense elevated stability operations to a priority comparable to combat operations, essentially answering Secretary Albright's implicit question in the affirmative.

Stability operations are a core mission that the military undertakes "when a state is under stress and cannot cope."[44] Such operations would normally be the responsibility of the state itself, but at times it may be in America's interest to provide stability, especially if the local government cannot do so because of a natural disaster, recent conflict, insufficient capacity, or some other reason. Defense Department doctrine explains that "the immediate goal of stability operations is to provide the local populace with security, restore essential services, and meet humanitarian needs. The long-term goal may be to develop the following: indigenous capacity for securing essential services, a viable market economy, rule of law, democratic institutions, and a robust civil society."[45] This conception of stability operations sets high goals for economic, political, and social development. In general, the more ambitious the US goals are in a given context, the more resources the United States will need to commit to an operation, and the longer it may need to remain involved.

In addition to being a component of a comprehensive counterinsurgency campaign, stability operations are important to several other forms of joint operations including conflict prevention, humanitarian assistance, and peace operations.

Conflict Prevention. As part of an overall US approach to a country or region, military actions to facilitate stability can contribute to preventing conflict. Stability operations can take place before a potential crisis to support security cooperation, security sector reform, dispute resolution, or other activities aimed at diminishing the risk of future hostilities. Security cooperation may include developing military relationships, conducting combined exercises, reforming or building security institutions, training partner forces, and facilitating foreign military sales. Additionally, the presence of US military forces in an area, through forward basing or deployments, may reduce the likelihood of conflict by shaping regional actors' perceptions. Military forces may be called upon to enforce sanctions or exclusion zones (such as a no-fly zone), which can be part of a comprehensive strategy to limit conflict escalation. The no-fly zones in Iraq after the 1991 Gulf War, for example, helped to prevent conflict between Saddam Hussein's military and Kurdish minorities in northern Iraq and Shiite citizens in southern Iraq.

Foreign Humanitarian Assistance. US military humanitarian assistance operations abroad are conducted to relieve or reduce the consequences of natural or manmade disasters or to alleviate the effects of endemic conditions such as disease, hunger, or other forms of privation. Foreign humanitarian assistance operations are generally limited in scope and duration and are intended to supplement or complement efforts of host-nation civil authorities or of other agencies of the US government, often the US Agency for International Development (USAID). For example, the US military provided extensive support after the 2010 earthquake devastated Haiti. While USAID was the lead US agency, it made use of military capabilities including logistics, security, communications, and planning.[46] Such humanitarian assistance supports long-term US foreign policy objectives by helping countries when they need it the most, and when the US military's significant capabilities can have a significant and positive effect.

Peace Operations. US military doctrine describes peace operations as "crisis response and limited contingency operations," which "normally include international efforts and military missions to contain conflict, redress the peace, and shape the environment to support reconciliation and rebuilding and to facilitate the transition to legitimate governance."[47] Two elements of this definition are especially noteworthy. First, just like the definition of stability operations, it suggests that military forces have a role to play within peace operations where they alone would be insufficient. Military operations must complement and support diplomatic and other efforts designed to facilitate a long-term political settlement. As a second and related point, the goal of peace operations is the reestablishment of legitimate governance. This definition sets a demanding standard for their execution, and peace operations must be specifically tailored to the individual situation.

Two major categories of peace operations involve primarily military forces. First, peacekeeping operations (PKO) are military operations to support implementation of an agreement such as a ceasefire or truce, with the concurrence of all parties, to facilitate a long-term political settlement.[48] The NATO deployment to Bosnia in support of the Dayton Peace Accords in 1995 is an example. Traditional peacekeeping operations are authorized under Chapter VI of the United Nations (UN) Charter, which covers the "Pacific Settlement of Disputes."

Second, peace enforcement operations (PEO) are the application of military force to compel compliance with resolutions or sanctions so as to impose the peace or the agreement on one or more of the parties in a conflict. Such operations are normally preceded by an international authorization, such as a UN resolution under Chapter VII of the UN Charter (which authorizes the UN Security Council to call on member states to respond with force to actions that threaten international peace and security). Military operations in Somalia in 1993 and in East Timor in 1999 are examples of PEO authorized by a UN Security Council resolution.

Current US doctrine includes three additional categories of peace operations: peacemaking, peace building, and conflict prevention. In the first two, the military plays a subordinate and supporting role to US diplomatic efforts; in conflict prevention operations, military force may be used to shape the environment so as to minimize the likelihood of future conflict.

UN Secretary General Dag Hammarskjold once said, "Peacekeeping is not a soldier's job, but only a soldier can do it."[49] Current US military doctrine reflects an acceptance of the logic behind this statement and goes even further by explicitly stating that peacekeeping is a soldier's job and that the US military should have the doctrine, training, and procedures it will need to execute peace operations when necessary. However, US military doctrine also points out the importance of leveraging all instruments of power to have the greatest prospects of success.

Looking Ahead

Confronting irregular threats through counterterrorism, counterinsurgency, or stability operations is extremely difficult. The US military has a mixed record in these endeavors, which contrasts with its history of more consistent success in conventional operations. This mixed record, in combination with the costs associated with military intervention, have led some to argue that the United States should not engage in stability operations or nation building overseas when there is a need for the US government to make investments at home.

While prioritizing domestic needs may be appealing, threats to the United States are likely to continue to come from terrorists, insurgents, or other groups posing irregular threats. The tradeoffs involved will remain difficult, as there will be uncertainty as to how much investment in the use of the military to counter or prevent overseas threats actually reduces the security risk to the United States and its allies. At some level, the call to use military forces in conjunction with other elements of power will likely continue. Policy makers who understand the potential contributions, challenges, and limitations of counterterrorism, counterinsurgency, and stabilization operations will be better equipped to make decisions that will advance US national interests.

Discussion Questions

1. If an irregular challenge does not directly threaten vital US national security interests, should the United States respond with military force?
2. What criteria should a policy maker use to determine whether or not to respond militarily to an irregular threat?
3. Are stability operations really as important as conventional combat operations? To what extent is there a risk that military forces will be distracted by irregular threats and lose focus on conventional (or nuclear) adversaries that may pose a greater threat?
4. How have counterterrorism operations conducted by the United States changed since 9/11?
5. Do the four goals of counterterrorism strategy (defend, defeat, deny, diminish) address the correct issues? What goal or goals should be added or emphasized more prominently?
6. In the effort to secure the homeland, how should policy makers balance privacy and transparency with the need for security? Does the United States have the balance right today?
7. In counterinsurgency, why should the focus be on the population and the legitimacy of the supported government rather than on the destruction of the enemy?
8. How do the principles of counterinsurgency guide military leaders as they decide how to balance offensive, defensive, and stability operations?
9. How much weight should policy makers give to public opinion in determining whether to conduct a counterinsurgency operation? How much can public opinion be influenced by policy makers or others?
10. Should the United States be involved in stability operations abroad while there are unmet needs at home? Why or why not?

Recommended Reading

Cassidy, Robert M. *Counterinsurgency and the Global War on Terror: Military Culture and Irregular War.* Westport, CT: Praeger Security International, 2006.

Department of the Army. *Counterinsurgency FM 3-24/MCWP 3-33.5.* Washington, DC: Department of the Army, 2006.

Galula, David. *Counterinsurgency Warfare: Theory and Practice.* Westport, CT: Praeger, 1964, 2006.

Gordon, Michael R., and Bernard E. Trainor. *The Endgame: The Inside Story of the Struggle for Iraq, from George W. Bush to Barack Obama.* New York: Vintage Books, 2013.

Hashim, Ahmed. *Insurgency and Counter-Insurgency in Iraq.* Ithaca, NY: Cornell University Press, 2006.

Hooker, Richard D., and Joseph J. Collins, eds. *Lessons Encountered: Learning from the Long War.* Washington, DC: National Defense University Press, 2015.

Irwin, Lewis G. *Disjointed Ways, Disunified Means: Learning from America's Struggle to Build an Afghan Nation.* Carlisle Barracks, PA: US Army Strategic Studies Institute, 2012.

Nagl, John. *Learning to Eat Soup with a Knife: Counterinsurgency Lessons from Malaysia and Vietnam.* Chicago: University of Chicago Press, 2005.

Robinson, Linda. *Tell Me How This Ends: General David Petraeus and the Search for a Way out of Iraq.* New York: PublicAffairs, 2008.

Schadlow, Nadia. *War and the Art of Governance: Consolidating Combat Success into Political Victory.* Washington, DC: Georgetown University Press, 2017.

Wilson, Isaiah. *Thinking beyond War: Civil-Military Relations and Why America Fails to Win the Peace.* Rev. ed. New York: Palgrave Macmillan, 2013.

Zusman, Lynne, ed. *The Fundamentals of Counterterrorism Law.* Chicago: American Bar Association, 2014.

Internet Resources

Combating Terrorism Center at West Point, ctc.usma.edu
Institute for the Study of War, www.understandingwar.org
The Long War Journal, www.longwarjournal.org
Small Wars Journal, www.smallwarsjournal.com

Notes

1. The only counterterrorism actions taken after the 1998 attacks were Tomahawk cruise missile strikes. See Steven Strasser, *The 9/11 Investigations: Staff Reports of the 9/11 Commission* (New York: PublicAffairs, 2004), 104.

2. Chief of Staff of the Army Matthew Ridgway said, "We could have won, if we had been willing to pay the tremendous cost in men and money that such intervention would have required." Ridgway's warning of the significant cost involved was decisive in persuading President Eisenhower not to intervene. See Matthew B. Ridgway, *Soldier* (New York: Harper and Brothers, 1956), 275–77.

3. General John M. Shalikashvili, foreword in Joint Chiefs of Staff, *Joint Pub 3-07, Joint Doctrine for Military Operations Other than War* (Washington, DC: The Joint Staff, June 16, 1995), inside cover (unnumbered).

4. Joint Chiefs of Staff, *Joint Pub 3-07*, I-7 (emphasis in the original).

5. Department of Defense, *Directive, Subject: Military Support for Stability, Security, Transition, and Reconstruction (SSTR) Operations* (Washington, DC: Department of Defense, November 28, 2005), 2 (emphasis added).

6. These goals are taken from the 2003 *National Strategy for Combating Terrorism* (https://fas.org/irp/threat/ctstrategy.pdf), and articulated in Wayne A. Downing, "The Global War on Terrorism: Re-Focusing the National Strategy," in *Terrorism and Counterterrorism*, ed. Russell D. Howard and Reid Sawyer (Dubuque, IA: McGraw Hill, 2006), 435–53. The Obama administration's 2011 *National Strategy for Counterterrorism* had the same basic goals, but articulated them slightly differently. The 2011 strategy explicitly focused on al Qaeda. It added separate goals of preventing access to WMD, eliminating safe havens, and partnering with foreign nations (which were part of the "deny support" goal in the 2003 strategy document); and it added the goal of degrading links between al Qaeda and its adherents (which was part of "diminishing underlying conditions" in the 2003 document). The White House, *National Strategy for Counterterrorism* (Washington, DC: The White House, June 2011).

7. The White House, *National Strategy for Counterterrorism* (2011), 5.

8. Robert M. Gates, *Duty: Memoirs of a Secretary at War* (New York: Knopf, 2014), 542.

9. David E. Sanger, *Confront and Conceal: Obama's Secret Wars and Surprising Use of American Power* (New York: Crown Publishers, 2012), 243.

10. For an excellent analysis of the legal issues, see Maritza S. Ryan, "A Game of Drones," in *The Fundamentals of Counterterrorism Law*, ed. Lynne Zusman (Chicago: American Bar Association, 2014), 185–211.

11. The documentation of secret drone strikes is inherently difficult, but an excellent unclassified resource is the Long War Journal, http://www.longwarjournal.org/.

12. Barack Obama, "Remarks by the President at the National Defense University" (Washington, DC: The White House, May 23, 2013).

13. The White House, *National Strategy for Counterterrorism* (2011), 7.

14. For a detailed discussion of the use of finance for counterterrorism, see Patrick D. Buckley and Michael J. Meese, "The Financial Front in the Global War on Terrorism," in *Defeating Terrorism: Shaping the New Security Environment*, ed. Russell D. Howard and Reid L. Sawyer (New York: McGraw Hill, 2003), 51–61; and Juan Zarate, *Treasury's War: The Unleashing of a New Era of Financial Warfare* (New York: PublicAffairs, 2013).

15. Lauren Ploch, *Africa Command: U.S. Strategic Interests and the Role of the U.S. Military in Africa*, RL 34003 (Washington, DC: Congressional Research Service, July 22, 2011), 20–21.

16. Scott Helfstein, Nassir Abdullah, and Muhammad al-Obaidi, *Deadly Vanguards: A Study of al-Qa'ida's Violence against Muslims* (West Point, NY: USMA, Combating Terrorism Center, December 2009).

17. Reports from the Combating Terrorism Center at West Point are available at ctc.usma .edu. Publications of the CIA's Open Source Center are available on a limited basis to government employees or contractors deemed to have an appropriate need to know.

18. The White House, "Fact Sheet: The White House Summit on Countering Violent Extremism" (Washington, DC: The White House, February 18, 2015).

19. Nigel F. Aylwin-Foster, "Changing the Army for Counterinsurgency Operations," *Military Review* 86, no. 6 (2005): 2–3.

20. Department of the Army, *Counterinsurgency FM 3-24/MCWP 3-33.5* (Washington, DC: Department of the Army, December 15, 2006), vii.

21. Department of the Army, *Counterinsurgency*, 1–21. This description of counterinsurgency is adapted from Tania Chacho and Michael Meese, "What Is the Mission? Why Is Counterterrorism So Difficult?," in *The Fundamentals of Counterterrorism Law*, ed. Lynne Zusman (Chicago: American Bar Association, 2014), 33–48.

22. George W. Bush, "War Update," Fort Bragg, NC, June 28, 2005, http://www.presidentialrhetoric.com/speeches/06.28.05.html.

23. For example, during 2005–2006, coalition soldiers were ordered to consolidate from 112 forward operating bases to 50. The central tenet of American commander General George Casey's strategy involved "shifting responsibility to the nascent Iraqi Forces." See Michael R. Gordon and Bernard Trainor, *The Endgame: The Inside Story of the Struggle for Iraq, from George W. Bush to Barack Obama* (New York: Pantheon, 2012), 181, 192.

24. Michael O'Hanlon and David Petraeus, "America's Awesome Military," *Foreign Affairs* 95, no. 5 (2016): 13.

25. General Charles C. Krulak, "The Strategic Corporal: Leadership in the Three Block War," *Marines Magazine* 83, no. 1 (1999): 26–32.

26. Colin S. Gray, "Irregular Warfare: One Nature, Many Characters," *Strategic Studies Quarterly* 1, no. 2 (2007): 43.

27. The listed principles are taken from Department of the Army, *Counterinsurgency*, 1–21 to 1–24. See also Eliot Cohen, Conrad Crane, Jan Horvath, and John Nagl, "Principles, Imperatives, and Paradoxes of Counterinsurgency," *Military Review* 86, no. 2 (2006): 49–51.

28. Cohen, Crane, Horvath, and Nagl, "Principles, Imperatives, and Paradoxes of Counterinsurgency," 50.

29. Cohen, Crane, Horvath, and Nagl, "Principles, Imperatives, and Paradoxes of Counterinsurgency," 50.

30. Imperatives are from Department of the Army, *Counterinsurgency*, 1–24 to 1–26.

31. Clark A. Murdock and Michèle A. Flournoy, *Beyond Goldwater-Nichols: U.S. Government and Defense Reform for a New Strategic Era*, Phase II Report (Washington, DC: Center for Strategic and International Studies, 2005), 55.

32. Murdock and Flournoy, *Beyond Goldwater-Nichols*, 56.

33. Nina M. Serafino, "Peacekeeping and Related Stability Operations: Issues of U.S. Military Involvement," *CRS Issue Brief for Congress*, updated March 27, 2006, CRS-9.

34. Robert M. Gates, "Landon Lecture," November 26, 2007, http://archive.defense.gov/Speeches/Speech.aspx?SpeechID=1199.

35. Gates, "Landon Lecture."

36. Nicholas Kralev, "State Doubles Military Advisors," *Washington Times*, January 18, 2008, 1.

37. Murdock and Flournoy, *Beyond Goldwater-Nichols*, 55–57.

38. Amy Belasco, *The Cost of Iraq, Afghanistan, and Other Global War on Terror Operations since 9/11*, RL33110 (Washington, DC: Congressional Research Service, December 8, 2014), 5.

39. Sara Thannhauser and Christoff Luehrs, "The Human and Financial Costs of Operations in Afghanistan and Iraq," Annex A, in *Lessons Encountered: Learning from the Long War*, ed. Richard D. Hooker and Joseph J. Collins (Washington, DC: National Defense University Press, September 2015), 421–40. These figures include deaths that occurred outside Iraq or Afghanistan, but were related to operations in those nations, as in the case of those who sustained wounds in Iraq and subsequently died in the United States.

40. Ryan C. Crocker, "Report to U.S. House of Representatives on the Situation in Iraq: Ambassador Crocker," Joint Hearing of the Committee of Foreign Affairs and the Committee on Armed Services, September 10, 2007, 1, https://2001-2009.state.gov/p/nea/rls/rm/2007/91941.htm.

41. An ABC News/Washington Post Poll taken October 15–18, 2015, asked people about this statement: "As you may know, Obama has halted the withdrawal of U.S. forces from Afghanistan, saying the current force of 9,800 troops will remain in place through most of next year, and 5,500 will stay into 2017." Of those surveyed, 50 percent supported the stated policy, 39 percent opposed it, and 12 percent were unsure. See http://www.pollingreport.com/afghan.htm.

42. See Isaiah Wilson III, *Thinking beyond War: Civil-Military Operations and Why America Fails to Win the Peace* (New York: Palgrave Macmillan, 2013).

43. Colin Powell, *My American Journey* (New York: Random House, 1995), 576–77.

44. Joint Chiefs of Staff, *Joint Publication 3-07: Stability* (Washington, DC: Government Printing Office, October 17, 2007), x.

45. Joint Chiefs of Staff, *Joint Publication 1: Doctrine for the Armed Forces of the United States* (Washington, DC: Department of Defense, October 17, 2007), 1–16.

46. Gary Cecchine et al., *The U.S. Military Response to the 2010 Haiti Earthquake: Considerations for Army Leaders* (Santa Monica, CA: RAND, 2013).

47. Joint Chiefs of Staff, *Joint Publication 3-07.3: Peace Operations* (Washington, DC: Department of Defense, August 1, 2012), vii.

48. Joint Chiefs of Staff, *Joint Publication 3-07.3*, viii.

49. As quoted in Joint Chiefs of Staff, *Joint Publication 3-07.3*, II-1.

17

Nuclear Policy

Throughout the Cold War, nuclear weapons formed the backbone of Western defense policy. The United States and its NATO allies, unable to fully match the conventional military strength of the former Soviet Union and the Warsaw Pact, used the threat of nuclear escalation to help avert what US policy makers saw as a serious risk of Soviet military adventurism, as well as to deter the use of the Soviet nuclear arsenal. In support of this policy, the United States and its allies built tens of thousands of strategic and tactical nuclear weapons and deployed them throughout Europe, in Korea, and at sea. The policy was fraught with risks—some believed that the nuclear arms race placed the very survival of the human race in jeopardy—but Western leaders thought that the threat justified those risks.

In the years since the end of the Cold War, the Soviet nuclear threat has been replaced by a range of challenges posed by new and aspiring nuclear weapon states, including North Korea, Iran, Pakistan, and India, as well as by nonstate actors looking to acquire a nuclear device to strike at Western targets. Particularly in the case of nonstate actors, US strategic planners confront potential adversaries that most analysts believe cannot be deterred or contained by threats of nuclear reprisal, but that might inflict catastrophic damage if they were able to use a nuclear weapon. This chapter considers the catastrophic threat of nuclear weapons (shown in the lower right box, figure 13.1 in chapter 13) and policies designed to prevent the spread of nuclear weapons to actors who might use them against the United States or its allies.

US Nuclear Strategy during the Cold War

As the leader of the free world during the Cold War, the United States acted as the principal guardian against communist expansionism. The American nuclear arsenal served as the linchpin of containment by providing military strength and deterrence essential to US and NATO conventional military strength and political unity. On many occasions the United States enunciated or endorsed doctrines explicitly relying on the threat of nuclear war to achieve US strategic aims (see chapter 3). The vast US nuclear arsenal included more than 12,000 strategic warheads, thousands of tactical nuclear weapons at locations throughout Europe and the Far East, extremely accurate counterforce weapons targeted at Soviet missile sites, the satellites and command systems to help guide them, and heavy bombers built specifically to penetrate enemy airspace. The United States spent trillions of dollars on the strategic triad—a combination of nuclear missiles, bombers, and submarines—that comprised the US nuclear posture. That nuclear posture was designed to accomplish one key goal: to ensure a stable system that minimized the probability of nuclear conflict. How this stability was maintained varied over time depending on the strategic theory employed and the relative strengths and weaknesses of the US nuclear triad.

Nuclear Deterrence. US policy throughout the Cold War reflected two basic strategic theories to deter an opponent from initiating a nuclear war. Initially, a concept known as "assured destruction" held that, so long as one side is seen as capable of responding in kind to a nuclear attack, it will deter aggressive action by the other. Nuclear targeting policy threatened civilian targets, such as cities and industries, in what is called a *countervalue* approach to targeting. A countervalue strategy does not require a large or extremely accurate nuclear arsenal; it needs only to ensure that any attack could be met by an unacceptably high level of retaliatory punishment. Any aggressor state would recognize that an attack would be suicidal and would therefore be deterred from initiating it. Assured destruction requires a secure second-strike capability—that is, a nuclear force capable of withstanding an enemy attack and responding.

When both sides achieve this critical capability, a situation known as *mutually assured destruction*, or MAD, would exist. Neither side could rationally begin a war because each would be vulnerable to planned and credible retaliation. The emphasis on credibility requires not merely the existence of nuclear weapons, but the command, control, training, and exercising of nuclear weapon delivery systems sufficient to convince an adversary that it would suffer retaliation if it initiated a nuclear attack.

A second strategic approach, known as a counterforce or warfighting nuclear strategy, is more ambitious than a countervalue or assured destruction approach. *Counterforce*, defined as "the ability to destroy an adversary's nuclear weapons before they can be used," is intended to deter an opponent whose leaders might otherwise believe that a nuclear war could be fought and won.[1] Military capability must go beyond retaliation and be able to prevail over an opponent in a nuclear conflict.[2] Counterforce strikes could be aimed at either nuclear or non-nuclear targets, such as command and control nodes or radar sites, but the concept is most commonly associated with counter-nuclear strikes. A counterforce strategy aims to destroy an opponent's nuclear weapons prior to their launch, limiting its ability to execute a second strike. This constitutes a *first-strike* capability; in other words, the state has the ability to execute an attack, potentially without fear of retaliation. Under the MAD policy of the Cold War, a counterforce policy created a dilemma: if a state were able to generate a counterforce capability, an opposing state's nuclear retaliatory capability would be rendered unusable. Therefore, if the United States were to develop a counterforce capability, this would give the Soviet Union an incentive to strike before the US counterforce capability could become operational. Rather than serving as a deterrent, therefore, a counterforce capability could destabilize the nuclear balance.

One common analogy for the nuclear superpowers during the Cold War portrayed two individuals with guns pointed at each other's heads. Assured destruction would have each side merely watch and wait, with the warning that it would pull the trigger if the other side did. Counterforce advocates maintained that such a mutual suicide pact might not be credible, arguing that instead each side must be prepared to win a gun duel rather than merely return fire. The distinction is between deterrence by threat of punishment and deterrence by displaying the capability to win a nuclear conflict. Fortunately, strategic nuclear policy during the Cold War successfully avoided a devastating duel for over forty years. However, the legacy of nuclear weapons and competing conceptions of deterrence still affect twenty-first century security challenges.

US Nuclear Policy after the Cold War

The end of the Cold War brought the demise of the previous central focus of US nuclear policy—the Soviet Union—and necessitated reexamination of the role of nuclear weapons in contemporary US national security policy. There are two distinct yet related issues for consideration by US strategic planners today. The first concerns the threats created by the proliferation of nuclear weapons technology to additional states or to nonstate actors. The second is the need to identify the nuclear capabilities that will most effectively enhance US national security in the current strategic environment. The two issues are related, in that the success of US efforts against nuclear proliferation may be affected by the approach that the United States takes towards the development of its own nuclear arsenal and concepts governing its potential use.

Current and Future Threats. While the end of the Cold War diminished the threat of an all-out nuclear war involving the United States, the threat of nuclear weapons, possessed by a handful of states and coveted by other states and nonstate actors, remains significant. Consideration of some of these states illustrates the complexity and interconnected nature of US nuclear policy.

Russia. At present, Russia still possesses the capability to destroy the United States with its nuclear arsenal in a matter of hours. However, despite recurring tensions in relations between the two countries, few observers believe that Russia intends to wage war against the United States or that it poses as significant a military threat to NATO or other US allies, as it did during the Cold War (see chapter 22). For many experts, concern over the potential for nuclear conflict has been rivaled by the potentially greater threat from the deteriorating condition of the Russian nuclear arsenal. Russia's nuclear forces were not exempt from the general collapse that occurred in the rest of the country's armed forces. Stories of broken equipment, lax security, Strategic Rocket Forces personnel unpaid for months at a time, and rumored attempts at black-market sales of nuclear warheads became commonplace by the late 1990s. Many analysts believe that the greatest threat from Russia now stems not from deliberate government action, but rather from a condition of "nuclear anarchy," in which a lack of effective control could lead to an accidental, unintentional, or unauthorized use of nuclear weapons.[3] In both 2006 and 2011, the director of national intelligence reported to Congress that the United States could not determine the amount of material that had been lost since the dissolution of the Soviet Union, and that undetected smuggling of weapons-grade material had occurred.[4]

China. As of 2016, China's nuclear arsenal remains modest, with several hundred nuclear warheads.[5] Chinese delivery options include fifty to sixty intercontinental ballistic missiles (ICBMs), an unknown number of submarine-launched ballistic missiles that could be based on China's four nuclear ballistic-missile submarines, and several other intermediate-range missiles, gravity bombs, and tactical nuclear weapons. To counteract US and other countries' defense systems, China is developing multiple technologies such as maneuvering reentry vehicles, decoys, chaff, jamming, and thermal shielding.[6]

During the Cold War, China never sought to match the nuclear arsenals of the United States or the Soviet Union, nor does it do so today. Instead, China follows a strategic policy of *minimum deterrence.* It maintains a force structure large enough to survive an attack and to respond with sufficient strength to destroy a number of major cities of any state that attacked its homeland, thereby inflicting "unacceptable damage on the enemy."[7] The question remains whether Chinese military leaders will continue to be content with this approach or will seek to expand their nuclear arsenal to achieve parity with the United States and Russia. China's current nuclear plans, like those for the rest of the People's Liberation Army, points to more of the same; it has declared a preference for modernizing its small force rather than increasing its size. However, the US development of increased force-projection capacity, intended to maintain access to the western Pacific, may prompt further Chinese development of ballistic missile technology.

North Korea. On October 9, 2006, North Korea detonated its first nuclear device. This detonation came after years of diplomacy among six parties: the United States,

North Korea, South Korea, China, Japan, and Russia. Throughout the diplomatic process, North Korea made promises not to pursue nuclear weapons, but continued to do so in secret. After that first test, North Korean continued its weapons development with five additional tests—in 2009, 2013, two in 2016, and one in 2017.[8] Each test increased in power, with the 2017 test potentially exceeding one hundred kilotons—more than six times larger than the US bomb dropped on Hiroshima in 1945. The US intelligence community estimated that North Korea had up to sixty nuclear weapons and had the technology to miniaturize nuclear weapons so that they could fit inside a ballistic missile.[9] North Korea successfully tested intercontinental ballistic missiles (ICBMs) in July and November 2017, which demonstrated the capacity to reach the continental United States with the Hwasong-15 ICBM.[10] In spite of the potential to threaten the US mainland, likely targets of a North Korean nuclear weapon would be South Korea, Japan, or US forces deployed in the region.

One worrisome side effect of a nuclear North Korea is the specter of a nuclear arms race in Asia. It is possible that both South Korea and Japan would want to acquire nuclear weapons to deter a North Korean attack. If South Korea or Japan acquired nuclear weapons, China might seek to develop more robust nuclear capabilities in response. A destabilizing arms race could spread beyond the immediate region and engulf much of Asia.

India and Pakistan. In 1998, both India and Pakistan conducted underground nuclear tests and became declared nuclear weapon states. This situation raises at least three significant concerns. First, relations between the two states are still marked by tensions—particularly over the contested region of Kashmir—and they have already fought one war with each other since becoming nuclear powers (see chapter 19).[11] Second, the nuclear programs of these states could become a source of proliferation of nuclear technologies to other states or to nonstate actors. In November 2013, for example, the British Broadcasting Corporation reported that Saudi Arabia had invested in Pakistani nuclear weapons development programs and might seek to purchase a weapon to counter Iran's nuclear weapons program.[12] Third, domestic political instability—particularly in Pakistan—could result in risky nuclear posturing or loss of control over the country's nuclear arsenal, constituting another possible source of "nuclear anarchy." The bilateral relationship between India and Pakistan, as well as their nuclear postures, will continue to raise serious concerns for national security policy makers.

Iran. Preventing Iran from obtaining a nuclear weapon has been a consistent US policy objective for the past two decades, but the approach toward that objective has varied widely. Iran had successfully pursued nuclear weapons in secret for nearly twenty years until 2002, when the National Council of Resistance of Iran provided information on nuclear activities at Natanz and Arak. Despite conducting its nuclear research in secret, Iran claimed that its nuclear ambitions were peaceful, and that nuclear energy would be required to meet rising domestic energy requirements.[13] The November 2007 US National Intelligence Estimate (NIE) on Iranian nuclear intentions and capabilities reported that Iranian military entities had been "working under government direction to develop nuclear weapons" until the fall of 2003, when they stopped their nuclear weapons program "in response to international pressure."[14] The NIE judged that if Iran's policy changed again, it could restart the nuclear program and could produce a nuclear weapon between 2010 and 2015. In 2013, the Director of National Intelligence, James R. Clapper, stated that Iran was developing nuclear capabilities to enhance its regional power and influence.[15] Iran currently possesses a limited ballistic missile capability, as well as a burgeoning space program, both prerequisites for the development of an ICBM. Iran views the development of nuclear capability as key to its ability to project power and to deter outside intervention in the region.

The United States and the international community have applied a series of increasingly expansive and effective sanctions to address Iran's actions, beginning soon after the seizure of the US embassy in Tehran in 1979. Since the 1990s, these sanctions have increasingly focused on the Iranian energy sector. Both Democratic and Republican administrations have approved these sanctions; some have been implemented by presidential order, others have been imposed by congressional action, and many have been coordinated with the international community.[16] After continued, increasing, and effective pressure on the Iranian economy, in November 2013, the Iranian government agreed to a "Joint Plan of Action" that "would halt progress on Iran's nuclear program and roll it back in key respects" in exchange for temporary relief from sanctions. After eighteen months of negotiations, on July 14, 2015, the United States along with China, France, Germany, Russia, the United Kingdom, and the European Union finalized a "Joint Comprehensive Plan of Action" with Iran that "will ensure that Iran's nuclear programme will be exclusively peaceful, and [under which] Iran reaffirms that under no circumstances will Iran ever seek, develop or acquire any nuclear weapons."[17] President Obama and other supporters argued that this long-sought and historic agreement rolls back current nuclear programs and prevents future Iranian nuclear developments for at least the ten years specified in the treaty. Opponents of the treaty, including President Donald Trump in his statements during the 2016 presidential campaign, have argued that it removes sanctions while not going far enough to restrict Iran's nuclear ambitions, support of terrorism, or other actions that are inimical to American interests. Debate will likely continue over whether this agreement is a success in nuclear nonproliferation or instead an unwise concession facilitating increased Iranian power throughout the region.

The stakes are high because a nuclear Iran could initiate a nuclear arms race in the region. Threatening statements from Iranian leaders raise particular concerns for Israel.[18] Should Iran complete, or even nearly complete, a nuclear device, Israel might decide to take action similar to the 1981 Israeli air force preemptive strike against the Osiraq nuclear reactor in Iraq. A Shiite Iran with nuclear weapons could threaten Sunni Arab states; these states might take collective military action against Iran or pursue their own nuclear weapons with funding from their extensive oil wealth. Such fears are reflected in Saudi Arabia's potential acquisition of Pakistani nuclear technology. Terrorist groups operating in the region, such as Hezbollah, Hamas, and ISIL, increase the possibility that terrorists might gain access to nuclear weapons. Some of the most dangerous people in the world could become armed with the most dangerous weapons in the world. Each of these potential occurrences highlights the importance of controlling any potential Iranian nuclear program.

Nonstate Actors. The rise of terrorism in the post–Cold War era has been marked by an increase in violence towards nonmilitary targets. Many terrorism experts agree that nuclear weapons would exacerbate this trend (see chapter 15). The obstacles that hinder a terrorist organization such as al Qaeda or ISIL from attaining a nuclear capability include difficulties in acquiring, securing, maintaining, transporting, and detonating a nuclear weapon. The more likely scenario would be for a nonstate actor to acquire sufficient radiological and explosive material to fashion a radiological dispersion device, commonly referred to as a *dirty bomb*, for use against targets in the United States or elsewhere.[19] This type of device, easier to acquire, transport, and use than a nuclear weapon, could inflict significant physical and psychological damage.

Managing the Nuclear Challenge in a New Era. As this brief survey reflects, the challenges to US national security created by nuclear technology have become much more diverse in the twenty-first century. US policy makers can no longer focus on the threat posed by a single rival superpower, but must seek effective ways to minimize the threat posed by new nuclear weapon states as well as nonstate actors. Traditional nuclear deterrence strategy must be supplemented with other tools of foreign policy such as arms control and nonproliferation strategies.

Arms Control. In 1961, the United States established the Arms Control and Disarmament Agency (ACDA) to advise the president on arms control and to build expertise on negotiated measures for dealing with international conflict. When the United States was focused on the problems of military strategy and international conflict in a nuclear age, *arms control* was defined as having three purposes: to reduce the likelihood of war by enhancing communication and crisis stability; to limit the damage if war were to occur; and to reduce the economic burdens of preparing for war.[20] These purposes continue, but between 1997 and 1999, ACDA was dissolved as an independent agency, and its bureaus and functions were incorporated into the State Department.

During the Cold War, arms control agreements were an important component of US nuclear policy. They can be grouped into three broad categories: confidence-building measures, restrictions on the development of weapons, and limitations on the weapons themselves. Examples of *confidence-building measures* include the "Hot Line Agreement" of 1963, which established a direct communications link between the leaders of the United States and the Soviet Union, or the on-site inspections by foreign teams instituted by the 1986 Stockholm Conference on Confidence and Security-Building Measures and Disarmament in Europe. Examples of *testing restrictions* include the 1963 Limited Test Ban Treaty, which banned nuclear tests in the atmosphere, outer space, and under water, and the 1974 Threshold Test Ban Treaty, which committed the superpowers to limit the size of underground nuclear weapons tests. *Weapons limitations* include the Nuclear Nonproliferation Treaty (NPT, 1970), discussed below; the Strategic Arms Limitation Talks (SALT I), which constrained certain offensive strategic systems (1972); the Anti–Ballistic Missile (ABM) Treaty, which limited the superpowers' development of defensive capabilities (1972); SALT II (1979), which sought to begin arms reductions between the superpowers (although the US Senate never ratified it, the United States followed its restrictions throughout the 1980s); the Intermediate Nuclear Forces (INF) Treaty, which eliminated US and Soviet intermediate range nuclear systems (1989); and the Strategic Arms Reduction Treaty (START), which reduced US and Soviet deployed nuclear forces and established robust verification measures (1991).

Since the end of the Cold War and the dissolution of the Soviet Union, bilateral arms control has continued in a more limited way. In May 2002, US President George W. Bush and Russian President Vladimir Putin signed the Strategic Offensive Reductions Treaty (SORT, or the "Treaty of Moscow"), which committed each side to reducing its forces to not more than 2,200 operationally deployed warheads by the end of 2012. SORT critics noted its lack of verification measures and that it allowed the storage rather than destruction of warheads not operationally deployed. Consequently, in 2010 President Obama and then-President Dmitry Medvedev signed Measures for the Further Reduction and Limitation of Strategic Offensive Arms, known as the New START Treaty, in Prague. New START became a replacement for SORT in February 2011; it reduced the number of nuclear weapons and launchers and established new verification and transparency measures between the two countries. This new treaty's duration is ten years, taking it to 2021, unless it is extended or superseded by a subsequent agreement.[21] Although President Trump has publicly criticized the New START Treaty, he has not taken formal steps to change or abrogate it.[22]

Further considerations for the US-Russia nuclear relationship include US withdrawal from the Anti–Ballistic Missile (ABM) Treaty in 2002, a US focus on ship-based rather than ground-based missile systems, and efforts to locate missile-defense radar stations internationally. From the US perspective, these initiatives recognize the end of the Cold War and the existence of new threats—such as the possibility of Iranian missile launches—in a new strategic environment. However, Russian officials have repeatedly expressed concern about these developments and future US intentions. According to one Russian foreign ministry statement, "One cannot ignore the fact that US offensive weapons, combined with the missile defense being created, can turn into a strategic complex capable of delivering an incapacitating blow."[23] After Putin returned to the Russian presidency in 2012, he expressed openness to arms control as a key issue on the global agenda, and the sentiment was echoed by President Obama in a major policy speech at the Brandenburg Gate in Berlin in 2013.[24] Nevertheless, given challenges posed by Russia in Eastern Europe and elsewhere, the next steps in this complex and evolving bilateral relationship remain uncertain.

Nuclear Nonproliferation Treaty. The most significant multilateral agreement regarding nuclear weapons is the Treaty on the Nonproliferation of Nuclear Weapons. Commonly referred to as the NPT, it was signed by the United States in 1968 and entered into force in 1970. Its three "pillars" include nuclear nonproliferation, disarmament, and the peaceful uses of nuclear energy. The treaty calls for a review by signatories every five years to monitor and evaluate performance. As of 2018, 191 states were party to the treaty, including five recognized nuclear weapons states (China, France, Russia, the United Kingdom, and the United States).[25] Nonsignatory states include India, Israel, Pakistan, and South Sudan. North Korea withdrew from the NPT in 2003, prompting condemnation and sanctions from the UN Security Council for violations including testing nuclear devices.[26] India, Pakistan, and North Korea openly possess nuclear weapons, while Israel remains an undeclared nuclear weapons state.

The NPT commits the non–nuclear weapon states to not build or use nuclear weapons, and it commits the nuclear weapon states—the five states that had exploded a nuclear device by January 1, 1967—to the eventual elimination of their own weapons. In addition, all parties to the NPT agree to accept International Atomic Energy Agency (IAEA) safeguards on all nuclear activities; to not export nuclear equipment or materials to non–nuclear weapons states except under IAEA safeguards; and to give notice ninety days before withdrawing from the NPT (only North Korea has withdrawn).[27] The NPT has played an important role in limiting the spread of nuclear weapons to just the four additional states in the five decades since its inception. (South Africa had a nuclear weapons program from 1977–1989, but later dismantled the program; it signed the NPT in 1991.)[28] The relatively small growth in nuclear weapons states is particularly impressive in light of the fact that the NPT has no means of punishing those that violate its provisions, aside from referring the matter to the UN Security Council.

The NPT is the centerpiece of the global nonproliferation regime, but it is criticized by some in the international community. One tension derives from the fact that the NPT enshrined the status of the five nuclear weapon states, which some perceive as preserving their long-term military dominance. This concern is partially mitigated by the commitment of the recognized nuclear weapon states to eventual disarmament by signing the NPT. However, they are regularly criticized "for not disarming fast enough and [for] abandoning nuclear arms control, increasing reliance on nuclear weapons, and especially for developing new types of weapons."[29] A second source of tension relates to compliance. The inability of IAEA inspectors to monitor potential Iraqi nuclear production adequately prior to the Iraq war in 2003 and Iranian nuclear production prior to the 2015 treaty raises questions about the ability of the international community to enforce NPT provisions.

Cooperative Threat Reduction. In November 1991, in response to deteriorating conditions in the Soviet Union, the US Senate passed the bipartisan Nunn-Lugar Cooperative Threat Reduction Act, with the intent "to assist the states of the former Soviet Union in dismantling weapons of mass destruction (WMD) and establishing verifiable safeguards against the proliferation of those weapons."[30] The objectives of Cooperative Threat Reduction (CTR), housed within the Defense Threat Reduction Agency (DTRA), are fourfold:

- Dismantle the former Soviet Union's weapons of mass destruction, and concomitant infrastructure;
- Consolidate and secure weapons, and related materials and technology;
- Increase transparency; and
- Support international cooperation to prevent proliferation.[31]

Initial support included assisting in the transport of nuclear warheads from Kazakhstan, Ukraine, and Belarus back to Russia; converting the Soviet-era method of tracking nuclear warheads from a time-consuming and often inaccurate manual system to a rapid, automated system; and providing upgraded security equipment at weapons storage sites.[32]

In addition to securing nuclear weapons, CTR efforts focused on securing the material that would be necessary to construct a nuclear weapon. Russia still possesses the world's largest stock of fissile material (highly enriched uranium and plutonium).[33] The need to keep this material out of the hands of terrorists became more urgent after the events of September 11, 2001. In response, DTRA has expanded programs beyond the former Soviet Union to South Asia, Iraq, Afghanistan, and China, as well as to African nations such as Djibouti, Kenya, South Africa, and Uganda.[34] A 2012 Belfer Center for Science and International Affairs progress report explains that "many of the world's highest-risk nuclear stocks are either receiving significant security improvements or have been eliminated entirely. The risk of [future] nuclear theft and terrorism is lower as a result . . . but major challenges remain."[35]

The Proliferation Security Initiative. Originally launched in 2003, the Proliferation Security Initiative (PSI) is a global effort to stop the international shipment of nuclear weapons, weapons materials, and related technology. The focus of PSI is on interdicting nuclear materials during transit between the country of origin and the country or nonstate actor that is the intended recipient. States that are party to PSI voluntarily agree to provide intelligence, law enforcement, and diplomatic cooperation to combat the spread of nuclear weapons, utilizing force if necessary. Membership in the PSI and the types and levels of participation by the signatories are not widely publicized because of the political sensitivity of these activities.

Reviews of the effectiveness of the PSI are mixed. On the one hand, it has raised awareness of illicit trafficking in WMD-related materials, has probably constrained traffickers, and has "increased national capacities for coordinated detection and interdiction of suspect shipments" through its exercises.[36] On the other hand, the initiative is characterized by a lack of transparency, which reflects the political sensitivity of interdiction activities and the ambiguous status of such interdiction under international law. These characteristics of the PSI make its potential success difficult to verify.[37]

Missile Defense

Given the security challenges posed by nuclear weapons, as well as the difficulty faced by each of the approaches mentioned above in meeting those challenges, a perennial concern is the development of an effective defense against nuclear weapons. This has been an issue since the development of nuclear weapons and has become increasingly important with the advent of missile defense technology.

During the superpower rivalry of the Cold War, the United States accepted limits on the creation of anti–ballistic missile defenses by becoming a party to the 1972 ABM Treaty. In doing so, the United States acknowledged the situation of mutually assured destruction and accepted its own vulnerability as necessary to preserving stability in its nuclear competition with the Soviet Union. The first significant challenge to this posture came in January 1984, when President Ronald Reagan issued National Security Decision Directive (NSDD) 119. The purpose of NSDD 119 was to establish the Strategic Defense Initiative (which became known as "Star Wars") to "investigate the feasibility of eventually shifting toward reliance upon a defensive concept. Future deterrence should, if possible, be underwritten by a capability to defeat a hostile attack."[38] The original proposal has evolved since its inception because of budgetary constraints, the evolution of technology, and the changing nature of global threats.

A test for missile defense technology came during the 1991 Gulf War with Iraq. US Patriot missiles were deployed against incoming Iraqi SCUD missiles aimed at Saudi Arabia and Israel. Although the SCUD missiles carried only conventional warheads and were often inaccurate, and the Patriot missiles had limited success in actually defeating the SCUD missiles, these engagements demonstrated the possibility of defeating ballistic missiles while in flight. Subsequent administrations have continued to explore missile defense.

In 2002, President George W. Bush directed the Department of Defense to develop a Ballistic Missile Defense System (BMDS) as a layered "system of systems" designed to destroy ballistic missiles in each of three stages of flight: the boost phase, the mid-course phase, and the terminal phase.[39] Under President Barack Obama, the US Defense Department request to Congress for the fiscal 2015 budget included $8.3 billion for BMDS over the subsequent five years, with nearly $1 billion to fund a new homeland defense radar in Alaska.[40] This emphasis on missile defense increased with President Trump's 2019 budget request, which included $12.9 billion for missile defense overall and $9.9 billion in fiscal year 2019 for BMDS.[41]

The Case for Ballistic Missile Defense. The primary reason for the United States to acquire a defense against ballistic missiles is to secure and sustain stability throughout the international community. Considerations include the threat posed by hostile states to the national security of the United States, the safety of deployed troops, and the security of US allies and interests abroad. According to a State Department report, some twenty-seven states possess or are in the process of obtaining ballistic missiles.[42] The report cites missile technology in North Korea and Iran as the greatest threat to the "US, its forces deployed abroad, and allies and friends."[43] US preeminence in world affairs, says the report, may cause its adversaries to seek ballistic missiles as a means to deliver chemical, biological, radiological, or nuclear weapons (CBRN). These adversaries would seek to use CBRN weapons to "deter the U.S. from intervening in, or leading coalitions against, their efforts at regional aggression, or these states may believe that such capabilities would give them the ability to threaten allied countries in order to dissuade them from joining such coalitions."[44] A viable BMDS would mitigate the threat posed by states or nonstate actors possessing ballistic missiles. A functioning antimissile capability could also protect the United States and its allies against an accidental nuclear launch by any other state.

The Case against Ballistic Missile Defense. Opponents argue that BMDS cannot protect the United States, provides a false sense of security, and requires great expenditures for a program of uncertain effectiveness. If BMDS were to work by destroying a hostile warhead with an interceptor, then the United States would need to launch multiple interceptors for every single hostile warhead. For example, the United States would need to launch far more than one thousand interceptors against one thousand incoming warheads, plus any decoy warheads or other countermeasures that would likely accompany any attack. Moreover, since the BMDS is a layered system of systems consisting of elements that acquire targets, computer systems to analyze the data, and interceptor missiles to destroy the incoming missiles, it is extremely difficult to test. Like the concept of mutually assured destruction, even if a very expensive missile defense might be effective in theory or in simulations, it would be difficult or impossible ever to know whether it would work in practice. Moreover, a successful strategic ballistic missile defense system could be problematic or even destabilizing: other states might perceive US strategic invulnerability as a permissive condition for greater US aggression against other states.

Two additional issues are opportunity cost and appropriateness to current threats. With regard to opportunity cost, investments in missile defense systems are likely to come at the expense of other defense or homeland security priorities, particularly when the United States faces constrained defense and homeland security budgets. A second and related issue concerns the nature of the threat: missiles are not the only CBRN threat. Thus, some analysts argue that other homeland security measures, such as cargo inspection at US ports, might actually be more effective than missile defense in providing protection against the most probable uses of CBRN in the United States.

The possibility of defensive weapons integrated into a system that reduces vulnerability will always be appealing, despite costs, technical challenges, and potential strategic ramifications. Thus, whether to deploy strategic or theater ballistic missile defenses, and if so, which kind of defense to deploy, will continue to be a central debate in US nuclear policy.

Toward a New Nuclear Posture and Strategy

The Department of Defense (DoD) periodically conducts a Nuclear Posture Review (NPR) to determine the role of nuclear weapons in US security strategy. Previous reviews were completed in 1994, 2002, and 2010. In January 2017, President Trump directed DoD to initiate a new NPR, which was released in February 2018. The report noted that "the United States remains committed to its efforts in support of the ultimate global elimination of nuclear, biological, and chemical weapons," and has deployed no new nuclear capabilities in over two decades while reducing its nuclear weapons stockpile by over 85 percent. However, the report observes, "global threat conditions have worsened markedly since the most recent 2010 NPR, including increasingly explicit nuclear threats from potential adversaries. . . . This rapid deterioration of the threat environment since the 2010 NPR must now shape our thinking as we formulate policy and strategy, and initiate the sustainment and replacement of U.S. nuclear forces."[45] The 2018 NPR calls for the modernization of Cold War legacy nuclear forces, command and control systems, laboratories, and other infrastructure.

Recognizing the evolving and uncertain international security environment, the NPR reaffirmed the critical role that US nuclear forces play in national security strategy. Nuclear forces contribute to:

- Deterrence of nuclear and non-nuclear attack;
- Assurance of allies and partners;
- Achievement of US objectives if deterrence fails; and
- Capacity to hedge against an uncertain future.[46]

In contrast to the objectives of the 2010 NPR, which included reducing the numbers of and the reliance on nuclear weapons as part of US national security strategy, the 2018 NPR has no such objectives. While recognizing the need to prevent proliferation and deny terrorists access to nuclear weapons, material, or expertise, the Trump administration has focused its nuclear strategy on threats from state actors, such as Russia, China, North Korea, and Iran.

Maintaining a credible "ultimate deterrent" by continuing to invest in nuclear weapons infrastructure will be costly. Secretary of Defense Jim Mattis estimates that, in addition to the 3 percent of the defense budget currently committed to nuclear weapons, an additional 3 to 4 percent will be required over a decade to replace aging systems.[47] For a variety of reasons, US spending on the development of its nuclear arsenal is viewed with a critical eye. Some argue that US investment in nuclear weapons—especially given the status of the arsenals of Russia and China—might be seen as an effort by the United States to obtain a threatening first-strike capability, rather than helping to maintain international stability and security.[48] Some policy advocates, concerned about the effect of continued US nuclear weapons development on arms control and nonproliferation efforts, argue that the current US nuclear arsenal is more than capable of meeting contemporary and future threats to national security. Others believe that the United States has a moral obligation not to pursue new nuclear technology, especially in light of its treaty obligations and its commitment to limiting the spread of nuclear weapons. Another argument relates to resources, with some analysts asserting that, rather than devoting money to researching and developing new nuclear weapons, spending it to secure "loose" nuclear weapons in the former Soviet Union or to fund other CTR programs would be more effective contributions to US national security.

The end of the Cold War reduced the profile of nuclear weapons in international politics, at least among the major powers. Currently, with Russia and China modernizing their nuclear arsenals, North Korea joining the "nuclear club," and the recent US NPR calling for the revitalization of US nuclear weapons, the role of nuclear weapons will again become more important. Whether it reaches the prominent status observed during the Cold War is an open question.

Looking Ahead

After the end of the Cold War, the United States faced a new strategic environment in which the specific characteristics of its nuclear arsenal became less relevant. Policy makers and analysts concerned with diverse new challenges—such as the threat of cross-border networks of nonstate actors—had been able to devote less attention to matters of nuclear policy. As a result, significant reductions in the US nuclear arsenal since the end of the Cold War have not received much attention in national security policy discussions. Even the Trump administration's NPR, which indicated a major change in policy, received relatively limited attention in policy circles or in the media.

The serious issues that the United States must address in this area would likely benefit from a vigorous and broad-ranging debate, which thus far has been lacking. National security policy makers will have to think carefully about the characteristics of the nuclear arsenal the United States still needs, keeping in mind the impact that these choices may have on stability, arms control, and nonproliferation efforts. A modernized American arsenal may be necessary, but these changes might need to be accompanied by more energetic and effective US leadership in multilateral disarmament efforts to support overall nuclear policy.

The vision of a world in which nuclear weapons play a diminishing and ultimately nonexistent role has had broad worldwide appeal for decades. The extent to which this vision is achievable, and the extent to which the United States should pursue it, are issues US policy makers will continue to confront in the years ahead.

Discussion Questions

1. What is the difference between a countervalue and a counterforce nuclear strategy? Which strategy requires more nuclear weapons? Which strategy would better suit US national security needs? Why?
2. What is counter-proliferation? What is nonproliferation? What are the similarities and differences between the two policies?
3. Will traditional methods of deterrence used during the Cold War work against modern adversaries such as Iran and North Korea and nonstate actors such as al Qaeda or ISIL? Why or why not?
4. Which poses the greater threat to US security: possession of nuclear weapons by "rogue" states (such as North Korea and Iran) or by nonstate actors (such as al Qaeda, ISIL, or cyberterrorists)? Why?
5. Has the Nuclear Nonproliferation Treaty been a success, or does the spread of weapons to at least four more states since 1970 constitute a failure?
6. How does North Korea's acquisition of nuclear weapons impact security in Asia?
7. To what extent has the threat posed by Iran's nuclear program been diminished by the 2015 nuclear deal with Iran? What are the long-term implications of the treaty for nuclear weapons in the Middle East?
8. Should the United States focus its efforts on preventing the spread of nuclear weapons, or on developing the capabilities to defend itself and its allies from a nuclear attack?
9. What is the role of nuclear weapons in US defense policy today? Should the United States develop new nuclear weapons as new threats emerge? Why or why not?
10. With respect to adherence to nuclear treaties, how might the international community balance issues of transparency with issues of sovereignty?

Recommended Reading

Ball, Desmond, and Jeffrey Richelson, eds. *Strategic Nuclear Targeting.* Ithaca, NY: Cornell University Press, 1986.

Campbell, Kurt M., Robert J. Einhorn, and Mitchell B. Reiss, eds. *The Nuclear Tipping Point: Why States Reconsider Their Nuclear Choices.* Washington, DC: Brookings Institution Press, 2004.

Cirincione, Joseph. *Nuclear Nightmares: Securing the World Before It Is Too Late.* New York: Columbia University Press, 2015.

Gavin, Francis J. *Nuclear Statecraft: History and Strategy in America's Atomic Age.* Ithaca, NY: Cornell University Press, 2012.

Lieber, Keir A., and Daryl G. Press. "The End of MAD? The Nuclear Dimension of U.S. Primacy." *International Security* 30, no. 4 (2006): 7–44.

Nolan, Janne E., Bernard I. Finel, and Brian D. Finlay, eds. *Ultimate Security: Combating Weapons of Mass Destruction.* New York: Century Foundation Press, 2003.

Office of the Secretary of Defense. *Nuclear Posture Review.* Washington, DC: Department of Defense, February 2018.

Sagan, Scott D., and Kenneth N. Waltz. *The Spread of Nuclear Weapons: An Enduring Debate.* New York: W. W. Norton, 2012.

The White House. *National Strategy to Combat Weapons of Mass Destruction.* Washington, DC: The White House, December 2002.

Recommended Internet Resources

The Arms Control Association, www.armscontrol.org
Carnegie Endowment for Peace, www.carnegieendowment.org
The International Atomic Energy Agency, www.iaea.org
The Missile Defense Agency, www.mda.mil
The Nuclear Age Peace Foundation, www.nuclearfiles.org
The Nuclear Threat Initiative, www.nti.org
The Programme for Promoting Nuclear Non-Proliferation, www.ppnn.soton.ac.uk

Notes

1. Keir A. Lieber and Daryl G. Press, "The Nukes We Need," *Foreign Affairs* 88, no. 6 (2009): 39–61, http://www.foreignaffairs.com/articles/65481/keir-a-lieber-and-daryl-g-press/the-nukes-we-need.

2. Lieber and Press, "The Nukes We Need."

3. Bruce G. Blair, "Lengthening the Fuse," *Brookings Review* 13, no. 3 (1995): 28–31.

4. National Intelligence Council, "2006 Annual Report to Congress on the Safety and Security of Russian Nuclear Facilities and Military Forces," https://www.fas.org/irp/nic/russia0406.html; National Intelligence Council, "2011 Annual Report to Congress on the Safety and Security of Russian Nuclear Facilities and Military Forces," http://fas.org/irp/nic/russia-2011.pdf.

5. Estimates of the number of Chinese nuclear weapons vary widely; a recent commander of US Strategic Command estimated that the Chinese arsenal is "in the range of several hundred weapons," while others put the number in the thousands. See Hans M. Kristensen, "STRATCOM Commander Rejects High Estimates for Chinese Nuclear Arsenal," August 22, 2012, http://fas.org/blogs/security/2012/08/china-nukes.

6. Department of Defense, *Military and Security Developments Involving the People's Republic of China 2015*, November 1, 2015, http://www.defense.gov/Portals/1/Documents/pubs/2015_China_Military_Power_Report.pdf.

7. Department of Defense, *Military and Security Developments*, 31.

8. Eleanor Albert, "North Korea's Military Capabilities," *Council on Foreign Relations Backgrounder*, January 3, 2018, https://www.cfr.org/backgrounder/north-koreas-military-capabilities.

9. Joby Warrick, Ellen Nakashima, and Anna Fifield, "North Korea Now Making Missile-Ready Nuclear Weapons, U.S. Analysts Say," *Washington Post*, August 8, 2017.

10. Eleanor Albert, "North Korea's Military Capabilities."

11. S. Paul Kapur, "Nuclear Proliferation, the Kargil Conflict, and South Asian Security," *Security Studies* 13, no. 1 (2003): 80.

12. Mark Urban, "Saudi Nuclear Weapons 'On Order' from Pakistan," BBC.com, November 6, 2013, http://www.bbc.com/news/world-middle-east-24823846.

13. Sharon Squassoni, *Iran's Nuclear Program: Recent Developments*, RS21592 (Washington, DC: Congressional Research Service, September 6, 2006), 2.

14. National Intelligence Council, *Iran: Nuclear Intentions and Capabilities* (Washington, DC: Director of National Intelligence, November 2007), 6.

15. James R. Clapper, Director of National Intelligence, *Worldwide Threat Assessment of the US Intelligence Community*, March 12, 2013, https://www.dni.gov/index.php/newsroom/testimonies/217-congressional-testimonies-2016/1313-statement-for-the-record-worldwide-threat-assessment-of-the-u-s-ic-before-the-senate-armed-services-committee-2016.

16. Kenneth Katzman, *Iran Sanctions*, CRS Report RS20971 (Washington, DC: Congressional Research Service, December 2, 2011).

17. *Joint Comprehensive Plan of Action*, July 14, 2015, 1, https://www.state.gov/documents/organization/245317.pdf.

18. In 2005, Iranian President Mahmoud Ahmadinejad reportedly threatened that Iran would "wipe Israel off the map." Subsequent analysis of the translation raises questions about whether that is exactly what he said, but enough statements have been made by senior Iranian leaders to give Israel reason to believe that Iran could have the intention to attack if it had nuclear weapons capability. See Carl Herman, "Iran to 'Wipe Israel off the Map'?" Washington's Blog, March 9, 2015, http://www.washingtonsblog.com/2015/03/iran-wipe-israel-map-read-600-words-confirm-usisrael-criminal-war-lies.html.

19. Charles D. Ferguson and William C. Potter, "Improvised Nuclear Devices and Nuclear Terrorism," the Weapons of Mass Destruction Commission, Paper Number 2, 17, 2004, http://www.wmdcommision.org.

20. US Arms Control and Disarmament Agency (ACDA), *Arms Control Report* (Washington, DC: ACDA, 1976), 3. See also Bernard Brodie, "On the Objectives of Arms Control," *International Security* 1, no. 1 (1976): 17–36.

21. Department of State, *New Strategic Arms Reduction Treaty* (Washington, DC, 2010), http://www.state.gov/t/avc/newstart/index.htm.

22. Andrei Akulov, "President Trump Decries New START Treaty," *Strategic Culture* (Online Journal), February 2, 2017, https://www.strategic-culture.org/news/2017/02/27/president-trump-decries-new-start-treaty.html.

23. Quoted in Wade Boese, "Missile Defense Five Years after the ABM Treaty," *Arms Control Today* 37, no. 5 (2007): 34. See also Daryl G. Kimball, "Missile Defense Collision Course," *Arms Control Today* 37, no. 6 (2007): 3.

24. President Barack Obama, "Remarks by President Obama at the Brandenburg Gate," Berlin, June 19, 2013, https://obamawhitehouse.archives.gov/the-press-office/2013/06/19/remarks-president-obama-brandenburg-gate-berlin-germany.

25. United Nations Office for Disarmament Affairs, Treaty on the Non-Proliferation of Nuclear Weapons, March 2018, http://disarmament.un.org/treaties/t/npt.

26. United Nations, "Security Council Tightens Sanctions on DPR Korea in the Wake of Latest Nuclear Blast," *UN News*, March 7, 2013, https://news.un.org/en/story/2013/03/433722-security-council-tightens-sanctions-dpr-korea-wake-latest-nuclear-blast.

27. Joseph Cirincione, *Nuclear Nightmares: Securing the World Before It Is Too Late* (New York: Columbia University Press, 2015), 28.

28. Roy E. Horton, *Out of (South) Africa: Pretoria's Nuclear Weapons Experience*, INSS Occasional Paper 27 (Colorado Springs: US Air Force Institute for National Security Studies, August 1999), http://www.fas.org/nuke/guide/rsa/nuke/ocp27.htm.

29. Oliver Meier, "NPT Preparatory Meeting Scores Some Success," *Arms Control Today* 37, no. 5 (2007): 24.

30. Richard Lugar, "Statement on Introduced Bills and Joint Resolutions," *Congressional Record*, March 18, 2002 (Senate), S2009–S2014, https://www.congress.gov/congressional-record/2002/03/18/senate-section/article/S2009-1.

31. Defense Threat Reduction Agency, *Cooperative Threat Reduction* (Washington, DC, December 2002), http://www.dtra.mil/Missions/Nunn-Lugar/GlobalCooperationInitiative.aspx.

32. Cirincione, *Nuclear Nightmares*, 131.

33. Cirincione, *Nuclear Nightmares*, 132.

34. Justin Bresolin, "Fact Sheet: The Nunn-Lugar Cooperative Threat Reduction Program" (Washington, DC: The Center for Arms Control and Nonproliferation, July 2013).

35. Matthew Bunn, Eben Harrell, and Martin B. Malin, "Progress on Securing Nuclear Weapons and Materials: The Four-Year Effort and Beyond" (Cambridge, MA: The Belfer Center for Science and International Affairs, John F. Kennedy School of Government, Harvard University, March 2012), 1.

36. Mark J. Valencia, "The Proliferation Security Initiative: A Glass Half-Full," *Arms Control Today* 37, no. 5 (2007): 18.

37. Valencia, "The Proliferation Security Initiative," 18–21.

38. The White House, National Security Decision Directive (NSDD) Number 119, January 6, 1984, http://www.fas.org/spp/starwars/offdocs/nsdd119.htm.

39. Missile Defense Agency, "History of the Agency," March 2018, http://www.mda.mil/mdalink/html/basics.html.

40. The White House, "Budget of the United States Government, Fiscal Year 2015," http://www.whitehouse.gov/omb/budget/Overview.

41. Office of the Under Secretary of Defense (Comptroller), *Defense Budget Overview, Fiscal Year 2019 Budget Request* (Washington, DC: Department of Defense, February 2018), 3–3, 3–8.

42. Department of State, "The Emerging Ballistic Missile Threat," September 1, 2001, https://2001-2009.state.gov/t/ac/rls/fs/2001/4892.htm.

43. Department of State, "The Emerging Ballistic Missile Threat."

44. Department of State, "The Emerging Ballistic Missile Threat."

45. Office of the Secretary of Defense, *Nuclear Posture Review* (Washington, DC: Department of Defense, February, 2018), v.

46. Office of the Secretary of Defense, *Nuclear Posture Review*, vii.

47. Jim Mattis, "Secretary's Preface," in Office of the Secretary of Defense, *Nuclear Posture Review*, iii.

48. Keir A. Lieber and Daryl G. Press, "The End of MAD? The Nuclear Dimension of U.S. Primacy," *International Security* 30, no. 4 (2006): 7–44.

IV

International and Regional Security Issues

18

East Asia

East Asia is as culturally varied as it is politically volatile. In the early twenty-first century, the possibility persists that it could be a battleground for the world's great powers. Most countries that make up Northeast Asia—including Russia, China, Taiwan, North Korea, South Korea, and Japan—have significant military capabilities and are in close proximity to significant US military forces stationed in the area.[1] After the United States, Northeast Asian countries led the world in military spending in 2015, with China second, Russia fourth, Japan eighth, and South Korea tenth.[2] Russia, China, and North Korea have demonstrated nuclear weapons capabilities. Taiwan, South Korea, and Japan have robust civilian nuclear power industries and, if they so desire, the technological capability to become nuclear weapons states rapidly. The countries of Southeast Asia, including the Philippines and Indonesia, as well as peninsular Southeast Asia, although not as developed as their northern neighbors, are undergoing significant economic, social, and political changes (figure 18.1).

The legacies of World War II and the Cold War—combined with new dynamics created by China's growing might—make great-power conflict an ever-present possibility. In Northeast Asia, many of the security challenges that divided the region throughout the Cold War maintain their salience. These include the security standoff between China and Taiwan, the absence of a permanent peace on the Korean peninsula, ongoing territorial disputes, China's continuing defense buildup, and varying degrees of deeply rooted mistrust and nationalism among the countries of the region. Northeast Asia's lack of strong international institutions to handle these security challenges makes the region even more volatile, although international trade relationships have significantly strengthened in the past decade.

FIGURE 18.1 East Asia

American Interests

In the mid-1800s, before the arrival of the "black ships" of Commodore Matthew Perry that are credited with opening Japan to the West, the US Navy was already present in East Asia. Four key interests, outlined below, help to explain America's long-standing concern with East Asia: economic access, regional hegemony, regional stability, and human rights and democracy.

Table 18.1 US Trade Figures in 2016 (in $ Millions and Share of World Total)

	US exports ($ millions)		*US imports ($ millions)*	
China (including Hong Kong)	$128,001	10.4%	$467,813	21.5%
Japan	57,140	4.7%	131,543	6.1%
South Korea	39,943	3.3%	71,579	3.3%
Russia	5,330	0.4%	14,318	0.7%
Taiwan	23,696	1.9%	39,177	1.8%
Northeast Asia subtotal	254,164	20.7%	724,441	33.3%
ASEAN subtotal	63,980	5.2%	158,500	7.3%
All of East Asia	318,144	25.9%	882,941	40.6%
World total	$1,226,482	100%	$2,173,617	100%

Source: Calculations based on https://relatedparty.ftd.census.gov/, August 2017. Trade with North Korea is negligible, but it is included in the Northeast Asia subtotal.

Economic Access. The enormous potential of Asian economic markets has held special appeal to the United States since the dawn of the Industrial Age. Recent trade figures highlight Asia's current economic importance to the United States. Table 18.1 presents data for US trade in 2016 with the countries of Northeast Asia and with the Association of Southeast Asian Nations (ASEAN), compared to US trade totals with the world overall. Exports to Northeast Asia accounted for approximately 21 percent of US total exports. The share rises to 26 percent of US global exports with the inclusion of the ASEAN member states.[3] Imports also reveal a robust trade relationship. In 2015, over 33 percent of total US imports came from Northeast Asia. The number grows to over 40 percent when US imports from ASEAN countries are also included.

In addition to the economic benefits from trade, US leaders have also hoped that economic ties with countries in the region would foster political reform. This is especially true in the case of China. For instance, the United States actively supported China's entry into the World Trade Organization (WTO) in 1999, partly in the hope that WTO membership would provide incentives for China to continue economic and political reforms.

Deter the Rise of a Regional Hegemon. To secure international waters for free trade and to maintain its influence in the region, the United States has sought to prevent the rise of any great power that could dominate the region—that is, a *regional hegemon.* The rise of such a power could constrain US freedom of action and could also cause other countries to react, sparking arms races or other forms of competitive behavior that could disrupt regional stability or hamper economic growth. During the Cold War, this objective of preventing a regional hegemonic power meant containing Soviet influence. In the twenty-first century, China is the potential hegemon of most concern. Table 18.2 presents more information on relative power within the region.

Table 18.2 East Asia Key Statistics

Country	*Total population (millions)*	*Life expectancy at birth*	*GDP US$ (billions)*	*GDP/ capita US$*	*Population living in poverty (%)*	*Military expenditure (% of GDP)*	*Military spending US$ (millions)*	*Human Development Index (HDI) ranking (of 188)*
Brunei	0.4	77.2	10.4	79,700	na	3.8	402	30
Cambodia	15.9	64.5	19.4	3,700	17.7	3.24	628	143
China	1,373.5	75.5	10,730.0	14,600	3.3	1.3	145,039	90
Hong Kong, China	7.2	82.9	316.1	58,100	19.6	na	na	12
Indonesia	258.3	72.7	941.0	11,700	10.9	0.9	8,171	113
Japan	126.7	85.0	4,730.0	38,900	16.1	1.0	47,342	17
North Korea (DPRK)	25.1	70.4	28.0	1,700	na	na*	na*	na
South Korea (ROK)	50.9	82.4	1,411.2	37,900	12.5	2.4	33,778	18
Laos	7.0	64.3	13.8	5,700	22.0	0.2	24	138
Malaysia	30.9	75.0	302.7	27,100	3.8	1.4	4,218	59
Mongolia	3.0	69.6	11.2	12,200	21.6	1.1	117	92
Myanmar (Burma)	56.9	66.6	68.3	6,000	25.6	3.3	2,264	145
Papua New Guinea	6.7	67.2	19.9	3,500	37.0	0.4	83	154
Philippines	102.6	69.2	311.7	7,700	21.6	0.8	2,538	116
Singapore	5.8	85.0	296.6	87,100	na	3.5	10,249	5
Taiwan	23.3	80.1	519.1	49,500	1.5	1.9	9,825	na
Thailand	68.2	74.7	406.8	16,800	7.2	1.5	5,717	87
Timor-Leste	1.3	68.1	2.5	4,200	41.8	1.1	26	133
Vietnam	95.3	73.4	200.5	6,400	11.3	2.0	4,010	115

na = not available.

* Although accurate information is unavailable, the US State Department estimated that the government of North Korea spent 14.8–23.9 percent of its GDP on defense during 2002–2012; World Military Expenditures and Arms Transfers 2015, April 2017, https://www.state.gov/documents/organization/251076.xlsx.

Sources: Data on population and economy is from the CIA World Factbook 2017, https://www.cia.gov/library/publications/the-world-factbook. Military expenditure data from International Institute for Strategic Studies (IISS), *The Military Balance 2017* (London: IISS, 2017). HDI rankings are from *Human Development Report 2016*, http://hdr.undp.org/en/data. Most figures are from 2016 (otherwise latest available data is listed). GDP is reported at the official exchange rate. GDP per capita is using Purchasing Power Parity rates.

Discourage Conflict and Maintain Regional Stability. Stability within East Asia is important not only for the long-term economic growth of the United States and the countries in the region, but also for continuing regional peace. A key concern remains the potential for conflict between China and Taiwan. China is also an important player in both the East China Sea and the South China Sea, where conflicting territorial claims and China's efforts to assert its economic and military power have heightened tensions. Another potential source of conflict is the continuing standoff on the Korean peninsula. The United States has been concerned about a possible resumption of hostilities between North and South Korea since the Korean War armistice of 1953. In addition, after the September 11, 2001, terrorist attacks in the United States, regional manifestations of transnational security issues, such as nuclear proliferation and terrorism, have increased in salience.

Promote Human Rights and Democracy. Another American interest is the promotion of democracy and human rights in East Asia. President Barack Obama's National Security Advisor Susan Rice stated in 2013 that "strengthening our shared security and promoting our shared prosperity are vital elements of America's commitment to the Asia Pacific region. So too is advancing respect for the rights and values we hold dear. . . . In the early years of this new century, we must help to consolidate and expand democracy across Asia to enable more and more people to participate fully in the political life of their countries."[4] The importance of protecting and promoting human rights was reiterated in the National Security Strategies of 2010,2015, and 2017. The 2010 document, for example, states that "America's commitment to democracy, human rights, and the rule of law are essential sources of [US] strength and influence in the world."[5] The 2017 strategy states, "We support, with our words and actions, those who live under oppressive regimes and who seek freedom, individual dignity, and the rule of law."[6]

History of US Policy toward East Asia

The United States has had a sustained interest in East Asia since well before the twentieth century, but it has faced stiff competition from other Western powers for regional influence. It did not emerge as the primary regional power until the end of World War II, a result that accompanied three related developments: the defeat of Imperial Japan, the resurgence of civil war in China, and the end of European colonization.

The Origins of Containment in East Asia. After Japan surrendered on September 2, 1945, the United States supported the transition of former European and Japanese colonies to self-rule throughout most of Asia. The United States also became involved in efforts to end the civil war in China between Mao Zedong's Chinese Communist Party (CCP) and Chiang Kai-shek's Nationalist Kuomintang (KMT) party. These competing factions—each of which claimed all of China—presented a policy dilemma for the United States. Chiang Kai-shek had been an ally during World War II, but the KMT had established a pattern of corruption and harsh governance that weakened its claim on US support. Mao ultimately drove Chiang and the KMT off the mainland to Taiwan; he proclaimed the People's Republic of China (PRC) as a unified communist state for all of China on October 1, 1949. Staking a competing claim, Chiang Kai-shek declared his government in Taiwan—the Republic of China (ROC)—to be the official government for all of China.

Initially, the United States did not take an official position on which government it would recognize. This ambiguity ended when North Korea invaded South Korea in June 1950. This attack, and the PRC's support of it, was a catalyst for the United States to extend into East Asia the main "containment" principles of the Truman Doctrine, which had originated primarily from a US fear of the spread of communism in Europe. The United States deployed vessels from the US Navy's Seventh Fleet to the Taiwan Strait and publicly announced its willingness to support Taiwan and assist in its defense. The US schism with the PRC deepened in late 1950, when Chinese communist forces entered the Korean War, attacking US forces that had advanced deep into North Korea and were approaching the Chinese border.

The Truman Doctrine also affected US policy toward Japan and South Korea. Prior to the Korean War, General Douglas MacArthur, commander of US occupation forces in Japan, focused on the promotion of liberal democracy and comprehensive demilitarization of Japan. Article 9 of the US-drafted 1947 Japanese constitution reflected this goal of demilitarization. The first paragraph states that the Japanese "forever renounce war as a sovereign right of the nation and the threat or use of force as means of settling international disputes"; its second paragraph permits Japan to have only a self-defense force (SDF).[7] American enthusiasm for Article 9 diminished with the onset of the Korean War: the United States came to perceive Japan as a bulwark against the spread of communism and as a potentially useful ally, rather than as a possible future threat. Accordingly, the United States concentrated on strengthening Japan economically, politically, and militarily. Amid similar concerns after the Korean War, the United States gave priority to strong governance in South Korea over liberal democratic reform.

These policies formed the foundation of a broad containment strategy to deter Soviet and Chinese aggression and to stop various communist revolutionary movements in the region, many of which were emboldened or supported outright by Mao's government in China. Ho Chi Minh launched the Viet Minh guerrilla forces against French colonists in Indochina from 1946 to 1954; the Hukbalahap rebellion, which began during World War II, simmered in the Philippines; communist insurgencies also occurred in Indonesia, Malaya (now Malaysia), and Burma (now Myanmar). The US pursuit of containment in the region was based on the underlying assumption that if communist states emerged throughout Asia, they would be allied ideologically, militarily, and politically with the Soviet Union and China. Regional containment set the stage for increased US security assistance to East Asia and led to US military involvement in Vietnam.

The primary diplomatic dimension of containment policy in East Asia was the creation of a system of bilateral alliances that came to be known as the *San*

Francisco System.[8] The name originated after many such alliances were created at the Japan peace treaty conference held in San Francisco in September 1951. At that conference, the United States signed separate bilateral defense accords with Australia, Japan, and the Philippines. Over the next few years, additional treaties with South Korea, Taiwan, and Thailand supplemented these original agreements. In each of these alliances, American interests were focused less on political reforms aimed at liberal democratic ideals than on developing strong, stable, anticommunist states willing and able to support US interests.

In addition to these bilateral alliances, the United States actively encouraged the development of regional security pacts. The first of these was the 1951 Australia, New Zealand, and United States Security Treaty (ANZUS), which provided for mutual aid in the event of aggression. The second was the Southeast Asia Treaty Organization (SEATO), established in 1954 by the United States, the United Kingdom, Australia, New Zealand, France, Pakistan, the Philippines, and Thailand. The creation of SEATO was a direct response to the perceived threat of communist expansion in Southeast Asia.

Meanwhile, China continued to support communist insurgencies in Asia and to engage in various military ventures. It invaded Tibet in 1950, fought the United States and United Nations (UN) forces during the Korean War (1950–1953), conducted operations against Taiwan over the smaller islands of Quemoy and Matsu in 1954 and 1958, and fought a brief war with India over border disputes in 1962 (see chapter 19). In 1979, China attacked Vietnam in response to Hanoi's military overthrow of the Khmer Rouge regime in neighboring Cambodia. China became a nuclear state in 1964, when it conducted its first successful nuclear test. All of these developments contributed to a growing US perception of China as an aggressive military power, much as it had long viewed the Soviet Union. Moreover, military cooperation between the two communist states and the seemingly close personal relationship between Mao and Soviet leader Joseph Stalin contributed to the appearance of a unified Sino-Soviet bloc. However, the so-called bloc began to unravel into Sino-Soviet rivalry after Stalin's death in 1953, which eventually provided the opportunity for a new direction for US foreign policy.

Evolution of the US Containment Policy in East Asia. By the late 1960s, the United States was ready to reexamine its policy of containment in Asia. The Sino-Soviet rivalry had evolved into a split; tensions between the two states had escalated into military conflict along their shared border. Domestic factors in the United States, such as growing public discontent with the Vietnam War, provided further impetus for a new approach. After pledging, while running for office, to end US military involvement in Vietnam, President Richard Nixon sought alternative ways to pursue the policy of containment in Asia.

Regional factors also played a role in promoting change in US policy, including the economic development of Japan and, increasingly, of South Korea. As these important regional allies became major economic powers, the US perception of danger from communist expansion decreased, and the ability of others to share the burden of regional defense increased. In this context, Nixon announced a new policy for the region. According to the Nixon Doctrine, the United States would keep its treaty commitments, but, should a security threat arise, it would look first to the threatened state to assume primary responsibility for its own defense, assisted by regional neighbors. This emphasis on burden-sharing set the stage for the withdrawal of approximately twenty thousand troops from South Korea in 1971, leaving a single combat division as the main US ground force component in Korea.

Seeking to further this doctrine and to exploit the now evident Sino-Soviet split, Nixon ushered in a new era of détente in Sino-US relations with his visit to Beijing in 1972. This meeting and future visits by other US presidents produced communiqués in 1972, 1979, and 1986 that continue to form the foundation of US policy toward China and Taiwan. Each new communiqué dealt with the issue incrementally. In the aggregate, they declare that the United States acknowledges that Chinese on both sides of the Taiwan Strait claim there is only one China and that Taiwan is part of China; that the PRC government is the sole *legal* government of China; and that the United States will continue to maintain cultural, commercial, and "other unofficial relations" with Taiwan.[9] The United States closed its official embassy in Taiwan in 1979 and established one in Beijing.

It is important to note that these communiqués do not necessarily mean that the United States officially recognizes that Taiwan is part of the PRC; they mean only that the United States acknowledges that both sides claim all of China and Taiwan. This intentionally vague wording formed the basis for what became known as America's "one China" policy. The United States intended the strategic ambiguity of this approach to deter both sides from taking unilateral steps that could provoke a renewal of conflict. Although the United States proclaimed its legal recognition of the PRC in 1979, its passage of the Taiwan Relations Act that same year clarified that this recognition did not imply US toleration of the use of military force by the PRC against Taiwan. That legislation authorized the US government to sell arms to Taiwan for its defense and stated that the United States would maintain the capacity of Taiwan to resist any Chinese use of force that would jeopardize Taiwan's security.[10]

This legislation did much to quell Taiwan's fears of abandonment by the United States, but other developments, including the withdrawal of US forces from Vietnam and the downsizing of US forces in South Korea, created a growing sense of anxiety among the states of the region that relied on US security commitments. This anxiety increased when President Jimmy Carter ordered the withdrawal of additional forces from Korea in 1979.[11]

It was not long until other events diminished these concerns. After the failure of Mao's economic policies—the Great Leap Forward in 1958 caused the deaths of at least forty-five million Chinese, while Mao's effort in the 1960s to establish political and social control with the Cultural Revolution resulted in chaotic upheaval—the PRC instituted major changes to its economic and foreign policies.[12] After Mao's death in 1976, Deng Xiaoping and subsequent Chinese leaders initiated a remarkable wave of reforms that stressed capitalist principles, initially limited to designated special economic zones (SEZs). They also gradually reshaped

China's foreign policy, from one that actively promoted revolutionary movements throughout the developing world to one that promoted regional stability for the purpose of furthering China's economic growth.

Meanwhile, in 1986, Soviet leader Mikhail Gorbachev initiated a major set of political and economic reforms, known as *glasnost* and *perestroika* (see chapter 22), and adopted a new approach toward East Asia that emphasized mutual security, balanced force reductions, and economic cooperation. This approach improved Soviet relations with China, South Korea, and Japan, as well as with the United States. Then, just five years later, the Soviet Union disintegrated, ending the Cold War.

The Post–Cold War Period: Brief Euphoria. With the collapse of the Soviet threat, improved US relations with China, and growing domestic demands for a peace dividend, the United States began cutting its defense budget and reducing the number of military forces deployed in the region. President George H. W. Bush ordered steep reductions in defense spending. A further withdrawal of 33,000 service members from East Asia, a 25 percent decrease, left approximately 100,000 US forces in the region.

The declines in defense spending and in forward troop presence stopped, however, after new regional developments overshadowed the initial post–Cold War euphoria. China's defense budget increased at an alarming rate as the country achieved an astonishing 8–10 percent annual growth rate in its gross domestic product (GDP).[13] Japan entered into a prolonged economic slump in 1990, and it became increasingly worried about the commitment of the United States to its security, especially in light of China's growing power and of problematic developments in North Korea.

In 1993, a standoff over North Korea's nuclear program created tensions. The administration of President Bill Clinton temporarily improved the situation in 1994 with a negotiated compromise called the Agreed Framework.[14] Then, in June 1995 and again in July 1996, China conducted a series of missile tests and military exercises in Fujian, the province of China nearest to Taiwan. The United States responded by deploying two aircraft carrier battle groups to the area as a deterrent show of force.[15] These developments convinced the United States that many of the prominent Cold War security issues in East Asia would, unlike the situation in Europe at that time, persist in the post–Cold War era. In response, the United States stopped reducing its military presence in the region and maintained the force at about one hundred thousand.[16] The United States also made clear its intentions to maintain its security commitments as outlined in the San Francisco System of bilateral alliances formed in the 1950s.

Terrorist Attacks, Economic Crisis, and a Rebalance to the Asia-Pacific Region. The terrorist attacks against the United States on September 11, 2001, fundamentally altered US perceptions of the world. The approach of the administration of President George W. Bush to this new security situation came to be known as the Bush Doctrine.[17] (For a more detailed discussion of the Bush Doctrine, see chapter 3.) This doctrine's focus on combating terrorism and nuclear proliferation and its embrace of preemptive—even preventive—uses of military force affected the East Asian security environment in several ways. One was that it created increased demands on US allies in the region. The United States reduced its troop presence on the Korean peninsula by approximately twelve thousand so that it could support operations in the Middle East and Central Asia. The United States also requested military support from both South Korea and Japan for military operations in Afghanistan and Iraq. A second effect was related to the Bush Doctrine's focus on rogue states and nuclear proliferation: George W. Bush's declaration that North Korea, along with Iraq and Iran, was part of an "axis of evil" caused concern in the region that the United States might take military action against North Korea.[18]

In 2008, an economic crisis that began in the US financial sector spread worldwide, sparking a deep recession in the United States and abroad. The resulting decline in developed-country imports from China contributed to a slowdown in the Chinese economy. Because China had adopted a strategy of growth based on its exports, with state-owned industrial enterprises playing a leading role, China was hit particularly hard by the worldwide recession.[19] Recovery was slower in developing countries, including those in Asia, than in developed states; lingering effects were felt for many years after the onset of the recession.[20]

When President Obama assumed office in January 2009, he was determined to raise the importance of East Asia as a US national security priority.[21] He laid out his vision in a speech in Australia in November 2011:

> As the world's fastest-growing region—and home to more than half the global economy—the Asia Pacific is critical to achieving my highest priority, and that's creating jobs and opportunity for the American people. . . . Asia will largely define whether the century ahead will be marked by conflict or cooperation, needless suffering or human progress. As President, I have, therefore, made a deliberate and strategic decision—as a Pacific nation, the United States will play a larger and long-term role in shaping this region and its future, by upholding core principles and in close partnership with our allies and friends.[22]

Though the media tended to portray this "pivot" or "rebalance" to Asia as a response to the increasing military power and assertiveness of China, that was only one motivation for a new approach. It also sought a number of goals: to strengthen multilateral arrangements and international institutions in Asia that serve US interests; to increase trade and economic growth; to enhance security for the United States and its allies and partners; and to promote democracy and human rights.[23] Perhaps the most significant results of this new policy orientation were the new trade deals, including a new trade agreement between the United States and South Korea that went into force in March 2012, and the multilateral Trans-Pacific Partnership (TPP), a major free-trade agreement between the United States and eleven other countries in Asia and the Americas. The TPP, however, faced significant domestic political opposition in the United States, causing both major 2016 presidential candidates to pledge to abrogate the agreement instead of submitting it for ratification. President Donald Trump withdrew US participation in the TPP in his first week in office in 2017.

Emerging Trends Affecting East Asia's Security Environment

Because East Asia is a region in which major powers—the United States, Russia, China, and Japan—border one another, great-power conflict has been a longstanding possibility, and the region is characterized by significant defense spending and military rivalry.[24] Four key trends will affect the region's security environment: the rise of China; Taiwan's position on its independence; changes in Japan's national security policy; and security developments on the Korean peninsula, including North Korea's nuclear program.

The Rise of China. China's transformation has been vast in scope and nature. As it continues to rise in terms of economic power, military power, and foreign influence, China is also struggling to manage growing domestic challenges. The success with which the Chinese Communist Party (CCP) can handle these challenges, while simultaneously maintaining stability and economic growth, will have a major impact on the regional security environment, as well as on China's relations with the United States and other western countries.

Economic Growth. Following the catastrophic failures of Mao's Great Leap Forward and the Cultural Revolution, the CCP leadership under Deng initiated bold economic reforms in 1978–1979. These reforms strayed far from the original ideological underpinnings of Maoism and represented a more pragmatic capitalistic approach that stressed the importance of effectiveness over political ideology. This sentiment is captured by Deng's analogy: "A cat, whether it is white or black, is a good one as long as it is able to catch mice."[25] Deng's reforms produced dramatic results: China's economy grew at an extraordinary rate of 8–10 percent annually for over two decades. By 2016, China boasted the second highest GDP in the world at $11.2 trillion, outpacing Japan (the world's third highest GDP at $4.9 trillion) and trailing only the United States ($18.6 trillion).[26]

The rapid pace of China's economic growth has had both global and domestic effects. Internationally, increased demand in China resulted in a worldwide scramble for oil and other materials. Domestically, economic change has been accompanied by rapid urbanization, increases in inequality, and environmental degradation. The last of these has become increasingly severe in recent years. A scientific study released in 2015 found that air pollution was responsible for approximately 1.6 million deaths in China a year, which amounts to 4,400 people a day.[27] Responding to the "thick, gray smog filling its cities and millions of residents commuting behind surgical masks," Chinese leaders declared "war on pollution" in 2014.[28] Scarcity of clean water is also a significant concern: "50 percent of water isn't good to fish in, while 25 percent is unfit for agricultural use. Half of China's cities have polluted ground water."[29] The public health system in China that must respond to these challenges—currently undergoing reforms intended to increase the role of the private sector—will also have to deal with significant demographic challenges as "the population aged sixty and older is projected to increase from 13 percent in 2012 to 34 percent in 2050."[30] In part, this demographic challenge is due to many years under China's "one-child" policy: fewer and fewer workers are available to support the retired and elderly.

Although China has made tremendous progress, it still faces many of the challenges of a developing country with an emerging economy. Its income per capita in 2016 of $15,470, for example, ranks just ninety-second in the world.[31] Given the imbalances created by an export-based strategy as well as environmental and demographic challenges, China's leaders recognize the need for change if growth is to be sustained. The World Bank reported that

> China's 12th Five-Year Plan (2011–2015) and the newly approved 13th Five-Year Plan (2016–2020) . . . highlight the development of services and measures to address environmental and social imbalances, setting targets to reduce pollution, to increase energy efficiency, to improve access to education and healthcare, and to expand social protection. The annual growth target in the 12th Five-Year Plan was 7 percent and the growth target in the 13th Five-Year Plan is 6.5 percent, reflecting the rebalancing of the economy and the focus on the quality of growth.[32]

Although China is the home of one of the world's oldest societies, modern capitalism is relatively new there. Whether China's leaders can maintain the country's state-centered ethos while continuing to foster economic growth will have a profound impact on Sino-US relations in the coming years.

Domestic Challenges. The CCP's shift away from Marxist and socialist ideals has undercut the original ideological base of CCP legitimacy, which has come to depend increasingly on China's economic performance. Although China's economy continues to expand, its 6.9 percent GDP growth rate in 2015 was the lowest in more than twenty-five years.[33] A significant challenge for the CCP will be to make needed adjustments in the economy to maintain sufficient economic growth and stability to meet rising Chinese expectations.

The 1989 pro-democracy demonstrations in Tiananmen Square remain a pointed reminder of the danger of domestic discontent. Since then, the CCP has methodically cracked down on demonstrations and weathered the ensuing international backlash. Although the size and seriousness of subsequent demonstrations have not repeated those of Tiananmen, incidents of social unrest occur with growing frequency.[34] According to Chinese law enforcement sources, public-order disturbances grew from 8,700 incidents in 1993 to 60,000 in 2003 and to 120,000 by 2008. The Chinese Academy of Social Science estimated in 2012 that "mass incidents now regularly exceeded 100,000 per year."[35] China has continued its crackdown on domestic dissidents. Until August 2014, the CCP held in prison one of China's prominent dissident lawyers, Gao Zhisheng; he was detained for eight years and repeatedly tortured due to his record as "one of China's most combative human rights advocates."[36] Even after release, Chinese dissidents such as Zhisheng may remain under police surveillance indefinitely. In 2014, the chairman of the CCP and president of the PRC, Xi Jinping, took steps to reassert more control over social order, becoming "the most 'hands on' CCP leader" in decades.[37] In 2018, President Xi received even further authority when the Chinese National People's Congress abolished term limits, thereby allowing him to remain as president beyond the previous limit of two five-year terms.[38]

The demonstrations and dissidence reflect major, deep-seated social issues. Although focused efforts by the Chinese government since 2005 have begun to reduce the economic inequality that had been growing in China for decades, a Pew poll in 2012 found that "most Chinese (81 percent) agree that today the rich just get richer while the poor get poorer, including 45 percent who *completely* agree."[39] This same poll, which repeated a survey that Pew had initially conducted in 2008, found double-digit increases over those four years "in the percentage of the Chinese public that considers old age insurance, education, corrupt officials, corrupt business people, health care, and conditions for workers as very big problems for their country."[40] In addition, "a 57 percent majority say their traditional way of life is getting lost. . . . Fully 71 percent believe their way of life needs to be protected from foreign influence."[41] Other pressures on Chinese society stem from economic and infrastructure differences between the coastal and interior provinces, a migrant workforce of around 250 million individuals who have left the countryside and now live in the cities, an expansion of the number of foreign nongovernmental organizations (NGOs) operating in China, and the explosive growth of information available through the Internet.[42] In 2014, the number of Internet users in China was estimated at 649 million, more than double the population of the United States.[43] Government efforts seem to have had an impact, particularly on the ability of ordinary Chinese to access non-CCP media sources, but not all Internet usage can be effectively censored.

In addition to economic performance, the CCP has increasingly resorted to nationalism as the country's ideological glue. Relying on nationalism carries its own set of risks. If populist nationalism were to grow too powerful, the CCP could lose its ability to control it, risking its relations with other countries. For example, resurgent nationalism could lead to excessive reactions to future regional security challenges, such as another Taiwan crisis or a South China Sea conflict.[44]

Military Modernization. China is actively modernizing and strengthening its military, the People's Liberation Army (PLA). The largest military force in the world, the PLA comprises four services: ground forces (PLA); naval forces (PLAN), which include the marines and naval aviation; air forces (PLAAF); and the PLA Rocket Force (formerly known as the Second Artillery), which is in charge of the PRC's nuclear arsenal. Although the Chinese government does not publicize official statistics, observers estimate that, as of 2015, the active force totaled approximately 2.3 million personnel, with a significant majority serving in the ground forces.[45]

Military reform has been an issue throughout China's post–World War II history, but the perceived need to change intensified in the 1990s. China's observations of US military performance during the 1991 Gulf War had a profound effect on PLA leaders.[46] Although they had known that the PLA was not yet a modern force, these military leaders had not expected to see such a wide performance gap between their forces and those of the United States. The ability of the United States to project a massive force over long distances, to incorporate high technology in adverse terrain, and to perform deep surgical strikes supported by aerial and space reconnaissance was alarming to Chinese observers. The relative ease with which the United States toppled the Taliban regime in Afghanistan in 2001 and Saddam Hussein's regime in Iraq in 2003 heightened China's sense of urgency about military modernization.

Chinese military spending grew at approximately 9.5 percent a year between 2005 and 2014. However, the gap in capabilities between the Chinese and US militaries continues to be reflected in the difference in defense expenditures between the two countries.[47] In 2014, the United States spent $610 billion on its military, while China spent an estimated $216 billion.[48] Consequently, rather than competing directly with the United States in all areas, the PLA has been focused on preparing to fight and win short-duration, high-intensity conflicts along China's periphery in defense of its territorial sovereignty. China has also prioritized development of what the US military calls "anti-access, area-denial" (A2/AD) capabilities, with which China intends to create "a zone around its coastal regions that could be potentially too dangerous for US forces to operate in, thus limiting the offensive capabilities that the United States could bring to bear in a conflict."[49]

The PLA's primary focus is on developing the capacity to prevent Taiwanese independence and to compel Taiwan to negotiate a settlement on Beijing's terms. This priority was reinforced in March 2005, when China's National People's Congress passed an anti-secession law to deter Taiwan's leaders from taking steps to proclaim independence. The PLA regularly holds amphibious exercises that deal explicitly or implicitly with a conflict over Taiwan. It has deployed over one thousand ballistic missiles in the region directly opposite Taiwan.[50] A 2015 US Defense Department report notes that "preparation for a Taiwan conflict with the possibility of US intervention continues to dominate China's military modernization program."[51]

China's military modernization efforts do not reflect an intent to compete with the United States on a symmetric basis. Instead, China is focusing on needs specific to its geographic situation and interests, as well as on disruptive, asymmetric capabilities that could operate against potential US vulnerabilities, especially in the domains of cyberspace and space. In addition to an aggressive Chinese program of cyber espionage, there are indications that Chinese military cyber forces have probed the critical infrastructure of potential future adversaries, seeking vulnerabilities that could be exploited in the event of conflict.[52] China also looks to its electronic warfare capabilities to erode US advantages in information-related technologies in the event of a future conflict.[53] China has made significant improvements to its space and counter-space programs in recent years, with the dual goals of advancing its own capabilities and countering those of an adversary.[54]

China has increasingly sought to develop force-projection capabilities and to use its military to enhance its international influence. For example, the PLA launched its first aircraft carrier, the *Liaoning*, in September 2012 and invited US Secretary of Defense Chuck Hagel to visit it in April 2014.[55] The PLA has increased the number of training events it engages in with foreign militaries. Between 2006 and 2010, it held thirty-two bilateral or multilateral exercises with other countries; in 2014 alone it held fourteen.[56] Perhaps China's most remarkable effort to use the PLA to increase its international influence has been in land reclamation processes to create new islands from reefs in disputed territories in the Spratly chain in the South China Sea and the development of these artificial islands to support military activities. In early 2016, the PLA was reported to have deployed missiles on the disputed Woody Island in the Paracel chain. These developments have raised concerns in the United States and among its regional partners about China's militarization of the South China Sea and implications for freedom of navigation.[57]

Diplomatic Initiatives. Deng articulated an approach to China's foreign policy that would support the priority he placed on internal economic development by fostering a peaceful external environment. Eventually codified as the "24 character" guideline, this policy called for China's leaders to "observe calmly; secure our position; cope with affairs calmly; hide our capacities and bide our time; be good at maintaining a low profile, and never claim leadership."[58] Deng's successors continued to abide by this approach, which was essentially reaffirmed twice under Hu Jintao, president of China from 2003 to 2013, in "white papers released by the Ministry of Foreign Affairs in 2005 and 2011 on 'China's Peaceful Development.'"[59] Guided by these central ideas, China has enhanced ties with important countries in virtually every region of the world and has resolved or diminished a number of border disputes with its regional neighbors. This success is all the more extraordinary when one considers China's history of troubled regional relations: during the 1960s and 1970s, it engaged in land wars with the Soviet Union, India, and Vietnam, and it supported Maoist insurgencies in several countries of Southeast Asia.[60]

Deng's ideas remain influential, but China's growing strength and the financial crisis that began in the United States in 2008 appear to have sparked increased debate in China about the appropriateness of a more active and insistent pursuit of China's interests abroad. A series of events in 2010 led some external observers to conclude that China's approach to the world had already become more assertive. These included strong Chinese statements in response to US arms sales to Taiwan in January; Chinese opposition to the visit of the Dalai Lama to the United States in February; China's increasingly strong rhetoric in its assertion of territorial claims in the South China Sea in March; Chinese support for North Korea after it took violent actions against South Korea in March and November; and China's confrontational response to Japan's detention of a Chinese ship captain after he had sought to ram Japanese coast guard vessels in September.[61]

China scholar Iain Johnston argues that concern that these incidents may represent a new Chinese assertiveness takes them out of historical and contemporary context. China has long been firm on issues that China views as impinging on its sovereignty, such as US arms sales to Taiwan, and during the same period China continued a policy of multilateral engagement in many other issue areas.[62] Others agree that these particular incidents should not be taken as evidence that China has become more aggressive; they believe, however, that China will inevitably become more engaged and assertive abroad as the country's power continues to grow and as the regime continues to rely on nationalism as a major source of its legitimacy.[63] Interpretations of these events vary, but there is general agreement that China has recently been doing more to reinforce its disputed maritime claims than in prior decades.

Under Xi Jinping, who became president in 2013, China's approach to foreign policy reflects important continuities with Deng's focus on attracting foreign investment and fostering an international environment conducive to the country's peaceful economic development. However, what may prove to be Xi's most significant strategic initiative—known in China as the *One Belt, One Road* (OBOR) policy or the *Belt and Road Initiative* (BRI)—also reflects China's intention to increasingly shape its international environment. Announced by Xi in a speech in 2013, this initiative calls for China to lead efforts to build "the 'Silk Road Economic Belt' and a counterpart '21st Century Maritime Silk Road'" that will enable the better integration of the economies of South, Central, and East Asia through increased investment in infrastructure and other supportive policies.[64] This initiative reflects the continuing significance of domestic development and represents an important means through which Xi aims to realize "the great rejuvenation of the Chinese nation" by achieving two important goals: "doubling GDP per capita for urban and rural residents by 2020, and turning China into a 'socialist modernized country . . . rich, strong, democratic, culturally advanced, and harmonious' by 2050."[65] At the same time, this strategic framework is meant to provide a constructive basis for enhanced relations with China's neighbors, as all stand to gain economically from better infrastructure and fewer barriers to trade. The impact on US interests will in part be shaped by the degree to which China seeks to create "exclusive 'Asian only' economic institutions dominated by China, or will instead lend its energy and support to [a] more open and inclusive Asia-Pacific institutional architecture."[66]

China seems intent on preserving a peaceful international environment to continue its economic progress, but important points of friction remain. China's success in its OBOR initiatives will rest, in part, on its ability to convince its partners that projects will truly be mutually beneficial, rather than directed at solving China's internal problems—such as pollution and excess industrial capacity—at the expense of China's neighbors. In addition, warns analyst Christopher Johnson, "Xi's unflinching assertion of China's sovereignty claims over disputed territories in both the East and South China Seas . . . is generating a pervasive level of insecurity among China's bordering nations that risks invalidating Beijing's good neighbor policy mantra."[67]

In terms of US national security, one can find reasons for optimism as well as reasons for concern in recent developments in Chinese foreign policy. On the one hand, Chinese leaders' view that great-power conflict remains unlikely in the near term enables a focus on economic development, and suggests a recognition that provocative actions toward the United States would be unproductive. In addition, a more activist foreign policy by China could be helpful to the United States in some areas, as exemplified by China's recent willingness to contribute more to UN peacekeeping missions.[68] On the other hand, if China's approach to regional economic development seeks to exclude the United States, this could be harmful to US interests; it would demand an integrated and comprehensive US policy response, which could be difficult for the US government to create and sustain.

China is very aware that it did not write the rules of the current international order, and it may therefore seek to rewrite them to pursue its interests without being taken advantage of and humiliated by outside powers, as it has been in the past. It is also likely that the United States will have to proceed carefully to avoid escalation as it takes steps to uphold freedom of navigation and to reassure its allies in the face of strong Chinese rhetoric and activism regarding disputed Chinese territorial claims in the East and South China Seas.[69]

Democratization and Sentiment Favoring Independence in Taiwan. The danger of war across the Taiwan Strait has been present since Chiang Kai-shek and the KMT party fled to the island of Taiwan in 1949. The US policy of "strategic ambiguity" has sought to deter conflict by providing assurances to China and Taiwan simultaneously. This strategic ambiguity has two primary elements: "(1) clear, credible commitments to transfer defensive capabilities to Taiwan and, if necessary, to intervene on Taiwan's behalf; and (2) political reassurances that the United States does not plan to use its superiority now or in the future to harm Beijing's core security interests by promoting the independence of Taiwan."[70] The first element works to deter China from a unilateral attack on Taiwan, and the second element aims to ensure that Taiwan does not unilaterally provoke a change in the status quo.

Taiwan's successful democratization complicates this policy of dual deterrence. Beginning in 1949, Taiwan was essentially a one-party, authoritarian state ruled by the KMT. From the 1950s through the 1970s, the KMT ruled with absolute power, dominating Taiwan's indigenous people as well as the Han people who had inhabited the island prior to 1949. In the 1980s, however, opposition parties emerged and offered a series of political reforms, which eventually led to the election of a new national assembly in 1991. This new legislative body passed a number of further reforms, leading to Taiwan's first direct presidential election in 1996. This expansion of democratic practices and the suspected pro-independence leanings of the ultimately successful KMT presidential candidate in these elections, Lee Teng-hui, alarmed China to the point that it resorted to military provocations that included military exercises and the firing of missiles that landed within thirty-five miles of major Taiwanese ports. The United States responded to these Chinese actions with the deployment of a carrier battle group in what became known as the 1995–1996 Taiwan Strait crisis.[71]

China considers Taiwan to be a renegade province within its sovereign domain, so it opposes any words or actions, in Taiwan or elsewhere, that promote the island's independence. This is why friction between China and Taiwan increased in 2000, when Chen Shui-bian won Taiwan's presidential election: Chen belongs to the Democratic Progressive Party (DPP), the only major party in Taiwan "that has a plank for pursuing Taiwan's de jure independence."[72] During his campaign and at various times during his presidency, President Chen's expressions of support for constitutional reforms or referenda were viewed by mainland China as unacceptable political challenges.

After poor performance by Taiwan's government and a series of scandals involving President Chen and his family, the DPP experienced significant electoral losses in elections in 2008. The party won only 27 out of 113 seats in the national legislature in January, and its candidate for the presidency was defeated by KMT candidate Ma-Jing Jeou in March.[73] During President Ma's eight years in office (2008–2016), efforts to strengthen diplomatic and economic relations with mainland China resulted in new official channels of communication, increased tourism to Taiwan from mainland China, and a significant new trade deal called the Economic Cooperation Framework Agreement.[74] These improved relations resulted in the first-ever meeting between the presidents of Taiwan and China in Singapore in 2015.[75]

While President Ma was successful in improving cross-strait relations, his presidency saw the accumulation of domestic difficulties. The global financial crisis in 2008 damaged Taiwan's export-oriented economy, which experienced a slow recovery. In addition, President Ma's diplomatic rapprochement with the PRC, the increasing integration of the two economies, and a perceived lack of transparency sparked domestic discontent. This culminated in the "Sunflower Movement" protest, during which various pro-democracy groups joined forces to occupy the national legislature in Taiwan for twenty-four days in March and April 2014. The spark that set off this protest was apparently a move by President Ma to push for legislative approval of a new Cross-Strait Services Trade Agreement (CSSTA) with the PRC without a detailed review of its provisions in the legislature. Disparate groups came together to block the CSSTA, unified around a variety of concerns that included objections to a process perceived as undemocratic; fears of economic penetration by the mainland and the impact on businesses in Taiwan; risks to media independence and freedom of expression in Taiwan; and potential negative implications for Taiwan's security.[76]

In 2016, discontent with the KMT and President Ma paved the way for the return to power of the DPP. It achieved unprecedented success in elections for the national legislature, winning 68 out of 113 seats, and regained the presidency through the election of Taiwan's first female executive, President Tsai Ing-wen.[77] Although President Tsai has been cautious in her discussions of cross-strait relations, her election is viewed negatively by PRC officials. They have criticized her for insufficient acknowledgment of the principle that there is only "one China."[78]

The management of cross-strait relations promises to remain a continuing challenge, as the PRC remains dedicated to eventual unification while public opinion in Taiwan is increasingly hostile to the idea: "In 2015, a record-low 9.1 percent of respondents in the annual poll conducted since 1992 by National Chengchi University's Election Study Center favored unification either now or in the future, compared to 20 percent in 2003. In the same poll, 59.5 percent wanted to maintain the status quo for the time being or indefinitely, and 21.1 percent favored independence now or eventually."[79] Taiwanese have increasingly abandoned the historic ROC goal of reunification and favor the status quo, at least for the present. It is unclear how hard the Taiwanese people might eventually push to establish a fully independent Taiwan, and what steps in this direction might provoke the PRC to respond with force.

Japan's Evolving Approach to National Security. After catastrophic defeat in World War II, including the psychological and physically devastating atomic bombing of Hiroshima and Nagasaki, Japan took drastic steps to ensure that its former aggressive nature would not reemerge. The legal foundation for this was Article 9 of Chapter 2, "The Renunciation of War," of the 1947 Japanese Constitution:

> Aspiring sincerely to an international peace based on justice and order, the Japanese people forever renounce war as a sovereign right of the nation and the threat or use of force as means of settling international disputes.
>
> In order to accomplish the aim of the preceding paragraph, land, sea, and air forces, as well as other war potential, will never be maintained. The right of belligerency of the state will not be recognized.[80]

At first glance, this article provides an impressive legal obstacle against the creation of any military capability. However, the second portion of the article, which starts with the words "In order to accomplish the aim of the preceding paragraph," allows for an interpretation that permits Japan to maintain military forces as long as they are not for the purpose of settling international disputes. Japanese governments have subsequently interpreted Article 9 as allowing Japan to exercise the right of self-defense and to develop and maintain the Japanese SDF for that purpose. This interpretation has evolved over time, from a narrow one that concentrated on the territorial defense of Japan toward a broader concept that allows some limited participation in multinational operations that further international peace and security.

During the first half of the Cold War, Japanese leaders favored the narrow interpretation. This was expressed in the Yoshida Doctrine, named after Japan's first postwar prime minister, Shigeru Yoshida. That doctrine stressed the primacy of economic development, while making only limited military improvements, in order to reduce the possibility of entanglement in security issues that did not directly threaten Japan's sovereignty. An important concern was that Japan's provision of bases to US forces, a key obligation of the US-Japan alliance, could make Japan a proxy target for enemies of the United States.[81] Japanese leaders were also concerned that the United States might pressure them to support the US-led containment strategy more directly in a role that would exceed strict national defense.

Japan's perspective changed rather significantly as a result of the Nixon Doctrine. Because the Nixon administration stressed détente with China and the Soviet Union and greater burden-sharing between the United States and its allies, Japanese fears of entanglement shifted to fears of abandonment. Growing trade and economic disputes between the United States and Japan in the 1980s further aggravated these concerns. As a result of these various developments, Japan began a qualitative buildup of its defense forces and published its first National Defense Program Outline in 1976.[82] For the first time, Japan not only identified its security strategy but also outlined the military force structure necessary to support it. This and subsequent plans led to the development of a sophisticated defense-industrial complex and a small but relatively advanced military force.

Concern over a declining US commitment to Japan's security rose even higher after the 1991 Gulf War. Many in the United States and some US coalition partners criticized Japan's decision not to make a military contribution to coalition forces during that conflict. Citizens and policymakers in Japan were unpleasantly surprised at the lack of US appreciation for the estimated $11 billion that Japan had spent to support the multinational force in the conflict and to aid countries in the region, as well the minesweepers it sent to the Persian Gulf after the end of hostilities. These efforts were not even mentioned by Kuwait in its full-page "thank-you" advertisement in the *New York Times* after the war.[83] At the time, the US government was also under significant domestic pressure to decrease its forward military presence and reduce defense spending. These dynamics suggested the possibility of a lesser US commitment to Japan, even as the rise of China and North Korea's developing missile and nuclear weapons programs served as powerful reminders to Japan of the dangers it could face. Such concerns provided the impetus for a shift away from focusing only on territorial self-defense and toward an acceptance of a broader, if still strictly limited, international role.

In June 1992, the Japanese Diet passed the International Peace and Cooperation Law, permitting the deployment of Japanese troops in support of UN peacekeeping operations. The law specifically allowed the deployment of Japanese SDF to Cambodia and East Timor. Although these forces did not take part in combat, their deployment outside of Japan signaled Japan's increased willingness to contribute militarily to collective efforts to further international peace and security abroad.

This trend accelerated following the September 11, 2001, terrorist attacks in the United States. Just a few months afterward, the Japanese Diet passed the Anti-Terrorism Special Measures Law, which enabled the dispatch of Japanese maritime SDF to the Indian Ocean to provide logistical support to US and coalition forces engaged in Operation Enduring Freedom in Afghanistan. In 2003, the Diet passed the Law Concerning Special Measures on Humanitarian and Reconstruction Assistance to enable the deployment of Japanese ground SDF to Iraq.[84] In 2005, the United States and Japan issued a joint "Security Guidelines" statement, declaring that their alliance plays "a vital role in ensuring the security and prosperity of both the United States and Japan, as well as in enhancing regional and global peace and stability."[85] The statement listed twelve shared regional objectives and six shared global strategic objectives common to both countries. (The inclusion of the peaceful resolution of the Taiwan Strait security dilemma did not go unnoticed by China.) In 2009, as Japan's SDF participated in a multinational antipiracy operation in the Gulf of Aden, it established Japan's first overseas logistics base since World War II. Special legislation passed by the Japanese Diet permitted the SDF to protect ships of any nationality.[86]

Recent years have continued to see gradual changes in Japan's approach to defense policy. In 2014, Japan approved a defense white paper that expressed a need to improve its defense capacity as a means of negotiating its increasingly complex security environment.[87] Although it highlighted potential threats from North Korea and Russia, the white paper was particularly focused on China, discussing increased Chinese naval activity in the East China and South China Seas. As just one indicator of increased Chinese activity, the Japanese Defense Ministry reported that it had deployed its aircraft to intercept Chinese military aircraft approaching or intruding into Japanese airspace a record 571 times in fiscal year 2015.[88]

On April 27, 2015, representatives from Japan and the United States released new "Guidelines for U.S.-Japan Defense Cooperation."[89] Negotiated over the course of several years, these guidelines provide enhanced coordination and planning mechanisms to improve the ability of the United States to come to the defense of Japan: "The two governments will take measures to ensure Japan's peace and security in all phases, seamlessly, from peacetime to contingencies, including situations when an armed attack against Japan is not involved."[90] These measures respond to Japan's longstanding concern about US abandonment by enhancing planning and operational coordination and adding detail about the roles of the two countries' armed forces in the event of an attack on Japan. At the same time, the guidelines also articulate an expanded role for Japan in regional and international security efforts. They seek to enhance Japan's value to the United States as a security partner by establishing conditions under which Japan might participate in collective defense in the event of an attack on the United States or a third country and by setting forth ways in which Japan and the United States could further regional and global security cooperation.[91] In September 2015 Japan's Diet passed two new national security laws that enable Japan to come to the defense of an ally and to provide logistical support to multinational operations abroad.[92]

It is not altogether clear how far Japan will go with its new security outlook and its corresponding development of military forces. Although the new guidelines and laws passed in 2015 mark change, the conditions under which Japan's SDF may play an expanded role are very restrictive (its own survival must be at stake before Japan may become involved in the defense of an attacked ally). There is little popular support within Japan for an expanded role for the SDF.[93] The future evolution of Japan's defense policy will be shaped by a number of factors, including the nature of China's rise; North Korea's nuclear and other military capability and intentions; Japan-US relations; Japanese relations with other countries, especially China and South Korea; and domestic political support for such policies.

Changing Security Conditions on the Korean Peninsula. In many ways, the Korean Peninsula remains caught in the military stalemate created during the Korean War, which still has not been concluded with a formal peace treaty. Important developments that will shape the future of the Korean peninsula include the changing military balance between the two Koreas, North Korea's demonstration of a nuclear weapons capability, evolution in the US-South Korean alliance, and intermittent thawing and refreezing of North-South relations.

The Changing Military Balance on the Peninsula. The conventional military balance on the Korean peninsula has changed from one that favored North Korea during the early part of the Cold War to one that is far less favorable to the North. This situation has likely increased North Korea's motivation to develop and maintain nuclear weapons as a deterrent. Currently, North Korea (officially known as the Democratic People's Republic of Korea, or DPRK) is the world's most militarized nation, with over one million troops on active duty from a population of just over twenty-five million.[94] Approximately two-thirds of these troops are deployed fewer than sixty miles away from the demilitarized zone that separates the two Koreas. Despite the fact that most of its population lives in extreme poverty, the North Korean government is estimated to have spent somewhere between 14.8 and 23.9 percent of its GDP on defense in the decade from 2002 to 2012.[95] The current leader of North Korea, Kim Jong-un, oversees a Stalinist political system and command economy that operate according to a political ideology known as *Juche*. Originally formulated by the country's founder, Kim Jong-un's grandfather Kim Il-sung, *Juche* emphasizes socialism, extreme nationalism, and self-reliance.[96]

Since North Korea lost one of its two major patrons—the Soviet Union—at the end of the Cold War, it has become increasingly isolated from the rest of the international community. Its remaining patron, China, provides significant fuel and food aid to North Korea. Despite Kim's continued bellicosity and the political leverage one would expect to accompany this supply relationship, China has been hesitant to put much pressure on Kim, for two main reasons. First, China would not like to see North Korea destabilized, which could result in chaos, massive refugee flows into China, and perhaps a resumed peninsular war. Second, China does not like the prospect that a collapse of North Korea could result in a unified Korean peninsula with a US troop presence in a country on its border.

On the other side of the demilitarized zone, South Korea's political system has evolved from an authoritarian republic into a flourishing liberal democracy. Its economic development has been equally dramatic. South Korea (or the Republic of Korea, ROK) has a GDP almost 50 times that of the North and roughly twice the population (see table 18.2). South Korea's military, although smaller in size, would present a formidable challenge to North Korea's military, given the quality of its training and weapons and the availability of energy resources.[97] South Korea has renounced nuclear weapons development, although it has the technological capability; it relies on its alliance with the United States for its nuclear deterrent.

North Korea still presents a formidable conventional threat, especially to the city of Seoul, which is within range of North Korean artillery and short-range rockets and missiles. However, many experts conclude that it would be unable to unify the peninsula by force. This is not only because of South Korea's increased military capabilities, augmented by US forces, but also because North Korea lacks the necessary external support for such an operation.

North Korea's Pursuit of Nuclear Weapons. Over the past four decades, North Korea has sought to acquire nuclear weapons to offset its shrinking conventional military advantage and to deter possible US attack. In the 1970s, North Korea received technical assistance on nuclear power from the Soviet Union, including the provision of a research reactor. This reactor was placed under International Atomic Energy Agency (IAEA) safeguards in 1977, but by then North Korea had already begun developing a small 5-megawatt (MWe) nuclear reactor at Yongbyon.[98] It finished the Yongbyon reactor in 1987 and began construction of two more reactors, a 50-MWe reactor at Yongbyon and a 200-MWe reactor at Taechon. At the time, it claimed that these reactors were dedicated solely to the production of energy for peaceful civilian use.

These developments raised serious concerns in the United States and among its regional allies and led to a nuclear crisis in 1993. Although it had signed the Nuclear Nonproliferation Treaty (NPT) in 1985, North Korea did not allow IAEA inspectors into its reactor sites until 1992, when the Yongbyon reactor had already been operational for five years. Western intelligence agencies estimated that during that time, North Korea could have produced enough fissile material for one or two nuclear weapons.[99]

When the inspections finally began in 1992, the inspectors encountered numerous discrepancies. In 1993, North Korea responded by blocking further inspections and threatening to withdraw from the NPT. In 1994, after protracted negotiations, the United States and North Korea reached a bilateral agreement, the Agreed Framework, which stated that North Korea would freeze any further production of fissile material in return for energy and economic concessions.[100] Over time, it became evident that North Korea was not honoring the Agreed Framework; by early 2003, these escalating suspicions resulted in US nullification of the Agreed Framework. As a result, North Korea withdrew from the NPT and announced that it had resumed reprocessing spent nuclear fuel rods to extract plutonium.

These developments alarmed the United States as well as states in the region. In 2003, diplomatic negotiations involving China, Japan, North Korea, Russia, South Korea, and the United States sought to resolve the crisis. Over the next four years, these Six-Party Talks generated multiple largely fruitless rounds of negotiations, during which time Western intelligence officials estimated that North Korea could have produced enough fissile material for six to eight additional nuclear weapons.[101] The crisis reached a new peak on October 9, 2006, when North Korea conducted its first successful nuclear test. Despite these discouraging developments, the Six-Party Talks continued, and a deal was announced on February 13, 2007. It featured another freeze of North Korea's nuclear program in return for energy and economic aid, much like the previous Agreed Framework.

The new agreement was short-lived: North Korea pulled out of the Six-Party Talks in April 2009, expelled IAEA inspectors, and officially restarted its nuclear program. The Foreign Ministry affirmed that North Korea would "never again take part in such talks [nor] be bound by any agreement [from] the talks."[102] Since restarting its nuclear program, North Korea could have stockpiled as many as sixty nuclear weapons. It has conducted five more nuclear weapons tests, for a total of six: one each in 2006, 2009, 2013, two in 2016, and one in 2017. The test of September 2017 was North Korea's largest to date, estimated to be over one hundred kilotons, which gives credence to North Korea's claim that it was a hydrogen bomb.[103] Although North Korea's nuclear capabilities remain opaque, they are undoubtedly improving and appear to be accelerating. The situation is enough of a threat to its regional neighbors and to the US mainland to remain a significant US policy challenge in the coming years.

The US–South Korean Alliance. After the Korean War ended with an armistice, the United States and South Korea signed a mutual defense treaty in 1953. As the alliance was formed, US motivations were mixed. On the one hand, the United States sought to ensure that South Korea would be able to defend itself against any future aggression from North Korea and to prevent communist expansion in accordance with the US strategy of containment. On the other hand, the United States also wanted to discourage South Korea's leader, Syngman Rhee (president from 1948 to 1960), from seeking to reunify the Korean peninsula through an invasion of North Korea, which could set off a wider war.[104] For South Korea, the intense desire for a US security guarantee and the pursuit of military effectiveness led to a decision to place South Korean forces under UN command even after the 1953 armistice. In 1978, the UN command was replaced by a ROK-US Combined Forces Command, which continues to be led by a US four-star general. A further change occurred in 1994, when an agreement between the United States and South Korea retained the wartime combined structure, but placed South Korean forces under South Korean command in peacetime.[105]

The end of the Cold War caused a strategic reassessment by both parties to the treaty. More significant changes began after a series of former opposition leaders assumed the presidency of South Korea (Kim Dae-jung from 1998 to 2003 and Roh Moo-hyun from 2003 to 2008). In the first decade of the twenty-first century, US and South Korean perceptions of the threat posed by North Korea diverged somewhat as the terrorist attacks of September 11, 2001, changed US strategic priorities and President Roh of South Korea placed an increased emphasis on asserting the country's sovereignty. Some in South Korea came to view the United States as a potentially dangerous source of instability on the peninsula due to US rhetoric that placed North Korea in an "axis of evil" and contemplated regime change. In this context, the South Korean public expressed greater support for military independence from the United States, which many believed would be made possible and desirable by defense reform efforts and improving relations with North Korea.[106]

During the presidency of Barack Obama, which began in 2009, the alliance was again reaffirmed as important to the security of both countries. Changes to the command structure of the alliance, which had been considered in previous years, were deferred indefinitely. In part, this may have been due to the election of two conservative and more pro-US presidents in South Korea, Lee Myung-bak in 2008 and Park Geun-hye in 2013. However, it was probably also due to a closer convergence in threat perceptions in the wake of the nuclear tests and other provocative North Korean actions, and a mutual willingness to adapt the alliance to new security demands in the twenty-first century. In the May 2013 "Joint Declaration in Commemoration of the 60th Anniversary of the Alliance between the Republic of Korea and the United States of America," the two parties declared that "the US-ROK Alliance is an increasingly global partnership, and the United States welcomes the Republic of Korea's leadership and active engagement on the world stage, including in international fora."[107] In September 2016, in a joint press conference with South Korea's President Park, Obama declared:

> As we all know, the ROK is one of America's oldest and closest allies. Our alliance remains the linchpin of peace and security not just on the Korean Peninsula, but across the region. . . . North Korea needs to know that provocations will only invite more pressure and further deepen its isolation, but that if it is willing to recognize its international obligations and the importance of denuclearization in the Korean Peninsula, the opportunities for us to dialogue with them are there. . . . Beyond the region, our alliance is a global one. We stand together against ISIL. We stand together in providing humanitarian assistance for the Syrian people and for refugees, promoting global health and fighting climate change. The ROK has been an excellent partner in helping Afghanistan stabilize. It has been an outstanding partner on global health and security issues.[108]

A long-term challenge for South Korea will be to continue to derive security benefits from its alliance with the United States even as China has become its single most important trading partner. Leaders of South Korea are likely to do their best to avoid being caught up in tensions between the United States and China as they pursue relationships with both countries that are beneficial in different ways.[109]

Relations between the Koreas. The strength of the US-ROK alliance has been in part affected by relations between the DPRK and ROK. Following the Korean War, South Korea's emphasis was defense against North Korea and early reunification. In the post–Cold War period, South Korea's policy toward North Korea came to emphasize economic engagement to promote gradual change in the North's political and economic policies.

In 1998, South Korea became a major source of aid to the North as it pursued a policy of engagement with North Korea, known as the *Sunshine Policy*. (The name refers to Aesop's fable in which only sunlight, and not harsh wind, was able to cause a traveler to take off his coat.) According to the South Korean government, total humanitarian aid provided to the North rose from $4.6 million in 1996 to $185 million by 2006.[110] In 2003, after the joint construction of a major industrial park just north of the Demilitarized Zone (DMZ), in Kaesong, North Korea, North-South trade reached $724 million.[111] In this industrial park, fifteen South Korean firms produced manufactured goods, largely for South Korean markets, employing approximately eight thousand North Korean workers.[112] The opening of limited rail links across the DMZ in 2007 also signaled warming.

Despite these positive developments, the relationship between the two Koreas grew frosty again because of both the nuclear weapons tests (in 2006 and 2009) and other belligerent actions, including the North Korean sinking of the South Korean naval vessel *Cheonan* in March 2010, and North Korean shelling of the South Korean island of Yeonpyeong in November 2010. When South Korea's President Lee took office in 2008, he ended the Sunshine Policy and significantly decreased humanitarian aid to the DPRK. By some estimates, South Korean aid to the North plummeted by 95 percent between 2008 and 2013.[113] In the wake of North Korea's fifth nuclear test, in September 2016, Lee's successor, Park, accused Kim Jong-un of displaying "maniacal recklessness" and called for additional sanctions and isolation by the international community.[114]

After a corruption scandal engulfed the presidency of Park, in May 2017 South Koreans once again elected a liberal politician as their president. Although election debates largely revolved around domestic economic matters, the Democratic Party of the new president, Moon Jae-in, has long favored improved relations with the DPRK.[115] In the midst of tensions between the DPRK and United States, heightened by the DPRK's September 2017 nuclear test and several long-range missile tests, the 2018 Winter Olympics in South Korea seemed to offer the possibility of rapprochement between the two Koreas. For the first time since the division of the peninsula, DPRK and ROK athletes competed on the same teams and, in a further sign of goodwill, Kim Jong-un sent his sister, Kim Yo-jong, to lead the DPRK's delegation. While in South Korea, Kim Jong-un's sister delivered an invitation to President Moon to participate in a summit. Although these are positive developments, previous summits have not resulted in significant, enduring change in North-South relations and many points of friction remain.[116] While South Korea has a strong interest in eventual, peaceful unification of the two Koreas, a constructive path toward that end remains elusive.

Challenges and Choices for Future US Policy

The key challenge for US policy makers in East Asian policy remains deciding how to interact with and respond to a rising, powerful China. The two broad choices are containment or engagement. Proponents of containment seek to prevent China from gaining strategic preponderance in the region, because they are wary that it would undermine US interests and undercut US economic and strategic access to the region. The containment approach emphasizes the value of a strong US-Japan alliance, a strengthened US-ROK alliance, and improved relations with India and the ASEAN countries.

Proponents of US engagement with China believe that containment policies would result in a hostile relationship. Instead, they argue, the United States should facilitate Chinese participation in the mechanisms that constitute the current international order. China would thereby gain an appreciation for how these rules and institutions serve its own interests. Proponents of engagement argue that a China that is fully integrated in the international community would become dependent on international trade and cooperation to sustain its economic growth and would not support measures that could disrupt regional stability.

The future of US-Chinese relations will also depend upon developments in cross-strait relations between China and Taiwan. The US policy of "strategic ambiguity" worked in past decades to deter China and Taiwan from taking unilateral steps that would overturn the status quo.[117] As Taiwan continues democratizing, a political compromise with the mainland that would be acceptable to both governments seems less likely. Furthermore, the military balance between China and Taiwan has tipped toward the mainland's favor. China has deployed ballistic missiles directly opposite Taiwan, and it has acquired and developed precision-strike munitions. Its doctrine, training, procurement, and development seem geared primarily to a Taiwan Strait scenario. Of course, capabilities that China develops for the strait could be directed elsewhere—for example, to settle territorial disputes with other neighbors. Meanwhile, Taiwanese defense spending has generally declined in real terms over the past two decades. Peaceful resolution of the Taiwan Strait issue will continue to be an important US strategic goal.

The United States also continues to grapple with the evolution of Japan's security policy. The US-Japanese alliance has been critical to enhancing regional stability. However, there are dangers in relying too heavily on this strategic relationship, because increases in Japan's military capabilities could aggravate historical grievances in East Asia. The United States might press Japan to make greater efforts to achieve regional reconciliation as it continues to develop its military capabilities, or to take more military responsibility in the international arena, but US pressure might come at a high price in terms of US-Japanese relations or other US alliances in the region. American efforts to encourage greater Japanese military strength could also affect US-Chinese relations.

Finally, the United States will continue to wrestle with the problem of North Korea's nuclear weapons. As North Korea continues to improve and test its nuclear and ballistic missile technology, the United States and other countries in the region will need to intensify their efforts to confront the threat posed by North Korea. Both in the nuclear context and, more broadly, in seeking regional stability, the US-South Korean relationship will continue to be of significant importance.

Discussion Questions

1. Was the Obama administration correct in pursuing a rebalancing toward East Asia? What is the case for this shift in focus in US national security policy?
2. To what extent does China's rise in power present a strategic threat to the United States?
3. Should the United States seek to contain or to engage China? Why? Can the two approaches be pursued simultaneously?
4. Can the United States have a positive impact on political and economic developments within China?

5. Given the rise in China's military power and a simultaneous rise in pro-independence sentiment in an increasingly democratic Taiwan, should the United States change its policy toward Taiwan?

6. How should the United States seek to influence Japan's changing national security policy? To what extent should US officials encourage Japan to focus on broader regional security issues? Are there dangers in or limits to this approach?

7. What can the United States do to try to prevent increased tensions and an intensified arms race among the countries of East Asia?

8. How should the United States respond to the challenge posed by a nuclear North Korea?

9. Can the United States influence economic and political developments within North Korea?

10. Should the United States change its alliance relationship with South Korea? If so, how?

Recommended Readings

Berteau, David, Michael J. Green, and Zack Cooper. *Assessing the Asia-Pacific Rebalance*. Lanham, MD: Rowman & Littlefield, 2014.

Cha, Victor D. *The Impossible State: North Korea, Past and Future*. New York: Ecco, 2012.

Christensen, Thomas J. *Worse than a Monolith: Alliance Politics and Problems of Coercive Diplomacy in Asia*. Princeton, NJ: Princeton University Press, 2011.

Friedberg, Aaron L. *A Contest for Supremacy: China, America, and the Struggle for Mastery in Asia*. New York: W. W. Norton, 2011.

Johnson, Christopher K. *President Xi Jinping's "Belt and Road" Initiative: A Practical Assessment of the Chinese Communist Party's Roadmap for China's Global Resurgence*. Washington, DC: Center for Strategic and International Studies, March 2016.

Johnston, Alastair Ian. *Cultural Realism: Strategic Culture and Grand Strategy in Chinese History*. Princeton, NJ: Princeton University Press, 1995.

Kissinger, Henry. *On China*. New York: Penguin, 2011.

Pyle, Kenneth B. *Japan Rising: The Resurgence of Japanese Power and Purpose*. New York: PublicAffairs, 2007.

Samuels, Richard J. *Securing Japan: Tokyo's Grand Strategy and the Future of East Asia*. Ithaca, NY: Cornell University Press, 2007.

Shambaugh, David L. *China Goes Global: The Partial Power*. Oxford; New York: Oxford University Press, 2013.

———. *Tangled Titans: The United States and China*. Lanham, MD: Rowman & Littlefield, 2013.

Swaine, Michael D. *America's Challenge: Engaging a Rising China in the Twenty-First Century*. Washington, DC: Carnegie Endowment for International Peace, 2011.

Recommended Internet Resources

Asia News Network, www.asianewsnet.net

Asia-Pacific Area Network, Pacific Command, Department of Defense, https://community.apan.org/support/apan-info/w/apan-info/

China Leadership Monitor, www.hoover.org/publications/china-leadership-monitor

Comparative Connections (online journal run by the Center for Strategic and International Studies), http://csis.org/program/comparative-connections
East-West Center, www.eastwestcenter.org
National Bureau of Asian Research, www.nbr.org

Notes

1. Mongolia is the only other country included in Northeast Asia, and it does not have significant military forces in proximity to US forces. Additionally, despite disagreement over its sovereign status and the US "one China" policy, Taiwan is treated as a country for the purposes of this discussion.

2. International Institute for Strategic Studies (IISS), "Chapter Two: Comparative Defence Statistics," *Military Balance* 116, no. 1 (2016): 19.

3. ASEAN states include Brunei, Cambodia, Indonesia, Laos, Malaysia, Myanmar, Singapore, Thailand, and Vietnam.

4. The White House Office of the Press Secretary, "America's Future in Asia," Remarks as Prepared for Delivery by National Security Advisor Susan E. Rice, November 21, 2013, https://www.whitehouse.gov/the-press-office/2013/11/21/remarks-prepared-delivery-national-security-advisor-susan-e-rice.

5. The White House, *National Security Strategy* (Washington, DC: The White House, May 2010), 2.

6. The White House, *National Security Strategy of the United States of America* (Washington, DC: The White House, December 2017), 42.

7. Full text of the Japanese constitution is available in English on the website of the National Library of the Japanese Diet, http://www.ndl.go.jp/constitution/e/etc/c01.html.

8. For more on US reliance on bilateral alliances in Asia, see Eric Heginbotham and Christopher P. Twomey, "America's Bismarckian Asia Policy," *Current History* 104, no. 683 (2005): 243–50; and Michael H. Armacost and Daniel I. Okimoto, eds., *The Future of America's Alliances in Northeast Asia* (Washington, DC: Brookings Institution Press, 2004).

9. The texts of all three communiqués are available from the Taiwan documents project, http://www.taiwandocuments.org/doc_com.htm.

10. "Taiwan Relations Act," *Public Law 96-8*, 96th Congress of the United States, April 10, 1979, https://www.congress.gov/bill/96th-congress/house-bill/2479.

11. President Carter actually wanted to order the complete withdrawal of all US forces—it was a prominent campaign pledge he made during the 1976 presidential election—but the proposal was rescinded after objections were raised by various policy advisors and security experts.

12. The estimate of forty-five million deaths is from Frank Dikötter, *Mao's Great Famine: The History of China's Most Devastating Catastrophe, 1958–1962* (New York: Walker, 2010), 2.

13. For more information about China's economic growth, see David Hale, "China Takes Off," *Foreign Affairs* 82, no. 6 (2003): 36–53.

14. In the Agreed Framework, North Korea agreed to freeze its nuclear program, initially for a number of economic and energy concessions including fuel shipments, have talks toward normalization of relations, and the provision of two light-water reactors. The agreement also included a North Korean promise to dismantle its nuclear program once the promised light-water reactors were delivered. See Jonathan D. Pollack, "The United States,

North Korea, and End of the Agreed Framework," *Naval War College Review* 56, no. 3 (2003): 11–49.

15. See Ashton B. Carter and William J. Perry, *Chapter 3 in Ashton B. Carter and William J. Perry, Preventive Defense: A New Security Strategy for America* (Washington, DC: Brookings Institution Press, 1999), 92–122.

16. Department of Defense, "United States Security Strategy for the East Asia–Pacific Region," *East Asian Strategy Report 1998* (Washington, DC: Office of the Secretary of Defense, 1998).

17. For a more in-depth analysis of the Bush Doctrine, see Robert Jervis, "Understanding the Bush Doctrine," *Political Science Quarterly* 118, no. 3 (2003): 365–88.

18. President George W. Bush first used the term "axis of evil" publicly in his 2002 State of the Union Speech to the US Congress on January 29, 2002.

19. Ian Bremmer, *The End of the Free Market* (New York: Penguin, 2010), 51–72.

20. The World Bank, "Anemic Recovery in Emerging Markets to Weigh Heavily on Global Growth in 2016," January 6, 2016, http://www.worldbank.org/en/news/press-release/2016/01/06/anemic-recovery-in-emerging-markets-to-weigh-heavily-on-global-growth-in-2016.

21. Kenneth Lieberthal, "The American Pivot to Asia: Why President Obama's Turn to the East Is Easier Said than Done," *Foreign Policy*, December 21, 2001, http://foreignpolicy.com/2011/12/21/the-american-pivot-to-asia/.

22. The White House Office of the Press Secretary, "Remarks by President Obama to the Australian Parliament," November 17, 2011, https://www.whitehouse.gov/the-press-office/2011/11/17/remarks-president-obama-australian-parliament.

23. The White House Office of the Press Secretary, "Remarks by President Obama to the Australian Parliament." See also Lieberthal, "The American Pivot to Asia."

24. See Anthony H. Cordesman and Ashley Hess, *The Evolving Military Balance in the Korean Peninsula and Northeast Asia* (Washington, DC: Center for Strategic and International Studies [CSIS], June 2013), http://csis.org/publication/evolving-military-balance-korean-peninsula-and-northeast-asia.

25. Suisheng Zhao, "China's Pragmatic Nationalism: Is It Manageable?" *Washington Quarterly* 29, no. 1 (2005–2006): 134.

26. See International Monetary Fund, World Economic Outlook, October 2017, http://www.imf.org/external/datamapper/datasets/WEO. These figures are based on the official exchange rate, which is most useful when examining the relative aggregate power of countries in the world. If purchasing power parity (PPP) calculations are used instead, China surpassed the United States as the world's largest economy in 2014. See Joseph E. Stiglitz, "The Chinese Century," *Vanity Fair*, January 2015, http://depthome.brooklyn.cuny.edu/bcchina/documents/ChineseCentury.pdf.

27. Dan Levin, "Study Links Polluted Air in China to 1.6 Million Deaths a Year," *New York Times*, August 13, 2015, http://www.nytimes.com/2015/08/14/world/asia/study-links-polluted-air-in-china-to-1-6-million-deaths-a-year.htm.

28. Madison Park, "Top 20 Most Polluted Cities in the World," CNN, May 10, 2014, http://www.cnn.com/2014/05/08/world/asia/india-pollution-who/.

29. Xing Xing, "Stress and Challenges: What's Facing China's 'Nine Dragons of Water,'" *Global Asia* 10, no. 1 (2015): 22.

30. Arthur Daemmrich, "The Political Economy of Healthcare Reform in China: Negotiating Public and Private," *SpringerPlus* 2 (2013), http://www.ncbi.nlm.nih.gov/pmc/articles/PMC3776089/.

31. The World Bank, "GNI per Capita, PPP (Current International $)," 2018, https://data.worldbank.org/indicator/NY.GNP.PCAP.PP.CD?year_high_desc=true.

32. The World Bank, *China Overview*, March 28, 2017, http://www.worldbank.org/en/country/china/overview.

33. Leslie Shaffer, "China's Economy Grew 6.9 Percent in 2015, a 25-Year Low," CNBC, January 18, 2016, http://www.cnbc.com/2016/01/18/china-reveals-key-q4-2015-gdp-data.html.

34. Murray C. Tanner, "China's Social Unrest Problem," testimony before the US-China Economic and Security Review Commission, May 15, 2014, 1, http://www.uscc.gov/sites/default/files/Tanner_Written%20Testimony.pdf.

35. Tanner, "China's Social Unrest Problem," 2.

36. Chris Buckley, "China: Lawyer Released from Prison," *New York Times International*, August 8, 2014, A9.

37. Tanner, "China's Social Unrest Problem," 1.

38. James Griffiths and Steven Jiang, "China's Top Paper Says Xi Jinping Won't Necessarily Serve For Life," CNN, March 1, 2018, https://www.cnn.com/2018/03/01/asia/china-peoples-daily-xi-jinping-term-limits-intl/index.html.

39. Organization for Economic Cooperation and Development (OECD), *China in Focus: Lessons and Challenges* (Paris: OECD, 2012), 16; Pew Research Center, "Growing Concerns in China about Inequality, Corruption," October 16, 2012, http://www.pewglobal.org/2012/10/16/chapter-1-domestic-issues-and-national-problems/ (emphasis in the original).

40. Pew, "Growing Concerns in China."

41. Pew, "Growing Concerns in China."

42. "China's Cities: The Great Transition," *Economist*, March 22, 2014, http://www.economist.com/news/leaders/21599360-government-right-reform-hukou-system-it-needs-be-braver-great.

43. "China's Online Users More than Double Entire U.S. Population," CNN, February 4, 2015, http://www.cnn.com/2015/02/03/world/china-internet-growth-2014/.

44. For more information about the potentially precarious relationship between CCP legitimacy and Chinese nationalism, see Peter Hayes Gries, "Chinese Nationalism: Challenging the State?" *Current History* 104, no. 683 (2005): 251–56.

45. Edward Wong, Jane Perlez, and Chris Buckley, "China Announces Cuts of 300,000 Troops at Military Parade Showing Its Might," *New York Times*, September 2, 2015, http://www.nytimes.com/2015/09/03/world/asia/beijing-turns-into-ghost-town-as-it-gears-up-for-military-parade.html.

46. For more information on the impact of US performance in the Gulf War on PLA reforms, see David Shambaugh, *Modernizing China's Military: Prospects, Problems, and Prospects* (Berkeley: University of California Press, 2004).

47. Office of the Secretary of Defense (OSD), *Annual Report to Congress: Military and Security Developments Involving the People's Republic of China* (Washington, DC: Department of Defense, 2015), i.

48. Stockholm International Peace Research Institute (SIPRI), 2014 data, http://www.sipri.org/research/armaments/milex/recent-trends.

49. David W. Kearn Jr., "Air-Sea Battle and China's Anti-Access and Area Denial Challenge," *Orbis* 58 (December 2014): 134.

50. Kearn, "Air-Sea Battle," 133.

51. OSD, *Annual Report to Congress*, 2015, 59.

52. Larry M. Wortzel, "China's Military Modernization and Cyber Activities," *Strategic Studies Quarterly* 8, no. 1 (2014): 11–12.

53. OSD, *Annual Report to Congress*, 2015, 38.

54. OSD, *Annual Report to Congress*, 2015, 35.

55. Associated Press, "Secretary of Defense Chuck Hagel Gets Rare Tour of China's New Aircraft Carrier," NYDailyNews.com, April 7, 2014, http://www.nydailynews.com/news/politics/secretary-defense-chuck-hagel-rare-tour-china-new-aircraft-carrier-article-1.1748237.

56. OSD, *Annual Report to Congress: Military and Security Developments Involving the People's Republic of China* (Washington, DC: Department of Defense, 2013), 1; OSD, *Annual Report to Congress*, 2015, 16.

57. Chun Han Wong, "China Appears to Have Built Radar Facilities on Disputed South China Sea Islands," *Wall Street Journal*, February 23, 2016, http://www.wsj.com/articles/china-appears-to-have-built-radar-gear-in-disputed-waters-1456198634; Michael Forsythe, "Missiles Deployed on Disputed South China Sea Island, Officials Say," *New York Times*, February 17, 2016, http://www.nytimes.com/2016/02/18/world/asia/china-missiles-south-china-sea.html.

58. Christopher K. Johnson, *President Xi Jinping's "Belt and Road" Initiative: A Practical Assessment of the Chinese Communist Party's Roadmap for China's Global Resurgence* (Washington, DC: Center for Strategic and International Studies, March 2016), 5.

59. Johnson, *President Xi Jinping's "Belt and Road" Initiative*, 5.

60. Graham Hutchings, *Modern China: A Guide to a Century of Change* (Cambridge, MA: Harvard University Press, 2001), 38.

61. Alastair Iain Johnston, "How New and Assertive Is China's New Assertiveness?" *International Security* 37, no. 4 (2013): 9.

62. Johnston, "How New and Assertive Is China's New Assertiveness?," 45–48.

63. Dingding Chen and Xiaoyu Pu, "Correspondence: Debating China's Assertiveness," *International Security* 30, no. 3 (2013/2014): 176–83.

64. Johnson, *President Xi Jinping's "Belt and Road" Initiative*, 1.

65. Johnson, *President Xi Jinping's "Belt and Road" Initiative*, 6, 14.

66. Johnson, *President Xi Jinping's "Belt and Road" Initiative*, 5.

67. Johnson, *President Xi Jinping's "Belt and Road" Initiative*, 12.

68. Rosemary Foot, "'Doing Some Things' in the Xi Jinping Era: The United Nations as China's Venue of Choice," *International Affairs* 90, no. 5 (2014): 1085–100.

69. Sukjoon Yoon, "Implications of Xi Jinping's 'True Maritime Power,'" *Naval War College Review* 68, no. 3 (2015): 40–63.

70. Thomas J. Christensen, "The Contemporary Security Dilemma: Deterring a Taiwan Conflict," *Washington Quarterly* 25, no. 4 (2002): 7.

71. J. Michael Cole, "The Third Taiwan Strait Crisis: The Forgotten Showdown Between China and America," *The National Interest*, March 10, 2017, http://nationalinterest.org/feature/the-third-taiwan-strait-crisis-the-forgotten-showdown-19742.

72. T. Y. Wang and S. F. Cheng, "Presidential Approval in Taiwan: An Analysis of Survey Data in the Ma Ying-Jeou Presidency," *Electoral Studies* 40 (December 2015): 36.

73. Alex Chuan-hsien Chang, "The 2016 Presidential and Legislative Elections in Taiwan," *Electoral Studies* 43 (September 2016): 176.

74. Chang, "The 2016 Presidential and Legislative Elections in Taiwan," 176.

75. Bonnie S. Glaser, "The Future of U.S.-Taiwan Relations," statement before the House Foreign Affairs Committee Subcommittee on Asia and the Pacific, February 11, 2016,

http://docs.house.gov/meetings/FA/FA05/20160211/104457/HHRG-114-FA05-Wstate-GlaserB-20160211.pdf.

76. Ian Rowen, "Inside Taiwan's Sunflower Movement: Twenty-Four Days in a Student-Occupied Parliament, and the Future of the Region," *Journal of Asian Studies* 74, no. 1 (2015): 1–15.

77. Wang and Cheng, "Presidential Approval in Taiwan," 177.

78. Javier C. Hernandez, "China Suspends Diplomatic Contact with Taiwan," *New York Times*, June 25, 2016, http://www.nytimes.com/2016/06/26/world/asia/china-suspends-diplomatic-contact-with-taiwan.html.

79. Glaser, "The Future of U.S.-Taiwan Relations," 5.

80. Full text of the Japanese constitution is available on the website of the National Library of the Japanese Diet, http://www.ndl.go.jp/constitution/e/etc/c01.html.

81. For a more thorough discussion concerning the risks inherent in security alliances, see Glenn H. Snyder, "The Security Dilemma in Alliance Politics," *World Politics* 36, no. 4 (1984): 461–95.

82. David Fouse, "Japan's FY 2005 National Defense Program Outline: New Concepts, Old Promises," *Asia-Pacific Center for Security Studies* 4, no. 3 (2003): 2.

83. William C. Middlebrooks Jr., *Why Japan Must Become a "Normal" Nation* (Westport, CT: Praeger Security International, 2008), 39.

84. James Przystup, "U.S.-Japan Relations: Progress Toward a Mature Relationship," *INSS Occasional Paper 2* (Washington, DC: National Defense University Press, 2005).

85. "Joint Statement: U.S.-Japan Consultative Committee," Japanese Ministry of Foreign Affairs, February 19, 2005, http://www.mofa.go.jp/region/n-america/us/security/scc/joint0502.html.

86. Adam P. Liff, "Japan's Defense Policy: Abe the Evolutionary," *Washington Quarterly* 38, no. 2 (2015): 81–82.

87. Ministry of Defense, "Defense of Japan," 2014, white paper, http://www.mod.go.jp/e/publ/w_paper/2014.html.

88. Franz-Stefan Gady, "Japan's Fighter Jets Intercepted Chinese Aircraft 571 Times in 2015," *Diplomat*, April 26, 2016, http://thediplomat.com/2016/04/japans-fighter-jets-intercepted-chinese-aircraft-571-times-in-2015/.

89. US Department of State, "A Stronger Alliance for a Dynamic Security Environment: The New Guidelines for U.S.-Japan Defense Cooperation," April 27, 2015, http://www.state.gov/r/pa/prs/ps/2015/04/241125.htm.

90. "The Guidelines for Japan-U.S. Defense Cooperation," April 27, 2015, http://www.mofa.go.jp/files/000078188.pdf.

91. Tomohiko Satake, "The New Guidelines for Japan-U.S. Defense Cooperation and an Expanding Japanese Security Role," *Asian Politics & Policy* 8, no. 1 (2016): 32–33.

92. Franz-Stefan Gady, "Why China Should Not Worry about Japan's New Security Laws," *Diplomat*, March 31, 2016, http://thediplomat.com/2016/03/why-china-should-not-worry-about-japans-new-security-laws/.

93. Gady, "Why China Should Not Worry about Japan's New Security Laws." See also Liff, "Japan's Defense Policy," 94.

94. CIA World Factbook, "North Korea," July 2017, https://www.cia.gov/library/publications/the-world-factbook/geos/kn.html.

95. US Department of State, "WMEAT 2015 Table I—Military Expenditures and Armed Forces Personnel, 2002–2012," *World Military Expenditures and Arms Transfers 2015*, April 2017, http://www.state.gov/documents/organization/251076.xlsx.

96. For more information regarding the domestic political ideology of North Korea, see Kong Dan Oh and Ralph C. Hassig, *North Korea through the Looking Glass* (Washington, DC: Brookings Institution Press, 2000).

97. Jin H. Pak and Michael Kim, "How Can the United States Take the Initiative in the Current North Korea Nuclear Crisis?" *Pacific Focus* 20, no. 2 (2005): 112.

98. MWe is a power rating that represents millions of watts of electricity produced per day. A reactor with a 5MWe rating is considered very small. Modern nuclear reactors typically yield about 500 to 2,000 MWe.

99. Sharon A. Squassoni, "North Korea's Nuclear Weapons: How Soon an Arsenal?" *CRS Report RS21391*, February 2, 2004.

100. The deal stipulated that as concessions for disarmament, energy and economic aid, North Korea would receive an agreement by all parties to respect each other's national sovereignty, and a promise of future negotiations at an "appropriate time" over the provision of a light-water nuclear reactor. See US State Department, Bureau of Nonproliferation, *US-DPRK Agreed Framework: Fact Sheet*, February 15, 2001, http://2001-2009.state.gov/t/isn/rls/fs/2001/5284.htm.

101. Larry A. Niksch, "North Korea's Nuclear Weapons Program," *CRS Report RL33590*, August 1, 2006.

102. Mark Landler, "North Korea Says It Will Halt Talks and Restart Its Nuclear Program," *New York Times*, April 15, 2009, http://www.nytimes.com/2009/04/15/world/asia/15korea.html.

103. Eleanor Albert, "North Korea's Military Capabilities," *Council on Foreign Relations Backgrounder*, January 3, 2018, https://www.cfr.org/backgrounder/north-koreas-military-capabilities.

104. Victor D. Cha, "Powerplay: Origins of the U.S. Alliance System in Asia," *International Security* 34, no. 3 (2009/2010): 173–77.

105. Park Hwee-rhak, "An Analysis and Lessons on South Korea's Attempt and Postponement of the OPCON Transition from the ROK-U.S. Combined Forces Command," *Korean Journal of Defense Analysis* 27, no. 3 (2015): 349.

106. Hwee-Rhak, "An Analysis and Lessons on South Korea," 352–55.

107. The White House Office of the Press Secretary, "Joint Declaration in Commemoration of the 60th Anniversary of the Alliance between the Republic of Korea and the United States of America," May 7, 2013, https://www.whitehouse.gov/the-press-office/2013/05/07/joint-declaration-commemoration-60th-anniversary-alliance-between-republ.

108. The White House Office of the Press Secretary, "Remarks by President Obama and President Park of the Republic of Korea after Bilateral Meeting," September 6, 2016, https://www.whitehouse.gov/the-press-office/2016/09/06/remarks-president-obama-and-president-park-republic-korea-after.

109. For a good discussion of these dynamics, see Ellen Kim and Victor D. Cha, "Between a Rock and a Hard Place: South Korea's Strategic Dilemmas with China and the United States," *Asia Policy* 21 (January 2016): 101–21.

110. "The Status of Humanitarian Assistance toward North Korea (as of June 30, 2006)," Ministry of Unification, Facts and Figures (Republic of Korea government website), June 5, 2006, http://www.unikorea.go.kr/english/ENK/ENK0301R.jsp.

111. Mark E. Manyin, "Foreign Assistance to North Korea," *CRS Report RL31785*, May 2005.

112. Seongji Woo, "North Korea–South Korea Relations under Kim Jong-Il," in *North Korea: The Politics of Regime Survival*, ed. Young Whan Kihl and Hong Nack Kim (New York: M. E. Sharpe, 2006), 227.

113. Choe Sang-Hun, "South Korea Pledges Millions in Aid for North," *New York Times*, July 28, 2013, http://www.nytimes.com/2013/07/29/world/asia/south-korea-pledges-humanitarian-aid-for-north.html.

114. "North Korea Claims Success in Fifth Nuclear Test," BBC News, September 9, 2016, http://www.bbc.com/news/world-asia-37314927.

115. J. Weston Phippen, "Moon Jae In Wins South Korea's Persidential Election," *The Atlantic*, May 9, 2017, https://www.theatlantic.com/news/archive/2017/05/south-korea-presidential-election/525942/.

116. Robert Kelly, "Have the Winter Olympics Repaired North-South Korea Relations?" BBC News, February 20, 2018, http://www.bbc.com/news/world-asia-43063399.

117. Christensen, "The Contemporary Security Dilemma," 7.

19

South Asia

The Indus Valley peoples and their modern descendants in South Asia represent some of the world's oldest civilizations. America's relatively recent arrival on the region's stage injected a powerful element into the local mix, but US involvement has not radically altered the fundamental factors that shape relations among the region's states. These factors include competition for regional influence between India and Pakistan, religious differences, and internal political and security challenges within each country. While US involvement has not profoundly altered these dynamics, globalization and the rise of transnational threats, including nuclear proliferation and international terrorism, have increased their importance to the United States.

For the purposes of this chapter, South Asia includes India, Pakistan, the Maldives, Sri Lanka, Bangladesh, Bhutan, and Nepal (figure 19.1). The primary focus here is on US interactions with and developments within India and Pakistan, the largest and most powerful regional actors. Although not usually considered part of South Asia, neighboring Afghanistan is also treated in this chapter because of its close relationship with Pakistan, and its role as a battleground for competition between New Delhi and Islamabad.

This chapter begins by identifying US interests in South Asia and then reviews the history of US policy in the region. With this as background, the chapter discusses the ongoing regional dynamics that affect US policy in South Asia today. The chapter concludes with issues for future consideration.

The authors would like to thank Mr. Don Rassler for his significant contributions to this chapter.

FIGURE 19.1 South Asia

US Interests in South Asia

American global priorities clearly dominated US policy in South Asia for decades following World War II. Developments in South Asia were seen through the lens of the Cold War and evaluated according to their impact on the standoff between the United States and the Soviet Union.

In the early twenty-first century, the United States has had several reasons to focus more directly on its interests in South Asia. First, the United States retains an interest in avoiding conflict escalation stemming from the rivalry between India and Pakistan. Given that both India and Pakistan have become declared nuclear weapon states, the potential cost of conflict between them has escalated dramatically. A second and related interest pertains to the way in which India and Pakistan handle their nuclear weapons technology and the implications of their actions for the global nonproliferation regime. Third, the terrorist attacks in the United States on September 11, 2001, brought the importance of nonstate actors in South Asia into sharp relief. This is unlikely to be a transient US interest, as instability in Afghanistan or worsening conditions in Pakistan would recreate conditions in which al Qaeda or similar groups could thrive. Finally, South Asia's developing economies present important economic opportunities and challenges. India, in particular, is clearly rising in economic significance, and an increasingly diverse group of Americans (including government policy makers, investment managers, and directors of large corporations) are taking note of the opportunities and challenges that stem from India's growing significance in the international economy.

Preventing Regional Conflict. Preventing regional conflict in South Asia and limiting the escalation of conflicts when they occur have long been key national security interests for the United States. As a result, the United States has a history of diplomatic engagement in the region's most volatile conflict, that between India and Pakistan. During the Cold War, US relationships with India and Pakistan were shaped by the extent to which these two countries affected the global balance of power between the United States and the Soviet Union. Since the end of the Cold War, US policy has been shaped by concern over the potential escalation of conflict between two states with nuclear weapons. India demonstrated its first device in 1974; Pakistan conducted nuclear tests and declared itself a nuclear weapon state in 1998.

Preventing Nuclear Proliferation. Along with limiting conflict that might precipitate nuclear war, the United States has an interest in limiting the proliferation of nuclear weapons and technology. Particularly in relation to Pakistan, with its established history of proliferation (discussed further below), there is concern that members of its nuclear bureaucracy or military might transfer nuclear technology or material to another state or violent nonstate actor. Given the chronic political instability in Pakistan, the possibility that Pakistan's nuclear weapons could fall into irresponsible hands is especially important. Because of these concerns, Pakistan has been called "the most crucial node of the nexus of terrorism and WMD proliferation."[1]

Combating Terrorism. A third major US interest in South Asia is countering threats from terrorist groups in the region. American counterterrorism efforts since the attacks of September 11, 2001, have exacerbated the challenges of regional security because the war in Afghanistan has had spillover effects in Pakistan and has affected the Indo-Pakistan relationship. The United States has also sought to counter other terrorist groups throughout the region.

Promoting Prosperity. A final major US interest in South Asia is economic. The United States stands to benefit from expanding commercial relationships with the countries of South Asia. This interest has also motivated US support for the economic development of South Asian countries and the integration of their economies into the global economy. The growing significance of South Asia, especially India, as a market and as a provider of manufactured goods and services presents both opportunities and challenges (table 19.1).

History of US Policy in the Region Since World War II

After the departure of the British from India and its partition into two states in 1949, the United States looked to Pakistan (then consisting of East Pakistan, later Bangladesh, as well as what is now known as Pakistan) and to newly democratic India for support in its struggle against the spread of communism and the global influence of the Soviet Union. Pakistan proved an eager and willing ally, primarily because it sought help from the most powerful country in the world against the most powerful country in its region, that is, India. Pakistan sought a protective patron throughout the Cold War and continues to do so to this day.[2] India, by contrast, due to its colonial history, size, and relative military advantage, was concerned mostly with preserving its national prerogatives against those who might infringe upon them. Its cooperative relations with the Soviet Union and its self-appointed role as spokesman for the world's developing countries combined to alienate India from successive US administrations.[3] For decades, the results were warm relations between the United States and Pakistan and a diplomatic chill between the United States and India.

As discussed in chapter 3, in the 1950s and 1960s the Eisenhower administration created and encouraged a series of Cold War alliances with countries in South Asia. In 1954, after the French departure from Vietnam, the United States, Pakistan, and six other countries formed the Southeast Asian Treaty Organization (SEATO) to oppose further communist expansion into South and Southeast Asia. Due to the threat it perceived from India, Pakistan sought explicit wording in the organizing documents that SEATO's mutual defense obligations would be invoked upon the attack of a member from any quarter.[4] The United States, however, limited the mutual obligation solely to an attack by communist forces.

In 1955, the United States organized the creation of what was to become the Central Treaty Organization (CENTO) to deter Soviet expansion toward Central Asia. Full members were the United Kingdom, Turkey, Iraq, Iran and Pakistan, with the United States joining the military committee in 1958. One practical benefit for the United States was Pakistan's willingness to allow intelligence operations

Table 19.1 South Asia Key Statistics

Country	*Total population (millions)*	*Life expectancy at Birth*	*GDP US$ (billions)*	*GDP/ capita US$*	*Population living in poverty (%)*	*Military expenditure (% of GDP)*	*Military spending US$ (millions)*	*Human Development Index (HDI) ranking (of 188)*
Afghanistan	33.3	51.3	18.4	2,000	35.8	14.0	2,581	169
Bangladesh	156.2	73.2	226.8	3,900	31.5	1.2	2,705	139
Bhutan	0.8	70.1	2.1	8,100	13.3	na	na	132
India	1,266.9	68.5	2,251.0	6,700	21.9	2.3	51,052	131
Maldives	0.39	75.6	3.3	15,300	16.0	na	na	105
Nepal	29.0	70.7	21.1	2,500	25.2	1.6	338	144
Pakistan	202.0	67.7	298.1	5,100	29.5	2.7	7,471	147
Sri Lanka	22.2	76.8	82.2	11,200	6.7	2.4	1,958	73

na = not available.

Sources: Data on population and economy is from the CIA World Factbook 2017, https://www.cia.gov/library/publications/the-world-factbook. Military expenditure data is from International Institute for Strategic Studies (IISS), *The Military Balance 2017* (London: IISS, 2017). HDI rankings are from *Human Development Report 2016*, http://hdr.undp.org/en/data. Most figures are from 2016 (otherwise latest available data is listed). GDP is reported at the official exchange rate. GDP per capita is using Purchasing Power Parity rates.

on its territory. It was from a Pakistani airbase, for example, that US Air Force pilot Francis Gary Powers took off in his U-2 surveillance aircraft in 1960 on his way to being shot down over the Soviet Union—an incident that exposed these US intelligence operations to international scrutiny.

Neither SEATO nor CENTO survived beyond the 1970s, but both arrangements reflected a US tilt toward Pakistan due to its support of the US policy of containment. Pakistan had become America's "most allied ally in Asia," as Pakistani military ruler Ayub Khan wrote in his autobiography.[5] In 1954, to reward Pakistan for joining the fight against communism and to help it prepare for that struggle, President Dwight Eisenhower approved the first sale of military hardware to Pakistan.[6] India reacted with anger and warned that Pakistan would use the US arms against India rather than against communist adversaries. Eisenhower expressed a willingness to give similar support to India, but Prime Minister Jawaharlal Nehru rejected such support, opting to preserve India's independent foreign policy stance and its amicable relations with the Soviet Union.[7]

Throughout the 1950s and early 1960s, US relations with Pakistan were generally good, but US relations with India were not. In addition to Indian dislike of the US arms flow to Pakistan, India's previous colonial experience made its leaders particularly sensitive to any paternalistic actions by Western powers or infringements upon the country's sovereignty. One reflection of these sentiments was India's leadership in the Non-Aligned Movement, a grouping of newly independent states that declared its desire to abstain from the competition and conflict that stemmed from the Cold War standoff between the United States and the Soviet Union. For their part, US policy makers were also troubled by India's military cooperation, limited though it was, with the Soviet Union.

Despite these dynamics, the United States responded to India's requests for military aid after its brief, disastrous 1962 border war with China.[8] The Soviet Union, its erstwhile military equipment supplier, refused to help.[9] From the US perspective, this experience showed that India could be a useful, if limited, ally in the global struggle against communism. India, on the other hand, took away a different lesson. Its rough handling by China and the necessity of requesting US aid indicated the need for a nuclear weapon capability, an indication that was reinforced by China's nuclear test in 1964.

In the mid-1960s, American relations with Pakistan deteriorated. In 1965, Pakistan launched an invasion into the Indian-controlled portion of the disputed region of Kashmir. Although Pakistan initially benefited from moving first, the conflict quickly turned in India's favor. The resulting ceasefire saw restoration of the preconflict status quo. President Lyndon Johnson's subsequent decision to end ten years of US military aid to Pakistan revealed the latter's dependence on that aid and left it at a serious disadvantage relative to India. As a result, Pakistan turned to China, deepening a security relationship that has since flourished.[10]

The beginning of the 1970s saw Pakistan serving as an interlocutor for the United States as the Nixon administration made overtures to China. However, Pakistan's attentions were soon drawn inward. Long dissatisfied with their relationship with West Pakistan, the people of East Pakistan, encouraged by India, declared their separation and independence in March 1971. The situation quickly escalated, and India intervened in November 1971. Despite US efforts to counter the intervention, India forced the surrender of the Pakistani Army in East Pakistan in December 1971, which led to the creation of the state of Bangladesh. American support of Pakistan against India increased the animosity between the United States and India, with little benefit to US relations with Pakistan.[11]

By 1979, several policy issues further complicated US relations with Pakistan. Intelligence assessments indicating that Pakistan was actively developing nuclear weapons caused the United States to cease its long-running support of the Pakistani nuclear energy program. This could have been a fatal blow to the US-Pakistan relationship, but the Soviet invasion of Afghanistan in late December 1979 fundamentally changed the dynamic. The Soviet effort to restore stability in a bordering country, as well as to restrain what it viewed as the dangerous and erratic leadership of a shaky communist government, provoked a decade-long insurgency by Afghan resistance fighters.[12] The United States enlisted Pakistan's help to aid these resistance fighters. Pakistan thus regained its status as a "front-line" anti-Soviet state and recipient of American aid.[13]

By 1989, the Soviets had withdrawn from Afghanistan, and shortly thereafter the Soviet Union collapsed. The end of the Cold War again profoundly altered the US estimation of its interests in South Asia. Most notably, Pakistan was no longer a necessary ally in the fight against communism. In 1985, Congress passed the Pressler Amendment to the Foreign Assistance Act, which required the president to certify that a country was not actively seeking nuclear weapons before that country could receive US aid. In 1990, President George H. W. Bush determined that he could not certify Pakistan and thus ended a substantial US aid program. The effect of this reversal was similar to that of America's earlier decision to end aid in 1979. Once again, Pakistan perceived that the United States was a fickle and untrustworthy ally.[14]

In May 1998, India and Pakistan each conducted a series of nuclear tests and declared themselves the newest members of the nuclear arms club. The Clinton administration quickly launched an intense diplomatic effort to sanction and curtail both countries' weapons programs. Strobe Talbott, the US deputy secretary of state, conducted protracted but futile shuttle diplomacy for two years, traveling frequently between the Pakistani and Indian capitals and meeting with senior officials of both countries to prevent further escalation of this regional arms race.

Several other developments shaped US policy toward South Asia in the closing years of the twentieth century. First, in May 1999, Pakistani-backed forces crossed the Line of Control in Kashmir and sparked the Kargil conflict between Pakistan and India. (The Line of Control is the de facto border separating the portions of Kashmir controlled by India and Pakistan.) In July 1999, the conflict ended with a restoration of the Line of Control, but almost five hundred Indians and eight hundred Pakistanis had died.[15] In October, an attempt by Pakistani Prime Minister Nawaz Sharif to replace Chief of the Army Staff Pervez Musharraf instead ended in a military takeover of the government, led by Musharraf. This coup resulted in additional US sanctions against Pakistan.[16]

As US-Pakistani relations deteriorated, the US relationship with India improved. Bilateral commercial ties between the two countries deepened and the Indian-American community became an increasingly important domestic political voice in the United States.[17] Reflecting the status of US relations with the region, President Bill Clinton's visit in 2000 to the subcontinent included five festive days in India and just five constrained and difficult hours in Pakistan.[18] During the visit, Clinton and Indian Prime Minister Atal Behari Vajpayee signed a five-page "Vision for the 21st Century" to create a "closer and qualitatively new relationship" between the two countries.[19]

After the terrorist attacks of September 11, 2001, US policy toward South Asia underwent another dramatic shift. In the weeks after 9/11, analysts connected the attacks to al Qaeda, which was being hosted and provided safe-haven by the Taliban in Afghanistan. The Taliban regime rejected US demands to turn over its al Qaeda guests. As America's preparations for war went into high gear, Musharraf offered Pakistan's support to the coming US-led assault. Pakistan was richly rewarded for this support with the return of robust US aid. Most of this aid took the form of security payments or reimbursements for Pakistani military operations that supported the US war on terror. In 2002, the US Agency for International Development (USAID) also reentered Pakistan, disbursing large sums to support Musharraf's regime and for activities aimed at diminishing the attractiveness of radical Islamist groups. By the end of the decade, the United States had provided Pakistan $20 billion in aid.[20]

Despite this initial support after the invasion of Afghanistan, US relations with Pakistan continued to be problematic. Some Pakistanis supported a foreign policy favorable to US interests, but many others did not, including some members of Pakistan's military and political establishment.[21] The rift in US-Pakistan relations was highlighted in the wake of the cross-border raid into Pakistan that killed al Qaeda leader Osama bin Laden in May 2011, a US Central Intelligence Agency operation undertaken without first informing the government of Pakistan. Connections between the two countries deteriorated further some months later, after a NATO airstrike inadvertently killed twenty-four Pakistani soldiers near the Afghan border. These setbacks, along with Pakistan's support for the Afghan Taliban and the Haqqani network (an Afghan and Pakistani insurgent group), and the contentious issue of drone strikes in Pakistan's northwest tribal areas, have strained the US-Pakistan relationship.[22]

US relations with India have continued to improve steadily since President Clinton's visit in 2000 and an Indian outpouring of sympathy after the 9/11 attacks. Although India condemned the US invasion of Iraq in 2003, Indian leaders were circumspect in their criticism, seeking to avoid significant damage to India-US relations.

Key to efforts to strengthen the US strategic partnership with India were the steps taken by President George W. Bush and President Barack Obama to resume nuclear energy cooperation with India, while stopping short of supporting India's accession to the Nonproliferation Treaty as a sixth recognized nuclear weapon state. The Obama administration's efforts to strengthen a strategic partnership with

India became part of a US strategy of rebalancing toward the Asia-Pacific region. This trend was continued with the Trump administration, whose first national security strategy called for the United States to "deepen our strategic partnership with India and support its leadership role in Indian Ocean security and throughout the broader region."[23] For India, engagement provides "opportunities for US investments in higher education, the retail market sector, and the insurance and aerospace industries."[24] Recognizing the benefits of these opportunities, the United States and India are likely to continue to pursue a robust partnership.

Key Developments within South Asia's Security Environment

Analysis of future US national security policies relevant to South Asia has to take into account not only the history of US engagement since World War II, discussed above, but also the dynamics of ongoing regional developments. These developments include continuing tensions between India and Pakistan; the risk of nuclear proliferation; the continued presence of transnational terrorist groups; the ongoing conflict in Afghanistan; and the internal stability and economic development of key states in the region.

Relations between India and Pakistan. A deep level of mistrust between India and Pakistan is rooted in the historical experience of these two countries, which includes violence and mass migration as independence from Britain resulted in the formation of the two states in 1947. The resulting distrust and animosity significantly influences each state's actions and strategic decisions, fuels interstate rivalry, and threatens regional stability. India and Pakistan have fought four wars since 1947; significant tension continues over the general geostrategic disposition of each country and especially the contested region of Kashmir.

Kashmir, one of the so-called princely states that was acrimoniously divided during partition in 1947, has been the cause of three of the four wars between India and Pakistan.[25] India and Pakistan both currently claim—and each partially controls—Kashmir. One of the reasons that the issue of Kashmir has been so intractable is that it is fundamentally related to the identities of the two states. Pakistan believes that it should control Kashmir, a Muslim-majority state, because Pakistan was created as a homeland for Muslims in South Asia. India believes Kashmir should be part of India because India was founded as a democracy where the rights of religious and ethnic minorities are protected, and because Hari Singh, a Hindu who ruled the princely state of Kashmir at the time of independence, opted for it to become part of India.

The first war over Kashmir occurred in 1947, almost immediately after independence, when Pakistan sent irregular forces into the province.[26] India also deployed forces to the region and won the largest and wealthiest share of the territory in the armed conflict that followed. UN resolutions then called for specific actions from both parties, which each side claims the other has failed to implement.[27] Since that time, the territory has had recurring periods of war, peace, and insurgent violence. Wars over Kashmir in 1965 and 1999 did little to resolve the conflict.

From the 1990s until 2001, Pakistan's intelligence and military services used battle-hardened mujahedeen groups as proxies to wage asymmetric warfare against Indian forces operating in Kashmir, hoping to raise the costs of war for India so much that it would cede control of the state.[28] This strategy was not successful. India and Pakistan have been locked in a protracted stalemate ever since, and the Line of Control within Kashmir continues to serve as a border between them. Although India retains a rhetorical claim over the portion of Kashmir on the Pakistani side of the Line of Control (often referred to as *Pakistan-administered Kashmir*), it has expressed willingness to recognize this line as a permanent international boundary.[29] Pakistan, however, is not satisfied with the current division and still lays claim to all of Kashmir.[30]

In the early years of the twenty-first century, the situation in Kashmir was less volatile. India and Pakistan agreed to a ceasefire in 2003, which has largely held despite some skirmishes and occasional larger outbreaks of violence. A critical component of this new understanding was a partial devolution of power from New Delhi to Srinagar, the capital of Indian Kashmir. This increased the legitimacy of the provincial government in the eyes of the local population and reduced the pressure on Pakistani officials to take action in support of their co-religionists. Nevertheless, stress on the ceasefire has been growing since 2013, with increasing numbers of incidents and incursions. Both India and Pakistan blame one another, and since there is no consistent, impartial monitoring of the border, it is difficult to verify claims.[31] As of 2018, the situation in Kashmir remains in a stasis of mutual mistrust punctuated by outbursts of violence.

The greatest current threats to the peace between India and Pakistan are cross-border terrorist attacks conducted by militant groups, such as Jaish-e-Muhammad and Lashkar-e-Taiba, which have been active in Kashmir and have historically been supported by Pakistan. These have included a December 2001 terrorist attack against India's Parliament in New Delhi; November 2008 terrorist attacks in Mumbai; and a September 2016 attack against India's Army base in Uri.[32] While India has generally been restrained in its response to these incidents, its mass mobilization of troops in Kashmir after the December 2001 attack indicates how cross-border terrorism might provoke a broader conflict between India and Pakistan. India's strikes against facilities in Pakistan-administered Kashmir after the 2016 Uri incident suggest that New Delhi's restraint might diminish.

The other war between India and Pakistan took place in 1971 in East Pakistan, now the independent country of Bangladesh. The loss of East Pakistan in the 1971 war was a significant territorial blow for Islamabad; it instilled, and in some ways reinforced, Pakistan's fears over a lack of strategic depth, which is the ability to trade space for time in any future conflict with the larger and stronger armed forces of India.

Pakistan's concerns over the vulnerability of its borders and its lack of strategic depth are exacerbated by the long-standing interest, reaching back to the 1940s, of some Pashtun nationalists in Afghanistan to create "Pashtunistan," a home for the Pashtun ethnic group. This issue has historically been of concern to Islamabad, because the Pashtun community lives on both sides of the Afghan-Pakistan border; the potential loss of Pakistan's mountainous Pashtun areas would further erode Pakistan's strategic depth. Even though the creation of a "Pashtunistan" is not currently likely, the issue—along with India's meddling in Afghanistan—has stoked Pakistan's fears of Indian encirclement and of vulnerability along its western and northern border. These concerns were increased by India's support during the 1990s and early 2000s for the Northern Alliance, a primarily Tajik and Uzbek political-military alliance led by Ahmed Shah Massoud, which fought against the Afghan Taliban (which Pakistan backed). This dynamic, and Pakistan's desire for a western neighbor that is friendly to its interests, or which it can influence directly or via proxies, helps to explain why Pakistan has tacitly provided sanctuary for the Afghan Taliban and the Haqqani network since 9/11.

Nuclear Nonproliferation. India and Pakistan are among a handful of countries in the world that have refused to sign the Nuclear Nonproliferation Treaty (NPT), which entered into force in 1970.[33] India has long argued that the NPT is an unjust arrangement that legitimizes the status of the five declared nuclear weapon states (United States, United Kingdom, France, Russia, and China) while preventing others from taking similar measures to ensure their own security.

India was influenced to reject the NPT by the specifics of its own security situation. China became a nuclear power in 1964, only two years after its 1962 border war with India. As a leader of the Non-Aligned Movement during the Cold War, India had no superpower patron to protect it from this Chinese capability.[34] India was also concerned about China's strategic partnership with Pakistan. In mid-May 1974, India conducted its first underground nuclear test. Decades later, in May 1998, it conducted two more tests; right away, Pakistan conducted nuclear tests of its own. By the end of the month, both India and Pakistan had declared themselves members of the nuclear club.

Because the two states are not parties to the NPT, their nuclear facilities and programs are not subject to the International Atomic Energy Agency (IAEA) safeguards that govern the nuclear programs of the five declared nuclear weapon states. The risk created by this lack of safeguards was brought into stark relief when Abdul Qadeer Khan, the "father" of Pakistan's nuclear weapons program, admitted on television in January 2004 that he had been involved in transferring uranium enrichment technologies to Libya, Iran, and North Korea.[35] This history of proliferation raises concern that members of Pakistan's nuclear bureaucracy or military might transfer additional nuclear technology, materiel, or know-how to another state or to a violent nonstate group. Given the chronic political instability in Pakistan, there is also a risk that control over its own nuclear weapons might fall into irresponsible hands. For these reasons, the "security of Pakistan's nuclear arsenal, materials, and technologies continues to be a top-tier US concern."[36]

In October 2008, the US Congress approved the US-India Civil Nuclear Cooperation Initiative, an agreement to facilitate nuclear cooperation. This initiative lifted a "three-decade U.S. moratorium on nuclear trade with India," gave IAEA inspectors access to India's civilian nuclear sites, and made these sites subject to IAEA safeguards.[37] (India's military nuclear facilities and its nuclear material produced before the agreement were not covered by the arrangement.) Under the agreement, India also pledged to continue its moratorium on nuclear weapons testing.[38] The deal is noteworthy because it places part of India's nuclear program under IAEA oversight, even though India is not party to the NPT. However, the deal is also controversial because some fear that the benefits it bestows on a nonmember of the NPT could undermine the nonproliferation regime itself (for more on the NPT, see chapter 17).

Counterterrorism. Al Qaeda's attack on the United States in September 2001 brought the threat of transnational terrorism to the forefront of US actions, strategy, and policy in South and Central Asia. Since then, confronting and defeating terrorist groups in the region has been a core US national security interest. US counterterrorism policy in the region has been driven primarily by two counterterrorism goals: to degrade and defeat transnationally oriented terror groups, especially al Qaeda, whose senior leadership has long been based in the region; and to prevent future attacks on the US homeland from al Qaeda and other groups based in the region. To achieve these objectives, the United States overthrew the Afghan Taliban regime; conducted an aggressive counterterrorism campaign in both Pakistan and Afghanistan; and engaged in other actions that have sought to deny areas of safe haven for al Qaeda and other armed militant groups.

To support counterterrorism objectives, the United States has deployed conventional and special operations forces in Afghanistan and executed a bilateral counterterrorism partnership with Pakistan. In addition, in partnership with the North Atlantic Treaty Organization (NATO), the United States has built, trained, and equipped the Afghan national security forces and sought to support the development of governance structures capable of providing for the country's security.

The United States has made significant progress toward removing al Qaeda's senior leadership and degrading its capabilities in the region. Through its campaign of targeted drone strikes and other operations, the United States has placed pressure on al Qaeda; killed its leader, Osama bin Laden, in Abbottabad, Pakistan, in May 2011; and prevented it from launching other strategic attacks on the US homeland. The al Qaeda organization in Afghanistan and Pakistan still poses a threat to the United States and its allies, however, because the group continues to plan attacks against the West and serves as both an inspiration and a partner for other militant groups.[39] Moreover, the US terrorism challenge in the region has grown more complex due to the attacks conducted by militant groups such as Lashkar-e-Taiba, which opposes India's presence in Kashmir and its influence in the region more broadly, and the creation of the Pakistani Taliban and similar organizations that have declared their intent to attack the United States and the symbols of Western influence both inside and outside the region.

The fraught relationship between the United States and Pakistan adds to these complexities. Since 9/11, Pakistan has been a key ally and counterterrorism partner for the United States, yet Pakistan has repeatedly been criticized for providing sanctuary and support for the Haqqani network and the Afghan Taliban, entities that actively fight US and Afghan forces in Afghanistan.[40] This has led some to label Pakistan a "perfidious partner."[41] For example, the fact that bin Laden's compound was located very close to Pakistan's military academy raised questions about what Pakistani military and intelligence officials knew about the al Qaeda leader's presence.

Stability and Security of Afghanistan. The United States continues to support the stability of Afghanistan and retains a counterterrorism capability in that country. Although Afghanistan has been unified since the eighteenth century, its stability has frequently been challenged by ethnic and tribal conflict, military coups, and regional power politics. Civil war erupted after the decade-long Soviet effort to bring communist order to the country ended in 1989. Then, after several years of fighting, the Taliban succeeded in controlling the Afghan government and nearly 90 percent of the nation's territory.[42] During Taliban rule, Osama bin Laden and his al Qaeda cohorts set up headquarters and jihadist training camps across Afghanistan, primarily in the southeastern part of the country.

After al Qaeda's bombing of two US embassies in Africa in 1998, bin Laden was indicted on terrorism charges by a US federal grand jury. In light of the mounting evidence of al Qaeda's terrorist activities and following the Taliban's refusal to deliver bin Laden to the United States for prosecution, the UN Security Council imposed sanctions on Afghanistan in 1999.[43] After al Qaeda's terrorist attacks of 9/11, the United States and the United Kingdom launched an air assault against Afghanistan on October 7, 2001. With US ground and air support, the opposition Northern Alliance attacked southward, routed the Taliban, and retook Kabul in little more than a month of fighting. Shortly thereafter, the anti-Taliban factions agreed on a coalition government under Hamid Karzai, who was later elected president in 2004.

The United Nations authorized a small International Security Assistance Force (ISAF, of which NATO took control in 2003) in support of the Karzai government. However, the Taliban were able to reconstitute and increasingly carried out offensive operations and suicide bombings. By 2008, the Afghan national army was being developed, and approximately 43,000 foreign troops (25,000 American and 18,000 from other NATO countries) were available to train it and conduct operations. Despite these efforts, the Taliban continued a robust insurgency, drawing support from and finding a safe haven among Pashtun tribes on the Afghan-Pakistan border.

In December 2009, President Obama ordered additional US troops to Afghanistan to reverse the insurgency's momentum. At its peak, from 2010 to 2012, there were over 130,000 troops from 51 NATO and NATO partner countries serving in Afghanistan.[44] The US "surge" of additional forces led to a total of more than

100,000 US service members in Afghanistan at its peak in 2011.[45] This US surge was part of a plan that also involved a timeline for withdrawal, which has since been extended. As of February 2017, there were 8,400 US troops and another 5,000 from NATO countries in Afghanistan; the Commander of US forces in Afghanistan indicated that he could use more.[46] In August 2017, President Donald Trump announced that his administration would continue military activities in Afghanistan to "stop the resurgence of safe havens that enable terrorists to threaten America" and base future decisions on troop presence on conditions on the ground rather than timetables set in advance.[47]

While counterterrorism objectives in the region have remained consistent since 9/11, American interests in Afghanistan have evolved considerably since the initial US invasion of Afghanistan in 2001.[48] What started as a broad goal of rebuilding the Afghan state has shifted to a more limited mission to train, advise, and equip the Afghan national security forces so they can stand on their own and defend their country. According to a 2017 report by the US Special Inspector General for Afghanistan Reconstruction, despite the fact that the United States spent over $70 billion to build Afghan National Defense and Security Forces between 2002 and 2016, "the Afghan security forces are not yet capable of securing their own nation."[49] Despite progress toward bolstering and institutionalizing Afghan security force capabilities, considerable challenges remain, especially given the resiliency of the Afghan Taliban.[50]

The insurgency in Afghanistan also constitutes a critical, lingering problem for the government of Pakistan. After being defeated by US forces in 2001–2002, the Taliban and al Qaeda retreated to the tribally ruled mountains of the Afghan-Pakistan border region. From havens on both sides of the border, the resurgent Taliban have fought a deadly insurgency that threatens to destabilize Afghanistan's regime. A number of factors have also led to the creation of other militant and terrorist groups in the region, and a considerable amount of violence has spilled over, deeply affecting Pakistan. A broad campaign of violence against the Pakistani state started in the early 2000s and picked up steam throughout the decade. It is tied to the perpetuation of the Afghan war; spillover associated with Pakistan's support for various militants; local frustration with Pakistani military actions in the Federally Administered Tribal Areas, which some have criticized as being indiscriminate; the continued presence of US forces in the region; the US drone campaign; and other concerns about Pakistan's alliance with the United States and its support for America's counterterrorism objectives.

While Pakistan has long had a diverse and complicated militant landscape, the primary driver of violence against Pakistan has been the Pakistani Taliban, an alliance of various Pakistan-based militant groups formed in 2007. Anti-state activity associated with the Pakistani Taliban and other like-minded militants has been costly for Pakistan. Estimates from Brown University's Costs of War project suggest that more than 8,000 members of Pakistan's security forces and more than 22,000 Pakistani civilians have lost their lives as a result of conflict in the country since 9/11, many due to operations by the Pakistani Taliban.[51]

Internal Political Stability and Economic Development of States in the Region. The cohesiveness and effective functioning of the region's major states, India and Pakistan, are of key importance to the United States. In addition to the tensions between these two states, discussed above, Bangladesh may also become a source of regional instability. The interactions among all major states in South Asia are also significantly influenced by China's significant political, economic, and military role in the region.

India: Great-Power Aspirations and Economic Growth. As the world's largest democracy and its second most populous nation, India has long held high aspirations concerning its place in the world. For many decades, India's economic and military capabilities limited the country's growth and its influence beyond the region. This has been changing, however. India's fortunes have improved dramatically, particularly since its adoption of economic reforms in the early 1990s. Its military forces have expanded India's influence and reach to the Middle East and Central Asia.

Economically, India has the world's seventh largest economy, with an estimated gross domestic product (GDP) of $2.26 trillion and a growth rate of 7.1 percent in 2016.[52] It has emerged as a critical player in the global information technology business, a source of personnel and talent for world-leading industrial firms, and a consumer whose demand for raw materials has an appreciable impact on global commodity prices. Overall, India's long-term economic outlook is generally positive, with a young population and increasing integration in the global economy.[53]

As India's economy has grown, so has its relationship with the United States. The United States is India's largest export market and is a lucrative source of financial and technological support.[54] As an example of the mutual benefits that flow from this relationship, US airplane manufacturer Boeing sells commercial aircraft to India's expanding private-sector airlines, and American high-technology firms are expanding their already considerable access to India's knowledge workers and information technology infrastructure.[55]

The Indian community in the United States has become increasingly important to this bilateral relationship. Between 1995 and 2005, Indian immigrants formed more engineering and technology companies in the United States than immigrants from any other nation. Clear evidence is seen in Silicon Valley, where, according to this same survey, Indians founded approximately 15.5 percent of start-ups between 1995 and 2005.[56] An estimated 30,000 Indian information technology professionals work in Silicon Valley, and many exercise significant political influence. Indians enjoying success in the United States also affect developments in India, as they invest resources back into India in a number of ways, including remittances, parallel businesses, and impact investing. US and Indian firms work to influence their governments to prevent political obstacles from unduly interfering in these burgeoning business ties.[57]

The US-India economic relationship benefits both parties, but it also poses challenges. Politically sensitive issues include the competition of low-cost Indian manufacturers with American firms and the outsourcing of business processes to well-educated, English-speaking Indian engineers, call-center operators, and high-technology firms. In addition, India's economic growth is increasing the global competition for raw materials, which boosts commodity prices, and also leads to greater energy demand across South Asia. As of 2013, India was the world's third largest consumer of energy, even though approximately 19 percent of India's people still lacked access to electricity.[58] Indian consumption of oil, driven by increased transportation and industrial demand, more than doubled between 2000 and 2016; despite its own vast fossil fuel resources, India is becoming increasingly dependent on foreign oil.[59] Greater demand for energy influences global markets as well as the environment. India is the third largest coal producer in the world after the United States and China; it relied on coal for approximately 44 percent of its energy in 2013.[60] As a result, India is also one of the world's largest carbon emitters. All of these issues have the potential to affect the United States and the global economy.

Despite indicators of strength, India faces significant challenges in sustaining rapid economic progress. First, its domestic market is hampered by a sclerotic bureaucracy, tight labor rules, and inefficiencies in its finance, housing, and educational sectors.[61] Second, India needs to ensure that more Indians benefit from economic growth; almost 22 percent of Indians live at or below the international poverty line (see table 19.1). Many Indians are paying a heavy price in economic as well as human terms as India transitions from a primarily agrarian economy to industrial and even postindustrial forms of production. Finally, India's infrastructure needs dramatic improvements, as evidenced by a massive electrical outage in the summer of 2012: a catastrophic failure across three of India's main power grids caused a blackout affecting approximately 670 million people, or nearly one-tenth of the world's population.[62] Environmental issues in the country pose similar challenges.

The United States bolstered its political ties with India during the Obama administration, as President Obama and Prime Minister Narendra Modi forged a personal connection that carried over to the formal relationship between the nations. Obama became the first president to visit India twice during his time in office. Nowhere did the enhanced status of the relationship evidence itself more than in India's agreement to be included, along with China, among the countries committing to reduce greenhouse gases as an outgrowth of the landmark 2015 Paris Agreement on Climate Change. Although the Trump administration has since announced its withdrawal from this agreement, it has also declared a desire to work with India on "fighting terrorism, promoting economic growth and reforms, and expanding security cooperation in the Indo-Pacific region."[63]

Pakistan: Fragile Politics and Struggling Economy. Pakistan, founded as a home for British India's Muslim population, has had great difficulty reconciling Islam and democracy ever since its creation. Until 2013, military and civilian governments alternated in power and no elected government had completed its term of office before being ousted by a military coup. Elections in May 2013 represented the first time since 1947 that an elected civilian government successfully ended its term and was replaced by an elected civilian government of the opposing party.[64] However, with the ouster of Prime Minister Nawaz Sharif in mid-2017, none of Pakistan's elected leaders has completed a full five-year term. Pakistan's government faces significant internal challenges, most notably from anti-state terrorism originating along Pakistan's western border and violent sectarian attacks conducted against religious and ethnic minorities across the country.

These challenges, along with the levels of defense spending needed to confront terrorism and compete with India (more than six times its size), have left Pakistan unable to create the conditions for stable, sustainable, and politically acceptable levels of economic growth. Pakistan's economy averaged approximately 3.5 percent growth between 2008 and 2014, a slow rate for a developing country.[65] Its economy remains dominated by agricultural products and textiles, and by the political interests these sectors represent.[66] High levels of defense spending have diverted resources from educational, medical, nutritional, and other social programs.[67] The scale of tax evasion and avoidance in Pakistan has compounded these issues.[68] In the face of these challenges, Pakistan is fighting an uphill battle as it seeks to modernize its economy and improve its economic prospects.

A brief period of stronger economic progress raised hopes and expectations in the mid-2000s. However, this was closely tied to unsustainable or one-time stimuli such as massive debt forgiveness (sponsored by the United States as compensation for Pakistan's support after the 9/11 terrorist attacks); increased International Monetary Fund lending; access to private lending that such funds supported (again at US instigation); and a surge in remittances from Pakistanis living abroad.[69] These measures might have helped Pakistan address long-term problems stemming from uncompetitive industries, an overly rigid economy, and severe market inefficiencies, but instead they simply created unsustainable short-term gains. According to a recent Asian Development Bank report, "Key challenges impeding stronger economic growth" in Pakistan include "inadequate infrastructure and transport connectivity, weak governance and institutions, and limited access to finance."[70] The report noted that "low investment in human development has also left the country with a workforce lacking the skills needed to help the country compete in global markets and to increase productivity by producing goods with higher value."[71] Pakistan will need to sustain political stability and economic reforms to improve the quality of life of its citizens.

The US-Pakistan relationship is important both politically and economically. Cooperation in support of common counterterrorism objectives as well as military assistance is necessary for Pakistan's stability. In 2015, Pakistan received $280 million in US military assistance, a sum exceeded only by US military aid to Afghanistan, Israel, Egypt, and Jordan.[72] Should Pakistan fall from US favor, its military capability, overall economy, and potentially its political stability could suffer significantly. The Trump Administration has said that Pakistan will need to take action to prevent this from happening, noting that "we have been paying Pakistan billions and billions of dollars at the same time they are housing the very terrorists that we are fighting. . . . It is time for Pakistan to demonstrate its commitment to civilization, order, and to peace."[73] In 2018, the Trump administration suspended $255 million of foreign military financing to Pakistan in an effort to seek greater Pakistani support to target groups that attack US and Afghan forces from safe havens in Pakistan.[74]

Bangladesh: Potential for Ongoing Challenges. Bangladesh may also become a source of regional instability and extremism. With a population of 156 million people crowded into an area about the size of Illinois and situated on the deltas of the great Ganges and Brahmaputra Rivers, Bangladesh perpetually faces natural disasters. In 1991, a cyclone killed over 130,000 people. In 1998, massive floods put two-thirds of the country under water and made thirty million people homeless. In 2007, monsoons caused massive flooding that covered most of the country, leaving thousands dead and millions homeless. Similarly, in 2017, floods across Bangladesh, India, and Nepal killed more than 1,200 people and devastated the farming industry that Bangladesh depends upon.[75] Rising sea levels tied to climate change and the melting of the polar ice caps may create additional challenges. The resulting displacement of Bangladeshis and loss of land could fuel additional competition for food, water, and other resources and could thus trigger both internal violence and broader regional conflict.[76]

Since it became independent from Pakistan in 1971, the politics within Bangladesh have been as unsettled as its weather. Ineffective, corrupt civilian rule has frequently given way to military coups; the country has had nineteen such coups in its forty-five year history.[77] The January 2014 parliamentary elections were marred by violence; many members of major opposition parties boycotted the election and fought openly in the streets after the ballots were counted.[78] The continuing ineffectiveness of civilian governance will make checking future Islamic extremism in Bangladesh particularly difficult.

The vast majority of Bangladesh's more than 120 million Muslims have long practiced a relatively moderate form of Islam, but extremism has grown in recent years.[79] Extremists have violently executed a number of well-known secular bloggers, and the government has responded with repressive measures.[80] If major natural catastrophes continue to afflict the country, as is likely, and if civilian governments continue to be ineffective, those motivated by radical conceptions of Islamist ideology could gain more influence in Bangladesh. Roughly 8 percent of the population of Bangladesh is Hindu, making Hinduism the second most prominent religion in the country; this gives India a stake in its neighbor, as well as prompts concerns about ethnic violence.

South Asia and China. No discussion of regional dynamics in South Asia would be complete without considering the rise and influence of China. Commercial rivalry between India and China naturally swings between cooperation and competition, but for the most part it is based on the established rules of the marketplace. Despite their common interest in stability, tensions may yet resurface over the border between the two countries, which was fought over once and is still disputed.[81] While India could be a valuable partner in helping the United States offset China's growing power, US expectations of its relationship with India tend to be tempered, given India's demonstrated preference for an independent foreign policy. The United States cannot expect Indian support unless India's regional and increasingly global aspirations are also furthered by US policies.

China's role in US-Pakistan relations has been and will continue to be complicated. China was implicated in the early sale of nuclear and missile technology to Pakistan, a relationship that grew out of security cooperation agreements from the 1960s.[82] China will likely continue to provide Pakistan with strategic support and with weapons technology as long as Pakistan is willing to side with China when called upon.[83] For its part, Pakistan will undoubtedly continue to seek political, economic, and material support from China to strengthen it in its continuing rivalry with India and to maintain a hedge against loss of US support.[84]

Looking Ahead

There are numerous challenges ahead for US security policy in South Asia. A successful, stable, and moderate Pakistan is key to maintaining stability in the region. The perpetuation of the Afghan conflict and associated spillover violence, which could threaten the political-military status quo in Pakistan and erode Pakistanis' confidence in the state, have made the balancing act more challenging for Pakistan's leaders as they seek to maintain national stability. Pakistan's economic challenges, a rise in sectarianism, and other key issues add to the difficulties with which Pakistani leaders must grapple. US policy towards Pakistan will continue to face its own set of challenges because of the complexity of Pakistan's security environment, Pakistan's relationships with militant groups like the Haqqani network, and the high level of anti-American sentiment in the country.[85]

A second major regional challenge facing the United States is how to support India's integration as a great power into the global political and economic system. As US policy makers strive to forge a new strategic partnership with India, they will need to pay greater attention to India's perspectives and national interests. Indian support could be crucial in dealing with global issues such as trade and investment, competition for raw materials, transnational threats, and the economic, political, and military rise of China. This will require delicate diplomacy, because a strengthening of US-India ties and a bolstering of that relationship are not likely to be viewed favorably by Pakistan and could affect US-Pakistani relations.

American relations with South Asian countries will also be shaped by other developments in the region, including conflict in Kashmir and in Afghanistan, nuclear and other weapons proliferation, and how each country handles domestic challenges such as sectarianism in Pakistan, communal violence in India, and responses to health pandemics and environmental crises. A decline in tensions between Pakistan and India over Kashmir would be a significant positive development, but it is still unclear how this outcome could be achieved and whether outside states can play a significant role.

Acts of terrorism in, or tied to, South Asia, and especially the presence of terrorist groups in Pakistan, will continue to jeopardize security within the region and beyond. US policy makers will be challenged, particularly in relations with Pakistan, to develop collaborative and effective responses to terrorist threats. Given the distrust between the United States and Pakistan over the issue of terrorism, this will require careful deliberation regarding what type of relationship with Pakistan would be best for the United States. Such deliberation would include evaluating whether it makes sense for the United States to "stay the course" and continue to hold Pakistan close as a key ally, offering various forms of assistance as incentives, or whether it would make more sense for the United States to shift course and adopt a much harder stance toward the country, even a policy of containment. A related challenge for US policy makers lies in creating mechanisms to mitigate the effects of terrorism in the region and to punish state actors that facilitate cross-border terrorist activity by groups like Lashkar-e-Taiba and Jaish-e-Muhammad. American engagement with Pakistan on issues related to terrorism will likely remain quite complicated into the foreseeable future.

Nuclear proliferation and the security of nuclear facilities and materiel in the region will remain a significant US and global concern. The United States must continually consider its interest in the credibility and effectiveness of the global nonproliferation regime in its policies and interactions with Pakistan and India as they pursue their nuclear ambitions.

Finally, the vast and growing population in the region, and the limited and interconnected supply of fundamental resources such as clean drinking water, could exacerbate existing social and environmental problems and thus lead to broader conflict. The rising sea levels that are a product of global climate change will also have a significant impact on countries in the region. American policy makers must be prepared to deal with the consequences of natural disasters and the dynamics created by natural resource competition.

Discussion Questions

1. How did US policy toward the Soviet Union during the Cold War affect US relations with India and Pakistan? To what extent did these dynamics persist beyond the Cold War?
2. What is the origin of the conflict between India and Pakistan? Why has the conflict and distrust between the two counties not been resolved? What is the most likely flashpoint for a renewal of armed conflict today?
3. Why is Afghanistan a battleground on which Pakistan and India compete with one another for influence?
4. What policies should the United States adopt toward India and Pakistan to minimize the risk of further proliferation of nuclear weapons technology?
5. How has the fact that India and Pakistan have become declared nuclear weapon states affected US policy toward South Asia?
6. What should be the most important considerations for US policy toward India: economic relations, regional policy toward Pakistan, nuclear nonproliferation, environmental issues, or other concerns?

7. How would you characterize the nature of the relationship between the United States and Pakistan? Would you recommend that the United States take a more conciliatory approach or a harder line in its relations with Pakistan? Why?

8. What forces contribute to political instability within Pakistan? How might the United States promote greater stability there? What are the limits to US power and influence in this regard?

9. How can the United States best contribute to political moderation and economic progress in Bangladesh?

10. What dynamics have shaped the relationships between China and the countries of South Asia?

Recommended Reading

Blank, Stephen. *Natural Allies? Regional Security in Asia and Prospects for Indo-American Strategic Cooperation*. Carlisle, PA: US Army War College, September 2005.

Chaudhuri, Rudra. *Forged in Crisis: India and the United States since 1947*. New York: Oxford University Press, 2014.

Cohen, Stephen P. *The Future of Pakistan*. Washington, DC: Brookings Institution Press, 2011.

———. *Shooting for a Century: The India-Pakistan Conundrum*. Washington, DC: Brookings Institution Press, 2013.

Cordesman, Anthony, and Varun Vira. *Pakistan: Violence vs. Stability*. Washington, DC: Center for Strategic and International Studies, 2011.

Haqqani, Husain. *Magnificent Delusions: Pakistan, the United States, and an Epic History of Misunderstanding*. New York: PublicAffairs, 2013.

International Crisis Group. *Political Conflict, Extremism and Criminal Justice in Bangladesh*, Report No. 277. Brussels: International Crisis Group, 2016.

Kaplan, Robert D. *South Asia's Geography of Conflict*. Washington, DC: Center for a New American Security, 2010.

Kux, Dennis. *The United States and Pakistan, 1947–2000: Disenchanted Allies*. Baltimore, MD: Johns Hopkins University Press, 2001.

Lamb, Robert, Sadika Hameed, and Kathryn Mixon. *South Asia Regional Dynamics and Strategic Concerns*. Washington, DC: Center for Strategic and International Studies, 2014.

Raju, Subramanyam. *Democracies at Loggerheads: Security Aspects of U.S.-India Relations*. Denver, CO: International Academic Publishers, 2001.

SarDesai, D. R., and Raju G. C. Thomas, eds. *Nuclear India in the Twenty-First Century*. New York: Palgrave-Macmillan, 2002.

Schaffer, Teresita. *Bangladesh in the Balance*. Washington, DC: Center for Strategic and International Studies, 2007.

———. *Kashmir: The Economics of Peace Building*. Washington, DC: Center for Strategic and International Studies, 2004.

———. *Pakistan's Future and U.S. Policy Options*. Washington, DC: Center for Strategic and International Studies, 2004.

Talbott, Strobe. *Engaging India: Diplomacy, Democracy, and the Bomb*. Rev. ed. Washington, DC: Brookings Institution Press, 2006.

Recommended Internet Resources

Afghanistan Analysts Network, www.afghanistan-analysts.org
Brookings Institution, www.brookings.edu/articles/south-asia
Bureau of South and Central Asian Affairs, US State Department, www.state.gov/p/sca
Council on Foreign Relations, www.cfr.org/asia
International Atomic Energy Agency, www.iaea.org
International Crisis Group, www.crisisgroup.org/asia/south-asia
International Institute for Strategic Studies, www.iiss.org/en/research/south-s-asia-s-security
US Institute of Peace, www.usip.org/regions/asia

Notes

1. Sharon Squassoni, *Nuclear Threat Reduction Measures for India and Pakistan* (Washington, DC: Congressional Research Service, updated February 17, 2005), 1.

2. For background on the US-Pakistan relationship, see Husain Haqqani, *Magnificent Delusions: Pakistan, the United States and an Epic History of Misunderstanding* (New York: PublicAffairs, 2013); and Daniel S. Markey, *No Exit from Pakistan: America's Tortured Relationship with Islamabad* (New York: Cambridge University Press, 2013).

3. For background on the US-India relationship, see Rudra Chaudhuri, *Forged in Crisis: India and the United States since 1947* (New York: Oxford University Press, 2014).

4. A. Subramanyam Raju, *Democracies at Loggerheads: Security Aspects of U.S.-India Relations* (Denver, CO: International Academic Publishers, 2001), 31.

5. Dennis Kux, *The United States and Pakistan: 1947–2000* (Baltimore, MD: Johns Hopkins University Press, 2001), 74.

6. Dwight D. Eisenhower, "Statement by the President on Military Aid to Pakistan," February 25, 1954, in American Presidency Project, ed. Gerhard Peters and John T. Woolley, http://www.presidency.ucsb.edu/ws/?pid=10171.

7. Dwight D. Eisenhower, "Letter to Prime Minister Nehru of India Concerning U.S. Military Aid to Pakistan.," February 25, 1954, in American Presidency Project, ed. Gerhard Peters and John T. Woolley, http://www.presidency.ucsb.edu/ws/?pid=10170.

8. Jeff M. Smith, "A Forgotten War in the Himalayas," *Yale Global Online*, September 14, 2012, http://yaleglobal.yale.edu/content/forgotten-war-himalayas.

9. Smith, "A Forgotten War in the Himalayas."

10. Kux, *The United States and Pakistan, 1947–2000*, 343.

11. Raju, *Democracies at Loggerheads*, 64.

12. David N. Gibbs, "Reassessing Soviet Motives for Invading Afghanistan: A Declassified History," *Critical Asian Studies* 38, no. 2 (2006): 259.

13. Dennis Kux, *Pakistan: Flawed Not Failed State* (New York: Foreign Policy Association, 2001), 20.

14. Strobe Talbott, *Engaging India: Diplomacy, Democracy, and the Bomb*, rev. ed. (Washington, DC: Brookings Institution Press, 2006), 57.

15. S. Paul Kapur, "Nuclear Proliferation, the Kargil Conflict, and South Asian Security," *Security Studies* 13, no. 1 (2003): 85.

16. "U.S. Condemns Pakistan Presidency Move," CNN, June 20, 2001, http://edition.cnn.com/2001/WORLD/asiapcf/south/06/20/pakistan.usa/.

17. Talbott, *Engaging India*, 57.

18. Jane Perlez, "Clinton Decides to Visit Pakistan, after All," *New York Times*, March 8, 2000, http://www.nytimes.com/2000/03/08/world/clinton-decides-to-visit-pakistan-after-all.html.

19. William J. Clinton, "Joint Statement on United States–India Relations: A Vision for the 21st Century," March 21, 2000, in American Presidency Project, ed. Gerhard Peters and John T. Woolley, http://www.presidency.ucsb.edu/ws/?pid=58271.

20. Aliza Litchman, "Shifting Allegiances: Rethinking U.S.-Pakistan Relations," Council on Foreign Relations, April 17, 2015, http://blogs.cfr.org/zenko/2015/04/17/guest-post-shifting-allegiances-rethinking-u-s-pakistan-relations/.

21. Zeeshan Haider, "Anti-Americanism Rife in Pakistan Army Institution: Wikileaks," Reuters, May 25, 2011, http://www.reuters.com/article/us-anti-americanism-rife-in-pakistan-arm-idUSTRE74O1EA20110525.

22. Don Rassler and Vahid Brown, *The Haqqani Nexus and the Evolution of al-Qa'ida* (West Point, NY: Combatting Terrorism Center, 2011), https://ctc.usma.edu/v2/wp-content/uploads/2011/07/CTC-Haqqani-Report_Rassler-Brown-Final_Web.pdf.

23. The White House, *National Security Strategy of the United States of America* (Washington, DC: The White House, December 2017), 50.

24. Ashok Sharma, "The U.S.-India Strategic Partnership: An Overview of Defense and Nuclear Courtship," *Georgetown Journal of International Affairs*, July 4, 2013, http://journal.georgetown.edu/the-u-s-india-strategic-partnership-an-overview-of-defense-and-nuclear-courtship-by-ashok-sharma/.

25. The official name of the state is Jammu and Kashmir, but it is more frequently referred to as Kashmir, the name used in this book.

26. "A Brief History of the Kashmir Conflict," *Telegraph*, September 24, 2001, http://www.telegraph.co.uk/news/1399992/A-brief-history-of-the-Kashmir-conflict.html.

27. UN Security Council, "Resolution of 21 April 1948," http://www.un.org/en/ga/search/view_doc.asp?symbol=S/RES/47(1948).

28. Husain Haqqani, *Pakistan: Between Mosque and Military* (Washington, DC: Carnegie Endowment for International Peace, 2005).

29. "The Future of Kashmir," BBC News, http://news.bbc.co.uk/2/shared/spl/hi/south_asia/03/kashmir_future/html.

30. "The Future of Kashmir."

31. Ajai Shukla, "Viewpoint: India and Pakistan Up the Ante on Disputed Border," BBC News, January 30, 2018, http://www.bbc.com/news/world-asia-india-42856494.

32. Jason Overdorf, "Analysis: Are India and Pakistan Headed for War?" *Global Post*, August 15, 2013, http://www.globalpost.com/dispatch/news/war/conflict-zones/130814/analysis-are-india-and-pakistan-headed-war.

33. George Bunn, "The Nuclear Nonproliferation Treaty: History and Current Problems," *Arms Control Today* 33, no. 10 (2003): 4.

34. Jaswant Singh, "Against Nuclear Apartheid," *Foreign Affairs* 77, no. 5 (1998): 42.

35. Paul Kerr, "New Details Emerge on Pakistani Networks," *Arms Control Today* 35, no. 4 (2005): 35.

36. K. Alan Kronstadt, "Pakistan-U.S. Relations: Issues for the 114th Congress," Congressional Research Service, May 14, 2015, 11.

37. Jayshree Bajoria and Esther Pan, "The U.S.-India Nuclear Deal," *Council on Foreign Relations Backgrounder*, November 5, 2010, http://www.cfr.org/india/us-india-nuclear-deal/p9663.

38. Bajoria and Esther Pan, "The U.S.-India Nuclear Deal."

39. Nick Patton Walsh, "Al Qaeda 'Very Active' in Afghanistan: U.S. Commander," CNN, April 13, 2016, http://www.cnn.com/2016/04/13/middleeast/afghanistan-al-qaeda/.

40. "Haqqani Network Enjoys Sanctuary in Pakistan, Claims U.S. Commander," *News* (Karachi), December 4, 2016, https://www.thenews.com.pk/print/169703-Haqqani-Network-enjoys-sanctuary-in-Pakistan-claims-US-commander.

41. See Ashley J. Tellis, "Pakistan's Impending Defeat in Afghanistan" (Washington, DC: Carnegie Endowment for International Peace, June 22, 2012), http://carnegieendowment.org/2012/06/22/pakistan-s-impending-defeat-in-afghanistan-pub-48633.

42. Zachary Laub, "The Taliban in Afghanistan," *Council on Foreign Relations Backgrounder*, July 4, 2014, https://www.cfr.org/backgrounder/taliban-afghanistan.

43. Colum Lynch, "U.S. Seeks Embargo on Taliban: Russia Joins in Effort to Seize bin Laden," *Washington Post*, October 7, 1999, http://www.washingtonpost.com/wp-srv/WPcap/1999-10/07/005r-100799-idx.html.

44. North Atlantic Treaty Organization, "ISAF's Mission in Afghanistan (2001–2014)," September 1, 2015, http://www.nato.int/cps/en/natohq/topics_69366.htm.

45. Danielle Kurtzleben, "CHART: How the U.S. Troop Levels in Afghanistan Have Changed under Obama," National Public Radio, July 6, 2016, http://www.npr.org/2016/07/06/484979294/chart-how-the-u-s-troop-levels-in-afghanistan-have-changed-under-obama.

46. Jeremy Herb, "U.S. Commander Tells Congress: More Troops Needed in Afghanistan," *Politico*, February 9, 2017, http://www.politico.com/story/2017/02/additional-troops-afghanistan-john-nicholson-234844.

47. The White House Office of the Press Secretary, "Remarks by President Trump on the Strategy in Afghanistan and South Asia," August 21, 2017, https://www.whitehouse.gov/the-press-office/2017/08/21/remarks-president-trump-strategy-afghanistan-and-south-asia.

48. For a timeline, see Council on Foreign Relations, "The U.S. War in Afghanistan, 1999–2018," 2018, https://www.cfr.org/timeline/us-war-afghanistan.

49. John F. Sopko, *Reconstructing the Afghan National Defense and Security Forces: Lessons From The U.S. Experience In Afghanistan* (Arlington, VA: Special Inspector General for Afghanistan Reconstruction, September 2017), 3, https://www.sigar.mil/pdf/lessonslearned/SIGAR-17-62-LL.pdf.

50. For background, see Bennett Seftel, "Mounting Security Challenges in Afghanistan," *Cipher Brief*, August 11, 2016, https://www.thecipherbrief.com/article/middle-east/mounting-security-challenges-afghanistan-1091.

51. For a more precise breakdown of terrorist incidents in Pakistan since 9/11, see the Global Terrorism Database, https://www.start.umd.edu/gtd/.

52. The World Bank, "Gross Domestic Product 2016," December 15, 2017, http://databank.worldbank.org/data/download/GDP.pdf; The World Bank, "GDP Growth (Annual %)," 2018, https://data.worldbank.org/indicator/NY.GDP.MKTP.KD.ZG.

53. See India Country Management Unit, *India Development Update: Unlocking Women's Potential* (New Delhi: The World Bank, May 2017), http://documents.worldbank.org/curated/en/107761495798437741/pdf/115297-WP-P146674-PUBLIC.pdf.

54. For background see Alyssa Ayres, "Economic Relations with India," statement before the Committee on Foreign Affairs, Subcommittee on Asia and the Pacific, United States House of Representatives, 2nd Session, 114th Congress, March 15, 2015.

55. Greg Waldron, "AERO INDIA: Boeing Looks beyond Indian Offset Work," *FlightGlobal*, February 13, 2017, https://www.flightglobal.com/news/articles/aero-india-boeing-looks-beyond-indian-offset-work-434098/.

56. Vivek Wadha, AnnaLee Saxenian, Ben A. Rissing, and Gary Gereffi, "American's New Immigrant Entrepreneurs," Duke Science, Technology, and Innovation Paper No. 23, January 2007, http://ssrn.com/abstract=990152.

57. Robert D. Hof, "India and Silicon Valley: Now the R&D Flows Both Ways," *Business Week*, December 8, 2003, 74.

58. US Energy Information Administration, "India: Overview," June 14, 2016, https://www.eia.gov/beta/international/analysis.cfm?iso=IND.

59. US Energy Information Administration, "India: Overview."

60. US Energy Information Administration, "India: Overview."

61. "A Growing Indian Empire," *Economist*, October 20, 2006, 1.

62. "India Blackouts Leave 700 Million without Power," *Guardian*, July 31, 2012, https://www.theguardian.com/world/2012/jul/31/india-blackout-electricity-power-cuts.

63. The White House Office of the Press Secretary, "Statement from the Press Secretary on the Visit of Prime Minister Narendra Modi of India," June 12, 2017, https://www.whitehouse.gov/the-press-office/2017/06/12/statement-press-secretary-visit-prime-minister-narendra-modi-india.

64. Gerald Hyman, "Nawaz's Decisive Victory Opens Doors for Rethinking Pakistan Security Policy," Center for Strategic and International Studies, May 21, 2013, https://csis.org/publication/nawazs-decisive-victory-opens-door-rethinking-pakistan-security-policy.

65. For background, see Asian Development Bank, "Country Partnership Strategy: Pakistan 2015–2019," August 2015, https://www.adb.org/documents/pakistan-country-partnership-strategy-2015-2019.

66. JPMorgan Chase, "Pakistan's Economic Momentum Ahead of 2007 Elections," JPMorgan Chase Bank, Economic Research, Global Data Watch, September 8, 2006. See also Asian Development Bank, "Country Partnership Strategy: Pakistan 2015–2019."

67. See Shane Mason, *Military Budgets in India and Pakistan: Trajectories, Priorities, and Risks* (Washington, DC: Stimson Center, 2016), https://www.stimson.org/content/military-budgets-india-and-pakistan-trajectories-priorities-and-risks-0.

68. See Sakib Sherani, "Pakistan's Taxation Crisis," *Dawn*, August 7, 2015, http://www.dawn.com/news/1198899.

69. Mason, *Military Budgets in India and Pakistan.*

70. Asian Development Bank, "Pakistan Economic Outlook Positive but Challenges Remain," March 30, 2016, http://www.adb.org/news/pakistan-economic-outlook-positive-challenges-remain.

71. Asian Development Bank, "Pakistan Economic Outlook Positive but Challenges Remain."

72. See US Department of State, "Foreign Military Financing Account Summary," n.d., https://2009-2017.state.gov/t/pm/ppa/sat/c14560.htm.

73. The White House Office of the Press Secretary, "Remarks by President Trump on the Strategy in Afghanistan and South Asia," August 21, 2017, https://www.whitehouse.gov/briefings-statements/remarks-president-trump-strategy-afghanistan-south-asia/.

74. Missy Ryan and Carol Morello, "Trump Administration Suspends Most Security Aid to Pakistan," *Washington Post*, January 4, 2018.

75. Jatindra Dash and Ruma Paul, "Worst Monsoon Floods in Years Kill More than 1,200 across South Asia," August 25, 2017, https://www.reuters.com/article/us-southasia-floods-idUSKCN1B510Z.

76. See Gardiner Harris, "Borrowed Time on Disappearing Land: Facing Rising Sea Levels, Bangladesh Confronts the Consequences of Climate Change," *New York Times*,

March 28, 2014, https://www.nytimes.com/2014/03/29/world/asia/facing-rising-seas-bangladesh-confronts-the-consequences-of-climate-change.html.

77. Joshua Kurlantzick, "A Look at Bangladesh's Steady Descent into Chaos," *National*, August 20, 2015, https://www.thenational.ae/arts-culture/a-look-at-bangladesh-s-steady-descent-into-chaos-1.50372.

78. Mahfuz Sadique, "Clashes and Boycott Mar Bangladesh Election," BBC News, January 5, 2014, http://www.bbc.com/news/world-asia-25602436.

79. See Joseph Allcin, "The Rise of Extremism in Bangladesh: Who Is Responsible for the Killings?" *Foreign Affairs*, June 9, 2016, https://www.foreignaffairs.com/articles/bangladesh/2016-06-09/rise-extremism-bangladesh.

80. Kurlantzick, "A Look at Bangladesh's Steady Descent into Chaos."

81. See Ishaan Tharoor, "The Sino-Indian War: 50 Years Later, Will India and China Clash Again?" *Time*, October 21, 2012, http://world.time.com/2012/10/21/the-sino-indian-war-50-years-later-will-india-and-china-clash-again/.

82. See William Burr, ed., "China, Pakistan, and the Bomb: The Declassified File on U.S. Policy 1977–1997," National Security Archive Electronic Briefing Book No. 114, March 5, 2004, http://nsarchive.gwu.edu/NSAEBB/NSAEBB114/; and Alex Kingsbury, "Why China Helped Countries like Pakistan, North Korea Build Nuclear Bombs," *U.S. News and World Report*, January 2, 2009, http://www.usnews.com/news/world/articles/2009/01/02/why-china-helped-countries-like-pakistan-north-korea-build-nuclear-bombs.

83. See, for example, China's support for the development of Pakistan's Gwadar port, discussed in Ayaz Gul, "China Turning Pakistan Port into Regional Giant," Voice of America, October 24, 2017, https://www.voanews.com/a/pakistan-china-gwadar-port/4084175.html.

84. Kux, *The United States and Pakistan*, 333.

85. On Pakistani views of the United States, see "A Less Gloomy Mood in Pakistan," Pew Research Center, August 27, 2014, http://www.pewglobal.org/2014/08/27/a-less-gloomy-mood-in-pakistan/.

20

The Middle East

The Middle East is as vital to US interests as it is vexing for US policy.[1] The region is marked by persistent upheaval and potential transformation. In the second decade of the twenty-first century, the Israeli-Palestinian peace process is again stalled, as violence increases among the major players. The United States withdrew combat troops from Iraq in 2011, signifying a decrease in American force presence in the region, but subsequently reengaged due to the growth of the militant Islamic State in Iraq and the Levant (ISIL). Iran's nuclear program, despite a nuclear deal in July 2015, continues to concern states in the region and beyond. Most significantly, the Arab Spring, which began in Tunisia in December 2010, was followed by protests in other Middle Eastern states with dramatic consequences. Initially interpreted as a hopeful sign of peaceful democratization, the Arab Spring protests have resulted in heightened instability and uncertainty in an already volatile region. In Syria, protests in 2011 sparked the country's rapid descent into a devastating civil war that has created a significant regional security challenge that also has implications for Europe, Russia, and the United States. (See figure 20.1 for a map of the Middle East.)

In 1993, through their signatures on the Oslo Accords, Israel and the Palestinians indicated their acceptance of a peace settlement based on the concept of a two-state solution. However, lack of tangible progress during the rest of the decade produced a Palestinian rebellion in September 2000 against the continued Israeli occupation and the corrupt Palestinian Authority (PA), which had gained control of newly autonomous Palestinian areas. This Palestinian uprising, known as the Al

The authors would like to thank Professor Ruth Beitler for her significant contributions to this chapter.

Aqsa Intifada ("Al Aqsa" after the mosque in Jerusalem and "Intifada" for uprising), unraveled previous progress and left the peace process in tatters.[2]

A year after this renewal of violence between Israelis and Palestinians, deadly terrorist attacks in the United States triggered a series of events prompting significant changes in the Middle East itself and the US presence in the region. The United States attacked Afghanistan in October 2001 to root out the al Qaeda operatives behind the attacks of September 11, including those who had established training camps with the assistance of Afghanistan's Taliban regime. In March 2003, with the stated intent of preventing a rogue regime from possessing weapons of mass destruction (WMD), the United States launched an invasion of Iraq that resulted in the overthrow of its brutal dictator, Saddam Hussein. In the aftermath of the invasion, the United States sought to establish a democracy in Iraq that would serve as an exemplar to other societies in the Middle East and help stem the growth of regional extremism by addressing one of its important root causes—political disaffection and unrepresentative governance. In the years after 2003, however, violence and political instability in Iraq diminished prospects for the successful establishment of a representative democracy and upset the regional balance of power by eliminating Iraq as a counterbalance to Iran.

The deep and increasingly difficult US involvement in Iraq and the creation of a Shiite-majority government in that country emboldened Iran to take a more assertive stance in the region. President Mahmoud Ahmadinejad, supported by Iran's powerful religious establishment, pursued strongly anti-Western foreign policies following his 2005 election. Iran activated and supported terrorist groups, such as the Shiite Hezbollah, which operates primarily in southern Lebanon. In July 2006, Hezbollah crossed the border into Israel and kidnapped two Israeli soldiers and killed six others, precipitating a thirty-three-day war. Israel's air strikes killed numerous Lebanese civilians and massively damaged Lebanese infrastructure without significantly degrading Hezbollah's capabilities. Hezbollah launched hundreds of rockets against civilian targets in northern Israel and emerged from the inconclusive conflict claiming victory. Despite pressure from the international community, Iran continued to advance its uranium enrichment program, prompting fears that it intended to develop nuclear weapons. By 2007 it was clear that Iran was providing arms and training to Shiite militias and extremists in Iraq.[3]

To combat the turbulent situation and the increasing number of American casualties, the United States implemented a "surge" of troops into Iraq. Although the strategy decreased violence and allowed for an increase in training for Iraq's military and its police, this relative peace and stability did not endure. After US troops withdrew in 2011, levels of violence and Iraqi civilian deaths increased; towns previously won in hard-fought battles were taken over by ISIL, an extremist organization that declared a new Islamic caliphate in the lands it controlled in Syria and Iraq. A coalition involving the United States had retaken most of these areas by early 2018, but the region remains unsettled.

In December 2010, protests erupted in Tunisia and then spread throughout the Middle East, toppling long-standing rulers in Tunisia, Egypt, Libya, and Yemen.

FIGURE 20.1 The Middle East

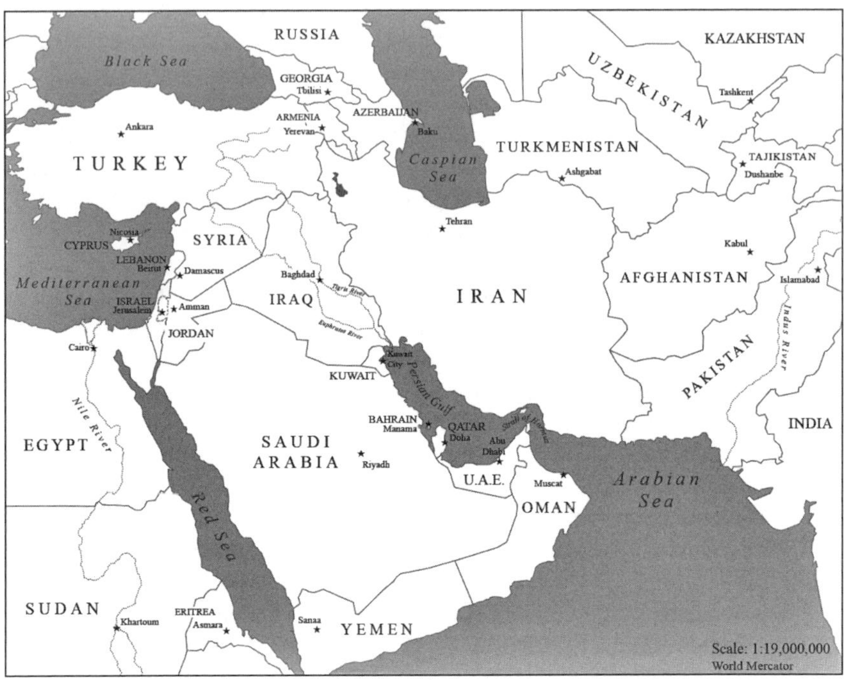

Although the United States was hopeful that democratic regimes would replace authoritarian ones, it quickly came to appreciate the challenges faced by transitioning governments and became aware that new democratic regimes might not be as pro-American as some of the former authoritarian governments. Furthermore, no Arab state other than Tunisia has transitioned to democracy. In Egypt, Mohamed Morsi was elected president in 2012, but the military, led by General Abdel Fattah al-Sisi, removed him from power in July 2013. The Syrian civil war had its origins in pro-democracy protests in 2011, but grew to involve Russia, the United States, and countries and their proxies from across the region. Having become "the biggest humanitarian and refugee crisis of our time," by December 2017 an estimated 5.4 million people had fled Syria—with ripple effects in bordering states and beyond. An additional 6.1 million people were displaced within Syria.[4] Yemen has been in the throes of a civil war since 2015, prompting a humanitarian crisis with widespread blackouts, a cholera outbreak, food scarcity, and refugees fleeing the country.

US Interests

Despite these new and complicated dynamics, US interests in the region, as reflected in the 2017 *National Security Strategy*, the first of President Donald Trump's administration, continue to center on energy, the security of Israel, curtailing Iran's nuclear program, countering jihadi ideology, and retaining influence in this strategically important, highly volatile region.[5]

Oil. Despite recent shifts in oil production and usage, the Middle East remains the world's most important source of oil exports. While the United States now produces more crude oil than Saudi Arabia, Persian Gulf countries still produce 33 percent of the world's oil, and they hold 66 percent of the world's oil reserves.[6] Although the Persian Gulf countries are no longer important suppliers of oil to the United States, the importance of the Middle East as an oil-producing region persists due to global demand.

Since 2005, the United States has experienced a dramatic decline in its domestic consumption of imported oil. In 2016, about 25 percent of the petroleum consumed by the United States was imported from foreign countries. The lowest level of consumption of foreign oil since 1970 was 24 percent in 2015.[7] Despite this change, the global oil market is so integrated that the loss of Persian Gulf oil due to armed conflict or terrorism would greatly affect world energy supplies. Three-fourths of Japan's oil imports and two-thirds of Western Europe's oil imports originate in the vicinity of the Persian Gulf. Without these supplies, these countries would be required to seek other sources. Additionally, China's demand for oil has increased tremendously since the 1990s; it has overtaken Japan as the world's second largest consumer of oil, after the United States. China is now the world's largest net importer of oil, with 19 percent of its oil coming from Saudi Arabia alone.[8] In all, China imports 52 percent of its oil from the Middle East.[9] Rapid development in many countries, including India and China, will continue to fuel increased global demand for oil for decades to come.

The Security of Israel. US relations with Israel have always been complicated. Prior to Israel's creation in 1948, members of the US government clashed over whether recognizing the nascent Jewish state would be a liability given existing US relationships with the Arab world, especially the Persian Gulf states.[10] Despite competing interests, President Harry Truman ultimately decided to back the creation of the new state.

Since 1948, commitment to the security of Israel has been one of the most enduring features of US policy in the Middle East. This is true despite periodic disputes between the two countries over issues such as Israel's participation with Britain and France in the Suez War in 1956 and Israel's continued settlement of the West Bank and Gaza after its occupation of the Palestinian territories in 1967. An important motivation for enduring US support is that Israel is the only enduring democracy in the Middle East. US support for Israel is also consistently bolstered by the continuing efforts of the American Israel Public Affairs Committee (AIPAC), widely recognized as the most powerful US lobbying organization focused on foreign affairs, as well as by various influential Christian groups.

Despite early political support, US military support for Israel did not become truly significant until the mid-1960s. Until then, France and Britain had been its major arms suppliers. In 1966, responding to Israel's fears of increased Soviet arms deliveries to Egypt and Syria, the United States agreed to provide it with large quantities of modern military equipment. Due to this continuing arms relationship, as well as the terms of the 1979 Camp David Peace Accords (discussed later in this chapter), Israel remains "the largest cumulative recipient of US foreign assistance since World War II."[11]

Iran and the Proliferation of Weapons of Mass Destruction. There are four reasons why keeping Iran from developing nuclear weapons is another key US national security goal in the Middle East. First, Iran may deliberately, or accidentally through an inadequate system of controls, transfer a nuclear device to a nonstate actor who cannot be deterred in the same manner as a state. Second, Iran's possession of a nuclear arsenal may spark an effort at military preemption by another country such as Israel. Third, Shia-dominated Iran's possession of nuclear weapons may set off a dangerous regional nuclear arms race among neighboring Sunni-dominated states. A fourth concern relates to the possibility that Iran might decide to use nuclear weapons if it comes into possession of them. There is an ongoing debate over the severity of this threat; it is likely (although hardly certain) that Iran could be deterred from deliberate use through the threat of retaliation, just as nuclear-armed states have been deterred in the past. However, Iran's possession of nuclear weapons could lead to their use by miscalculation or accident, and Iran's possession of a nuclear deterrent could embolden its other malign foreign activities, such as its support for the violent activities of Iranian proxies abroad.

The totality of these concerns led to a concerted effort begun in 2012 by President Barack Obama's administration and the European Union to increase existing sanctions on Iran, while simultaneously pushing for a diplomatic means to prevent Iran from developing nuclear weapons. On November 24, 2013, after intense negotiations with the United States, France, the United Kingdom, China, Russia, and Germany, Iran agreed, in exchange for some sanctions relief, to restrain its uranium enrichment program for six months so that a comprehensive agreement could be reached. In a report from February 2014, the International Atomic Energy Agency (IAEA) found that Iran had fulfilled its interim commitment; consequently, the United States released some of the Iranian assets that had been frozen following the hostage crisis in 1979.[12] In July 2015, despite significant domestic opposition from Congress and foreign opposition from Israel, the United States joined France, Germany, the United Kingdom, China, Russia, and the European Union in reaching a final status agreement with Iran, which increased Iran's breakout time to build a bomb from a few months to a year. Additionally, the agreement stipulated that international inspectors would have access to previously closed Iranian nuclear sites. Despite the new agreement, complex issues persist, including international sensitivity toward the choices that Iran makes as it spends its unfrozen assets, and concerns over how Iran will behave when the agreement expires in fifteen years. During his campaign for president in 2016, Trump pledged to renegotiate this agreement once elected; in October 2017 after he became president, Trump declared that Iran was not in compliance with the agreement. In May 2018, Trump announced that the United States would end participation in the agreement, leaving the effect on Iran and other signatories to be determined.

Combating Terrorism and Countering Jihadist Ideology. US interests in the Middle East include protecting the United States and its citizens from acts of terrorism inspired by an extreme ideology that justifies public violence, and even the targeting of noncombatants, in the name of jihad. (*Jihad* is often translated as "struggle," which may imply nonviolent means, but the term is also used to connote violent action.) Countering such extremists involves capturing or killing terrorists and ending the willingness of states such as Iran and Syria to harbor and support terrorist groups. An even more difficult, but essential, task in achieving long-run success is delegitimizing jihadists' claims that their violent acts are natural outgrowths of Islam.

As with all religions, the tenets of Islam are interpreted differently by different followers. Competing interpretations of Islam vie for legitimacy and popular support throughout the Muslim world. Islam, the world's second largest religion, directs its followers to submit to the will and ultimate sovereignty of God (Allah) as communicated through Mohammed, believed to be the final prophet of God, and set out in its holy book, the Koran.[13] In Mecca in 622 CE, Mohammed proclaimed that there is only one God and that all humanity is subject to God's authority. Islam ultimately unified the previously fractured, tribal cultures of pre-Islamic Arabia. For many Muslims, the subsequent rapid spread of the Islamic caliphate throughout the region and into Europe and Asia during an Islamic "Golden Age" serves as historical validation of the authenticity of God's revelations. Inherent in this sense of authenticity is the belief that the early generations of Muslims flourished because of their devoutness and adherence to Islamic law and traditions.[14] The fact that many in the Muslim world today live in relative powerlessness and poverty, especially compared with the West, constitutes a source of humiliation for some believers who ask, as Western scholar Bernard Lewis put it in his well-known text about Islam, "What Went Wrong?"[15]

A fundamentalist strain of Islamic political thought answers this question by blaming a diminished devoutness among subsequent generations of Muslims for the Western exploitation and domination of the region.[16] Accordingly, restoration of the Muslim world to its rightful state of societal justice and strength requires that Muslims must reject corrupting Western influences and manmade political institutions, and must rise up to wage jihad against corrupt regional regimes and the West.[17] The United States is a particular target; adherents to this radical strain argue that the United States is at war with Islam. Some see US political, economic, and military engagement in the Middle East—particularly US support for Israel and military interventions in Afghanistan and Iraq—as confirmation of this narrative.

A competing approach, sometimes termed *Liberal Islam*, promotes pluralism, liberalization, freedom of conscience and political participation, rights for women and non-Muslims, and interpretation of Islamic law in light of modern political, economic, and social conditions.[18] Liberal Islam upholds the personal and political sovereignty of God (not popular sovereignty, as in the West) and insists that the restoration of societal justice, vitality, and strength in the Muslim world will require a return to Islam's true first principles, which include liberal principles interpreted in the context of modern political and economic institutions. According to this approach, Muslims should publicly oppose radical Islamists as misguided practitioners of an illegitimate doctrine in opposition to God. These liberal voices are, however, often drowned out by those of the extremists.

The United States has an interest in combating violent religious extremists and in countering the ideology that gives rise to violence. A challenge for the United States is to use its political, economic, and military engagement in the Middle East to strengthen liberal Islamic thought and institutions while discouraging extremism. However, the United States has only a limited ability to facilitate this process directly. Instead, developments within the region and interactions between extremist and moderate Muslims will largely dictate the success of this effort. The withdrawal of US troops from Afghanistan and Iraq coupled with the challenges and instability caused by the Arab Spring, especially in Syria, Libya and Yemen, allowed the foothold of extremist groups to increase in some locations. Additionally, the American withdrawal from Iraq in 2011, followed by a civil war in Syria beginning in 2012, led to a power vacuum that allowed ISIL to gain territory.

Some observers point to US support of Israel as a policy that may diminish the credibility of American efforts to delegitimize jihadi extremism.[19] However, while the Israeli-Palestinian issue is important, the sources of violent extremism are more varied, complex, and often local. One effort to address this was the 2015 Summit on Countering Violent Extremism convened by the Obama administration; it brought together "local, federal, and international leaders . . . to develop community-oriented approaches to counter hateful extremist ideologies that radicalize, recruit or incite to violence."[20] The *National Security Strategy* of 2017 expresses the Trump administration's intent to continue to engage local communities within the United States with a focus on "terrorism prevention" in concert with law enforcement and civic leaders.[21]

Continuing US Influence in the Region. With the 1968 withdrawal of British forces from the Middle East, the United States and the Soviet Union became the region's principal external influences. Using US support for Israel as the anvil, the Soviets continually sought to hammer out a solid anti-American Arab bloc. The Soviets relied mainly on military aid and advisors to various countries and also offered trade and civilian aid projects, such as support for Egypt's Aswan Dam. The Soviet approach was relatively successful in Iraq and Syria but yielded mixed results in other countries.

Table 20.1 Middle East Key Statistics

Country	*Total population (millions)*	*Life expectancy at birth*	*GDP US$ (billions)*	*GDP/ capita US$*	*Population living in poverty (%)*	*Military expenditure (% of GDP)*	*Military spending US$ (millions)*	*Human Development Index (HDI) ranking (of 188)*
Bahrain	1.4	78.9	31.8	50,300	na	4.8	1,523	47
Egypt	94.7	72.7	342.8	12,100	25.2	1.9	5,330	111
Iran, Islamic Republic of	82.8	71.4	412.3	18,100	18.7	3.9	15,882	69
Iraq	38.1	74.9	173.0	16,500	23	11.6	17,900	121
Israel	8.2	82.4	311.7	34,800	22	6.1	15,878	19
Jordan	8.2	74.6	39.5	11,100	14.2	4.4	I ,448	86
Kuwait	2.8	78.0	110.5	71,300	na	3.8	4,313	51
Lebanon	6.2	77.6	51.2	18,500	28.6	3.5	1,740	76
Oman	3.4	75.5	59.7	43,700	na	16.4	9,103	52
Qatar	2.3	78.7	185.4	129,700	na	2.8	4,404	33
Saudi Arabia	28.2	75.3	637.8	54,100	na	8.9	56,898	38
Syria	17.2	74.9	24.6	2,900	82.5	na	na	149
Turkey	80.3	74.8	856.8	21,100	21.9	1.2	8,764	71
United Arab Emirates	5.9	77.5	375.0	67,700	19.5	na	na	42
Yemen	27.4	65.5	31.3	2,500	54	na	na	168

na = not available.

Sources: Data on population and economy is from the CIA World Factbook 2017, https://www.cia.gov/library/publications/the-world-factbook. Military expenditure data is from International Institute for Strategic Studies (IISS), *The Military Balance 2017* (London: IISS, 2017). HDI rankings are from *Human Development Report 2016*, http://hdr.undp.org/en/data. Most figures are from 2016 (otherwise latest available data is listed). GDP is reported at the official exchange rate. GDP per capita is using Purchasing Power Parity rates.

The disappearance of the Soviet Union left the United States as the only major external actor in the region. In the absence of the Soviets, the United States showcased its military power during the 1990–1991 Gulf War and, in late 2001–2002, in Afghanistan. Awareness of and respect for US power remains, but setbacks in the Iraq war demonstrated its limits and drastically undercut the perceived legitimacy of American leadership in the region. Even in countries with strong ties to the United States, such as Saudi Arabia, Egypt, Jordan, and Morocco, distrust of US policy in the Middle East reached new peaks as the populations of these countries came to believe that the invasion of Iraq was intended "to control oil, protect Israel, and weaken the Muslim world."[22]

Beginning in 2010, the Arab Spring led to further challenges to US and Western influence in the region. When protests spread from Tunisia to Egypt, the United States was ambivalent in its support for President Hosni Mubarak and eventually sided with the protestors, some of whom called for a more representative government. This US withdrawal of support for the leader of an erstwhile ally—Egypt had long been the third largest recipient of US aid—damaged relations with rulers in Saudi Arabia and other regimes who feared American abandonment in the face of possible mass protests in their own countries. President Mubarak subsequently stepped down and Muslim Brotherhood candidate Mohammed Morsi was elected president in 2012. US-Egyptian relations cooled after the Egyptian military removed Morsi from power in July 2013 and then undertook a brutal crackdown on political opposition groups including Morsi's Muslim Brotherhood, an Islamist organization with extremist, often violent offshoots. Egypt was then offered substantial financial support from Saudi Arabia, Bahrain, and the United Arab Emirates, countries that supported the military takeover.[23] This financial aid has the potential to reduce US leverage in Egypt and the region.

The United States had hoped that its withdrawal from Iraq and Afghanistan and the effects of the Arab Spring would allow a shift in US strategic interests to a focus on Asia. However, since 2014, the United States has reintroduced combat troops and has conducted airstrikes in the region to combat the threat of ISIL. Delicately balancing the interests of its partners in an environment characterized by complex relationships, the United States also sought to counter Russian influence as Russia intervened in Syria in 2015 to support the regime of President Bashar al-Assad.

History of US Involvement in the Region

Starting in the mid-1960s, a series of political and economic changes in the Middle East and the rest of the world steadily increased the importance of the region to US national security. These developments included a dramatic increase in global oil consumption, the Israeli occupation of the West Bank and Gaza during the 1967 war, the British withdrawal from the Persian Gulf area in 1968, and the broadening influence of the Soviet Union in the region.

Increased US Engagement and the Importance of Oil. The rapid increase in world oil consumption in the decades after World War II fundamentally altered the conditions governing the production and distribution of oil. Before 1965, the major global oil companies had been able to ensure that the supply of oil met or slightly exceeded demand. By 1970, however, the supply of oil was not increasing fast enough to meet escalating demand, and competition among consumers for available oil intensified. Furthermore, in 1970, first Libya and then others began to pressure foreign oil companies for improved concessions and payments. As producing states gradually realized that the market for oil had become a seller's market, they nationalized the oil business and raised prices.

Between 1968 and 1975, the average price of oil increased from less than $2 per barrel to roughly $11 per barrel. Most of this increase occurred at the end of 1973 and early in 1974, when prices quadrupled following an embargo by Arab producers against the United States and the Netherlands because of their support for Israel during the 1973 Arab-Israeli War. In the United States and other importing states, such steep increases led to serious balance-of-payments problems and contributed to inflation. At this point it became clear that America had a strong interest in ensuring access to Middle Eastern oil at acceptable prices.

The 1980–1988 Iran-Iraq War posed a renewed threat to oil supplies as each side attacked the other's production and refinery facilities. Despite the loss of about three million barrels per day of exports, oil was initially plentiful due to unprecedented standby production capacity, primarily in Saudi Arabia. Nor did the years of conflict, including Iraq's and Iran's targeting of tanker ships in the Persian Gulf beginning in 1984, seriously threaten overall oil flows from the Gulf. Pipelines could, to a limited extent, divert Saudi and Iraqi oil to ports on the Red Sea. However, concerns arose that potential closure of the Persian Gulf's twenty-eight-mile-wide Strait of Hormuz could wreak havoc on the global economy, as the approximately eight million barrels per day exported through the Gulf accounted for over 40 percent of world trade in oil.

After only a short period of peace, Iraq invaded Kuwait in August 1990. The resulting Persian Gulf crisis of 1990–1991 posed risks beyond interruption of the oil supply. Observers worried that if Saddam Hussein took control of most Persian Gulf oil reserves and the choke point of the Strait of Hormuz, he would be able to set a monopoly price on the world's oil. Thus the US intervention in 1991 was prompted not only by the desire to return sovereignty to Kuwait but also by the potential threat to the health of the US and international economy.

The price of oil began to increase at the turn of the century due to increased demand and to limitations in global refining capacity. By 2012, the figure peaked at more than $110 per barrel. However, oil prices have plunged in more recent years, averaging $43 per barrel in 2016, due to increased US oil production from hydraulic fracturing (fracking) and a slowdown in global energy demand.[24] Despite its decreasing dependence on Middle Eastern oil, complete regional disengagement is not a viable option for the United States. The Middle East is still a major player in the global oil market, fulfilling much of the demand from China, India, and many developing nations.[25] The global economy necessitates continued US efforts to establish partnerships with governments in the Middle East into the foreseeable future.

Support for Israel. As noted earlier, it was not until the mid-1960s that Jerusalem began to receive large amounts of military and financial aid from Washington. In response to Soviet support for Egypt and Syria prior to the 1967 war, the United States began providing substantial arms and equipment to Israel. Since that time, a continuing challenge for US foreign policy in the Middle East has been to balance its relations with Israel and the Arab states.

In 1973, Egyptian President Anwar Sadat launched a surprise attack against Israel, jeopardizing the existence of the small state. After being informed of a Soviet airlift of arms to Syria, President Richard Nixon authorized a full-scale US airlift to Israel.[26] Israel received an emergency package of US arms worth a total of $2 billion during the crisis. Although the Arab states initially inflicted severe casualties on the Israelis, they were unable to retain control of the territory they gained early in the war.

Despite the continuing flow of US arms, Israel soon recognized that excessive reliance on US goodwill could restrict its freedom of action. As a result, it embarked on a program to acquire and manufacture enough military equipment to enable its forces to wage a war against the combined forces of Egypt, Syria, Jordan, Iraq, and Saudi Arabia for three weeks without exhausting its supplies. Strategically, the Camp David Accords and the Egyptian-Israeli peace treaty of 1979 helped Israel achieve this goal. The United States facilitated the acceptance of the 1979 peace treaty with pledges of massive financial and military aid to both Egypt and Israel. This assurance of supply, combined with Israel's own production and military predominance in the region, seriously reduced the possibility that the United States would be able to pressure Israel in a future crisis. Israel also gained flexibility through the removal of Egypt as a possible opponent.

An important test came when Israel preemptively and successfully struck Iraq's Osirak nuclear facility in 1981. The Arab world was outraged at what they perceived to be a mild American response to an attack on Iraq's sovereignty, even though President Ronald Reagan had condemned Israel's attack in the United Nations (UN) Security Council and temporarily suspended the delivery of F-16 aircraft that Israel had already purchased. Israel further demonstrated its strategic independence by invading Lebanon in June 1982 in response to Palestinian guerilla attacks launched into Israel from southern Lebanon. Eventually, Israeli troops laid siege to West Beirut, forcing the Palestinian Liberation Organization (PLO) to withdraw from its sanctuary in Lebanon. Only after the Reagan administration threatened a breach in relations did the Israelis call off their siege. Nevertheless, Israel and the United States were drawn into the quagmire of Lebanon's civil war, and both incurred serious human and political costs before they were able to withdraw. Israeli troops remained in Lebanon until Israeli Prime Minister Ehud Barak's unilateral withdrawal in 2000.

Reagan's successor, President George H. W. Bush, sought to distance himself somewhat from the right-wing Likud government of Israeli Prime Minister Yitzhak Shamir. The first Gulf War in 1991 and America's aid to Kuwait also helped restore some US credibility in the Arab world. Consequently, President Bush was able to convince key Arab states to participate in the Madrid Conference and to undertake bilateral and multilateral negotiations with Israel. He also opened talks with the Palestinians. His threat to withhold financial aid from Israel in an effort to pressure Shamir to cease construction of Israeli settlements in the West Bank and Gaza Strip was, however, fruitless.

Following Bush's acrimonious relationship with Israel's leadership, President Bill Clinton fostered warmer ties with Prime Minister Yitzhak Rabin. Clinton actively sought to build a sustained peace based on the 1993 Oslo Accords between Israel and the Palestinians. His efforts culminated in the US-sponsored Camp David summit in July 2000 between Rabin and Palestinian Chairman Yassir Arafat, but it failed to resolve final status issues for the creation of a Palestinian state.

When President George W. Bush assumed office in January 2001, he initially neglected the Israeli-Palestinian peace process, but moved firmly to back Israel following the terrorist attacks on the United States later that year. To many in the Bush administration, Israel's war against suicide bombers and the US struggle against international terrorists constituted the basis for deeper cooperation between the two countries. A complication later arose when Hamas, an organization that refused to recognize Israel or to renounce violence, won a majority in the 2006 Palestinian parliamentary elections. Despite these challenges, Secretary of State Condoleezza Rice increased US activism in the peace process during the second term of the Bush administration.

The Arab world was hopeful that the United States would take a more balanced approach to the Israeli-Palestinian peace after President Barack Obama took office in 2009. In June 2009 in Cairo, Obama spoke of seeking "a new beginning between the United States and Muslims around the world, one based on mutual interest and mutual respect, and one based upon the truth that America and Islam are not exclusive and need not be in competition."[27] In that same speech, Obama reaffirmed America's commitment to Israel but also clearly stated firm support for a Palestinian state.

The Obama administration continued to pursue peace talks, but efforts at a peace treaty collapsed in April 2014. A six-week-long war erupted between Israel and Gaza after three Jewish Israeli teenagers were kidnapped and murdered in the West Bank in June 2014. Israel cracked down on Hamas members in the West Bank accused of orchestrating the kidnapping and murders of the Israelis. Hamas then increased its rocket attacks into Israel; Israel undertook intense bombing raids into Gaza and a ground invasion to destroy the intricate system of tunnels from Gaza that had been used to carry out terrorist attacks inside Israel. Since that war, no real efforts have emerged to reignite the peace process.

The Trump administration has expressed a commitment to finding a resolution to the ongoing conflict. However, the 2017 *National Security Strategy* states that the Israel-Palestinian discord is not the key impediment to peace in the region, and the document does not include language on a two-state solution, a departure from previous administrations.[28] In December 2017, President Trump signaled another shift when he recognized Jerusalem as the capital of Israel and announced his intention to build an American embassy in the city. This move complicates future efforts to seek a peace agreement because Palestinians lay claim to East Jerusalem and plan to use it as the capital for their future state. The announcement was widely embraced by Israelis and denounced by Palestinians; in its aftermath, President of the Palestinian Authority Mahmoud Abbas vowed that he would never again participate in peace negotiations brokered by the United States.[29]

Operation Desert Storm: The First Gulf War and Its Aftermath. On August 2, 1990, still reeling from the manpower losses and economic dislocations of a stalemated eight-year war with Iran, Iraq invaded the tiny sheikdom of Kuwait. The United States led most of the world in responding with condemnations and a variety of economic sanctions. By the end of 1990, most countries supported military action unless Iraq immediately and unconditionally withdrew its troops. Last-minute diplomatic efforts failed to resolve the crisis, and a US-led coalition attacked Iraq in January 1991. Coalition forces from thirty-four countries, with more than 750,000 troops, thousands of aircraft, and nearly two hundred warships, liberated Kuwait in a forty-four-day campaign.

Within two weeks of the start of hostilities, the Iraqi army in Kuwait was cut off from its command and control linkages and most of its logistical lifelines. Only the continuing threat of Iraqi Scud missiles aimed at key Israeli and Saudi cities remained a danger; by the third week of the air campaign, there were no more Iraqi Scud launches. The complex ground campaign began in February 1991, and in a one-hundred-hour assault and flanking maneuver, allied forces encircled and defeated the Iraqi army.

Concerned with maintaining the coalition and fearful that complete destruction of Iraq's forces would result in chaos and create a power vacuum that Iran could exploit, the US-led coalition allowed a substantial portion of the Iraqi army to escape. As a consequence, and in defiance of ceasefire agreements, Saddam Hussein reconstituted a sizable force that he used a few months later to quell uprisings of internal opponents, including Kurds in the north and Shiites in the south. After much Kurdish suffering, the United Nations imposed a protective area in Iraqi Kurdistan and provided humanitarian relief there. In 1992, the international community imposed a "no fly zone" over Iraqi territory south of the 36th parallel to protect the mostly Shiite local communities from Saddam Hussein's army. Despite these measures and continuing economic sanctions that were painful for Iraq's people and damaging to its economy, Saddam Hussein resisted full compliance with the ceasefire agreement's call for the destruction of all of Iraq's missiles and chemical, biological, and nuclear weapons manufacturing facilities.

The UN sanctions against Iraq were an important component of the overall US policy of "dual containment" in the Persian Gulf. This policy, articulated in 1993, was designed to contain and isolate both Iran and Iraq. There were different objectives for each country: a change in regime became a prerequisite for resumption of US relations with Iraq, while the United States demanded that Iran terminate its support for terrorism and end its efforts to develop WMD.

After the Gulf War of 1991, the United States became, for the first time, extensively involved in military actions on the ground in the Middle East. Some Western observers contended that the war's end provided an opportunity for a "new world order" that would see enhanced cooperation among the great powers. Others saw the war's conclusion as an opportunity to transform traditional political structures in the Middle East through the spread of pluralism and democracy. One immediate effect was that the United States achieved new credibility within the region. It took advantage of this opportunity to press for international peace talks to resolve the Arab-Israeli conflict, which led to a regional peace conference in 1991 at Madrid.

The Madrid Conference constituted the first direct negotiations between Israel and any of its Arab neighbors other than Egypt (which had signed a peace agreement with Israel in 1979). This Arab recognition of Israel's right to exist, although only implicit, set the stage for agreements between Jerusalem and a number of regional actors and states, most notably in the Oslo Accords with the PLO in 1993 and a peace treaty with Jordan in 1994. In addition, Arab states in the Persian Gulf and North Africa established commercial relations with Israel.

US Military Operations in Afghanistan and Iraq. Following the September 2001 terrorist attacks in the United States, President George W. Bush declared a "global war on terrorism," substantially altering dynamics in the region. Fifteen of the nineteen hijackers were from Saudi Arabia, resulting in a deterioration of US-Saudi relations. In October 2001 the United States attacked Afghanistan to force from power the Taliban regime that had supported al Qaeda with financing and training bases (discussed further in chapter 19). By the spring of 2002, US and Afghan forces had largely suppressed Taliban and al Qaeda elements and had succeeded in establishing a pro-US government in Kabul headed by Hamid Karzai. Although the ramifications of the war continue to play out, the creation of a pro-American government in this initial period was considered a victory.

After this apparent early success in Afghanistan, the United States focused its attention on Saddam Hussein's regime in Iraq. Although the United States had considered ousting Saddam during the first Gulf War, George H. W. Bush had opted to end the war once Iraq withdrew from Kuwait. The primary considerations behind that decision included concerns about the cohesiveness of the international coalition that had fought the war and the obligations that the United States would assume if it decided to overthrow the Iraqi government.[30] Slightly more than a decade later, in the wake of the large-scale terrorist attacks on US soil, the calculus had changed. President George W. Bush was convinced that Iraq's noncompliance with UN resolutions on the elimination of WMD meant that Iraq had such weapons; moreover, he was more willing than his father to accept the risks associated with changing the Iraqi regime.

In his 2002 State of the Union address, President Bush labeled Iran, Iraq, and North Korea an "axis of evil," alleging that those states supported terrorist groups and were pursuing WMD. His administration spent the next year arguing the case that Iraq possessed WMD and had connections with al Qaeda and other terrorist organizations. While seeking international support for regime change, the United States made it clear that it was willing to act unilaterally.

After considerable internal debate, the Bush administration opted to present its case to the United Nations. The Security Council passed Resolution 1441, which called on Iraq to admit UN weapons inspectors and threatened severe repercussions in the event of its refusal to comply. The Iraqi government then permitted UN inspectors access to purported weapon sites and delivered some documents ostensibly revealing the status of Iraq's weapons programs. The United States, however, emphasized the Iraqi government's untrustworthiness by pointing to Saddam's repeated noncompliance with earlier UN resolutions and lack of full compliance with current demands.

In a televised address in March 2003, President Bush presented an ultimatum, demanding that Saddam Hussein and his sons leave Iraq within forty-eight hours. When the deadline passed and Saddam remained, the United States and the United Kingdom moved prepositioned troops from Kuwait into southern Iraq and began air strikes on key targets. Within two weeks, the United States and other coalition forces had gained control of southern Iraq and were preparing to move on to Baghdad. Some resistance slightly slowed the advance, including from irregular fedayeen fighters, but Baghdad fell in April 2003. In the north, Kurdish militia took over key cities including Mosul, Kirkuk, and Erbil. Bush declared the end of major combat operations in a dramatic speech on an aircraft carrier in the Persian Gulf in May 2003.

With this declaration, postconflict requirements rose to the fore, such as sealing borders, maintaining order, rebuilding Iraqi infrastructure, and administering the country until a new Iraqi government could be established. With insufficient numbers of forces in country, the initial US response to these requirements was grossly inadequate.[31] The first civilian entity charged with establishing an administration until the Iraqis were prepared to take over the governance of their country was the Office of Reconstruction and Humanitarian Assistance (ORHA), established in January 2003 and led by retired Lieutenant General Jay Garner. Garner's prewar expectation that his work in Iraq would take only three months lends credence to a pervasive view that the Bush administration did not plan sufficiently for "worst-case scenarios" for postwar Iraq.[32] By the time Garner arrived in Baghdad in April, significant destruction had already occurred from widespread looting. He left Baghdad at the beginning of June, and ORHA was dissolved a few weeks later.

By May 2003, George W. Bush had selected former Ambassador L. Paul Bremer III to head a new Coalition Provisional Authority (CPA), which would replace ORHA and assume responsibility for reconstruction and political transition. Bremer arrived in Iraq later in May. He made two key decisions within his first thirty days in Baghdad: to disband the Iraqi Army and to engage in a "de-

Baathification" of the Iraqi government by purging Saddam loyalists from all positions of authority. Although there were arguments in favor of both of these decisions, their impact proved to be disastrous. They increased the number of opponents of the occupation and vastly heightened the difficulty of creating order and stability.

After little more than a year, in June 2004, the CPA handed sovereignty back to the Iraqis. In December 2003, Saddam had been captured near his hometown of Tikrit. He was later tried by the Iraqi government and executed in 2006. In December 2005, elections were held to select the Iraqi legislature. Although these elections indicated progress, most people voted along sectarian lines, and after the elections, it took almost five months for a government to form. Bush administration hopes that Saddam's capture and Iraqi elections would limit the violence proved to be misplaced. Postinvasion challenges grew and violence intensified. In addition to the mostly Sunni insurgents, other violent actors entered the fray, including Shiite militias, foreign fighters, and criminals.

As a consequence of deterioration in security conditions during 2006, American strategy shifted in early 2007. US forces switched from a focus on finding and fighting insurgents to a "clear and hold" approach: they sought to clear selected areas (Baghdad initially) of insurgents and then hold those areas with a continuing troop presence. Many of the troops needed to execute the new strategy were provided by additional Iraqi units, supplemented by about 30,000 more US troops who were also "surged" to Iraq, bringing total US forces in country to over 160,000.

By the end of the second term of President Bush's administration, US fatalities in Iraq numbered more than 4,200. Estimates of the number of Iraqi insurgents and civilians killed ranged from 100,000 to 600,000.[33] Neither new WMD nor signs of a substantive weapons program were found. American popular support for the war plummeted, and Congress sought to restrict the president's capability to continue American involvement in Iraq by attaching various exit requirements to funding provisions. Public debate over continued US military involvement in Iraq escalated. Although successful in toppling Saddam Hussein, the US-led invasion had not led to a stable, effective successor regime capable of maintaining internal order or protecting Iraq from external interference. Indeed, the continued US presence in Iraq itself proved to be a problem in that it served as a sign of Arab humiliation and perceptions that the United States intended to dominate and exploit the region.

President Barack Obama came into office in January 2009 having campaigned on a promise to bring the war in Iraq to a responsible close. Legislative elections in Iraq in 2009–2010 had a high voter turnout, and the Iraqi military and police provided security for voters. However, the disputed results, and the US and British troop withdrawal in 2011, signaled trouble. Shia militias, funded by Iran, began to take control of areas in the south.[34] By 2012, growing discontent among Sunnis, who resented an increasingly sectarian Shia-dominated government, also led to an upsurge in violence. ISIL eventually took over some territory. In June 2014, the United States sent a small number of troops to advise and arm Kurdish fighters opposing ISIL and began an aerial campaign against ISIL in Iraq. By September 2014, in concert with some of its Arab allies, the United States began bombing

ISIL in Syria as well. Although ISIL was later substantially defeated in both Syria and Iraq, the shape of an enduring political settlement remains unclear as the underlying grievances of the Sunni population in Iraq and Syria remain unresolved.

Factors Affecting Regional Stability

The history described above significantly affects the ability of the United States to protect its national interests in the Middle East. However, highly visible, specific developments and events are only part of the challenge. Important underlying factors can be found in the sources of political and social instability that continue to characterize much of the region.

State Strength. Many Middle Eastern states were either created or significantly altered after World War I in a highly arbitrary fashion by the European powers that dominated the region. The political systems established to govern the new entities reflected European, rather than local, interests and values; borders were drawn largely to satisfy the interests of the European powers. As a result, some ethnic and cultural groups that thought of themselves as separate were incorporated into single states. In other cases, cohesive linguistic or religious groups were divided into several states dominated by their traditional antagonists. Most prominent among these are the Kurds, who are dispersed in a large geographic area that includes parts of Turkey, Iraq, Syria, and Iran.

As a result of these artificial boundaries, levels of national cohesion and political solidarity tended to be low in these newly independent states. Throughout the region, the focal points of loyalty were the family, village, tribe, and ethnic group. Religion and ties of ethnic and cultural solidarity competed vigorously with the new state governments for popular allegiance.

Complicating these internal political dynamics was the widespread appeal of Arab nationalism. Egypt's charismatic leader, Gamal Abd al-Nasser, used Arab nationalist rhetoric in the 1950s and 1960s to galvanize Arab masses across the Middle East against "reactionary" regimes in Jordan and Saudi Arabia, Zionism, and continued Western colonialism. In the competition among Arab states in the Middle East, Arab nationalism itself became a contentious issue. Border clashes and attempts to subvert rival regimes by means of propaganda and the distribution of arms and subsidies to potential dissidents were common.[35] Tensions stemming from rapid economic change further exacerbated conflicts among Arab states. After World War II, countries of the Middle East saw land reforms, the development of heavy industry, and the growth of state ownership and bureaucratic controls over the economy. Increased taxes, scarcities, and severe inflation accompanied the new economic policies. Economic dissatisfaction was converted into political unrest.

In the oil-producing countries of the Middle East, different problems caused by different patterns of economic development were no less acute. The vast funds generated by the oil industry enabled governments to initiate major economic development programs. However, local technical expertise required to undertake these programs was largely absent; thus by the late 1970s, Americans, Europeans, Egyptians, and Palestinians played key roles in the economies, bureaucracies, and educational systems of the oil-producing countries of the Arabian Peninsula, while Yemenis, Pakistanis, and Indians made up much of the unskilled labor force. This foreign presence became a politically sensitive issue and a source of grievances. American relationships with regimes friendly to US interests but unresponsive to the needs of their own populations became a source of widespread resentment.

The eruption of the Arab Spring in Tunisia in 2010, leading to the departure of long-time president Zine El-Abidine Ben Ali in January 2011, precipitated widespread change across the region. Massive protests in Egypt, Libya, and Yemen forced long-standing authoritarian leaders out of power. Libya, Syria, and then Yemen erupted into violent civil wars that have yet to be resolved.

Egypt. In Egypt, after the overthrow of Mubarak in January 2011, a twenty-one-member council composed of senior military leaders, known as the Supreme Council of the Armed Forces (SCAF), assumed control of the country. It promised to hand over authority to a civilian government once elections were held. From November 2011 to January 2012, parliamentary elections took place, and a new parliament was seated; SCAF retained executive control until Morsi was elected president in July 2012. Some in the United States were concerned about Morsi's election, as he had been a member of the Muslim Brotherhood. As Morsi began to consolidate executive and legislative power, the Egyptian population and external players worried about the future of democracy in Egypt.

In July 2013, after protests erupted objecting to Morsi's consolidation of power, the Egyptian military, led by Field Marshal Abdel Fattah el-Sisi, conducted a coup and began a brutal crackdown on the Muslim Brotherhood and other opposition groups. The United States withheld military aid from Egypt because of the military's oppression of political opponents and its move away from democracy. Illustrating its ambivalence on how to deal with Egypt, however, and despite some protests in Congress, the United States also delivered helicopters to Egypt, citing their use in combating terrorists in the Sinai.[36] Egypt remains an important US ally, and the fact that it is one of the few Arab countries to maintain diplomatic ties with Israel is a stabilizing factor in the region. However, concerns about the Egyptian government's respect for human rights are likely to continue to be a constraint on US-Egyptian relations.

Libya. Caught up in the energy of the Arab Spring, pro-democracy protestors spilled onto the streets of Benghazi in February 2011. By March 17, 2011, the United Nations authorized the use of force in Libya; a few days later the United States and other NATO allies established a no-fly zone to protect civilians. By October, and with Western military support, rebel forces gained control of the country and killed former Libyan leader Muammar al-Qaddafi.[37] The operation was initially hailed as a victory and a model for low-cost military intervention that did not involve ground troops. But this early assessment was flawed, as noted by President Obama, who later expressed regret for not managing Libya's transition after the removal of Qaddafi.[38] Despite democratic elections in 2012, the country quickly unraveled and became a failed state and a new home for ISIL.

Radical jihadist groups, which had formed militias to rebel against Qaddafi, were supported by Qatar, Sudan, and other countries.[39] The new Libyan government was too weak to disarm them. Additionally, a rival group established a parallel government in the eastern part of Libya. The state's lack of a monopoly on force was blatantly visible on September 11, 2012, when jihadists attacked the US Embassy in Benghazi, killing four Americans including US Ambassador Christopher Stevens. By 2015, radical jihadist groups controlled the city of Sirte, in proximity to Libya's oil facilities, which they attacked to disrupt the flow of revenue to the government. The jihadist groups captured Egyptian Coptic Christian workers near Sirte and publicized their beheading in a widely circulated video. By August 2016, with US support, the forces of the Government of National Accord, an interim Libyan government supported by the United Nations, retook Sirte from ISIL forces. Whether the UN-backed government will manage to forestall a return of ISIL and rebuild functioning institutions remains an open question.

Syria. The protests in Syria that began as part of the Arab Spring, the reponse of the Assad regime to them, and the subsequent internationalization of the conflict had a catastrophic impact on people of Syria. By March 2016, at least 460,000 Syrians had been killed.[40] In 2011, protests began in the Syrian city of Deraa; they were met by a brutal regime response in an attempt to deter an outcome like that in Egypt or Tunisia, where long-standing rulers fell. Exacerbating Syria's divisions, Saudi Arabia and Turkey began supplying arms and Islamist fighters to defeat Bashar al-Assad, Syria's president. Iran, along with its proxy, Hezbollah, entered the conflict to support the Assad regime. Sunni militants, whose power had been weakened in Iraq after the US surge in 2007, took advantage of the unrest in Syria. Many of these militants joined ISIL, which gained new adherents and a new operating base in Syria. Violence extended across the Syrian-Iraqi border, as ISIL succeeded in capturing Iraqi cities that included Mosul and Tal Afar.[41]

At the beginning of Syria's unrest, the United States had contemplated intervention, but, having just withdrawn from Iraq and anticipating a withdrawal of troops from Afghanistan, the United States refrained from military intervention in Syria. In 2012, however, President Obama declared "a red line": "seeing a whole bunch of chemical weapons moving around or being utilized" by the Syrian regime "would change my calculus."[42] After Syria used chemical weapons in 2013, however, the United States did not take military action. Russia, an ally of Syria since the Cold War, used the opportunity to gain a stronger foothold in the region and to help keep Assad in power by negotiating a framework under which Syria agreed to destroy its chemical arsenal. In return, the United States decided to defer indefinitely its bombing of Syria.[43] After that accord, Russia built an airbase in Latakia and began bombarding both rebel forces and ISIL. Due to Russia's support of

Assad's regime and the US insistence on regime change, some observers have described Russia's role in Syria as transforming the "civil war there into a proxy U.S-Russian conflict."[44] A further complication stems from US support for the Kurdish People's Protection Units (YPG) from Syrian Kurdistan, which have been effective in combating ISIL. Close ties between the YPG and a domestic Kurdish terrorist group in Turkey, the Kurdistan Workers' Party (PKK), has caused tensions between the United States and longstanding ally Turkey.

Syria's civil war is proving to be intractable and complicated; its myriad external actors exacerbate the tensions. At present, Syria no longer exists as a viable state. More than half of its pre-war population of approximately 20.7 million has been forcibly displaced, and its economy has been devastated with long-term consequences. According to a World Bank report, "the losses in [Syrian] GDP between 2011 and 2016 sum to about four times the size of the Syrian GDP in 2010."[45] In Syria, as throughout the Middle East, the issue of state strength continues to be a pressing problem. Monarchies and authoritarian structures endure even as the ramifications of the Arab Spring are still unfolding.

Relations between Israel and its Arab Neighbors. One of the most profound and persistent of the many regional problems in the Middle East is the Arab-Israeli conflict. In 1947, the United Nations called for the partition of Palestine to create a Jewish state and an Arab state to alleviate tension between the two groups. The United States voted in favor of the UN partition plan for a two-state solution, with Jerusalem to be placed under international administration. On May 14, 1948, David Ben-Gurion proclaimed the formation of the state of Israel and became its first prime minister. Full-scale war immediately broke out, with the armies of five neighboring Arab states intervening on the side of the Palestinians.

By April 1949, Israel had defeated the combined Arab forces and had gained control of additional territory that had not been assigned to it in the original partition plan. More than 700,000 Palestinian Arabs had been expelled or had fled from their homes and were living as stateless refugees in neighboring Arab countries. Jordan took control of the West Bank, and Egypt maintained authority over the Gaza Strip, both areas that had been assigned to the Palestinians in the original plan.

Arab-Israeli hostility was deepened by Israel's inconclusive 1956 attack on Egypt, which was conducted in concert with the British and French following Nasser's nationalization of the Suez Canal. A number of hostile Arab moves in the spring of 1967—including Nasser's ejection of UN peacekeeping forces that had been present in the Sinai since 1956, Egypt's closing of the Straits of Tiran at the Gulf of Aqaba to Israeli shipping, and the massing of Syrian forces on the Golan Heights—precipitated a surprise preemptive strike by the Israeli air force. The June 1967 war, in which Israel defeated Egypt, Syria, and Jordan on three fronts in six days, radically altered the political and military balance in the Middle East. The combined Arab forces suffered a humiliating defeat as Israel occupied the Sinai Peninsula, the Gaza Strip, the West Bank, and Syria's Golan Heights. Continued

Israeli occupation of those lands increased antagonism toward Israel to the point that this animosity took precedence over various inter-Arab disputes.

The resulting inter-Arab rapprochement was demonstrated by a joint Egyptian-Syrian surprise attack on Israel in October 1973. The Saudis and other oil-producing states in the region supported the Arab cause with oil embargoes against the United States and the Netherlands. Despite early Arab successes, however, once again the Israelis were victorious.

On the Arab side, the Egyptian-Israeli peace treaty, signed in March 1979 in Washington, DC, signaled Egypt's shift away from pan-Arab military confrontation toward policies of political accommodation and economic cooperation with Israel. In return, Egypt regained control over the Sinai, captured by Israel in 1967. As a consequence, however, the Saudis joined the other Arab states in opposing Egypt's separate peace with Israel.

The early to mid-1980s saw no serious progress toward resolving the Palestinian problem. In December 1987, an Israeli army vehicle hit a car and killed four Palestinian passengers. This incident sparked the first intifada, a spontaneous wave of mass demonstrations and violent riots in the Israeli-occupied territories, which lasted in varying degrees of intensity for several years.[46] In December 1988, PLO Chairman Yassir Arafat formally recognized Israel's existence and renounced the use of terrorism, satisfying US preconditions for talks with the PLO. Over the objections of the Israeli government and the American Jewish community, the Reagan administration began meeting with PLO leaders in Tunis. The talks, which were intended to lay the groundwork for Israeli-Palestinian negotiations, broke down in March 1989 after a planned Palestinian attack on a Tel Aviv beach was thwarted at the last moment by an Israeli coastal patrol.

The overall record on reconciliation between Israel and its Arab neighbors is mixed, with much hinging on resolution of the Israeli-Palestinian conflict. The 1994 Jordan-Israel peace agreement set out an ambitious agenda of cooperative relations between the two countries in diverse fields, including economic development, tourism, environmental protection, cultural exchanges, and even security.[47] Although official relations have developed, popular Jordanian opposition to the agreement remains strong. Because a majority of Jordanians are of Palestinian origin, Jordanians are particularly resistant to the development of normal relations with Israel until there is a resolution of the Israeli-Palestinian conflict.

In May 1999, Ehud Barak became the Israeli prime minister and formed a coalition that championed a final resolution to the Arab-Israeli conflict. He began direct negotiations with Syria on the future of the Golan Heights, but those talks were suspended when Israel and Syria hit a key obstacle: Israel wanted security guarantees, while Syria required Israel to agree to full withdrawal from the Golan Heights before it would make any concessions.

On Israel's northern border, Syria controlled Lebanon's foreign policy and limited Lebanon's ability to make a separate peace treaty with Israel. After the assassination of former Lebanese Prime Minister Rafik Hariri in February 2005, Lebanese protesters poured into the streets, demanding the withdrawal of Syrian troops that had been present in Lebanon since 1976.[48] By April 2005, Syria had withdrawn its troops, and it appeared that Lebanon was on the road to building a new, more independent parliamentary democracy. Yet Hezbollah's continued control of Lebanon's southern border, as well as the July 2006 kidnapping of two Israeli soldiers, prompted a destructive war fought on Lebanese soil. Israeli air strikes caused tremendous destruction in Lebanon (an estimated $4 billion of damage); more than 750,000 refugees were created by the conflict. As a result, peace between Israel and Lebanon has appeared as only a distant possibility. In 2008, in a bid to become a power broker in the region, Turkey initiated peace talks between Syria and Israel concerning the future of the Golan Heights. However, talks were suspended when Israel conducted military operations in Gaza at the end of 2008. With the outbreak of the Arab Spring in 2010 and the subsequent chaotic civil war in Syria, any movement on the Arab-Israeli peace process in the foreseeable future seems improbable.

The Israeli-Palestinian Peace Process. Israel's 1992 national election returned the left-of-center Labor Party to power after fifteen years in opposition. The new prime minister, Yitzhak Rabin, a hero of the June 1967 war, with impeccable credentials as a tough-minded security hawk, represented the mainstream of an Israeli electorate who wanted peace but did not want to compromise security or capitulate to Arab terror. The lack of progress of other efforts eventually convinced a number of leading political figures in Israel that the path to peace lay in direct negotiations with the PLO, which had been designated by the Arab League in 1974 to be the "sole, legitimate representative of the Palestinian people." With Labor's victory, the Israeli parliament was persuaded to lift the ban on private contacts with the PLO.[49] Direct negotiations between the PLO and Israel began in earnest in a secluded farmhouse outside the Norwegian city of Oslo in January 1993.

The Oslo negotiations resulted in the *Declaration of Principles*, also known as the Oslo Accords, signed by Rabin and Arafat in an extraordinary ceremony on the White House lawn in September 1993. The agreement was a framework for negotiation intended to build trust between the two parties through incremental steps, the most prominent of which would be an Israeli withdrawal from significant portions of the West Bank and Gaza Strip. These redeployments did not include relinquishing control of external security or the security of the 140 Jewish settlements in the occupied territories. The Oslo Accords were followed by the Cairo Agreement in May 1994, which committed Israel to withdraw from the Gaza Strip and the West Bank town of Jericho, paving the way for Arafat's first return to Palestine since the late 1960s. Further negotiations yielded a third agreement in September 1995, dubbed *Oslo B*. Cumulatively, these agreements promised the Palestinians limited autonomy, with authority over 90 percent of the Palestinian population in the West Bank and Gaza Strip. But by early 1998 Israel had ceded full control of only about 3 percent of the territory and shared control over an additional 24 percent.

Despite progress, extremists on both sides continued to oppose reconciliation. Terrorism and retaliation continued. Israeli extremists made their opposition known through the assassination of Rabin in November 1995. In the May 1996 elections, the Israeli public returned the Likud party to power under the leadership of hard-liner Binyamin Netanyahu, who ran on a platform of "peace with security" and demanded that the Palestinian Authority root out and destroy Palestinian extremist organizations. In Netanyahu's first year in power, the peace process ground to a halt. The Palestinians lacked faith in an Israeli political party that adamantly opposed the Oslo Accords and that advocated the continuation of Jewish settlement in disputed areas, including East Jerusalem, which the Palestinians considered their future capital.

By 2000, two years after the Palestinians were supposed to have reached final status agreements with Israel, they still lacked an independent state. The slow pace of the peace process, along with the Palestinians' deteriorating economic and political situation, set the stage for another rebellion. In this charged environment, the head of the Likud Party, Ariel Sharon, entered the mosque enclave above the Temple Mount on September 28, 2000, despite warnings that his visit would exacerbate tensions.[50] Sharon's symbolic assertion of Israeli sovereignty over one of the most holy places in Islam (as well as Judaism) at a sensitive stage in negotiations triggered a new escalation of violence. The Palestinians embraced more violent means than in the first intifada, including the use of firearms. It was clear that the Oslo Accords were dead.

To quell the heightened violence in the Middle East, the United States, Russia, the European Union (EU), and the United Nations—known as the Middle East Quartet—drafted a road map for peace in December 2002. Although deferring complex issues, such as the return of refugees or the status of Jerusalem, the proposal called for a Palestinian state by 2005.[51] The road map led to a ceasefire in June 2003. However, on August 14, 2003, Israel assassinated a Palestinian militant, a member of a group called Islamic Jihad. Israel claimed he was responsible for planning suicide attacks and was in the midst of planning a new assault.[52] In response, the Islamic resistance movement Hamas carried out an attack that killed twenty Israelis. The ceasefire was over, and the peace process was again in tatters. Two years later, however, Israel began to withdraw from Gaza and parts of the West Bank, reflecting Prime Minister Sharon's new acceptance of a two-state solution to the continuing crisis.

The death of Palestinian leader and national symbol Arafat in November 2004, coupled with the waning of the Al Aqsa Intifada that had begun in September 2000, ushered in a period with the potential for peace and the consolidation of a democratic Palestine. The Palestinian Authority (PA) sought to stem the appeal of more violent organizations such as Hamas, the Islamic Jihad, and a secular group known as the Al Aqsa Martyrs Brigade. However, the PA did not reform sufficiently before the January 2006 elections, leading to Hamas's victory at the polls. Israel, the United States, and the European Union have refused to negotiate with Hamas until the organization recognizes Israel's right to exist, honors all previous agreements between the PA and Israel, and renounces terrorism. Hamas has adamantly refused to do so.

Fresh American efforts to reinvigorate the road map were launched near the end of the second term of the George W. Bush administration. These led to a major conference in Annapolis, Maryland, in 2007, attended by Israelis, Palestinians, and the Middle East Quartet, as well as by a number of Arab states. The talks ended in January 2009 after the Israeli military launched a ground assault in Gaza in response to rocket attacks into Israeli territory. After an uneasy truce between Israel and Hamas took hold, Obama sent Middle East Envoy George Mitchell to infuse new life into the talks. Although there was only indirect contact between Israelis and Palestinians at this point, Obama convinced Netanyahu to accept a ten-month partial freeze in settlements to begin in November 2009 as a confidence-building measure and to allow direct negotiations to occur.

In September 2010, Secretary of State Hillary Clinton arranged for direct negotiations between Israelis and Palestinians toward achieving a final status agreement within one year. However, when the Israelis did not renew the settlement freeze at the end of September, talks were suspended. Mitchell continued to work towards a peace deal until 2011. Palestinian President Mahmud Abbas, frustrated by what he perceived as unconditional US support of Israel, declared his intention to seek full membership in the United Nations, hoping that this move would put international pressure on both Israel and the United States to create a Palestinian state.[53] The United States, however, made it clear that it would veto any Security Council measure regarding Palestinian membership in the United Nations.

Throughout 2013, Secretary of State John Kerry worked with Israelis and Palestinians to restart direct negotiations, and in July 2013, the two sides met after a hiatus of almost three years. The peace talks collapsed in April 2014, however, after Israel failed to release a fourth group of Palestinian prisoners called for in a prior agreement, because the Palestinians would not commit to peace talks after an April 29 deadline to create a framework for negotiations. Complicating matters further, after seven years of division, in June 2014 Abbas's political party, Fatah, signed a unity agreement with Hamas that called for elections for a unified Palestinian government (although those elections had not yet occurred by early 2018). Hamas has neither recognized Israel, nor renounced violence, nor agreed to the Oslo Accords, so Israel refuses to continue negotiations unless Abbas disavows the unity agreement with Hamas. It is also unclear whether a unified government that included Hamas would agree to negotiate with Israel. The scarcity of progress toward peace indicates that the conflict is likely to endure.

The Role of Iran. Arabs and Persians have coexisted uneasily within the framework of Islam since the Arab conquest of Persia in the seventh century. Subsequent Persian empires dominated Arab lands on both sides of the Persian Gulf. When they weakened, local Arabs quickly threw off Iranian control. Arab-Iranian tension in recent decades stems partly from Arab fears that an increasingly strong Iran will seek to reassert its past regional hegemony.

After World War II, US military assistance to thwart Soviet influence in Iran enabled its shah, Mohammad Reza Shah Pahlavi, to expand and strengthen Iran's armed forces considerably. In the late 1960s, the shah began to purchase large quantities of arms designed to provide Iranian forces with significant offensive capability. To the Arabs, and most significantly to Iraq, it seemed that these forces were oriented directly at them. From the Iranian point of view, such a military buildup was necessary to provide security for vital Persian Gulf oil fields and tanker facilities. Iranian diplomats worked to convince Arab rulers that Iran's military power posed no threat. However, the Shah used force to seize three Arab islands in the Persian Gulf in 1971, and Iran provided military support to Kurdish rebels in Iraq.[54]

The Iranian revolution of 1978–1979 upset all the old assumptions in Iran and elsewhere in the region. The shah's accelerated economic development program, carried out largely along Western lines with a heavy infusion of Western technicians and values, was profoundly destabilizing. However, the precipitating cause of the shah's downfall was his attempt to crush religious opposition to his rule. Although Iran's rulers had traditionally shared power with its religious leaders, the shah was convinced that they opposed his modernization efforts. The shah's actions provoked a genuine popular revolution under the banners of resurgent Islam, which was exacerbated by his increasingly repressive and authoritarian rule, to which a growing and politicized middle class objected.

Unwilling to share power with the middle class and alienated from traditional sources of support, the shah relied more heavily on repression to maintain control. In Tehran and other major cities, there were massive demonstrations and street riots. This instability culminated in the shah's flight from Iran in early 1979. The Ayatollah Khomeini triumphantly returned from exile in France, declaring his intention to establish a "pure Islamic state."[55] Despite this regime change, chaos ensued throughout much of 1980, due both to the disintegration of the once large and well-armed Iranian military and to the start of the Iran-Iraq War. The new government sought to antagonize and humiliate the United States: several hundred students stormed the US embassy in Tehran in November 1979 and captured more than fifty American diplomats and Marine guards, holding them hostage for 444 days. The United States was able to rally international opinion and invoke international law on its side, but the Iranians ignored the pressure. Western technicians, essential to maintaining the advanced weapons systems the shah had purchased, were pushed out of the country. The once large and well-armed Iranian military went into decline.

To exploit Iran's weakened, isolated condition and also to preempt possible Iranian incitement of Iraq's large Shiite population, Iraq launched a series of ground and air assaults against Iran in September of 1980. The resulting war lasted for eight years. Despite some initial territorial gains, Iraq was unable to prevail over Iran's weakened forces, and it was forced to withdraw in 1982. Iranian counteroffensives began immediately, and they resulted in massive casualties, particularly on the Iranian side. The credibility of US attempts to help terminate the war suffered sharply with the revelation of covert US arms sales to Iran in 1985 and 1986 (the Iran-Contra affair).[56] In 1988, after suffering hundreds of thousands of total casualties, Iran and Iraq finally agreed to halt the fighting.

After the Ayatollah Khomeini died in 1989, the climate in Iran began to change. While Khomeini's charisma as well as his increased use of repression staved off opposition, once he passed from the scene, reformist tendencies began to surface. Elected in 1989, President Ali Rafsanjani embarked on policies to improve Iran's relations with Western powers. In 1997, Iran elected reformist President Mohammed Khatami, who ran on a platform that called for liberalization of the mass media, freedom of expression, civil rights, and pluralism. Relations between Iran and the United States finally began to thaw.

Unfortunately, this trend proved short lived. Hard-liner Mahmoud Ahmadinejad prevailed in the 2004 presidential elections, due in part to the slow pace of domestic reforms, as well as the manipulation of the electoral system by hardline mullahs in the Guardian Council, who had banned reformist candidates from running. Ahmadinejad took an antagonistic approach to the West, called for Israel to be "wiped off the map," and accelerated aspects of Iran's nuclear program. In December 2006, the United Nations agreed to sanctions against Iran for its pursuit of uranium enrichment. The sanctions were strengthened in March 2007 by UN Resolution 1747, which banned Iranian arms exports and levied financial and travel restrictions on Iranians involved in suspected proliferation-related activities. Yet the effect of these sanctions was weakened by the lack of uniform support. For example, China signed an energy contract with Iran in 2005 that made it reluctant to implement effective sanctions. Support for sanctions was further eroded by the late 2007 release of American intelligence that found that Iran had stopped its program to weaponize uranium in 2003.

In 2009, the United States was hopeful that relations between the two countries would improve, and Obama reached out to the Iranian regime to engage in direct talks. However, that same year, it was revealed that Iran had built a secret uranium enrichment facility, although US intelligence organizations did not believe Iran was building a nuclear weapon.[57] Iran held presidential elections in June 2009 after an unprecedented campaign in which candidates had televised debates and an opposition candidate, Mir Hossain Mousavi of the Green Movement, campaigned with his wife. Mousavi contested the election results after Mahmoud Ahmedinajad was declared the winner, and the Green Movement brought protesters into the streets. They were met by a repressive governmental crackdown. After hundreds of arrests and trials, stability in Iran was restored, and the Green Movement has remained, for the most part, underground.

Iran continued to expand its uranium enrichment program, which the international community feared could readily be adapted to produce weapons grade material. The United States and Iran held secret negotiations to solve the nuclear dilemma. The June 2013 election of a more moderate Iranian president, Hassan Rouhani, facilitated the signing of the November 2013 Joint Plan of Action agreed upon by the P5+1 (the United States, United Kingdom, France, China, Russia, and Germany), the European Union, and Iran in Geneva. Despite the obstacles to completing a deal, an international agreement to curb Iran's nuclear program was signed in July 2015 and formally adopted by the parties in October. Israel and Saudi Arabia have vigorously opposed the agreement because they mistrust the Iranians and preferred any final status agreement to leave Iran without any nuclear program. In May 2018, President Trump announced that the United States would withdraw from the agreement. The future of the agreement and the Iranian nuclear program remains unclear.

Developments in Turkey. Turkey occupies a key position in the Middle East, geographically and functionally. It is a land bridge between Europe and Asia, and during the Cold War it was also a barrier between the Soviet Union and the Mediterranean. Since 1951, Turkey has been an important member of the North Atlantic Treaty Organization (NATO), serving as a security bulwark on the alliance's southeastern flank. Although Turkey's strategic significance to the United States temporarily waned after the demise of the Soviet Union, it was restored following the catastrophic attacks of September 11, 2001.

In 2003, Turkey's refusal to allow US forces to transit the country to invade Iraq from the north soured relations. Tensions persist between the two countries as the growing independence of the Iraqi Kurds increases Turkey's anxiety about the aspirations of its own Kurdish population. Nevertheless, Turkey remains an important US strategic partner. The continued value that the United States places on this relationship is reflected in US efforts to pressure Europe into accepting Turkey as a member of the European Union: from the US perspective, admission of a Muslim country into the European Union would have profound and positive effects on US security and other regional interests.[58]

Since the Arab Spring, relations between the United States and Turkey have oscillated. During 2010–2013, Obama established a strong relationship with Prime Minister Recep Tayyip Erdogan and spoke with him frequently regarding policy options during this turbulent period. However, competing priorities in the conflict in Syria increased tensions between the two allies. Moreover, to deflect attention from a corruption scandal within Turkey, Erdogan blamed the United States for fostering the scandal, thereby further straining the relationship.[59] Tensions escalated in the summer of 2016 when a failed military coup in Turkey left many Erdogan supporters suspicious of US involvement.[60]

US-Turkish relations did not improve when President Trump took office. In April 2017, Erdogan won a narrow victory in a referendum providing him with sweeping authority as the country's president. Additionally, the government's repression and arrests of journalists and opposition politicians signaled a dramatic move away from democratic values. Another blow to relations occurred in early 2018 when Turkish troops attacked US-backed Kurds in Syria. Despite these difficulties, the United States recognizes Turkey's important role in the region and will likely continue to search for ways to pursue mutual interests.

Looking Ahead

Despite its attempt to decrease its footprint in the Middle East, the United States retains important national security interests that necessitate its continued engagement in regional affairs. Undoubtedly, the Middle East will be turbulent for years to come. The lack of progress on the Palestinian-Israeli front, the continuing threat from militant groups, and political instability in the wake of the Arab Spring are grounds for pessimism. It remains to be seen whether the nuclear agreement between the international community and Iran can be salvaged, and if so, whether this agreement will relieve an important source of friction in the region.

Middle Eastern leaders recognize American economic and political power and in many cases they aim to retain close relationships with the United States. Virtually every significant political group in the Middle East has found some area—economic, political, scientific, or military—from which it can derive benefits by maintaining good relations with the United States. The resulting US ability to exert influence on both sides of regional disputes is a major diplomatic and security asset. Nevertheless, the legitimacy of US involvement in the region is seen with increasing skepticism by much of the population, and this skepticism will be difficult for the United States to overcome.

The high stakes and persistent instability in the Middle East make it a critical and difficult region for US national security policy. However, the United States still possesses formidable assets with which it can promote peace and further its interests in this region.

Discussion Questions

1. How have US economic interests in the Middle East changed during the past forty years?
2. How has the recent growth of US oil production affected relationships between the United States and oil-producing countries in the Middle East?
3. What advantages and disadvantages does Iran possess in its relationships with other states in the Middle East? Could it become a regional superpower in the twenty-first century? What would the implications be for US national security interests in the region?
4. What major interests does Russia have in the region? What other non–Middle Eastern states have interests in the region? How might they attempt to exert their influence?
5. How important is it for the United States to be closely involved in searching for a settlement to the Israeli-Palestinian conflict? Can the United States be an honest broker in the dispute?
6. Why might domestic political considerations and interest groups such as AIPAC have more influence on US foreign policy in this region than in others?
7. What impacts did the September 11, 2001, terrorist attacks have on US interests in the region?
8. How has the US involvement in Iraq since 2003 impacted regional stability?
9. How has the Arab Spring affected US interests and relationships in the region? How has it affected the political stability of traditional US allies such as Egypt?
10. What are the likely long-term consequences of the civil war in Syria? What US national interests are at stake?

Recommended Reading

Ajami, Fouad. *The Arab Predicament: Arab Political Thought and Practice since 1967.* New York: Cambridge University Press, 1992.

Andersen, Roy R., Robert F. Seibert, and Jon G. Wagner. *Politics and Change in the Middle East.* 8th ed. Upper Saddle River, NJ: Pearson Prentice-Hall, 2006.
Diamond, Larry. "Lessons from Iraq." *Journal of Democracy* 16, no. 1 (2005): 9–23.
Hourani, Albert. *A History of the Arab Peoples.* Cambridge, MA: Harvard University Press, 1991.
Hunter, Shireen T. *Iran and the World: Continuity in a Revolutionary Decade.* Bloomington: Indiana University Press, 1990.
Lust, Ellen, ed. *The Middle East.* 13th ed. Los Angeles: Sage/CQ Press, 2013.
Lynch, Mark. *The Arab Uprising: The Unfinished Revolution in the Middle East.* New York: PublicAffairs, 2012.
Milani, Mohsen M. *The Making of Iran's Islamic Revolution: From Monarchy to Islamic Republic.* 2nd ed. Boulder, CO: Westview Press, 1994.
Piscatori, James, and Dale Eikelman. *Muslim Politics.* Princeton, NJ: Princeton University Press, 1996.
Quandt, William B. *Decade of Decisions: American Policy toward the Arab-Israeli Conflict, 1967–1976.* Berkeley: University of California Press, 1977.
Robinson, Glenn E. *Building a Palestinian State: The Incomplete Revolution.* Bloomington: Indiana University Press, 1997.
Tessler, Mark. *A History of the Israeli-Palestinian Conflict.* Bloomington: Indiana University Press, 2009.

Recommended Internet Sources

Bureau of Near Eastern Affairs, US Department of State, www.state.gov/p/nea
Cooperation Council for the Arab States of the Gulf, www.gcc-sg.org/eng
Energy Information Administration, Department of Energy, www.eia.doe.gov
International Atomic Energy Agency, www.iaea.org
League of Arab States, www.lasportal.org/Pages/Welcome.aspx
United States Central Command, www.centcom.mil

Notes

1. The term "Middle East" in this chapter includes Egypt, Israel, Jordan, Lebanon, Syria, Turkey, Iraq, Saudi Arabia, Kuwait, Bahrain, Qatar, the United Arab Emirates, Iran, Oman, and Yemen.

2. The first uprising or intifada erupted in 1987; it ended after the Persian Gulf War in 1991.

3. General David H. Petraeus, Commander, Multi-National Force–Iraq, *Report to Congress on the Situation in Iraq*, September 10–11, 2007, http://iipdigital.usembassy.gov/st/english/texttrans/2007/09/20070911183028eaifas0.4634363.html#axzz3xGumbKrn.

4. United Nations High Commissioner for Refugees, "Syria Emergency," December 7, 2017, http://www.unhcr.org/en-us/syria-emergency.html.

5. The White House, *The National Security Strategy of the United States* (Washington, DC: The White House, December 2017).

6. Robert S. Strauss Center for International Security and Law at the University of Texas at Austin, "Oil in the Persian Gulf," August 2008, https://www.strausscenter.org/hormuz/oil-in-the-persian-gulf.html; Bloomberg News, "U.S. Seen as Biggest Oil Producer after Overtaking Saudi," July 4, 2014, http://www.bloomberg.com/news/articles/2014-07-04/u-s

-seen-as-biggest-oil-producer-after-overtaking-saudi; Organization of Petroleum Exporting Countries, "OPEC Share of World Crude Oil Reserves, 2014," July 2015, http://www.opec.org/opec_web/en/data_graphs/330.htm.

7. US Energy Information Administration, "Frequently Asked Questions: How Much Oil Consumed by the United States Comes from Foreign Countries?" Preliminary net petroleum import estimate as of April 4, 2017, http://www.eia.gov/tools/faqs/faq.cfm?id=32&t=6.

8. US Energy Information Administration, "China Is Now the World's Largest Net Importer of Petroleum and Other Liquid Fuels," March 24, 2014, https://www.eia.gov/todayinenergy/detail.cfm?id=15531.

9. Keith Johnson, "China Tops U.S. as Biggest Oil Importer," *Foreign Policy*, May 11, 2015, http://foreignpolicy.com/2015/05/11/china-tops-u-s-as-biggest-oil-importer-middle-east-opec-sloc/.

10. H. W. Brands, *Into the Labyrinth: The United States and the Middle East, 1945–1993* (New York: McGraw-Hill, 1994), 19.

11. Jeremy M. Sharp, *U.S. Foreign Aid to Israel* (Washington, DC: Congressional Research Service, April 11, 2014), i.

12. International Atomic Energy Association (IAEA), "Implementation of the NPT Safeguards Agreement and Relevant Provisions of Security Council Resolutions in the Islamic Republic of Iran," February 20, 2014, https://www.iaea.org/sites/default/files/gov2014-10.pdf.

13. The Koran, formally compiled under Islam's third caliph, Uthman (644–656 CE), is said to be an exact translation of God's revelations to Mohammed without error or omission. Islamic law (*sharia*) consists primarily of dictates in the Koran, *hadith* (sayings of Mohammed), and the *sunnah* (examples or ways of Mohammed).

14. The seventh through the thirteenth centuries represented a "Golden Age" of Islam. The same period in Europe is known as the Dark Ages and early Middle Ages.

15. See Bernard Lewis, *What Went Wrong? The Clash Between Islam and Modernity in the Middle East* (New York: Harper Perennial, 2002).

16. Prominent advocates of the strict-adherence approach in political Islam include Muhammad ibn Abd-al-Wahhab, Hassan Al Banna, Sayyid Abul Ala Mawdudi, and Sayyid Qutb.

17. See Muhammad Bin Ahmad al-Salim, *39 Ways to Serve the Jihad and Take Part in It*, At-Tibyan Publications, 2003, https://www.cia.gov/library/abbottabad-compound/2D/2D06F676D114500575E4A970D5915C33_39_WAYS_(LAST_PART).pdf.

18. Charles Kurzman, ed., *Liberal Islam: A Sourcebook* (Oxford: Oxford University Press, 1998).

19. Geoffrey Aronson, "Policy Options in a Time of Transition: The US and the Israel-Palestine Conflict," *Middle East Journal* 67, no. 2 (2013): 250.

20. The White House Office of the Press Secretary, "FACT SHEET: The White House Summit on Countering Violent Extremism," February 18, 2015, https://www.whitehouse.gov/the-press-office/2015/02/18/fact-sheet-white-house-summit-countering-violent-extremism.

21. The White House, *The National Security Strategy of the United States* (Washington, DC: The White House, December 2017), 11.

22. F. Gregory Gause III, "Can Democracy Stop Terror?" *Foreign Affairs* 84, no. 5 (2003): 72.

23. Liz Sly, "Backing Egypt's Generals, Saudi Arabia Promises to Fill Financial Void," *Washington Post*, August 19, 2013, https://www.washingtonpost.com/world/middle_east

/backing-egypts-generals-saudi-arabia-promises-to-fill-financial-void/2013/08/19/9d91384a-0901-11e3-9941-6711ed662e71_story.html.

24. European Brent Spot Pricing FOB, US Energy Information Administration, release date March 23, 2018, https://www.eia.gov/dnav/pet/hist/LeafHandler.ashx?n=PET&s=RBRTE&f=A.

25. Clifford Krauss, "'Saudi America': Mirage? Challenges Lie Ahead for North American Oil Production," *New York Times*, April 21, 2014, F4.

26. Dana Allin and Steven Simon, "The Moral Psychology of U.S. Support for Israel," *Survival* 45, no. 3 (2003): 126.

27. Barack Obama, "Remarks by the President on a New Beginning," Cairo, Egypt, June 4, 2009, http://www.whitehouse.gov/the_press_office/Remarks-by-the-President-at-Cairo-University-6-04-09/.

28. The White House, *The National Security Strategy of the United States* (Washington, DC: The White House, December 2017), 49.

29. Mark Landler, "U.S. Presses to Relocate Embassy to Jerusalem by 2019," *New York Times*, January 18, 2018, https://www.nytimes.com/2018/01/18/us/politics/trump-israel-embassy-jerusalem.html.

30. Michael Sterner, "Closing the Gate: The Persian Gulf War Revisited," *Current History* 96 (January 1997): 15.

31. Larry Diamond, "Lessons from Iraq," *Journal of Democracy* 16, no. 1 (2005): 10.

32. Trudy Rubin, "Bush Never Made Serious Postwar Plans," *Knight Ridder*, June 23, 2003, http://articles.philly.com/2003-06-26/news/25448395_1_jay-garner-postwar-plans-iraq-war.

33. Brian MacQuarrie and Bryan Bender, "Disputed Study Says 600,000 Iraqis Killed during War," *Boston Globe*, October 12, 2006, A16.

34. Eric Davis, "Iraq," in *The Middle East*, 13th ed., ed. Ellen Lust (Los Angeles: Sage/CQ Press, 2013), 527.

35. For complete coverage of this topic, see Malcolm Kerr, *The Arab Cold War*, 3rd ed. (London: Oxford University Press, 1971).

36. Steve Kenny, " Egypt: US to Deliver Helicopters, *New York Times*, April 23, 2014.

37. Alan J. Kuperman, "Obama's Libya Debacle: How a Well-Meaning Intervention Ended in Failure," *Foreign Affairs* 94, no. 2 (2015): 66–77.

38. Thomas Friedman, "Obama on the World," *New York Times*, August 8, 2014, https://www.nytimes.com/2014/08/09/opinion/president-obama-thomas-l-friedman-iraq-and-world-affairs.html.

39. Kuperman, "Obama's Libya Debacle."

40. Anne Barnard, "Death Toll from War in Syria Now 470,000, Group Finds, "*New York Times*, February 11, 2016, https://www.nytimes.com/2016/02/12/world/middleeast/death-toll-from-war-in-syria-now 470000-group-finds.html.

41. Kenneth Katzman et al., "Iraq Crisis and U.S. Policy," Congressional Research Service, June 20, 2014.

42. Remarks by the President to the White House Press Corps, August 20, 2012, https://www.whitehouse.gov/the-press-office/2012/08/20/remarks-president-white-house-press-corps.

43. Michael R. Gordon, "U.S. and Russia Reach Deal to Destroy Syria's Chemical Arms," *New York Times*, September 14, 2013, https://www.nytimes.com/2013/09/15/world/middleeast/syria-talks.html.

44. Angela Stent, "Putin's Power Play in Syria: How to Respond to Russia's Intervention," *Foreign Affairs* 95, no. 1 (2016): 106.

45. World Bank Group, *The Toll of War: The Economic and Social Consequences of the Conflict in Syria*, 2017, vi–vii, http://www.worldbank.org/en/country/syria/publication/the-toll-of-war-the-economic-and-social-consequences-of-the-conflict-in-syria.

46. See Ruth Margolies Beitler, *The Path to Mass Rebellion: An Analysis of Two Intifadas* (Lanham, MD: Lexington Books, 2004).

47. See Steven A. Cook, *Jordan-Israel Peace, Year One: Laying the Foundation* (Washington, DC: The Washington Institute for Near East Policy, 1995).

48. Syria is suspected of having carried out the assassination of Prime Minister Hariri, who had called for the removal of Syrian troops and influence from Lebanon.

49. David Makovsky, *Making Peace with the PLO: The Rabin Government's Road to the Oslo Accord* (Boulder, CO: Westview Press, 1996), 14.

50. The Temple Mount, sacred to both Muslims and Jews, is the site of the Dome of the Rock and Al-Aqsa mosque as well as the Second Jewish Temple. A day before Sharon's visit to the Temple Mount, Adnan Husseini, chairman of the Islamic Trust, met with Jerusalem Police Chief Yair Yitzhaki to try to convince him to have the visit canceled. See Lee Hockstader, "Street Army Spearheads Arab Riots," *Washington Post*, October 4, 2000, A1.

51. Neil King Jr. and Jeanne Cummings, "Road Map Seeks Palestinian State within a Year," *Wall Street Journal*, February 28, 2003, A7. For a full discussion of the roadmap, see US Department of State, "A Performance-Based Roadmap to a Permanent Two-State Solution to the Israeli-Palestinian Conflict," April 30, 2003, http://2001-2009.state.gov/r/pa/prs/ps/2003/20062.htm.

52. Guy Chazan, "Militant Is Killed, Further Clouding Truce in Mideast," *Wall Street Journal*, August 15, 2003, A6.

53. Mark Tessler, "The Israeli-Palestinian Conflict," in *The Middle East*, 13th ed., ed. Ellen Lust (Los Angeles: Sage/CQ Press, 2013), 365.

54. Shahram Chubin and Sepehr Zabih, *The Foreign Relations of Iran* (Berkeley: University of California Press, 1974), 178–81.

55. Amos A. Jordan, "Saudi Pillar on Firmer Soil," *Washington Star*, February 18, 1979, D1.

56. Paul Pillar, "The Role of Villain: Iran and U.S. Foreign Policy," *Political Science Quarterly* 128, no. 2 (2013): 221.

57. Ken Dilanian, "U.S. Does Not Believe Iran Is Trying to Build a Weapon," *Los Angeles Times*, February 23, 2012, http://articles.latimes.com/2012/feb/23/world/la-fg-iran-intel-20120224.

58. Steve Wood and Wolfgang Quaisser, "Turkey's Road to the EU: Political Dynamics, Strategic Context and Implications for Europe," *European Foreign Affairs Review* 10, no. 2 (2005): 150.

59. Tim Arango, "Growing Mistrust between the U.S. and Turkey Is Played Out in Public," *New York Times*, December 23, 2013, A9.

60. Tim Arango and Ceylan Yeginsu, "Turks Can Agree on One Thing: U.S. Was Behind Failed Coup," *New York Times*, August 2, 2016, http://www.nytimes.com/2016/08/03/world/europe/turkey-coup-erdogan-fethullah-gulen-united-states.html?_r=0.

21

Sub-Saharan Africa

The historical place of Sub-Saharan Africa in the context of US national security interests is often described as "peripheral." Africanist Christopher Alden noted in 2000 that the US approach to Sub-Saharan Africa might even be described as one of outright neglect.[1] These assessments might have been apt at times over the past two centuries, but since the end of the Cold War in 1991, US national security interests in Sub-Saharan Africa have grown and US activities in the region have become integral to broader US strategic initiatives.

Today, the forty-eight states of Sub-Saharan Africa present extremely challenging national security issues (figure 21.1).[2] Since the first years of the twenty-first century, the subcontinent has hosted a growing number of insurgent and terrorist groups, some of them aligned with al Qaeda and the Islamic State of Iraq and the Levant (ISIL). The transnational nature of these groups, coupled with the weakness of the states in which they operate, makes their mitigation profoundly challenging. In Somalia, for example, the jihadist al Shabaab insurgency has, since 2006, contributed to the prolonged fragility of that country. In 2015, Boko Haram in Nigeria was called the world's deadliest insurgency. Across the Sahel, in a network of militant groups primarily aligned with al Qaeda, new groups form and disintegrate almost monthly; they have launched deadly attacks in Mali, Niger, and Burkina Faso. The Uganda-based Lord's Resistance Army is a theocratic antigovernment insurgency that uses child soldiers; although now weakened, it has presented a pernicious regional security issue for much of the past two decades. The threats that these groups pose to civilians, states, and regional stability have led the United

The authors would like to thank Professor Jason Warner for his significant contributions to this chapter.

FIGURE 21.1 Sub-Saharan Africa

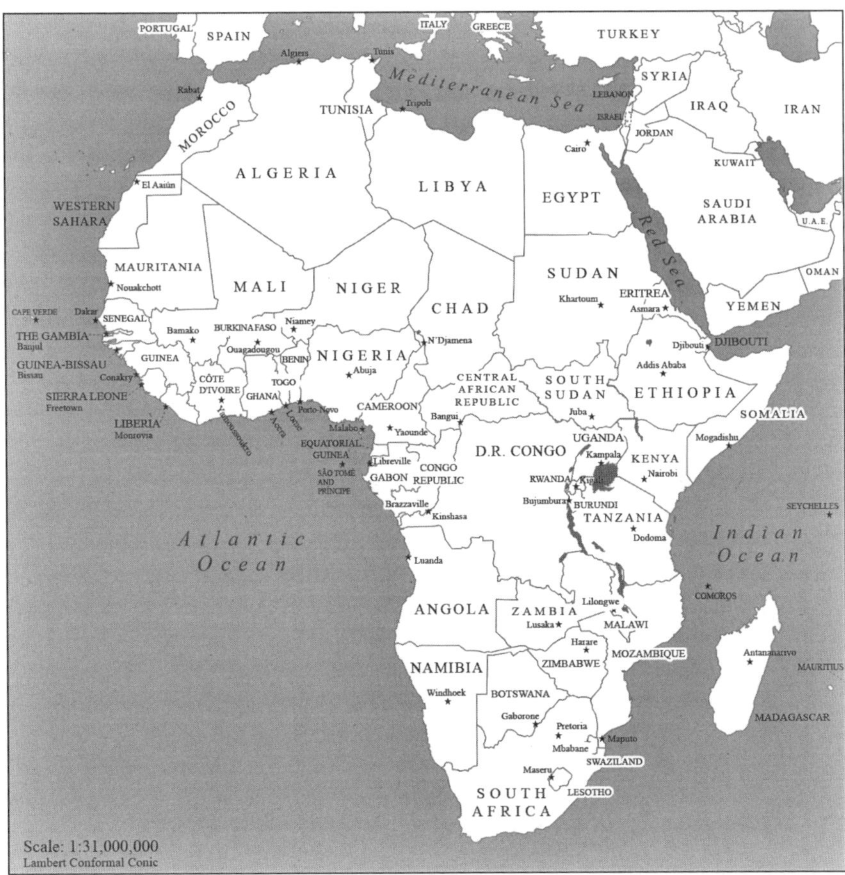

States to develop, quietly, a substantial if patchy presence throughout Sub-Saharan Africa, offering training and equipment, advisory, and even operational assistance in Nigeria, Somalia, Uganda, Niger, Chad, Kenya, and Djibouti, among others. The US military presence has become the open secret of the contemporary Sub-Saharan African security landscape.

In addition to kinetic missions that target mostly transnational terrorism and insurgency, US interests are also affected by other nonmilitary threats on the continent. These include combating poverty by encouraging economic development, mitigating authoritarian rule through democracy promotion, and reversing threats to human security (in areas such as gender, health, education, human rights, and the environment; see table 21.1). These efforts affect security in more traditional domains. More broadly, the primary US national security interest in Sub-Saharan Africa has been to cement its position as the leading non-African power on the African continent. It has attempted to accomplish this by means of ideological and

Table 21.1 Sub-Saharan Africa Key Statistics

Country	*Total population (millions)*	*Life expectancy at birth*	*GDP US$ (billions)*	*GDP/ capita US$*	*Population living in poverty (%)*	*Military expenditure (% of GDP)*	*Military spending US$ (millions)*	*Human Development Index (HDI) ranking (of 188)*
Angola	20.2	56.0	91.9	6,800	40.5	3.0	2,778	150
Chad	11.9	50.2	10.4	2,600	46.7	2.6	269	186
Congo, Democratic Republic of	81.3	57.3	39.8	800	63.0	2.2	875	176
Congo, Republic of	4.9	59.3	8.8	6,800	46.5	6.4	565	135
Djibouti	0.8	63.2	1.9	3,400	23.0	na	na	172
Eritrea	5.9	64.9	5.4	1,300	50.0	na	na	179
Ethiopia	102.4	62.2	69.2	1,900	29.6	0.7	451	174
Ghana	26.9	66.6	42.8	4,400	24.2	0.5	195	139
Kenya	46.8	64.0	69.2	3,400	43.4	1.8	1,219	146
Liberia	4.3	59.0	2.1	900	54.1	0.7	13	177
Nigeria	186.1	53.4	415.1	5,900	70.0	0.4	1,734	152
Rwanda	13.0	60.1	8.3	1,900	39.1	1.1	88	159
Senegal	14.3	61.7	14.9	2,600	46.7	1.7	256	162
Sierra Leone	6.0	58.2	4.3	1,700	70.2	0.3	14	179
Somalia	10.8	52.4	5.9	400	na	na	na	na
South Africa	54.3	63.1	280.4	13,500	16.6	1.1	3,090	119
South Sudan	12.5	57.3	2.6	1,700	50.9	2.9	76	181
Sudan	36.7	64.1	94.3	4,500	46.5	na	na	165
Tanzania	52.4	62.2	46.7	3,100	22.8	1.1	520	151
Zimbabwe	14.6	58.0	14.2	1,700	72.3	2.5	358	154

na = not applicable.

Sources: Data on population and economy is from the CIA World Factbook 2017, https://www.cia.gov/library/publications/the-world-factbook. Military expenditure data is from International Institute for Strategic Studies (IISS), *The Military Balance 2017* (London: IISS, 2017). HDI rankings are from *Human Development Report 2016*, http://hdr.undp.org/en/data. Most figures are from 2016 (otherwise latest available data is listed). GDP is reported at the official exchange rate. GDP per capita is using Purchasing Power Parity rates.

normative soft power, on one hand, and military capacity and realpolitik gamesmanship, on the other. Although the United States faces no existential threat from any possible coalition of states in Sub-Saharan Africa, the prevalence and freedom of action of nonstate actors on the subcontinent have given Sub-Saharan Africa a growing role in US national security policy. The asymmetric nature of the security challenges presented by actors on the subcontinent means that Sub-Saharan Africa is no longer "peripheral" to US national security interests, if it ever was.

History of US Involvement in Sub-Saharan Africa

The United States has a long history with Africa. In the eighteenth and nineteenth centuries, US national security, especially in the economic sense, was grounded in the trans-Atlantic slave trade. This process, in which kidnapped humans were sold into slavery and forced to work mainly on plantations in the southern United States, was integral to the preindustrial economic development of the early American republic. The economies of Virginia, North Carolina, South Carolina, Georgia, and other agrarian states relied on the labor of a perpetual flow of enslaved persons from major West African ports, including Dakar in Senegal, Freetown in Sierra Leone, and Cape Coast in Ghana.

Beginning in 1820, groups of freed slaves from the United States returned to Africa, where they contributed to the intellectual development of nineteenth-century Black Nationalist impulses.[3] People returning from the United States eventually founded the country of Liberia, the first globally recognized independent state in Sub-Saharan Africa. The returning freed slaves from the United States intermingled with and subsequently overtook the existing Liberian population. Although this engendered a new form of colonialism, it also created the first cultural and geopolitical US foothold on the continent.

The European Colonial Period and Decolonization. In the years directly following the US Civil War (1861–1865), which was in no small part waged over the fate of enslaved people of primarily Sub-Saharan African descent, the subcontinent remained peripheral to US national security interests, and broad indifference marked US attitudes toward Sub-Saharan Africa. For Europe, however, the subcontinent became the new battleground for European states competing for power and territory during the latter half of the nineteenth century. At the Berlin Conference (1884–1885), European powers officially allocated the lands of Sub-Saharan Africa to various European states in an attempt to prevent war between European powers over their various African claims. While the United States remained generally indifferent to the Berlin Conference, a century later, it began to grapple with the consequences of the colonially imposed divisions created by it.

The European colonies in Sub-Saharan Africa began to crumble at the end of World War II in 1945. A confluence of factors led to the decolonization process in Sub-Saharan Africa and throughout the world. Erstwhile European colonial powers, especially France and Britain, were greatly weakened after World War II and became unable to maintain the bureaucratic infrastructure required for the management of their overseas colonies, none of which had been as economically productive as their colonies in the Caribbean. Simultaneously, the stage was set for African independence by new global normative commitments to independence, sovereignty, and a right to self-determination, embedded in the Charter of the nascent United Nations. Such new global thinking around normative equity allowed African independence to occur through bureaucratic and thus bloodless means in many cases, such as in the wave of independence for fourteen Francophone African countries between April and December of 1960. Independence movements elsewhere, however, involved violence, including the National Liberation Front insurgency in Algeria and the so-called Mau-Mau rebellion in Kenya.[4]

The United States was eager for Sub-Saharan Africa's decolonization, both for ideological reasons and reasons of power and prestige. The US understanding of the need for African decolonization was predicated on the call for the dismantling of European empires in the 1941 Atlantic Charter that outlined goals for the post–World War II world order. Moreover, as the United States was assisting European reconstruction through the Marshall Plan, US leaders sought a global order in which the United States would not be overshadowed by a Europe that retained its colonies around the world. The United States quickly found itself at the forefront of the Allied Western world order, a role that would define its approach to the African continent for much of the Cold War. As the colonial powers left Africa, the United States and the Soviet Union vied for influence and resources in a series of proxy conflicts across the continent.

The Cold War. During the Cold War, Sub-Saharan Africa began to assume a greater role in US national security policy, primarily as an arena where geopolitical antipathies towards the Soviet Union could play out. US interests in African states remained low in the immediate post-independence period of the 1960s, but the United States nevertheless cultivated a range of African client states that gave at least declaratory support for American liberal values. As a result, throughout the Cold War, the United States was engaged with a series of strange bedfellows in Sub-Saharan Africa. Its presence on the continent was a consequence of the global struggle with the Soviet Union. The United States saw little intrinsic strategic interest in maintaining a presence on the continent beyond that of serving as an ideological foil to the presence of the Soviets. Yet this role had an impact, given that winning this ideological battle was the cornerstone of US grand strategy between the 1950s and late 1980s.

Seeking to keep communism at bay in Sub-Saharan Africa, the United States sought to forge ties with willing African states. Targeted bilateral efforts included airlifting Zairian troops to take action against secessionists in 1964 and 1967; covert support for anticommunist insurgencies such as Jonas Savimbi's National Union for the Total Independence of Angola (UNITA) in the 1970s; and financial and logistical support to the Chadian army in the 1980s.[5] Other instances of direct US funding included $500 million to Samuel Doe in Liberia from 1980 to 1985,

$1 billion to Mobutu Sese Seko in Zaire between 1965 and 1997, and $1.5 billion to Jaafar Nimeiri in Sudan from 1969 to 1985.[6] While these relationships were at times beneficial for the United States, they often proved to be troublesome.

The Soviet Union was playing the same game. As the United States promoted democracy and free-market liberalism, the Soviet Union touted popular communist and neo-Marxist economic ideologies, which many Africans saw as compatible with traditional African concepts of communalism and rejection of individualism. Throughout the Cold War, the Soviet Union's communist rhetoric found adherents in Afro-Marxist regimes in Benin, Burkina Faso, Guinea, and elsewhere, perhaps most notably in the rise of Mengistu Haile Mariam and his Communist "Derg" regime in Ethiopia in 1974. With the impending independence of the Lusophone (Portuguese-speaking) countries of Angola, Mozambique, and Cape Verde in 1975, US fears of the establishment of Marxist regimes led Washington to become deeply engaged in supporting one set of insurgents in each civil war, while the Soviets supported the other. This led to a series of decades-long proxy conflicts in the region, as the United States and the Soviet Union supported or undermined many heads of state throughout Africa.

The influence of the Cold War on US national security policy in Sub-Saharan Africa was reflected in Washington's approach to the apartheid government in South Africa in the 1980s. The United States adhered to a policy of "constructive engagement," led by Under Secretary of State for Africa Chester Crocker. It declined to offer much of a critique of the race-based policy that vested power in minority white South Africans ruling over blacks. It was thought to be in the US interest to quietly help a repressive but stable and friendly regime, rather than to advocate for a new regime that might lean toward the Soviet Union. In response to US inaction, a group of primarily African American civil rights activists in the United States formed the Free South Africa movement. Protests outside of the South African embassy in Washington were a daily occurrence for more than a year beginning in November 1984, with activists demanding that the United States help end apartheid. In 1986, in response to this and other lobbying efforts including hunger strikes, sit-ins, and divestment campaigns on US college campuses, Congress placed a trade embargo on South Africa. International pressure helped lead to the end of apartheid by 1991.[7]

It may be said that the African component of the Cold War ended symbolically on December 22, 1988: officials of South Africa, Cuba, and Angola met in New York to sign agreements that initiated the departure of approximately 50,000 Cuban troops from Angola, a step that was tied to Namibia's UN-monitored transition to independence. The United States negotiated these agreements over a period of several years, with critical Soviet support in the latter stages. They embodied an implicit recognition by both Washington and Moscow that neither would gain from further military competition in Africa.

Post–Cold War to 9/11. Between the end of the Cold War and the attacks of September 11, 2001, the United States experienced a decade of unparalleled global hegemony. Taking stock of the new and expanded foreign policy exigencies facing the United States, President George H. W. Bush commissioned "the most comprehensive review" of US policy towards Africa in over a decade. In the "National Security Review 30: American Policy Toward Africa in the 1990s," which was released in June 1992, the United States began to recognize Africa as more than a Cold War arena: it posed its own unique security challenges.[8]

Despite its new role as global leader, the United States quickly found itself facing a paradox that continues to affect contemporary US security strategy in Sub-Saharan Africa. The international community expects US action and leadership to quell African conflicts, while Congress, the public, and US leaders generally do not wish to dedicate troops or money to conflicts in which they perceive no US interests. Thus the central question that has defined the post–Cold War approach to Sub-Saharan national security policy has been how to reconcile the imperatives of serving as an engaged global leader while devoting minimal resources to the endeavor.

Two events exemplify this paradox: the 1993 Battle of Mogadishu in Somalia (vividly described in the book and movie *Black Hawk Down*) and the US failure to act against the 1994 Rwandan genocide. In Somalia, after the central government collapsed in 1991, a series of clan-based clashes ensued, resulting in widespread famine and no single group being able to hold the capital of Mogadishu. In August 1992, the United States sent military transports to support multinational UN relief efforts and later launched a major coalition operation to assist and protect these relief efforts. This work to restore peace and stability was unsuccessful, in part because of disruption by warlord Mohammed Farah Aidid and his followers. In October 1993, a team of US special operations forces was deployed to Mogadishu to capture two of Aidid's advisors. The operation was supposed to last no more than an hour, but it met heavy resistance from Somali militias. Intense fighting in downtown Mogadishu lasted over two days and required a rescue operation; eighteen US soldiers were killed, and seventy-five were injured, along with hundreds of Somali casualties.[9] News and images of the debacle in Mogadishu were broadcast in the United States. President Bill Clinton was criticized for allowing "mission creep," while broad swaths of the US public reacted negatively to the loss of US life and treasure in a faraway country.[10] The mood in the United States turned inward: US citizens and their representatives in Congress no longer had an appetite for American incursions into African countries caught up in civil wars.

In the aftermath of Somalia, the United States officially began retrenchment from African security affairs. President Clinton signed Presidential Decision Directive 25 (PDD 25), which restricted US deployments abroad generally—and in Africa specifically—to instances where US interests were in jeopardy, implicitly precluding US intervention for humanitarian purposes.[11] The change of policy had haunting consequences just months later in Rwanda: PDD 25 would forestall US involvement as extremist ethnic Hutus orchestrated a genocide that would kill an estimated 800,000 Tutsis, moderate Hutus, and others in mid-1994.

"African Solutions to African Problems" and US Attempts to Foster African Collective Security. Turmoil in Somalia in 1993 and in Rwanda in 1994, as well as recognition of the limits of US capacity to moderate conflict, led policy makers to reconsider approaches to Sub-Saharan Africa.[12] They sought to reconcile the US desire to show global leadership by remaining involved in African security affairs with the desire to avoid responsibility for outcomes that could be largely beyond US control.

The resulting US approach to African security during the last years of the twentieth century came to be known as *African solutions to African problems*, or ASTAP. This diplomatic shorthand between Western states and their African counterparts indicated that the United States recognized the deeply challenging security landscape faced by African states and remained willing to support African partner states, while both sides recognized—each for its own political, economic, and strategic reasons—that African states should be at the forefront of such efforts, with Western nations in a primarily supporting role.[13] Scholars have written about the notion of ASTAP in relation to such themes as the degree of "Africanization" of ASTAP efforts;[14] innovations in the institutionalization of ASTAP in regional peacekeeping;[15] the capacity of the African Union to fulfill its ASTAP mandate;[16] and the manner in which powerful African states such as South Africa[17] and Rwanda[18] approach ASTAP in their own foreign policy.

American ASTAP policy spurred the United States to attempt to help institutionalize African schemes of collective security. France had urged the creation of a regional intervention mechanism for Africa that would be similar to the Organization for Security and Cooperation in Europe (OSCE), and, in 1996, the United States under the leadership of Secretary of State Warren Christopher, together with France and Britain, inaugurated the African Crisis Response Force (ACRF).[19] The new African force was planned to consist of five to ten thousand African troops drawn from around the continent, aided by US and European equipment, training, and logistical support. The ACRF was intended to enable US and European support for the resolution of future conflicts without the need to put US or European boots on the ground.[20]

However, the ACRF met with detractors as soon as it was announced. First, African leaders were fundamentally opposed to the "force" component of the ACRF.[21] "A spate of criticism" came from African partners who saw the ACRF as an indication that the United States would train a standing African army over which, they feared, the United States would exert too much control.[22] Second, there was concern over ambiguities in the ACRF proposal, as well as the haste with which it had been created.[23] Third, many African leaders were displeased with what they saw as its heavy-handed US presentation; for example, the United States asked Kenya's President Daniel Arap Moi to sign on to the ACRF initiative in the very same meeting at which it was presented to him.[24] Africans criticized the United States for doing little to inform or consult with leaders prior to the unveiling, and they felt that the new plan afforded them little ownership or control.[25] In short, "the ACRF proposal was not well received by most African states."[26]

The United States then returned with a new plan for African collective security, called the African Crisis Response Initiative (ACRI).[27] Unlike the ACRF—which would have included a standing force—the ACRI was presented as a capacity-building initiative to help selected bilateral African partners to train battalion-level contingents for effective peacekeeping operations. While some states were supportive of the "new" ACRI proposal, the most vocally dissident ones included the continent's major powers, South Africa and Nigeria, and pariah states such as Zimbabwe, which were "skeptical of America's motives."[28] Various critiques of ACRI emerged. First, given concerns over regime security that have historically underpinned many African grand strategies, many African leaders worried that US-trained troops might turn on them, perhaps at the request of the United States.[29] Second, the program was criticized for proposing to train only certain units, rather than augmenting the broader military apparatus. Another criticism was that the US commitment offered ACRI training only to governments with exclusive civilian control of the military and with positive human rights records, which was seen as hypocritical.[30] Fourth, after the Cold War vagaries of US policy ("to many Africans the US looks like a fair-weather friend"[31]), many African leaders had begun to think that it "would be unwise to rely upon external donors whose priorities were notoriously fickle."[32] Some African leaders disliked the timing of the announcement of the ACRI: as Alden notes, ACRI was "rushed into prominence" in a "last-minute whirlwind tour of the continent by outgoing Secretary of State Warren Christopher" in 1996.[33] Eric Berman and Katie Sams attribute this to Washington's need to "devise a quick-fix response in mid-1996 to the anticipated bloodbath in Burundi and to avoid having to commit American troops."[34]

ACRI also had its detractors at the Pan-African and subregional levels because it disregarded efforts by African institutions that were formulating their own collective security initiatives. For example, as early as 1993, the Organization of African Unity (OAU) was in the process of operationalizing its institutions for intervention, in the form of the OAU Mechanism on Conflict Prevention, Management, and Resolution (the precursor to today's African Standby Force). Representatives from the Economic Community of West African States (ECOWAS) were also dismayed at the announcement of the ACRI, given their organization's demonstrated efficacy at launching regional peacekeeping missions including ECOMOG I in Liberia (1990) and ECOMOG II in Sierra Leone (1997). Once the ACRI did eventually get off the ground, members of participating countries complained of patronizing attitudes of US officers toward African partners and of US hypocrisy in working with nondemocratic partners.[35] Before the ACRI was terminated, about nine thousand troops from eight countries were trained, and some of these forces participated in UN peacekeeping operations in the region.

Africa in the Post-9/11 Period

The George W. Bush Administration. The George W. Bush administration continued to view Africa through the lens of its larger geopolitical goals, which came to be called the *Global War on Terror.* As its 2002 *National Security Strategy of the United States* noted: "In Africa, promise and opportunity sit side by side with disease, war, and desperate poverty. This threatens both a core value of the United States—preserving human dignity—and our strategic priority—combating global terror. . . . Together with our European allies, we must help strengthen Africa's fragile states, help build indigenous capability to secure porous borders, and help build up the law enforcement and intelligence infrastructure to deny havens for terrorists."[36]

In this period, the United States began attempts to enhance the counterterrorism capabilities of African militaries through two notable programs: the Trans-Saharan Counterterrorism Partnership (TSCTP), created in 2005, and the Partnership for East African Counterterrorism (PREACT), created in 2009. The TSCTP was designed to help integrate military and law enforcement agencies of partner states in Northern and Western Africa to carry out counterterrorism activities more effectively, and to reduce the threat of violent extremism by improving human security for those populations in vulnerable or neglected regions who were thought to be at risk of adopting extremist attitudes. Partner states for the TSCTP are Algeria, Burkina Faso, Cameroon, Chad, Mali, Mauritania, Morocco, Niger, Nigeria, Senegal, and Tunisia. PREACT was largely designed to accomplish similar goals, focusing on countries in East Africa and the Horn. Active members of PREACT are Djibouti, Ethiopia, Kenya, Somalia, Tanzania, and Uganda; other members include Burundi, Comoros, Rwanda, Seychelles, South Sudan, and Sudan.[37] Eritrea, which the United States has long treated as a pariah state, is noticeably absent.[38]

At the same time that the Global War on Terror was emerging as an organizing feature of US national security policy, African states themselves were making significant changes. In 2001, the Organization of African Unity became the African Union (AU), led by Nigeria, South Africa, Libya and, to a lesser extent, Senegal.[39] At the core of the AU was a new set of collective security institutions that the United States would come to support as an ASTAP alternative to the US-initiated ACRF and ACRI. At its center, led by the AU's Peace and Security Council, was the African Standby Force, intended to serve as a rapid-reaction force to quell continental conflicts at early stages.[40] The United States established the only standalone mission to the AU and gives it direct funding.[41]

The United States also seeks to assure peace, in Africa and elsewhere, through conflict mitigation and peacekeeping efforts. To that end, in 2005 the Bush administration introduced the Global Peace Operations Initiative (GPOI) to provide $660 million over five years to train, equip, and support forces in states willing to participate in peace operations. The plan increased US coordination with the United Nations, the European Union (EU), and the AU, and improved regional training centers. GPOI's mandate was renewed for a second five-year period beginning in 2010, and again in 2015. By 2015, the GPOI had devoted more than $1 billion in assistance to peacekeeping worldwide, with approximately $700 million destined for Africa.[42]

The George W. Bush administration's promotion of US national security in Africa, widely viewed as a success, was capped by two initiatives: the Millennium Challenge Account (MCA) and the President's Emergency Preparedness Fund for

AIDS Relief (PEPFAR). Announced by Bush in 2002, the goal of the MCA was to tie grants and aid to progress toward specific goals on economic and political reform, including opening competitive markets and fighting internal corruption. The program, overseen by the Millennium Challenge Corporation (MCC), has provided over $10 billion in grants and programs to qualifying countries (of which African nations are a plurality). The MCC creates the general guidelines for applicant nations, but each individual country determines and implements its own programs, which can include, for example, educational initiatives, infrastructure improvements, and programs to curb political corruption.

A lasting legacy of George W. Bush's presidency is the US effort to help stem the spread of disease in Africa, especially the PEPFAR initiative aimed at helping the countries hit hardest by HIV/AIDS. In 2003, Bush launched PEPFAR, committing the United States to allocate $15 billion over five years. A particular focus was to increase the number of individuals receiving antiretroviral treatments; at the start of PEPFAR, only fifty thousand people living in Sub-Saharan Africa were receiving these medicines. The program aimed to increase this number to two million in five years. In 2017, PEPFAR reported that it was providing antiretroviral treatments to more than eleven million people living with HIV/AIDS, mostly in Africa; this represented a 50 percent increase since 2014.[43] PEPFAR has also provided medication to protect almost one million infants from being infected with HIV from their mothers. PEPFAR was reauthorized in 2008, some of its authorities were extended again in 2013, and President Obama incorporated the program into his Global Health Initiative.

The Creation of AFRICOM. The most significant articulation of post–Cold War recognition of the importance of Sub-Saharan Africa to US national security interests was the establishment of a unified US military command for the continent. In 2007, President George W. Bush authorized the creation of a new Africa Command (AFRICOM), which assumed responsibility for the African theater of operations in October 2008. According to its mission statement, AFRICOM "disrupts and neutralizes trans-national threats, protects US personnel and facilities, prevents and mitigates conflict, and builds African partner capacity in order to promote regional security, stability, and prosperity."[44] As one of the US military's six geographic combatant commands, AFRICOM is responsible for all US military cooperation, training exercises, and other operations with all African states—not just those in Sub-Saharan Africa—apart from Egypt (responsibility for which lies with Central Command).

From AFRICOM's inception, there have been critics from both Africa and the United States. African states—especially those who viewed the US presence on the continent as inimical to their interests—lambasted the announcement as representing a wave of "US neocolonialism" primarily intended to grab African oil and to counter China's influence. In the United States, progressive groups such as TransAfrica made similar critiques. Across the continent, many regimes declared their refusal to host a US military base; behind the scenes, the real motivation was public opinion. Eventually, the United States located the new AFRICOM headquarters in Stuttgart, Germany.

Despite these controversies, AFRICOM swiftly began to help the United States pursue both its military and its nonmilitary national security interests. On the military front, AFRICOM's objective is to develop the military capacities of African states, especially through the conduct of joint exercises. The most well-known of these is the annual Flintlock counterterrorism exercise, which has taken place in northwest Africa since 2005. Seeking to streamline cooperative efforts among countries, the Flintlock exercises bring together regional and non-African entities to focus on the protection of civilians and counterterrorism.[45]

In addition to AFRICOM, the most prominent US military foothold in Sub-Saharan Africa is the Combined Joint Task Force–Horn of Africa (CJTF-HOA), based in Djibouti City, Djibouti, and housed at the former French base, Camp Lemonnier, the only permanent US base in Sub-Saharan Africa. CJTF-HOA was initially established in 2002 as a counterterrorism initiative and now helps to build defense capability and capacity among its partner nations in the fight against violent extremism.

The Barack Obama Administration and Beyond. Many Africans assumed that the inauguration of Barack Obama as the forty-fourth president of the United States would, given his family connections to Kenya, bring a new, more robust relationship with Africa. Instead, the Obama administration's relationship with countries of Sub-Saharan Africa was marked more by consistency than by radical change. Four pillars—strengthening democratic institutions, encouraging trade and investment, promoting peace and security, and advancing development—made up a status quo agenda. These goals have "been pursued in Africa as a matter of stated policy or actual practice by every US administration—both Republican and Democrat—since the end of the Cold War."[46]

While continuing and even extending many of the counterterrorism activities and African military training programs inaugurated under President George W. Bush, the United States under President Obama showed a broader commitment to peace support operations, especially those led by the United Nations and the African Union. The United States became the largest bilateral donor for peace support operations in Africa and has used its role on the UN Security Council to expand African peace operations. The United States also contributed to numerous UN missions based in Sub-Saharan Africa. The United States offered approximately 120 personnel to support missions to Somalia, and another approximately 300 to the AU-led Regional Cooperation Mission aimed at the elimination of the Uganda-based Lord's Resistance Army. A US officer served as the chief of staff of the UN mission to Liberia. As of January 2015, forty-two uniformed US personnel were serving in UN peacekeeping missions in Sub-Saharan Africa.[47]

The strategy of contributing to UN and AU peacekeeping missions is logical for the United States, as such missions are cheaper alternatives than direct US deployments, and they allow the United States to have a useful impact in theaters where direct deployments might be politically sensitive. Given the preference for ASTAP, the United States under President Obama was generally reluctant to commit ground troops. Instead it sent police officers or military observers, or assisted in African peace support missions through train-and-equip and other assistance programs. At the US-Africa Leaders Summit in 2014, Obama announced the African Peacekeeping Rapid Response Partnership, through which the United States committed $110 million per year over three to five years to train African militaries to respond more effectively to emerging conflicts. That same year, AFRICOM created the Africa Logistics Council to facilitate rapid deployments of peacekeepers and necessary materiel.[48] This approach has largely continued with the Trump administration, which has provided small numbers of trainers and other troops to work with military forces in various African countries.

US Interests in Sub-Saharan Africa

Mitigating Transnational Terrorism. The most pressing US priority in Sub-Saharan Africa today is addressing transnational terrorism. Across Sub-Saharan Africa, violent Islamist extremist groups have become a primary US focus. Concern rose after August 1998, when al Qaeda–affiliated groups working with Osama bin Laden (who had been based in the Sunni Islamist republic in Sudan during the mid-1990s) orchestrated the bombings of the US embassies in Dar es Salaam, Tanzania, and Nairobi, Kenya. After 9/11, when bin Laden became US enemy number one, the Horn of Africa and especially Sudan and Somalia became primary areas of US concern because they had sheltered and abetted suspected al Qaeda–linked terrorists. The United States remains deeply involved in the fight against violent Islamic extremist groups from around the continent.

In Somalia, the top US concern has been the al Shabaab insurgency. In a bid to restore order to a country that had been generally lawless since its collapse in 1991, al Shabaab emerged in 2006 as a radical and violent wing of the Union of Islamic Courts. It has ravaged Somalia, seeking to unseat a succession of shaky national governments backed by the international community. The African Union and its African Union Mission in Somalia (AMISOM) force have been at the forefront of the fight against al Shabaab; the United States has assisted through training, logistical, and surveillance support. Al Shabaab has continued to demonstrate its potency even outside of Somalia with, for example attacks in Kenya at Westgate Mall, which killed 68 people in 2013, and on Garissa University College, which killed 158 in 2015.

Among the Islamic State–affiliated groups emerging as threats in the Horn of Africa has been the Islamic State in Somalia. Based in the northern Puntland region of the country, it occupied the port town of Qandala in October 2016. Other affiliates of the Islamic State in Iraq and the Levant (ISIL) include the Islamic State in Somalia, in Kenya, in Tanzania, and in Uganda.[49] Al Qaeda–affiliated al Shabaab has become displeased with the presence of these Islamic State affiliates in its area of operation, sparking concern about a potential inter-jihadi war whose outcome could further exacerbate instability in Somalia.[50]

In West Africa, in the Sahara and Sahel, the United States has been attempting to mitigate the influence of interrelated Islamic insurgent groups that are allied both to al Qaeda and to the Islamic State. Of primary concern is the Boko Haram insurgency in northeastern Nigeria, sometimes called the Islamic State West Africa Province. This insurgency, which has spilled over into neighboring Cameroon, Chad, and Niger, has as its goal the recreation of the fabled nineteenth-century Sokoto Caliphate and the institution of sharia law across northern Nigeria and neighboring provinces. The group's brutal campaign has targeted the Nigerian government, Christians, Muslims, and civilians. As of March 2017, the group had killed more than 15,600 people, and remains one of the deadliest terror groups in the world.[51] It is notorious for its 2013 kidnapping of 276 schoolgirls, the so-called "Chibok Girls," as well as its use of female and child suicide bombers.[52] The United States has sent special operations forces to the area to advise Nigerian and multinational coalitions, an undertaking made more difficult by the tumultuous relations between Nigeria and the United States. In October 2017, four US soldiers, in addition to four Nigerian soldiers and an interpreter, were killed in an ambush in Niger, raising public awareness about the presence of US forces in Africa to help mitigate terrorist threats.

Other al Qaeda–affiliated groups have also drawn US concern. Following the collapse of Libya in 2011, arms flowed south into the Sahara, fueling differences based on long-standing grievances among historically marginalized groups living in Mali, Niger, Burkina Faso, and southern Algeria and Libya. New coalitions of jihadist groups arose, including al Qaeda in the Islamic Maghreb (across the Sahara and Sahel); Ansaru (Nigeria); al-Mourabitoun (Mali); Ansar Dine (Mali); and the Macina Liberation Front (Mali). Having pledged fidelity ("bayat") to ISIL in October 2016, a group known as the Islamic State in Greater Sahara is one of the new threats to US national security.

Although none of these Africa-based groups has made an attack on American soil, the United States remains concerned about dimensions of African security that could affect the safety of its homeland and of its citizens abroad. In addition to the 1998 US embassy bombings, individual US citizens have been targeted in Sub-Saharan Africa. US economic interests in African oil, especially in Nigeria, have led to concern about the decades-long waves of militancy in the Niger Delta region. Locals have become insurgents, joining groups such as the Movement for the Emancipation of the Niger Delta (MEND) and the Niger Delta Avengers (NDA), which seek greater equity in the massive oil profits of multinationals such as Exxon and Chevron.[53] US economic interests were put at risk during recent years when pirates from Somalia had a considerable presence in the Gulf of Aden, attacking and hijacking boats and shipping. Between 2001 and mid-2015, forty-three Americans were held hostage in Sub-Saharan Africa: one in Chad; another in Mauritania; a third in Sudan; two in Kenya; six in Somalia; and thirty-two in Nigeria. As of mid-2017, however, no US citizen has died at the hands of kidnappers in Sub-Saharan Africa during the twenty-first century.[54]

Addressing Sub-Saharan African Immigration. Displacement of globally vulnerable populations and their immigration to the United States and to Europe remains one of the most vexing and contentious security issues facing many countries. During the 2016 presidential campaign and his early administration, President Donald Trump articulated public fears of potential threats from citizens from Islamic countries. Citizens of Somalia, Sudan, and Chad were among those barred from entering the United States by executive orders issued in January, March, and September 2017.[55] Additionally, members of Sub-Saharan African diasporas who are already in the United States might pose threats to the US homeland, not through direct affiliations with terrorist groups, but through "lone wolf" attacks inspired by transnational terrorist groups or ideology. For example, the so-called "underwear bomber," Nigerian immigrant Umar Farouk Abdulmutallab, planned to detonate a bomb on a Christmas Day 2009 flight from Amsterdam to Detroit, which could have killed 289 people. In 2016, Abdul Razak Ali Artan, a Somali immigrant resettled in the United States as a permanent resident, attacked people by automobile and knife at Ohio State University, injuring thirteen before he was killed by police; although a "lone wolf" attacker, he was said to have been inspired by terrorist propaganda from ISIL and Anwar al-Awlaki. In grappling with this issue, the United States is confronted with a double-edged sword: how to maintain its ideals as a global moral leader based on respect for human rights, dignity, and the value of diversity, while simultaneously protecting its citizens from the few who seek to do harm.

Maintaining Relationships with Regionally Powerful African States. In pursuit of its goal to be the leading non-African country in Sub-Saharan Africa, the United States has sought to maintain relationships with regional anchors across the continent. In a landscape of forty-eight countries, it emphasizes its strategic relationships with the "power players." In West Africa, the United States prioritizes its relationship with Nigeria, the most powerful country in that region in terms of economic strength, military power, and population size. The United States also views Ghana, a fairly stable country, which has West Africa's highest standard of living, and Senegal, a stable majority-Muslim Francophone democracy open to cooperation, as important allies. In Southern Africa, the United States has viewed post-apartheid South Africa as key to promotion of its national security interests in the region. Pretoria is southern Africa's economic anchor; moreover, for a time after 1979, it was the only country in Africa that could theoretically have posed an existential threat to the United States (in 1989, it became the first country ever to dismantle its nuclear weapons program voluntarily). The United States and Angola do not have a robust relationship despite US strategic interest in Angola's oil wealth. In the Horn of Africa, the United States has emphasized national security in its relationship with Ethiopia, a staunch ally on terrorism but domestically repressive; Kenya, a reliable if corrupt Anglophone ally; Uganda, another pseudo-democratic country that has worked with the United States to combat the Lord's Resistance Army; and Rwanda, a strategic peacekeeping ally, but one whose authoritarian tendencies complicate relationships with the United States.

In contrast to these working relationships with partner nations, several African states pose threats to US national security interests. The primary countries of concern are Somalia, whose lack of effective governance since 1991 has permitted the rise of insurgent al Shabaab jihadists and of piracy off the coast;[56] the Democratic Republic of Congo, whose tumultuous northeast conflicts in Kivu and Ituri followed "Africa's World War" of 1998–2003, which killed between 2.4 and 5.7 million; Eritrea, which is known, perhaps hyperbolically, as "Africa's North Korea"; and Sub-Saharan Africa's newest state, South Sudan, which has been embroiled in civil conflict since shortly after its independence in 2011. Other recent flashpoints for US national security interests include the collapse of Mali in 2012, the collapse of the Central African Republic in 2013, the intractable Boko Haram insurgency in Nigeria, and social and political instability in Burundi, Ethiopia, Côte d'Ivoire, the Gambia, and Burkina Faso.

Assuring Leadership. To position itself as the leading non-African country in Sub-Saharan Africa, the United States must manage its relations with other would-be contenders for the role. The United States has historically worked fairly harmoniously with France and Britain: both states, as former colonial powers and close US allies, are mostly willing to let the United States lead the effort. France remains the more culturally and ideologically powerful partner in its former colonies in Francophone West Africa, including Senegal, Côte d'Ivoire, Guinea, Mauritania, Mali, Niger, Benin, Burkina Faso, and Cameroon, as well as in Gabon and Congo in Central Africa. The former and current British presence is more strongly felt in Nigeria, Ghana, Kenya, Zimbabwe, and Sierra Leone. Less powerful although still influential Western allies that support US national security interests in Africa include other Western European countries such as Germany, Denmark, and Sweden, as well as, to a lesser degree, Canada and Japan. The United States has been an influential member of the United Nations and has acted in concert with the European Union with regard to Sub-Saharan Africa. Other countries including India, Brazil, and Venezuela have also attempted to establish stronger relationships in the region.

Most US attempts at informal hegemony in Africa are accepted by Western European nations, but China is a different story. Its interest in Africa has been a prominent US concern since the early 2000s, when China ascended in the global political economy. China's approach to promoting its own ideological influence in Africa significantly diverges from standard US strategy.[57] In contrast to the US neoliberal agenda of promoting democratization, human rights, and free markets, China has instead engaged various countries on the continent predominantly with infrastructure and public-private inducements, including large-scale dam projects in Ethiopia, bridges in Niger, uranium projects in Namibia, and funding for the 2013 construction of a brand-new African Union headquarters in Addis Ababa, Ethiopia.

Perhaps more powerful than what China gives is what China says, and does not say, as it engages with the region. China refrains from discussions of human rights and democracy in African nations. It funds large-scale economic projects without critique of the African governments receiving its funding. Instead, China touts its relationships with African states as partnerships among equals, leveraging notions of global South solidarity and harmonious friendship. This contrasts with US approaches, which are often seen as more paternalistic.

This low-level struggle for African hearts and minds can be seen playing out throughout the continent. For instance, while the United States was for many years the only non-African country to have a separate mission to the African Union in Addis Ababa, China now plans to open its own standalone mission. It also announced that it will build a new military base in Djibouti, near the US base at Camp Lemonnier. While the Chinese entry as an ideological counterweight to the United States has not been wholly welcomed by Washington, it has not caused the relationship between the two countries to devolve into open hostility.

Encouraging Economic Development and Good Governance. The United States has long maintained its commitment to encouraging economic development and democratization, based on the rationale that free and economically prosperous societies are more peaceful societies. US trading partners in Africa include Nigeria, South Africa, Angola, and Kenya. Major US economic interests are particularly affected by conditions in those African states that hold significant natural resources, such as natural gas, oil, diamonds, gold, coltan, and rare earth minerals. Until recently, the United States was the world's largest consumer of African oil: in 2008, nearly 18 percent of US oil imports came from Africa, almost as much as the United States received from Saudi Arabia. However, between 2010 and 2015, the United States cut its African oil imports by 90 percent due to increased domestic oil production.[58]

The key US program to foster economic national security in Africa, the African Growth and Opportunity Act (AGOA), was established in 2000. AGOA has been at the vanguard of Washington's efforts to encourage open African markets by granting selected African countries preferential access to US markets through duty-free entry of certain products. African states can qualify to participate in AGOA by having a market-based economy with limited government interference, democratic governance or tangible movement toward it, assurances against corruption, and a general tendency not to undermine US interests and foreign policy, among other stipulations.[59] AGOA has been credited with diversifying US imports from Africa; it accounted for approximately $25.6 billion, or just over 1 percent of total US trade in 2014. African states agreed unanimously to seek the renewal of AGOA when it came up for consideration in 2015.[60] Nevertheless, detractors criticize AGOA's emphasis on duty-free African oil (apparel imports come in a distant second).[61] Perhaps to counter Chinese approaches to African engagement, the Obama administration announced in 2013 the Power Africa initiative, a public-private partnership designed to create upwards of 60 million new electricity connections and to generate 30,000 megawatts of clean power in Africa.[62] The program's rationale is that access to electricity engenders numerous societal benefits such as education and health outcomes that are intrinsically worthwhile and that may also reduce the extent of disaffected and potentially radicalized populations.

The United States has long sought to encourage the deepening of democracy in Sub-Saharan Africa, and it has begun to interpret the absence of democratic values as a threat. For instance, when in 2015 Burundian President Pierre Nkurunziza attempted to extend his term in office and violence erupted from both detractors and supporters, President Obama issued an executive order stating that the crisis in Burundi "constitutes an unusual and extraordinary threat to the national security and foreign policy of the United States."[63] Although that statement was perhaps hyperbolic, the point remains that underdeveloped democracy in Sub-Saharan Africa is seen as giving rise to threats to the United States.[64]

Promoting Human Security. In recent years, the United States has begun to consider human security as part of its national security interests in Sub-Saharan Africa. The United States, like the African Union, sees threats relating to issues such as gender, health, education, human rights, and the environment as potential drivers of conflict. In 2010, the US government introduced the "Feed the Future" initiative to enhance sustainable global food security for vulnerable populations, particularly in Sub-Saharan Africa and Southeast Asia. In the same year, it introduced the Young African Leaders Initiative, which seeks to provide professional development, training, and networking opportunities to the region's next generation.

The United States has long considered potential epidemiological catastrophes to be threats to its national security, and just such a potentially dire scenario was seen in Sub-Saharan Africa in 2014 with the outbreak of Ebola. The most deadly global threat to come out of Sub-Saharan Africa in recent history, it had great likelihood of affecting the lives and health of US citizens. Starting in 2013, the Ebola virus spread throughout three West African countries—Liberia, Sierra Leone, and Guinea—none of which had a public health sector capable of containing the outbreak. A global response was mounted, slowly, by the World Health Organization, the United Nations, Médecins Sans Frontières, the African Union, and other bilateral partners, although individual African countries mostly remained in the lead. After public fears rose over the potential impact of Ebola in the United States, the Obama administration deployed three thousand "health-keeping troops" to West Africa to help prevent further spread of the virus before it could establish a presence in the United States.[65] These efforts were eventually successful, and the Ebola epidemic was largely contained by 2016.

US Policy Challenges for the Future

The role of Sub-Saharan Africa in US national security interests under the new Donald J. Trump administration is uncertain. President Trump's stated foreign policy outlook of "America first" suggests an overall retrenchment in global affairs, while increasing the focus on terrorism and continuing a realpolitik attitude toward adversaries such as Iran and China; the effects of such policies might well be felt in Sub-Saharan Africa. Upon assuming the post, President Trump sent a list of questions to US government Africa experts on the status of US Africa policy. Among other concerns, he asked why the United States had failed to eradicate al Shabaab in Somalia, and he questioned the logic of many of the developmental assistance programs that the United States provides in Sub-Saharan Africa.[66] The Trump administration gave an early signal that Sub-Saharan Africa would figure in considerations of US national security interests by the inclusion of three states from the region, Somalia, Chad, and Sudan, on the list of majority-Muslim countries affected by various versions of proposed US travel bans. Under President Trump, the US relationship with Sub-Saharan Africa may be viewed primarily through dual lenses: countering terrorism and augmenting US business ties for the benefit of American corporations and consumers. Efforts focused on democracy promotion and humanitarian programs associated with the United States Agency for International Development are likely to receive lower priorities than under previous administrations.

While the broad contours of the US national security strategy toward Sub-Saharan Africa remain opaque, issues that are likely to remain top priorities include transnational terrorism and criminality, improving relationships with selected African states and with Africa's international organizations, managing relationships with other foreign actors in Africa, and addressing environmental degradation and demographic pressures.

Transnational terrorism may be the most challenging issue facing the United States in Sub-Saharan Africa. Difficult problems include the splintering and proliferation of al Qaeda–aligned groups throughout the Sahara and the Sahel, the continued carnage wrought by al Shabaab in the Horn of Africa, and outcroppings of new Islamic State–affiliated cells in both West Africa and the Horn. US national security interests will also be focused on the connections between terrorist groups and criminality, such as drug smuggling, human trafficking, arms dealing, the circulation of diamonds, minerals, and ivory, and the illegal diversion, theft, and smuggling of oil. Cybercrime will also be an important US national security interest in the twenty-first century. While Sub-Saharan Africa is presently one of the least connected world regions, its connectivity is growing. African governments and their intelligence agencies may themselves not yet be capable of launching damaging attacks on US cyber-infrastructure, but nonstate actors, particularly those located in Anglophone portions of the continent including Nigeria, Ghana, Kenya, Tanzania, and South Africa, may give rise to an increased cybercriminal presence.

Another enduring challenge for US national security interests in Sub-Saharan Africa is effective cooperation with African international organizations that are at the forefront of the fight to protect collective security. These include the AU and regional economic communities such as the Economic Community of West African States and the Intergovernmental Authority on Development. US support in training and assisting members of the African Standby Force, the pan-African rapid-response team, and potentially the African Capacity for Immediate Response to Crises would help to ensure that they have adequate capabilities for potential engagements.

An important consideration for the Trump administration will be relationships with other non-African actors on the African continent, not all of whom support US agendas. The United States currently works with France as it pursues counter-terror efforts jointly with regional nations in the Sahara and Sahel and elsewhere in their former colonies. The United Kingdom, Germany, and the Scandinavian countries are traditionally important allies for the United States on the continent. The United States must decide how to interpret and respond to the presence of China. While for the past decade a number of African states have been eager to make use of China's presence and its noncritical approach to their internal affairs, the honeymoon appears to be weakening on both sides. African states have complained about the poor quality of many of China's large-scale investment projects; China has abandoned its noninterference policy and has contributed its largest contingent of UN peacekeepers to date in Mali. Perhaps the Chinese military venture that will most affect the United States is China's construction of a new base in Djibouti, in proximity to the US presence at Camp Lemonnier.

Environmental issues may become a priority for US security in Sub-Saharan Africa. Across the continent, ecological pressures such as access to potable water and loss of arable land due to desertification are linked to conflict. For instance, in eastern Nigeria, Fulani herders from the north are grazing farther and farther south on the lands of historically sedentary non-Fulani herding people, leading to bloody clashes between groups for whom sharing land had historically never been an issue.[67] Elsewhere, a decrease in potable water has led to clashes; in Sudan, although such clashes were not the main reason for the conflict in western Darfur, they were a contributing factor. For the United States, helping African partner nations mitigate the impact of environmental degradation, both as an end in itself and to forestall future conflict, will continue to be an important policy consideration.

In the coming years, demographic pressures arising from rapid population growth in Sub-Saharan Africa will present significant challenges. As development outcomes have improved, with reductions in child mortality and in deaths from disease along with better nutrition, the population has grown faster in Sub-Saharan Africa than in any other world region. The population is expected to explode from 1.05 billion people in 2016 to approximately 2.8 billion by 2060. Of particular concern is the so-called youth bulge, an expanding base of citizens under the age of thirty. In Sub-Saharan Africa in 2012, approximately 40 percent of the population was under the age of fifteen and 70 percent under the age of thirty; these percentages are far higher than in older and more developed societies.[68] The African youth bulge heightens the risks of insecurity in various ways; the most discussed concern is the prevalence of young males who are unemployed or underemployed and whose societal disaffection might lead them to join insurgencies or terrorist groups.

As a result of demographic pressures, "mega-cities"—urban spaces with more than ten million people—may form throughout Sub-Saharan Africa in the coming years. Two such mega-cities already exist in Sub-Saharan Africa: Lagos in Nigeria and Kinshasa in Democratic Republic of Congo. Other metropolitan areas, including Dar es Salaam, Tanzania, Johannesburg, South Africa, and Luanda, Angola, are expected to become mega-cities by 2050.[69] The emergence of poor and crowded mega-cities throughout Sub-Saharan Africa poses numerous problems: competition for limited resources such as potable water, affordable food, and consistent electricity has the potential to spark conflict, while lack of public sanitation services can lead to a proliferation of infectious diseases, which can spread all the more quickly in crowded tropical urban spaces. Such dangers, and the likely scarcity of employment for rural newcomers to urban spaces, could lead to greater dependence on religious or ethnic sources of social support. The concern is that such conditions might result in radicalization and violence.

US national security interests in Sub-Saharan Africa are at an inflection point. Sub-Saharan Africa has never occupied a dominant role in US national security interests, but the beginning of the twenty-first century has highlighted the need for more focus on this dynamic region.

Discussion Questions

1. Explain the historical place of Sub-Saharan Africa in the pursuit of US national security interests.
2. What arguments support the view that Sub-Saharan Africa now has a more important place in US national security interests than ever before? Why might Sub-Saharan Africa be of lesser importance than other regions to US national security?
3. What arguments support the view that terrorism is the primary national security threat the United States faces from Sub-Saharan Africa? What are some other threats?
4. Who are the key US allies and adversaries in Sub-Saharan Africa?
5. How will the increasing influence of China influence US behavior in Sub-Saharan Africa?
6. What is or should be the role of the African Union in US security policy?
7. How can the United States reconcile international pressures to involve itself as an "honest broker" to quell conflicts in Sub-Saharan Africa with its goal of maintaining a leadership position there, given the US public's unwillingness to expend blood and treasure on the continent?
8. Under what conditions is the US public willing to apply resources in Sub-Saharan Africa?
9. How will the rise of mega-citics influence US strategy surrounding human security in Sub-Saharan Africa?
10. What do you consider the most pressing American national security issue in Sub-Saharan Africa today?

Recommended Reading

Berkeley, Bill. *The Graves Are Not Yet Full: Race, Tribe, and Power in the Heart of Africa*. New York: Basic Books, 2001.

Brigety, Reuben E. "The New Pan-Africanism: Implications for U.S. Africa Policy." *Survival* 58, no. 4 (2016): 159–76.

Buss, Terry, et al., eds. *African Security and the African Command: Viewpoints on the U.S. Role in Africa*. Sterling, VA: Kumarian Press, 2011.
Cooke, Jennifer G., and J. Stephen Morrison. *U.S. Africa Policy beyond the Bush Years: Critical Challenges for the Obama Administration*. Washington, DC: Center for Strategic and International Studies (CSIS), 2009.
Francis, David J., ed. *U.S. Strategy in Africa: AFRICOM, Terrorism and Security Challenges*. Repr. ed. New York: Routledge, 2011.
Keenan, Jeremy. *The Dark Sahara: America's War on Terror in Africa*. New York: Pluto Press, 2009.
Schraeder, Peter J. *United States Foreign Policy toward Africa: Incrementalism, Crisis and Change*. Cambridge: Cambridge University Press, 1994.
Williams, Paul D. *Enhancing U.S. Support for Peace Operations in Africa*. New York: Council on Foreign Relations, 2015.

Recommended Internet Sources

African Union, https://au.int/
Millennium Challenge Corporation, www.mcc.gov
United States Africa Command (AFRICOM), www.africom.mil
United States President's Emergency Plan for AIDS Relief (PEPFAR), www.pepfar.gov

Notes

1. Chris Alden, "From Neglect to 'Virtual Engagement': The United States and Its New Paradigm for Africa," *African Affairs* 99, no. 396 (2000): 355–71.

2. Here, we use the term "Sub-Saharan Africa" for the landmass of Africa apart from the northern African countries of Morocco, Algeria, Tunisia, Libya, and Egypt. In addition, while they do not emerge as topics in this chapter, the island nations of Cape Verde, São Tomé and Príncipe, Madagascar, Comoros, Seychelles, and Mauritius are also considered to be parts of Sub-Saharan Africa.

3. For more on how nineteenth-century African American populations understood Africa's role in relation to their own security, see the compendium edited by Wilson Moses, *Classical Black Nationalism: From the American Revolution to Marcus Garvey* (New York: New York University Press, 1996).

4. Martin Meredith, *The Fate of Africa: A History of Fifty Years of Independence* (New York: PublicAffairs, 2006).

5. D. G. Jamieson, "AFRICOM: A Threat or an Opportunity for African Security?" *South African Journal of International Affairs* 16, no. 3 (2009): 311–29. A. Carl LeVan, "The Political Economy of African Responses to the U.S. Africa Command," *Africa Today* 57, no. 1 (2010): 3–23.

6. Bill Berkeley, *The Graves Are Not Yet Full: Race, Tribe, and Power in the Heart of Africa* (New York: Basic Books, 2001), 65, 80, 213.

7. See Richard J. Payne and Eddie Ganaway, "The Influence of Black Americans on U.S. Policy towards Southern Africa," *African Affairs* 79, no. 317 (1980): 585–98.

8. Emmanuel K. Aning, "African Crisis Response Initiative and the New African Security (Dis)order," *African Journal of Political Science/Revue Africaine de science politique* 6, no. 1 (2001), 43–67. To demonstrate its newfound concern about threats emanating from Africa, on July 1, 1990 (a month prior to the Iraqi invasion of Kuwait), the US Special

Operations Command (SOCOM) established the US Army Third Special Forces Group (Airborne) (3rd SFG) based at Fort Bragg, North Carolina. A major rationale for the establishment of the 3rd SFG was to contribute to resolving African crises. See also The White House, "National Security Review 30," June 15, 1992, https://bush41library.tamu.edu/files/nsr/nsr30.pdf.

9. Benedikt Franke, *Security Cooperation in Africa: A Reappraisal* (Boulder, CO: First-ForumPress, 2009), 77.

10. "Mission creep—the temptation commanders feel to chase success and perhaps glory around the next corner by expanding their mandate and rolling over anyone in their way—threatens to take hold in Mogadishu." Jim Hoagland, "Beware 'Mission Creep' in Somalia," *Washington Post*, July 20, 1993.

11. Alden, "From Neglect to 'Virtual Engagement,'" 355–71.

12. See Eric G. Berman and Katie E. Sams, *Constructive Disengagement:Western Efforts to Develop African Peacekeeping* (Pretoria, South Africa: Institue for Security Studies, 1998), 9–10.

13. The "ASTAP" rhetoric has also extended into nonsecurity related discussions, including governance, development, and protection of human rights.

14. Benedikt Franke and Stefan Gänzle, "How 'African' Is the African Peace and Security Architecture? Conceptual and Practical Constraints of Regional Security Cooperation in Africa," *African Security* 5, no. 2 (2012): 88–104.

15. Katharina P. Coleman, "Innovations in 'African Solutions to African Problems': The Evolving Practice of Regional Peacekeeping in Sub-Saharan Africa," *Journal of Modern African Studies* 49, no. 4 (2011): 517–45.

16. Phillip Apuuli Kasaija, "The African Union (AU), the Libya Crisis and the Notion of 'African Solutions to African Problems,'" *Journal of Contemporary African Studies* 31, no. 1 (2013): 117–38.

17. Laurie Nathan, "African Solutions to African Problems: South Africa's Foreign Policy," SAFPI Policy Brief No. 51 (South African Foreign Policy Institute, 2013).

18. Danielle Beswick, "Peacekeeping, Regime Security and 'African Solutions to African Problems': Exploring Motivations for Rwanda's Involvement in Darfur," *Third World Quarterly* 31, no. 5 (2010): 739–54.

19. Aning, "African Crisis Response Initiative and the New African Security (Dis)order," 48.

20. Eric G. Berman and Katie E. Sams, *Peacekeeping in Africa: Capabilities and Culpabilities* (New York: United Nations Publications, UNIDIR, 2000), 78.

21. LeVan, "The Political Economy of African Responses to the U.S. Africa Command," 10.

22. Aning, "African Crisis Response Initiative and the New African Security (Dis)order," 49.

23. Aning, "African Crisis Response Initiative and the New African Security (Dis)order," 49.

24. Berman and Sams, *Peacekeeping in Africa*, 271.

25. Solomon Hailu, *Promoting Collective Security in Africa: The Roles and Responsibilities of the United Nations, African States, and Western Powers* (Lanham, MD: University Press of America, 2011), 44.

26. Franke, *Security Cooperation in Africa*, 78.

27. Franke and Gänzle, "How 'African' Is the African Peace and Security Architecture?," 91.

28. Alden notes that "the United States and the interested member states of the European Union put great stock in winning the support and/or adherence of Pretoria for their initiatives to reformulate their Africa policies, be it the African Crisis Response Initiative (and its European variants)." Alden, "From Neglect to 'Virtual Engagement,'" 364, 369.

29. Aning, "African Crisis Response Initiative and the New African Security (Dis)order," 60.

30. Alden, "From Neglect to 'Virtual Engagement,'" 364.

31. Adam Cobb, "Don't Stop with Joint Forces Command . . . Cut AFRICOM Too," *African Security Review* 20, no. 1 (2011): 134–40.

32. Paul D. Williams, *War and Conflict in Africa* (Cambridge, UK: Polity, 2011), 191.

33. Alden, "From Neglect to 'Virtual Engagement,'" 364.

34. Berman and Sams, "Constructive Disengagement," 15.

35. Aning, "African Crisis Response Initiative and the New African Security (Dis)order," 59–60.

36. The White House, *The National Security Strategy of the United States of America, 2002* (Washington, DC: The White House, September 17, 2002).

37. US State Department, "Bureau of Counterterrorism and Countering Violent Extremism: Programs and Initiatives," 2017, https://www.state.gov/j/ct/programs/index.htm.

38. For more on the US-Eritrea relationship, see Bronwyn Bruton, "It's Bad in Eritrea, but Not That Bad," *New York Times*, June 23, 2016; Jason Warner, "Eritrea's Military Unprofessionalism and U.S. Security Assistance in the Horn of Africa," *Small Wars and Insurgencies* 24, no. 4 (2013): 696–711.

39. Thomas Kwasi Tieku, "Explaining the Clash and Accommodation of Interests of Major Actors in the Creation of the African Union," *African Affairs* 103, no. 411 (2004): 249–67.

40. Jason Warner, "Complements or Competitors? The African Standby Force, the African Capacity for Immediate Response to Crises and the Future of Rapid Reaction Forces in Africa," *African Security* 8, no. 1 (2015): 56–73.

41. Paul D. Williams, *Enhancing U.S. Support for Peace Operations in Africa* (New York: Council on Foreign Relations, 2015), 16.

42. Williams, *Enhancing U.S. Support for Peace Operations in Africa*, 18.

43. The United States President's Emergency Plan for AIDS Relief, "Thirteenth Annual Report to Congress (2017)," https://www.pepfar.gov/press/2017annualreport/index.htm.

44. United States Africa Command, "About the Command," n.d., http://www.africom.mil/about-the-command.

45. United States Africa Command, "Flintlock," n.d., http://www.africom.mil/what-we-do/exercises/flintlock.

46. Reuben E. Brigety,"The New Pan-Africanism: Implications for U.S. Africa Policy," *Survival* 58, no. 4 (2016): 159–76.

47. Williams, *Enhancing U.S. Support for Peace Operations in Africa*, 11–17.

48. Williams, *Enhancing U.S. Support for Peace Operations in Africa*, 11–17.

49. Jason Warner, "Sub-Saharan Africa's Three 'New' Islamic State Affiliates," *CTC Sentinel* 10, no. 1 (2017): 28–32.

50. Jason Warner and Mohammed al-'Ubayidi, "Inter-Jihadi Violence: Understanding the Battle between Al-Shabaab and the Islamic State" (West Point, NY: US Military Academy, Combating Terrorism Center, forthcoming 2017).

51. Institute for Economics and Peace, *Global Terrorism Index 2016* (Sydney, Australia, 2016), 27.

52. Jason Warner and Hilary Matfess, *Exploding Stereotypes: The Unexpected Operational and Demographic Characteristics of Boko Haram's Suicide Bombers* (West Point, NY: Combatting Terrorism Center, 2017).

53. Omolade Adunbi, *Oil Wealth and Insurgency in Nigeria* (Bloomington: Indiana University Press, 2015).

54. Hostage Project Database (West Point, NY: US Military Academy, Combating Terrorism Center, 2017).

55. Sudan was listed on the executive orders issued in January and March 2017 but was dropped from the September executive order. Chad was not on the first two executive orders but was added to the September executive order.

56. AFP, "Somali Piracy Is Down, Not Out," *Daily Mail*, April 7, 2016.

57. See Chris Alden, *China in Africa: Partner, Competitor or Hegemon?* (London: Zed Books, 2007); Howard W. French, *China's Second Continent: How a Million Migrants Are Building a New Empire in Africa* (New York: Knopf, 2014); Deborah Brautigam, *The Dragon's Gift: The Real Story of China in Africa* (Oxford, UK: Oxford University Press, 2009).

58. Brock R. Williams, *African Growth and Opportunity Act (AGOA): Background and Reauthorization* (Washington, DC: US Congressional Research Service, 2015).

59. American Growth and Opprtunity Act, "About AGOA: The African Growth and Opportunity Act," 2018, https://agoa.info/about-agoa.html.

60. Brigety, "The New Pan-Africanism."

61. Williams, *Enhancing U.S. Support for Peace Operations in Africa*, 12.

62. US Agency for International Development, "About Us: Power Africa," March 2018, https://www.usaid.gov/powerafrica.

63. The White House, "Executive Order—Blocking Property of Certain Persons Contributing to the Situation in Burundi," November 22, 2015, https://obamawhitehouse.archives.gov/the-press-office/2015/11/23/executive-order-blocking-property-certain-persons-contributing-situation.

64. Kayla Ruble, "The New 'Extraordinary Threat' to U.S. National Security Is a Landlocked Country in Africa," *VICE News*, November 23, 2015, https://news.vice.com/article/the-new-extraordinary-threat-to-us-national-security-is-a-landlocked-country-in-africa.

65. Williams, *Enhancing U.S. Support for Peace Operations in Africa*.

66. Helene Cooper, "Trump Team's Queries about Africa Point to Skepticism about Aid," *New York Times*, January 13, 2017.

67. Andrew McGregor, "The Fulani Crisis: Communal Violence and Radicalization in the Sahel," *CTC Sentinel* 10, no. 2 (2017): 34–40.

68. Justin Yifu Lin, "Youth Bulge: A Demographic Dividend or a Demographic Bomb in Developing Countries?" in World Bank blog, *Let's Talk Development*, January 5, 2012, http://blogs.worldbank.org/developmenttalk/youth-bulge-a-demographic-dividend-or-a demographic-bomb-in-developing-countries, accessed on September 12, 2017.

69. Mark Jackson, "Africa's Emerging Mega-Cities," UrbanAfrica.Net, 2015. https://www.urbanafrica.net/urban-voices/the-future-of-african-mega-cities/.

22

Russia

Russia's international power and influence have varied dramatically in recent years, and so have its relations with the United States. The post–World War II relationship was marked by confrontation. Then, expectations of partnership arose following the 1991 Soviet collapse. The first decades of the twenty-first century, however, brought renewed friction over Russia's behavior and its standing in the international political, economic, and strategic order. Throughout these fluctuations, Russia has remained important to US policy makers concerned with national security (figure 22.1).

The dissolution of the Soviet Union eliminated what may have been the single greatest external threat to the United States. The threat was more than strategic; it was foundational. The Soviets offered a profoundly different set of values and institutions, which formed an alternative political, economic, and cultural system. An appreciation for the history of this threat remains valuable for the perspective it provides on current US national security challenges, including the problems of terrorism, weapons of mass destruction, and geostrategic stability. As the primary heir of the Soviet Union, Russia is shaped by this legacy and, moreover, remains a nuclear superpower with an arsenal capable of destroying the United States.

Russia's failure to establish authentic democratic institutions and a market economy after the Soviet collapse means that, for the foreseeable future, cooperation between Washington and Moscow will rest less on shared values than on perceptions of shared interests. In recent years, however, Russia's increased assertiveness in global politics has severely impeded cooperation based on even the most basic

The authors would like to thank Professor Rob Person for his significant contributions to this chapter.

FIGURE 22.1 Russia

mutual interests. Russia might play the role of spoiler or of supporter of US foreign policy, depending on how it defines its interests. Its recent actions suggest that it is more likely to play the role of spoiler for the foreseeable future.

The rest of this chapter reviews, briefly, US-Soviet relations during the Cold War, then the Soviet collapse, followed by the subsequent relationship between the United States and Russia in the contemporary era.

The Cold War

From the end of the Second World War until the collapse of communist regimes in Eastern Europe and the Soviet Union in 1989–1991, the Cold War—the intense geopolitical competition between the United States and the Soviet Union—was the overwhelming focus of American national security policy. It was the conceptual framework through which both American and Soviet policy makers interpreted and understood their security environments. Strategists on both sides saw nearly all of the globe as a grand chessboard on which the two superpowers competed for influence and interests.

This fact gives rise to one of the great paradoxes of the Cold War: that it could also be described as "the long peace."[1] With this term, historian John Lewis Gaddis points out that the Cold War represented the longest period in the history of the modern state system without direct warfare between great powers.[2] The Cold War period cannot, however, be described as peaceful: many conflicts were fought outside the European theater in Asia, Africa, and Latin America. These proxy wars, many of them fought by one superpower or the other against or with third parties, were generally seen as part of the global competition between the United States and the Soviet Union.

Two dominant narratives describe the fundamental causes of conflict between the United States and the Soviet Union during the Cold War. The first is captured by the realist school of international relations theory, which portrays the Cold War as a competition for security—and ultimately for survival—between great powers.[3] Such competitions have long been characteristic of the international state system. Although the presence of only two superpowers in a bipolar system made the Cold War period unique (compared to the multipolar systems of earlier epochs), realists would say that it is not particularly surprising that the superpowers were locked in a global struggle for security. The logic behind this zero-sum view of power is described as the *security dilemma*: "Many of the means by which a state tries to increase its security decrease the security of others."[4] According to this framework, the United States and Soviet Union were destined to forge a conflictual relationship characterized by competition, mistrust, and arms races as each pursued security at the expense of the other.

A second and contrasting narrative sees the origins of the conflict in the ideological struggle of Soviet Marxism-Leninism versus US liberal democracy and market capitalism. Each ideology offers a distinct vision of how to organize the economic, political, and social life of a society. These ideologies both laid claim to universal validity and embodied inherent opposition along many dimensions. For example, Karl Marx and Friedrich Engels had argued that the capitalist order contained the seeds of its own destruction and would eventually be replaced by its antithesis, communism. Messianic overtones could be discerned in the claims of each side to represent the pinnacle of social organization. Adherents to both ideologies would come to view the world in terms of an existential ideological struggle between good and evil. Marxism-Leninism was part of the genetic code of the Soviet Union, while liberalism had guided the United States since its founding.

More than a quarter of a century after the end of the Cold War, the debate continues over which framework—great-power politics or ideology—better explains the dynamics of superpower competition during the Cold War. It is likely that both contributed to the animosity between the two great antagonists. George Kennan, writing anonymously in 1947 from his position in the State Department, argued that Stalin's aggressive and expansionist postwar policies were shaped by the Marxist-Leninist ideology and by the nature of the totalitarian Soviet system.[5] This ideology was layered on an older Russian identity that had long been plagued by feelings of insecurity and a strong conviction that the outside world was hostile. In Soviet leaders' conviction that expansionism was necessary to security, "the powerful tradition of Russian history and tradition reached up to sustain them."[6] Kennan advocated a sharply US realist response: "In these circumstances it is clear that the main element of any United States policy toward the Soviet Union must be that of a long-term, patient but firm and vigilant containment of Russian expansive tendencies."[7] From this view was born the Cold War policy of *containment*, which sought to check Soviet territorial and security advances wherever they might manifest themselves. (See also chapter 3.)

The Collapse of the Soviet Union and the End of the Cold War

This section describes broad factors leading to the demise of the Soviet Union, as Kennan had predicted forty-four years earlier: "Soviet power, like the capitalist world of its conception, bears within it the seeds of its own decay. . . . The sprouting of these seeds is well advanced."[8] Scores of volumes have been written on the collapse of communism in Eastern Europe and its culmination in the crumbling of the Soviet political system in late 1991.[9] First and foremost, the Soviet planned economy, with all industry under state ownership, was moribund by the time Mikhail Gorbachev came to power in 1985.[10] The broken economic system and its inability to provide the better future that had been promised by Soviet leaders since Lenin had severely undermined the legitimacy of the entire socialist system—and the state that embodied it—in the eyes of the Soviet people. What little legitimacy the Marxist-Leninist ideology had maintained through the stagnant and corrupt era of Leonid Brezhnev (1964–1982) had evaporated entirely by the late 1980s. This economic crisis drove Gorbachev's attempt to reform the socialist economy through *perestroika*, or "restructuring," and to slow the costly Cold War arms race through a series of arms control agreements with the United States.

Second, a complex legacy of ethnic, national, and territorial politics meant that the Soviet Union was a multiethnic empire. As such, it was vulnerable to awakening nationalist movements that became particularly strong in western Ukraine, the Caucasus, and the Baltic republics of Estonia, Latvia, and Lithuania.[11] Gorbachev's liberalizing political reforms, known as *glasnost*—"transparency" or "openness"—made room for such nationalist movements to emerge and grow, and ultimately they destabilized the Soviet Union.[12]

By 1991, a crumbling economy, a defunct ideology, and increasingly assertive nationalist movements seeking independence made for an explosive mixture. Gorbachev's attempts to save the Soviet system through reform could not halt the momentum of change; Lenin's grand social experiment was swept away with breathtaking speed. A coup by hardliners failed in August 1991. Then, on December 25, 1991, Gorbachev resigned; days later, the Soviet Union was no more. Soviet citizens were instead citizens of fifteen independent countries. The global geopolitical landscape was fundamentally reshaped.

US-Russian Relations in the Post-Soviet Period. American foreign policy toward Russia in the early post-Soviet period was marked by optimism that the United States and Russia could cooperate on shared interests abroad. However, actual results have been mixed. While the ideological component of Cold War antagonisms declined with the collapse of the Soviet regime, international competition between the United States and Russia remains a reality as each country pursues its own national interests. The bilateral relationship is characterized by periods of cooperation as well as periods of considerable competition and friction. The prospect of military conflict is much reduced in the post–Cold War era, but persistent challenges in US-Russian relations have hindered cooperation.

The gradual deterioration in US-Russian relations in the post-Soviet period is due in part to the emergence of an increasingly authoritarian and illiberal political regime in Moscow. It is also attributable to the emergence of significant and seemingly irreconcilable tension in the international community relating to Russia's international status. Four broad themes reflect the changing character of US-Russian relations in the post-Soviet period: (1) the gradual weakening of the integration of post-Soviet Russia into the West, including reversals in democratization; (2) the revival of Russia as a regional power and as an international actor increasingly able to assert its interests, potentially through the use of force; (3) the declining ability of the United States, despite its superpower status, to shape Russian behavior in the international and domestic spheres; and (4) the tendency of the United States to pursue its national security interests in a unilateral manner, viewed in Moscow as an attempt to undermine Russian security, sometimes even in Russia's own backyard.

The Yeltsin Era

The leadership of Boris Yeltsin was prominent in the collapse of the Soviet Union and in the course of US-Russian relations in the first post-Soviet decade. Yeltsin was a product of the Soviet communist system, having climbed the ladder of the Soviet bureaucracy from provincial party leader to Politburo member in Moscow. In 1991, after a break with Gorbachev and the Communist Party over the pace and nature of Soviet reform, Yeltsin was elected president of the Russian Soviet Federated Socialist Republic, at that time one of the constituent republics of the Soviet Union. That position gave him enormous legitimacy and political power, with which he emerged from the demise of the Soviet Union as the head of the newly born Russian Federation.

In the immediate post-Soviet period, Washington viewed support of Boris Yeltsin, the first president of the new Russian state, as the most effective way to promote US interests and its values.[13] On almost all foreign policy issues of importance to the United States, Yeltsin backed Washington's initiatives or at least did not obstruct them. Yeltsin's positions reflected his tacit recognition of the overwhelming power of the United States and the relative weakness of the new Russian state. Debate continues over whether Yeltsin was truly a liberal democrat and market capitalist, or whether he was rather a political opportunist who declared fealty to these ideals to garner power and the economic and political support from the West that he needed for his own survival. Episodes throughout Yeltsin's turbulent presidency support both explanations.

One of Yeltsin's most significant contributions to US interests was his rejection of Russian and Soviet imperial policies. He did not seek to block the states of Eastern and Central Europe as they reoriented their foreign policies toward the West, and he permitted the new states of the former Soviet Union to establish their independence and pursue their own paths of political development. These policies may have reflected Russia's weak geopolitical and economic situation after the Soviet collapse, but they also may have been driven by Yeltsin's genuine political ideals: if the first Russian president had been an ultra-nationalist or an unreformed communist, developments in Eastern Europe and the post-Soviet space might have looked very different.[14]

Dramatic progress occurred in arms control and disarmament during Yeltsin's administration. International concern about the safety and security of the former Soviet nuclear stockpile, plus cost considerations, prompted a 1992 decision by the individual nuclear powers among the new post-Soviet states—Russia, Belarus, Kazakhstan, and Ukraine—to have Russia retain centralized command and control over the vast former Soviet arsenal. Encouragement and financial aid came from the United States, particularly through the Nunn-Lugar Cooperative Threat Reduction (CTR) programs (see also chapter 17 on CTR and arms control). The four nuclear successor states signed a protocol in Lisbon in May 1992 assuming the responsibilities of the defunct Soviet Union under the 1991 Strategic Arms Reduction Treaty (START). Belarus, Kazakhstan, and Ukraine further committed themselves to joining the Nuclear Nonproliferation Treaty (NPT) as non–nuclear weapon states, although Ukraine refused to return its Soviet-era nuclear weapons to Russia until it received assurances of respect for its sovereignty and territorial integrity from Moscow. In the 1994 Budapest Memorandums on Security Assurances, the leaders of Ukraine, Russia, the United States, and Great Britain committed to respecting Ukraine's independence, its sovereignty, and its post-1991 borders.[15] Some prominent scholars questioned the wisdom of Ukraine's voluntary loss of a nuclear deterrent capability at the time, but Kiev ultimately handed over all nuclear weapons on its territory.[16]

The denuclearization of Russia's neighbors was completed with the removal of the last Russian SS-25 intercontinental ballistic missiles (ICBMs) from Belarus on June 30, 1997. Driven by concerns over the possible theft of nuclear materials and their sale to terrorists, CTR programs had improved employment opportunities and working conditions for former Soviet nuclear scientists and had provided more secure storage facilities for Russian nuclear materials. Many in both countries saw CTR as one of the most significant and successful cases of US-Russian security cooperation in the post-Soviet era. However, CTR cooperation came to an end in 2013 after a 2012 announcement by the Russian government that it was terminating its participation in the program, a move symptomatic of the chill then emerging in US-Russian relations.[17]

Fears about smuggling, mishaps, and accidental launches of nuclear weapons stimulated and sustained interest in Moscow and Washington in continued strategic arms reduction. START, signed by President George H. W. Bush and President Gorbachev in 1991, put a cap on the number of nuclear delivery systems held by both sides and required both parties to reduce the number of nuclear warheads in their arsenals from existing levels of 10,000 to 12,000 to no more than 6,000 each.[18] START II, signed by President George H. W. Bush and President Yeltsin in January

1993, reduced the number of deployed nuclear warheads even further. START II was ratified by the US Senate in 1997 and by the Russian Duma in 2000, after several years of delay stemming from Russian opposition to the expansion of the North Atlantic Treaty Organization (NATO) and to NATO's military campaign in Kosovo. In 2001, Russia suspended its adherence to START II following the declaration of US withdrawal from the Anti-Ballistic Missile (ABM) Treaty of 1972. However, this was a relatively minor setback to the arms control agenda; START II was soon superseded by the Strategic Offensive Reductions Treaty (SORT, signed May 2002) and then by the New START agreement (signed April 2010).[19]

The high tide of US-Russian cooperation occurred in 1997. Yeltsin insisted on compensation for Washington's plans to expand NATO into Eastern and Central Europe. Clinton offered the Russian president, then facing rising political opposition at home, significant inducements that brought Russia closer to the West: Russia became a partner in the prestigious annual Group of Seven (G7) summits (thereafter the G8). The United States also promised to press for Russia's inclusion in important international institutions such as the World Trade Organization (WTO) and the Organization for Economic Cooperation and Development (OECD). In May 1997, Russia and NATO signed the NATO-Russia Founding Act in Paris, establishing a formal mechanism to promote cooperation and to the "maximum extent possible . . . joint decisions and joint action with respect to security issues of common concern."[20]

The United States had thrown its support to Yeltsin largely because he was—at least initially—an advocate of Russian democratization. Russian progress toward democracy could advance American values and strengthen American security interests according to the widely held view that democracies do not fight wars with each other.[21] However, Russia drifted from the democratic ideal. Throughout the Yeltsin era, Russia struggled to define its post-Soviet and post-empire national identity. It is telling that, for the first post-Soviet decade, Russia's new national anthem lacked lyrics, a reflection of the absence of national consensus on Russia's identity.[22]

The problematic nature of Russia's political identity and its failure of democratization are due in large part to the political, economic, and social upheavals that convulsed Russia in the first decade of independence. Yeltsin's wrenching economic program of marketization and privatization impoverished many Russians, while a small group of oligarchs came to control much of Russia's national wealth.[23] As Russia descended further into economic and political instability and corruption in the 1990s, Yeltsin became increasingly unpopular. Undemocratic strands became more prominent in his leadership as he struggled to maintain control of the Russian political system.

By the close of the twentieth century, both Russia's elites and its masses widely believed that the West, particularly the United States, opposed vital Russian interests. This perspective was fueled by accumulated grievances against the West and by Russian fears of international isolation and even encirclement. Against the backdrop of Russia's weakness and America's unchallenged global power, Russian elites (liberal and otherwise) criticized the United States for its early advocacy of rapid Russian marketization and privatization, as well as for supporting Yeltsin despite the rampant corruption and ineffectiveness of his regime.

The expansion of NATO during the 1990s and NATO's 1999 military campaign in support of the Kosovar Albanians against Serbia, a traditional Russian ally, were especially contentious issues.[24] Both were stark reminders that Russia was simply too weak to object effectively to Western policies. This was particularly painful for Russia's political and military elites, many of whom had only recently stood at the helm of Soviet power. Believing that the West had pledged at the end of the Cold War not to expand NATO, Russians were understandably concerned for their security as Poland, the Czech Republic, and Hungary—states that had previously provided a buffer between the Soviet Union and the West—became members of one of the most powerful alliances in history. Even committed Russian democrats increasingly believed that the United States was behaving like a "rogue hegemon," exploiting Russia's weakness, challenging its core national interests, and undermining the Russian state as a viable institution.[25] By the late 1990s Yeltsin, now deeply unpopular, was unable to insulate Russian foreign policy from growing nationalism. A decade of economic, political, and social instability had generated mass demand for a strong leader who could restore order to Russia and return the country to the ranks of the world's great powers.

The Rise of Putin and Competitive Authoritarianism

With Yeltsin's abrupt resignation on December 31, 1999, Prime Minister Vladimir Putin, a former lieutenant colonel in the Committee for State Security (KGB), was elevated to acting president. Putin was elected president the following March. If Russian democratization under Yeltsin had suffered from mismanagement and frequent neglect, under Putin it began to be subjected to direct assault.

Under Yeltsin most Russian elites had—at least in principle—accepted the concepts of elections, markets, and private property. However, the most influential elites—the oligarchs—had done much to corrupt these values, especially by pressuring the Russian state to favor their private interests. Putin quickly moved to diminish the power of the oligarchs. In effect, he transferred their political influence to the *siloviki*, top state officials with backgrounds in the Interior Ministry, the military, and the Federal Security Service (FSB, the successor to the KGB). These "uniformed bureaucrats" now formed a "militocracy" that shared Putin's desire to create a strong Russian state and to revive Russian patriotism.[26] Largely hostile to political pluralism and highly vigilant against domestic and external enemies (real or imagined), this group reflected and supported Putin's worldview. Putin clamped down on the media and worked to control and contain Russian civil and political institutions. He restricted the activities of nongovernmental organizations. After the politicized arrest in October 2003 of the oil tycoon Mikhail Khodorkovsky, charged with economic crimes, even the once-powerful Russian oligarchs retreated from any oppositional role in politics.[27]

Political scientists Steven Levitsky and Lucan Way define competitive authoritarian regimes as

> civilian regimes in which formal democratic institutions exist and are widely viewed as the primary means of gaining power, but in which incumbents' abuse of the state places them at a significant advantage vis-à-vis their opponents. Such regimes are competitive in that opposition parties use democratic institutions to contest seriously for power, but they are not democratic because the playing field is heavily skewed in favor of incumbents. Competition is thus real but unfair.[28]

This is an apt description of Russian politics during the first decade of Putin's rule.

Despite Putin's assault on the political freedoms of the Yeltsin period, the Kremlin's efforts to restore the power of the Russian state, internally and externally, buoyed his popularity among Russian elites and the mass public.[29] Many Russians regretted the collapse of the Soviet Union, both for the loss of domestic economic and political stability and for the loss of Russia's global power and prestige. When asked in a survey after the American-led invasion of Iraq in 2003—which Russia vocally but unsuccessfully opposed—how they wanted Russia to be perceived by other nations, 48 percent of survey respondents said "mighty, unbeatable, indestructible, a great world power." Only 3 percent of the respondents said that they wanted Russia to be viewed as "peace-loving and friendly," and only 1 percent said "law-abiding and democratic."[30] Although other surveys reveal strong support for democratic values among most Russians, in practice democratization in Russia has suffered significant setbacks under Putin, in part because of the acquiescence of much of Russian society.[31]

Public acquiescence can be primarily attributed to the significant economic recovery that took place during Putin's presidency from 2000 to 2008. While most external experts attribute this to rising oil prices rather than to Putin's economic policies, Putin received the credit domestically.[32] After the tumultuous decade under Yeltsin, many citizens sought basic order, stability, and predictability in their lives. Putin delivered these outcomes, albeit with increased restrictions on political choice, rights, and freedoms.

Putin's immense popularity among ordinary Russians has also been shaped by increased Russian nationalism. Russian nationalism, a restoration of Russia's great-power status internationally, the reassertion of Russian interests in its former imperial lands, and social conservatism are the basis of the Kremlin's vision of Russian identity in the twenty-first century. This is fostered by the Kremlin-controlled media, which asserts that the government is protecting Russia from Western—particularly American—encirclement and attempts at regime change. Putin's vision of Russia's "national idea" became apparent during his first two terms, from 2000 to 2008, and it intensified following his return to the presidency in 2012.

The Crisis in Chechnya. Putin's approach to the crisis in Chechnya, which reflected his efforts to rebuild the power of the Russian state, was the primary source of his initial popularity and authority.[33] The secessionist movement in Chechnya, and Moscow's brutal and ineffective efforts to reign it in during the 1990s, had sharpened Russia's sense of insecurity and even sparked fears of the collapse of the newborn Russian state. Under Yeltsin, the weakness of the Russian state had been on full display during the disastrous Russian-Chechen war of 1994–1996. Well-organized and highly motivated Chechen rebels halted the ill-prepared conscripts of the Russian Army and eventually forced a humiliating Russian withdrawal from Chechen soil. Although the end of the conflict reflected a Chechen victory in some ways, the war left Chechnya in ruins, wracked by violent feuds among rival warlords, the collapse of social order, and the rise of Islamic radicalism and terrorism.[34]

Convinced that Russia was merely a "paper tiger" after its defeat in Afghanistan and the humiliation of the first Chechen War, Chechen radicals believed that a second war could destroy the political center in Chechen politics and propel them to power at the head of an independent trans-Caucasus Islamic state. To this end, Chechen militants undertook deadly bombings of residential buildings in Moscow and an armed incursion into neighboring Dagestan. These provocations prompted Moscow to launch the second Russian-Chechen War in 1999, during Putin's brief tenure as Yeltsin's prime minister.[35] This time Russian forces, better organized and facing a divided Chechen opposition, scored significant successes in the field, eventually pacifying most of the countryside. Although Chechen separatists committed several spectacular and brutal acts of terrorism during the early 2000s, by 2006 many radicals had been killed or captured or had accepted amnesty. At this point, Moscow installed an oppressive and corrupt government in Chechnya, led by Ramzan Kadyrov, the leader of a prominent and rapacious Chechen militia.[36]

The Kremlin finally claimed victory in Chechnya in 2007, but radical elements continued to spread to neighboring regions, including Ingushetia, North Ossetia, and Dagestan. These regions have served as launching points for terrorist attacks in Russia, particularly in its southern areas.[37] The terrorist attacks, particularly the tragic 2004 hostage crisis at a school in Beslan, North Ossetia, served as a justification for institutional changes in Russia that have further undermined democracy and reinforced Putin's centralized authority.[38] Due primarily to its competing foreign policy priorities, the United States has been unwilling to level consistent or significant criticism against the Kremlin for the extreme violations of Chechen human rights by Russian security forces and their proxies.

Russian Foreign Policy after 9/11. After the tragic events of September 11, 2001, and despite some worsening of relations as the 1990s drew to a close, the United States and Russia once again seemed to be on a path toward cooperation.[39] Putin was the first foreign leader to contact President George W. Bush after the terrorist attacks on US soil. He offered support for the US invasion of Afghanistan and the establishment of US bases in former Soviet Central Asia. In exchange, Russia expected greater deference to its interests in the former Soviet space, particularly a recognition that the region was within Russia's legitimate sphere of influence. Furthermore, Moscow expected that its support of the United States after 9/11 would ensure the preservation of the ABM Treaty, which Russia saw as the cornerstone of strategic stability, but which the George W. Bush administration viewed with increasing skepticism.[40] Putin also hoped to gain US assurances that

NATO expansion would not continue eastward, particularly not to the Baltic states of Estonia, Latvia, and Lithuania, or to Ukraine or Georgia.

Moscow provided significant assistance to the United States and to the Afghan Northern Alliance in defeating the Taliban in Afghanistan, but Washington's response to Putin's overtures fell far short of the full partnership sought by the Kremlin. Warming relations between Moscow and Washington began to cool significantly when George W. Bush decided, in December 2001, to pull out of the ABM treaty and pursue missile defense.[41] In 2007, Washington announced plans to field a limited ABM system, including a radar installation and ten interceptor missiles, in Poland and the Czech Republic. Although Washington declared that the system was intended to defend Europe against the missiles of a "rogue" state, such as Iran or North Korea, the Kremlin strongly condemned the proposal and warned that, as a consequence, Russia might again target Europe with its nuclear arsenal. The proposed systems were significantly reduced and revised by President Barack Obama in 2009, but ongoing US efforts to deploy missile defense systems in Eurasia continued to be a major source of friction between the United States and Russia.

Russia's opposition to American foreign policy goals gradually crystalized during the run-up to the second Iraq War. In 2002, Russia joined Germany and France in opposing Washington's efforts to obtain support from the United Nations for an invasion of Iraq.[42] Moscow's opposition was based on two factors. The first was Putin's concern that the unilateralism of the George W. Bush administration, within the context of American unipolarity and in the absence of a strategic partnership with the United States, was undercutting efforts to restore Russia's status as a great power. The second factor was Moscow's long-standing relationship with Baghdad. Iraq had been a Soviet client during the Cold War; the resounding defeat of Saddam Hussein's Soviet-equipped army in 1991 was viewed as a humiliation by the Soviet political elite and the leadership of the Red Army. Moscow maintained close ties with Baghdad in the post-Soviet period, largely due to economic motivations, particularly arms sales. In the 2003 crisis over Iraq, Russia sought to support its old client and to resist the expansion of US power in the Middle East.

In 2004 Russia suffered another blow to its national security interests, when Estonia, Latvia, Lithuania, Bulgaria, Romania, Slovakia, and Slovenia were admitted into NATO. Although NATO officials maintained that the latest round of enlargement did not threaten Russian security, the incorporation of the Baltic states, which had been constituent republics of the Soviet Union from 1940 to 1991, brought the alliance to Russia's doorstep. It also left open the possibility of further NATO expansion into Ukraine and Georgia, a development that would be viewed by Moscow as a grave threat to Russian national security.[43]

The Near Abroad: The "Color Revolutions." Other developments also complicated Russia's relationship with its "near abroad." Even under Yeltsin, Russian elites had assumed that the former Soviet space would be part of Russia's sphere of interest. This assumption was based on the history of Russian imperialism in Eurasia and the long-standing socioeconomic and cultural ties between Russia and the people of the new post-Soviet states. That up to twenty-five million ethnic Russians resided in the near abroad reinforced Russia's strong interest in the region.

Russia was far weaker than the United States, but its economic and military strength overshadowed other post-Soviet countries, and so it could continue to view itself as the dominant regional power. This was challenged by the enlargement of NATO, by the establishment of American bases in Central Asia after 9/11, and, most importantly, by an unexpected wave of mass uprisings and regime change. Georgia had its "Rose Revolution" of 2003, Ukraine the "Orange Revolution" of 2004, and Kyrgyzstan the "Tulip Revolution" of 2005.[44] In Georgia and Ukraine, electoral fraud by the semi-authoritarian regimes had mobilized broad-based opposition. Events there were of particular concern because of their proximity to Russia, Russia's unsuccessful efforts to tilt the elections, the pro-Western tenor of the political upheavals, and Western support for democratic forces in those countries. This support included direct aid by Western governments to local actors in civil society, as well as the involvement of Western nongovernmental organizations (NGOs) in civic and political education.[45]

After the "color revolutions," Ukraine, Georgia, and Kyrgyzstan struggled to establish stable democracies committed to the rule of law. Russia's elites nevertheless viewed with concern the threat posed by mass movements supported by Western entities. The active involvement of Western NGOs and governments in encouraging and supporting the overthrow of pro-Russian leaders in former Soviet states—viewed by Moscow as firmly within Russia's sphere of influence—were seen as direct threats to Russia's interests and another example of American-led encirclement.

Fearing the spread of democratic contagion to Russia itself, the Kremlin characterized the political upheavals as meddling by an unsavory alliance of domestic opposition groups and foreign interests seeking to destabilize the region. On this basis, Moscow denounced the Organization for Security and Cooperation in Europe (OSCE), which had uncovered and publicized electoral fraud in the pivotal elections in Ukraine. Within Russia, the Kremlin placed more stringent controls on the media, civic organizations, NGOs, and opposition groups and parties. These authoritarian measures prompted Western criticism, leading to further mutual recriminations.

Russia's Authoritarian Shift. Having seen pro-Russian incumbents fall at the hands of popular protest movements in the "color revolutions," Putin left nothing to chance as Russia entered the 2007–2008 electoral cycle.[46] Although he was barred from running for a third consecutive term by the Russian constitution, Putin chose his successor, Dmitri Medvedev, for the presidency, while continuing to exercise influence as the prime minister. The 2007 parliamentary elections and 2008 presidential elections were characterized by sophisticated electoral fraud, despite high levels of popular support for both leaders, who would have won anyway.[47]

Putin's carefully orchestrated transition—including increased restrictions on the media and popular protest—was carried off relatively smoothly. In 2011–2012, Medvedev declined to seek reelection, making way for Putin to return to the presidency. This confirmed what many had suspected, that Russia's political future had been decided behind closed doors long before.

Such manipulation provoked a significant mass reaction after the fraudulent 2011 parliamentary elections.[48] In 2012, parties loyal to the Kremlin retained the majority, and Putin went on to win the presidency, but Moscow and other major cities were again shaken by mass protests. This brought a harsh crackdown on the organized political opposition, civil society, and individuals openly expressing dissent from Putin's rule. Several notable political dissidents, including anti-corruption blogger Alexei Navalny and the protest punk band Pussy Riot, were harassed, arrested, and jailed during Putin's second presidency.[49] If from the late 1990s to 2012 Russia might have been described as a competitive authoritarian regime, Russia thereafter became a case of consolidated authoritarianism, tightly controlled by Putin and his inner circle.

Russia Resurgent. In the first decade of the twenty-first century, Russia's increasing assertiveness in the near abroad and on the international stage became a mark of Putin's leadership.[50] On several occasions Russia utilized its position as the dominant supplier of natural gas to exact political and economic concessions from Ukraine, Belarus, and Georgia and to punish them for pursuing policies deemed contrary to Moscow's interests.[51] The so-called gas wars of the 2000s had significant implications beyond Russia's immediate neighborhood: much of Europe depends on Russian gas and on the pipelines crossing the post-Soviet countries, so many European countries found themselves in the middle of these disputes. Dependence on Russian natural gas has at times made the European Union (EU) reluctant to criticize or punish Russia for its domestic and international transgressions.

One particularly notable instance of Russia's increasing assertion of its interests in the post-Soviet region was its 2008 invasion of Georgia and its occupation of the separatist regions of South Ossetia and Abkhazia within Georgia. After the 2003 Rose Revolution brought a strongly pro-Western government to power under President Mikheil Saakashvili, relations between Russia and Georgia rapidly deteriorated. The separatist regions of South Ossetia and Abkhazia had long been outside the control of the Georgian government, looking instead to Russia for support. Following an ill-conceived Georgian military assault on South Ossetia in August 2008, Russian forces quickly invaded and occupied portions of Georgian territory.[52] The Russian justification for the invasion was based on the protection of Russian peacekeepers and the protection of civilians, many of whom held Russian passports.[53] Some observers viewed the invasion as an attempt to destabilize the Saakashvili government and to draw a line against any proposals of NATO membership for Georgia. Russia declined the separatists' request for annexation, but Russian troops remained in the occupied regions as "peacekeepers," which kept them outside of Georgian control. The conflict brought US-Russian relations to a new post–Cold War low. Western countries viewed Russia's actions as illegitimate aggression that violated the territorial integrity of a sovereign nation. Nonetheless, no significant long-term punishments were imposed on Moscow for its actions—a situation that reflected the limits of Western leverage over Russia in the former Soviet space.

Reset: A New US Approach to Relations with Russia. Following the 2008 US presidential election, President Barack Obama was determined to set a new course in American relations with Russia and move beyond historical and recent antagonisms in the bilateral relationship.[54] Obama's "reset policy" with Russia, announced in 2009, coincided with the presidency of the somewhat more liberal-minded Medvedev. The policy, although controversial, produced some important advances in US-Russian relations and a reduction in the tensions that had characterized the later years of the Putin-Bush relationship. One of the first achievements of the reset with Russia was the 2009 announcement that Russia would permit US troops and weapons to be transported through Russian airspace in transit to Afghanistan. This Northern Distribution Network, a key alternative to routes through Pakistan in support of the American war effort in Afghanistan, was a major breakthrough in the US bilateral relationship with Russia. The warmer relationship of Obama and Medvedev also paid off in the 2010 signing of the "New START" treaty in Prague. The treaty limited each country to 700 deployed nuclear-capable bombers and land-based and submarine-based nuclear missiles, 1,550 deployed warheads, and 800 additional deployed and nondeployed delivery vehicles (such as ICBMs, submarine-launched ballistic missiles, and heavy bombers).[55] The signing of the New START treaty may, in retrospect, have been the high point of US-Russia relations since 2008.

A chill returned to the relationship as Putin returned to the presidency in 2012, bringing back his authoritarian domestic tendencies and assertive foreign policy approach. The United States and Russia attempted cooperation on specific issues of mutual and global concern such as terrorism, drug trafficking, the civil war in Syria, and the perennial issue of Iranian nuclear weapons proliferation, but progress became increasingly difficult.

The underlying causes of this continual deterioration in US-Russian relations are complex and open to debate. The Obama administration pursued some American national security concerns in a more multilateral manner than the preceding administration of George W. Bush. However, Russian elites, and Putin himself, continued to perceive US actions as constituting active and deliberate efforts to undermine Russian security, especially within Russia's self-claimed sphere of influence in the former Soviet space. The ruling elite in Moscow may still view the world through the lens of bipolar competition with the United States: what is good for America is bad for Russia and vice versa. This view, although perhaps oversimplified, is accompanied by a resurgence in Russia of state-directed nationalism and the desire to restore Russia to great power status. Some observers have charged that Russia seeks nothing less than a restoration of the Soviet empire without the socialism. There is little doubt that Moscow has been seeking to defend and advance its primacy in the former Soviet region with an assertiveness not seen since the days of Brezhnev.

The Ukrainian Crisis. The deepest crisis between Russia and the United States since the Soviet invasion of Afghanistan in 1979 began unfolding in Ukraine in November 2013. Under enormous pressure from Moscow, the government of President Viktor Yanukovych (the former antagonist of pro-Western demonstrators during the Orange Revolution) suspended negotiations on an agreement that would have laid the political and economic groundwork for eventual Ukrainian membership in the European Union (EU).[56] Fearful that Ukraine was on the verge of escaping from its orbit, Russia offered Ukraine membership in the emerging Eurasian Economic Union, a customs union consisting of Russia, Belarus, and Kazakhstan, with additional former Soviet states expected to join in the future. The European Union and Russia saw their respective trade agreements with Ukraine as incompatible and mutually exclusive; the government in Kiev must choose one or the other.

Yanukovych's decision to stand with Russia was heavily influenced both by Moscow's pressure and by a desperate need for immediate Russian economic aid. The choice to forego closer relations with Europe in favor of tighter links with Russia upset a delicate balance between the population of the more nationalist-minded western portion of the country and the population in Eastern Ukraine that has traditionally identified more closely with Russia. Overlaid are complex regional divisions between ethnic Ukrainians and ethnic Russians and between Ukrainian speakers and those whose first language is Russian.[57]

Fearing that Yanukovych's turn toward Moscow marked a turn toward Ukrainian subordination to Russia, pro-European citizens—largely Ukrainian-speaking ethnic Ukrainians from Western and Central Ukraine—took to the streets in protest.[58] Over the next three months, protests of 50,000–800,000 disorganized and diverse participants were punctuated by episodes of violence as the Yanukovych government tried to regain control. In February 2014, the city of Kiev experienced its worst days of violence since World War II, with at least eighty-eight people killed over two days. On February 21, 2014, in a tacit concession that government forces were unable to bring the protests to a halt, Yanukovych reached an EU-mediated compromise with leaders of the opposition movement to deescalate the crisis.

However, any illusion of compromise or a return to normalcy was quickly dispelled on the next day when Yanukovych, who had been effectively abandoned by most of his political supporters, was forced to flee Ukraine. His residence and the presidential administration building were overtaken by opposition forces, and Yanukovych himself took refuge in Russia. An interim government in Kiev, consisting of leaders of the various opposition groups, attempted to consolidate control by stripping Yanukovych of his position, naming an interim president, and appointing other supporters to key government positions.

Not surprisingly, the crisis in Kiev was viewed far differently in Washington and in Moscow. The Obama administration hailed the ouster of Yanukovych as a step forward for Ukrainian democracy (despite the entirely undemocratic means by which he lost power) and praised the opportunity for Ukraine to return to its path toward the West. The Kremlin, on the other hand, saw this as yet another instance of Western interference in a region considered to be of vital strategic interest to Russia. The fall of Yanukovych—and the possibility that Ukraine had been lost to the West for good—was seen in Moscow as a dire threat to Russia's security and interests.[59]

The crisis then entered a new phase of interstate conflict. On February 27–28, well-armed pro-Russian fighters began seizing key buildings in Crimea, a peninsula on the Black Sea in Southern Ukraine. Crimea had been part of Russia until Nikita Khrushchev made a "gift" of the region to Ukraine in 1954. It has continued to serve as the base of the Russian Navy's Black Sea Fleet—a situation that has been a long-standing point of friction in Russian-Ukrainian relations. Crimea is the only region of Ukraine with an absolute majority of ethnic Russians, many of whom retained Russian citizenship. Over the next several days, more Russian military forces, authorized by Putin, invaded and occupied Crimea.

There is disagreement over the motives behind Russia's occupation of Crimea, but it appears that it was simultaneously a reaction to the wider threat posed by Yanukovych's ouster, an opportunity to secure the Russian fleet's position in Crimea, and a chance to reverse the "gift" and rectify what many Russians saw as a mistake of the Soviet era. On March 16, 2014, Crimean separatists, under the watch of Russian troops, carried out a dubious referendum for secession with a ballot that offered no opportunity to vote in favor of remaining with Ukraine. After a purported 97 percent approval vote for secession, Crimea was officially absorbed into the Russian Federation two days later.[60]

Separatist movements soon spread across many of Ukraine's pro-Russian regions in the eastern part of the country, populated by many ethnic Russians who speak primarily Russian and have strong cross-border ties with Russia. Pro-Russian protests took place across a wide swath of eastern Ukraine and several attempts to occupy government buildings were successful. Significant violence took place between pro-Russian separatists, pro-government demonstrators, and Ukrainian military forces loyal to Kiev in the regions of Kharkiv, Odessa, Luhansk, and Donetsk. Moscow used the uprisings to undertake a strategy of hybrid warfare against Ukraine, exacerbating the conflict.[61] By supplying advisors, weapons, intelligence, and even active-duty Russian military personnel to the separatist movements, Moscow's intervention has kept the conflict burning despite its repeated pledges to support ceasefires. Russia's apparent unwillingness to commit fully to achieving a peaceful political solution to the conflict in Ukraine has caused Washington to distrust Moscow's motives elsewhere in the post-Soviet region and beyond.

The United States has been unable to compel Russia to reverse its policies in Ukraine. Having decided against large-scale direct military assistance lest it escalate the conflict, the United States and the European Union (along with several other countries) have primarily sought to use instruments of economic power to press Russia to end the conflict in Ukraine and reverse its occupation of Crimea.

These sanctions have targeted individuals and private and government entities that facilitated, contributed to, or otherwise provided material support of Russian military activities in Ukraine. Punitive measures include Russia's expulsion from the G8 forum, travel bans for implicated officials, trade restrictions on military goods and equipment used in the oil industry, and asset freezes. Sweeping restrictions on Russia's finance, energy, and defense industries effectively cut off many Russian enterprises from access to global financial networks and much-needed foreign capital. These sanctions, along with a dramatic decline in the price of oil and the weak ruble, plunged Russia into a severe recession that, since 2013, has eroded the Putin regime's ability to deliver promised economic prosperity. Although regime collapse as a result is far from likely today, there is a risk that the regime will turn to more provocative means of shoring up its public support and legitimacy if the economy does not improve soon.

By some standards, Western sanctions against Russia and associated financial weapons have been a failure in that they have not compelled Russia to end its support of rebels in Eastern Ukraine, nor have they forced Russia to withdraw from Crimea and return the peninsula to Ukrainian control. However, sanctions can also have an important deterrent effect: when the threat of economic pain has been credibly demonstrated by initial sanctions, the target country may refrain from further provocations in order to avoid additional painful sanctions. In more concrete terms, Russia may have been deterred from further aggression in Ukraine by the threat of additional punitive measures. While there is no way to determine whether Russia would have behaved more aggressively in the absence of sanctions, Russian officials' surprise both at the resolve of the West in applying and maintaining sanctions and at the economic pain they caused suggests that the measures may have averted further Russian belligerence in Ukraine (see chapter 12 on the use of sanctions more generally).

Ukraine elected a new pro-Western president, Petro Poroshenko, in May 2014, but immense challenges to stabilizing the country persist. Ukraine remains deeply divided by language, nationality, and culture; plagued by a domestic economic crisis; hampered by deep systemic corruption; pulled in opposite directions by powerful external actors; and unlikely to be reunified territorially or socially in the near future. The military conflict in Ukraine simmers as a series of cease-fires are broken by violations on both sides. This will continue to complicate relations between the United States and Russia and is likely to hinder their cooperation on other interests.

Russian Military Intervention in Syria. In September 2015, Vladimir Putin once again took the world by surprise with Russia's military intervention in the Syrian civil war. Russia's intervention, consisting mostly of airstrikes and missile strikes, was ostensibly intended to counter militant Islamic groups such as the Islamic State in Iraq and the Levant (ISIL) and the al-Nusra Front.[62] However, Russia's strikes were directed more broadly at the range of forces opposed to Syrian President Bashar al-Assad, Moscow's last ally in the Middle East. Some armed groups targeted by Russian forces had been trained and supplied by the United States in a US attempt to support moderate opposition groups fighting Assad's repressive regime. Such strikes, along with the Turkish downing of a Russian jet over Turkey, significantly escalated the tension between the United States and Russia.[63]

American objectives in Syria have been twofold: defeating ISIL and forcing Assad to relinquish power, in order to pave the way for free elections in Syria. Russia's objectives have been harder to discern. Moscow has a stake in the global struggle against terrorism: the North Caucasus region (including the regions of Chechnya, Ingushetia, and Dagestan) have long been fertile recruiting grounds for outside extremist groups as well as launching pads for terrorist attacks in Russia. Thus Russia, too, has an interest in seeing ISIL defeated.

Yet most of Russia's airstrikes were directed not against ISIL targets, but rather against more moderate opposition forces that had been fighting Assad since 2011. This suggests that Russia sought to ensure that its ally, Assad, regained political and military control over the country. By such a metric, the Russian intervention was largely successful, in that it stabilized and shored up Assad's position and that of the forces loyal to him. Russia's intervention did not terminate the civil war in Assad's favor, but it put the dictator back on more solid footing.

Russia's intervention also guaranteed Moscow a strong influence over the future course of the Syrian conflict and its eventual settlement. After ending direct military missions in Syria in February 2016, Russia remains a central player in the multilateral negotiations to bring the civil war to an end. Putin proved adept at seizing an opportunity to fulfill several core national security interests at once. While Russia's intervention in Syria targeted the terrorist threat posed by ISIL, it also ensured the survival of Russia's only ally in the Middle East, and the preservation of the only Russian naval base outside the former Soviet Union, at Tartus in Syria. It also returned Moscow to a role as a significant power broker in the Middle East for the first time since Soviet influence in the region began eroding in the early 1970s. It succeeded in constraining unilateral US pursuit of its interests, a key objective of Putin's "multipolar" foreign policy doctrine. Although Russia's intervention in Syria is not likely a harbinger of further military intervention or expansion around the globe, it highlights Moscow's ability and willingness to balance against US interests in key regions and conflicts.

Russian Efforts to Undermine the Political Institutions of the West. According to Russia experts Paul Stronski and Richard Sokolsky, "Having long embraced the narrative that the West was seeking to weaken and remove the Russian regime, the Kremlin evidently decided that what goes around comes around."[64] In a campaign that has escalated since the Ukrainian crisis in 2014, Russian targets have included the European Union and the North Atlantic Treaty Organization and their member states. More specifically, using economic, political, and informational tools, Russia has sought to foster political divisions and to further Russian interests with operations against and within at least the following countries: the former Soviet Baltic states of Lithuania, Latvia, and Estonia; the Netherlands; Spain; Germany; France; the United Kingdom; and the United States.[65] As just two examples, in an effort to sow division within a German society already split over the issue of refugee flows into the country, Russia provided support to a far-right political party in Germany's 2017 federal elections and, to foster fear of migrants, Russian media and Russian Foreign Minister Sergey Lavrov disseminated "a false story about a Russian-German girl abducted by Syrian refugees."[66] In France, Putin and Russian information operatives supported anti-European and far-fight candidate Marine Le Pen in France's 2017 presidential election.[67]

From the perspective of American national security, the most significant aspect of this Russian campaign has been Russia's interference in the US presidential election of 2016. According to a January 2017 assessment by the US intelligence community, as an expression of Moscow's long-held desire to undermine the "US-led liberal democratic order . . . Russian President Vladimir Putin ordered an influence campaign in 2016 aimed at the US presidential election. Russia's goals were to undermine public faith in the US democratic process, denigrate Secretary [Hillary] Clinton, and harm her electability and potential presidency. We further assess Putin and the Russian Government developed a clear preference for President-elect [Donald] Trump."[68] In a finding that is perhaps at least as disconcerting, the report observes that "Moscow will apply lessons learned from its Putin-ordered campaign aimed at the US presidential election to future influence efforts worldwide, including against US allies and their election processes."[69]

While it is not clear that Russian efforts in 2016 actually affected the outcome of the election, they clearly succeeded in fostering divisions within the US political system. Concerned about the integrity of US elections, both houses of Congress launched investigations into Russian election meddling. The investigation in the House of Representatives was particularly plagued by partisan acrimony over its proceedings and findings. Moreover, the US Justice Department appointed a former director of the Federal Bureau of Investigation, Robert S. Mueller III, as a special prosecutor to look into "any links and/or coordination between the Russian government and inviduals associated with the campaign of President Donald Trump."[70] By February 2018, the Mueller team had leveled criminal charges against nineteen individuals, to include Trump's first national security advisor, Michael Flynn, and his former campaign chairman, Paul Manafort.[71] In addition to the potential impact of Russian actions on US elections, Russian interference in 2016 has created a specter of doubt concerning US policy toward Russia. Trump administration policies toward Russia have been consistently viewed through a partisan lens, further exacerbating political divisions among Americans.

Future Challenges in US-Russian Relations

Areas of concern in US-Russian relations and American national security are revealed by the recent crises in Ukraine and Syria, as well as Russian efforts to undermine the unity and internal political stability of Western liberal democracies. Unfortunately, the United States has yet to find a compelling way to influence

Russia's actions in the international sphere. Despite repeated warnings, pleas, and increasingly painful economic sanctions imposed by the United States and the European Union, Russia has been undeterred from pursuing its interests in Ukraine and elsewhere. Any leverage over Russia is further diluted by the fact that the West depends on Russia for many things, including Russian energy exports, as well as its political and diplomatic support in resolving conflicts with Syria, Iran, and North Korea. Although the United States has been able to operate freely for much of the post–Cold War era, the limits to American influence are laid bare when US actions bump up against the core national security interests of other great powers.

Russia's actions in the post–Cold War period can be seen as a reaction to what it sees as the erosion of its security caused by US actions (whether intentional or not), including NATO expansion into Eastern Europe and then the Baltics; development of US ballistic missile defenses; support of pro-Western opposition forces in the "color revolutions" of Georgia, Ukraine, and Kyrgyzstan; US actions against Moscow's allies in Iraq, Libya, and Syria; and an American unwillingness to recognize the former Soviet region as Russia's special sphere of influence. These episodes—and Moscow's reactions to them—serve as a reminder that all great powers have their own interests and that they will defend them—sometimes with force—when they are threatened.[72]

The Ukrainian crisis has confirmed that the era of meaningful post–Cold War cooperation between the United States and Russia is over. Although the bilateral relationship has, all along, been plagued by tensions and disputes, key areas of mutual interest in nonproliferation, arms control, counterterrorism, preventing drug trafficking, and economic integration showed some progress despite flare-ups elsewhere in the relationship. However, the mutual animosity and mistrust arising from events in Ukraine suggest that, absent a major common threat, Russia and the United States may find little common ground in coming years.

Syria is a striking example of the challenges facing US-Russian rapprochement and cooperation even in the face of a common threat. While the United States and Russia share an interest in ending the Syrian civil war, restoring political stability, and eliminating the threat posed by ISIL, they differ sharply on how best to do so. Both countries have intervened militarily in Syria, but their disagreements and distrust prevent them from operating in a coordinated fashion.

Russia may instead turn to other partners who are less likely to threaten Russian interests and to criticize Russian policy. Of particular importance will be Russia's relationship with China, which it began to strengthen long before the current nadir in relations between Russia and the West, and can be expected to pursue further in the coming years.[73] However, while Russia and China have a shared goal of curbing US global influence, "The brakes on closer bilateral cooperation against U.S. interests involve the growing asymmetry between China and Russia in terms of economic and military power and influence, increasingly relegating Russia to the role of a junior partner—a status causing concern in Moscow."[74]

As illustrated by its efforts to sow division within and among the Western democracies that have provided key support to the liberal international order,

Moscow will continue to try to achieve Putin's vision for a multipolar world.[75] The multipolar world is not based on cooperative relationships mediated through international institutions; rather, it is one in which each great power has its sphere of influence within which it can pursue its national interests without interference from outside powers. Putin's multipolar world is one in which the United States is constrained from taking the unilateral actions around the globe that Russians believe have characterized American foreign policy since 1991. Putin's vision is at odds with the national security strategy of the United States, and it is sure to generate friction between the two countries in the coming years.

Discussion Questions

1. What are America's national security interests in the post-Soviet region?
2. Should the United States concede to Russia its own version of the Monroe Doctrine with regard to former Soviet countries? Why, or why not?
3. Should NATO grant membership to Georgia or Ukraine? What are the arguments for and against such membership?
4. How can the United States enhance its influence in Eastern Europe, the South Caucasus, Central Asia, and elsewhere in the former Soviet space? What responses should the United States anticipate from Russia?
5. What are the most effective US instruments for supporting stability in the former Soviet space?
6. To what extent—and with what instruments—should the United States promote democratization in the post-Soviet region?
7. Assess the prospects for meaningful cooperation between Russia and the United States in the coming decade. What are the most significant challenges to cooperation, and how might they be overcome?
8. How should the United States, and other liberal democracies, respond to Russia's efforts to interfere in their domestic political affairs?
9. How might the United States counter malicious Russian actions in cyberspace? What are the advantages and risks associated with these actions?
10. In 1947, George Kennan argued that the Soviet system was plagued by internal contradictions that might undercut its long-term pursuit of power. Is this also true of contemporary Russia? What domestic political, economic, and social challenges are present in the Russian system today?

Recommended Reading

Åslund, Anders, and Michael McFaul, eds. *Revolution in Orange: The Origins of Ukraine's Democratic Breakthrough*. Washington, DC: Carnegie Endowment for International Peace, 2006.

Asmus, Ronald D. *A Little War That Shook the World: Georgia, Russia, and the Future of the West*. New York: Palgrave Macmillan, 2010.

Beissinger, Mark R. *Nationalist Mobilization and the Collapse of the Soviet State*. Cambridge: Cambridge University Press, 2002.

Cornell, Svante E., and S. Frederick Starr, eds. *The Guns of August 2008*. Armonk, NY: M. E. Sharpe, 2009.

Fish, M. Steven. *Democracy Derailed in Russia: The Failure of Open Politics.* New York: Cambridge University Press, 2005.
Gaddis, John Lewis. *We Now Know: Rethinking Cold War History.* Oxford: Oxford University Press, 1997.
Galeotti, Mark. *Russia's Wars in Chechnya, 1994–2009.* Oxford: Osprey Publishing, 2014.
Gessen, Masha. *The Man without a Face: The Unlikely Rise of Vladimir Putin.* New York: Riverhead Books, 2012.
Kaplan, Lawrence S. *NATO Divided, NATO United: The Evolution of an Alliance.* Westport, CT: Praeger, 2004.
Kotkin, Stephen. *Armageddon Averted: Soviet Collapse, 1970–2000.* Oxford: Oxford University Press, 2008.
Mankoff, Jeffrey. *Russian Foreign Policy: The Return of Great Power Politics.* 2nd ed. Lanham, MD: Rowman & Littlefield, 2011.
McFaul, Michael. *Russia's Unfinished Revolution: Political Change from Gorbachev to Putin.* Ithaca, NY: Cornell University Press, 2002.
Nation, R. Craig. *Black Earth, Red Star: A History of Soviet Security Policy, 1917–1991.* Ithaca, NY: Cornell University Press, 1992.
Remnick, David. *Lenin's Tomb: The Last Days of the Soviet Empire.* New York: Vintage, 1994.
Sakwa, Richard. *Frontline Ukraine: Crisis in the Borderlands.* London, UK: I. B. Tauris, 2014.
Sherlock, Thomas. *Historical Narratives in the Soviet Union and Post-Soviet Russia.* New York: Palgrave-Macmillan, 2007.
Shevtsova, Lilia. *Putin's Russia.* Washington, DC: Carnegie Endowment for International Peace, 2010.
Stent, Angela E. *The Limits of Partnership: US-Russian Relations in the Twenty-First Century.* Princeton, NJ: Princeton University Press, 2015.
Suny, Ronald Grigor. *The Revenge of the Past: Nationalism, Revolution, and the Collapse of the Soviet Union.* Stanford, CA: Stanford University Press, 1993.
Tsygankov, Andrei P. *Russia's Foreign Policy: Change and Continuity in National Identity.* Lanham, MD: Rowman & Littlefield, 2013.
Wilson, Andrew. *Ukraine's Orange Revolution.* New Haven, CT: Yale University Press, 2006.

Recommended Internet Sources

Carnegie Moscow Center, www.carnegie.ru/en
Eurasia Daily Monitor, Jamestown Foundation, www.Jamestown.org/edm
Johnson's Russia List, Institute for European, Russian, and Eurasian Studies (IERES), George Washington University, http://russialist.org/
Moscow Times, www.themoscowtimes.com
"NATO-Russia Relations," NATO LibGuide, www.natolibguides.info/nato-russia
"NATO-Ukraine Relations," NATO LibGuide, www.natolibguides.info/nato-ukraine
The Program on New Approaches to Research and Security in Eurasia (PONARS Eurasia), Institute for European, Russian, and Eurasian Studies (IERES), George Washington University, www.ponarseurasia.org
Radio Free Europe/Radio Liberty, www.rferl.org
"Russia," Freedom House, https://freedomhouse.org/country/russia

"Russia," US Department of State,www.state.gov/p/eur/ci/rs
VoxUkraine, http://voxukraine.org/en/

Notes

1. John Lewis Gaddis, "The Long Peace: Elements of Stability in the Postwar International System," *International Security* 10, no. 4 (1986): 99–142. See also the classic argument by international relations theorist Kenneth Waltz on why a bipolar distribution of power between two superpowers should theoretically be a stable distribution without "hot" wars between the superpowers: Kenneth Waltz, "The Stability of a Bipolar World," *Daedalus* 93, no. 3 (1964): 881–909. The principles of nuclear deterrence and mutually assured destruction have also been offered as a compelling explanation for why the superpowers refrained from open warfare throughout the Cold War period. See Kenneth Waltz, "Nuclear Myths and Political Realities," *American Political Science Review* 84, no. 3 (1990): 731–45.

2. For an authoritative history of the Cold War and a useful bibliography, see John Lewis Gaddis, *We Now Know: Rethinking Cold War History* (Oxford: Oxford University Press, 1997).

3. Kenneth Waltz, *Theory of International Politics* (New York: McGraw-Hill, 1979).

4. Robert Jervis, "Cooperation under the Security Dilemma," *World Politics* 30, no. 2 (1978): 167–214.

5. "X" [George Kennan], "The Sources of Soviet Conduct." *Foreign Affairs* 25, no. 4 (1947): 566–82.

6. "X" [George Kennan], "The Sources of Soviet Conduct," 569.

7. "X" [George Kennan], "The Sources of Soviet Conduct," 575.

8. "X" [George Kennan], "The Sources of Soviet Conduct," 580.

9. An insightful account of the collapse of communist regimes in the Eastern Europe satellite states and their subsequent post-communist development is Gale Stokes, *The Walls Came Tumbling Down: Collapse and Rebirth in Eastern Europe* (Oxford: Oxford University Press, 2011). For an account of the Gorbachev era and Soviet collapse, see David Marples, *The Collapse of the Soviet Union, 1985–1991* (New York: Routledge, 2004). Analyses of the central role that nationalist movements played in the collapse of the Soviet Union can be found in Ronald Grigor Suny, *The Revenge of the Past: Nationalism, Revolution, and the Collapse of the Soviet Union* (Stanford, CA: Stanford University Press, 1993), and Mark Beissinger, *Nationalist Mobilization and the Collapse of the Soviet State* (Cambridge: Cambridge University Press, 2002). Broader looks at the collapse of the Soviet Union and its implications for Russia's post-Soviet political development are Stephen Kotkin, *Armageddon Averted: The Soviet Collapse, 1970–2000* (Oxford: Oxford University Press, 2001); and Michael McFaul, *Russia's Unfinished Revolution: Political Change from Gorbachev to Putin* (Ithaca, NY: Cornell University Press, 2001).

10. Janos Kornai, *The Socialist System: The Political Economy of Communism* (Oxford: Oxford University Press, 1992).

11. Suny, *The Revenge of the Past.*

12. Beissinger, *Nationalist Mobilization and the Collapse of the Soviet State.*

13. Comprehensive overviews of Russian foreign policy and US-Russian relations during the Yeltsin era include Celeste A. Wallander, ed., *The Sources of Russian Foreign Policy after the Cold War* (Boulder, CO: Westview Press, 1996); Michael Mandelbaum, *The New Russian Foreign Policy* (New York: Council on Foreign Relations, 1998); Ted Hopf,

ed., *Understandings of Russian Foreign Policy* (University Park, PA: Penn State Press, 1999); Michael McFaul, "Russia's Many Foreign Policies." *Demokratizatsiya* 7, no. 3 (1999): 393–412.

14. James M. Goldgeier and Michael McFaul, *Power and Purpose: U.S. Policy toward Russia after the Cold War* (Washington, DC: Brookings Institution Press, 2003), 362.

15. "Budapest Memorandums on Security Assurances, 1994," Council on Foreign Relations, December 5, 1994, http://www.cfr.org/arms-control-disarmament-and-nonproliferation/budapest-memorandums-security-assurances-1994/p32484.

16. John Mearsheimer, "The Case for a Ukrainian Nuclear Deterrent," *Foreign Affairs* 72, no. 3 (1993): 50–66. Such a warning was seen as prescient following Russia's 2014 annexation of the previously Ukrainian territory of Crimea. As their annexation occurred, the 1994 Budapest Memorandum offered little solace to the government in Kiev.

17. David M. Herszenhorn, "Russia Won't Renew Pact on Weapons With U.S.," *New York Times*, October 11, 2012, A10.

18. Nuclear Threat Intiative, "Treaty Between the United States of America and the Union of Soviet Socialist Republics on Strategic Offensive Reductions (START I)," October 26, 2011, http://www.nti.org/learn/treaties-and-regimes/treaties-between-united-states-america-and-union-soviet-socialist-republics-strategic-offensive-reductions-start-i-start-ii/.

19. Amy F. Woolf, "The New START Treaty: Central Limits and Key Provisions," Congressional Research Service, April 8, 2014, http://oai.dtic.mil/oai/oai?verb=getRecord&metadataPrefix=html&identifier=ADA601564.

20. For a discussion of the NATO-Russia Founding Act, see Goldgeier and McFaul, *Power and Purpose*, 208.

21. Bruce Russett, *Grasping the Democratic Peace: Principles for a Post–Cold War World* (Princeton, NJ: Princeton University Press, 1993).

22. Putin's 2000 decision to revive the Soviet anthem with new words, scrubbed of communist imagery, settled the question, at least on a symbolic level. J. Martin Daughtry, "Russia's New Anthem and the Negotiation of National Identity," *Ethnomusicology* 47, no. 1 (2003): 42–67.

23. See Cynthia Roberts and Thomas Sherlock, "Bringing the Russian State Back In: Explanations for the Derailed Transition to Market Democracy," *Comparative Politics* 31, no. 4 (1999): 477–98.

24. Oksana Antonenko, "Russia, NATO and European Security after Kosovo," *Survival* 41, no. 4 (1999): 124–44.

25. Alexei K. Pushkov, "Don't Isolate Us: A Russian View of NATO Expansion," *National Interest* 47 (Spring 1997): 58–63.

26. See Daniel Treisman, "Putin's Silovarchs," *Orbis* 51, no. 1 (2007): 141–53.

27. Richard Sakwa, *Putin and the Oligarch: The Khodorkovsky-Yukos Affair* (New York: I. B. Tauris, 2014).

28. Steven Levitsky and Lucan Way, *Competitive Authoritarianism: Hybrid Regimes after the Cold War* (Cambridge: Cambridge University Press, 2010), 5.

29. See Thomas Sherlock, *Historical Narratives in the Soviet Union and Post-Soviet Russia* (New York: Palgrave-Macmillan, 2007), chap. 7.

30. Richard Pipes, "Flight from Freedom," *Foreign Affairs* 83, no. 3 (2004): 14–15.

31. See Vladimir Petukhov and Andrei Ryabov, "Public Attitudes about Democracy," in *Between Dictatorship and Democracy*, ed. Michael McFaul, Nikolai Petrov, and Andrei Ryabov (Washington, DC: Carnegie Endowment for International Peace, 2004), 290–91. See also Robert Person, "Nothing to Gain But Your Chains," PhD dissertation (Yale University, 2010).

32. Michael McFaul and Kathryn Stoner-Weiss, "The Myth of the Authoritarian Model—How Putin's Crackdown Holds Russia Back," *Foreign Affairs* 87, no. 1 (2008): 68–84.

33. For a more complete discussion of these issues, see chapter 4 in Cindy Jebb, Peter Liotta, Thomas Sherlock, and Ruth Beitler, *The Fight for Legitimacy: Democracy versus Terrorism* (Westport, CT: Praeger, 2006).

34. Carlotta Gall and Thomas De Waal, *Chechnya: A Small Victorious War* (London: Pan Original, 1997).

35. Matthew Evangelista, *The Chechen Wars: Will Russia Go the Way of the Soviet Union?* (Washington, DC: Brookings Institution Press, 2004).

36. For harrowing assessment of the Chechen tragedy, see Anna Politkovskaya, *A Small Corner of Hell: Dispatches from Chechnya* (Chicago: University of Chicago Press, 2003).

37. For a comprehensive list of terrorist attacks in Russia from 1994 to 2014, see William Robert Johnston's archive: http://www.johnstonsarchive.net/terrorism/terr-russia.html.

38. Robert Person, "Potholes, Pensions, and Public Opinion: The Politics of Blame in Putin's Power Vertical," *Post-Soviet Affairs* 31, no. 5 (2015): 420–47.

39. For an assessment of the role of the September 11 attacks in US-Russian relations, see Anatol Lieven, "The Secret Policemen's Ball: The United States, Russia and the International Order after 11 September," *International Affairs* 78, no. 2 (2002): 245–59.

40. John Newhouse, "The Missile Defense Debate," *Foreign Affairs* 80, no. 4 (2001): 97–109.

41. James M. Lindsay and Michael E. O'Hanlon, "Missile Defense after the ABM Treaty," *Washington Quarterly* 25, no. 3 (2002): 161–76.

42. Galia Golan, "Russia and the Iraq War: Was Putin's Policy a Failure?" *Communist and Post-Communist Studies* 37, no. 4 (2004): 429–59.

43. See Martin A. Smith, *Russia and NATO since 1991: From Cold War through Cold Peace to Partnership?* (London: Routledge, 2006).

44. Joshua A. Tucker, "Enough! Electoral Fraud, Collective Action Problems, and Post-Communist Colored Revolutions," *Perspectives on Politics* 5, no. 3 (2007): 535–51.

45. Adrian Karatnycky, "Ukraine's Orange Revolution," *Foreign Affairs* 84, no. 2 (2005): 35–52.

46. Clifford G. Gaddy and Andrew C. Kuchins, "Putin's Plan," *Washington Quarterly* 31, no. 2 (2008): 117–29.

47. Mikhail Myagkov, Peter Ordeshook, and Dimitri Shakin, *The Forensics of Election Fraud: Russia and Ukraine* (Cambridge: Cambridge University Press, 2009).

48. For discussion of the 2011–2012 protests, see Denis Volkov, "The Protesters and the Public," *Journal of Democracy* 23, no. 3 (2012): 55–62; Graeme Robertson, "Protesting Putinism: The Election Protests of 2011–2012 in Broader Perspective," *Problems of Post-Communism* 60, no. 2 (2013): 11–23; Karrie J. Koesel and Valerie J. Bunce, "Putin, Popular Protests, and Political Trajectories in Russia: A Comparative Perspective," *Post-Soviet Affairs* 28, no. 4 (2012): 403–23.

49. Regina Smyth and Irina Soboleva, "Looking beyond the Economy: Pussy Riot and the Kremlin's Voting Coalition," *Post-Soviet Affairs* 30, no. 4 (2014): 257–75.

50. See Celeste Wallander, "Russian Transimperialism and Its Implications," *Washington Quarterly* 30, no. 2 (2007): 107–22.

51. Bertil Nygren, "Putin's Use of Natural Gas to Reintegrate the CIS Region," *Problems of Post-Communism* 55, no. 4 (2008): 3–15.

52. For background and implications of the conflict, see Jim Nichol, "Russia-Georgia Conflict in South Ossetia: Context and Implications for US Interests," Congressional Research Service, October 24, 2008, http://www.dtic.mil/dtic/tr/fulltext/u2/a490073.pdf.

53. Roy Allison, "Russia Resurgent? Moscow's Campaign to 'Coerce Georgia to Peace,'" *International Affairs* 84, no. 6 (2008): 1145–71.

54. R. Craig Nation, "Reset or Rerun? Sources of Discord in Russian-American Relations," *Communist and Post-Communist Studies* 45, no. 3 (2012): 379–87.

55. Amy F. Woolf, "The New START Treaty: Central Limits and Key Provisions," Congressional Research Service, January 8, 2014, https://www.fas.org/sgp/crs/nuke/R41219.pdf.

56. Serhiy Kudelia, "The House that Yanukovych Built," *Journal of Democracy* 25, no. 3 (2014): 19–34.

57. Karina V. Korostelina, "Mapping National Identity Narratives in Ukraine," *Nationalities Papers* 41, no. 2 (2013): 293–315.

58. See *Russian Politics & Law* 53, no. 3 (2015), a special issue of the journal devoted to the revolution in Ukraine.

59. John J. Mearsheimer, "Why the Ukraine Crisis Is the West's Fault," *Foreign Affairs* 93, no. 5 (2014): 77–89.

60. Steven Lee Myers and Ellen Barry, "Putin Reclaims Crimea for Russia and Bitterly Denounces the West," *New York Times*, March 18, 2014.

61. John J. McCuen, "Hybrid Wars," *Military Review* 88, no. 2 (2008): 107.

62. Some would argue that Russia's targeting choices reveal the anti-ISIL justification to be window dressing. However, Moscow's prior actions and rhetoric suggest that it sees strengthening Assad's forces as the best way to ensure ISIL's defeat. Thus, the suggestion that Russia's intervention was at least partly motivated by concerns about terrorism is at least plausible.

63. As Turkey is a member of NATO, this prompted fear that the incident might spiral out of control and escalate into a more general standoff between Russia and NATO over Turkey.

64. Paul Stronski and Richard Sokolsky, "The Return of Global Russia: An Analytical Framework," Carnegie Endownment for International Peace, December 14, 2017, http://carnegieendowment.org/2017/12/14/return-of-global-russia-analytical-framework-pub-75003.

65. Paul Stronski and Richard Sokolsky, "The Return of Global Russia: An Analytical Framework."

66. Paul Stronski and Richard Sokolsky, "The Return of Global Russia: An Analytical Framework."

67. Paul Stronski and Richard Sokolsky, "The Return of Global Russia: An Analytical Framework."

68. National Intelligence Council, *Assessing Russian Activities and Intentions in Recent US Elections*, January 6, 2017, ii, https://www.dni.gov/files/documents/ICA_2017_01.pdf.

69. National Intelligence Council, *Assessing Russian Activities and Intentions in Recent US Elections*, iii.

70. Rod J. Rosenstein, "Order No. 3915-2017: Appointment of Special Counsel to Investigate Russian Interference with the 2016 Presidential Election and Related Matters," Office of the Deputy Attorney General, Washington, DC, May 17, 2017, https://www.justice.gov/opa/press-release/file/967231/download.

71. Philip Bump, "Mueller Team Has Leveled Over 100 Criminal Charges against 19 People," *Washington Post*, February 22, 2018, https://www.washingtonpost.com/news

/politics/wp/2018/02/22/muellers-team-has-leveled-over-100-criminal-charges-against-19-people/?utm_term=.3f8df93af85b.

72. Mearsheimer, "Why the Ukraine Crisis Is the West's Fault."

73. Fiona Hill and Bobo Lo, "Putin's Pivot: Why Russia Is Looking East," Brookings Institution, July 31, 2013, http://lionelingram.com/562_Putins%20Pivot_%20Why%20Russia%20is%20Looking%20East%20_%20Brookings%20Institution.pdf.

74. Michael S. Chase, Evan S. Medeiros, J. Stapleton Roy, Eugene B. Rumer, Robert Sutter, and Richard Weitz, "Russia-China Relations: Assessing Common Ground and Strategic Fault Lines," The National Bureau of Asian Research, July 2017, vi, http://carnegieendowment.org/files/SR66_Russia-ChinaRelations_July2017.pdf.

75. Vladimir Putin, "Speech and the Following Discussion at the Munich Conference on Security Policy," February 10, 2007, Munich, Germany, http://en.kremlin.ru/events/president/transcripts/24034.

23

Europe

Throughout the history of the United States, American national security policy has focused predominantly on US relations with the countries of Europe. Europe played a preeminent role in international relations for more than four hundred years after the Age of Exploration that started in the fifteenth century, and the countries of Europe dominated the colonization of North America. Although Europe no longer exercises such a uniquely outsized role in US global strategy and affairs, it remains a significant locus of international economic, military, and political power. Moreover, the United States continues to experience a high level of interdependence with the countries of Europe. The transatlantic economy is the most highly integrated and influential in the world. The North Atlantic Treaty Organization (NATO) is the world's most consequential formal military and political alliance, encompassing more countries and embracing more diverse missions in the twenty-first century than in the twentieth. Liberal democracies in Europe and the United States share common values that offer a foundation for sustaining existing relationships and building future partnerships.

US Interests in Europe

Developments in Europe were dominant influences on much of US foreign policy in the twentieth century. The two World Wars began in Europe and came to involve the United States. A third global conflict, the Cold War, saw Europe as its most crucial theater, with the United States making a substantial military commitment

The authors would like to thank Majors Jordan Becker and Seth Johnston for their significant contributions to this chapter.

to it throughout that period. In light of the dramatic transformations on the European continent since the fall of the Berlin Wall in 1989, and then the large-scale terrorist attacks in the United States and Europe in the early twenty-first century, the United States has continued to reassess its security interests in Europe (figure 23.1). These discussions are likely to be shaped by five major issues.

First, the United States has a continuing interest in peace and stability in Europe. NATO is the preeminent entity for the promotion of these interests, encompassing as it does twenty-seven European states, the United States, and Canada. Established in 1949, NATO successfully promoted the security of its members and prevented war in Europe during the forty years of the Cold War. Since the end of the Cold War, NATO has continued to grow and adapt beyond its original focus on the territorial defense of Western Europe. It now has more than thirty-five countries as nonmember partners in Europe, the Mediterranean, the Middle East, and elsewhere around the world. Since the end of the Cold War, it has conducted operations in the Balkans, Afghanistan, Iraq, North Africa, and elsewhere. From its founding, the NATO alliance has served as the foremost means by which the United States has cooperated with European partners in its initiatives relating to international peace and security. Its continuing operations suggest that it will remain a useful treaty organization into the foreseeable future.

Second, because of the large volume of trade and investment across the Atlantic, the stability of this region and security of transatlantic lines of communications

FIGURE 23.1 Europe

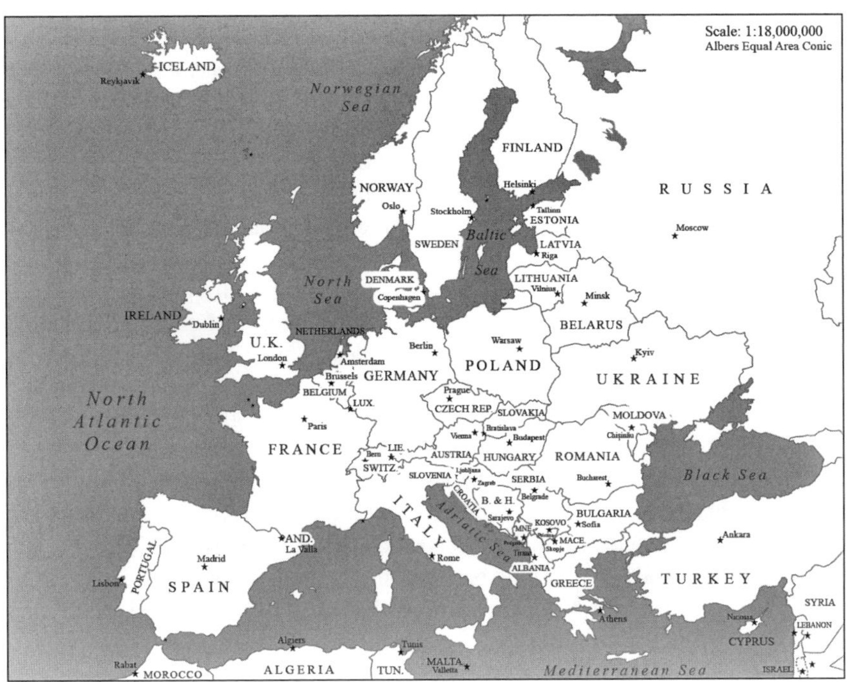

remain key to US economic interests. The common market of the European Union's twenty-eight member states is significant economically, with a gross domestic product (GDP) of $16.4 trillion, slightly smaller than that of the United States, in 2016 (table 23.1).[1] The United States and Europe are important economic partners, as well: the transatlantic economy accounts for as much as $5.5 trillion in total commercial activity per year and is responsible for approximately fifteen million jobs on both continents.[2] Trade disagreements between the United States and the European Union (EU) are common, and a comprehensive formal trade agreement has proved elusive. Despite these challenges, and despite the potential for some instability resulting from the United Kingdom's recent decision to withdraw from the European Union, no other economic relationship in the world is as intertwined or influential as this transatlantic economy.

Third, the United States has an interest in maintaining close ties in Europe to balance against the influence of the major successor state to the former Soviet Union, Russia. Russia retains a large conventional and nuclear weapons arsenal capable of threatening its neighbors and the United States. Russia's 2008 invasion of Georgia, its 2014 annexation of Crimea and military support of armed separatists in eastern Ukraine, and its 2015 military intervention in the Syrian civil war demonstrate its willingness to use military force and other instruments of power to coerce other actors in its vicinity and beyond. Many countries in Eastern and Central Europe and in Central Asia fear that Russia could threaten their security and autonomy. The United States has an interest in the continued political and economic development of these countries and in long-term peace and stability in Eurasia. (For more on Russia, see chapter 22.)

Fourth, Europe's geographic proximity to other regions in which the United States has vital interests—particularly the Middle East—adds to its strategic value for the United States. For example, in the 1990–1991 Gulf War and again during the Afghanistan and Iraq conflicts after 2001, US bases in Europe served as important logistical and training areas and as vital medical waypoints for wounded service members evacuated from combat theaters. Continued close cooperation with the countries of Europe can help the United States address security concerns beyond the European continent.

Finally, the United States has a continuing national security interest in cooperating with European partners to combat transnational challenges including terrorism; proliferation of weapons of mass destruction; trafficking in persons and narcotics and other forms of organized crime; malicious uses of cyberspace; and environmental change. US-European relations have global significance for the international system not only because of the combined material power of both regions but also because of their broadly shared values and interests. Democracy, capitalism, individual rights, and the rule of law are all core features of US and European governance models and national security objectives. The highly institutionalized relations between the United States and Europe influence global governance practices in ways that reflect these shared values and interests.

Table 23.1 Europe Key Statistics

Country	*Total population (millions)*	*Life expectancy at birth*	*GDP US$ (billions)*	*GDP/ capita US$*	*Population living in poverty (%)*	*Military expenditure (% of GDP)*	*Military spending US$ (millions)*	*Human Development Index (HDI) ranking (of 188)*
Albania	3.0	78.3	12.1	11,900	14.3	1.0	115	75
Austria	8.7	81.5	387.3	48,800	4.0	0.6	2,313	24
Belarus	9.6	72.7	48.1	17,500	5.7	1.1	509	52
Belgium	11.4	81.0	470.2	44,900	15.1	0.8	3,895	22
Bosnia-Herzegovina	3.9	76.7	16.6	11,000	17.2	1.2	191	81
Bulgaria	7.1	74.5	50.5	20,100	22.0	1.4	678	56
Croatia	4.3	75.9	49.9	22,400	19.5	1.2	588	45
Cyprus	1.2	78.7	19.9	34,400	na	1.8	356	33
Czech Republic	10.6	78.6	193.5	33,200	9.7	1.0	1,971	28
Denmark	5.6	79.4	306.1	46,600	13.4	1.2	3,547	5
Estonia	1.3	76.7	23.5	29,500	21.3	2.2	503	30
Finland	5.5	80.9	239.2	40,600	na	1.4	3,283	23
France	66.8	81.8	2,488.0	42,400	14.0	1.9	47,201	21
Germany	80.8	80.7	3,495.0	48,200	16.7	1.1	38,281	4
Greece	10.8	80.5	195.9	26,800	36.0	2.4	4,639	29
Hungary	8.9	75.9	117.1	27,200	14.9	0.9	996	43
Iceland	0.3	83.0	19.4	48,100	na	0.2	31	9
Ireland	5.0	80.8	307.9	69,400	8.2	0.3	1,003	8
Italy	62.0	82.2	1,852.0	36,300	29.9	1.2	22,309	26
Latvia	2.0	74.5	25.0	25,700	25.5	1.5	411	44
Lithuania	2.9	74.9	42.8	29,900	22.2	1.5	642	37

(*Continued*)

Table 23.1 (Continued)

Country	*Total population (millions)*	*Life expectancy at birth*	*GDP US$ (billions)*	*GDP/ capita US$*	*Population living in poverty (%)*	*Military expenditure (% of GDP)*	*Military spending US$ (millions)*	*Human Development Index (HDI) ranking (of 188)*
Luxembourg	0.6	82.3	61.0	102,000	na	0.4	220	20
Macedonia (FYROM)	2.1	76.2	10.5	14,500	21.5	1.1	107	82
Malta	0.4	80.4	10.5	37,900	16.3	0.6	58	33
Montenegro	0.6	76.1	4.2	17,000	8.6	1.6	70	48
Netherlands	17.0	81.3	773.9	60,800	8.8	1.2	9,193	7
Norway	5.3	81.8	376.3	69,300	na	1.6	5,968	1
Poland	38.5	77.6	467.4	27,700	17.6	1.9	9,073	36
Portugal	10.8	79.3	205.9	28,500	19.0	1.1	2,181	41
Romania	21.6	75.1	186.5	22,300	22.4	1.5	2,777	50
Serbia	7.1	75.5	37.5	14,200	8.9	1.4	507	66
Slovakia	5.4	77.1	90.3	31,200	12.3	1.1	983	40
Slovenia	2.0	78.1	44.0	33,100	14.3	1.0	450	25
Spain	48.6	81.7	1,252.0	36,600	21.1	1.0	12,222	27
Sweden	9.9	82.1	511.4	49,700	15.0	1.1	5,828	14
Switzerland	8.1	82.6	662.5	59,400	6.6	0.7	4,720	2
Turkey	80.3	74.8	856.8	21100	21.9	1.2	8764	71
Ukraine	44.2	71.8	87.2	8,200	24.1	2.5	2,165	84
United Kingdom	64.4	80.7	2,650.0	42,500	15.0	2.0	52,498	16

na = not available.

Sources: Data on population and economy is from the CIA World Factbook 2017, https://www.cia.gov/library/publications/the-world-factbook. Military expenditure data is from International Institute for Strategic Studies (IISS), *The Military Balance 2017* (London: IISS, 2017). HDI rankings are from *Human Development Report 2016*, http://hdr.undp.org/en/data. Most figures are from 2016 (otherwise latest available data is listed). GDP is reported at the official exchange rate. GDP per capita is using Purchasing Power Parity rates.

History of US Involvement in Europe

After World War II, the global distribution of power was bipolar: only the United States and the Soviet Union had sufficient capabilities to play significant leadership roles. When victory ended the antifascist wartime alliance between these two countries, their conflicting ideologies and interests led to direct US-Soviet competition in Europe. Faced with growing Soviet expansionism and bellicosity in Central and Eastern Europe, combined with Soviet threats directed against Western and Southern Europe, the United States responded with a series of peacetime foreign commitments that were unprecedented in US history.

First, on March 12, 1947, President Harry Truman announced what came to be known as the Truman Doctrine in reaction to the growing threat of communist insurgency in Greece and Turkey. The Truman Doctrine identified the expansion of totalitarianism to be a threat to US security and international peace, and it committed the United States to helping free peoples resist subjugation by militant minority groups and outside pressures. Within a year, the United States backed these words with action by sending military assistance and advisors to Greece and Turkey. As discussed in chapter 3, the Truman Doctrine was the opening move in a strategy of worldwide containment through which the United States sought to confine the Soviet Union to its existing boundaries and limit its influence abroad.

The European Recovery Program, better known as the Marshall Plan, was the second major US commitment to the continent. It grew from a realization that Europe's economic recovery from the effects of World War II would be vital to its political stability and security. By 1947, postwar recovery had proved slower and more difficult than expected. Between 1948 and 1951, the United States supplied more than $13 billion in economic aid (nearly 5 percent of US GDP at the time) to sixteen participating countries in Western Europe. It administered the program through an innovative structure known as the US Economic Cooperation Administration, which encouraged European aid recipients to help set their own priorities for recovery assistance. The Marshall Plan played an important role in repairing the massive physical devastation of the war; it still stands today as an oft-cited model for how to facilitate a postwar recovery.[3]

The creation of NATO as a lasting security alliance between the United States and Europe marked the third major post–World War II US commitment to the continent. The 1947 Dunkirk Treaty and the 1948 Brussels Treaty—pledges of mutual defense motivated by concern about the possibility of a resurgent Germany—were the first mutual security arrangements made by Western European countries after World War II. The Soviet-sponsored coup in Czechoslovakia in 1948 and the Soviet blockade of Berlin in 1948–1949 convinced Western Europeans and Americans alike that the Soviet Union was the greater threat and that US power would be needed to help contain it. In 1949, the United States, Canada, and ten Western European countries signed and ratified the treaty that created NATO. NATO was designed as a collective defense organization in which an attack on one would be considered an attack on all. West Germany joined NATO in 1955, thereby constraining German power within the American-led alliance while also making West Germany's resources available for the East-West struggle of the Cold War.

The Evolution of NATO during the Cold War. NATO has been a successful alliance, if not always a harmonious one. Geopolitical developments have at times tested intra-alliance relations but, at each such juncture, the alliance has been able to adapt and survive.

NATO was America's first peacetime military alliance, apart from the 1947 Rio Pact, which allied the United States with its Latin American neighbors (see chapter 24). The new alliance was at first focused on deterring a Soviet attack by increasing the Soviet perception of the costs of such a venture. However, this deterrence strategy rapidly evolved, especially after the North Korean invasion of South Korea in 1950. Many believed that the invasion was instigated by the Soviet Union and feared that it portended a similar Soviet move within Europe. NATO strategy began to emphasize defense as well as deterrence, and NATO countries sought—with limited success—to develop a substantial force on the European continent, which would be capable of repelling a massive attack with conventional as well as nuclear means.

The credibility of the US commitment to European security in the face of growing Soviet nuclear capability was tested in the late 1950s, when Europeans became concerned about US willingness to use its nuclear arsenal in the event of a Soviet attack on Europe.[4] After an attempt at building a European multilateral nuclear force failed in the mid-1960s, a NATO nuclear deterrent was developed, composed primarily of US nuclear forces placed in Europe, as well as the US strategic deterrent. The new presence of theater nuclear forces on the ground in Europe achieved an essential goal for the European allies by linking conventional defenses along the East-West frontier with American strategic forces.

Later modernization of theater nuclear systems, made necessary by the introduction of Soviet intermediate-range nuclear missiles aimed at Western Europe, caused renewed friction within the alliance. As a result, in 1979 NATO adopted a "two-track" policy: it modernized its theater nuclear forces while the United States negotiated with the Soviet Union to achieve reductions. The resulting 1987 Intermediate-Range Nuclear Forces (INF) Treaty between the United States and the Soviet Union also eased tensions among NATO members.

As NATO coped with changes in doctrine necessitated by technology and by an ever-shifting geopolitical environment, the allies also grappled with the fair distribution of the burden of providing for the common defense. Concerns over burden sharing were seemingly unavoidable for an alliance composed of a superpower, some medium powers, and some smaller powers, with occasionally divergent goals.[5] The smaller NATO states generally let their larger neighbors take the lead and pay the costs. The United States historically accounts for between two-thirds and three-quarters of combined NATO countries' military spending. Moreover, in 1966 the French developed and deployed their own nuclear weapons, the *force de frappe*, and withdrew their forces from the military command of

NATO, complicating efforts to establish a concerted flexible defense in Europe. Greece and Turkey have, since 1974, engaged in a longstanding dispute over Cyprus, which remains an issue today both within NATO and between NATO and the European Union. NATO initiatives and financial burdens have shifted increasingly to Germany, the United Kingdom, and the United States.

NATO and the End of the Cold War. Shifts in Soviet behavior began to change the European security landscape significantly in the late 1980s. The first demonstration of altered Soviet intentions occurred in the field of conventional arms control. NATO and the Warsaw Pact had held talks aimed at limiting conventional military forces in Europe for thirteen years, but with little result until 1986. Then, in response to a NATO proposal, Soviet General Secretary Mikhail Gorbachev called for phased reduction of ground and air forces in Europe. The resulting Conventional Forces in Europe (CFE) Treaty of 1990 was signed by the sixteen NATO member countries and the six countries that had belonged to the Warsaw Pact. Along with the INF, it reflected a rapid transformation of the European security environment. More than 125,000 battle tanks, armored combat vehicles, artillery pieces, combat aircraft, and attack helicopters would be removed or destroyed, greatly reducing the threat of large-scale surprise conventional attack.

However, the CFE Treaty was rapidly overtaken by events. By the conclusion of the conventional force negotiations, the Warsaw Pact had dissolved, and Germany was approaching unification. The collapse of the Soviet Union itself further challenged the conventional arms control regime established in 1990: it required additional negotiations among seven of the former republics—Russia, Belarus, Ukraine, Moldova, Georgia, Armenia, and Azerbaijan—before the CFE Treaty could be ratified and come into force in 1992. The treaty was renegotiated again and signed into effect in 1999, but the agreement was short-lived: amid tensions over a planned US missile shield, Russian President Vladimir Putin announced in 2007 that Russia would suspend its obligations under the CFE treaty. In 2015, Russia formally withdrew from the treaty entirely.

Evolution of NATO in the Early Post–Cold War Years. Just as the arms control process was forced to adapt to the changing political and security environment, so too was the western security framework that had evolved during more than four decades of East-West confrontation and the Cold War. In view of the declining threat from the Soviet Union—due to conventional arms control arrangements, unilateral Soviet military withdrawals, the dissolution of the Warsaw Pact, and the unification of East and West Germany—the policy of stationing military forces along the former border between NATO and the Warsaw Pact grew increasingly inappropriate. NATO responded to the new environment by establishing diplomatic liaison with the states of Central and Eastern Europe and by announcing a fundamental political and military review at the London Summit of July 1990. The process of change begun with this summit had two major consequences. First, a new relationship with the alliance's former enemies in the now-defunct Warsaw Pact was defined. Second, a new strategic concept was formulated, which enabled an alliance that found itself without an apparent adversary to reach beyond its borders to conduct operations and provide stability.

The essence of NATO's political approach to the former Warsaw Pact states was encapsulated in the 1991 NATO Copenhagen communiqué, which stated: "Our own security is inseparably linked to that of all other states in Europe. The consolidation and preservation throughout the continent of democratic societies and their freedom from any form of coercion or intimidation are therefore of direct and material concern to us."[6] Although NATO initially stopped short of providing a security guarantee to the states of Central and Eastern Europe, it gradually became clear that the alliance would consider eventual expansion eastward.

By 1994, NATO had formulated the Partnership for Peace (PfP) to promote official military contact at all levels among the former adversaries, as well as with traditionally neutral states. The PfP focuses on military matters, including transparency in defense planning; the democratic control of armed forces; the development of cooperative military ventures, such as peacekeeping and training exercises with NATO; and the training of troops better able to operate with NATO forces in the field.[7] Twenty-seven countries, for a variety of individual reasons, signed onto the program. Many undoubtedly hoped that membership in the PfP would lead to eventual membership in NATO itself. The PfP evolved until it became clear, at least unofficially, that it served two purposes: to prepare some countries for membership in NATO and to enhance cooperation between NATO and those partners not likely to be admitted.

Throughout 1996 and 1997, political debate raged over the possibility of NATO expansion. The reaction from Russia was a particular obstacle. Unsurprisingly, Russia saw eastward expansion of the alliance as a threat to its national security. NATO, however, believing that enlargement would produce a stronger, more stable Europe and that it should not cave in to Russian concerns, eventually decided to admit new members. When the Soviet Union collapsed in 1991, NATO had sixteen member states: the original twelve members had been joined by Greece and Turkey in 1952, West Germany in 1955, and Spain in 1982.[8] Since the end of the Cold War, an additional thirteen countries have become NATO members, beginning with three waves of enlargement. The alliance's ranks first grew to nineteen when the Czech Republic, Hungary, and Poland joined in 1999. In 2004, seven additional countries—Bulgaria, Estonia, Latvia, Lithuania, Romania, Slovakia, and Slovenia—formally joined the alliance. Albania and Croatia joined in 2009, and Montenegro became the twenty-ninth NATO country in 2017. Three other PfP countries have expressed interest in joining and remain in dialogue with NATO about membership: Bosnia and Herzegovina, Georgia, and the former Yugoslav Republic of Macedonia.

In addition to PfP, NATO established regional programs in the Mediterranean Dialogue and the Istanbul Cooperation Initiative, discussed further below. More recently, and mostly in connection with practical cooperation in NATO's operations outside Europe, NATO has established partnerships with countries in other regions, such as Australia and South Korea. Other partnership activities have sought to offer a level of inclusiveness to Russia and other nonmembers, including the North Atlantic Cooperation Council, which was established in 1991 and succeeded by the Euro-Atlantic Partnership Council in 1997. That same year, the NATO-Russia Founding Act established a forum for dialogue known as the Permanent Joint Council; it was succeeded by the NATO-Russia Council in 2002. Although these global partnerships have led to substantive and practical cooperation, relations between NATO and Russia have remained difficult.

Even as NATO was redefining its relationships with former adversaries and its basic security concept in the 1990s, it was also participating in an increasing number of security operations. Beginning with involvement in Bosnia-Herzegovina in the wake of the Dayton Accords in 1995, the alliance moved beyond its Cold War task of defending member states and into crisis management outside its borders. NATO's new strategic concept, defined at the Washington Summit in April 1999, acknowledged the need for alliance participation in out-of-area peace support operations. This provided the underpinnings for NATO's intervention in Kosovo in the spring of 1999 to halt a humanitarian catastrophe and to restore stability in a strategic region.[9]

Key Developments in NATO in the Twenty-First Century. Since its creation in 1949, NATO has been the preeminent security institution in Europe and the most institutionalized transatlantic link between the United States and Europe. NATO's charter has enabled the organization to adapt to meet the needs of its member countries in a changing world. Article 5 of NATO's founding document, the North Atlantic Treaty, proffers a classic alliance security guarantee that an attack on any one member state is considered an attack against all. However, it is the less prominent Article 4 that provides for the sort of political consultation on security affairs that has become increasingly common in NATO's activities in recent decades. The preamble to the treaty, which describes the basic purpose of the alliance—to "safeguard the freedom, common heritage, and civilization" of its peoples—makes no specific mention of an enemy. Instead, it anchors the alliance's rationale in the principles of the United Nations (UN) Charter. It has proven to be enduring but also flexible in response to new challenges. This adaptability is one of the important strengths of the alliance, but it does come with tensions.

The terrorist attacks on the United States of September 11, 2001, forced the alliance to come to terms with the implications of collective defense in a new era.[10] On September 12, 2001, the alliance moved to invoke Article 5 of the North Atlantic Treaty for the first time in its history.[11] Support provided to the United States in the aftermath of the terrorist attacks included deployment of five NATO Airborne Warning and Control Systems (AWACS) aircraft and the deployment of NATO's Standing Naval Force Mediterranean to the eastern Mediterranean to begin a counterterrorism mission.[12]

At NATO's Prague Summit of 2002, NATO member countries agreed to improve their military capabilities in a wide range of specific areas.[13] Particularly noteworthy is that member states called for a NATO Response Force of up to

25,000, which would be able to deploy within five days to crises anywhere in the world. NATO had never before had such a capability for worldwide force projection. The Prague Summit also committed NATO to a leadership role in the UN-mandated International Security Assistance Force (ISAF) operating in Afghanistan, which was the start of NATO's first and largest ground operation outside Europe. In October 2006, in another landmark step, the NATO headquarters in Afghanistan took command of all international military forces from the US-led coalition, expanding the alliance mission to the whole of Afghanistan.

Meanwhile, NATO continued establishing relationships with countries in other regions. The 2004 Istanbul Summit led to increased NATO responsibilities in Iraq. Although NATO did not assume a combat role, it provided equipment, training, and technical assistance to support the development of effective Iraqi security forces until its mission was discontinued in 2011. Further reforms sought to streamline and "Europeanize" NATO: the number of commands within NATO underwent a drastic reduction under the NATO Command Structure streamlining initiative of 2010, and European officers were given more consideration for major commands that had previously gone mostly to US officers.

As evidenced by NATO's leadership in military operations in Afghanistan, the alliance is capable of fairly large-scale deployments at a strategic distance. The political will to sustain these operations even in the face of casualties proved durable for years, even if they were not always popular. Although these developments may have increased the attractiveness of NATO to the United States, NATO's involvement in Afghanistan also highlighted weaknesses within the alliance. Many of the states that contributed troops placed constraints on their soldiers' involvement, limiting their ability to perform certain types of actions.

In addition, NATO countries have sought to keep defense spending limited, despite the existence of foreign commitments. Recent economic challenges highlight the sometimes painful trade-offs involved in choices over defense spending. Concerns about a mismatch between the capabilities required to reach NATO's level of ambition and the resources devoted to doing so helped drive the pledge on defense investment agreed to at the 2014 Wales Summit, where member countries reaffirmed that each should spend at least 2 percent of GDP on defense. President Donald Trump has made this commitment to increasing NATO defense spending a centerpiece of his administration's engagement with NATO states.[14] Observers increasingly call for a restructuring of the common funding program to allow NATO greater flexibility in financing its operations. The current system of letting "costs lie where they fall," which mandates that member countries pay their own way during operations, complicates decision making. Former NATO Secretary General Jaap de Hoop Scheffer described this arrangement as "a reverse lottery," noting that "if your numbers come up, you lose money. If the [NATO Response Force] deploys while you happen to be in the rotation, you pay the full costs of the deployment of your forces."[15]

For the time being, however, NATO remains the institution of choice in matters involving the coordinated use of military force among its members. The response to the Balkan crises, first in Bosnia-Herzegovina and then in Kosovo in the late

1990s, showed that the results of the search for an effective institutional response that had eluded both the United Nations and the Europeans when acting alone were successful. This pattern extended into the twenty-first century when, in 2011, NATO organized the European-led, US-supported air campaign to enforce an arms embargo on Libya and protect Libyan civilians from Muammar Qaddafi's regime.

The Continuing Search for US-European Security Consensus. While Cold War strategies emphasized nuclear deterrence and defense against the Soviet bloc to the east of the Iron Curtain dividing Europe, US efforts in the decades since have focused on a more expansive and inclusive approach to creating what President George H. W. Bush described in 1989 as "a Europe whole and free."[16] Despite agreement on overarching goals, the United States and allied European countries often disagree on the methods and the balance of leadership necessary to achieve and maintain this broad consensus. Moreover, although Russia is substantially weaker now than it was during the heyday of the Soviet Union, it continues to impede many of these efforts. In the immediate aftermath of the Cold War, it appeared to be democratizing and leaning more toward a Western style of government. However, strong nationalist and revisionist forces in Russia have since resisted and prevented fully cooperative relations with NATO members.

Efforts to create an inclusive approach to security in Europe date back more than forty years. In the 1975 Helsinki Final Act of the 1973–1975 Conference on Security and Cooperation in Europe (CSCE), signed by thirty-five countries including the United States, Soviet Union, and European states on both sides of the Iron Curtain, signatory states pledged themselves to the inviolability of frontiers in Europe, peaceful settlement of disputes, and respect for human rights. Although the Final Act did not have the full force of a treaty in international law, and although interpretations of its provisions varied widely, it was the first and most significant attempt during the Cold War to reach a comprehensive post–World War II settlement in Europe.

The end of the Cold War appeared to offer new opportunities to forge consensus on security and governance in Europe, as Western institutions extended eastward. The collapse of communist regimes in Eastern Europe after 1989 and a brief moment of US-Soviet cooperation in opposition to the 1990 Iraqi invasion of Kuwait gave rise to George H. W. Bush's discussion of a "new world order" and new hopes for the realization of peace and security goals outlined in the UN Charter. Following the collapse of the Soviet Union itself and moves toward democratic governance and market economies, Europe and Eurasia appeared to some observers to be at what Francis Fukuyama termed "the end of history," bringing to a close a twentieth century marked by ideological and military struggle.[17]

To consolidate these gains, the Organization for Security and Cooperation in Europe (OSCE) was established to institutionalize the aims of the CSCE and the Helsinki Final Act. At the same time, NATO and the European Union embarked on partnership and expansion programs to the east. The OSCE currently has fifty-seven member countries across Europe, North America, and Central Asia. The OSCE's inclusivity imbues it with legitimacy but also limits its capacity for action. Early hopes for a contribution by the OSCE to European security faded after 1992, when the organization was unable to deal effectively with the violent disintegration of Yugoslavia. The OSCE sponsored observer teams but delegated most of the mediation efforts to the forerunners of the European Union and peacekeeping duties to the United Nations. These efforts were also unsuccessful, and eventually NATO intervened in Bosnia in 1994 and again in Kosovo in 1999.

The integration of Central and Eastern European countries into NATO and the European Union, together with formalized dialogue and modest engagement with other powers in neighboring regions, seemed for a short time to offer the prospect of a European security consensus. However, Russia's opposition to this Western-led model has become increasingly apparent and forceful. Vladimir Putin, Russia's leading political figure since the end of the Cold War, has sought to reestablish Russian influence in the former Soviet space via alternatives to Western institutions, including the Eurasian Economic Union, the Collective Security Treaty Organization, and the Shanghai Cooperation Organization. Russia has also demonstrated an increasing willingness to turn to military force as an instrument of foreign policy. Faced with the prospect of Georgian and Ukrainian moves toward potential membership in NATO, Russia invaded both countries and supported local ethnic-Russian separatist movements to sustain instability and extend Russia's influence. Russia's 2014 annexation of Crimea from Ukraine was the first time since World War II that any country used force to seize territory and change international borders in Europe. Russia also undertook a significant military modernization program starting in 2010 and increased its military spending by more than 50 percent between 2009 and 2014. Given these events, it appears that Fukuyama's "end of history" has given way to what Robert Kagan calls "the return of history."[18]

Obstacles to consensus on security in Europe are not confined to disputes between a unified transatlantic bloc and external rivals. European states often have serious disagreements with one another and with the United States. Cold War examples include: the 1956 Suez Crisis, in which the United States opposed the invasion of Egypt by Britain, France, and Israel; the 1966 withdrawal of France from NATO's integrated military structure and ejection of NATO's headquarters from Paris to its present location in Belgium; and divergences over the deployment of medium-range nuclear missiles in Europe during the 1980s. In the twenty-first century, the 2003 US invasion of Iraq divided European governments and populations. More recent divisions among European countries over how to deal with a resurgent Russia have been less publicly acrimonious, but they nevertheless reflect divergent views, particularly between the Western European countries and the Eastern European countries, which view the potential threat of Russia with greater alarm.

Transatlantic Economic Relations. The economic ties that bind Europe and the United States are among the most significant of any two regions in the world. The relationship between the United States and democratic Europe has dominated the post-1945 economic global landscape. The United States is the primary destination for European exports, receiving as much as 20 percent of all goods exported from Europe in 2017, with China a distant second at 10.5 percent. Since 2006, China has been the leading exporter *to* Europe, with goods from China accounting in 2017 for 20.2 percent of European imports.[19] In all, goods trade between the United States and the European Union totaled $1.1 trillion in 2016.[20]

Over the post–World War II period, the transatlantic economy has been characterized by competitive cooperation between the United States and its European partners. Headlines from the last seventy years highlight myriad disputes between the United States and Europe in the economic sphere, from quarrels over banana import policies to disagreements over the safety of genetically modified foods. Negotiations over a Transatlantic Trade and Investment Partnership (TTIP) encompass two key issues in transatlantic trade: the extent to which the United States and the European Union will engage in bilateral or interregional trade agreements, rather than focusing on the global trading system, and the extent to which they can harmonize regulatory policy.[21] These negotiations were put on hold following the 2016 US presidential election but representatives from the Trump administration and European leaders expressed interest in resuming talks on the TTIP.

Although the relationship has not been without discord, the transatlantic community has been free of violent conflict throughout the postwar period. The United States and its European allies have created a dense network of formal and informal institutions to enhance their aligned economic interests while peacefully managing conflicting ones. This ability to capitalize on areas of agreement while minimizing the possible damage from disputes has enabled significant economic development on both sides of the Atlantic since World War II.

The system of institutions and norms that the United States and Europe created to further the transatlantic relationship has also enabled other nations and regional associations to thrive. Fareed Zakaria has termed this phenomenon the "rise of the rest."[22] The rise began with Europe: between 1950 and 1973, GDP growth rates among the member states of the European Economic Community (described below) were nearly twice the rates of the preceding and following quarter-centuries, with productivity increasing dramatically as well.[23] After a half-century of destructive conflict, Europe was economically revitalized during this period. Other regions and nations, most notably countries in East Asia, have since capitalized on the institutions and norms created by and for this increasingly globalized world. While the United States and the countries of Western Europe have received great benefits from the post–World War II international economic order, they have also set the stage for the rise of developing countries, whose higher growth rates have enabled rapid progress and resulted in a diffusion of power in the international system.

Developments within Europe

Analysis of future US national security policies relevant to Europe must consider not only the history of US engagement since World War II, but also a range of internal developments within Europe and transnational challenges that face both countries.

European Integration. Although the United States has played an important role in European security since the end of World War II, Europe's own efforts at institution building and integration remain vital to the region. The most prominent and important of these efforts is the European Union and its forerunners.

The process of European integration has shaped and will continue to shape the European political and security landscape in two significant ways: first, by encouraging neighboring countries to seek integration and membership in the European Union (known as *widening* in EU policy circles), and second, by aligning the foreign and domestic policies of the member states (known as *deepening*). Similar in intent to the Marshall Plan, these goals emphasize economic development and opportunities for European leadership. A unified Europe can have mixed implications for the United States, because a strong Europe is more effective as a partner but also more capable of resisting US leadership. However, in the history of US policy toward Europe since World War II, the former interest has generally won out over the latter in guiding US actions.

The Creation of the European Union. The European Union grew out of the European Coal and Steel Community (ECSC) proposed by French foreign minister Robert Schuman in 1950. The original goal was to ensure French access to German markets, while also dampening Franco-German competition, by organizing joint control of the strategic mineral resources required by the militaries of each country. The ECSC included Italy, Belgium, Luxembourg, the Netherlands, France, and Germany. Its success created an impetus for a larger common internal market among its members, leading to the 1957 Treaty of Rome and the resulting European Economic Community (EEC). The EEC worked to eliminate barriers to the free flow of goods, services, capital, and labor. The move toward European integration took a substantial step forward in 1992 when twelve nations signed the Maastricht Treaty, signaling their intent to create an economic and monetary union, which became known as the European Union.

Economic Integration. Under the auspices of the European Commission (established in 1958) and the European Central Bank (ECB, established in 1998), the European Union has grown into a significant player in international trade and commerce, primarily due to the development of the Single European Market and the Economic and Monetary Union (EMU). The concept of a single market, which enables the free flow of goods, capital, services, and people, is a central component of European integration, and in many ways has been a success in promoting growth and employment. Although it has faced periods characterized by stagnation, particularly in the 1970s, the single market has contributed significantly to European integration.

The EMU in Europe has been more challenging. Although the euro is the official currency of the European Union, only nineteen of the European Union's twenty-eight members use it.[24] All member states, except for the United Kingdom and Denmark, are legally bound to adopt the euro and aspire to do so; but EU members outside the eurozone must live by EU financial decisions, even though they are not full members of the decision-making process. For countries such as Denmark, which have chosen monetary independence over influence in the Eurogroup, the increasing demands for bailouts or other financial and economic measures needed to support the euro decrease the attractiveness of their relationship to the European Union.

The fact that individual member states continue to determine their own economic and fiscal policies places further strains on the EMU as an incomplete monetary union.[25] It is difficult to manage a monetary union in the absence of a budgetary union, which in many ways would amount to a political union. This type of union would represent a significant cession of sovereignty, and resistance to this explains, at least in part, the difficulty Europe has experienced in developing genuine economic governance.

By 2011, in the wake of the 2008 financial crisis, the most urgent item on the transatlantic agenda had become Europe's economic crisis. Indeed, Europe faced not one crisis, but four: (1) high debt and public deficits in eurozone countries; (2) a banking crisis affecting private European banks; (3) an economic recession and high unemployment in eurozone countries; and (4) persistent trade imbalances among Eurozone members.[26] At times, these crises appeared to threaten Europe's monetary union and even the entire EU project itself.

European policy makers weathered the storm through a combination of fiscal harmonization and further deepening of the economic union. By late 2013, the eurozone had made significant progress toward a European banking union. The ECB was functioning as a lender of last resort: a Single Supervisory Mechanism, granting the ECB oversight of Eurozone banks, had been approved by the European Parliament and the Council of the European Union.[27]

The resiliency of the European Union and of the eurozone during and after the 2008 crisis is due at least in part to the political foundations of the euro. In spite of criticisms of the monetary union, Europe's political leadership appears committed to the survival of the euro and the broader project of European integration. The dollar and the euro also remain dominant international reserve currencies, reinforcing the global importance of the monetary policies of the United States and the European Union.

EU Foreign and Defense Policy. By the late 1990s, the prospects for EU expansion and the development of a common European Security and Defense Policy (ESDP) positioned the European Union as a major international actor. A credible autonomous defense capability was an important part of this effort. The European Union advanced this prospect with agreements in the 1997 Amsterdam Treaty, the 1998 declaration at St. Malo between Britain and France, and the 1999 decision to create a European Rapid Reaction Force capable of humanitarian and peacekeeping missions.

These steps gave rise to US concern over whether the development of autonomous European security structures might conflict with the role of NATO in the region. In 1998, Secretary of State Madeleine Albright outlined American expectations towards the ESDP, referring to the "three Ds": (1) no duplication of what was done effectively under NATO, (2) no decoupling from the United States and NATO, and (3) no discrimination against non-EU members of NATO, such as Turkey.[28] By 2002, NATO and the European Union had worked out a partnership regarding crisis management activities, which is reflected in the March 2003 "Berlin-Plus Agreement": it allowed the European Union to use NATO structures, mechanisms, and assets to carry out military operations if NATO were to decline to act.

In the early twenty-first century, the European Union has taken steps to develop common foreign policy agendas as well as enhanced military capabilities. The Lisbon Treaty of 2007 expanded the European Union's institutional capacity for its renamed Common Foreign and Security Policy, including the new Common Security and Defense Policy. The post of High Representative of the Union for Foreign Affairs and Security Policy was established to lead a newly created EU diplomatic corps, European External Action Service, and European Defense Agency. The Lisbon Treaty also laid the groundwork for permanent structured cooperation on defense issues among member states that have significant military capabilities and are interested in enhanced coordination of efforts. EU operations in Bosnia (ongoing since 2004), Macedonia (2003), and the Democratic Republic of the Congo (2006) have shown that this capability is real, although it has shortcomings. For example, the European Union's ability to project and sustain a military force is questionable, given its reluctance to commit forces for an extended period of time. The European Union has also faced internal political setbacks, such as the failure to agree on a common response to the Arab Spring, and the eventual choice of NATO by the United Kingdom and France as a forum for organizing a response to the civil conflict in Libya. Despite these limitations, the European Union has acquired sufficient prominence to affect the calculus of US security policy.

Brexit. The largest set back to the general trend of European integration took place in June 2016, when British citizens voted for a referendum requiring the United Kingdom to become the first state to leave the European Union. This British exit, or *Brexit*, was caused by several factors. A significant part of the British population has long advocated independence from the European Union because of the belief that the EU push for continent-wide harmonization of standards can subordinate national sovereignty to the European Parliament and "bureaucrats in Brussels." Britain's continued use of the pound instead of the euro as its currency and insistence on other exemptions from EU centralized policies reflects this ongoing resistance to European integration.[29] The call for independence increased as Britain, like other nations, confronted significant immigration challenges, waves of asylum seekers, and the continued challenges of coordinating economic activity after the 2008–2009 financial crisis. By 2016, populists leaders had successfully rallied a majority in the nation to vote to leave the European Union, resulting in a narrow, 51.9 percent approval of the Brexit referendum and the subsequent resignation of British Prime Minister David Cameron, who campaigned against the referendum. Article 50 of the 2009 Lisbon Treaty specifies the formal process for the United Kingdom to leave the European Union, which is expected to be completed in 2019.

As the United Kingdom prepares to be the first state to leave the European Union, this departure has significant implications. Within the United Kingdom, there are significantly divergent perspectives on the economic impact of leaving. Some argue that separating from the world's largest economic union may be economically devastating, while others believe that trade will still take place on a bilateral basis and may actually improve because it will not be subject to EU regulations and constraints. Brexit was a watershed event within Europe causing euro-skeptics throughout the continent to consider whether other countries should follow the United Kingdom's example. Populist parties initially rallied with consideration of similar referendums, but other European nations have not had the same political, economic, and demographic circumstances that led to Brexit. For the United States, Brexit will mean that its bilateral special relationship with the United Kingdom is increasingly important. Additionally, there will be a relatively greater emphasis on NATO-oriented security policy as opposed to the growth of a separate EU security and defense policy. Nevertheless, it will be important to maintain a robust economic and political relationship with the European Union. The continuation of European integration, or the potential for further disintegration, will be significantly affected by the British departure from the European Union and its end result.

Ethnic Nationalism. The processes of political and economic transition have in many cases been accompanied by sharp political, economic, and ethnic tensions. Regional instability arising from ethnic and nationalist tensions erupted with the dissolution of Yugoslavia and again on the territory of the former Soviet Union in such places as Nagorno-Karabakh, South Ossetia, Moldova, and Chechnya. NATO has maintained a peace support operation in Kosovo for more than fifteen years. Even the peaceful "velvet divorce" of the Czech Republic and Slovakia in 1993 was a result of nationalist and ethnic disputes. In 2014, a competitive referendum vote in Great Britain nearly put Scotland on a path to independence; a similar movement in Spain continues to seek independence for Catalonia.

Ethnic nationalism is a growing force in the domestic politics of major European states, where anti-immigration and anti-EU political parties on the right have found increasing support and success at the polls. In addition to the success of the UK Independence Party with Brexit, in recent years the French Front National, Hungary's anti-Semitic Jobbik group, the Flemish nationalist Vlaams Belang in

Belgium, Greece's far-right Golden Dawn, Austria's Freedom Party, and Italy's Lega Nord have demonstrated increased prominence in public discourse and in electoral contests. Many of these parties are beginning to spread beyond the borders of their original countries to become influential in the broader EU system. They achieved notable success in the 2014 European Parliament elections.[30]

Demographic Challenges. Changing demographic trends and immigrant integration issues have the potential to create major long-term security issues on the European continent. Europe's population is the world's oldest and getting older, with a median age of forty and with more individuals over sixty years old than under fifteen.

By 2005, fertility across Eastern Europe was just 1.3 children per woman as young workers of reproductive age emigrated west.[31] European fertility has not reached replacement levels since 1975, despite various social policies aimed at promoting fertility through financial incentives and social services.[32] As a result, the population of Europe is expected to start shrinking in 2020. Population decline has already begun in a number of European countries and is expected to accelerate.[33] These demographic trends, coupled with increased immigration from outside of Europe facilitated by free labor movement within an integrated EU economic zone, have created economic, political, and social strains across much of the continent.

Immigration from North Africa and the Middle East has generated contentious debate over the cultural foundations of European states and whether Muslim immigrants, in particular, can (or should) become "European."[34] Concern over Muslim immigration led former French President Valery Giscard D'Estaing to declare that EU membership for Turkey would lead to the "end of the European Union."[35] Such comments suggest that Europe is a "Christian Club" that Muslims are not welcome to join.[36]

The integration of Muslims in Europe has security implications for Europe and for the United States. Some have even gone so far as to call the process "crucial to the future of Europe."[37] The vast majority of the European Union's thirteen million immigrant Muslims have no connection to the extremist offshoots of the religion, but many struggle to integrate into European society, nevertheless. The difficulty that many European countries have in integrating large Muslim immigrant populations has led to concerns that some European environments may serve as breeding grounds for extremists. The interconnectedness of debates over immigration and national security policy in both the United States and Europe is highlighted by the influence of recent terrorist attacks, including the 2015 terrorist attacks at multiple sites in Paris, the 2016 attacks in Belgium, the 2017 attacks in Spain, and an increasing unwillingness to take in Syrian refugees.

Energy. Energy and the security of energy infrastructure will challenge Europe in the coming decades. As the economies of larger developing countries such as China and India grow, competition for scarce natural resources will increase.

Unless and until they develop alternative energy sources, European nations will remain dependent on imports of fossil fuels. Given the variability of oil prices and concerns (particularly in Germany) about the safety of nuclear energy, this situation does not appear likely to change for the foreseeable future. It has profound implications for national security.

Conscious of their vulnerability as energy importers, European states view any confrontations with energy-rich countries as risky. Energy dependence could make it more difficult for Europe and the United States to find common ground when dealing with Russia, for example, which has shown a readiness to wield its energy exports as a political weapon. Russia's simmering disputes with Ukraine raise questions about the reliability of the source of much of Europe's fuel: Europe obtains a quarter of its gas from Russia, and around 90 percent of that supply crosses Ukraine by pipeline, a vulnerability that is impossible to mitigate in a short time.[38] Fears of a potential disruption in fuel supply may affect Europe's calculus when dealing with Russia on a wide array of policy issues.

Return of Great-Power Politics? Many of the political, military, and economic developments in Europe since 1945 have been closely associated with international institutions such as NATO and the European Union. Europe is the most highly institutionalized region of the world in terms of the number and scope of formal international organizations. No other military alliance is as powerful, durable, or highly organized as NATO. The European Union uniquely exerts such powerful forces of governance on its members that it transcends many of the functions of an international organization, approaching some of the competencies of a state. The broad inclusiveness of the OSCE, the Council of Europe, and similar consultative bodies has never existed to the same extent in other regions or other eras. Even the bipolar Cold War dynamic of security competition between a US-backed NATO bloc and a Soviet-backed Warsaw Pact was a highly structured form of strategic competition.

This system is unique to European affairs after World War II, and it is not certain to last. There have been other moments of European integration and peace, but those eras did not include international institutions: in the first half of the twentieth century, for example, efforts at European integration were undertaken through conquest, not institutions. The period between the Congress of Vienna at the end of the French Revolutionary Wars and the outbreak of the First World War (1815–1914) featured peace, prosperity, and relative stability in Europe; it was underpinned by the careful calibration of a balance of power in the Concert of Europe, not by international organizations.

The strength of the formal international institutions that have governed European affairs since 1945 may prove durable. Alternatively, states within these organizations may reassert themselves, believing cooperation in such large structures to be no longer as attractive as it once was. States on the outside may no longer pursue membership in these institutions as they once did. The assertiveness of Russia and a return to the use of military force to alter borders and achieve political objectives may signal a return to an era of realpolitik. The relative decline of Europe in light of the emergence or reemergence of developing countries in other regions may also affect European politics in unforeseen ways. The democratization of power and technology, the rising power of nonstate actors, and growing international networks of informal and nongovernmental organizations may decrease the impact of the kind of formal international organizations that have characterized European politics since World War II.

US Policy Challenges for the Future

Countries on both sides of the Atlantic will continue to evaluate the role and relevance of NATO. Burden sharing is likely to remain a politically salient issue and potential source of tension. Recent developments such as the splitting of the US military headquarters in Europe into two separate commands for Europe and for Africa, the Obama administration's efforts to rebalance US efforts toward the Asia-Pacific, and the Trump administration's criticism of insufficient defense spending by some NATO countries, are interpreted by many as a redirection of America's attention and investment away from Europe. US military presence in Europe has declined from approximately 300,000 troops at the end of the Cold War to fewer than 70,000 as of 2017.

Few European member countries meet the NATO target for military spending of 2 percent of GDP. Differences in spending between the United States and the majority of its European allies have led to interoperability problems. Advances in military technology that are supported by large amounts of US defense spending have left many European militaries struggling to operate effectively in combined operations with the US military, or requiring substantial assistance in training and materiel. However, seventeen member states increased their defense spending as a share of their GDP in 2016, coming closer to the 2 percent guideline. As a whole, NATO spent more on defense in 2016 than it did in either of the previous two years and more of that spending was targeted for equipment than in years past.

Meanwhile, the purpose of NATO is the subject of ongoing debates. Its 2010 Strategic Concept describes collective defense, crisis management, and politico-military security cooperation as core tasks, but relative priorities continue to evolve. After more than a decade of participating in the International Security Assistance Force in Afghanistan, some NATO members have been saying that it is time to reorient toward challenges closer to home. Following Russia's invasions of Georgia and Ukraine, these calls have been most urgent from Central and Eastern European members, states that are newer to NATO but have long-standing security concerns about Russia. At the same time, NATO's long list of military operations and political partnerships outside Europe reflect a continuing interest in having the alliance act on the broader international scene.

The future of trade between the United States and Europe will also have significant implications for American national security. Other states, including China and Brazil, play an increasing role in global economic governance and seek an even greater one. For example, the United States and the European Union play a key role in the management of global trade via the World Trade Organization (WTO). However, because the WTO works on a one-vote-per-member system, the increased engagement and influence of developing economies dilutes the influence of the transatlantic economic community. EU-US trade dispute settlements within the WTO process nevertheless remain economically and politically significant: they engage a large portion of global commerce, and often serve as precedents for the rest of the global system. The extent to which the United States and its European partners can successfully manage a relationship that is simultaneously interdependent and competitive could have significant effects on the entire global trading system.[39]

Finally, American national security interests will be affected by economic developments in Europe and the future of the European Union. Economic and monetary problems in Europe stemming from the 2008 global financial crisis strained the cohesion of the European Union and its common currency, the euro. These problems were most acute in Greece after 2009, but concern over the size of public debt in Portugal, Ireland, Spain, Italy, and even France continues to hang over Europe's economy. As of 2016, loan and bailout programs, a program of quantitative easing by the ECB, and cooperation from global financial institutions have lessened fears of a currency collapse. However, future problems for the euro remain possible so long as its basic design allows countries to share a common currency (and monetary policy) without a common fiscal authority for national budgets or a method of transferring payments among member countries.

Although some have proposed reinstituting some limited forms of monetary cooperation among separate national currencies, the short-term economic and political challenges make such a move unlikely.[40] Any dismantling or collapse of the euro would cause significant economic disruption for Europe and other regions, including the United States.

Ultimately, the United States will continue to involve itself with and in Europe, but the form and structure of transatlantic cooperation will continue to evolve. NATO will likely continue to be the most important part of the overall transatlantic security relationship, and the European Union will continue to play a significant role with regard to global economic relationships. As other European institutions develop and NATO and the European Union evolve, the United States may find itself relying more on bilateral relationships or ad hoc coalitions than on established multilateral arrangements.

Discussion Questions

1. What are the US security commitments under NATO?
2. After the dissolution of the Soviet Union and the end of the Cold War, is NATO still relevant today?
3. What factors have enhanced or limited the credibility of NATO?
4. How does the European Union's desire for common foreign and defense policies and an autonomous defense capability affect US interests?

5. What are the arguments for and against the future expansion of NATO and the European Union? How are US security interests affected if either organization expands further?

6. When dealing with global security concerns, including terrorism, should the United States approach European states on a bilateral basis or through international organizations such as NATO or the European Union? What are the advantages and disadvantages to each approach?

7. How might the changing demographics of Europe affect US security policies?

8. What does the future hold for transatlantic relations? Will the United States continue to view European states as key allies that are instrumental to American security interests?

9. What are the implications of the British vote to leave the European Union for US relations with both the United Kingdom and the European Union?

10. What are the merits and risks of further institutionalizing US economic relations with Europe?

Recommended Reading

Ash, Timothy Garton. *Free World: America, Europe, and the Surprising Future of the West.* New York: Vintage Books, 2005.

Calleo, David P. *Rethinking Europe's Future.* Princeton, NJ: Princeton University Press, 2001.

Clark, Wesley K. *Waging Modern War: Bosnia, Kosovo, and the Future of Combat.* New York: PublicAffairs, 2001.

Everts, Steven, Lawrence Freedman, Charles Grant, François Heisbourg, Daniel Keohane, and Michael O'Hanlon. *A European Way of War.* London: Centre for European Reform, 2004.

Giry, Stéphanie. "France and Its Muslims." *Foreign Affairs* 85, no. 6 (2006): 75–85.

Johnston, Seth. *How NATO Adapts: Strategy and Organization in the Atlantic Alliance since 1950.* Baltimore, MD: Johns Hopkins University Press, 2017.

Judt, Tony. *Postwar: A History of Europe Since 1945.* New York: Penguin, 2005.

Kagan, Robert. *Of Paradise and Power: America and Europe in the New World Order.* New York: Alfred A. Knopf, 2003.

Lindberg, Tod, ed. *Beyond Paradise and Power: Europe, America, and the Future of a Troubled Partnership.* New York: Routledge, 2004.

Moravcsik, Andrew. *Social Purpose and State Power from Messina to Maastricht.* Ithaca, NY: Cornell University Press, 1998.

Rühle, Michael. "NATO after Prague: Learning the Lessons of 9/11." *Parameters* 33, no. 2 (2003): 89–97.

Sloan, Stanley R. *NATO, The European Union, and the Atlantic Community: The Transatlantic Bargain Reconsidered.* Lanham, MD: Rowman & Littlefield, 2003.

Whitman, Richard. "NATO, the EU, and ESDP: An Emerging Division of Labor?" *Contemporary Security Policy* 25, no. 3 (2004): 430–51.

Recommended Internet Resources

European Union, http://europa.eu/index_en.htm
North Atlantic Treaty Organization, http://www.nato.int
Organization for Security and Co-Operation in Europe, www.osce.org
US Commission on Security and Cooperation in Europe, www.csce.gov

Notes

1. The World Bank, "European Union," n.d., http://databank.worldbank.org/data/reports.aspx?source=world-development-indicators. In June 2016, the United Kingdom voted to leave the European Union; however its contribution to GDP is still included in this the $16.3 trillion.

2. Daniel S. Hamilton and Joseph P. Quinlan. "The Transatlantic Economy 2015," Center for Transatlantic Relations, Johns Hopkins University, Paul H. Nitze School of Advanced International Studies, Washington DC, 2015, http://transatlanticrelations.org/books/transatlantic-economy-2015.

3. See Walt W. Rostow, "Lessons of the Plan: Looking Forward to the Next Century," in the Marshall Plan Commemorative Section, *Foreign Affairs* 76, no. 3 (1997): 205–12.

4. See Henry A. Kissinger, "The Future of NATO," *Washington Quarterly* 2, no. 4 (1979): 7.

5. For a discussion of the problems inherent in collective systems, see Mancur Olson Jr., *The Logic of Collective Action: Public Goods and the Theory of Groups* (Cambridge, MA: Harvard University Press, 1965).

6. "Partnership with the Countries of Central and Eastern Europe," statement issued by the North Atlantic Council, meeting in Ministerial Session in Copenhagen, June 6 and 7, 1991, Press Communique M-1(91)42 (Brussels: NATO, June 6, 1991).

7. Nick Williams, "Partnership for Peace: Permanent Fixture or Declining Asset?" *Survival* 38, no. 1 (1996): 102.

8. NATO's original twelve members were Belgium, Canada, Denmark, France, Iceland, Italy, Luxembourg, the Netherlands, Norway, Portugal, the United Kingdom, and the United States.

9. NATO, "NATO's Role in Kosovo," 2007, www.nato.int/kosovo/kosovo.htm.

10. On the discussion at NATO Headquarters on September 11 and 12, 2001, leading to the invocation of Article 5, see Edgar Buckley, "Invoking Article 5," *NATO Review* 2 (Summer 2006), www.nato.int/docu/review/2006/issue2/english/art2.html.

11. NATO, "NATO and the Fight against Terrorism," 2017, www.nato.int/terrorism/index.htm.

12. The NATO AWACS were deployed from Europe to the United States to assist in providing airspace control after 9/11 because many US aircraft were deployed to Afghanistan. See "NATO Aircraft Guard U.S. Skies," CNN, October 12, 2001, http://www.cnn.com/2001/US/10/12/ret.nato.awacs/index.html. See also Vice Admiral Roberto Cesaretti, "Combating Terrorism in the Mediterranean," *NATO Review* 3 (Autumn 2005), www.nato.int/docu/review/2005/issue3/english/art4.html.

13. See NATO Press Release 127 (2002), "Prague Summit Declaration," November 21, 2002, www.nato.int/docu/pr/2002/p02-127e.htm.

14. NATO, "Wales Summit Declaration," September 5, 2014, http://www.nato.int/cps/en/natohq/official_texts_112964.htm. See also "Tillerson Sets NATO Allies 2-Month 'Goal' on Spending," *CBS News*, March 31, 2017, http://www.cbsnews.com/news/rex-tillerson-nato-allies-defense-spending-russia-isis/.

15. Nicholas Fiorenza, "NATO Response Force—Ready for Action," *Jane's Defense Weekly*, September 21, 2006.

16. George H. W. Bush, "A Europe Whole and Free," remarks to the Citizens of Mainz, Federal Republic of Germany, May 31, 1989, http://usa.usembassy.de/etexts/ga6-890531.htm.

17. Francis Fukuyama, "The End of History?" *National Interest* 16 (Summer 1989): 3–18.

18. Robert Kagan, *The Return of History and the End of Dreams* (New York: Knopf, 2008).

19. Directorate General for Trade, European Commission, "Client and Supplier Countries of the EU28 in Merchandise Trade (Value %) (2017, Excluding Intra-EU Trade)" (Brussels: European Commission, 2017).

20. Office of the United States Trade Representative, "European Union," n.d., https://ustr.gov/countries-regions/europe-middle-east/europe/european-union.

21. Stephen McGuire and Michael Smith, *The European Union and the United States: Competition and Convergence in the Global Arena* (New York: Palgrave Macmillan, 2008).

22. Fareed Zakaria, *The Post-American World: Release 2.0* (New York: W. W. Norton, 2011).

23. Barry Eichengreen, *The European Economy since 1945: Coordinated Capitalism and Beyond* (Princeton, NJ: Princeton University Press, 2008).

24. There are nineteen EU member states that use the euro as their currency: Austria, Belgium, Cyprus, Estonia, Finland, France, Germany, Greece, Ireland, Italy, Latvia, Lithuania, Luxembourg, Malta, the Netherlands, Portugal, Slovakia, Slovenia, and Spain. The other EU members have yet to adopt the euro or have chosen not to do so.

25. Paul De Grauwe, *Economics of Monetary Union* (Oxford: Oxford University Press, 2012); Ian Bache, Stephen George, and Simon Bulmer, *Politics in the European Union* (Oxford: Oxford University Press, 2011).

26. Rebecca M. Nelson, Paul Belkin, Derek E. Mix, and Martin A. Weiss, *The Euro Zone Crisis: Overview and Issues for Congress* (Washington, DC: Congressional Research Service, 2012).

27. Paul De Grauwe, "The European Central Bank as Lender of Last Resort in Government Bond Markets," *CESifo Economic Studies* 59, no. 3 (2013): 520–35; Council of the European Union (press release), "Council Approves Single Supervisory Mechanism for Banking," October 15, 2013, http://www.consilium.europa.eu/uedocs/cms_data/docs/pressdata/en/ecofin/139012.pdf.

28. Secretary of State Madeleine Albright, "Albright to North Atlantic Council," December 8, 1998, http://fas.org/man/nato/news/1998/98120802_tlt.html.

29. For example, the United Kingdom did not join the border-free Schengen area, and it negotiated a reduced budget contribution. See James McBride, "What Brexit Means," *Council on Foreign Relations Backgrounder*, June 9, 2017, https://www.cfr.org/backgrounder/what-brexit-means.

30. "Eurobarbarians at the Gates: Forecasting the Seats Potentially Won by Anti-EU Parties," *Economist*, May 23, 2014, http://www.economist.com/blogs/graphicdetail/2014/05/european-parliament-elections; "Ultra-Nationalist Party Surges in Hungary," NPR, May 24, 2014, http://www.npr.org/2014/05/24/315445164/ultra-nationalist-party-surges-in-hungary; "UKIP Gains First Elected MP with Clacton Win," BBC, October 10, 2014, http://www.bbc.com/news/uk-politics-29549414.

31. European Union Center of North Carolina, "The EU's Demographic Crisis," *EU Briefings*, March 2008, https://europe.unc.edu/files/2016/11/Brief_EU_Demographic_Crisis_2008.pdf.

32. France has seen some success with policies to promote fertility, however, and Germany has recently copied some French policies. Tracy McNicoll, "France's Baby Boom," *Newsweek*, January 30, 2011, http://www.newsweek.com/frances-baby-boom-66713.

33. On European demographics generally, see Iris Hossmann et al., *Europe's Demographic Future: Growing Imbalances* (Berlin: Berlin Institute for Population and Devel-

opment, 2008) and Sarah Harper, "Aging Europe's Demographic Destiny: Framing the Challenges Ahead," *Current History* 110 (March 2011): 117–21.

34. For an intelligent and provocative statement of the pessimistic case, see Christopher Caldwell, *Reflection on the Revolution in Europe* (New York: Doubleday, 2009).

35. Garth Harding, "No Turkey for EU Says Giscard d'Estaing," UPI, November 8, 2002, http://www.upi.com/No-Turkey-for-EU-says-Giscard-dEstaing/61351036767928/.

36. "Too Big for Europe? The Turks Are at the Gates of Brussels," *Economist*, November 16, 2002, 47.

37. Anthony Browne, "Threat of Islamic Extremism that Stretches across Europe," *TimesOnline*, July 26, 2005, www.timesonline.co.uk/tol/news/uk/article548063.ece.

38. Thomas Catan, Javier Blas, Hugh Williamson, Gerrit Wiesmann, Robert Anderson, Jan Cienski, and Neil Buckley, "Stand-Off Cuts Gas Supplies to Europe," *Financial Times*, January 2, 2006.

39. See McGuire and Smith, *The European Union and the United States: Competition and Convergence in the Global Arena* (New York: Palgrave Macmillan, 2008), 67–95.

40. François Heisbourg, "The EU without the Euro" *Survival* 56, no. 2 (April/May 2014): 35.

24

Latin America

The nations that comprise Latin America share common geography but represent a highly diverse collection of sovereign states with an array of cultures and heritages. This chapter looks at two geopolitical regions of the western hemisphere: the Caribbean, along with its islands and perimeter territory, and South America (figure 24.1).[1] Within the Caribbean perimeter are Mexico, Central America (Belize, Guatemala, El Salvador, Honduras, Nicaragua, Costa Rica, and Panama), and the northern coast of South America (Colombia, Venezuela, Guyana, Suriname).[2] Major Caribbean island nations include Cuba, Dominican Republic, Haiti, Jamaica, Trinidad-Tobago, the commonwealth of Puerto Rico, the Dutch island of Curaçao, and France's Martinique. The Caribbean is sometimes referred to as America's *third border*.[3] The South American geopolitical arena encompasses the Southern Cone (Argentina, Chile, Paraguay, and Uruguay), the Andes (Ecuador, Peru, and Bolivia), and the vast landmass of Brazil. Approximately 633 million citizens, or nearly one-tenth of the earth's total population, call Latin America and the Caribbean home, 80 percent of them residing in urbanized areas. Spanish is the official language of twenty nations. Portuguese is the language of 207 million Brazilians. English, Spanish, Dutch, and French can be heard around the Caribbean.[4] Pre-Colombian indigenous languages are still spoken by significant populations in Bolivia, Guatemala, Mexico, and Peru.

Since the days of European conquest and colonization, Latin America economies have developed around exports. Latin America's abundant natural resources, including gold, silver, sugar, tobacco, soybeans, copper, and petroleum, have

The authors would like to thank Dr. Ray Walser for his significant contributions to this chapter.

FIGURE 24.1 Latin America

supplied the international economy for centuries. In recent decades, Latin America has supplemented exports with expanded industrial capacity and its nations experienced a period of sustained economic growth with an increasing middle class and substantial reductions in poverty, especially extreme poverty. Latin America generated $5.295 trillion in economic activity in 2016 (table 24.1).[5] Despite recent economic setbacks, Brazil remains the world's seventh largest economy, and joins

Table 24.1 Latin America Key Statistics

Country	*Total population (millions)*	*Life expectancy at birth*	*GDP US$ (billions)*	*GDP/ capita US$*	*Population living in poverty (%)*	*Military expenditure (% of GDP)*	*Military spending US$ (millions)*	*Human Development Index (HDL) ranking (of 188)*
Argentina	43.9	77.1	541.7	20,200	32.2	1.0	5181	45
Belize	0.4	68.7	1.8	8,200	41.0	1.2	21	103
Bolivia	11.0	69.2	34.0	7,200	38.6	1.2	443	118
Brazil	205.8	73.8	1,777.0	14,800	3.7	1.3	23545	79
Chile	17.7	78.8	234.9	24,000	14.4	1.4	3318	38
Colombia	47.2	75.7	274.1	14,100	27.8	3.4	8953	95
Costa Rica	4.9	78.6	57.7	16,100	21.7	0.7	413	66
Cuba	11.2	78.7	81.6	11,900	na	na	na	68
Dominican Republic	10.6	78.1	71.5	15,900	30.5	0.6	455	99
Ecuador	16.1	76.8	99.1	11,000	25.6	1.6	1565	89
El Salvador	6.2	74.7	26.6	8,900	34.9	0.6	146	117
Guatemala	15.2	72.3	68.4	7,900	59.3	0.4	268	125
Guyana	0.7	68.4	3.5	7,900	35.0	1.3	46	127
Haiti	10.5	63.8	8.3	1,800	58.5	0.1	7	163
Honduras	8.9	71.1	20.9	5,300	29.6	1.4	295	130
Jamaica	3.0	73.6	13.8	9,000	16.5	0.8	115	94
Mexico	123.2	75.9	1,064.0	18,900	46.2	0.5	5060	77
Nicaragua	6.0	73.2	13.4	5,300	29.6	0.5	73	124
Panama	3.7	78.6	55.2	22,800	23.0	1.4	751	60
Paraguay	6.9	77.2	32.2	9,500	22.2	1.0	267	110
Peru	30.7	73.7	180.3	13,000	22.7	1.2	2086	87
Uruguay	3.4	77.2	58.5	20,300	9.7	0.9	494	54
Venezuela	30.9	75.8	333.7	15,100	19.7	0.4	1444	71

na = not applicable.

Sources: Data on population and economy is from the CIA World Factbook 2017, https://www.cia.gov/library/publications/the-world-factbook. Military expenditure data is from International Institute for Strategic Studies (IISS), *The Military Balance 2017* (London: IISS, 2017). HDI rankings are from *Human Development Report 2016*, http://hdr.undp.org/en/data. Most figures are from 2016 (otherwise latest available data is listed). GDP is reported at the official exchange rate. GDP per capita is using Purchasing Power Parity rates.

Mexico and Argentina as members of the group of twenty industrialized nations, the G20.

Quality of life has improved along with the economy, but not uniformly. Life expectancy rose from 56 years in 1960 to 75 in 2015. Millions were lifted out of extreme poverty and many entered the middle classes from 2002 to 2012. In 2003, 41.3 percent of the region's people lived below the poverty line, but by 2013 this figure had fallen to 24.3 percent. Latin America's middle class, defined as people with incomes of $10–50 per day, grew from 21.3 percent to 35.0 percent of the population during this period.[6] Despite these improvements, considerable inequality, high levels of poverty, and significant crime persists. One-third of global homicides occur in Latin America; murder rates in Brazil and Venezuela are among the highest in the world.[7] Other factors that may inhibit equitable growth include corruption, legal insecurity, overregulation, lack of infrastructure, and extensive informal markets.

This chapter provides an overview of the conditions in Latin America and the role of US policy in the region. It begins with a review of the history of US relations in the western hemisphere, illustrating international political dynamics that still influence policy today. It then articulates seven major US policy objectives in the region and three factors that could diminish US influence. It then provides an overview of the major countries and sub-regions within Latin America. The chapter concludes with a look ahead at future US policy toward the Western Hemisphere.

History of US Involvement in Latin America

Sheltered by the Atlantic Ocean from the major European powers, the newly independent United States sought to define and protect its southern flank by establishing friendly relations with other American nations. In his 1823 annual message to Congress, President James Monroe articulated one of the first general principles of US foreign policy: "The American continents . . . are henceforth not to be considered as subjects for future colonization by any European powers."[8] At the time, the United States relied upon the tacit cooperation of its old enemy, Great Britain, whose interests and superior navy deterred other European powers, to maintain this policy.

As American economic and military might grew in the nineteenth century, the Monroe Doctrine, as it came to be known, represented an increasingly unilateral US assumption of hegemonic control, by establishing a US-dominated sphere of influence, particularly in the Caribbean and Central America. The Monroe Doctrine did not, however, prevent the United States from expanding at the expense of Mexico in the 1840s or engaging in frequent military interventions in the early twentieth century. Close ties within the Americas did, however, lead to the US construction of the Panama Canal from 1904 to 1914.

Seldom popular with Latin American nations, the implementation of the Monroe Doctrine has shifted over time. In the 1930s, the Good Neighbor Policy of President Franklin D. Roosevelt outlined an approach based on an end to interventions and greater respect for national sovereignty. The approach was generally short-lived: during the two World Wars and the Cold War, the United States took actions to counter possible German, Japanese, and Soviet gains in the Western Hemisphere. The Monroe Doctrine was revitalized during the Cold War. After the communist takeover of Cuba, the United States shifted back to the key tenets of the Monroe Doctrine to prevent other nations from following suit. In October 1962, a dangerous game of nuclear brinksmanship led to a naval blockade. The Cuban Missile Crisis was resolved with a compromise between the two superpowers: a US pledge not to invade Cuba and to withdraw missiles in Turkey in exchange for the removal of Soviet missiles from Cuba. The Cuban Missile Crisis, the nearest the United States has ever come to a nuclear exchange, highlighted the urgent US need to respond to security threats close to home. In the late 1960s, the United States helped Bolivia eliminate an insurgent threat led by Che Guevara; in the 1970s, the United States favored the bloody coup against Chile's leftist president, Salvador Allende.

US policy swung back closer to Roosevelt's Good Neighbor approach when President Jimmy Carter negotiated the Panama Canal Treaty, which initiated the process of turning over the Canal Zone to Panama by the end of the twentieth century. Following the armed overthrow of Nicaragua's right-wing dictator Anastasio Somoza in July 1979, a policy of conciliation advanced by President Carter failed to yield positive results. The radicalization of the Nicaragua Revolution and the advance of a guerilla insurgency in El Salvador led President Ronald Reagan's administration to pursue a hardline strategy in Central America. For more than a decade, the administrations of Reagan and George H. W. Bush were involved both directly and covertly in civil strife in Guatemala, El Salvador, Honduras, and Nicaragua. In 1983, violent instability on the small Caribbean island of Grenada prompted a military operation to protect American lives, restore order, and thwart Cuban and Russian designs on the island. The Cold War's final struggles included an assertive policy of "rollback" meant to demonstrate US resolve to support "freedom fighters" and weaken or oust potential Soviet allies. The Central American wars of the 1980s—costly in human lives, economically devastating, and morally debatable—ended in negotiated peace agreements, but left deep political, economic, and social scars that have remained for decades.

By the early 1990s, US fears of Soviet-inspired communist takeovers subsided, and increasing democratization in Latin America permitted Washington policy makers to focus on a broad range of shared interests, and to seek enhanced engagement concerning free trade, foreign investment, economic development, poverty reduction, democratic governance, and shared security. A vision of a mature hemispheric relationship based on solidarity, mutual respect, and a smoothly functioning inter-American system of peace and cooperation has served as a guiding beacon in recent decades as the nations of the hemisphere have worked cooperatively within the Organization of American States (OAS), the world's oldest regional body.[9] The United States and its hemispheric partners also share common security interests in stopping illicit trafficking in humans, firearms, and drugs; managing illegal migration; combatting international terrorism; and addressing recurring environmental and health challenges. In 1994, President Bill Clinton convened the first Summit of the Americas in Miami, where heads of state pledged to advance prosperity, democratic values, institutions, and security in the Western Hemisphere. Assigning priority to hemispheric ties, President Clinton also created the office of White House Special Envoy to Latin America. In 1999, the United States completed the transfer of the Panama Canal Zone and ownership of the canal to the Panamanian people. Secretary of State Colin Powell signed the OAS's Democratic Charter in Lima, Peru, in September 2001.[10] As the United States shifted away from concerns over security and fear of communism toward deepening inter-American security cooperation, "soft power" tools of statecraft increasingly took precedence over hard power.

In a 2013 speech at the OAS, President Barack Obama's Secretary of State John Kerry declared without equivocation that "the era of the Monroe Doctrine is over."[11] In its place, Secretary Kerry defined a new US vision for the region: "The relationship that we seek and that we have worked hard to foster is . . . about all of our countries viewing one another as equals, sharing responsibilities, cooperating on security issues, and adhering not to doctrine, but to the decisions that we make as partners to advance the values and the interests that we share. This new vision, treating Latin America as equal partners and not as subordinates, is increasingly demonstrated in US foreign policy in Latin America."[12] The Monroe Doctrine had become less relevant because the challenges to US interests were mostly from sources indigenous to the region rather than from European intervention.

President Donald Trump's concerns are not with European powers in Latin America but with Chinese "state-led investment and loans" and China and Russia "seeking to expand military linkages and arms sales across the region." The Trump administration vowed to work with Latin American states to "build a stable and peaceful hemisphere that increases economic opportunities for all, improves governance, reduces the power of criminal organizations, and limits the malign influence of non-hemispheric forces."[13] The challenge for the United States is to develop and implement policies in Latin America that can achieve US national security objectives in this contemporary environment.

National Interests and Policy Objectives

Despite the altered global and regional circumstances of the twenty-first century, US national interests in Latin America have remained largely consistent: protecting the US southern flank, advancing democracy and human rights, promoting economic growth, reducing the flow of illicit drugs, and limiting illegal migration. In the past two decades, two additional interests—responding to humanitarian crises and addressing the environmental effects of climate change—have become increasingly important aspects of US strategy in the region.

Protect the US Homeland through Hemispheric Security. Given the unequal power relationship between the United States and Latin American nations, the

United States has, apart from the 1962 Cuban Missile Crisis, been spared any direct military threat from its southern neighbors. Historically, this advantageous relationship close to home has provided the United States with greater freedom to engage diplomatically and militarily elsewhere, in Asia, Europe, and the Middle East. Nevertheless, Washington policy makers have also used the overwhelming US economic and military superiority in the Western Hemisphere to neutralize perceived security threats during the two World Wars and during the Cold War.

As part of its strategy of containment of Soviet expansion (see chapter 3), the United States advanced the Inter-American Treaty of Reciprocal Assistance (also known as the Rio Pact) in 1947. The Rio Pact specified that an attack on any of the signatories would be considered "an act of aggression against all other American states" and would be met by a concerted response to halt an attack.[14] In a parallel diplomatic move, the United States undertook to transform the Pan American Union (which had been formed in 1890 to promote cooperation among the countries of Latin America and the United States) into a more cohesive regional body; the Organization of American States (OAS) was established in 1948. The objective of the OAS was to promote a regional order of peace and justice, with solidarity and collaboration, and to defend the members' sovereignty, territorial integrity, and independence. Begun in Bogota, Colombia, with twenty-one members, the OAS has grown to include thirty-five member states focused on four main issue areas: democracy, development, human rights, and security.[15]

On the defense and security side, the Inter-American Defense Board was formed during World War II to foster military cooperation to counter Axis aggression. This cooperation continued during the Cold War; the Inter-American Defense College, located at Fort McNair in Washington, DC, was established in 1962 to support professional education and continued military cooperation. Today both organizations are linked to the OAS and its efforts to foster peace in the Americas. Sometimes overlooked, the 1967 Treaty of Tlatelolco is also important to US security interests: it declares all territory south of the Rio Grande to be a nuclear-weapon-free zone.[16]

Despite these strong institutional ties, United States and Latin American interests have sometimes been in conflict. While Latin American states have often accepted US financial and military support, they generally oppose US interventions in the internal affairs of other countries. Most Latin American nations have taken a dim view of interventions, such as the covert toppling of Guatemala's left-leaning President Jacobo Arbenz in 1954; the failed attempt at the Bay of Pigs to overthrow Fidel Castro's regime in 1961; the direct US military intervention in the Dominican Republic in 1965 to thwart a potential communist takeover; and the U.S involvement in the Central American wars of the 1980s.

Currently, two geographic combatant commands anchor US defense of its southern flank. US Northern Command (NORTHCOM), established in 2002, has responsibility for US relations with Mexico and with the Bahamas.[17] US Southern Command (SOUTHCOM), previously based in the Panama Canal Zone, is now headquartered in southern Florida and handles US security ties with the rest of Latin America and the Caribbean.[18] In 2017, SOUTHCOM's missions focused on countering transregional and transnational threat networks, building relationships to meet global challenges, and increasing partner capacity and capability.[19] Military-to-military training and education are supported by the Western Hemisphere Institute for Security Cooperation (formerly known as the School of the Americas), located at Fort Benning, Georgia, and the William J. Perry Center for Hemispheric Defense Studies at the National Defense University in Washington, DC. Another vehicle for security cooperation is the annual conference of ministers of defense of the Americas, begun in 1995, which is dedicated to preserving democracy, civilian-military dialogue, respect for human rights, and peaceful conflict resolution.[20]

Advance Democracy and Human Rights. Respect for basic human rights and the importance of democratic elections are enshrined in numerous UN and OAS declarations. The Inter-American Commission on Human Rights and the Inter-American Human Rights Court are designed to serve as watchdogs and defenders of the rights of citizens, as promised in the American Convention on Human Rights (also known as the Pact of San Jose, signed in Costa Rica in 1969).

Although there have been regressions, Latin American nations have generally moved toward electoral democracy and away from oligarchic rule, rule by military strongmen (*caudillos* and juntas), coups d'état, and revolutionary upheaval. By the late 1980s, military regimes in Argentina, Brazil, Chile, and other states had restored governance to elected civilians. Bipartisan consensus in the United States agreed that democratically governed nations were more likely to secure the peace, expand open markets, promote economic development, protect American citizens, uphold human rights, and avoid humanitarian crises. The United States intervened militarily in Panama (in 1989) and Haiti (in 1995 and 2001) to prevent power consolidation by leaders who sought to undermine democratic elections. All states in the hemisphere, except Cuba, signed the Inter-American Democratic Charter in 2001 and committed to collective action, including expelling those who violate the charter's fundamentals. This multilateral OAS approach to democracy promotion began to unravel in the past fifteen years, in large part because of a rise in influence of Venezuela's Hugo Chavez. Chavez's ideological concepts of "participatory democracy" and "twenty-first century socialism" facilitated the arbitrary use of executive power though authoritarian, one-party rule in the name of providing social justice for the previously marginalized.

Since the early 1990s, the United States has increasingly invested in bilateral programs to assist in democracy development, focusing on government-citizen relationships. These multidimensional programs link integrity, service delivery, accountability, transparency, and other aspects of government effectiveness with citizen involvement such as voting, forming political parties, advancing civil society, and fostering a free media. The US Agency for International Development (USAID) administers these programs through nonprofit nongovernmental organizations, such as the National Endowment for Democracy, the National Democratic Institute, and the International Republican Institute. In 1998, Congress established the Human Rights and Democracy Fund in the US State Department to monitor and extend democracy and protect human rights.

A history of human rights abuses in Latin America by military regimes and by security forces fighting insurgency and criminal networks has complicated US policy in the region. Grievous cases include the "Dirty Wars" of the 1970s in the Southern Cone, massacres and "death squads" in Central America in the 1980s and more recently in the 2000s, and the case of "false positives" in Colombia (civilians deliberately murdered to increase the body count of enemy dead). In each case, governments friendly to the United States faced radicalized, anti-American enemies. Questions arose over the US responses: whether it should withdraw important security assistance or instead overlook human rights abuses. The Leahy Law, initiated by Senator Patrick Leahy and passed by the US Congress in the late 1990s, stated that the United States would not tolerate or support foreign partners who violate the personal integrity, dignity, or due process of their citizens. The Leahy Law requires monitoring to ensure that US arms and military training are delivered only to foreign military professionals with records of good conduct, while being denied to individuals or units charged with violations of human rights and the rules of war.

A significant focus of recent US policy toward Latin America has been efforts to combat corruption. Specific steps have included measures directed at corrupt officials living in the United States and the seizure of illicit assets and properties held in the United States. Department of Justice enforcement of the Foreign Corrupt Practices Act and supervision by the Securities and Exchange Commission are tools employed to detect and punish corruption at the corporate and individual levels.

Promote Economic Growth and Stability. The economic health of Latin America is a vital regional interest for the United States. Sustained and predictable economic development that helps to reduce poverty, lessen inequality, and promote prosperity remains the most promising long-term answer to regional tensions over issues such as immigration, intrastate violence, illegal drug activity, and antidemocratic practices. Robust trade and financial engagement provide a sound foundation for stronger partnerships between the United States and the region.

Latin America is a major trading partner of the United States, providing several crucial goods. In recent years, trade with Latin America accounts for approximately 22 percent of US global trade. Mexico is America's third largest trading partner and second largest export market, accounting for 15 percent of total US trade.[21] Brazil, Venezuela, and Colombia are also major US trade partners within the region. Venezuela and Colombia are important oil exporters; Brazil and Colombia import substantial quantities of US agricultural products.

US commercial integration with Latin American economies has continued to expand during the past two decades, despite the 2008 recession. Economic drivers include joint manufacturing production, which often involves assembly platforms where labor costs are low (known as *maquiladoras*), and substantial US commodity imports, including metals, agricultural products, and petroleum products. The United States remains a major provider of financial, telecommunications, and other services to Latin America. US tourism is especially important for the economies of Mexico and the Caribbean islands. The regular flow of remittances sent from migrants in the United States to family members in Latin America is important to Latin America's economic health; totals reached $73 billion in 2016.[22] The United States is still the single largest source of foreign direct investment in Latin America and has historically supported robust capitalization of the World Bank and the Inter-American Development Bank (IADB). For example, the IADB has provided more than $260 billion in loans for projects in key sectors such as transportation, energy, education, health, water, and sanitation.[23] In addition to IADB loans, foreign direct investment helps diversify Latin American economies away from dependence on commodity exports, such as oil, copper, iron ore, soybeans, coffee, and beef, thereby reducing their vulnerability to the volatility of global commodity markets.

Recognition of the mutual benefits to be gained from strengthening economic relationships within the hemisphere led to proposals to accelerate economic integration and liberalize trade. Over the past five decades, the nations of the Western Hemisphere have attempted numerous free trade initiatives. While some have failed, others are major drivers of economic growth. From the US perspective, the most significant free trade agreement remains the North American Free Trade Agreement (NAFTA), which entered into force in January 1994. Between 1993 and 2015, trade among its three members—Canada, the United States, and Mexico—quadrupled from $297 billion to $1.14 trillion. Under NAFTA, agricultural exports among all three nations have surged, export-related jobs in goods and services have grown, and integrated production chains have increased the global competitiveness of a variety of manufactured products, particularly motor vehicles. Fiercely debated when first proposed, NAFTA remains a politically contentious topic with ongoing disputes about its advantages and disadvantages.[24] The Trump administration has argued that NAFTA is unfair to US workers and has proposed renegotiating or possibly ending it.

The United States, five Central American nations, and the Dominican Republic signed the Central America–Dominican Republic Free Trade Agreement (CAFTA-DR) in 2004. Fully in force by 2009, CAFTA-DR removed all tariff barriers by 2015. The United States entered into the agreement as "a way for America to support freedom, democracy, and economic reform in our neighborhood."[25] In 2014, the CAFTA-DR region was the thirteenth largest US export market and its third largest in Latin America, behind Mexico and Brazil. The United States exported $31.3 billion in goods to CAFTA-DR members in 2014, almost 86 percent more than in 2005, immediately before the agreement entered into force.[26] In addition to NAFTA and CAFTA-DR, the United States has concluded bilateral free trade agreements with Chile, Peru, Colombia, and Panama. These agreements constitute an important component of the US strategy of opening markets in the hemisphere through competitive liberalization.

Apart from agreements with the United States, Latin American nations have promoted economic integration with one another and reduction of barriers to mutual trade. The Common Market of the South (MERCOSUR), launched in 1991, drew together Argentina, Brazil, Paraguay and Uruguay. It sought to create an economic and political framework similar to that of the European Union and thus focused on removing trade barriers and coordinating policy; in addition, it even contemplated a common external tariff and currency.[27] MERCOSUR has promoted intraregional trade, but its member nations have been unable to reach consensus regarding policy coordination. Venezuela's entry into MERCOSUR in 2012 was initially welcomed, but relations between the original four members and Venezuela swiftly soured because of the latter's human rights violations and economic difficulties. In December 2016, the original four members suspended Venezuela from MERCOSUR for failure to comply with its requirements. The future of MERCOSUR will depend in large part on the actions of its two largest members—Brazil and Argentina—and on the ability to forge broader agreements, such as a proposed EU-MERCOSUR free trade agreement currently under negotiation.

Other regional economic integration mechanisms include the fifteen-member Caribbean Community (CARICOM), the Andean Community, and the Central American Integration System (SICA). In 2012 Peru, Chile, Colombia, and Mexico created the Pacific Alliance to deepen cooperation among members in support of closer relations with the Asia-Pacific region. A Free Trade Area of the Americas (FTAA), proposed at the first Summit of the Americas in 1994 would have created the world's largest free trade zone. When optimism ran high, proponents of the FTAA set a target date for completion in 2005. The FTAA failed to become reality for several reasons, including rejection by Venezuela's Hugo Chavez and other key leaders, fears of the impact of trade liberalization on fragile developing economies, and sharp divisions over US agricultural subsidies. Negotiations for the FTAA ended in acrimony at the 2005 Summit of the Americas in Argentina.

Reduce the Threat of Illicit Drugs. Latin America has been prominent in US attempts to limit the supply of opiates, heroin, cocaine, marijuana, and other illicit drugs into the United States. By the early 1980s, drug producers and traffickers operating in Medellín and Cali, Colombia, formed powerful cartels led by Pablo Escobar and other notorious kingpins. Colombia emerged as the center of cocaine production and export, accounting for 80 percent of the cocaine sent to the United States. The trade in cocaine and other illicit drugs fueled assassinations, homicides, insurgency, extortion, and corruption on a wide scale, traumatizing much of Colombia from the 1980s well into the twenty-first century.

US counter-narcotics initiatives eventually led to Plan Colombia (discussed further below), which evolved over time into a generally successful strategic partnership. Other key US counter-drug initiatives include the Mérida Initiative with Mexico, which has provided more than $2.5 billion to fight organized crime and drug trafficking since 2008; the Central American Regional Security Initiative (CARSI), with nearly $1 billion since 2008; and the Caribbean Basin Security

Initiative (CBSI), with $437 million in US support since 2010. These initiatives include programs to curtail cultivation of coca, poppy, and marijuana, as well as funding to strengthen law enforcement capacity, improve judicial processes, and enhance the rule of law. Funding is often complemented with measures to improve extradition procedures, share intelligence, track financial networks, improve interdiction capabilities, and enhance currency controls.

Consistent success in the drug war remains elusive.[28] Currently, criminal drug networks in Mexico represent the greatest threat because they are the principal wholesale suppliers of illicit drugs to the United States.[29] Director of National Intelligence Dan Coates explained in 2017 that "rising foreign drug production, the staying power of Mexican trafficking networks, and strong demand are driving the U.S. drug threat. In Mexico, the dominant source of U.S. heroin, potential heroin production doubled from 2014 to 2016. . . . Production of cocaine reached the highest levels on record for Colombia in 2016 and for Peru and Bolivia in 2015 . . . driven in part by a decline in coca eradication efforts."[30] Effective cooperation with Latin American nations to counter drugs will continue to be a challenge for the foreseeable future.

Limit Illegal Migration. Another major US interest in Latin America is to reduce illegal immigration into the United States. Economic and political conditions in Latin America significantly affect the number of persons who attempt to enter or remain in the United States. US immigration policy has significant economic, diplomatic, and political effects in Latin America. For example, in 2014, tens of thousands of women and children attempting to reach the United States, including many unaccompanied minors, set out from Central America, especially the violence-prone, gang-ridden Northern Triangle of El Salvador, Guatemala, and Honduras. Many came seeking asylum, in what President Obama labeled a humanitarian crisis. According to the US Border Patrol, the 2014 movement involved apprehension of 479,000 Central Americans, including 69,000 unaccompanied children.[31] Two years later, another Central American surge resulted in 408,000 apprehensions. The Central American outflow forced the Obama administration to toughen border enforcement, enhance cooperation with Mexico to discourage transit, and develop a more comprehensive effort to address poverty and lawlessness at the source. Cracking down on illegal immigration, to include the construction of a border wall between the United States and Mexico, was a central tenet of Trump's 2016 presidential campaign and his ensuing administration.

Latin America has a critical interest in US immigration policy. Mishandled immigration reform has the potential to sour key relationships with individual countries, to inflict needless hardships and costs, to crimp remittances, and to divert resources from countering drugs and other criminal activity. Ultimately, policy makers in the United States and in each Latin American nation must resolve the immigration issue. Until there are major improvements in Latin America's economy, especially for the desperately poor, immigration will continue remain challenging.

Respond to Humanitarian Crises. Hurricanes, earthquakes, and communicable diseases in the Americas inflict enormous costs in human lives, injury, and property damage, with spillover effects on the United States. US policy makers recognize that these events are inevitable, though unpredictable, and that the United States must be prepared to deal with such contingencies in a generous, proactive, interagency manner. In late October 1998, for example, Hurricane Mitch struck Central America, leaving more than 11,000 people dead, destroying hundreds of thousands of homes, causing more than $5 billion in damage, and triggering an increase in migration toward the United States. The January 2010 Haitian earthquake claimed over 220,000 lives, injured 300,000, and displaced 1.5 million Haitians. The US military was at the forefront of rescue and disaster relief efforts that became a "whole of government" undertaking.[32] USAID provided emergency food relief for nearly four million people in the first three months after the earthquake, the largest emergency food distribution ever. A crisis over the spread of the mosquito-borne Zika virus in 2016 broadly affected Latin America and the United States, triggering a wide range of responses at the national, state, and local levels, which underscored the complex policy responses needed to contain the ravages of a pathogen. In 2017, the one-two punch of Hurricanes Irma and Maria in the Caribbean decimated Puerto Rico and the US Virgin Islands as well as the British Virgin Islands, St. Martin, Barbuda, and Cuba. Future management of natural disasters will continue to influence a comprehensive regional security strategy for Latin America.

Address Effects of Climate Change. Climate change will contribute to increasing natural disasters, refugee flows, and conflicts over basic resources such as food and water in Latin America.[33] Challenges include rising sea levels, increasingly severe weather patterns, and the melting of Andean glaciers. Countries bordering the Pacific are particularly affected by El Niño events that alter rain patterns, causing heavy precipitation and flooding in some areas and drought in others. Climate models suggest that El Niño events will become larger over time. The 2015–2016 El Niño, the largest on record by some measures, aggravated Brazil's recent drought, its worst in almost a century, and affected issues as diverse as Sao Paolo's drinking water supply, hydropower production, and Zika virus transmission.[34] The effects of climate change in Latin America will be an increasingly important policy concern in the region.

Threats to US Influence

In additional to the inherent difficulty of pursuing the US objectives previously discussed, three significant developments affect US influence in Latin America: external actors, populism and anti-Americanism, and transnational criminal organizations.

Extra-Regional Actors. The rise of the People's Republic of China to global power and its status as a potential peer rival to the United States has had a major impact in Latin America. Just as the United States considers itself to be an Asian power, China is increasingly influencing the Americas. China has used its economic power in trading goods, supplying loans, and providing foreign direct investment to pursue its geostrategic interests in Latin America. One key Chinese objective is to increase recognition of the One China policy among Latin American countries in order to isolate Taiwan.[35] In June 2017, Panama became the latest to switch its diplomatic recognition from Taipei to Beijing. China's growing influence in Latin America also helps to amplify its voice in a variety of multilateral forums including the United Nations.

China pursues an active and generally positive approach to Latin America, describing the region as "a land full of vitality and hope."[36] During a November 2016 visit to the region, China's leader, Xi Jinping, pledged to increase trade with Latin America by $500 billion and investment by $250 billion by 2025. China's main development banks—the China Development Bank and the Export-Import Bank of China—already lend more in Latin America than do the World Bank, the Inter-American Development Bank, and the Andean Development Fund combined. China's evolving economic strategy is becoming more diversified, with less emphasis on mining and energy extraction and more attention devoted to infrastructure, manufacturing, telecommunications, finance, tourism, and even space.[37]

China also takes a keen interest in interoceanic canals. China is the second most frequent user of the Panama Canal, where the completion of a third set of locks in 2016 dramatically increased the size of cargo vessels that could transit the canal. Farther north, the Nicaraguan government of Daniel Ortega granted a massive concession to the Hong Nicaraguan Canal Development Investment, led by Chinese billionaire Wang Jing, to build a 161-mile canal from the Atlantic to Pacific at a cost of more than $50 billion. However, backing from the Chinese government remains uncertain, and the project appears to be on hold, with actual construction delayed indefinitely. Leaders of Cuba, Ecuador, and Venezuela have often turned to China to secure loans and financing without the economic and other strings normally attached by Western international financial institutions.[38] Stronger military-to-military ties and sales of Chinese-made arms are also making headway in the region.

Latin American nations recognize that ties to China can have negative implications. Inexpensive Chinese imports undercut many Latin American manufacturers; China's appetite for oil and minerals may increase environmental degradation and social conflict. A hands-off Chinese approach, with minimal concern for official transparency and accountability, tends to exacerbate corruption. A reduction in Chinese commodity purchases from Latin America has recently slowed Latin American economic growth.

Iran, too, seeks a stronger foothold in the Americas. Tehran's strategy includes traditional diplomacy, trade relations, public outreach, and religious diplomacy, including establishing Shia cultural centers to support and encourage Islamic converts. The biggest concerns for US policy are Iran's covert objectives. Its sponsorship of the foreign terrorist organization Hezbollah extends into Latin America, especially to seek financing for the terrorist group. Security experts have long considered the Tri-Border Area of Paraguay, Brazil, and Argentina to be a hub for lucrative illegal commerce that funds Hezbollah's militancy. To the south, Argentina continues to investigate Iran's responsibility for deadly bombings of Israel's embassy and a Jewish center in Buenos Aires in the mid-1990s. As president, Venezuela's late Hugo Chavez brazenly courted closer relations with Iran, dubbing the two countries' shared ties an "axis of unity" against the United States.

Russia under President Vladimir Putin has returned to more active engagement in Latin America in a way that harkens back to the Cold War. Trade between Russia and Latin America grew from $3 billion in 2000 to $24 billion in 2013. Russia's pursuit of oil and gas industry deals, particularly in Venezuela, is one of several facets of its economic policy toward Latin America. Russian interests, writes Diana Villiers Negroponte, reflect "the need to acquire exploration rights in diverse oil and gas fields, expand the market for arms sales, cultivate a subtle anti-US mindset in the region, and, finally, assert that Russia was a political actor on the world stage."[39] Russia wrote off $32 billion of debt that Cuba had owed since the 1980s. Former Soviet client Daniel Ortega of Nicaragua has actively renewed friendly ties with Moscow. For over a decade, Russia has armed Venezuela for defense against the alleged threat of US intervention, selling it a reported $11 billion in arms that include advanced fighter aircraft, main battle tanks, attack helicopters, and several thousand surface-to-air missile systems.[40] In October 2016, Venezuela's President Nicolas Maduro awarded Putin the first annual Hugo Chavez Peace Prize.[41]

Populism, Regionalism, and Anti-Americanism. One of the oldest political slogans in Latin America is "Yankee Go Home!" From the days of independence to the present, anti-Americanism has been a frequent aspect of US–Latin American relations. Hostility to the United States, whether based on cultural differences, ethnic divides, ideological clashes, or the history of US intervention, is reflected in what is often called Latin America's love-hate relationship with the United States.[42]

A powerful political current linking populism, nationalism, and statist or socialist economics with anti-Americanism emerged in the late 1990s. President Hugo Chavez of Venezuela embodied this new brand of authoritarianism, which he called the "Bolivarian Revolution," after Simon Bolivar, a nineteenth-century Venezuelan revolutionary leader. Rising to power on a populist and socialist platform, Chavez successfully rewrote the political playbook in Venezuela, governing in the name of the people at the expense of Venezuela's traditional party system and democratic constitutional order. Leveraging Venezuela's enormous oil resources at a time of high energy prices, Chavez used "social power diplomacy" to forge alliances with Cuba, Bolivia, Ecuador, Nicaragua, and others. Chavez's ambition was to unite Latin American nations as a bulwark against US power and influence.[43] Whether it required expelling agencies of the US government, protesting US security agreements with nations like Colombia, or courting friendship with US enemies such as Iran, the Chavez strategy emphasized the end of US primacy in the world. Chavez also championed new regional diplomatic and security bodies intended to undercut the OAS and exclude the United States and Canada. The Union of South American Nations (UNASUR) was created in 2004 and the Community of Latin American and Caribbean States (CELAC) were created in 2011, both as regional platforms for closer political cooperation and common security policies, without United States participation. While Chavez's death in 2013 and Venezuela's ongoing political and economic crisis have blunted the appeal of anti-American sentiments, a vision of "Latin America for Latin Americans" still resonates. US policies that are perceived to reflect arrogance and unchecked hubris, or that fail to take Latin Americans interests into account, will draw negative responses and provoke an uptick in anti-Americanism.

Transnational Criminal Organizations. Following the attacks of September 11, 2001, the global threat of illegal drugs became more complicated because of connections between the illegal drug trade, international terrorist groups, and transnational criminal organizations (TCOs). From the highlands of Peru and the urban *favelas* of Brazil to Central America's gang-ridden Northern Triangle and the Pacific slopes of Sinaloa, Mexico, criminal organizations and networks increasingly challenge the sovereignty of states and the safety of their citizens by exploiting institutional and human weaknesses to move anything and anyone across porous borders for great profit. Global networks that can move drugs can also facilitate the illegal transport of arms, explosives, human trafficking victims, or funds.

Moises Naim has identified "five wars of globalization" that pit the United States and other nation-states against "agile, well-financed networks of highly networked individuals" engaged in international trade in drugs, arms, intellectual properties, people, and money.[44] Policy makers and security analysts are increasingly looking at transnational criminal networks operating within and across the borders, threatening stability and sometimes converging in pursuit of multiple illegal ends.[45] With TCOs presenting a persistent challenge to US interests, they are the focus of agencies and institutions ranging from the United Nations and the OAS to the US Departments of Defense, Homeland Security, Justice, State, and Treasury, to federal, state and local law enforcement.

Subregional Overview

The US interests and challenges described above differ in each region and each nation in Latin America. This section identifies a number of the most important considerations with regard to US policy.

Mexico: Cooperation or Confrontation? Former US Ambassador to Mexico Anthony Wayne has said that "no relationship touches the daily lives of American citizens more than does the United States–Mexico relationship."[46] Interconnectivity begins with a two-thousand-mile border, more than thirty-four million individuals of Mexican birth or descent residing in the United States, a billion dollars of daily transborder commerce, a million daily individual border crossings, and increasingly integrated economies and production platforms. The sheer quantity of interactions engages much of America and virtually every part of the US and Mexican federal governments.

Two centuries of not always harmonious US-Mexican relations generate clashing narratives. From the US perspective, Mexico's northern territories were lands to be claimed and incorporated in the United States under the slogan "Manifest Destiny." From Mexico's perspective, the United States exercised aggressive power to take Texas, California, and much of the Southwest by force of arms. In the late 1800s, profit-hungry US companies and investors exploited Mexico's economy, favoring its oligarchs over the masses. The Mexican Revolution, from 1910 to 1920, forever altered Mexico; it provoked short-lived US interventions in 1914 and again in 1916. Out of the Mexican Revolution emerged a complex corporatist regime with a highly nationalist outlook presided over by the Revolutionary Institutional Party (PRI). Nationalization of the oil industry at the expense of United States and other foreign investors was a signature achievement of the PRI in the 1930s. Mexico supported the United States in World War II, but during the Cold War it favored more independent and self-sufficient foreign and economic policies. In the early 1980s, the United States and Mexico appeared to be working at cross-purposes during the Central American crisis; American journalist Alan Riding famously described the relationship as one of "distant neighbors."[47]

Starting in the late 1980s, reform-minded PRI presidents Salinas de Gortari (1988–1994) and Ernesto Zedillo (1994–2000) rejuvenated the PRI, overhauled the Mexican state, injected free-market dynamism, and drew Mexico closer to the United States by advancing mutual economic interests. NAFTA more closely integrated their economies and precipitated rapid change in Mexico. In 1995, the Clinton administration rescued Mexico from a financial crisis, helping to stabilize the peso and to avert major negative repercussions for US financial markets. In 2000, Mexico elected President Vicente Fox, candidate of the National Action Party (PAN), ending PRI's dominance. President George W. Bush forged deeper ties with Mexico by developing the Security and Prosperity Partnership for North America and convened regular summits of the leaders of Mexico, Canada, and the United States, dubbed "the Three Amigos." The Mérida Initiative intensified counter-drug cooperation and supported the fight of Mexico's President Felipe Calderon against drug traffickers.

The Obama administration worked to preserve a strong and cordial relationship. It augmented the Merida Initiative to fight drug lords and to reform and strengthen Mexico's law enforcement capabilities. President Obama also recognized that southward flows of firearms and cash along with money laundering in the United States contributed to lawlessness in Mexico and accepted co-responsibility for the perennial problem. The Obama administration also took executive action to advance immigration reform.

A reinvigorated PRI supported Enrique Peña Nieto, who was elected president of Mexico in 2012. He reformed the Mexican state-owned petroleum company

(PEMEX) to attract foreign investment in the oil industry and to explore deep-water fields in the Gulf of Mexico. He also challenged entrenched interest in areas such as the teachers' union to improve Mexico's educational performance. In January 2017, Mexico extradited Joaquin "El Chapo" Guzman, the notorious head of the Sinaloa Cartel, to the United States to stand trial. Nonetheless, Pena Nieto and the PRI were forced to grapple with mounting domestic ills: sluggish economic growth, fiscal deficits caused by falling energy prices, corruption, and unrelenting drug warfare.

Future US-Mexican relations could become problematic if US policy pulls back from the economic integration achieved under NAFTA, shifts resources from border infrastructure and connectivity to a contentious border wall, exacerbates US hostility to Mexican migrants, and triggers a potential trade war with a border adjustment tax or similar measures. A worsening of bilateral relations could undermine security cooperation, reduce Mexican help with Central America's migrant flows, and create new incentives for Mexico to strengthen its economic ties with China, Japan, and the European Union. US policy choices in the Trump administration will largely determine the extent to which positive US-Mexican cooperation continues or whether Mexico becomes a "distant neighbor" again.

Central America: Enduring Crises. The causes of Central American instability have deep roots in the history of the isthmus. From the 1920s until the early 1990s, Central America saw poverty, extreme inequality, and political violence, along with oligarchic and military domination of fragile export economies. The Sandino revolt and US intervention in Nicaragua (1927–1933), a peasant revolt known as "La Matanza" (the Massacre) in El Salvador in 1932, and the 1954 US-backed coup against Arbenz in Guatemala were followed by decades of insurgency, social revolution, and counterrevolution in Nicaragua (1961–1990), El Salvador (1980–1992), Guatemala (1960–1996), and Panama (1989). These and other struggles took an enormous toll in human lives, refugee outflows, and economic destruction. In all of Central America, only Costa Rica escaped debilitating civil strife after a brief "liberation struggle" in 1948, whereupon it became the "Switzerland" of Central America.

With a population of forty million, Central America can be divided into two zones. The more populous Northern Triangle (El Salvador, Guatemala, and Honduras) faces myriad governability challenges. Democratic order is frequently undermined by presidential removals and resignations—most recently Honduras in 2009 and Guatemala 2015—corruption scandals, popular protests, fragmented political parties, and weak government institutions. From the judiciary to law enforcement to prison systems, the administration of justice is often overwhelmed and unable to deliver citizen security. Homicide rates are among the highest in the world, and violent crime is widespread. Drug smugglers linked to Mexican transnational criminal organizations moving cocaine often make first landfall, by air or by sea, in the Northern Triangle. These three countries are also among the most impoverished in the Americas.

To the south, the security situation, although precarious, is less threatening. Nicaragua's troubled democracy has yielded to the authoritarian dominance of Sandinista leader Daniel Ortega, his wife, and his inner circle. Elected president in 2006, Ortega has twice engineered reelection, eliminated the checks and balances of an independent judiciary, and solidified support among the poor. Although leftist in orientation, Ortega has permitted substantial private sector development and maintains relative domestic peace.

Under President Luis Guillermo Solis, Costa Rica, always the more democratic and peaceful outlier, has enjoyed higher levels of economic growth thanks to tourism, strong agricultural exports, and investments in computer assembly and back-office services. Panama, too, enjoyed over 5 percent economic growth in 2017. With the opening of a third set of locks in 2016, revenues from its canal have increased. Panama is an international financial hub, benefits from high rates of foreign investment, and favors domestic policies that welcome immigration, especially for entrepreneurs. Similarly, Belize, having gained independence from Britain in 1981, has established strong economic and political relationships with the United States. The United States is the largest provider of economic and military assistance to Belize and coordinates on issues as varied as promoting tourism to fighting illegal narcotics trafficking.

US policy aims to build greater government strength, enhance public security, and improve economic well-being in Central America, particularly in the Northern Triangle. A major US interest is tackling the two major drivers of external migration: crime and poverty. In November 2015, the Obama administration launched the Alliance for Prosperity in the Northern Triangle with the objectives of improving prosperity, security, and governance. The alliance requires Central American government participation, private sector buy-in, and coordination among international donors. Targets include the reduction of poverty and youth unemployment, police and judicial reforms, and sustainable energy development. The Trump administration appears willing to continue the approach, but the final outcome will depend upon immigration policy and foreign assistance funding.

Colombia: Will Peace Hold? Security analysts and historians will debate who saved Colombia at the end of the twentieth century. Racked by violence for almost half a century, Colombia was on the precipice of state failure in the 1990s. Insurgent groups such as the Revolutionary Armed Forces of Colombia (FARC), the National Liberation Army (ELN), paramilitaries, drug traffickers, and common criminals were an increasing threat to the state and to democracy in Colombia. The FARC alone commanded a well-equipped army of 20,000, controlled territory the size of Switzerland, and generated as much as $1 billion annually from cocaine sales and other criminal activities. Paramilitary groups fielded as many as 30,000 combatants to battle the government and insurgents. The Colombian state lacked control in 169 of its 1099 municipalities. Since 2002, the conflict has displaced 4.7 million Colombians.[48]

Two factors helped save Colombia: determined Colombian leadership and steady, well-resourced US support for a multifaceted program commonly referred to as *Plan Colombia*. Under the leadership of President Alvaro Uribe (2002–2010), Colombia negotiated an end to the conflict with the paramilitaries, regained territorial control, and effectively countered FARC, which were increasingly viewed as narco-terrorists. Gaining broad national support, taxing the rich, and outlining a comprehensive strategy, known as the Democratic Security Policy, Uribe succeeded where others had failed. By the end of his second term in 2010, FARC was on the defensive and the Colombian government had gained major territorial control in areas formerly dominated by narco-terrorists.

Approved by Congress in July 2000, Plan Colombia included wide-ranging US cooperation with Colombia to counter drugs, guerrilla violence, and related institutional and social problems. Between 2000 and 2017, the United States spent over $10 billion on the initiative, more than it spent anywhere in the world except the Middle East and Afghanistan. While Plan Colombia prioritized counter-narcotics operations, specifically the eradication of coca in southern Colombia, it also included support for the judiciary and for economic development. As security expert David Spencer observed, "U.S. aid played an important enabling role, but did not drive Colombian policy and strategy."[49] Over the years, deep bonds of cooperation and trust developed among US and Colombian diplomats, military, and law enforcement leaders. The United States actively sought Colombian support and expertise in Mexico and Central America. In December 2016, Colombia signed a cooperation agreement with the North Atlantic Treaty Organization (NATO) to combat transnational crime, terrorism, and drug trafficking.

After the 2010 election of President Juan Manuel Santos, a former defense minister under President Uribe, the government felt sufficiently confident to embark upon peace negotiations with FARC. After four years of talks, a historic peace agreement was approved in 2016, ending the oldest insurgency in the Americas. In exchange for FARC laying down its arms and ending drug trafficking and other criminal activities, the Colombian government committed to a process of transitional justice, compensation for victims of civil violence, promises of rural land reform, and the right for FARC to participate in the electoral process. President Santos was recognized for his effort with the 2016 Nobel Peace Prize.

However, the transition to peace represents a costly, complex undertaking whose success hinges on the ability of the government to deliver on its peace promises. The Obama administration and Congress committed to continue support for Peace Colombia as a successor to Plan Colombia with $450–500 million per year. Such support is important both for the peace process and to counter those moving into FARC territory to continue coca production. Colombia remains the source of 90 percent of all cocaine seized in the United States, and it is the second largest supplier of heroin. Supporting the Colombian government in consolidating peace will be an important part of US policy toward Latin America.

Venezuela: On the Brink of Collapse? Once-democratic Venezuela faces a major crisis of governability. The Bolivarian Revolution governing model of authoritarian socialism, implemented by its charismatic, populist president, Hugo Chavez, has been under political and economic siege. After he won the presidency in 1999, six years after leading a failed coup attempt, Chavez, a former lieutenant colonel and an ardent admirer of Fidel Castro, ended Venezuela's traditional two political party system. Steps toward authoritarian control included concentrating state power in the hands of the executive, taking over directorship of Venezuela's national oil company (PDVSA), erosion of constitutional checks and balances, quashing political and media opposition, and successful manipulation of electoral outcomes. During a wave of high oil prices, Chavez and his political party, the United Socialist Party of Venezuela (PSUV), were able to distribute benefits—education, medical care, subsidized housing and food—to poor and marginalized Venezuelans who had felt betrayed by previous governments. With these policies, Chavez won the adulation of the masses and electoral victories.

However, the Chavez regime possessed a darker side involving crony business deals, large-scale corruption, and rumored drug trafficking, which amounted to the criminalization of the Venezuelan state. Chavez's increasingly close alliance with the dictatorial Castros in Cuba was also troubling for a country with a democratic tradition. Venezuela provided massive oil subsidies to Cuba in exchange for medical, educational, and security personnel. Chavez's fiery anti-neoliberalism, incendiary nationalism, and hostility toward the United States gained the attention of other anti-US leaders. Chavez employed petro-diplomacy to cement alliances in Central America and the Caribbean. Claiming that the OAS in Washington was subservient to US influence, Chavez worked to weaken the regional body by supporting alternate diplomatic alignments to counter US influence.

Chavez intended to govern Venezuela indefinitely, but he died in 2013 after a long battle with cancer. Executive power passed to his chosen successor, the less charismatic Nicolas Maduro. After being declared the winner of the April 2013 presidential elections, Maduro inherited a failing economy and a deluge of problems. With oil prices down to $45 a barrel and PDVSA's production flagging due to corruption and underinvestment, oil revenue—the source of 95 percent of Venezuela's foreign exchange earnings—plummeted; its foreign exchange reserves dropped; and its foreign debt service obligations became increasingly onerous. Economic growth turned sharply negative, while government takeovers of productive industries increased. The annual rate of inflation grew to as much as 700 percent, and food, medicine, and basic needs were increasingly scarce. As many as 80 percent of Venezuelans have fallen back into poverty.

Chavez's death ushered in deeper political polarization. To hold power, Maduro has been relying on support from hardline members of PSUV, recipients of state-granted benefits, senior military officials newly enriched via corruption or criminality, armed groups known as *colectivos*, and Cuban security personnel and advisers. An opposition coalition, the Democratic Unity Roundtable (MUD), was emboldened by its legislative victory in 2015, when it won a majority in the National Assembly. Nevertheless, efforts to find solutions to Venezuela's political and economic problems have so far been hindered by Maduro.

While popular support for Maduro has evaporated, opposition efforts to force democratic changes either through mediation, legislative, and electoral means or by street protests have hardened the ideological battle lines. In March 2017, the

Supreme Court, dominated by pro-Maduro judges, stripped the National Assembly of its powers. Responding to increased pressure from the OAS and the international community, Maduro announced Venezuela's intention to withdraw from the regional body. In August 2017, without a free or fair electoral process, he convened a constituent assembly to draft a new constitution that is expected to grant even greater power to the executive and to perpetuate PSUV dominance. The government has also been employing other tools of misrule—disqualifying candidates arbitrarily, taking political prisoners, using military tribunals, and conducting political violence—to intimidate the opposition.

US policy options for Venezuela remained limited. The United States has not had an ambassador in Caracas since 2008. Intermittent diplomatic talks have led nowhere. Working through the OAS, the United States and other democracies have criticized the Maduro regime and have pressed for international mediation, but these moves have produced no significant results. The United States implemented targeted sanctions against Venezuelan officials and members of the Supreme Court; in 2017 it designated the vice president, Tareck al Aissami, a "drug kingpin."[50] The Trump administration increased sanctions against Venezuela and banned the use of digital curriences introduced by Maduro to subvert these international sanctions. Further sanctions could be introduced to restrict the sale of Venezuelan crude oil in the United States, a move that could worsen Venezuela's economic crisis.[51] Regional players, including Brazil, Argentina, and Colombia, may be in a better position to avert a massive humanitarian crisis by promoting compromise, reconciliation, and reestablishment of genuine democratic practices.

Cuba: End of the Castros. The death of Fidel Castro in November 2016 at the age of ninety marked the passing of a historic figure in Latin America. Revolutionary *caudillo*, maximum leader, Fidel Castro was the Cuban Revolution's defiant driver. A thorn in the side to the United States, he was a hero to millions. Castro's brother Raul inherited a poor and aging but proud nation of ten million locked in a socialist, egalitarian authoritarianism. Under the younger Castro, the size of Cuba's state apparatus has been shrinking. Displaced workers have been scrambling to earn a living wage in the nonstate sectors, in small restaurants and hotels, agricultural cooperatives, taxis, and other limited businesses. The recent loss of Venezuelan oil subsidies and the cautious pace of reform have become significant drags on the economy, which contracted by one percent in 2016. Cuban officials are still quick to blame the US economic embargo for Cuba's economic woes.

Raul Castro's commitment to stepping down as head of state in 2018 will lead to the first Cuban government since 1959 without a Castro at the helm. On the other hand, his decree that the transfer of power will be orderly means that he—not the people—will determine the outcome. Cuba's Communist Party and its military, twin pillars of the regime, intend to remain in control, with the goal of preserving the longest-lasting dictatorship in Latin America.

While Cuba has introduced some market-based mechanisms and has granted individuals some new economic freedoms, the regime demonstrates scant tolerance for open dissent, rejects the formation of political parties and labor unions, and exerts censorship and control over national media. Despite several positive indicators in education, health, and social equality, Cuba's aging and increasingly dependent population faces a bleak economic future without a major transition to a more dynamic economic and political model.

In 2009, President Obama started to change US policy toward Cuba, beginning with removal of restrictions on travel by Cuban Americans to their homeland. The Obama administration argued that fifty years of anti-regime legislation and diplomatic isolation had failed to alter the nature of the Cuban regime and had simply resulted in more isolation for the United States, rather than Cuba, from the global community. Instead, economic empowerment for the nonstate sector and acceptance of the legitimacy of the Cuban regime stood a better chance for liberalizing Cuba from within, giving the Cuban people the means to propel peaceful changes. In December 2014, Obama reestablished full diplomatic relations, removed Cuba from the list of state sponsors of terrorism, and liberalized rules regarding travel to and investments in Cuba. President Obama's trip to Havana in March 2016 symbolized a new era in US-Cuba relationship.

The new Trump administration partially rolled back Obama's executive orders, which will have the effect of limiting individual tourism and reducing dollars flowing to hotels and other businesses owned and run by the Cuban military. This more punitive approach, favored by many Cuban Americas, will again distance Washington from the Castro regime; by applying renewed pressure for democratic change, it may lend greater support to dissidents and civil society. Policy adjustments in Washington, leadership changes in Havana, and the economic and social realities of the Cuban people will all influence the future of Cuba and the Cuban-American relationship.

Haiti and the Caribbean: Third Border Concerns. Apart from Cuba, the Caribbean subregion is characterized by small states with large humanitarian and economic problems. Haiti and the Dominican Republic, each with a population of about ten million, tensely share the island of Hispaniola. The fifteen members of the Caribbean Community (CARICOM) also include the Bahamas, Belize, Grenada, Guyana, Suriname, Jamaica, Barbados, Monserrat, Trinidad and Tobago, and microstates Antigua-Barbuda, St. Kitts and Nevis, St. Vincent and the Grenadines, and St. Lucia. Overall, these countries have few economic resources to sustain prolonged growth or development. Fluctuating tourism revenues and energy prices, coupled with a drop in demand and prices for their major exports, such as sugar and bauxite, have placed a tremendous strain on their economies. The Caribbean islands are also among the most heavily indebted in the world. Severe income disparities and rapid demographic growth have exacerbated a depressed socioeconomic situation, resulting in political turbulence and major population outflows. In a few cases, such as Haiti and Cuba, refugee flows have reached dramatic proportions.

Haiti has been the poorest country in the Western Hemisphere for decades, and it remains a source of significant concern. The ruthless and despotic misrule of the

Duvalier era (1957–1986) guaranteed that the road to economic viability and democratic governance would be long and difficult. The United States intervened in Haiti in 1994 to restore the government of Jean-Bertrand Aristide after a military coup in 1991 removed him from power. After being reelected in 2001, Aristide resigned in 2004, when armed insurgents threatened Haiti's capital and the United States expressed a lack of confidence in his presidency; once again US troops intervened. In a sign of increased regional cooperation, Brazil assumed leadership of an UN-sanctioned international peacekeeping force deployed in Haiti but drawn largely from Latin American countries later that year.

Although Haiti inaugurated a democratically elected government in 2006, its legacy of poverty and political violence present continuing challenges. The 7.0 magnitude earthquake that struck Haiti in 2010 devastated much of the country, especially the capital. The US military, along with other organizations from the international community, brought essential aid and expertise to the nation. Haiti is still dependent on external armed forces and financial aid to maintain domestic peace and civil order.

Caribbean nations fear both US inattention and a US overemphasis on security issues. They prefer an approach that addresses economic development, preferential market access, employment, external indebtedness, energy issues, and climate change mitigation. Two important US initiatives were developed during the Obama administration: the Caribbean Basin Security Initiative (CBSI) supports maritime and aerial security cooperation, law enforcement capacity enhancement, border and port security, firearms interdiction, justice sector reform, citizen security, and at-risk youth. The Caribbean Energy Initiative (CESI) aims to boost energy security and sustainable economic growth by attracting investment in energy technologies through a focus on improved governance, increased access to finance, and strengthened coordination among energy donors, governments, and stakeholders.

Brazil: A Rising Giant Hobbled. Brazil is the world's fifth largest nation-state (in territory and population). It intended the 2016 Summer Olympics to showcase its arrival as a major international player. While the Olympics games were generally successful, they unfolded in a nation undergoing severe political and economic growing pains.

Brazil's steady ascent dates back to the presidency of Fernando Henrique Cardoso (1995–2002), a centrist economist of the Brazilian Social Democratic Party (PSDB), who curbed his country's inflationary appetite, introduced spending limits, encouraged privatization, and reduced debt. After the 2003 presidential victory of Luiz Iancio Lula da Silva, a charismatic former labor leader of the leftist Workers' Party (PT), Brazil continued to enjoy years of economic success, helped by high commodity prices. Important industries emerged such as Embraer, an aviation leader, and Odebrecht, a construction and holding company giant. With steadily rising energy prices, Brazil's oil giant, Petrobras, excited global energy markets by promising to tap enormous reserves under Atlantic waters. Brazil reduced poverty through an innovative social program known as conditional cash transfers (*Bolsa Familia*). Between 2003 and 2014, inequality dropped significantly, and Brazil lifted twenty-nine million people out of poverty. While structural issues such as a bloated pension system, bureaucratic bottlenecks, and persistent crime hindered progress, the economy grew by 4.5 percent annually between 2006 and 2014, accounting for 60 percent of South America's total GDP. After Lula's two successful terms, he was succeeded by Dilma Rousseff, also of the PT. Brazil's first female president and winner of presidential elections in 2010, she won reelection by a narrow margin in 2014.

In President Rousseff's second term, economic headwinds developed. The Brazilian economy entered into recession in 2015, contracting by 3.8 percent in its worst annual performance since 1981. A series of corruption scandals involving senior PT members triggered arrests, resignations, clashes between the executive and legislature, and massive street protests. Petrobras and Odebrecht were at the center of widespread scandals involving kickbacks and political payoffs: the latter allegedly distributed more than $800 million in bribes between 2001 and 2016, and recently agreed to pay $2.6 billion in fines to the United States and Switzerland.

The Brazilian congress charged President Rousseff with manipulating the federal budget to conceal Brazil's economic woes. Impeachment proceedings culminated in August 2016 with her removal from office. Vice President Michel Temer of the opposition Brazilian Democratic Movement Party (PMDB) became interim president. Temer promised to back government reforms, create a more business-friendly environment, and limit government spending to reduce inflation, but he too faces investigation for receiving bribes. In July 2017, former President Lula da Silva was convicted on charges of corruption and money laundering, tarnishing his record of achievement.

Despite Brazil's internal political struggles and slumping economic performance, the United States continues to invest in its future diplomatically, financially, and militarily. Education, biomedical research, science, and technology, including Brazil's "Science without Borders" program, are important elements of a mutually beneficial relationship. Brazil and the United States share common security interests, including combating terrorism and transnational crime, supporting international peacekeeping, and protecting the Amazon Basin. In 2010, the United States and Brazil initialed a Defense Cooperation Agreement (DCA) and a General Security of Military Information Agreement (GSOMIA), both of which facilitate further cooperation. Brazil continues to show interest in obtaining advanced, highly sensitive military technologies.

Other Nations of Latin America. Each of the region's nations has its distinctive culture, history, economy, and geography, but all must be considered in regard to US policy toward the region. Argentina, Chile, Peru, Paraguay, and Uruguay currently have strong, stable relations with the United States. US relations with Ecuador and Bolivia remain more distant, in part because they are more closely aligned with Venezuela. In Ecuador, Lenin Moreno, the leftist candidate who was vice president for Rafael Correa, narrowly won election in February 2017, keeping the Pacific-Andean nation on a more leftward track. Bolivia under President Evo Morales is at odds with the United States; full diplomatic relations remain suspended.

Future Challenges in Latin America to US National Security

While the Monroe Doctrine may now be a historical artifact, Washington policy makers remain highly sensitive to security threats close to the homeland. Promoting regional security, politically stable democracies, and economic growth, while limiting the deleterious effects of illegal drugs and illegal immigration, will continue to shape US policy toward Latin America. US efforts to influence specific nations will increasingly compete with those of other state actors such as China, Russia, and Iran, as well as with nonstate actors, including narco-traffickers, transnational criminal networks, and terrorists. Due to its proximity, military resources, and economic power, the United States will likely continue to be indispensable as it responds to the inevitable environmental or humanitarian crises that will affect nations in the region.

How these factors will evolve in the Trump administration remains an open question. President Trump's "America First" agenda and proposals for construction of a border wall with Mexico and for cancellation or renegotiation of trade agreements reflect a readiness to distance the United States from previous multilateral initiatives. On the other hand, US interests in the region are enduring; many specific policy changes would require substantial international cooperation and long lead times. The increasing interconnectedness of all nations in the Western Hemisphere and the challenges from beyond the region will ensure that future American policy makers will receive rapid and insistent responses to proposed policy changes.

Discussion Questions

1. What are the historical national security interests of United States in Latin America? How have they changed in the twenty-first century?
2. In the 1980s, many countries in Latin America transitioned to democracy. What subsequent challenges have these democracies faced?
3. Should the United States play a role in supporting democratic consolidation in Latin America? If so, what specific policies should the United States adopt?
4. What policies or actions can the United States take to limit the propensity for and amount of corruption in Latin American nations?
5. What policies should the United States pursue in the countries of Latin America to increase their ability to confront nefarious nonstate actors such as drug traffickers, transnational criminal organizations, and terrorists?
6. Is Mexico a national security partner or a national security threat? What kind of relationship with Mexico will best support US interests in the long run?
7. What should US policy be with respect to Venezuela as its economic and political turmoil dramatically undermines Venezuelans' quality of life?

8. What can US policy makers learn from the success in Colombia that may be applicable elsewhere in the region and in the world?

9. Why has Central America played a central role in the formulation of US policy toward Latin America? What approaches have worked best in dealing with Central America's political, economic, and security challenges?

10. What are the prospects for the normalization of relations with Cuba in the coming years? What policy should the United States pursue toward Cuba?

Recommended Readings

Camp, Roderic Ai. *Politics in Mexico: Democratic Consolidation or Decline?* 6th ed. New York: Oxford University Press, 2013.

Corrales, Javier, and Michael Penfold. *Dragon in the Tropics: Venezuela and the Legacy of Hugo Chavez.* 2nd ed. Washington, DC: Brookings Institution Press, 2015.

Crandall, Russell C. *The United States and Latin America after the Cold War.* New York: Cambridge University Press, 2008.

Dominguez, Jorge I., and Michael Shifter, eds. *Constructing Democratic Governance in Latin America.* 4th ed. Baltimore, MD: Johns Hopkins University Press, 2013.

Feinberg, Richard E. *Open for Business: Building the New Cuban Economy.* Washington, DC: Brookings Institution Press, 2016.

Kline, Harvey A., Christine J. Wade, and Howard Wiarda. *Latin America Politics and Development.* 9th ed. New York: Westview, 2017.

Mares, David R., and Harold Trinkunas. *Aspirational Power: Brazil on the Long Road to Global Influence.* Washington, DC: Brookings Institution Press, 2016.

McPherson, Alan. *Intimate Ties, Bitter Struggles: The United States and Latin America since 1945.* Washington, DC: Potomac Books, 2006.

Miklaucic, Michael, and Jacqueline Brewer, eds. *Convergence: Illicit Networks and National Security in the Age of Globalization.* Washington, DC: National Defense University Press, 2013.

Reid, Michael. *Forgotten Continent: The Battle for Latin America's Soul.* New Haven, CT: Yale University Press, 2007.

Roett, Riordan. *Brazil: What Everyone Needs to Know.* New York: Oxford University Press, 2016.

Skidmore, Thomas, Peter H. Smith, and James N. Green. *Modern Latin America.* 8th ed. New York: Oxford University Press, 2013.

Smith, Peter H. *Talons of the Eagle: Latin America, the United States and the World.* 4th ed. New York: Oxford University Press, 2012

Tavares, Rodrigo. *Security in South America: The Role of States and Regional Organizations.* Boulder, CO: Lynne Rienner, 2014.

Recommended Internet Sources

Americas Quarterly, www.americasquarterly.org
Americas Society/Council of Americas, www.as-coa.org
Global Americans, http://latinamericagoesglobal.org
Inter-American Development Bank, www.iadb.org
The Inter-American Dialogue, www.thedialogue.org
Latin American Network Information Center, http://lanic.utexas.edu

Latin American Press, www.latinamericapress.org
Organization of American States, www.oas.org

Notes

1. Throughout this chapter, the term *Latin America* is used for Latin America and the Caribbean (that is, all states of the Western Hemisphere apart from Canada and the United States). Of the thirty-five member states of the Organization of America States (OAS), thirteen are Caribbean countries. The terms *Western Hemisphere* or the *Americas* refer in geostrategic terms to the entirety of North, Central, and South America, along with the Caribbean.

2. In Central America, only El Salvador has no territory bordering on the Caribbean.

3. The George W. Bush administration popularized the term "third border" in reference to the Caribbean, labeling US policies the "Third Border Initiative." See The White House, "Fact Sheet: President's Speech at the Summit of the Americas," April 21, 2001, https://georgewbush-whitehouse.archives.gov/news/releases/2001/04/20010423-1.html.

4. Creole French is spoken in Haiti.

5. The World Bank, Data, Latin America and the Caribbean, July 2017, http://data.worldbank.org/region/latin-america-and-caribbean.

6. National Intelligence Council, *Global Trends: Paradox of Progress: South America*, January 2017, https://www.dni.gov/index.php/the-next-five-years/south-america.

7. National Intelligence Council, *Global Trends.*

8. The Monroe Doctrine, Yale Law School, The Avalon Project: Documents in Law, History and Diplomacy, http://avalon.law.yale.edu/19th_century/monroe.asp.

9. At play are two approaches to US-Latin American relations. One seeks to discover common ground and shared values, as well as to continue the quest for liberty that set the New World apart from the Old World; this view has been called the *Western Hemisphere idea*, or the *Inter-American ideal*. See Arthur P. Whitaker, *The Western Hemisphere Idea: Its Rise and Decline* (Ithaca, NY: Cornell University Press, 1954). A second approach looks at the persistent cultural divide separating the United States, with its strongly Protestant, white, Anglo-Saxon roots, from Latin America, with its Catholic, racially mixed, Ibero-American foundations. See Lawrence Harrison, *The Pan American Dream: Do Latin America's Cultural Values Discourage True Partnership with the United States and Canada?* (New York: Basic Books, 1997).

10. Organization of American States, *Inter-American Democratic Charter*, September 11, 2001, http://www.oas.org/charter/docs/resolution1_en_p4.htm.

11. John Kerry, "Remarks on U.S. Policy in the Western Hemisphere," November 18, 2013, https://2009-2017.state.gov/secretary/remarks/2013/11/217680.htm.

12. Kerry, "Remarks on U.S. Policy in the Western Hemisphere."

13. The White House, *National Security Strategy of the United States of America* (Washington, DC: The White House, December 2017), 51.

14. Inter-American Treaty of Reciprocal Assistance (Rio Pact), September 2, 1947, Library of Congress, Documents, http://www.loc.gov/law/help/us-treaties/bevans/m-ust000004-0559.pdf.

15. The OAS rescinded Cuba's expulsion from the OAS in 2009, but Cuba has taken no steps to rejoin. In April 2017, Venezuela announced it intends to withdraw from the OAS.

16. The 1967 Treaty of Tlatelolco is officially known as the Treaty for the Prohibition of Nuclear Weapons in Latin America and the Caribbean; see treaty commentary and text, US State Department, https://www.state.gov/p/wha/rls/70658.htm.

17. Particularly pertinent to US-Mexico security relations are US Army North, stationed at Fort San Houston in San Antonio, Texas, and Joint Task Force (JTF) North, at Fort Bliss, Texas.

18. Components of SOUTHCOM include US Army South; Twefth US Air Force (Air Forces Southern); US Naval Forces Southern Command (Fourth Fleet); US Marine Corps Forces South; Special Operations Command South; Joint Interagency Task Force (JIATF) South; Joint Task Force (JTF)–Bravo (Honduras) and JTF-Guantánamo (Cuba).

19. Posture statement of Admiral Kurt W. Tidd, Commander, US Southern Command, April 6, 2017, https://www.armed-services.senate.gov/imo/media/doc/Tidd_04-06-17.pdf. See also Admiral Kurt W. Tidd and Tyler W. Morton, "U.S. Southern Command: Evolving to Meet 21st-Century Challenges," *Joint Forces Quarterly* 86, no. 3 (2017): 11–19.

20. First Conference of Ministers of Defense of the Americas, The Williamsburg Principles, July 24, 1995, https://www.state.gov/p/wha/rls/71542.htm.

21. US Census Bureau, "Top Trading Partners," December 2015, https://www.census.gov/foreign-trade/statistics/highlights/top/top1512yr.html.

22. World Bank, "Remittances to Developing Countries Decline for Second Consecutive Year," April 21, 2017, http://www.worldbank.org/en/news/press-release/2017/04/21/remittances-to-developing-countries-decline-for-second-consecutive-year. The $73 billion figure includes remittances from all sources, but most are from the United States,

23. Inter-American Development Bank, *2016 Annual Report: The Year in Review* (Washington DC: Inter-American Development Bank, April 2017), ii, iadb.org/wsdocs/getdocument.aspx?docnum=40862380.

24. See, for example, "Ready to Take Off Again?" *Economist*, January 4, 2014; and James McBride and Mohammed Aly Sergie, "NAFTA's Economic Impact," Council on Foreign Relations, October 4, 2017, https://www.cfr.org/backgrounder/naftas-economic-impact.

25. Office of the United States Trade Representative, "The Case for CAFTA: Growth, Opportunity, and Democracy in Our Neighborhood," February 2005, https://ustr.gov/archive/assets/Trade_Agreements/Regional/CAFTA/Briefing_Book/asset_upload_file235_7178.pdf.

26. Dominican Republic–Central America–United States Free Trade Agreement (CAFTA-DR), July 1, 2015, http://2016.export.gov/fta/cafta-dr/.

27. MERCOSUR started as a bilateral trade agreement between Argentina and Brazil and has since expanded to five member states: Argentina, Brazil, Paraguay, Uruguay, and Venezuela (currently suspended), and seven associate members: Bolivia, Chile, Colombia, Ecuador, Guyana, Peru, and Suriname.

28. Tidd and Morton, "U.S. Southern Command."

29. Drug Enforcement Agency, *2016 National Drug Threat Assessment Summary*, November 2016, https://www.dea.gov/resource-center/2016%20NDTA%20Summary.pdf.

30. Daniel R. Coats, Director of National Intelligence, "Statement for the Record: Worldwide Threat Assessment of the US Intelligence Community," Senate Select Committee on Intelligence, May 11, 2017, https://www.dni.gov/files/documents/Newsroom/Testimonies/SSCI%20Unclassified%20SFR%20-%20Final.pdf.

31. Statement by Secretary Jeh Johnson on Southwest Border Security, October 18, 2016, https://www.cbp.gov/newsroom/stats/southwest-border-unaccompanied-children/fy-2016.

32. See Gary Cecchine et al., *The U.S. Military Response to 2010 Haiti Earthquake: Considerations for Army Leaders* (Santa Monica, CA: RAND, 2013).

33. Department of Defense, Report to the Senate, "National Security Implications of Climate-Related Risks and a Changing Climate," July 23, 2015, http://archive.defense.gov

/pubs/150724-congressional-report-on-national-implications-of-climate-change.pdf?source=govdelivery.

34. National Intelligence Council, *Global Trends*.

35. Of the twenty-one nations that still recognize Taiwan, eleven are in Latin America and the Caribbean.

36. Ministry of Foreign Affairs of the People's Republic of China, "China's Policy Paper on Latin America and the Caribbean," November 24, 2016, http://www.fmprc.gov.cn/mfa_eng/zxxx_662805/t1418254.shtml.

37. Jose Cardenas, "China's Great Leap into Latin America," *Real Clear World*, May 2, 2017, http://www.realclearworld.com/articles/2017/05/02/chinas_great_leap_into_latin_america.html.

38. Ted Piccone, "The Geopolitics of China's Rise in Latin America," Brookings Institution, 2016, https://www.brookings.edu/wp-content/uploads/2016/11/the-geopolitics-of-chinas-rise-in-latin-america_ted-piccone.pdf.

39. Diana Villiers Negroponte, "What's Putin's Game in the Western Hemisphere?" *Americas Quarterly* 9, no. 1 (2015): 66–72.

40. Tass Russian News Agency, "Russian Weaponry Selling Best in Latin America," March 30, 2016, http://tass.com/defense/866023.

41. Reuters World News, "Venezuela Creates Hugo Chavez Peace Prize, Awards to Russia's Putin," October 7, 2016, http://www.reuters.com/article/us-venezuela-politics-idUSKCN12801I.

42. Carlos Rangel, *The Latin Americans: Their Love-Hate Relationship with the U.S.*, rev. ed. (New Brunswick, NJ: Transaction Books, 1987); Mark Falcoff, "Our Latin American Hairshirt," *Commentary* 62, no. 4 (1976): 58–65.

43. Javier Corrales, "Using Social Power to Balance Soft Power: Venezuela's Foreign Policy," *Washington Quarterly* 32, no. 4 (2009): 97–114.

44. Moises Naim, "Five Wars of Globalization," *Foreign Policy* 134 (January/February 2003): 29–37.

45. Michael Miklaucic and Jacqueline Brewer, eds., *Convergence: Illicit Networks and National Security in the Age of Globalization* (Washington, DC: National Defense University Press, 2013).

46. "Trade, Security, and the U.S.-Mexico Relationship," transcript, Washington, DC, the Brookings Institution, May 25, 2017, https://www.brookings.edu/wp-content/uploads/2017/06/fp_20170525_us_mexico_transcript.pdf.

47. Alan Riding, *Distant Neighbors: A Portrait of the Mexicans* (New York: Vintage, 1989).

48. Dan Restrepo et al., "The United States and Colombia: From Security Partners to Global Partners in Peace," Center for American Progress, February 2, 2016, https://www.americanprogress.org/issues/security/reports/2016/02/02/130251/the-united-states-and-colombia-from-security-partners-to-global-partners-in-peace/.

49. David E. Spencer, "Lessons from Colombia's Road to Recovery, 1982–2010," Center for Hemispheric Defense Studies, Occasional Paper, May 2012, http://chds.dodlive.mil/files/2013/12/pub-OP-spencer.pdf.

50. Ana Vanessa Herrero and Nicholas Casey, "U.S. Imposes Sanctions on Venezuela's Vice President, Calling Him a Drug 'Kingpin,'" *New York Times*, February 13, 2017.

51. US oil imports from Venezuela are declining, but still account for 8–9 percent of US total oil imports. Venezuela is the third largest foreign supplier of oil to the United States.

V

Current and Future Issues in American National Security Policy

25

Looking Ahead

As this book goes to print, the United States is in the second year of the administration of President Donald J. Trump. The Trump administration's approach to American national security has been articulated in its "America First Foreign Policy," which prioritizes combating Islamic terrorist groups, ensuring US military dominance, and crafting fair trade deals that will benefit US manufacturing.[1] Within national security circles, a vigorous debate is underway about the implications of Trump's approach. Critics raise concerns about the negative, isolationist echoes produced by the administration's use of the pre–World War II slogan, "America First" and, more fundamentally, about the possibility that Trump's foreign policy will reduce US leadership of and support for an international order that has served American interests since World War II.[2] Supporters of the Trump administration, on the other hand, argue that its foreign policy represents a needed correction because the foreign and military policies of the administration of President Barack Obama "left behind a far more dangerous world than the one he inherited in 2009," and that Trump policies will be more in line with traditional, conservative priorities than critics suggest.[3]

Underlying this debate are fundamental questions about the role of the United States in the world that are likely to remain significant as US national security policy makers look ahead to the coming decade and beyond. One of these questions is whether US national security interests are furthered by the existence of a rules-based international order in which potential conflicts in key issue areas are mitigated through participation in international institutions and the reinforcement of international laws and norms. A second, related issue is whether US national interests are advanced through American leadership on the international stage. In other words, do the benefits of US leadership in international affairs outweigh the costs? Or has the United States unwisely sacrificed its own interests in the service of international security or economic prosperity abroad?

To provide some perspective on these questions, this chapter provides a brief overview of the lessons of the interwar period that informed the American approach to foreign and national security policy in the post–World War II era. As discussed in chapter 2, the traditional American approach to national security changed in important ways during this timeframe as a consensus developed that advancing US interests in an interconnected world required sustained American engagement in international affairs. The chapter then discusses the mechanisms and policies adopted to advance US interests in an environment in which isolation no longer appeared to be a realistic option and US leadership in many issue areas appeared necessary. The chapter then surveys major developments over recent decades that may have contributed to a decline in the postwar consensus. Looking ahead, US policy makers will need to decide whether the historical lessons that have underpinned American leadership on the world stage for the past seventy years are still relevant in light of new opportunities and challenges. They will also need to determine whether the international mechanisms developed after World War II are still useful and, if they are, how they should be adjusted to advance American interests in the very complex and dynamic strategic environment of the twenty-first century.

The Origins of the Post–World War II Order

In retrospect, it may seem natural to attribute the leadership role that the United States played in international affairs after World War II to the imperatives of the Cold War standoff with the Soviet Union. Certainly, the Cold War provided the United States with additional motivation to engage internationally and led the United States to a more active role than that envisioned by the early American architects of the postwar international order, including wartime President Franklin Delano Roosevelt. However, policy-makers began to consider the desirable characteristics of postwar international affairs well before the Cold War began; in fact, early expressions of an American internationalist vision predate the entry of the United States into World War II.

Two examples of this early thinking about the characteristics of the postwar order can be found in the 1941 Atlantic Charter and in President Roosevelt's famous "Four Freedoms" speech. The Atlantic Charter was a joint declaration by President Roosevelt and British Prime Minister Winston Churchill after their meeting on the USS *Augusta* off the coast of Newfoundland in August 1941, which took place four months before the Japanese attack on Pearl Harbor and US entry into the war. In addition to a common commitment that they would forgo future territorial expansion, this declaration included seven principles that the two countries would support in the postwar world. They agreed "to seek the liberalization of international trade; to establish freedom of the seas, and [to set] international labor, economic, and welfare standards. Most importantly, both the United States and Great Britain were committed to supporting the restoration of self-governments for all countries that had been occupied during the war and allowing all peoples to choose their own form of government."[4]

President Roosevelt had laid some of the groundwork for this postwar internationalist vision seven months earlier, in his January 1941 State of the Union address. In that speech he argued that more than at any other time in US history, "The future and the safety of our country and our democracy are overwhelmingly involved in events far beyond our borders."[5] Thus, the world order that the United States ought to help usher into existence was one in which all human beings, "everywhere in the world," would enjoy freedom of speech and of worship and freedom from want and fear.[6] To symbolize America's goals in the war, the military medal presented to every soldier, sailor, airman, and marine who served in World War II was inscribed: "FREEDOM FROM FEAR AND WANT, FREEDOM OF SPEECH AND RELIGION."

Lessons of the 1920s and 1930s. Both President Roosevelt's 1941 State of the Union speech and the Atlantic Charter reflect fundamental lessons that would inform the efforts of the United States and its allies as they sought to create new mechanisms to shape international affairs in the postwar period. These lessons were a response to grave and dangerous interwar developments, including a severe global Great Depression, which began in 1929 and had effects that persisted through the 1930s, the rise of totalitarianism in the Communist Soviet Union and of dictatorships in Fascist Italy and Germany, and the expansion of the Empire of Japan in Asia. The surprise attack by the Japanese Navy on the US naval base at Pearl Harbor, Hawaii, in December 1941 merely provided additional evidence that the United States could not avoid the effects of these developments. The attack dramatically diminished support for isolationism in the United States and raised expectations that policy makers would create a national security apparatus to prevent such attacks in the future.[7] After Pearl Harbor, "the massive isolationist movement within the United States evaporated overnight. Immediately following the attack, Charles Lindbergh, the most well-known spokesman of the America First Movement, issued a press release in which he called upon Americans to unite in support of the war effort."[8]

The US failure between the two World Wars to assume a leadership role commensurate with its power came to be seen as having allowed the rise of authoritarianism, international aggression, and global economic distress. Historian E. H. Carr points out that "in 1918 world leadership was offered, by almost universal consent, to the United States . . . [and] was declined."[9] Carr argues that the tendency of the United States and Great Britain to take a legalistic and moralistic approach to foreign policy after World War I—an approach that failed to account for the realities of power politics—bore considerable responsibility for the breakdown of international peace and security in the interwar period. With regard to the global economy, economist Charles Kindleberger points out that "the 1929 depression was so wide, so deep and so long because the international economic system was rendered unstable by British inability and United States unwillingness to assume responsibility for stabilizing it."[10]

Efforts by American statesmen to create a postwar environment that would foster American prosperity and security were influenced by several interpretations of the interwar experience. The first of these is that deprivation leads to political extremism, as demonstrated by the collapse of the Weimar Republic and the rise of Nazi Germany in the early 1930s. German statesman Erich Koch-Weser explained the political forces in Germany in 1931: "Economic depression and political radicalism go hand in hand. . . . When a man is driven to despair, he is ready to smash everything in the vague hope that a better world may arise out of the ruins."[11] Three years before Adolf Hitler declared himself to be the fuhrer of a German "Third Reich," Koch-Weser identified Germany's National Socialists (or Nazis) to be a major concern, because they drew support from formerly middle-class citizens who "have been uprooted from a satisfactory social position by war, revolution and inflation, and thrust out to seek an uncertain and penurious existence."[12]

A second major lesson from the interwar period was that security issues and economic issues were intrinsically linked. As US Secretary of the Treasury Henry Morgenthau Jr. observed in 1944, "All of us have seen the great economic tragedy of our time. We saw the world-wide depression of the 1930s. We saw currency disorders develop and spread from land to land, destroying the basis for international trade and international investment and even international faith. In their wake, we saw unemployment and wretchedness—idle tools, wasted wealth. We saw their victims fall prey, in places, to demagogues and dictators. We saw bewilderment and bitterness become the breeders of fascism and, finally, of war."[13] Economic dislocation could cause domestic political instability and might trigger international conflict.

Facing economic difficulties at home, countries resorted to protectionist measures to assist their domestic producers. As countries around the world increased trade barriers, international trade declined, further deepening the impact and duration of the Great Depression. One example was the Smoot-Hawley Tariff Act of 1930, which focused primarily on protecting American farmers but also increased protection of US manufacturers. Although its precise economic impact on the US economy is still debated, it set off a series of retaliatory tariff increases by other countries.[14] The drive by some countries to create exclusive economic blocs also contributed to reductions in free trade in the interwar period. In Europe, Nazi Germany created exclusive commercial relationships within its sphere of influence; imperial Japan behaved similarly in East Asia. Again in the words of Morgenthau: "Economic aggression can have no other offspring than war."[15]

A third major lesson was that isolationism could no longer advance American national interests or protect US national security. Many policy makers recognized this even prior to US entry into World War II, as Roosevelt's January 1941 speech reflects. However, the Japanese attack at Pearl Harbor revealed in a striking way to some who had previously been unconvinced that the United States could not remain secure by confining itself to the territory and concerns of its hemisphere. Speaking just two days after that attack, President Roosevelt told the country, "We have learned a terrible lesson. . . . We have learned that our ocean-girt hemisphere is not immune from severe attack—that we cannot measure our safety in terms of miles on any map." Roosevelt went on to explain the interrelatedness of events in Asia and Europe, indicating that the future security of Americans would also depend on the success of the Soviet Union and Great Britain against Fascist Italy and Germany. Beyond winning the war, he asserted, "We are going to win the peace that follows."[16]

Founding the Institutions of the Postwar International Order. In response to the lessons of the 1920s and the 1930s, the United States played a leading role in the development of international institutions to foster economic and political cooperation in a new postwar order. These efforts started before the conclusion of World War II. On the economic front, a major milestone was an international conference at Bretton Woods, New Hampshire, in July 1944. Forty-four countries participated in these discussions, including the Soviet Union.[17] On the security front, a major milestone was a meeting from August to October 1944 among representatives of China, Great Britain, the Soviet Union, and the United States at the Dumbarton Oaks mansion in Washington, DC.[18]

Bretton Woods. The overall goal of the Bretton Woods Conference was to create "an international monetary system that would ensure exchange rate stability, prevent competitive devaluations, and promote economic growth."[19] The primary accomplishments of the gathering, which was preceded by several years of preparation, were the creation of the International Monetary Fund (IMF) to promote the currency stability essential to international economic activity and the International Bank for Reconstruction and Development (IBRD) (which remains a component of the World Bank) to assist postwar reconstruction and economic development through the provision of loans. Both institutions constituted responses to the lessons of the 1920s and 1930s in that they provided forums for cooperation in international financial management and tools for preventing and ameliorating economic distress (see chapter 12 for more on the IMF).

In addition to international monetary policy and reconstruction, American statesmen also sought to address the issue of trade. An important lesson of the interwar period was that the effects of the Great Depression had been exacerbated by trade barriers and by the creation of exclusive economic blocs. In response, the United States led negotiations that culminated in talks in Havana from November 1947 to March 1948 and produced the International Trade Organization (ITO). The ITO was ambitious in the sense that the countries involved "rejected the idea that it was possible to maintain a firewall between trade, development, employment standards, and domestic policy."[20] The ITO sought to go beyond reducing international barriers to trade by incorporating affirmative goals such as full employment and by establishing a standing mechanism for the arbitration of international trade disputes. Despite early US leadership in the creation of the ITO, however, the US Senate failed to ratify the ITO treaty, largely because of fears that the ITO would interfere in domestic issues.

As a result of the US failure to ratify the ITO, the General Agreement on Tariffs and Trade (GATT) became the primary mechanism in the decades after World War II to facilitate multilateral efforts to reduce international barriers to trade. Economist Douglas Irwin argues that "the nascent postwar consensus about America's global leadership responsibilities" led to bipartisan support for GATT in 1947 as a "necessary component of Europe's economic recovery and America's national security."[21] Initially intended as a provisional mechanism, GATT dramatically reduced tariffs through a series of multilateral rounds of trade negotiations from 1948 until the creation of its successor, the World Trade Organization, in 1995.[22]

Dumbarton Oaks. In addition to these economic institutions, the United States also sought to create a mechanism to further international peace and security. President Roosevelt's efforts in this area were affected profoundly by President Woodrow Wilson's failure to bring the United States into the League of Nations after World War I. Roosevelt's approach to avoiding a repeat of that failure included early efforts to reach out to Republicans and to earn popular support.[23] After the meeting at Dumbarton Oaks, President Roosevelt continued to advance discussions of the proposed United Nations at the February 1945 Yalta Conference with Prime Minister Churchill and Soviet Premier Joseph Stalin, which resulted in invitations to Allied nations to attend a conference in San Francisco in April 1945. Although President Roosevelt died before the April 1945 conference, his successor, President Harry Truman, embraced the effort. In July 1945, as he urged the US Senate to adopt the UN Charter that had been drafted by the San Francisco Conference, Truman pointed out that "it comes from the reality of experience in a world where one generation has failed twice to keep the peace. The lessons of that experience have been written into this document."[24]

Ultimately, the Charter of the United Nations, drawn up by the fifty countries attending the San Francisco Conference, reflected a compromise between the need to recognize the significance of the great powers and the inclusiveness that would be necessary for domestic and international legitimacy. The outsize role of the great powers was recognized in the establishment of a Security Council with five permanent members—the United States, the Soviet Union, the United Kingdom, France, and China—each of which could veto resolutions involving international peace and security. The need for inclusiveness and the importance of the sovereign equality of states was realized through the creation of a General Assembly in which each country would have an equal vote.[25] Affirming the interrelatedness of economic and security issues and developments, the UN structure also included an Economic and Social Council with a charter to foster economic development.

In light of contemporary criticisms of the United Nations that are occasionally voiced by American policy makers and the public, it is interesting to note the depth of American support for the institution at its founding. For example, as John Ruggie details, "Just before the San Francisco conference, a Gallup poll reported that 81 percent of Americans favored U.S. entry into a 'world organization with police power to maintain world peace'; of those responding affirmatively, 83 percent described entry as 'very important.'"[26] Support among the country's elected representatives was similarly high, with the US Senate ultimately approving the UN Charter by a vote of 89–2. Perhaps the best indicator of congressional support was the willingness of the US Congress to cede a portion of its war power to the United Nations. "Congress decided in December 1945 that, once it had ratified the basic forces agreement with the United Nations, making U.S. troops available to the UN on call, the president would require no additional congressional authorization to commit them to specific UN missions."[27]

Ruggie's 1996 book *Winning the Peace* makes two key observations about the postwar system. First, the international security and economic institutions were intended to be, and have remained, explicitly multilateral. As Ruggie explains, "In its pure form, a multilateral world order would embody rules of conduct that are commonly applicable to all countries, as opposed to discriminating among them based on situational exigencies or particularistic preferences."[28] Ruggie argues that this approach was adopted not just because it served US interests, but also because of its consistency with American identity. Just as the United States is a political community that is in principle open to everyone and bound together by citizenship rather than racial or ethnic origin, the international order that the United States sought to create after World War II is similarly "a universal or general foundation open in principle to everyone."[29] A further benefit of this system was its potential attractiveness to other states: its principles of openness and nondiscrimination offered other countries a strong prospect of joint gains, and its encompassing nature enhanced its durability in the face of change.[30]

Second, Ruggie argues that the international economic architecture of the postwar era constituted a compromise he calls *embedded liberalism*: "Unlike the economic nationalism of the thirties, it would be multilateral in character; unlike the liberalism of the gold standard and free trade, its multilateralism would be predicated upon domestic interventionism."[31] This approach was the product of a broad decline in international support for the idea that a purely laissez-faire approach to markets would produce socially acceptable outcomes.[32] Beginning in the late nineteenth century, governments were increasingly expected to play a role in promoting domestic economic stability. Although many countries had returned to a more laissez-faire approach in the early years after World War I, by the 1930s, "governments everywhere had developed increasingly active forms of intervention in the domestic economy in order to affect the level of prices and employment, and to protect them against external sources of dislocation."[33] The postwar system would seek the benefits in overall growth and productivity that were offered by free trade, while also allowing states to take measures to manage their vulnerabilities and minimize adjustment costs. In the long run, these two purposes would be interdependent: government "efforts to moderate the deleterious consequences of unfettered market forces and corporate deployments" would be necessary to preserve political support for the liberal international economic order.[34]

The Impact of the Cold War. As discussed in chapter 3, the end of World War II was accompanied by a strong desire to "return to normalcy" in the United States with a very rapid military demobilization. However, developments in Europe and Asia caused a deepening distrust between the United States and the Soviet Union and created a new sense of confrontation. The United States came to see aggressive Soviet intentions at work in Iran, Eastern Europe, Greece, Turkey, and East Asia. The Soviet Union failed to honor wartime commitments to the principle of self-determination, which would have permitted all nations to choose their own forms of government. Particularly salient events in the early years after World War II included the continued presence of Soviet military forces in northern Iran after 1945; a failure by Soviet forces to allow a return to self-government in Eastern Europe at the end of the war; external support for communist forces in Greece; Soviet postwar territorial claims against Turkey; the forced communization of Czechoslovakia and the Soviet blockade of the Western sector of occupied Berlin in 1948; the Soviet demonstration of atomic weapon capabilities and the communist victory in the Chinese civil war in 1949; and Communist North Korea's invasion of South Korea in 1950. Important components of the American response include the declaration of the Truman Doctrine in 1947; the launch of the Marshall Plan in 1948; the creation of the North Atlantic Treaty Organization in 1949; and a US-led UN intervention to defend South Korean sovereignty and push North Korean forces back above the 38th parallel on the Korean peninsula in 1950.

The onset of the Cold War had at least three major implications for the multilateral, rules-based international order that the United States worked to build after World War II. First, this order would be only partially rather than universally implemented.[35] The institutions the United States helped found after World War II were, in principle, open to all countries. However, despite Soviet participation in the Bretton Woods Conference in 1944, there was an unresolvable tension between the economic principles that informed its proceedings and the command economy of the Soviet Union. Without a fundamental change in its government, society, and economy, the Soviet Union would not fit within the financial and trade systems created by the United States and its other World War II allies. On the security side, as a permanent member on the Security Council, the Soviet Union held veto power over important UN decisions on international peace and security. Under these circumstances, the Soviet Union saw its interests as being served by participation in the United Nations, but confrontation between the permanent members of the Security Council—with the United States on one side and the Soviet Union on the other—would greatly impede the ability of the United Nations to act throughout the Cold War.[36]

The deterioration in relations among the World War II Allies would force the United States to adjust its postwar plans to new realities. American diplomat Charles Bohlen wrote in 1947:

> The United States is confronted with a condition in the world which is at direct variance with the assumptions upon which, during and directly after the war, major United States policies were predicated. Instead of unity among the great powers—both political and economic—after the war, there is complete disunity between the Soviet Union and the satellites on one side and the rest of the world on the other. There are, in short, two worlds instead of one. Faced with this disagreeable fact, however much we may deplore

> it, the United States in the interest of its own well-being and security and those of the free non-Soviet world must reexamine its major policy objectives.[37]

A 1950 National Security Council report, which came to be known as NSC 68, concluded that the United States would therefore have to pursue two policies simultaneously: "a policy of attempting to develop a healthy international community" and a "policy of 'containing' the Soviet system."[38]

A second impact of the Cold War was that the United States would have to make much greater investments and play a much more active managerial role than America's postwar planners had hoped.[39] Two important examples of this include the Marshall Plan and the North Atlantic Treaty Organization (NATO). Early architects of the postwar order had not foreseen the need for a massive aid package for Europe; however, the combination of slower-than-expected recoveries among US allies and a fear that economic distress could cause political instability and opportunities for communist parties in Western Europe motivated the United States to launch the European Recovery Act, which became known as the Marshall Plan. Ultimately, the Marshall Plan was a response to security concerns in the face of apparent Soviet aggressive intent, as well as an effort to foster economic recovery.

Another important example of the way in which the Cold War drew the United States into a more extensive and activist role was the founding of the North Atlantic Treaty Organization (NATO) in 1949. American planners had hoped, early on, that the United Nations might provide the necessary institutional framework to promote international peace and security. However, after the events of the early post–World War II years, the United States also sought to encourage European unity as a counterweight to the Soviet Union. For their own distinct reasons, the countries of Western Europe were not content with this approach and sought a greater US commitment to their security.[40] The response was the creation of NATO, with the United States as a leading member. However, after the treaty was signed, many US policy makers hoped that even without a significant US military presence, NATO's mere existence would deter aggression against its members and would provide political and psychological reassurance to the populations of the member states of Western Europe. It was not until after the beginning of the Korean War in 1950 that the United States significantly increased its forces in Western Europe and NATO began the practice of designating a US general as the supreme allied commander to lead all NATO military forces.[41] As described in chapter 3, the 1950s also saw a vast expansion in America's peacetime alliances around the world.

A third impact of the Cold War was that it prompted an added degree of discipline in relations among the United States and its allies and gave them a further incentive to cooperate.[42] International relations scholar G. John Ikenberry argues that an American decision to exercise "strategic restraint" was critical to the success of the postwar international order. Rather than maximize the immediate gains that might have been won through the exercise of its disproportionate power at the end of World War II, the United States sought to establish a framework that would serve its long-term interests. This framework also offered other states the possibility that their interests, too, could be served through participation.

The "constitutional characteristics" of this order mitigated "the implications of power asymmetries" and fostered "consensual and reciprocal" relations among states.[43] However, while institutions may help participants cooperate despite competing interests, they do not eliminate all sources of friction. The broader strategic context of the Cold War standoff with the Soviet Union helped keep conflict among the United States and its economic and security partners from escalating to the point that it would have caused a fundamental breach in relations.

The creation of the postwar multilateral order was not dependent on the onset of the Cold War, although it was closely related in time. As Ikenberry points out, "Although the Cold War reinforced this order, it was not triggered by it or ultimately dependent on the Cold War for its functioning and stability."[44] This basic insight goes a long way toward explaining why the basic norms and institutions of the postwar international order, including the United Nations, the IMF, the IBRD/World Bank, GATT/WTO, and even NATO have continued beyond the end of the Cold War.

Persistent Tensions in the US Role in the World

Chapter 3 of this volume traces the post–World War II history of US national security policy, focusing especially on the effects of international political and military developments, domestic priorities, and technological advances on American policies and actions. Even though chapter 3 is not comprehensive—no single account of seven decades can be—it is clear that not all US policies and actions recounted there can be explained as those of a country playing the role of restrained builder and defender of a rules-based, liberal international order. In fact, some observers argue that this relatively benign image of the United States and its actions in the world is fundamentally flawed. Historian Andrew Bacevich, for example, argues that the record of US foreign policy during this timeframe does not reflect "a nation committed to liberalism, openness, or the rule of law"; to pretend that it does would be to "whitewash the past."[45] Bacevich and others argue instead that the United States behaved in the way that great powers have always behaved: "following the rules when it serves their interest to do so; disregarding the rules whenever they become an impediment."[46]

Morality and Foreign Policy. Although Bacevich's account slights the critical role that the United States played as an architect of the institutions that underpin the postwar international order, his critique provides some useful reminders. The first is to be wary of assuming that US actions to build a multilateral order after World War II were fundamentally guided by morality rather than interest. In fact, the architects of the postwar order saw their plans as advancing, rather than sacrificing, the national interest. On the last day of the Bretton Woods Conference, Treasury Secretary Morgenthau declared:

> I am perfectly certain that no delegation to this Conference has lost sight for a moment of the particular national interest it was sent here to represent. The American delegation,

> which I have the honor of leading, has been, at all times, conscious of its primary obligation—the protection of American interests. And the other representatives here have been no less loyal or devoted to the welfare of their own people. Yet none of us has found any incompatibility between devotion to our own country and joint action. Indeed, we have found on the contrary that the only genuine safeguard for our national interests lies in international cooperation.[47]

In fostering the development of a rules-based, international order that would facilitate cooperation, American diplomats and policy makers sought to create a sustainable framework in which US prosperity and security could best be secured in an increasingly interconnected and interdependent world.

Unilateralism versus Multilateralism. A second useful reminder that Bacevich provides is that the history of US foreign policy since World War II is also marked by significant incidences of what Ruggie calls "American exemptionalism," which is the idea that because the United States is a special case, it should be considered "exempt" from certain aspects of international law.[48] As discussed in chapter 2, Americans tend to view the founding of the Republic as constituting a fundamentally new and unique human experiment in governance that serves as a model for other societies around the world. This notion of the unique nature of the United States contributes to the idea of "American exceptionalism." Ruggie explains that "American exemptionalism" has similar roots in that it stems from "a perceived need to safeguard the special features and protections of the US Constitution from external interference."[49] Historically, "the 'exemptionalist' resistance has been anchored in Congress. It has been most pronounced and consequential in the area of human rights and related social issues, where it has typically been framed in terms of protecting states' rights against federal treaty-based incursions."[50] In the early decades after World War II, for example, southern Democrats in Congress were worried about the potential impact of international human rights agreements on the Jim Crow laws that perpetuated racial segregation. Today, exemptionalists are "animated by a more diffuse set of social issues including capital punishment, abortion, gun control, unfettered property rights, and the role of religion in politics and policy."[51] In addition to this focus on social issues, Ruggie points out that in recent decades other groups have embraced variations of American exemptionalism. For example, a "nationalist" school of lawyers raises questions about the domestic applicability of international law; and some neoconservatives argue that due to the unique power status and identity of the United States, US freedom of action abroad should not be constrained by the institutions or international laws that limit the actions of other states (see also chapter 1).[52]

When it comes to foreign policy choices, there are likely to be continuing debates about the relative merits of unilateral and multilateral action. Unilateralism involves fewer constraints and offers greater freedom of action. It will probably always be the case that when its vital national interests are at stake, the United States cannot forgo the option of proceeding alone. Multilateralism, on the other hand, offers three key advantages: (1) it provides a framework for organizing interstate relations and fostering stability; (2) it allows for sharing the burden while pursuing common purposes; and (3) it generates international legitimacy for a state's foreign policy. The ultimate goal for any state that accepts multilateral principles is to serve its own interests by supporting a system that regulates the behavior of the other participating states, thereby reducing uncertainty and establishing certain practices others should respect.[53]

In addition to their varied costs and benefits, unilateralism and multilateralism also entail different risks. For example, unilateralism may tend to lead to isolationism, even when that is not the initial goal. As Ruggie points out, the experience of the United States in the interwar period "suggests that it was not necessary to be a political isolationist, or to harbor such objectives, in order to contribute to the isolationist outcome. Among political leaders, it was enough initially to favor unfettered unilateralism; among the public at large it sufficed initially to give tacit approval."[54] Multilateralism, on the other hand, conjures up concerns about overreach and overextension. In the article in which Bacevich calls into question the image of the United States as the founder and supporter of a liberal international order, his real target seems to be those who want the United States to be an aggressive hegemon "that forces other nations to bend to its will."[55] A question facing proponents of multilateralism is whether a foreign policy based on that approach can remain prudent, restrained, and carefully attuned to a reasonable definition of the national interest.

Contemporary Challenges to the Postwar International Order

The purpose of this section is not to evaluate the relative merits of multilateral or unilateral approaches in serving particular US national security interests. Instead, this section introduces a few of the most significant developments since World War II that have implications for the postwar international order and its ability to continue to serve US interests. Some may see these developments as constituting reasons that the United States should continue to lead in reinforcing and sustaining the post–World War II system of economic and security institutions; others may see them as reasons why a fundamentally new strategic approach is needed. Either way, they are factors that US policy makers must consider as they look ahead.

The Post–Cold War Experience. Even though the post–World War II, rules-based international order was not rooted in the Cold War, the onset of the Cold War enhanced the incentives of participating states to cooperate and invest in the order. Since the Cold War's end, this urgency has lessened, and the approach of the United States—the key founder and a critical supporter of this system—has fluctuated between efforts to reinforce its utility and actions that reject its constraints.

A high point in the US embrace of multilateralism occurred in the years immediately after the end of the Cold War, as the end of the US-Soviet standoff brought hopes for greater cooperation. According to Brent Scowcroft, President George H. W. Bush's national security advisor, the administration's "core premise" from August 1990 forward was that the United States "would be obligated to lead the world community to an unprecedented degree . . . and that we should attempt to pursue our national interests, whenever possible, within a framework of concert with our friends and the international community."[56] This was evident in the case of the Gulf War of 1990–1991, which followed Iraq's invasion and attempted annexation of Kuwait. The subsequent multilateral security operation to expel Iraq from Kuwait, led by the United States, marked the first time since the Korean War that the UN Security Council had been able to reach the consensus needed to authorize such an action.

A low point in American multilateralism occurred just over a decade later, again involving a war against Iraq. In early 2003, the administration of President George W. Bush confronted a stark choice over how to pursue its goals of removing Iraqi President Saddam Hussein and his regime from power in Iraq and disarming Iraq of suspected weapons of mass destruction (WMD). In November 2002, the UN Security Council unanimously demanded Iraqi compliance with disarmament obligations stretching back to the Gulf War of 1991. This collective demand, which threatened "serious" if unspecified consequences should Iraq refuse to cooperate, was a powerful symbol of international support for the administration's objectives.[57] By January 2003, however, the George W. Bush administration had grown impatient with what it deemed continuing deception by the Iraqi regime, as well as with the ongoing inspections that had yet to locate evidence of alleged Iraqi WMD stockpiles or a capability to manufacture them. After several fruitless attempts to persuade the Security Council of the necessity for force, in March 2003 the administration invaded Iraq without explicit Security Council authorization.[58] Although the United States and the ad hoc coalition it assembled rapidly defeated Hussein's regime, debate over the war's legitimacy and its effects has continued. In large part because its action was unilateral, America's international reputation suffered. In contrast to the substantial support that the United States had received in the first Gulf War, most of the political, military, and financial burden of its second war in Iraq was borne by the United States alone. (See also chapters 3, 16, and 20.)

Since the administration of President George W. Bush, America's embrace of the principle of multilateralism has continued to fluctuate. At least rhetorically, the administration of President Barack Obama doubled down on the postwar order. The last chapter of its 2015 *National Security Strategy* was devoted to multilateralism:

> The modern-day international system currently relies heavily on an international legal architecture, economic and political institutions, as well as alliances and partnerships the United States and other like-minded nations established after World War II. Sustained by robust American leadership, this system has served us well for 70 years, facilitating international cooperation, burden sharing, and accountability. It carried us through the Cold War and ushered in a wave of democratization. It reduced barriers to trade, expanded free markets, and enabled advances in human dignity and prosperity.[59]

The Obama administration's actions, however, were more unilateral than its declared policy. For example, however well justified it may have been, the unilateral 2011 raid into Abbottabad, Pakistan, to kill Osama bin Laden was undertaken without coordination with Pakistan. President Obama's decision to rely more than his predecessor did on drone strikes, most of which were conducted unilaterally (see chapter 16), is another example of the United States exempting itself from multilateralism.

Many analysts see the foreign policy of the Trump administration, including the slogan "America First," as deemphasizing the importance of the postwar international architecture to America's prosperity and security.[60] Among the early indications that this rhetorical stance will translate into policy are the administration's decisions to withdraw from the Trans-Pacific Partnership, a trade deal that involved twelve countries, and from the Paris Agreement on climate change, which involves 197 countries.[61] It is important to recall, however, that most presidential administrations since World War II have adopted both unilateral and multilateral approaches to serve US national interests. It would be premature to attempt an overall assessment of the Trump administration at this early date.

Diffusion of Power in the International System. At the end of World War II, the concentration of political and economic power in the hands of the United States was unprecedented. The United States, on the winning side of a global conflict, had military bases around the world. In addition, the United States had a monopoly on atomic weapons and had demonstrated its capability during the war against Japan. These diplomatic and military strengths were underpinned by its economic power. As historian Melvyn Leffler observes, "In 1945, the United States had two-thirds of the world's gold reserves, three-fourths of its invested capital, half of its shipping vessels, and half of its manufacturing capacity. Its gross national product was three times that of the Soviet Union and more than five times that of Great Britain."[62] The territory of the United States had been largely untouched by a war that had devastated the economies and infrastructure of both its wartime allies and its adversaries. The possession of this concentration of power helped to give the United States the means, the will, and the incentive to be the leading architect of the postwar international order.

More than seven decades later, the strategic position of the United States remains enviable in many ways. It has the world's largest economy and, by most measures, it has the world's most powerful military.[63] In addition, it is in formal alliance agreements with six of the top ten most economically powerful countries.[64] Despite these US strengths, however, power has become more diffuse within the international system. An increasing number of states and, in some issue areas, nonstate actors have become consequential and must be taken into account. One economic measure of this diffusion of power is the US share of global economic output. In 1945, US economic output constituted over 50 percent of the world's total; in 2016 US output was less than 25 percent of the world's total.[65]

Scholars and analysts disagree about what this shift means for America's future strategic choices. Robert Keohane, G. John Ikenberry, and others argue that this shift makes it even more worthwhile for the United States to reaffirm the rules-based, liberal international order it helped to create after World War II.

Keohane points out that it is less costly to maintain international institutions than it is to create them, and that even in the absence of a liberal hegemon—the role played by the United States after World War II—these institutions can continue to facilitate cooperation.[66] Ikenberry also argues that in a world in which new security challenges have arisen and power has become diffuse, the real dividing line "will be between those who want to renew and expand today's system of multilateral governance arrangements and those who want to move to a less cooperative order built on spheres of influence." He argues that it is in the US interest to support those who take the former approach.[67]

Others see the diffusion of power within the international system as necessitating a change in the US role in the world. Scholars who hold this view generally focus on international peace and security and argue that the United States should not continue to assume a disproportionate share of the global burden.[68] The concern that multilateralism will lead to overextension is often accompanied by a skepticism about the efficacy of international institutions and a concern that joint gains from multilateral institutions may disproportionally disadvantage the United States, with implications for national security.[69] For example, John Mearsheimer points out that Chinese economic gains can be translated into other forms of power that could threaten US interests. He argues that "if China continues its impressive economic growth over the next few decades, the United States and China are likely to engage in an intense security competition with considerable potential for war."[70] Although Mearsheimer acknowledges that "there is no practical way of slowing the Chinese economy without also damaging the American economy," an implication of his analysis is that the relative economic gains experienced by other states that participate in a liberal, rules-based international economic order can have long-term negative implications for US security.[71] The international system that allowed China to enjoy sustained high levels of economic growth also facilitated its emergence as a great power whose ambitions may run contrary to the interests of the United States and its allies.

Support for Free Trade within the United States. Variations in American attitudes toward free trade also have implications for US global leadership. An important principle of the postwar economic institutions is that openness in the global economy offers the greatest gains in overall welfare. These gains are maximized in a system that includes the greatest number of participants who all obey common rules and operate according to the principles of reciprocity and nondiscrimination. Although each state will include some who gain from trade and some who lose, aggregate gains in each state should be sufficient to allow the winners to compensate the losers, creating an overall improvement in each state's welfare. The "embedded liberalism" compromise means that, out of concern for domestic economic stability and social welfare, postwar international economic institutions include provisions that allow states to manage their vulnerabilities and to mitigate adjustment costs. In ensuring that political and social goals would be given priority over pure market forces and economic rationality, these provisions would also help to sustain the system itself by preserving public support in the countries involved.

In recent years, American public opinion on the issue of free trade has been somewhat volatile. On the one hand, a February 2017 poll found that 72 percent of Americans viewed foreign trade as an opportunity, and only 23 percent viewed it as a threat.[72] On the other hand, in a poll during the 2016 election campaign, most Americans reported a belief that "free trade has cost the US more jobs than it has created"; those agreeing with that statement included 85 percent of the Republicans surveyed and 54 percent of the Democrats.[73]

There are probably at least two dynamics at work in this polling data. The first is an increasing tendency for many Americans to view public policy issues, including foreign policy issues, through a partisan lens. As candidate Trump denounced foreign trade deals, including the North American Free Trade Agreement and the proposed Trans-Pacific Partnership, many Republican voters adopted a negative view of them.[74] Partisanship, in the form of trust in a president of the same party, may also explain why Democrats became more positive about trade than Republicans beginning in 2012, under the administration of Democratic President Obama, while during the administration of Republican President George W. Bush, "the opposite was true."[75] A second issue relates to how polling questions are framed; if they ask about whether trade protectionism is justified to protect jobs, this probably increases the tendency of respondents to favor restrictions on trade.[76] In any event, in the 2016 presidential election, major candidates from both parties campaigned against free trade agreements, and both the Democratic and Republican nominees adopted the position that the United States should withdraw from the Trans-Pacific Partnership.

The significance of variations in the country's support for free trade lies in what Ruggie calls "the fragile domestic basis of the international economic order."[77] As early as 1996, he expressed concern that "the combined effects of wage stagnation, widening income gaps, increasingly kaleidoscopic labor markets, and the growing inability or unwillingness by the government to moderate the deleterious consequences of unfettered global market forces and corporate deployments" might lead to populist calls for protection and "economic neo-isolationism."[78] It is the case that wage stagnation has increased in the United States since the early 1970s, and income inequality in the United States has been growing for the past fifty years.[79]

These developments likely stem from a complex set of dynamics, including public policy choices and technological trends. However, the large impact of expanded trade with China on the US economy—especially since 1999—may have played an important role. This "China Shock" continues to plague those affected by foreign imports:

> Alongside the heralded consumer benefits of expanded trade are substantial adjustment costs and distributional consequences. These impacts are most visible in the local labor markets in which the industries exposed to foreign competition are concentrated. Adjustment in local labor markets is remarkably slow, with wages and labor-force participation rates remaining depressed and unemployment rates remaining elevated for at

> least a full decade after the China trade shock [commenced]. Exposed workers experience greater job churning and reduced lifetime income. At the national level, employment has fallen in US industries more exposed to import competition, as expected, but offsetting employment gains in other industries have yet to materialize.[80]

As recent developments in international trade have produced greater distributional consequences and adjustment costs than those seen in previous decades, governments that wish to continue to gain the aggregate benefits from trade may need to implement policies that better address the political and social costs.

Intrusive Global Governance Regimes. Recent efforts to increase multilateral trade and to advance global governance have intruded increasingly into issue areas that were previously considered matters of domestic politics. With regard to trade, this dynamic is in part the product of the success of GATT and its successor organization, the WTO, in reducing tariffs and other external barriers to trade. Remaining obstacles are often more complex and are the products of domestic policy choice. Issues such as government procurement, state-owned enterprises, intellectual property rights, and labor standards may now be the subjects of multilateral trade negotiations. The importance of these issues issues will differ across different domestic political economies and, within countries, they will affect politically sensitive institutions and practices.[81] International negotiations on issues such as human rights and climate protection may also reach more deeply into the domestic sphere than existing agreements. As Ruggie points out, "Not only has the global governance agenda become more crowded and diverse, but it also projects more deeply into the domestic policy sphere of states."[82]

The increasing intrusiveness of international agreements may produce a domestic backlash, as populations around the world resent infringements on sovereignty. Within liberal democracies, the concern may be over legitimacy, if the processes that produce global rule-making are not as democratic as those that are in effect in national institutions. In any event, the implications for popular support for a rules-based, international order might be that policy makers who want to preserve and strengthen existing international institutions should approach their expansion into new issue areas with restraint and caution.

The Rise in Populist Movements in the United States and Abroad. The rise of populist movements in the United States and Western Europe is one manifestation of a backlash against efforts at global governance and the impacts of international market forces. Political commentator John Judis explains that populist movements in these countries generally seek to gain political power by working through the democratic system, rather than by subverting it. He distinguishes between left-wing populists, whose approach is a "politics of the bottom and the middle against the top," and right-wing populists, who "champion the people against an elite that they accuse of coddling a third group, which can consist, for instance, of immigrants, Islamists, or African American militants."[83] Exemplifying a rise in populism in recent years are the 2016 presidential candidacies of Senator Bernie Sanders, who ran as a Democrat, and Donald Trump, who ran as a Republican. Both were populist candidates who challenged the mainstream of the parties with which they were associated. Examples from abroad include the British vote to leave the European Union in 2016 and the increasing success of several populist political parties across Europe.[84]

Although the causes and implications of populist movements are debated, most are generally nativist and nationalist and therefore do not generally support robust international institutions or international cooperation.[85] Left-wing populism, manifested in the Sanders campaign, attacked the "billionaire class," denounced rising income inequality, and opposed trade agreements that would benefit the owners of capital and harm labor and the environment.[86] Right-wing populist movements in Western Europe also opposed "supranational formations" and emphasized the reassertion of "national control over their currency, fiscal policy, and borders."[87] Populist politics are likely to be a challenge for policy makers seeking to advance their countries' national interests in a globally interconnected world characterized by an increasingly diverse set of transnational challenges, many of which cannot be addressed effectively without international cooperation.

Increasing Partisanship in American Politics. A final challenge to the rules-based postwar international order, as well as to American leadership in foreign policy, may be increasing partisanship in US politics, which inhibits cooperation among elected political leaders from the country's two major political parties. One notable feature of early US efforts to construct the postwar international order was that bipartisan consensus underpinned the endeavor. This was followed by a strong bipartisan consensus behind the overall approach to the Cold War, which involved containment of the Soviet Union. In 1947, Republican Senator Arthur Vandenberg famously declared the need to stop "partisan politics at the water's edge."[88] For the remainder of the decade, as chair of the Senate Foreign Relations Committee, Vandenberg supported efforts by Democratic President Harry Truman to respond to the onset of the Cold War.

Since the end of the Cold War, however, bipartisan consensus and cooperation has declined substantially. Using data on American military interventions since 2002, political scientist Robert Leiber points out that, while presidents have still benefited from an initial "rally around the flag" effect when embarking on foreign military interventions (see chapter 2), popular and elite opinion about ongoing conflicts soon divide along partisan lines, with support influenced by whether or not the individual concerned is of the same political party as the president. Lieber concludes that "in today's polarized climate, politics can be delayed at the water's edge, but it certainly doesn't stop for long."[89]

While recent decades have seen partisan identification increasingly shape attitudes regarding foreign policy, as of 2016 a majority of Republicans, Democrats, and Independents all continued to favor an active role for the United States in international affairs.[90] Translating this underlying consensus into a constructive agenda for American engagement that serves US interests will remain a significant challenge for policy makers in the years to come.

Conclusion

As World War II drew to a close, American statesmen sought to create a rules-based, liberal international order. As they did so, they were responding to the lessons of the 1920s and 1930s, which taught them that economic deprivation leads to political extremism, that economic and security affairs are intrinsically linked, and that isolationism is not an adequate approach when seeking to foster the prosperity of the United States and ensure its security. They sought to take advantage of a moment in which American power was unrivaled to build an international architecture that would serve US national interests long into the future.

Seventy years later, much has changed. Nevertheless, the challenges confronting today's policy makers are at least as complex. In an increasingly interconnected world, it is useful to consider the lessons of the 1920s and the 1930s and to determine which of them retain relevance. As policy makers navigate a host of specific issues relating to international economics, politics, and security, it will be valuable to consider the costs and benefits associated with adopting a multilateral approach. In cases where multilateral approaches offer the best prospects for serving the national interest, policy makers will also have to build and protect the domestic political foundation on which a sustained, multilateral approach must rest.

Discussion Questions

1. What lessons from the 1920s and 1930s shaped the American approach to foreign policy after World War II?
2. What international economic institutions were created in the immediate postwar period, and what were they intended to accomplish?
3. As revealed in the initial failure of the International Trade Organization, or debates about multilateral trade agreements today, on what grounds are these treaties opposed?
4. Is the United Nations a useful mechanism for promoting international peace and security? Why or why not?
5. What aspects of American political identity seem more consistent with a multilateral approach to international affairs? What aspects of American identity seem more consistent with a unilateral approach?
6. How should policy makers evaluate whether or not multilateral agreements have gone too far in affecting domestic conditions, laws, and rights?
7. If generally open trade improves the overall prosperity of a country in the aggregate, why would many vocal groups oppose such trade? What can or should be done to address those who are disadvantaged by trade agreements?
8. What is populism? What impact might it have on a country's foreign policy?
9. What factors have led to increasingly partisan approaches to US national security policy? Can the United States return to a condition where partisan politics "stop at the water's edge"?
10. Under what circumstances is it best for the United States to adopt a multilateral approach to advancing its national interests? When would unilateralism be more appropriate?

Recommended Reading

Alden, Edward. *Failure to Adjust: How Americans Got Left Behind in the Global Economy*. Lanham, MD: Rowman & Littlefield, 2017.

Brooks, Stephen G., and William C. Wohlforth. *America Abroad: The United States' Role in the 21st Century*. Oxford: Oxford University Press, 2016.

Fromkin, David. *In the Time of the Americans: The Generation that Changed America's Role in the World*. New York: Vintage, 1995.

Fukuyama, Francis. *America at the Crossroads: Democracy, Power, and the Neoconservative Legacy*. New Haven, CT: Yale University Press, 2006.

Haass, Richard N. *A World in Disarray: American Foreign Policy and the Crisis of the Old Order*. New York: Penguin, 2017.

Ikenberry, G. John. *After Victory: Institutions, Strategic Restraint, and the Rebuilding of Order after Major Wars*. Princeton, NJ: Princeton University Press, 2001.

———. *Liberal Leviathan: The Origins, Crisis, and Transformation of the American World Order*. Princeton, NJ: Princeton University Press, 2011

Judis, John B. *The Populist Explosion: How the Great Recession Transformed American and European Politics*. New York: Columbia Global Reports, 2016.

Kindleberger, Charles P. *The World in Depression, 1929–1939*. Berkeley: University of California Press, 2013.

Luce, Edward. *The Retreat of Western Liberalism*. London, UK: Little, Brown Book Group, 2017.

Packer, George. *The Unwinding: An Inner History of the New America*. New York: Farrar, Strauss and Giroux, 2013.

Ruggie, John Gerard. *Winning the Peace: America and World Order in the New Era*. New York: Columbia University Press, 1996.

Internet Resources

Council on Foreign Relations, www.cfr.org
International Monetary Fund, www.imf.org/external/index.htm
United Nations, www.un.org/en/index.html
The World Bank, www.worldbank.org
World Trade Organization, www.wto.org

Notes

1. The White House, "America First Foreign Policy," n.d., https://web.archive.org/web/20170220151548/https://www.whitehouse.gov/america-first-foreign-policy. See also Melvyn P. Leffler, "The Worst 1st Year of Foreign Policy Ever," *Foreign Policy*, September 19, 2017, http://foreignpolicy.com/2017/09/19/the-worst-first-year-of-foreign-policy-ever/.

2. See, for example, Brian Bennett, "'America First,' a Phrase with Loaded Anti-Semitic and Isolationist History," *Los Angeles Times*, January 20, 2017, http://www.latimes.com/politics/la-na-pol-trump-america-first-20170120-story.html; and G. John Ikenberry, "The Plot against American Foreign Policy: Can the Liberal Order Survive?" *Foreign Affairs* 96, no. 3 (2017): 2–9.

3. Matthew Kroenig, "The Case for Trump's Foreign Policy: The Right People, the Right Positions," *Foreign Affairs* 96, no. 3 (2017): 30; Eliott Abrams, "Trump the Traditionalist: A Surprisingly Standard Foreign Policy," *Foreign Affairs* 96, no. 4 (2017): 10–16.

4. Office of the Historian, Department of State, "The Atlantic Conference & Charter, 1941," https://history.state.gov/milestones/1937-1945/atlantic-conf.

5. Franklin Delano Roosevelt, "Message to Congress, 1941," 5, https://fdrlibrary.org/documents/356632/390886/readingcopy.pdf/42234a77-8127-4015-95af-bcf831db311d.

6. Roosevelt, "Message to Congress, 1941," 20–21.

7. Douglas T. Stuart, *Creating the National Security State: A History of the Law that Transformed America* (Princeton, NJ: Princeton University Press, 2008), 40–42.

8. Stuart, *Creating the National Security State*, 40.

9. Edward Hallett Carr, *The Twenty Years Crisis, 1919–1939: An Introduction to the Study of International Relations*, 2nd ed. (London: Macmillan, 1946), 234.

10. Charles P. Kindleberger, *The World in Depression, 1929–1939* (Berkeley: University of California Press, 2013), 292.

11. Erich Koch-Weser, "Radical Forces in Germany," April 1931, reproduced in "How We Got Here: The Rise of the Modern Order," *Foreign Affairs* 91, no. 1 (2012): 18–19.

12. Koch-Weser, "Radical Forces in Germany," 20.

13. Henry Morgenthau Jr., "Address by the Honorable Henry Morgenthau, Jr., at the Inaugural Plenary Session," July 1, 1944, http://www.cvce.eu/obj/inaugural_address_by_henry_morgenthau_jr_1_july_1944-en-34c4153e-6266-4e84-88d7-f655abf1395f.html.

14. Kindleberger, *The World in Depression, 1929–1939*, 132.

15. Kindleberger, *The World in Depression, 1929–1939*, 132.

16. Franklin Delano Roosevelt, "On the Declaration of War with Japan," December 9, 1941, http://docs.fdrlibrary.marist.edu/120941.html.

17. Kurt Schuler and Mark Bernkopf, "Who Was at Bretton Woods?" (New York: Center for Financial Stability, 2014), http://www.centerforfinancialstability.org/bw/Who_Was_at_Bretton_Woods.pdf.

18. United Nations, "Dumbarton Oaks and Yalta: 1944–1945," n.d., http://www.un.org/en/sections/history-united-nations-charter/1944-1945-dumbarton-oaks-and-yalta/.

19. US Federal Reserve, "Creation of the Bretton Woods System," November 22, 2013, https://www.federalreservehistory.org/essays/bretton_woods_created.

20. Daniel Drache, *The Short but Significant Life of the International Trade Organization: Lessons for Our Time* (Coventry, UK: Center for the Study of Globalisation and Regionalisation, November 2000), 2, http://wrap.warwick.ac.uk/2063/1/WRAP_Drache_wp6200.pdf.

21. Douglas A. Irwin, "From Smoot-Hawley to Reciprocal Trade Agreements: Changing the Course of U.S. Trade Policy in the 1930s," in *The Defining Moment: The Great Depression and the American Economy in the Twentieth Century*, ed. Michael D. Bordo, Claudia Goldin, and Eugene N. White (Chicago: University of Chicago Press, 1998), 326

22. World Trade Organization, "The GATT Years: From Havana to Marrakesh," n.d., https://www.wto.org/english/thewto_e/whatis_e/tif_e/fact4_e.htm.

23. John Gerard Ruggie, *Winning the Peace: America and World Order in the New Era* (New York: Columbia University Press, 1996), 29.

24. Harry S. Truman, "Address before the Senate Urging Ratification of the Charter of the United Nations," July 2, 1945, https://www.trumanlibrary.org/publicpapers/index.php?pid=76.

25. Ruggie, *Winning the Peace*, 30–34.

26. Ruggie, *Winning the Peace*, 33.

27. Ruggie, *Winning the Peace*, 34.

28. Ruggie, *Winning the Peace*, 20.

29. Tracy B. Strong, "Taking the Rank with What Is Ours: American Political Thought, Foreign Policy, and Questions of Rights," in *The Politics of Human Rights*, ed. Paula R.

Newberg (New York: New York University Press, 1980), 50, as cited by Ruggie, *Winning the Peace*, 25.

30. Ruggie, *Winning the Peace*, 48.

31. John Gerard Ruggie, "International Regimes, Transactions, and Change: Embedded Liberalism in the Postwar Economic Order," *International Organization* 35, no. 2 (1982): 393.

32. Ruggie, "International Regimes, Transactions, and Change," 387.

33. Ruggie, "International Regimes, Transactions, and Change," 390.

34. Ruggie, *Winning the Peace*, 161.

35. G. John Ikenberry, *Liberal Leviathan: The Origins, Crisis, and Transformation of the American World Order* (Princeton, NJ: Princeton University Press, 2011), 107.

36. The UN was able to act against North Korea in June 1950 because the two countries most likely to issue a veto were not present. At this time, China was still represented by the Nationalists on Taiwan rather than by the government of the communist People's Republic of China (PRC), which had won the Chinese civil war in 1949. The Soviet Union was absent because it had undertaken a boycott to protest the failure of the PRC to have been granted China's seat.

37. Charles Bohlen, Memorandum dated August 30, 1947, *Foreign Relations of the United States 1947* (Washington, DC: Brookings Institution, 1963), chap. 1, as cited by G. John Ikenberry, "Rethinking the Origins of American Hegemony," *Political Science Quarterly* 104, no. 3 (1989): 386.

38. James S. Lay Jr., "A Report to the National Security Council on United States Objectives and Programs for National Security (NSC 68)," April 14, 1950, 21, https://www.trumanlibrary.org/whistlestop/study_collections/coldwar/documents/pdf/10-1.pdf.

39. Ikenberry, "Rethinking the Origins of American Hegemony," 385–94; see also Ikenberry, *Liberal Leviathan*, chap. 5.

40. Ikenberry, "Rethinking the Origins of American Hegemony," 391–94.

41. The First NATO supreme allied commander was General of the Army Dwight D. Eisenhower. There has been an American general (or admiral) as the supreme allied commander since 1951.

42. G. John Ikenberry, "Institutions, Strategic Restraint, and the Persistence of American Postwar Order," *International Security* 23, no. 3 (1998–1999): 44.

43. Ikenberry, "Institutions, Strategic Restraint, and the Persistence of American Postwar Order," 45, 4.

44. Ikenberry, "Institutions, Strategic Restraint, and the Persistence of American Postwar Order," 46.

45. Andrew J. Bacevich, "The 'Global Order' Myth: Teary-Eyed Nostalgia as Cover for U.S. Hegemony," *American Conservative*, June 15, 2017, http://www.theamericanconservative.com/articles/the-global-order-myth/.

46. Bacevich, "The 'Global Order' Myth."

47. Henry Morgenthau Jr., "Bretton Woods and International Cooperation," *Foreign Affairs* 23, no. 2 (1945): 193.

48. John Gerard Ruggie, "American Exceptionalism, Exemptionalism, and Global Governance," in *American Exceptionalism and Human Rights*, ed. Michael Ignatieff (Princeton, NJ: Princeton University Press), 305–38.

49. Ruggie, "American Exceptionalism, Exemptionalism, and Global Governance," 305.

50. Ruggie, "American Exceptionalism, Exemptionalism, and Global Governance," 305.

51. Ruggie, "American Exceptionalism, Exemptionalism, and Global Governance," 324.

52. Ruggie, "American Exceptionalism, Exemptionalism, and Global Governance," 325–26.

53. See John Gerard Ruggie, "Multilateralism: The Anatomy of an Institution," *International Organization* 46, no. 3 (1992): 561–98.

54. Ruggie, *Winning the Peace*, 18.

55. Bacevich, "The 'Global Order' Myth."

56. George Bush and Brent Scowcroft, *A World Transformed* (New York: Knopf, 1998), 400.

57. Neil MacFarquhar, "Iraq Inspections Receive Approval from Arab League," *New York Times*, November 11, 2002, A1; Patrick E. Tyler, "NATO Leaders Say Iraq Must Disarm," *New York Times*, November 22, 2002, A1; Richard Bernstein, "Threats and Responses: Brussels Summit; European Union Says Iraq Must Disarm Quickly and Fully," *New York Times*, February 18, 2003, A1.

58. John Tagliabue, "Threats and Responses: Europe; France and Germany Draw a Line, against Washington," *New York Times*, January 23, 2003, A10.

59. The White House, *National Security Strategy* (Washington, DC: The White House, February 2015), 23.

60. Examples include Ikenberry, "The Plot against American Foreign Policy," 2–9; and Douglas A. Irwin, "The False Promise of Protectionism: Why Trump's Trade Policy Could Backfire," *Foreign Affairs* 96, no. 3 (2017): 45–56.

61. Mireya Solis, "Trump Withdrawing from the Trans-Pacific Partnership," *Brookings Institution,* March 24, 2017, https://www.brookings.edu/blog/unpacked/2017/03/24/trump-withdrawing-from-the-trans-pacific-partnership/; Andrew Restuccia, "Trump Administration Delivers Notice U.S. Intends to Withdraw from Paris Climate Deal," *Politico*, August 4, 2017, http://www.politico.com/story/2017/08/04/trump-notice-withdraw-from-paris-climate-deal-241331; United Nation Framework Convention on Climate Change, "Paris Agreement—Status of Ratification," n.d., http://unfccc.int/paris_agreement/items/9444.php.

62. Melvin P. Leffler, "The Emergence of an American Grand Strategy, 1845–1952," in *Cambridge History of the Cold War*, ed. Melvin Leffler and Odd Arne Westad (New York: Cambridge University Press, 2010), 1:67–89, as cited by Ikenberry, *Liberal Leviathan*, 163.

63. International Monetary Fund, "Nominal GDP," October 2017, http://www.imf.org/external/datamapper/NGDPD@WEO/OEMDC/ADVEC/WEOWORLD/USA; Jeremy Bender, "Ranked: The World's 20 Strongest Militaries," *Business Insider*, October 3, 2015, http://www.businessinsider.com/these-are-the-worlds-20-strongest-militaries-ranked-2015-9.

64. International Monetary Fund, "Nominal GDP"; Jeremy Bender, "Ranked: The World's 20 Strongest Militaries."

65. The World Bank, "GDP (Current US$)," n.d., http://data.worldbank.org/indicator/NY.GDP.MKTP.CD.

66. Robert O. Keohane, *After Hegemony: Cooperation and Discord in the World International Economy* (Princeton, NJ: Princeton University Press, 1984, 2005).

67. G. John Ikenberry, "The Future of the Liberal World Order: Internationalism after America," *Foreign Affairs* 90, no 3 (2011): 68.

68. Eugene Gholz, Daryl G. Press, and Harvey M. Sapolsky, "Come Home, America: The Strategy of Restraint in the Face of Temptation," *International Security* 21, no. 4 (1997): 5–48.

69. John J. Mearsheimer and Stephen M. Walt, "The Case for Offshore Balancing: A Superior U.S. Grand Strategy," *Foreign Affairs* 95, no. 4 (2016): 70–83.

70. John J. Mearsheimer, "China's Unpeaceful Rise," *Current History* 105, no. 690 (2006): 160.

71. John J. Mearsheimer, "Can China Rise Peacefully?" *National Interest*, October 25, 2015, http://nationalinterest.org/commentary/can-china-rise-peacefully-10204.

72. Art Swift, "In U.S., Record-High 72% See Foreign Trade as Opportunity," Gallup, February 16, 2017, http://www.gallup.com/poll/204044/record-high-foreign-trade-opportunity.aspx.

73. Benjamin Oreskes, "POLITICO-Harvard Poll: Amid Trump's Rise, GOP Voters Turn Sharply Away from Free Trade," *Politico*, September 24, 2016, http://www.politico.com/story/2016/09/politico-harvard-poll-free-trade-trump-gop-228600.

74. Oreskes, "POLITICO-Harvard Poll."

75. Swift, "In U.S., Record-High 72% See Foreign Trade as Opportunity."

76. Frank Newport, "American Public Opinion on Foreign Trade," Gallup, April 1, 2016, http://www.gallup.com/opinion/polling-matters/190427/american-public-opinion-foreign-trade.aspx.

77. Ruggie, *Winning the Peace*, 6.

78. Ruggie, *Winning the Peace*, 160–61.

79. Ajay Chaudry et al., *Poverty in the United States: 50-Year Trends and Safety Net Impacts* (Washington, DC: Department of Health and Human Services, March 2016), 4–6, https://aspe.hhs.gov/system/files/pdf/154286/50YearTrends.pdf.

80. David H. Autor, David Dorn, and Gordon H. Hanson, "The China Shock: Learning from Labor Market Adjustment to Large Changes in Trade," Institute of Labor Economics, February 2016, http://hdl.handle.net/10419/141507.

81. Rashmi Banga, "New Issues in Multilateral Trade Negotiations," *Economic and Political Weekly* 51, no. 21 (2016): 28–32.

82. Ruggie, "American Exemptionalism," 311.

83. John B. Judis, *The Populist Explosion: How the Great Recession Transformed American and European Politics* (New York: Columbia Global Reports, 2016), 14–15.

84. Judis, *The Populist Explosion*, 12–13.

85. See, for example, E. J. Graff, "Everything You Need to Know about the Worldwide Rise of Populism," *Washington Post*, November 10, 2016, https://www.washingtonpost.com/news/monkey-cage/wp/2016/11/10/heres-what-we-know-about-the-spread-of-populism-worldwide; and Larry Bartels, "The 'Wave' of Right-Wing Populist Sentiment Is a Myth," *Washington Post*, June 21, 2017, https://www.washingtonpost.com/news/monkey-cage/wp/2017/06/21/the-wave-of-right-wing-populist-sentiment-is-a-myth.

86. Judis, *The Populist Explosion*, 82–83.

87. Judis, *The Populist Explosion*, 156.

88. US Senate, "Featured Bio Vandenberg," n.d., https://www.senate.gov/artandhistory/history/common/generic/Featured_Bio_Vandenberg.htm.

89. Robert J. Leiber, "Politics Stops at the Water's Edge? Not Recently," *Washington Post*, February 10, 2014, https://www.washingtonpost.com/news/monkey-cage/wp/2014/02/10/politics-stops-at-the-waters-edge-not-recently.

90. Dina Smeltz, Ivo Daalder, Karl Friedhoff, and Craig Kafura, *2016 Chicago Council Survey: America in the Age of Uncertainty* (Chicago: The Chicago Council on Global Affairs, 2016), 26–27.

Index